Medieval Buda in Context

Brill's Companions to European History

VOLUME 10

The titles published in this series are listed at *brill.com/bceh*

Medieval Buda in Context

Edited by

Balázs Nagy
Martyn Rady
Katalin Szende
András Vadas

BRILL

LEIDEN | BOSTON

Cover illustration: Woodcut of Buda, Schedel'sche Weltchronik, Blatt 138v/139r.
https://commons.wikimedia.org/wiki/File:Nuremberg_chronicles_-_BVJA.png Accessed 19 February 2016

Library of Congress Cataloging-in-Publication Data

Names: Nagy, Balázs, editor of compilation.
Title: Medieval Buda in context / edited by Balázs Nagy, Martyn Rady, Katalin Szende, and András Vadas.
Description: Leiden ; Boston : Brill, [2016] | Series: Brill's companions to
  European history ; volume 10 | Includes bibliographical references and
  index.
Identifiers: LCCN 2016014148 (print) | LCCN 2016015094 (ebook) | ISBN
  9789004307681 (hardback : alk. paper) | ISBN 9789004307674 (E-book)
Subjects: LCSH: Buda (Hungary)--Civilization. | Buda (Hungary)--History. |
  Buda (Hungary)--Politics and government. | Hungary--History--1000-1699.
Classification: LCC DB984 .M44 2016 (print) | LCC DB984 (ebook) | DDC
  943.9/12--dc23
LC record available at https://lccn.loc.gov/2016014148

Want or need Open Access? Brill Open offers you the choice to make your research freely accessible online in exchange for a publication charge. Review your various options on brill.com/brill-open.

Typeface for the Latin, Greek, and Cyrillic scripts: "Brill". See and download: brill.com/brill-typeface.

ISSN 2212-7410
ISBN 978-90-04-30768-1 (hardback)
ISBN 978-90-04-30767-4 (e-book)

Copyright 2016 by Koninklijke Brill NV, Leiden, The Netherlands.
Koninklijke Brill NV incorporates the imprints Brill, Brill Hes & De Graaf, Brill Nijhoff, Brill Rodopi and Hotei Publishing.
All rights reserved. No part of this publication may be reproduced, translated, stored in a retrieval system, or transmitted in any form or by any means, electronic, mechanical, photocopying, recording or otherwise, without prior written permission from the publisher.
Authorization to photocopy items for internal or personal use is granted by Koninklijke Brill NV provided that the appropriate fees are paid directly to The Copyright Clearance Center, 222 Rosewood Drive, Suite 910, Danvers, MA 01923, USA.
Fees are subject to change.

This book is printed on acid-free paper and produced in a sustainable manner.

Contents

Acknowledgements   IX
List of Figures   X
List of Abbreviations   XIII
Notes on Contributors   XVII

Introduction   1

PART 1
Buda: History, Sources, Historiography

1 The Budapest History Museum and the Rediscovery of Medieval Buda   25
   Zoltán Bencze

2 The Fate of the Medieval Archives of Buda and Pest   52
   István Kenyeres

PART 2
Buda before Buda

3 Buda before Buda: Óbuda and Pest as Early Centers   71
   Enikő Spekner

4 'A castle once stood, now a heap of stones…' the Site and Remains of Óbuda in Medieval Chronicles, National Epics, and Modern Fringe Theories   92
   József Laszlovszky and James Plumtree

5 A Royal Forest in the *Medium Regni*   115
   Péter Szabó

PART 3
The Topography of Buda

6 Royal Residences in Buda in Hungarian and European Context   133
   Károly Magyar

7   Buda-Pest 1300 – Buda-Pest 1400. Two Topographical Snapshots   169
    András Végh

8   The Monastic Topography of Medieval Buda   204
    Beatrix F. Romhányi

9   Sacred Sites in Medieval Buda   229
    Gábor Klaniczay

10 Merchants, Markets, and Shops in Late Medieval Buda,
    Pest and Óbuda   255
    Judit Benda

11 Commercial Contacts of Buda along the Danube and beyond   278
    István Draskóczy

PART 4
Buda as a Power Center

12 The Government of Medieval Buda   303
    Martyn Rady

13 Diets and Synods in Buda and Its Environs   322
    János M. Bak and András Vadas

14 Royal Summits in and around Medieval Buda   345
    Balázs Nagy

15 Buda, Medieval Capital of Hungary   366
    András Kubinyi

PART 5
Court Culture of a 'Capital'

16 Made for the King: Sigismund of Luxemburg's Statues in Buda and
    Their Place in Art History   387
    Szilárd Papp

17   The Court of the King and Queen in Buda in the
      Jagiellonian Age   452
        Orsolya Réthelyi

18   Buda as a Center of Renaissance and Humanism   472
        Valery Rees

      PART 6
      Buda beyond Buda

19   Buda: From a Royal Palace to an Assaulted Border Castle,
      1490–1541   497
        László Veszprémy

20   The Last Medieval King Leaves Buda   513
        Antonín Kalous

21   Buda and the Urban Development of East Central Europe   526
        Katalin Szende

      Appendices   555
      Select Bibliography on the History of Medieval Buda   559
      Index of Geographic Names   562
      Index of Personal Names   569

Acknowledgements

The idea behind the present volume goes back to a discussion at the International Medieval Congress in Leeds some years ago. János M. Bak of the Central European University and Julian Deahl on behalf of Brill agreed that there was a lack of a comprehensive English-language volume on the history of medieval Buda. The editors' first thanks go therefore to János and Julian who provided the inspiration for the present volume.

We also wish to express our gratitude to all the contributors. The studies in the present volume were partly submitted in Hungarian and partly in English. Many of the studies were translated by Alan Campbell, and the names of the other translators are indicated at the beginning of each paper. Frank Schaer and Judith Rasson acted as proof readers and we gratefully acknowledge their contribution. Béla Nagy kindly allowed us to use some of the maps that he had prepared. We are thankful to Andra Juganaru for helping with compiling the indexes. At Brill both Julian Deahl and then Marcella Mulder were always at our disposal and helped us resolve a number of editorial questions. The quality of the studies was significantly developed by the careful reviews of Derek Keene and Laurenţiu Rădvan. Despite the number of persons listed here, there will still be errors, infelicities and omissions, for which the editors take responsibility.

Finally, the book could never have been completed without the generous financial support of a number of institutions. Brill set the project in motion by financing much of the translation work and of the initial tidying of the text; the remainder of the translation costs was covered by a special grant under the "Budapest Bank for Budapest" scheme. The Budapest City Archives also contributed significantly to the completion of the volume by financing the drawing of the maps and additional editorial work. The Budapest History Museum kindly gave permission to reproduce images from their collection. The Department of Medieval Studies at Central European University, Budapest, the home institution to three of the editors and several authors, has provided time to work on the manuscript and served as a focus for the large network of scholars who have contributed to this project.

We dedicate this work to the memory of the most knowledgeable and enthusiastic scholar of medieval Buda and the urban history of Hungary in the Middle Ages, the late András Kubinyi, who we hope would have been very satisfied with this volume.

The Editors

List of Figures

0.1	The medieval kingdom of Hungary with the main trade routes and towns	11
0.2	The *medium regni* with the medieval settlements	12
0.3	Medieval settlements in the territory of present-day Budapest	13
0.4	The view of Buda in the Schedel Chronicle, printed in 1493	14
1.1	The Lapidarium in the building of the Fishermen's Bastion	28
1.2	The Lapidarium in the building of the Fishermen's Bastion	29
1.3	Archaeological excavations in the Castle District up to 2013	39
3.1	The most important elements of the topography of Óbuda	73
4.1	The view of Óbuda in the *Epistolae itinerariae* of Jakob Tollius, Amsterdam, 1700	95
4.2	Present-day Óbuda with the medieval buildings excavated in the area	108
5.1	The number of settlements in the Pilis by century	126
5.2	Medieval settlements in the Pilis	128
6.1	Ground plan of the buildings of Prague Castle around 1180	136
6.2	Ground plan of the pre-Romanesque and Romanesque buildings of Cracow's Wawel	137
6.3	The ground plan of Buda Castle around 1350	146
6.4	The ground plan of Buda Castle around 1390	152
6.5	The ground plan of Buda Castle around 1440	153
6.6	The royal palace of Buda in the late fifteenth century	159
6.7	Buda from the west on Erhard Schön's engraving. The siege of Buda (1541)	165
7.1	Buda around 1300	171
7.2	Buda-Pest and their surroundings c. 1300	178
7.3	Buda-Pest and their surroundings c. 1400	195
7.4	Division of the house of János Garai and Miklós Garai in the medieval St George Street	202
8.1	Monasteries and monastic estates on the territory of Buda before 1241	206
8.2	The monastic topography of Buda, Pest and Óbuda around 1300	212
8.3	The monastic topography of Buda, Pest and Óbuda around 1400	213
8.4	The monastic topography of Buda, Pest and Óbuda around 1500	216
8.5	Monasteries and friaries in the *medium regni* around 1500	217
8.6	Monasteries in the countryside owning houses in Buda	224
9.1	Sacred sites within the borders of present-day Budapest	230
9.2	The Margaret Island in 1542 (Enea Vico's etching)	239
9.3	View of Óbuda in the early seventeenth century	240

LIST OF FIGURES   XI

9.4   The *medium regni* with Budaszentlőrinc (S. Paulus), map of Lazarus
       secretarius from 1528   249
10.1   The topography of Buda and Pest with commercial buildings and market
       places   257
10.2   The market of Tárnok Street on the medieval market square, end of the
       nineteenth century   260
10.3   The medieval market hall before its demolition (late nineteenth
       century)   262
10.4   Úri Street 31, Budapest, 1st District. House of a wholesaler   266
10.5   Úri Street 13/Anna Street 2, Budapest, 1st District. Retailers' shops   272
10.6   Lajos Street 158, Budapest, 3rd District. Shambles   274
11.1   The medieval communication networks of Europe with the geographic names
       referred to in the article   282
11.2   The medieval communication networks of Hungary with the geographic
       names referred to in the article   289
13.1   The surroundings of Pest-Buda and the Field of Rákos   326
16.1   Buda, the southern end of the Castle Hill with the buildings of the royal
       palace and the find spots of the statues   426
16.2   Fragment of an apostle's/prophet's head   427
16.3   Torso of a knight figure   428
16.4   Torso of a knight figure   429
16.5   Figure of a helmet-carrying herald   430
16.6   *Chaperone* male head   427
16.7   Saint Ladislas (?)   431
16.8   Gold coin of King Sigismund (1402–1437), reverse side   431
16.9   Torso of a royal (?) figure   432
16.10 Rogier van der Weyden: Columba altar, central panel, detail   432
16.11 Fragment of a head with hair tied up with a roll of cloth   433
16.12 Rogier van der Weyden: Bladelin Triptych, right wing, detail   433
16.13 Saint Bartholomew (?)   434
16.14 Claus Sluter: Madonna   435
16.15 Torso of an apostle/prophet   437
16.16 Torso of an apostle/prophet   436
16.17 Torso of an apostle/prophet   438
16.18 Claus Sluter: Angel   439
16.19 Torso of an apostle/prophet   440
16.20 Mourner on the tomb of Philip the Bold, detail   441
16.21 Head fragment of an apostle/prophet   442
16.22 Detail of a prophet from the so-called Matthias calvary   442
16.23 Torso of an apostle/prophet   443

16.24	Console with the figure of a prophet/apostle	443
16.25	Madonna	444
16.26	The Madonna of Jeanne d'Evreux	445
16.27	Wilton diptych, right wing, detail	445
16.28	Courtier figure	447
16.29	Torso of a knight figure	446
16.30	Courtier	447
16.31	Fragment of a *Chaperone* male head	448
16.32	Charles VI, king of France, detail from the Goldenes Rössl	448
16.33	Mary from the Annunication ensemble	449
16.34	Torso of a bishop	450
16.35	Bishop	451
16.36	Bishop from the Bergenfahrer chapel	451
18.1	Frontispiece for Antonio Averulino, *De architectura libri XXV, ex Italico traducti et Matthiae regi dicati ab Antonio de Bonfinis*	490
18.2	The House of Virtues and Vices, crowned by a statue of Virtue. Cutaway plan. Antonio Averulino, *Trattato di Architettura*	491
18.3	The House of Virtues and Vices, plan and elevation. Antonio Averulino, *Trattato di Architettura*	492
20.1	The pageant of Louis II's army when leaving Buda on 20 July 1526	520
21.1	Residences referred to in the article	527
21.2	The Prague agglomeration in the early thirteenth century	530
21.3	Medieval Cracow: the Wawel, the Old Town, Okół, Kazimierz, and Kleparz	531
21.4	Medieval Wrocław with the Cathedral Island	532
21.5	Medieval Vienna with the old (Herzogshof) and new (Hofburg) princely residences	536
21.6	Suceava in the fifteenth century	538
21.7	Smederevo, castle and walls built between 1428 and 1459	539
21.8	Siret in the fourteenth and fifteenth centuries	545

List of Abbreviations

ÁMTF	Györffy, György, *Az Árpád-kori Magyarország történeti földrajza*, 4 vols [in progress] [Historical geography of Hungary in the Árpádian period] (Budapest: Akadémiai, 1963–1998)
AO	*Anjoukori okmánytár. Codex diplom. Hungaricus Andegavensis*, 7 vols, eds Nagy, Imre and Tasnádi Nagy, Gyula (Budapest: MTA Könyvkiadó Hivatala, 1878–1920)
AOklt	*Anjou-kori oklevéltár. Documenta res Hungaricas tempore regum Andegavensium illustrantia*, 30 vols [in progress], eds Kristó, Gyula and Almási, Tibor (Budapest–Szeged: JATE – Csongrád Megyei Levéltár, 1990–2014)
ÁÚO	*Árpádkori új okmánytár. Codex diplomaticus Arpadianus continuatus*, 12 vols, ed. Wenzel, Gusztáv (Pest–Budapest: M. Tud. Akadémia Tört. Bizottmánya, 1860–1874)
BFL	Budapest Főváros Levéltára/Budapest City Archives
Bonfini, *Decades*	Antonius de Bonfinis, *Rerum Ungaricarum decades*, 4 vols (Bibliotheca Scriptorum Medii Recentisque Aevorum Saeculum XV), eds Fógel, Iosephus, Iványi, Béla, Juhász, Ladislaus (Leipzig–Budapest: Teubner – Egyetemi Nyomda, 1936–1941) vol. iv/2 (Bibliotheca Scriptorum Medii Recentisque Aevorum. Series Nova, 1), eds Kulcsár, Margarita and Kulcsár, Petrus (Budapest: Akadémiai, 1976)
Bp. tört.	*Budapest története*, 5 vols [The history of Budapest], ed. Gerevich, László (Budapest: Budapest Főváros Tanácsa, 1975–1980)
BTM	Budapesti Történeti Múzeum/Budapest History Museum
BTOE	*Budapest történetének okleveles emlékei*, 3 vols in 4 parts [Charters to the history of Budapest], eds Gárdonyi, Albert and Kumorovitz, L. Bernát (Budapest: A Székesfőváros kiadása – BTM, 1936–1988)
Budapest im Mittelalter	*Budapest im Mittelalter. Ausstellungskatalog* (Veröffentlichungen des Braunschweigischen Landesmuseums, 62), ed. Biegel, Gerd (Braunschweig: Braunschweigisches Landesmuseum, 1991)
CD	*Codex diplomaticus Hungariae ecclesiasticus ac civilis*, 11 vols in 44 parts, ed. Fejér, Georgius (Buda: Typis Typogr. Regia Universitatis Ungaricae, 1829–1844)

DF	Collection of Diplomatic Photographs (preserved in MNL OL)
DL	Collection of Diplomatics (preserved in MNL OL)
DRH 1301–1457	*Decreta regni Hungariae 1301–1457* (A Magyar Országos Levéltár kiadványai, ii. Forráskiadványok, 11), eds Döry, Franciscus, Bónis, Georgius and Bácskai, Vera (Budapest: Akadémiai, 1976)
DRH 1458–1490	*Decreta regni Hungariae 1458–1490* (A Magyar Országos Levéltár kiadványai, ii. Forráskiadványok, 19), eds Döry, Franciscus, Bónis, Georgius, Érszegi, Geisa and Teke, Susanna (Budapest: Akadémiai, 1989)
DRMH	*Decreta regni mediaevalis Hungariae. The Laws of the Medieval Kingdom of Hungary*, 5 vols (The laws of East Central Europe The laws of Hungary. Series 1), eds Bak, János M., Bónis, György, Sweeney, James R., Domonkos, Leslie S., Engel, Pál, Harvey, Paul B., Banyó, Péter and Rady, Martyn (Budapest–New York–Salt Lake City–Los Angeles–Idyllwild: Schlacks – Department of Medieval Studies, Central European University, 1992–2012)
EFHU, iii/2	*Elenchus fontium historiae urbanae* (Elenchus fontium historiae urbanae, iii/2), ed. Kubinyi, András (Budapest: Balassi, 1997)
Györffy, *Budapest*	Györffy, György, "Budapest története az Árpád-korban," [The history of Budapest in the Árpádian period] in *Bp. tört.*, i, pp. 217–349.
Italy & Hungary	*Italy & Hungary: Humanism and Art in the Early Renaissance*, eds Farbaky, Péter and Waldman, Louis A. (Florence: Villa i Tatti, 2011)
Kubinyi, *Anfänge Ofens*	Kubinyi, András, *Die Anfänge Ofens* (Osteuropastudien der Hochschulen des Landes Hessen. Reihe i. Giessener Abhandlungen zur Agrar- und Wirtschaftsforschung des europäischen Ostens, 60) (Berlin: Duncker & Humblot, 1972)
Kubinyi, *Budapest*	Kubinyi, András, "Budapest története a későbbi középkorban Buda elestéig (1541-ig)," [The history of Budapest in the late Middle Ages until the fall of Buda (1541)] in *Bp. tört.*, ii, pp. 7–240.
Kubinyi, *Tanulmányok*	Kubinyi, András, *Tanulmányok Budapest középkori történetéről*, 2 vols [Studies in the history of medieval Budapest] (Várostörténeti Tanulmányok), eds Kenyeres, István, Kis, Péter and Sasfi, Csaba (Budapest: BFL, 2009)

Mary of Hungary	*Mary of Hungary: The Queen and Her Court 1521–1531*, eds Réthelyi, Orsolya, F. Romhányi, Beatrix, Spekner, Enikő and Végh, András (Budapest: Budapest History Museum, 2005)
Matthias Corvinus, the King	*Matthias Corvinus, the King. Tradition and Renewal in the Hungarian Royal Court 1458–1490*, eds Farbaky, Péter, Spekner, Enikő, Szende, Katalin and Végh, András (Budapest: Budapest History Museum, 2008)
Medium regni	Altmann, Julianna, Biczó, Piroska, Buzás, Gergely, Horváth, István, Kovács, Annamária, Siklósi, Gyula and Végh, András, *Medium regni. Medieval Hungarian Royal Seats* (Budapest: Nap, 1999)
Mon. Vat.	*Monumenta Vaticana historiam regni Hungariae illustrantia*, 9 vols, eds Ipolyi, Arnold, Fraknói, Vilmos, Pór, Antal and Fejérpataky, László (Budapest: [Szent István Társulat], 1884–1909, repr. Budapest: METEM, 2000–2001)
MNL OL	Magyar Nemzeti Levéltár Országos Levéltára/Hungarian National Archives, State Archive (Budapest)
MTA	Magyar Tudományos Akadémia/Hungarian Academy of Sciences (Budapest)
OSt	*Das Ofner Stadtrecht. Eine deutschsprachige Rechtssammlung des 15. Jahrhunderts aus Ungarn* (Monumenta Historica Budapestinensia, 1), ed. Mollay, Karl (Budapest: Akadémiai, 1959)
OSZK	Országos Széchényi Könyvtár/Széchényi National Library (Budapest)
RA	*Az Árpád-házi királyok okleveleinek kritikai jegyzéke. Regesta regum stirpis Arpadianae critico-diplomatica*, 2 vols, eds Szentpétery, Imre and Borsa, Iván (Budapest: MTA – Akadémiai, 1923–1987)
Rady, *Buda*	Rady, Martyn C., *Medieval Buda: A Study of Municipal Government and Jurisdiction in the Kingdom of Hungary* (East European Monographs, 182) (Boulder: East European Monographs, 1985)
Sigismundus Rex et Imperator	*Sigismundus Rex et Imperator: Kunst und Kultur zur Zeit Sigismunds von Luxemburg 1387–1437*, ed. Takács, Imre (Budapest–Mainz am Rhein: Philipp von Zabern, 2006)

SRH	*Scriptores rerum Hungaricarum tempore ducum regumque stirpis Arpadianae gestarum*, 2 vols, ed. Szentpétery, Emericus (Budapest: MTA, 1937–1938, repr. Budapest: Nap, 1999)
Végh, *Buda*	Végh, András, *Buda város középkori helyrajza*, 2 vols (Monumenta Historica Budapestinensia, 15–16) [The topography of medieval Buda] (Budapest: Budapesti Történeti Múzeum, 2006–2008)
ZsO	*Zsigmondkori oklevéltár*, 12 vols [in progress] [Register of the Sigismund period] (A Magyar Országos Levéltár kiadványai, ii. Forráskiadványok, 1, 3–4, 22, 25, 27, 32, 37, 39, 41, 43, 49, 52), eds Mályusz, Elemér, Borsa, Iván, C. Tóth, Norbert, Neumann, Tibor and Lakatos, Bálint (Budapest: Akadémiai – MOL, 1951–2014)

Notes on Contributors

János M. Bak
is Professor Emeritus of Medieval Studies at the University of British Columbia, Vancouver and Central European University, Budapest. His main field of interest is legal and institutional history (above all of rulership), and he has edited, among much else, the five-volume bi-lingual edition of the medieval laws of the kingdom of Hungary (*Decreta Regni Mediaevalis Hungariae*) and the English translation of several narrative sources from medieval Central Europe.

Zoltán Bencze
is an archaeologist in the Medieval Department of the Budapest History Museum where he was the head of the Department for 25 years. He has conducted excavations at a number of sites spanning from the Conquest period to the Ottoman times in the territory of present-day Budapest including the medieval Pauline monastery at Budaszentlőrinc (in present-day Budapest), the results of which he published with György Szekér (*A budaszentlőrinci pálos kolostor* [The Pauline monastery of Budaszentlőrinc], 1993).

Judit Benda
is an archaeologist at the Medieval Department of the Budapest History Museum. Her main research interests are medieval trade, crafts and economic history. She was the leading archaeologist of the Carmelite friary in Buda as well as a number of other sites in the Castle District and the Water Town of Buda.

István Draskóczy
is Professor of Medieval History at the Eötvös Loránd University, Budapest. His main research interest is the economic and social history of late medieval Hungary. He published a number of studies on personnel in the financial administration of the kingdom and on the royal income. In the last two decades he has extensively published on the history of mining and trade in medieval Hungary with special regard to salt. Currently he is working on the university peregrination of Hungarian students. He is the head of the joint research group of the Hungarian Academy of Sciences and the Eötvös Loránd University on this topic.

Antonín Kalous
is Associate Professor in Medieval History at the Palacký University, Olomouc. His field of interest is late medieval ecclesiastical, cultural and political history with special attention to Central Europe, Italy and the papacy. He is the author of *Matyáš Korvín, 1443–1490: uherský a český král* [King Matthias, 1443–1490, Hungarian and Czech king] (2009) and *Plenitudo potestatis in partibus?: papežští legáti a nunciové ve střední Evropě na konci středověku (1450–1526)* [Legates and papal nuncios in Central Europe in the late Middle Ages (1450–1526)] (2010) and ed. *The Transformation of Confessional Cultures in a Central European City: Olomouc, 1400–1750* (2015).

István Kenyeres
is General Director of the Budapest City Archives. His main research interest is late medieval and early modern economy, administration, finance and urban history. His publications include the edition of *XVI. századi uradalmi utasítások. Utasítások a kamarai uradalmak prefektusai, udvarbírái és ellenőrei részére* [Instructions of the Hungarian Chamber Estates from the Sixteenth Century] (2002) and of the German Butchers' Guild book (*Zunftbuch und Privilegien der Fleischer zu Ofen aus dem Mittelalter*, 2008). He authored the monograph *Uradalmak és végvárak. A kamarai birtokok és a törökellenes határvédelem a 16. századi Magyar Királyságban* [Lordships and border castles. Estates of the Hungarian Chamber and the anti-Ottoman border protection in the sixteenth-century kingdom of Hungary] (2008).

Gábor Klaniczay
is Professor of Medieval Studies at the Central European University, Budapest. His research interests comprise historical anthropology of medieval and early modern Christianity (sainthood, miracle beliefs, visions, stigmatics, magic, witchcraft) and the comparative history of 'medievalism'. His books include *The Uses of Supernatural Power* (1990); *Holy Rulers and Blessed Princesses* (2002); and he is the editor of *Saints of the Christianization Age of Central Europe (Tenth–Eleventh centuries)* (2013).

András Kubinyi
(1929–2007) was Professor of Medieval Archaeology at the Eötvös Loránd University in Budapest and member of the Hungarian Academy of Sciences. His main research interest was late medieval urban, social, ecclesiastical and economic history, the history of everyday life and material culture. He dedicated a number of works to the history of medieval Buda, Pest and Óbuda as well as of their suburbs. His works include: *Die Anfänge Ofens* (1972); and *König*

und Volk im spätmittelalterlichen Ungarn. Städteentwicklung, Alltagsleben und Regierung im mittelalterlichen Ungarn (1998). His collected studies on the history of Budapest were published posthumously in two volumes: *Tanulmányok Budapest középkori történetéről* [Studies on the medieval history of Budapest] (2009).

József Laszlovszky
is Professor of Medieval Studies at the Central European University, Budapest and director of its Cultural Heritage Program. He is also a regular guest lecturer at the Eötvös Loránd University, Budapest. His research interests span the archaeology of the countryside and monastic landscape through the preservation of cultural heritage to the history of English–Hungarian relations in the Middle Ages. He has conducted a number of excavations in medieval sites such as the Cistercian grange at Pomáz-Nagykovácsi and the Franciscan friary at Visegrád.

Károly Magyar
is an archaeologist at the Medieval Department of the Budapest History Museum. His main research interests are medieval archaeology and the architectural history of royal residences. He has published several studies on the excavations that he led in the area of the Buda palace complex and his works also analyze the relationship of residences and towns in Central Europe.

Balázs Nagy
is Associate Professor of Medieval History at the Eötvös Loránd University and visiting faculty at the Department of Medieval Studies at the Central European University, Budapest. His main research interests is the medieval economic and urban history of Central Europe. He is co-editor of the Latin-English bi-lingual edition of the autobiography of Emperor Charles IV (ed. with Frank Schaer, 2001); and has edited with Derek Keene and Katalin Szende, *Segregation – Integration – Assimilation: Religious and Ethnic Groups in the Medieval Towns of Central and Eastern Europe* (2009).

Szilárd Papp
is art historian at the Museum of Fine Arts in Budapest. His principal research focus is the art, architecture and sculpture of the Gothic period in Hungary and Central Europe. His works include a monograph: *A királyi udvar építkezései Magyarországon 1480–1515* [The architecture of the royal court in Hungary, 1480–1515] (2005). He is currently leading a research project on the re-evaluation of the Buda Gothic sculpture find.

James Plumtree
is Assistant Professor at the American University of Central Asia, Bishkek. He was awarded his PhD from the Central European University, Budapest, in 2014 with a thesis on "How the Corpse of a Most Mighty King… The Use of the Death and Burial of the English Monarch (From Edward to Henry I)". His research interests include historiography, textual communities, modern interpretations and manipulations of the past, and literature.

Martyn Rady
is Masaryk Professor of Central European History at the School of Slavonic and East European Studies, University College London. He was for ten years part of the team that edited and translated the corpus of the laws of medieval Hungary together with János M. Bak (*Decreta Regni Mediaevalis Hungariae*). His previous books include *Medieval Buda. A Study of Municipal Government and Jurisdiction in the Kingdom of Hungary* (1985); *Nobility, Land and Service in Medieval Hungary* (2000) and *Customary Law in Hungary: Courts, Texts, and the Tripartitum* (2015). He has also edited and translated a number of Hungarian and Czech medieval chronicles.

Valery Rees
is a senior member of the Renaissance faculty of the School of Economic Science in London, working on a complete edition of the *Letters of Marsilio Ficino*. She has published widely on Ficino, on Renaissance philosophy, the Renaissance in Hungary and a recent monograph *From Gabriel to Lucifer: A Cultural History of Angels* (2013). She contributed to the publication of *Brill's Encyclopaedia of the Neo-Latin World* (2014).

Orsolya Réthelyi
is Assistant Professor at the Department of Dutch Studies at the Eötvös Loránd University, Budapest. Her main research interests include medieval and early modern cultural history and literature, comparative court studies, early modern literature, cultural transmission, cultural contacts between Hungary and The Netherlands, reception studies, modern medievalism and theatre studies. Her publications include an exhibition catalogue ed. with Beatrix Romhányi, Enikő Spekner and András Végh, *Mary of Hungary, Widow of Mohács. The Queen and her Court 1521–1531* (2005) and ed. with Martina Fuchs, *Maria von Ungarn, eine europäische Persönlichkeit zu Anbruch der Neuzeit* (2007) and ed. with Ton van Kalmthout and Remco Sleiderink, *Beatrijs de wereld in. Vertalingen en bewerkingen van het Middelnederlands verhaal* [Beatrijs worldwide. Translations and adaptations of the Middle Dutch story] (2013).

Beatrix F. Romhányi
is Associate Professor at the Department of Medieval History at Károli Gáspár Calvinist University, Budapest. Her fields of interest and range of publications include medieval ecclesiastical history, especially the history of monasticism, economic history, and historical demography. Her recent research focuses on the economic activity of the Paulines and the mendicant orders in Hungary and in Central Europe. Her most recent monograph is '*A lelkiek a földiek nélkül nem tarthatók fenn.' Pálos gazdálkodás a középkorban* ['*Spiritualia* cannot be sustained without *temporalia*': Pauline economy in the Middle Ages].

Enikő Spekner
is a historian at the Medieval Department of the Budapest History Museum. Her research focuses on the ecclesiastical institutions of medieval Buda and the history of Buda and Pest within the kingdom of Hungary. Her works include ed. with Péter Farbaky, Dániel Pócs and András Végh, *Mattia Corvino e Firenze. Arte e Umanesimo alla corte del re di Ungheria* (2013) and a recent monograph *Hogyan lett Buda a középkori Magyarország fővárosa* [How did Buda become the capital of medieval Hungary] (2015).

Péter Szabó
is Deputy Head at the Department of Vegetation Ecology, Institute of Botany of the Czech Academy of Sciences in Brno. His main research interest is historical ecology, especially the history of Central European woodlands and landscapes from the beginning of the Holocene until the present. His research is based on the examination of written sources (from the Middle Ages onwards) as well as on landscape archaeological fieldwork. His works include *Woodland and Forests in Medieval Hungary* (2005) and ed. with Radim Hédl, *Human Nature: Studies in Historical Ecology and Environmental History* (2008)

Katalin Szende
is Associate Professor of Medieval Studies at the Central European University, Budapest. Her research concentrates on medieval towns in the Carpathian Basin and Central Europe, with particular regard to society, demography, literacy, everyday life, and topography. Her previous publications include *Otthon a városban. Társadalom és anyagi kultúra a középkori Sopronban, Pozsonyban és Eperjesen* [At home in the town: Society and material culture in medieval Sopron, Pressburg and Prešov] (2004); ed. with Finn-Einar Eliassen, *Generations in Towns: Succession and Success in Pre-industrial Urban Societies* (2009); and ed. with Derek Keene and Balázs Nagy *Segregation – Integration – Assimilation:*

Religious and Ethnic Groups in the Medieval Towns of Central and Eastern Europe (2009).

András Vadas

is Assistant Professor of Medieval History at the Eötvös Loránd University, Budapest. His research interest is environmental and economic history of the Middle Ages and the Early Modern Period. His works discuss the problem of the environmental change brought by military activities in the Carpathian Basin as well as on mills and milling in medieval Hungary. His monograph *Körmend és a vizek. Egy település és környezete a korai újkorban* [Körmend and the waters. A settlement and its environment in the Early Modern period] was published in 2013.

András Végh

is an archaeologist and Head of the Medieval Department of the Budapest History Museum and Associate Professor at the Department of Archaeology of the Pázmány Péter Catholic University, Piliscsaba. His main research interests include urban topography, architectural history and medieval Jewish architecture. He published amongst others *Buda város középkori helyrajza* [The topography of medieval Buda] (2006–2008); ed. with Péter Farbaky, Dániel Pócs and Enikő Spekner, *Mattia Corvino e Firenze. Arte e Umanesimo alla corte del re di Ungheria* (2013) and ed. with Péter Farbaky et al., *Mátyás-templom – A budavári Nagyboldogasszony-templom évszázadai (1246–2013)* [Matthias Church – Centuries of the Virgin Mary Church in Buda (1246–2013)] (2015).

László Veszprémy

is Director of the Institute of Military History, Budapest and Head of the Research Group in Medieval Studies of the Hungarian Academy of Sciences. His research interests include medieval and early modern military history, Latin and German historiography, and intellectual history. He is the translator from Latin into English and Hungarian of a number of narrative sources from medieval Hungary.

Introduction

Buda, Pest and Óbuda

Present-day Budapest is a young city, less than 150 years old: its territory was unified only in 1873. Before that it consisted of three major and several minor settlements, the most important ones being Buda, Pest, and Óbuda. This cluster of settlements already functioned in the Middle Ages as an agglomeration, with its members complementing – and sometimes also competing with – each other. This is why in this volume, principally dedicated to medieval Buda, all of these settlements will be considered in due course, although their relationship has to be clarified at the outset.

In terms of age, Óbuda (meaning literally 'Old Buda', originally simply called Buda), on the right bank of the Danube, north of the later Castle Hill, has chronological precedence, being founded in the tenth century on the ruins of Roman Aquincum, at a site where the Danube could be easily crossed. One of the former royal residences of the Árpád dynasty in the *medium regni* (the geographical as well as political center of the kingdom of Hungary), its southern half including the royal castle became the queen's possession from the mid-fourteenth century onwards. The northern part was owned from the mid-eleventh century by the rich and influential Buda Chapter, one of the ecclesiastical institutions authorized to issue authentic documents in secular matters pertaining to any place in the country. The significance of Óbuda decreased when a 'new' Buda was founded further south.

The second oldest was the town of Pest, on the left bank of the Danube, built on a strategically very important site, where all the roads of the Hungarian plain converged in order to reach the most favorable point to cross the Danube by ferry. This site, where in Roman times a small military outpost in the Barbaricum was located, attracted a good number of merchants, Hungarian and foreign (Muslims and Germans) alike. Both Óbuda and Pest were destroyed by the Mongol invasion of 1241–1242, after which they recovered only slowly and partially. Pest had been practically degraded to a suburb of Buda, its magistrates being delegated from among Buda's councillors. It was only from the mid-fourteenth century that Pest regained some of its former cultural and economic potential, reaching the rank of a free royal town – on a par with Buda and six other merchant towns – from 1498 onwards.

The great winner in the urbanization process, however, was the youngest partner, Buda. This city was founded by King Béla IV in the aftermath of the Mongol invasion of 1241, when he instructed the few surviving citizens of the devastated town of Pest and Óbuda to move to the hill on the right bank of the Danube, bringing their charters of liberty with them. The ground plan of the new settlement indicates that it was a planned foundation, although on account of the contours of the hilltop, the city's streets and the arrangement of its plots did not follow a regular grid pattern. The new city was, however, strongly fortified, with walls reaching altogether five kilometers in extent. By the late Middle Ages a further wall had been built to enclose the suburb area. The population of Buda, or of the New Mount of Pest as it was known, was dominated by a substantial German elite of merchants and patricians, in which respect Buda counted as the easternmost settlement on the Danube with a large German presence.[1]

The new Buda hosted a royal house from its foundation onwards, the *Kammerhof* on the north part of the hilltop. From the mid-fourteenth century onwards the royal palace of Buda stood at the strategically most important southern tip of the Castle Hill, but it did not become the prime royal residence until the reign of King Sigismund, in the 1410s. Until then (from 1323 onwards), a fourth town on the Danube Bend, Visegrád (the eponymous settlement of the 'Visegrád countries' in contemporary politics), about 40km north of the agglomeration described above, was the main royal seat. The urban potential of Visegrád was strongly restricted by the Pilis Hills, which left only a narrow strip on the riverbank for human habitation; nevertheless, the rulers of the Angevin dynasty, Charles I and Louis I, and even the young Sigismund, held their courts there. The question of which town fulfilled the role of the capital and how issues of the display of royal power and prestige were arranged between Buda and Visegrád in the second half of the fourteenth century was complex and will be addressed in some of the studies to follow.

The new city of Buda – like its left-bank predecessor, Pest – was situated on a convenient crossing-point of the Danube and mediated commerce between Italy and southern Germany on the one side, and the towns of Transylvania and modern-day Slovakia on the other.[2] Its economic significance was bolstered by the close proximity of Óbuda and Pest, the second of which became particularly active in the cattle trade. On account of its hot springs, a further settlement at Budafelhévíz, which lay just north of the city by the road leading to Óbuda, had watermills that functioned all year round. It became an industrial center serving the city, while the warm waters also made it suitable for a

---

1 For the name of Buda, see the chapters below by András Végh as well as by József Laszlovszky and James Plumtree.
2 On Buda's place in international trading relations, see the chapter below by István Draskóczy.

hospital.[3] The main commercial driver of urban wealth was, however, the royal court and administration, which became firmly based in Buda from the early fifteenth century and was located in the palace situated on the southern part of the hilltop. Buda was, however, sacked by the Ottomans in the immediate wake of the battle of Mohács in 1526. Although it survived the assault, the city was eventually occupied by the Ottomans in 1541 and it would remain in Turkish occupation until 1686. Following the city's capture, Hungary's royal seat moved nominally to Pressburg (called Bratislava only in modern times), although the kingdom was effectively administered from Habsburg Vienna and Prague. Buda only gradually recovered its status as a capital city from the late eighteenth century onwards, with the moving of more and more central offices and institutions from Vienna and Pressburg to Buda or Pest.[4]

Despite its status as the kingdom's premier city and, from the fifteenth century, the seat of its kings, Buda was not an episcopal center. The kingdom's primatial see, the archbishopric of Esztergom, was instead located fifty kilometers to the north-west. Nor was Buda the royal coronation city. Although the principal church in Buda, the Church of Our Lady, is now sometimes called the Coronation Church, this is by virtue of the coronations of 1867 and 1916, and not on account of any medieval coronation, which took place as a rule at Székesfehérvár. (The occasional description of Buda's biggest parish church as the Matthias Church is equally misnamed, being based only on the fact that Matthias Corvinus celebrated his enthronement and two marriages there and had his coat of arms placed on the tower.) The kingdom's diet, moreover, only rarely convened in Buda. On account of the numerousness of its composition, the diet usually met on the opposite side of the Danube, on the plain beside Pest known as the field of Rákos.[5]

Nor was Buda a center of manufacture. The craftsmen of the city were overwhelmingly engaged in providing for the local market and, increasingly, for the palace. Thus, whereas we know of large quantities of cloth coming to Buda from all across Europe, including England, we cannot point to any specific goods that were manufactured in the city for export. Of course this did not mean that crafts and craftsmen were absent from Buda, Pest and Óbuda. András Kubinyi identified 40 different crafts organized in 29 guilds in Buda, and 43 crafts (with some overlap) in Pest.[6] Most of these, however, belonged to the most common crafts pursued for satisfying local demand: bakers, tailors, shoemakers, potters,

---

3   Kubinyi, *Budapest*, p. 160.
4   For Buda's role as a capital city, see the chapter below by András Kubinyi.
5   See the chapter below by János M. Bak and András Vadas.
6   Kubinyi, *Budapest*, pp. 111–127.

blacksmiths, furriers, and so on. Their representatives were settled typically in the suburbs of Buda, especially in the area between the Castle Hill and the Danube (the Water Town – Víziváros); increasingly so because of the need to house the prelates and barons on the Castle Hill after the definitive move of the royal court to the Buda palace. The two significant exceptions were the row occupied by the goldsmiths opposite the Dominican friary of Buda (probably connected to Buda's role as a central minting chamber), and the shearers in a street west of the main market place, who were also textile merchants.[7]

Beyond this basic level one can find some crafts connected to the long-distance trade of agricultural commodities. Some of them provided containers or vehicles for the trade itself, such as cartwrights or coopers; others used the raw materials 'left behind' by large-scale local consumption, such as turners and tanners using the bones and hide of the animals slaughtered locally; others again, most notably the butchers, combined local business with international trading ventures. Another group of local craftsmen made their living from putting the finishing touch to imported goods – the shearers, the hatters and the cutlers. Representatives of all these crafts sat from time to time on the local councils of Buda, Pest and Óbuda.[8]

Courtly life encouraged the development of luxury crafts. Indeed, besides the goldsmiths and a gemstone-carver (*gemmifisor*) found in the written evidence, archaeological finds testify to majolica production, a scriptorium and bookbinders' workshop, architects, sculptors, book-illuminators and other artists in courtly service. On the whole, however, courtly consumption relied mostly on the import of high-quality goods by special court purveyors such as Florentine and, to a lesser extent, Venetian textile merchants. Even most of the court-workshops were a special form of this import, whereby not the goods but the craftsmen or artists producing them were invited to Buda from abroad and employed there for a while.[9] It was rather the second tier of prominent consumers, the members of the nobility and high clergy residing in Buda, who relied on and promoted the development of locally-based specialist craftsmen.

7   See the chapters by András Végh and Judit Benda in the present volume.
8   András Kubinyi, "Die Zusammensetzung des städtischen Rates im mittelalterlichen Königreich Ungarn," *Südostdeutches Archiv* 34–35 (1991–1992), pp. 23–42. For Óbuda, see: Ferenc Kanyó, "A késő középkori Óbuda város magisztrátusa 1526-ig," [The magistracy of the late medieval town of Óbuda (until 1526)], in *Micae mediaevales IV. Fiatal történészek dolgozatai a középkori Magyarországról és Európáról* [Studies of young historians on medieval Hungary and Europe], eds Judit Gál *et al*. (Budapest: ELTE BTK Történelemtudományok Doktori Iskola, 2015), pp. 133–156, esp. pp. 141–142.
9   See the chapter by Szilárd Papp in the present volume.

The spatial distribution of crafts between Buda, Pest and Óbuda shows a conscious division of labor. As excavations in the last few decades have revealed, the flat landscape of Pest provided a better setting for dangerous or polluting crafts that needed ample space, such as a huge tannery by the Danube or a glassmaker's workshop close to the town walls.[10] The industrial center of Budafelhévíz sustained communities of fullers, tanners, armorers, goldsmiths, and perhaps even paper-makers. The mills, which underpinned Budafelhévíz's economy, were kept in use even after the Ottoman occupation of Buda as the new overlords adapted the site for the production of gunpowder.[11]

A Hub of Ethnic Diversity

The craft organization of medieval Buda was often split between competing guilds, which were arranged by national criteria. We thus know of separate guilds for German and Hungarian butchers, tailors, coopers and skinners. This circumstance reflects the ethnic divisions within the city itself. The original settlement at Pest was described in the 1240s as a *magna et ditissima Theutonica villa* and the new foundation on the Buda Hill was similarly German in character.[12] The wealthier citizens, who dominated the city's commerce, were thus of predominantly German descent and they controlled the main institutions of Buda's government. Although there is some evidence of bilingualism, the German and Hungarian communities were largely endogamous in their marriages, with Germans frequently marrying into German families living abroad or in other Hungarian towns, but rarely into Hungarian families. Increasingly too, the two communities occupied separate spaces within Buda, with Hungarians occupying the northern part of the city and Germans the middle and southern parts.[13]

---

10 See the forthcoming works of Eszter Kovács and Judit Zádor.
11 András Kubinyi, "Budafelhévíz topográfiája és gazdasági fejlődése," [The topography and economic development of Budafelhévíz] in Kubinyi, *Tanulmányok*, i, pp. 115–182, esp. pp. 153–160; Judit Benda, "Malmok, pékek és kenyérszékek a késő-középkori Budán," [Mills, bakers and bread-stalls in late medieval Buda] *Tanulmányok Budapest Múltjából* 38 (2013), pp. 7–31, esp. pp. 8–11.
12 Master Roger, *Epistle to the Sorrowful Lament upon the Destruction of the Kingdom of Hungary by the Tatars* (Central European Medieval Texts, 5), eds János M. Bak and Martyn Rady (Budapest–New York: Central European University Press, 2010), pp. 160–161 (cap. 16).
13 Katalin Szende, "Integration through Language: The Multilingual Character of Late Medieval Hungarian Towns," in *Segregation – Integration – Assimilation. Religious and Ethnic Groups in the Medieval Towns of Central and Eastern Europe* (Historical Urban Studies),

Antagonism between the German and Hungarian communities led to rioting in 1439, after which an agreement was reached and parity observed in the allocation of offices and of places on the city council.[14] Nevertheless, German merchants retained their leading role in the city's commerce until the 1520s. In 1529, following the city's recapture by Ottoman forces (it was first taken by the Turks in 1526, in the aftermath of the battle of Mohács), many Germans were slain, including the judge, Wolfgang Freiberger.[15] Some Germans remained in the city and continued to serve on the city council, but they were forced to flee in 1541, following a failed attempt to hand Buda over to the Habsburg forces encamped outside the city. Even after the city's occupation and absorption into the Ottoman Empire in August 1541, a city council continued to function, using the old seal of Buda.[16] Its competence was, however, greatly circumscribed. As far as we may ascertain, its membership was almost entirely Hungarian.[17]

The ethnic composition of the city was diverse. Buda was located at the southern end of a strip of Slavonic settlement, which reached southwards from modern-day Slovakia and across the Pilis Hills.[18] The hamlet of Tótfalu (literally Slav Village), which was located on the northern slope of the Buda Hill, may bear witness to an older Slavonic population. Slavonic immigration into the new city must have continued, since Buda's population continued to be fed by immigration from the north. Doubtless, the newcomers were swiftly absorbed into the numerically preponderant Hungarian community. During the later sixteenth and seventeenth centuries, there was an influx of Orthodox Slavs, known as 'Illyrians', into Ottoman Buda, some of whom later settled nearby on the islands of the Danube as well as at Szentendre, a mostly Serbian settlement some twenty kilometers north of Buda.[19]

---

eds Derek Keene, Balázs Nagy and Katalin Szende (Farnham: Ashgate, 2009), 205–233, here pp. 206 and 216–217; András Végh, "Buda: The Multi-Ethnic Capital of Medieval Hungary," in *Segregation – Integration – Assimilation*, pp. 89–99, esp. pp. 94–99.

14 See the chapter below by Martyn Rady.
15 For the sieges and occupations of Buda after 1526, see the chapter below by László Veszprémy.
16 Miklós Jankovich, "Buda város keresztény tanácsa a török hódoltság korában," [Buda's Christian Council during the Turkish Occupation] *Tanulmányok Budapest Múltjából* 14 (1961), pp. 147–161, here p. 147.
17 *Bp. tört.*, ii, p. 398.
18 ÁMTF, iv, p. 593. For the significance of the Pilis Hills and forest, see the chapter below by Péter Szabó.
19 Jankovich, "Buda város keresztény tanácsa," p. 155.

We have evidence in the early thirteenth century of settlements of Muslim traders in the vicinity of Pest, as well as of an As (Jász or Jazygian) community made up of Iranian-speaking nomads.[20] Neither of these groups is thought to have endured here beyond the middle of the century. There was, however, an Armenian community in Buda, which although small was significant enough to give its name to a street.[21] Immigration during the Turkish period resulted in an expanded Armenian population.[22] There was also in the later sixteenth century an influx of Gypsies, sufficient for the outer suburb of the city to be known as the *Zingarorum civitas*.[23] Italians remained numerous throughout the later Middle Ages and one of the principal streets in Buda, the present-day Országház Street, was named the *Platea Italicorum*. The Italians, who were mostly Florentines, dealt in cloth and luxury goods, as well as farming tithes and leasing the minting and mining chambers.[24] In the fourteenth century, they were a mostly transient population. Having made a profit, they returned home. In the fifteenth century, they were more likely to settle for longer periods in the city, although they rarely acquired citizenship. A few were involved with Hungarian partners in the cattle trade, driving herds southwards to the Adriatic and North Italian emporia.[25] Their numbers were swollen as a consequence of Matthias Corvinus's interest in Italian fashions, culture, philosophy, and political alliances.[26] During the Ottoman period, the few Italian merchants who stayed or arrived anew in the city increasingly turned away from

---

20 See below, the chapter by Enikő Spekner; on the As, see Nora Berend, *At the Gate of Christendom: Jews, Muslims and 'Pagans' in Medieval Hungary, c. 1000–c. 1300* (Cambridge: Cambridge University Press, 2001), pp. 57–58.

21 Kubinyi, *Budapest*, pp. 30 and 72. See also the chapter below by Beatrix Romhányi.

22 Aurel Littke, *Buda-Pest a török uralom korában* [Buda-Pest under the Turks] (Budapest: Fritz Armin, 1908), p. 41. See also: *Far away from Mount Ararat: Armenian Culture in the Carpathian Basin*, eds Bálint Kovács and Emese Pál (Budapest: Budapest History Museum – Hungarian National Széchényi Library, 2013).

23 As recorded in György Závodszky's diary, under 1598. See *Magyar Történelmi Tár* [Hungarian Historical Collection], 1859, p. 264.

24 Kubinyi, *Budapest*, p. 49; Krisztina Arany, *Florentine Families in Hungary in the First Half of the Fifteenth Century*, unpublished PhD Dissertation (Budapest: Central European University, 2014); eadem, "Generations Abroad: Florentine Merchant Families in the First Half of the Fifteenth Century," in *Generations in Towns: Succession and Success in Pre-Industrial Urban Societies*, eds Finn-Einar Eliassen and Katalin Szende (Newcastle: Cambridge Scholars Publishing, 2009), pp. 129–152.

25 Kubinyi, *Budapest*, p. 100. See also Katalin Prajda, "The Florentine Scolari Family at the Court of Sigismund of Luxemburg in Buda," *Journal of Early Modern History* 14 (2010), pp. 513–533.

26 Kubinyi, *Budapest*, p. 192. See further the chapter below by Valery Rees.

direct involvement in commerce and towards tax-farming and the leasing of revenues.[27]

A Jewish community developed in Buda during the later thirteenth century. An urban Jewry was a recent phenomenon in Hungary, since Jews had hitherto been mainly active in the kingdom either as itinerant, long-distance merchants or as specialists in the royal service, usually as minters or moneyers.[28] Within Buda, members of the Jewish community were mainly involved in money lending, not only to citizens of the city but also to nobles and even to peasants.[29] Since this activity often brought them into conflict with the borrowers, they were dependent upon the ruler for support in their business affairs. This dependence came, however, at the cost of special taxes levied on the community and was not always reciprocated. The royal will might choose just as much to cancel a loan, particularly if the debtor's plea was accompanied by a story of misfortune, as to enforce the strict terms of repayment.[30] Around 1350, the royal displeasure with the kingdom's Jews – possibly on account of their supposed responsibility for the spread of the Black Death – was sufficient for Louis I to seek their conversion. When this was not forthcoming, Jews in Hungary were expelled from the kingdom, only to be readmitted in 1364.

Buda's Jews were originally settled towards the south-western corner of the Castle Hill, where the ruins of a synagogue have been recently excavated.[31] They were moved during the first decades of the fifteenth century, probably to make way for the spreading royal palace. Their new quarter lay next to today's Táncsics Street, on the north-eastern side of the hill, where two new synagogues were built.[32] This was not, however, a ghetto, for Christians lived there

---

27 Kubinyi, *Budapest*, pp. 215; *Bp. tört.*, ii, p. 382.
28 See Katalin Szende, "Traders, 'Court Jews', Town Jews: Changing Roles of Hungary's Jewish Population in the light of Royal Policy between the Eleventh and the Fourteenth Centuries," in *Intricate Interfaith Networks: Quotidian Jewish-Christian Contacts in the Middle Ages*, eds Ephraim Shoham-Steiner and Gerhard Jaritz (Turnhout: Brepols, 2016, forthcoming).
29 *Magyar-Zsidó oklevéltár*, 18 vols [Hungarian Jewish Collection of Documents], eds Armin Friss *et al.* (Budapest: Izraelita Magyar Irodalmi Társulat, 1903–1980) (henceforth: MZsO), i, pp. 132–3; ibid., v/1, p. 59.
30 MZsO, i, pp. 148, 155–156, 212–214, 236, 321; MZsO, iv, p. 86.
31 András Végh, "The Remains of the First Jewish Quarter of Buda in the Light of Recent Excavations," in *Régészeti ásatások Magyarországon 2005* [Archaeological Excavations in Hungary 2005], ed. Júlia Kisfaludi (Budapest: Magyar Nemzeti Múzeum, 2006), pp. 125–148.
32 Táncsics Street was until 1948 Werbőczy Street. It is one of the few streets left in Budapest to retain its Communist designation.

as well, while Jews also owned properties in other parts of the city.[33] The Jewish population of Buda numbered between 300 and 500 persons and was augmented by refugees from persecution.[34] As the Burgundian traveler, Bertrandon de la Broquière, reported of Buda in the 1430s, "Many Jews live there, who speak French well, several of them being descendants of those driven formerly from France."[35] Buda's Jews were in their internal affairs subject to the authority of their own courts and, from the 1470s, to a prefect drawn from the Mendel family, who also had responsibility throughout the realm for collection of the Jewish tax. In their dealings with Christians, however, they were bound to proceed through the city council or one of the kingdom's high judges.[36] The city's Jews played an important part in urban ceremonial, being among the first to greet the ruler at entrées and forming part of the escort that accompanied the coronation procession. In a glittering ceremony in December 1476, Buda's Jews bade farewell to King Matthias, who was on his way to meet his bride, Beatrice of Aragon. The prefect, Mendel, rode into the inner courtyard of the royal palace, accompanied by a troop of horsemen, decorated with silver buckles and ostrich feathers.[37] Less happily, in September 1526 it was Jews who attended the entry of Suleiman into Buda and handed over to him the keys of the city. They departed with the Ottoman army, many moving to Thessaloniki.[38] Since

---

33 Jews might thus come into the possession of properties in Buda and its environs by pledge or delinquent debt. See BTOE, ii/1, p. 296 (no 571); BTOE, ii/2, pp. 53–53 (no 775). See also Végh, *Buda*, i, pp. 301–307.

34 László Zolnay, *Buda középkori zsidósága* [Medieval Buda's Jewry] (Budapest: Tudományos Ismeretterjesztő Társulat), 1968, p. 23, puts the population at 500. András Kubinyi accepts Ferenc Kováts's estimate of 320–400 persons: see András Kubinyi, "A magyarországi zsidóság története a középkorban" [The history of the Jews in Hungary in the Middle Ages], *Soproni Szemle* 49 (1995), pp. 2–27, here pp. 20–21.

35 *The Travels of Bertrandon de la Brocquiere*, trans. Thomas Johnes (Hafod: Hafod Press, 1807), p. 310.

36 Rady, *Buda*, pp. 81–85.

37 Sándor Scheiber, "Zsidó küldöttség Mátyás és Beatrix esküvőjén," [A Jewish Delegation at the Wedding of Matthias and Beatrice] *Múlt és Jövő* 33 (1943), pp. 107–108; see also: *Jewish Budapest: Monuments, Rites, History*, ed. Géza Komoróczy (Budapest: CEU Press, 1999), p. 10, Kubinyi, "A magyarországi zsidóság," pp. 17–18.

38 Katalin Szende, "Scapegoats or Competitors? The Expulsion of Jews from Hungarian Towns on the Aftermath of the Battle of Mohács (1526)," in *Expulsion and Diaspora Formation: Religious and Ethnic Identities in Flux from Antiquity to the Seventeenth Century* (Religion and Law in Medieval Christian and Muslim Societies, 5), ed. John V. Tolan (Turnhout: Brepols, 2015), pp. 51–83, here pp. 73–75.

only a few returned, most of the Jewish population of Turkish Buda comprised newcomers.[39]

The population of Buda and its immediate environs may in the late fifteenth century have numbered as much as 15,000.[40] The figure could hardly, however, have been stable, but subject to flux, depending upon whether the ruler was resident there and on the periodic assembly of the kingdom's law courts. Although we have many sources to rely on in respect of the city's leading elite, merchants, guildsmen, resident noblemen and aliens, the vast majority of the city's inhabitants have an anonymous existence. Day laborers, servants, petty clerks and the under-employed, they appear in the historical record only at moments of crisis. We know thus of rioting and of the looting of shops that accompanied the political conflict between Germans and Hungarians in 1439.[41] In 1496 on the occasion of the diet's assembly, scrumping in the orchards near Buda soon gave way to the plunder of Jewish homes and to attacks on foreigners and prelates.[42] Several bishops fled the city, while the king dared not leave the palace. Buda was not immune to the Peasants' Rebellion of 1514 when a number of noble homes in the city were destroyed. Again, in 1525, popular discontent over the debasement of the coinage led to the further plundering of Jewish properties, on this occasion with the excuse that the responsible treasury official, Imre Szerencsés, was of Jewish descent. It took cannon shot to disperse the mob. The next year, a convoy of wagons accompanying Louis II's Bohemian chancellor was robbed by a crowd in front of the royal palace. Only two of the 22 wagons were recovered.[43]

We do, occasionally, have glimpses of the city's ordinary womenfolk. The Buda *Stadtrecht* thus recorded the abuses that the market women were inclined to level at one another, and of the "stone of shame" (*Bagstein*) that female offenders were expected to drag on their backs in a public act of contrition.[44] It also noted the city's prostitutes, the distinctive yellow scarf they were obliged to wear, and enjoined their protection. "Poor, sad and fallen",

---

39   *Bp. tört.*, ii, p. 413.
40   Kubinyi, *Budapest*, p. 134.
41   See below the chapter by Martyn Rady.
42   Lipót Óváry, *A Magyar Tudományos Akadémia történelmi bizottságának oklevélmásolatai. Első füzet. A Mohácsi vész előtti okiratok kivonatai* [Copies of Documents of the Historical Committee of the Hungarian Academy of Sciences. First volume. Extracts of Documents from before the Mohács Disaster] (Budapest: MTA, 1890), p. 192.
43   Kubinyi, *Budapest*, pp. 150–153; Kubinyi, "A magyarországi zsidóság," pp. 24–25.
44   OSt, p. 115. (cap. 155) On this penalty more generally, see Eberhard v. Künssberg, *Über die Strafe des Steintragens* (Breslau: Marcus, 1907), pp. 15–17.

INTRODUCTION

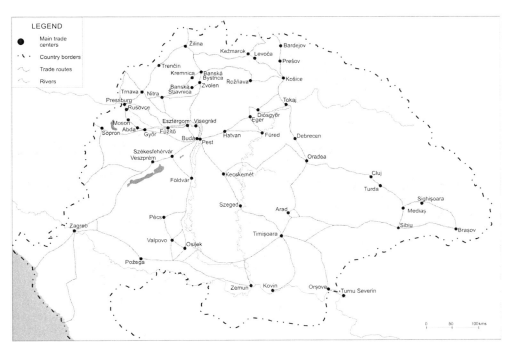

FIGURE 0.1 *The medieval kingdom of Hungary with the main trade routes and towns*

as the *Stadtrecht*'s author described them, they nonetheless lived under the city's protection – unlike their counterparts several centuries later, who might expect punishment.[45] For the most part, however, we know only of women belonging to the better-off sections of society, in particular those widows who on account of the city's customs of inheritance were entitled to a portion of their husbands' estate, on equal terms with their children. Widows such as these were not only a sought-after commodity, but they often also retained upon re-marriage their first husband's name, as a sign of their independent means.[46]

---

45 OSt, pp. 124–125, 155–166 (cap. 186 and 289). The colour of prostitutes' scarfs alternated in Hungary between yellow, red and black. We know of brothels in fifteenth-century Pressburg, Prešov and Levoča, but not in Buda. See Gyula Magyary-Kossa, *Magyar orvosi emlékek. Értekezések a magyar orvostörténelem köréből*, 4 vols [Hungarian Medical Records: Studies on Hungarian Medical History] (Budapest: Orvosi Könyvkiadó, 1929–1940), i, pp. 192, 209–210, 219, 222 and ii, p. 441.

46 Kubinyi, *Budapest*, pp. 135–138.

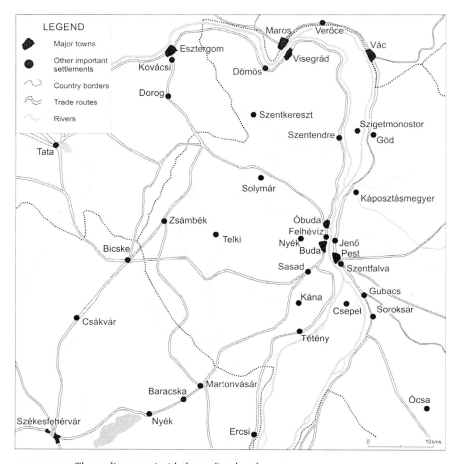

FIGURE 0.2 *The* medium regni *with the medieval settlements*

Civitas et ecclesia

The ecclesiastical organization of medieval Buda both reflected and contributed to social and ethnic tensions within the city.[47] The area of the Buda settlement had three parishes, with a fourth located to the south at St Gellért's (St Gerard's) Hill which served the Kreinfeld (Kelenföld) community. Of the three, the parish church of Our Lady (now the thoroughly 'Victorianized' Coronation Church or Matthias Church) claimed superiority as a royal foundation. It was also the parish church of Buda's Germans, who had by virtue of the city's

---

47 For the churches and religious organization of Buda, see the chapters below by András Végh and Beatrix Romhányi.

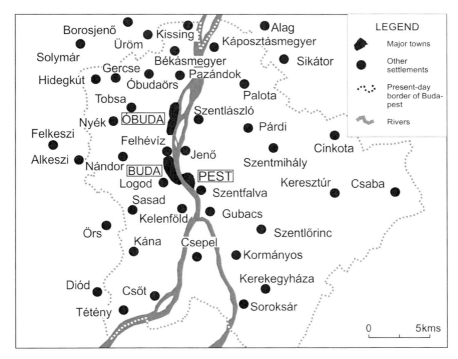

FIGURE 0.3 *Medieval settlements in the territory of present-day Budapest*

1244 charter the right to elect the church's priest. The church of Mary Magdalene, which lay about 400 metres to the north, acted as the parish church of Buda's Hungarians. The Schedel woodcut (Fig. 0.4) of 1493 shows it as occupying a larger territory and skyline than the German church. St Peter's Church in the suburbs also served a mainly Hungarian congregation. Conflicts over parish boundaries mirrored the competition between the city's German and Hungarian communities. In the fifteenth century Germans tended to cluster in the middle and southern parts of the city; Hungarians in the north, in the vicinity of the Magdalene Church.[48]

The majority of the city's religious houses belonged in respect of their membership to either nobles or members of the city's elite, including those belonging to the Beguines.[49] The Franciscan house, situated at the southern end of the Castle Hill, was little different, except that its Observant friars tended towards the sort of simpler religiosity that was bound to bring them into conflict

48 Végh, "Buda: The Multi-Ethnic Capital," pp. 97–98.
49 For the religious life of Buda, see the chapters below by Beatrix Romhányi and Gábor Klaniczay.

FIGURE 0.4 *The view of Buda in the Schedel Chronicle, printed in 1493*

with the church authorities. The sermons of the two Franciscans, Osvald of Lasko and Pelbart of Temesvár (Timişoara), contained elements inimical to the established order. Both condemned the luxury of the royal court, denounced the emptiness of ritual without faith, and promoted "a new terrestrial hierarchy, founded on merit and not on birth."[50] Neither was interested, however, in converting their teaching into an ideology of political revolution and social rebirth. Their less sophisticated followers, however, gave revolutionary meaning to their words. The contribution to the peasants' revolt of 1514 of "pretend, iniquitous and false preachers" with links to the Franciscan Observants, is attested to in correspondence, in contemporary accounts (as for instance in Taurinus's *Stauromachia*), in subsequent legislation and, indeed, in the topography of the revolt.[51] Following the suppression of the revolt, there was an investigation of the Observants' role in the conversion of what had originally been a crusade

50 Marie-Madeleine de Cevins, "The Influence of Franciscan Friars on Popular Piety in the Kingdom of Hungary at the End of the Fifteenth Century," in *Communities of Devotion: Religious Orders and Society in East Central Europe, 1450–1800* (Catholic Christendom, 1300–1700), eds Maria Crăciun and Elaine Fulton (Farnham and Burlington, VT: Ashgate, 2011), pp. 71–90, here p. 85. See also Zoltan J. Kosztolnyik, "Pelbartus of Temesvár: a Franciscan Preacher and Writer of the Late Middle Ages in Hungary," *Vivarium*, 5 (1967), pp. 100–110; idem, "Some Hungarian Theologians in the Late Renaissance," *Church History* 57 (1988), pp. 5–18, here pp. 8–18.

51 Jenő Szűcs, "A ferences observancia és a 1514. évi parasztháború. Egy kódex tanulsága," [The Franciscan Observants and the 1514 Peasants' War: an instructive codex] *Levéltári Közlemények* 43, no 2 (1972), pp. 213–263, here pp. 245–248. See further: Norman Housley,

against the Turks into an armed insurrection against the nobility and social hierarchy. The full extent of the friars' responsibility for the mayhem of 1514 remains uncertain, although it seems likely that their preaching provided one of the 'building blocks' on which a rudimentary ideology of social and political revolution was founded.[52]

Within Buda, the preaching orders were also responsible for the few institutions of higher education. Hungary was unusual in Central Europe in not having a durable university. Louis I founded a university at Pécs in 1367; Sigismund one at Óbuda in 1395, and again in 1410, the previous one having decayed; and Matthias the Academia Istropolitana in Pressburg in 1467. None of these lasted for more than a few years. Both the Franciscans and Dominicans established *studia generalia* in Buda during the fifteenth century (if not before), of which the Dominican school was the more eminent. Although modeled on Bologna, its curriculum was modest, being confined to theology and philosophy. Its teaching was, moreover, old fashioned, being mostly concerned with defending scholasticism against the new humanist scholarship. It is in this respect telling that one of the principal works of the *studium*'s rector, the Dominican Petrus Niger, was entitled 'The Shield of the Thomists' (*Clypeus thomistarum*, Venice, 1481). Niger was a leading scholar of Hebrew but his denunciation of Jewish belief and the Talmud was often banal and unsophisticated.[53] Although we know of several distinguished teachers with connections to the *studium*, it was no match for Cracow, Vienna, Prague and the Italian universities. The absence of a university in Buda, and in particular of a law faculty, had major consequences for the kingdom's legal and institutional development, for it served to isolate Hungary's courts from the scholarly Roman law reception. Partly as a consequence, Hungary remained a largely customary law jurisdiction until the modern period, uninfluenced by the new Romanized jurisprudence.[54]

Buda was, however, open to the new ideas of the Protestant faith. One conduit for the Reformation was the royal court, where Mary of Hungary (the Habsburg wife of Louis II) adopted a tolerant and open approach to the

---

"Crusading as Social Revolt: The Hungarian Peasant Uprising of 1514," *Journal of Ecclesiastical History* 49, no 1 (1998), pp. 1–28, here pp. 10–12.

52 Szűcs, "A ferences obszervancia," p. 216.
53 Maria Diemling, "Petrus Nigri (Peter Schwarz): Fifteenth-Century Polemicist, Preacher and Hebraist," in *Dominikaner und Juden – Dominicans and Jews*, eds Elias H. Füllenbach OP and Gianfranco Miletto (Berlin: De Gruyter, 2015), pp. 299–317, here p. 305.
54 On Roman law and Hungary in the Early Modern Period, see Martyn Rady, *Customary Law in Hungary: Courts, Texts and the Tripartitum* (Oxford: Oxford University Press, 2015), pp. 152–163.

new religion. It was at her bidding that Thomas Stoltzer, *magister capellae* in the royal court, set several of Luther's translations of the Psalms to music.[55] Mary's evident interest in the new religion was supported by George, margrave of Brandenburg-Ansbach, who acted as a tutor to her teenage husband. For a time, one of Mary's court chaplains may have been Conrad Cordatus, who otherwise served as a priest in the Church of Our Lady and was known by the first Hungarian reformers as 'our Luther'.[56] Following an outspoken sermon in which he denounced the pope and cardinals, Cordatus was replaced by Johann Henckel, who was an advocate of Erasmian humanism but who would in the 1530s embrace Protestantism.[57] A further channel of communication was the German language itself which rendered Buda open to the pamphlet literature of Wittenberg and to the proselytizing of reformers. Of these the most outstanding was Simon Grynaeus, originally from Swabia, who was rector of a church school in Buda until forced to flee the city in 1523. He subsequently joined Oecolampadius in bringing Basle over to the Reformation.[58] It may well be that the first wave of converts to Protestantism consisted of clergy and teachers.[59] Nevertheless, the appeal of the new faith soon ran deeper. Early in 1522 Paul Speratus was invited by citizens of Buda to serve as a priest, although his reputation was such that it proved impossible for him to remain there.[60] We also know that the income from the sale of plenary indulgences in the Jubilee of 1524–1525 fell considerably short of expectation, yielding only a few hundred florins from Buda. As the papal envoy to Hungary reported, "in place of money we found scurrilous broadsheets, mocking Your Holiness and us, one of which said, 'Take your Holy Year to Rome, and leave us our money.'"[61] After 1526, the new faith spread rapidly, being now openly preached within the

---

55 See the chapter below by Orsolya Réthelyi. For court politics during the reign of Louis II, see the chapter below by Antonin Kalous.

56 David P. Daniel, "Publishing the Reformation in Habsburg Hungary," in *Books have their own Destiny: Essays in Honor of Robert V. Schnucker*, 2 vols, eds Robin B. Barnes *et al.* (Kirksville, MO: Thomas Jefferson University Press, 1998), i, pp. 47–60, here p. 48.

57 R.R. Betts, "Poland, Bohemia and Hungary," in *The New Cambridge Modern History: Volume 2. The Reformation, 1520–1559*, ed. G.R. Elton (Cambridge: Cambridge University Press, 1990), pp. 198–222, here p. 206; Zoltán Csepregi, "Court Priests in the Entourage of Queen Mary of Hungary." in *Mary of Hungary*, pp. 49–61, here p. 53.

58 Peter G. Bietenholz, "Grynaeus, Simon," in *Contemporaries of Erasmus: A Biographical Register of the Renaissance and Reformation*, 3 vols, eds Beietenholz and Thomas B. Deutscher (Toronto: University of Toronto, 2003), ii, pp. 142–146.

59 Kubinyi, *Budapest*, p. 163.

60 Csepregi, "Court Priests in the Entourage of Queen Mary," p. 51.

61 Kubinyi, *Budapest*, p. 164.

city. The last judge of Buda before the Ottoman occupation of 1541, Nicholas Turkovith, was a Lutheran.[62]

Research Traditions and Perspectives

The collection and study of sources on medieval Buda, Pest and Óbuda has a long tradition, as indeed has the investigation of Buda's physical remains.[63] The earliest scholarship grew out of source publishing and archaeological research. In the 1830s, József Podhraczky transcribed many of the most important documents concerning the medieval history of Buda and Pest, some of which he included in his study on the early history of the two settlements (the majority remained, however, in manuscript).[64] In the next decade, Michnay and Lichner published the earliest edition of the *Ofner Stadtrecht* in the expectation that it might contribute to the kingdom's developing commercial law.[65] The unification of Buda, Pest and Óbuda in 1873 gave fresh impulse to publish a comprehensive synthesis on the history of Budapest.[66] Ferenc Salamon (1825–1892), professor of history at Budapest University, accepted the invitation to write the work. In his three-volume work, Salamon described the history of Budapest from antiquity to the close of the Middle Ages.[67] The first regular publication of scholarly essays on the history of Budapest focusing mainly on archaeological and architectural research with the title *Budapest Régiségei* (Antiquities of Budapest) was started in 1889.[68]

In 1911 a systematic and comprehensive new program was initiated by Dezső Csánki (1857–1933) to survey and edit the surviving medieval sources on the

---

62 Kubinyi, *Budapest*, p. 223.
63 János Gyalmos, "Bevezetés. Budapest története megírásának előzményei," [Introduction: Prelude to writing a history of Budapest] in *Bp. tört.*, i, pp. 9–15.
64 Jozsef Podhraczky, *Buda és Pest szabad királyi városoknak volt régi állapotjokról* [Previous stages in the history of the free cities of Buda and Pest] (Pest: Beimel, 1833). See also below, the chapter by István Kenyeres.
65 Endre Michnay and Pál Lichner, *Ofner Stadtrecht von MCCXLIV–MCCCCXXI* (Buda: Wigand, 1845).
66 After the unification of Budapest in 1873, most scholarly publications cover not only the history of medieval Buda, but usually the medieval territory of the modern Budapest, including Pest and Óbuda.
67 Ferencz Salamon, *Buda–Pest története*, 3 vols [The history of Budapest] (Budapest: Kocsi S. Nyomda – Athenaeum Nyomda, 1878–1885).
68 On-line access as of August 2015: http://library.hungaricana.hu/hu/collection/muze_orsz_bptm_budapest_regisegei.

history of the capital city of Hungary. The First World War and its consequences hindered the progress of the work, and Csánki's labours, which had been supplemented by Albert Gárdonyi, remained for the most part unpublished. The 250th anniversary in 1936 of the re-conquest of Buda from the Ottomans also increased the interest in the early history of Hungary's capital. In 1932 a new publication series entitled *Tanulmányok Budapest Múltjából* (Studies on Budapest's past) was launched on the initiative of the Budapest City Archives to make available the results of recent work to a wider scholarly audience.[69] Both this series and *Budapest Régiségei* are currently edited by the Budapest History Museum.

The publication of the charters relevant to the history of Budapest by Albert Gárdonyi in 1936 covered the years 1148–1301.[70] A later addition to this publication was the work of Bernát L. Kumorovitz (1900–1992), who used the previous collections of Csánki and Gárdonyi when publishing three volumes covering the period 1382–1439.[71] In 1942 and 1944 the first volumes of the new synthesis of the history of Budapest were published, but only the volumes covering the ancient period and the Ottoman period were made available; the volume on the Middle Ages has never been printed.[72]

Soon after the end of the Second World War the territory of Budapest was significantly increased by the incorporation in 1950 of twenty-three nearby settlements into Budapest. Thereafter most of the studies on the history of Budapest covered not only the development of Buda and Pest, but typically the territory of the so-called Greater Budapest.

In the decades after the Second World War the institutional background of the study of the history of Budapest was consolidated, being based on three main scholarly institutions. The Budapesti Történeti Múzeum (Budapest Historical Museum) embraced the Castle Museum on the site of the medieval royal residence and the Aquincum Museum, which presented the Roman heritage of Budapest.[73] The series *Monumenta Historica Budapestinensia* of

---

69 On-line access as of August 2015: http://library.hungaricana.hu/hu/collection/muze_orsz_bptm_tanulmanyok_budapest_multjabol/.

70 BTOE, i.

71 BTOE, iii/1–2.

72 Ferenc Tompa, András Alföldi and Lajos Nagy, *Budapest története az ókorban*, i/1 [History of Budapest in the Antiquity] (Budapest: Egyetemi Nyomda, 1942); András Alföldi, Lajos Nagy and Gyula László, *Budapest története az ókorban*, i/2 [History of Budapest in Antiquity] (Budapest: Egyetemi Nyomda, 1942); Lajos Fekete, *Budapest a törökkorban* [History of Budapest in the Ottoman Period] (Budapest: Egyetemi Nyomda, 1944).

73 See the article of Zoltán Bencze in the present volume.

the Budapest History Museum regularly publishes monographs and collective works on the history of the city. The most important surviving textual source of medieval Buda, the law code (*Ofner Stadtrecht*) was published by the eminent German philologist Károly Mollay in this series in 1959.[74]

The Budapest Főváros Levéltára (Budapest City Archives) collects the archival material on the history of Budapest, and the Budapest Gyűjtemény (Budapest Collection) of the Fővárosi Szabó Ervin Könyvtár (Szabó Ervin Metropolitan Library) is a special library collection on the local history of Budapest. The Budapest Collection established in 1913 edits various bibliographies on the history of Budapest.[75]

A new and ambitious scholarly enterprise, a comprehensive five-volume history of Budapest was initiated in the early 1950s, but the first volumes of the series were only published in 1972. Still today this is the most essential and detailed overview of the history of Budapest in Hungarian, not only because of the extent of this work, but also because of the excellence of its authors. The history of the Budapest in the Árpádian period was written by György Györffy (1917–2000) and the later period,[76] up to the Ottoman conquest of the city, by András Kubinyi (1929–2007).[77] László Gerevich (1911–1997) summarized in two chapters the most important art historical features of Buda in the Middle Ages.[78]

The publication of the earliest volumes in the new series took place against the background of the so-called "Buda debate", a protracted discussion from the 1960s to the early 1980s on the site and dating of the early royal residence in Buda that involved practically all historians and archaeologists working on Buda (László Gerevich, László Zolnay, Erik Fügedi, András Kubinyi, and others).[79] The questions whether the Castle Hill was inhabited before the Mongol invasion of 1241/42 and whether its southern tip already housed a royal

---

74   OSt.
75   *Budapest történetének bibliográfiája*, 7 vols [Bibliography of the History of Budapest], ed. László Berza (Budapest: Fővárosi Szabó Ervin Könyvtár, 1963–1974).
76   Györffy, *Budapest*.
77   Kubinyi, *Budapest*.
78   László Gerevich, "Budapest művészete az Árpád-korban," [The art of Budapest in the Árpádian period] in *Bp. tört.*, i, pp. 351–401; idem, "Budapest művészete a későbbi középkorban a mohácsi vészig," [The art of Budapest in the Later Middle Ages until the Battle of Mohács] in *Bp. tört.*, ii, pp. 241–334. Gerevich's chapters on the art history of Buda have been translated and edited as an English language book: László Gerevich, *The Art of Buda and Pest in the Middle Ages* (Budapest: Akadémiai, 1971).
79   For the palace, see the chapters below by Károly Magyar and Szilárd Papp.

residence in the thirteenth century generated a significant amount of historical, topographical, and morphological research.[80]

In the last decades, András Kubinyi was the leading expert of the medieval history of Buda, first as a head of the Medieval Department of the Budapest History Museum, later as a professor of medieval archaeology at the Eötvös Loránd University, Budapest.[81] With a deep knowledge both of written and archaeological sources and an outstanding overview of the comparative study of European urban history, he published dozens of scholarly articles on various aspects of urbanization of medieval Hungary and also on the history of Buda.[82]

The significance of the Budapest History Museum in Kubinyi's career in particular and in research on medieval Buda, Pest and Óbuda in general is fully understandable if one keeps in mind the large-scale destruction of the built fabric of the Hungarian capital over the centuries. The Castle Hill has been exposed to dozens of sieges since Buda's foundation, the last and perhaps most destructive one being the fighting in the winter of 1944–45. Therefore the task of recovering and presenting the material remains of the once glorious royal palace and the city beside it rest mostly with the archaeologists of this institution, the main expert authority for conducting excavations in the Hungarian capital. The fact that since 1987 Buda Castle and the Danube embankment area below it has been a UNESCO World Heritage Site increases their responsibility, but also the interest of scholars and visitors alike.

The amount of recent literature on the medieval history of Buda is too numerous to be overviewed here, but in an English language volume, the non-Hungarian literature should not be overlooked. Martyn Rady's volume concentrating on the administrative and legal aspects of Buda's history belongs to the very few English works on the topic.[83] The exhibition on the medieval history

---

80 The discussion is summarized in András Kubinyi, "Burgstadt, Vorburgstadt und Stadtburg (Zur Morphologie des mittelalterlichen Buda)," *Acta Archaeologica Academiae Scientiarum Hungaricae* 33 (1981), pp. 161–178.

81 For a short biography and full publication list see: Miklós Szabó and József Laszlovszky, "András Kubinyi (1929–2007)," *Acta Archaeologica Academiae Scientiarum Hungaricae* 60 (2009), pp. 535–550. See also: Katalin Szende, "Kubinyi András, a várostörténész," [András Kubinyi as urban historian] *Urbs. Magyar Várostörténeti Évkönyv* 3 (2008), pp. 15–38.

82 See his collected studies on the history of Budapest: Kubinyi, *Tanulmányok*. Some works of Kubinyi are available in German as well: Kubinyi, *Anfänge Ofens*; idem, *König und Volk im spätmittelalterlichen Ungarn: Städteentwicklung, Alltagsleben und Regierung im mittelalterlichen Königreich Ungarn* (Herne: Tibor Schäfer, 1998).

83 Rady, *Buda*.

of Buda in Braunschweig in 1991 was followed by the publication of a German-language catalogue and volume of scholarly essays.[84]

In recent years exhibition catalogues connected to rulers who had their seat in Buda (Sigismund, Matthias Corvinus, Mary of Hungary) have contributed through their German, French and English editions to a larger, international appreciation of medieval Buda's history, and especially of the royal palace.[85] Exhibitions of archaeological finds from the entire area of modern Budapest have drawn attention to what is under the city and only now coming to light as a result of intensive new construction.[86] The most detailed bilingual (Hungarian/English) presentation of Buda's topography, authored by András Végh, archaeologist at the Budapest History Museum, appeared in the series *Hungarian Atlas of Historic Towns* just as editorial work on the present volume was completed.[87] This series is planned to be continued and to include the other medieval predecessors of Budapest: Óbuda and Pest.

The present work builds on these achievements and aims to bring together the latest scholarship.[88] It also seeks to provide through its critical apparatus a guide to the literature, in both Hungarian and western languages, so that it may act in the manner of a handbook and work of reference. Compared to the medieval cities of Western Europe, those of Central Europe are less familiar to historians and they rarely feature in more general works on the growth and development of urban society and institutions in the Middle Ages. It is the purpose of this book to begin to redress this imbalance.

B.N. – M.R. – K.Sz. – A.V.

---

84   *Budapest im Mittelalter.*
85   See the chapter by Zoltán Bencze in the present volume.
86   *Kincsek a város alatt/Treasures under the City*, ed. Paula Zsidi (Budapest: BTM, 2004).
87   See also the magisterial work of András Végh on the topography of medieval Buda: Végh, *Buda.*
88   The results of a major research project directed by Elek Benkő on the settlements of the *medium regni* were published in a volume of collected essays that only became available after the completion of the manuscript of this volume. Their individual contributions are as a result not referred to in the chapters of the present work. See *In medio regni Hungariae. Régészeti, művészettörténeti és történeti kutatások "az ország közepén"* [Archaeological, art historical and historical research in the middle of the kingdom], eds Elek Benkő and Krisztina Orosz (Budapest: MTA Bölcsészettudományi Kutatóközpont, 2015). In the meantime another important volume on the formation of Buda as the capital of Hungary was published by Enikő Spekner that is also not referred to in the individual chapters: *Hogyan lett Buda a középkori Magyarország fővárosa? A budai királyi székhely története a 12. század végétől a 14. század közepéig* [How did Buda become the capital of medieval Hungary? The history of the Buda seat from the end of the 12th to the mid-14th century] (Monumenta Historica Budapestinensia, 17) (Budapest: BTM, 2015).

PART 1

Buda: History, Sources, Historiography

∴

CHAPTER 1

The Budapest History Museum and the Rediscovery of Medieval Buda

Zoltán Bencze

Why Archaeology?

Buda shares the sad fate of practically all medieval towns and cities in the central part of present-day Hungary: their buildings and archives suffered severe losses during the period of Ottoman occupation starting in the mid-sixteenth century, and the damage done to material assets and human lives in the battles accompanying the expulsion of the Ottomans in the late seventeenth century was often even greater. The scarcity of written evidence and the small number of buildings that still stand put archaeology in a key position when it comes to (re)constructing urban life in the medieval capital of Hungary, from the mightiest city walls to the tiniest bone needles used in the households of the Buda burghers.

However, Buda is also a bustling modern capital where archaeological research cannot as a rule set its own independent research agenda, but is instead constrained by the needs of modern life. This article follows the history of archaeological research into the remains of medieval Buda from its tentative beginnings, almost a century ago, through the large-scale reconstruction works of the city after the Second World War which revolutionized the quantity and quality of the available evidence, to the striking discoveries and painful compromises of the last few decades. The material thus brought to light forms the basis of many articles in this volume, and will continue to offer new insights into the history of medieval Buda as it is evaluated in the future. All this work would not have been possible without the firm institutional background provided by the Budapest History Museum, which (under varying names) has been the bulwark of research into the medieval history and archaeology of the Hungarian capital since 1885. This municipal museum is home to one of the most comprehensive departments of medieval urban archaeology in Central Europe. Therefore this presentation begins with a sketch of the development and work of this institution over time, followed by the enumeration of the main excavation projects concerning medieval Buda, and finally some thoughts on the evaluation of the material.[1]

Translated by Kyra Lyublyanovics.

1 Archaeological research into the remains of medieval Pest and Óbuda merits equally detailed overviews but such would unfortunately exceed the limits of the present article. Some

The Brief History of the Municipal Museum of Budapest and Its Medieval Department

On 25 November, 1802, Count Ferenc Széchényi decided to donate his antiquarian collection to the Hungarian nation. This material provided the basis for the present-day Hungarian National Museum and the National Széchényi Library. Later, in the second half of the nineteenth century, a number of city museums were founded.[2] Budapest came into existence with the union of Pest, Buda and Óbuda in 1873. The City Council declared on 13 November, 1885 that there was a need for a Museum of the Capital,[3] and so it accordingly decided to establish a Museum of City History on 20 October, 1887.[4] The task was assigned to Bálint Kuzsinszky, who also conducted the excavations at Aquincum from 1888 onwards. The Aquincum Museum was completed by 1894 among the ruins of the former town of Aquincum, and enlarged between then and 1896.[5] On 15 August, 1898, Kuzsinszky put forward the proposal to organize a Museum of the Capital and library.[6] The Museum finally opened in 1907 on Stefánia Road in the City Park (Városliget); its collection was later used as the basis of the Department of City History.[7] Miksa Schmidt, the owner of a factory that produced furniture, bequeathed the Kiscelli Castle, as well as the building that formed

---

of the literature quoted in the article gives insight into research on these parts of present-day Budapest.

2   *Múzsák kertje. A magyar múzeumok születése* [The garden of muses. The birth of museums in Hungary] (Budapest: Pulszky Társaság – Magyar Múzeumi Egyesület, 2002). The map on page 10 shows their locations.

3   The three major departments of the Budapest History Museum had already come into existence before the Second World War. These are the Medieval Department of the Castle Museum, located in the royal palace, the Ancient and Migration Period Department at Aquincum, and the Department of Modern Urban History and Metropolitan Gallery at the Kiscelli Museum. The formerly independent Budapest Gallery was recently attached to the Museum.

4   Andorné Lenkei, "A Budapesti Történeti Múzeum kialakulása," [The formation of the Budapest History Museum] *Tanulmányok Budapest Múltjából* 12 (1957), pp. 495–519, here p. 507.

5   Katalin K. Végh, *A Budapesti Történeti Múzeum az alapítástól az ezredfordulóig* [The history of the Budapest History Museum from its foundation to 2000] (Monumenta Historica Budapestinensia, 11) (Budapest: BTM, 2003), pp. 20–21.

6   Lenkei, "A Budapesti," pp. 514–515; K. Végh, *A Budapesti Történeti Múzeum*, pp. 24–26.

7   Ervin Seenger, "Az Újkori osztály – Kiscelli Múzeum története," [The history of the Modern Department – the Kiscelli Museum] *Tanulmányok Budapest Múltjából* 16 (1964), pp. 31–41, here pp. 31–33.

the Trinitarian abbey and church, to the Museum in 1935. Later the Museum's early modern collection and art gallery were housed here.[8]

Collecting medieval finds started in the period when these institutions were set up. Stone carvings recovered from the church of the Dominican friary[9] on the occasion of repairing a segment of wall in the Fishermen's Bastion were stored in the northern corner tower of the Bastion. The establishment here of a local museum had already been proposed in 1905, and in 1912 financial resources were secured;[10] however, it took another 20 years to actual implementation. Art historian Henrik Horváth founded the Medieval Lapidarium in 1932. The exhibition, put on display in the ground floor and the upper ambulatory of the northern corner tower of the Fishermen's Bastion, featured 367 stone-carvings (Figs. 1.1 and 1.2).[11] The lion's share of this material came from the medieval royal palace, the Church of Our Lady, and the church of the Dominican friary. Even though the Medieval Lapidarium was not yet an independent unit, its establishment may be seen as marking the birth of the Medieval Department of the Museum; nevertheless, the latter was officially founded only 10 years later. Henrik Horváth, a student of Bálint Kuzsinszky, worked as museum director between 1935 and 1941, and continued managing the Medieval Lapidarium as well. In 1936, the name Museum of the Capital was changed to Historical Museum of the Capital (*Székesfővárosi Történeti Múzeum*), while the Aquincum Museum, the Medieval Lapidarium, the Art Gallery of the Capital and the Early Modern Collection in the City Park (*Városliget*) became sub-divisions of it.[12] The Institute of Archaeology and Excavation was founded in the Károlyi Palace in the same year, under the leadership of Lajos Nagy, as a separate department of the Museum; it was the predecessor of the Department of Prehistory and the History of the Migration period.[13]

After the death of Henrik Horváth in 1941, Lajos Nagy succeeded as director. He appointed László Gerevich to supervise the Medieval Lapidarium, and also founded a Department of Medieval Excavations within the Institute

---

8   Seenger, "Az Újkori osztály," pp. 35–36; K. Végh, *A Budapesti Történeti Múzeum*, pp. 51–53.
9   János Szendrei, "A budavári domonkos templom kiásatása," [The archaeological excavation of the Dominican church at the Buda Castle] *Archaeologiai Értesítő* [NS] 22 (1902), pp. 395–400.
10 K. Végh, *A Budapesti Történeti Múzeum*, p. 38.
11 Henrik Horváth, *A Székesfővárosi Múzeum középkori lapidáriumának leíró lajstroma* [Catalogue of the medieval lapidary of the Capital Museum] (Budapest: [n. p.], 1932).
12 K. Végh, *A Budapesti Történeti Múzeum*, p. 51.
13 Tibor Nagy, "Az Ős- és Ókortörténeti Osztály története. Az Ásatási és Régészeti Intézet," [History of the Prehistoric and Ancient Department. The Institute of Excavation and Archaeology] *Tanulmányok Budapest Múltjából* 16 (1964), pp. 19–21.

FIGURE 1.1   *The Lapidarium in the building of the Fishermen's Bastion*
BTM, PHOTO COLLECTION

of Archaeology, for which Gerevich was chosen as director. The foundation charter of the Medieval Department was issued by the mayor of Budapest on 28 January, 1942.[14]

---

14   Mayoral resolution, No 220794/1942-XI.

FIGURE 1.2 *The Lapidarium in the building of the Fishermen's Bastion*
BTM, PHOTO COLLECTION

The Fishermen's Bastion was damaged in the Second World War. After its restoration in 1948, the exhibition in the Medieval Lapidarium was re-opened. For a short period of time this was called the Museum of Cultural History, and later it was re-named the Castle Museum.[15] It was of pivotal importance that the mayor, Zoltán Vas, proposed the restoration of the medieval town hall (2 Szentháromság Street in present-day Budapest) on 31 August, 1945, and ordered the Medieval Museum of the Capital to be housed in this building.[16] From 1 April, 1950, László Gerevich became director of the institute, which since 1951 has been called the Budapest History Museum.[17] In 1952, an exhibition focusing on the castle of Buda was organized at this new location, to which new finds were added in 1959, and the exhibition was renamed "Buda

15 Erzsébet Lócsy Erzsébet and András Kubinyi, "A Középkori osztály – Vármúzeum – története," [The history of the Medieval Department – Castle Museum] *Tanulmányok Budapest Múltjából* 16 (1964), pp. 22–30, here p. 26.
16 Mayoral resolution, No 223129/1945-XI, Lócsy and Kubinyi, "A Középkori osztály," p. 28.
17 For an overview of the collections of the Museum, see *The Budapest History Museum*, eds Géza Buzinkay and Péter Havassy (Budapest: Corvina, 1995). From that time on, the head of the Museum held the title of director-general: K. Végh, *A Budapesti Történeti Múzeum*, p. 90.

in the Middle Ages".[18] László Gerevich acted as director of the Budapest History Museum until January 1961, and during these years he also supervised the Medieval Department. The Medieval Department was led by Bernát L. Kumorovitz in 1961–1969, by András Kubinyi in 1969–1978, and by Emese Nagy in 1978–1987.[19]

The Medieval Department moved again in 1967, along with other departments and the director's office, to block E of the early modern palace building erected above the remains of the medieval royal palace, where it operates today. In April of the following year, the exhibition entitled "The medieval royal palace in the Buda Castle" opened in the cellar halls, to be followed by an exhibition in October 1968 that focused on the city's history, entitled "1000 Years of the Capital".[20] In December 1979 finds from the Roman times to 1945 were presented within the framework of an exhibition called "Two Millennia of Budapest".[21] The Museum also organized a large-scale display of medieval findings in the Braunschweigisches Landesmuseum, Braunschweig, in spring 1991.[22] The idea behind this exhibition in Germany served subsequently as the basis for a new city historical exhibition called "Budapest in the Middle Ages" which opened in October 1993, on the Budapest Museum's ground floor.[23] The first part of a new permanent exhibition on city history, entitled "Light and Shadow – A 1000 Years' History of Budapest", opened in autumn 2011. This exhibition provides an overview of life in the area of the present-day capital from the period of the Hungarian Conquest to 1990. Thematic showcases were added in November 2012, after which it is now considered complete.[24]

Beside the permanent exhibitions some temporary ones should also be mentioned, to which the Medieval Department contributed significantly. The

18 Lócsy and Kubinyi, "A Középkori osztály," p. 28.
19 Between 1988 and 1990 the head of the department was István Feld, and from 1991 to the present day the author of the present article.
20 After sketching the Migration Period the exhibition presented the history of the capital from the age of the Hungarian Conquest to 1945. See K. Végh, *A Budapesti Történeti Múzeum*, p. 122.
21 K. Végh, *A Budapesti Történeti Múzeum*, p. 142.
22 *Budapest im Mittelalter*.
23 The exhibition in a reduced form was relocated to the stairway of the Budapest History Museum in 1998. The reduced version still covers the whole exhibition floor, occupying two thirds of the ground floor. The curator was István Feld.
24 The curator of the medieval exhibition was András Végh and of the modern part, Roland Perényi.

exhibition "King Sigismund and His Time in Art History" was organized in 1987, on the 600th anniversary of Sigismund's accession to the throne.[25] "Centuries of the royal palace in the Buda Castle" opened in 2000,[26] and the material it exhibited was also put on display in Paris in 2001.[27] In 2002–2003 the collection "Layers of the Past: The history of the Szent György Square" was presented to the public.[28] "Mary of Hungary – The Queen and her Court, 1521–1531" was staged in 2005, and in the next year the exhibition went on tour to the National Gallery of Slovakia in Bratislava.[29] The exhibition "Matthias Corvinus the King" was hosted in 2008 as a celebration of the 550th anniversary of his ascent to the throne.[30]

In 1976, the principal fragments of the previously unearthed Gothic statues were displayed in the museum's Gothic hall and partly also in the chapel. In 1992 these were all displayed together on the museum's ground floor.[31] Significant finds brought to light by the excavations at Szent György Square were added to this collection in 2007,[32] such as the statues of the Church of St Sigismund, and finds recovered from well No 8 in the Teleki Palace, including a silk tapestry embellished with the coat of arms of the Hungarian Angevin dynasty.[33]

---

25 *Művészet Zsigmond király korában 1387–1437*, 2 vols [Art in the age of Sigismund, 1387 to 1437], eds László Beke, Ernő Marosi and Tünde Wehli (Budapest: MTA Művészettörténeti Kutató Csoport, 1987). The exhibition was organized jointly by the Budapest History Museum (curators: Emese Nagy, Júlia Altmann and Katalin Irásné Melis) and the Institute of Art History of the Hungarian National Academy (Ernő Marosi and Tünde Wehli).

26 *Centuries of the Royal Castle in Buda*, ed. Katalin Földi-Dózsa (Budapest: Budapest History Museum, 2000). The curator of the exhibition was Katalin F. Dózsa.

27 *Un château pour un royaume : histoire du château de Budapest : Musée Carnavalet, Histoire de Paris, 15 juin–16 septembre 2001* (Paris: Paris Musées, 2001).

28 The curator of the exhibition that presented the results of the excavations carried out at Szent György Square was Zoltán Bencze. No traditional exhibition catalogue was published, but most of the 31st volume of *Tanulmányok Budapest Múltjából* (pp. 7–268) is devoted to this exhibition.

29 *Mary of Hungary*. The curator of the exhibition was Orsolya Réthelyi, while Zuzana Ludiková contributed to the staging of the exhibition at Bratislava.

30 *Matthias Corvinus the King*. The curators of the exhibition were Péter Farbaky, Enikő Spekner and András Végh.

31 *Gothic Sculptures from the Royal Palace of Buda. Exhibition Catalog*, eds András Végh, Károly Magyar and Ernő Marosi (Budapest: Budapest History Museum, 1992).

32 On the excavations carried out here, see the overview in the later part of this study.

33 Dorotya B. Nyékhelyi, "Découverte d' un puits médiéval place Saint-Georges," in *Un château*, p. 73 and 101 (cat. no 8–9); eadem, Dorottya B. Nyékhelyi, *Középkori kútlelet a*

The Beginnings of Archaeological Research and the First Excavations at Medieval Sites

As with other countries in Europe, Hungary showed an interest in Roman history long before actual museums were established. A winegrower found the remains of a Roman hypocaust while working in the fields around Óbuda in 1778; István Schönwiesner conducted a planned excavation there (on present-day Flórián Square) and published the results in the same year.[34] Subsequent research clarified that these were the ruins of a bath used by the Roman *Legio II Adiutrix* that was stationed at Aquincum. Archaeological research in this area continued from 1778 until 1984, with temporary pauses.[35]

Among nineteenth-century archaeological projects, the grave identified back then as that of Catherine of Poděbrady (Matthias Corvinus' first wife who died young in childbirth), brought to light in Szent György Square in 1826–1827, should first be mentioned.[36] In 1838, the archaeological heritage of the Dominican nunnery on Margaret Island was robbed.[37] Research in the Pauline monastery of Budaszentlőrinc started in 1846–1847, conducted by one of the leading scholars of the time, Imre Henszlmann, who is now viewed as the pioneer of architectural history in Hungary, and who later led archaeological excavations in Székesfehérvár. Flóris Rómer's drawings documented

---

budavári Szent György téren [Finds in a medieval well at the Szent György Square] (Monumenta Historica Budapestinensia, 12) (Budapest: BTM, 2003).

34   Stephanus Schönwiesner, *De ruderibus laconici caldariique romani et nonnullis aliis monumentis in solo Budensi. Partim hoc primum anno M.DCC.LXXVIII. repertis partim nondum vulgatis liber unicus.* (Buda: Typys Regiae Universitatis, [1778]).

35   Melinda Kaba, *Thermae maiores legionis II. adiutricis* (Monumenta Historica Budapestinensia, 7) (Budapest: BTM, 1991).

36   Miklós Jankovich, "Budai Várban talált régi gazdag sírboltról, s benne hihetőleg helyheztetett Katalin királyné, Podiebrad lánya teteméről," [On the rich sepulchre found in the Buda Castle and on the remains presumably identifiable with Queen Catherine, the daughter of Podiebrad] *Tudományos Gyűjtemény* 11 (1827), pp. 15–16. Cf. Emese Nagy, "Jankovich Miklós régészeti és műemléki tevékenysége," [The archaeological and heritage activity of Miklós Jankovich] *Művészettörténeti Füzetek* 17 (1985), pp. 122–142, here pp. 132–133.

37   Ferenc Kubinyi, "A Margitsziget műemlékei," [The monuments of Margaret Island] *Archaeologiai Közlemények* 2 (1861), pp. 4–22; István Radványi, *A Margit-Sziget története* [The history of Margaret Island] (Pest: Beimel J. és Kozma Vazul, 1858), p. 95, Rózsa Feuerné Tóth, "V. István király sírja a margitszigeti domonkos apácakolostor templomában," [The burial of King Stephen V in the church of the Dominican nunnery on Margaret Island] *Budapest Régiségei* 21 (1964), pp. 115–131.

the remains of the monastery in 1864.[38] As regulations for archaeological rescue operations were nonexistent at this time, much discovered during construction work was inadequately recorded. Finds occasionally unearthed and identified as archaeological remains were in most cases transported to the National Museum.

No planned excavations were conducted in the capital until 1931. From this year, the engineer Sándor Garády[39] initiated archaeological excavations at several locations in Budapest and its vicinity, such as in the area of the former village of Nyék and its hunting lodge and in the Pauline monastery of Budaszentlőrinc. He also worked in the Water Town (*Víziváros*) and in Óbuda.[40] László Gerevich started unearthing the medieval village of Csút in 1941,[41] and conducted research at Albertfalva in 1943.[42]

---

38 *Pesti Hírlap* 800. 1846. dec. 22, p. 410; *Családi Lapok* I. 1852. 152, II. 1852. p. 48. Edit D. Matuz, "Adatok Rómer Flóris kéziratos hagyatékából Pest-Buda középkori történetéhez," [Information on the history of medieval Pest-Buda from the manuscript bequest of Flóris Rómer] *Budapest Régiségei* 29 (1992), pp. 11–32, here pp. 13–15.

39 Cf. *Magyar múzeumi arcképcsarnok* [Hungarian museological portrait gallery], eds Sándor Bodó and Gyula Viga (Budapest: Pulszky Társaság – Tarsoly, 2002), pp. 302–303 (by Anna Gyuricza).

40 Sándor Garády, "Budapest székesfőváros területén végzett középkori ásatások összefoglaló ismertetése. 1931–1941, i. Egyházi célú maradványok és temetők feltárása," [Overview of the archaeological excavations in the territory of Budapest, 1931 to 1941. The excavations of ecclesiastical buildings and cemeteries] *Budapest Régiségei* 13 (1943), pp. 167–254; idem, "Jelentés az 1936–1942. évben végzett ásatásokról," [Report on the excavations carried out between 1936 and 1942] *Budapest Régiségei* 13 (1943), pp. 401–438; idem, "Budapest székesfőváros területén végzett középkori ásatások összefoglaló ismertetése. 1931–1941, ii. Világi célt szolgáló építmények," [Overview of the archaeological excavations in the territory of Budapest, 1931 to 1941. Buildings with lay functions] *Budapest Régiségei* 14 (1945), pp. 397–448.

41 László Gerevich, "A csúti középkori sírmező," [The medieval grave field of Csút] *Budapest Régiségei* 13 (1943), pp. 103–166; idem, "A Középkori Múzeum kutatásai az 1941–42. évben," [The excavations of the Medieval Museum in 1941–1942] *Budapest Régiségei* 13 (1943), pp. 439–444.

42 See László Gerevich, "Budapest művészete az Árpád-korban," [The art of Budapest in the Árpádian period] in *Bp. tört.*, i, pp. 351–401, here pp. 397–398. Re-evaluation of the material suggests this may have been a manor house. See György Terei, "Az albertfalvai vár lokalizálása," [Location of the castle at Albertfalva] *Budapest Régiségei* 35 (2002), pp. 633–663; idem, "Exploration of the Medieval Mansion House at Albertfalva," in *Palaces, Monasteries, Villages. Medieval Excavations of László Gerevich (1911–1997)*, eds Judit Benda, Elek Benkő and Károly Magyar (Budapest: BTM, 2011), pp. 22–23.

New Research in the Aftermath of the Second World War

The Second World War severely damaged the early modern royal palace and the houses of the city. On the other hand, the restoration and rebuilding that followed presented an opportunity to conduct archaeological and cultural-heritage research, which has contributed to our present knowledge of medieval Buda, its palace and the surrounding settlements to an extent previously unimaginable. The first excavations that utilized modern archaeological methods were made possible by the rebuilding activity after 1945.[43] Between 1946 and 1958/1962 these focused on the systematic excavation of the medieval royal palace that had been situated at the same site where the Baroque and early twentieth-century royal palace was later built.[44] Additional information was gained through occasional surveys and observations connected to the restoration of individual dwelling houses in the Castle District.[45]

The research conducted in the royal palace was on a scale that was quite unprecedented and it continued in a more sporadic form after the upheaval in the 1950s. Now, local observations yielded results of pivotal importance. Finds enormous in terms of both their mass and variety were brought to light; in themselves these could have filled a whole museum. Besides, *in situ* architectural remains were now unearthed. With considerations of heritage protection in mind, their restoration and presentation to the public were now the main goal. Thus these remains were treated holistically when the Baroque palace wing (present-day block E) was restored. This building was transformed in order to host the Budapest History Museum from 1967, and it met the most rigorous standards of the time. However, archaeological research of the medieval palace remains was not comprehensive, as in the early 1950s the building complex was planned to house a center for the party and

---

43 In 2012 the author and Károly Magyar sketched out the excavations that had taken place since the Second World War and this outline was included in the 25-year development plan for the Castle of Buda. The project was conducted by the KÖZTI and involved many experts. This work is based on the structure of the study.

44 László Gerevich, "A budai Vár feltárt maradványainak leírása," [Description of the remains of the excavated part of the Buda Castle] in *Budapest műemlékei*, i [The monuments of Budapest] (Magyarország műemléki topográfiája, 4) (Budapest: Akadémiai, 1955), pp. 223–257; László Gerevich, *A budai vár feltárása* [The excavation of the Buda Castle] (Budapest: Akadémiai, 1966).

45 László Gerevich, "Gótikus házak Budán," [Gothic buildings in Buda] *Budapest Régiségei* 15 (1950), pp. 121–238.

the government,[46] and rapid rebuilding was a more important consideration than scientific research. Thus, the locations and ways in which excavations were conducted were defined by standards other than academic. Unfortunately, this mentality remained predominant also in the 'milder' political era in the 1970s and 1980s.

Excavations mainly focused on the palace's core area on the southernmost part of the plateau and on the dwelling wings and inner courtyards (closed gardens) around them, situated one level lower. Nevertheless, for the reasons mentioned above comprehensive excavations were not possible here either. Only key spots of the external courtyards and of the Zwinger (the open area between the two defensive walls) could be surveyed, and it was not possible to excavate larger areas.

From 1957 the Castle Museum was assigned an important role in the restoration of the Castle District. The museum was commissioned to conduct architectural and historical surveys preceding the restoration of the dwelling houses, most of which had medieval origins.[47] The results were regularly summarized in the journal *Budapest Régiségei* (Antiquities of Budapest).[48]

Excavations on a larger scale were first possible in the late 1950s in Kapisztrán Square, among the ruins of the Church of Mary Magdalene that was demolished after the war.[49] The main goal of this project was to pave the way for the restoration of architectural heritage in the area, and it continued

---

46   Endre Prakfalvi, "Adatok a budavári palotaegyüttes 1945 utáni építéstörténetéhez," [Information on the history of the construction of the palace complex of Buda Castle after 1945] *Tanulmányok Budapest Múltjából* 29 (2001), pp. 348–359.

47   Lócsy and Kubinyi, "A Középkori osztály," p. 29.

48   Anon., "A budai vár házainak 1957. évi műemléki kutatásai," [The archaeological survey of the houses of Buda in 1957] *Budapest Régiségei* 19 (1959), pp. 301–372; Anon., "A budai vár házainak 1959. évi műemléki kutatásai," [The archaeological research of the houses of the Buda Castle in 1959] *Budapest Régiségei* 20 (1963), pp. 489–527; Anon., "A Budapesti Történeti Múzeum leletmentései és ásatásai 1960–61-ben," [The archaeological rescue works and the excavations of the Budapest History Museum in 1960 and 1961] *Budapest Régiségei* 21 (1964), pp. 304–308.

49   Kálmán Lux prepared the object descriptions as well as the cost estimations instrumental in the reconstruction of the church in 1946. They are preserved in the files of the Hungarian Historical Museum. The reconstruction plans are kept in the Plan Collection of the Gyula Forster National Center for Cultural Heritage Management. Despite this, the church was pulled down, except for its tower. On the church in detail, see Andrea Szebeni and András Végh, "A budavári volt Helyőrségi templom," [The former garrison church of Buda Castle] *Budapest Régiségei* 35, no 2 (2002), pp. 427–457.

for many years (1958–1959, 1965, 1967 and 1974).[50] Excavations were conducted here more recently (2000–2001) as part of the planned reconstruction of the church.[51]

The next large excavation was organized in 1962 in 9–11 Táncsics Mihály Street, the so-called *Kammerhof* (marked as No 10 on the map). This building was identified by some scholars as the original royal dwelling of Buda, used before the Mongol invasion.[52] The survey, however, is treated today only as a preliminary excavation, because the site and the building are extremely complex and huge.[53] What makes this project special is that it is the only excavation so far organized specifically to obtain historical information and not for the purposes of restoration or rebuilding. Therefore, the presentation of the remains to the public was out of the question: they were subsequently reburied, which better served their preservation.[54]

Ruins of a synagogue came to light on the ground floor of 26 Táncsis Mihály Street (marked as No 12 on the map) in 1964, when a one-storey dwelling house was rebuilt.[55] A buttress was discovered when a water draining trench was dug

---

50   The excavations were led by Vilmosné Bertalan. See Anon., "A Budapesti Történeti Múzeum leletmentései és ásatásai az 1958. évben," [The archaeological rescue works and excavations of the Budapest History Museum in 1958] *Budapest Régiségei* 19 (1959), pp. 243–272, here p. 258; Anon., "A Budapesti Történeti Múzeum leletmentései és ásatásai az 1959. évben," [The archaeological rescue works and excavations of the Budapest History Museum in 1959] *Budapest Régiségei* 20 (1963), pp. 529–560, here pp. 550–551; Bertalan Vilmosné, "Mittelalterliche Baugeschichte der Maria Magdalena (später Garnisons-Kirche) in der Budaer (Ofner) Burg," *Acta Technica* 67 (1970), pp. 227–248; eadem, "Előzetes jelentés a Mária Magdolna templom ásatásairól," [Preliminary report of the excavations of the church of Mary Magdalene] *Budapest Régiségei* 22 (1971), pp. 419–428.

51   *Régészeti kutatások Magyarországon 2000* [Archaeological investigations in Hungary in 2000], ed. Júlia Kisfaludi (Budapest: Kulturális Örökségvédelmi Hivatal – Magyar Nemzeti Múzeum, 2003), p. 101 (Cat. no 37, by Zoltán Bencze); *Régészeti kutatások Magyarországon 2001* [Archaeological investigations in Hungary in 2001], ed. Júlia Kisfaludi (Budapest: Kulturális Örökségvédelmi Hivatal – Magyar Nemzeti Múzeum, 2003), p. 145 (Cat. no 41, by Zoltán Bencze).

52   László Zolnay, "Ásatások a budai I. Táncsics Mihály utca 9. területén," [Excavations at plot 9 Táncsics Mihály Street, Buda, 1st district] *Archaeologiai Értesítő* 94 (1967), pp. 39–47; idem, "Ásatások a budai I. Táncsics Mihály utca 9. területén," [Excavations at plot 9 Táncsics Mihály Street, Buda, 1st district] *Archaeologiai Értesítő* 95 (1968), pp. 40–60.

53   The excavations covered only about 8 percent of the whole area.

54   The Hungarian state reacquired the plot from the United States in 2014, so in the near future it may be possible to conduct archaeological excavations at this site.

55   Melinda Papp, "Baudenkmäler im mittelalterlichen Judenviertel der Budaer (Ofner) Burg," *Acta Technica* 67 (1970), pp. 205–225.

in the street in connection with the rebuilding of a house at 23 Táncsics Street (marked as No 11). Archaeological research in 1964–1965 revealed that the remains were those of the late medieval double-nave synagogue used by the Jews of Buda and built in 1461. It was partially excavated and then reburied.[56]

The next location excavated was the area of the early modern Carmelite friary (marked as No 17 on the map) in Színház Street (under the northern and eastern wings) and the adjoining promenade. This survey in the 1960s was again made possible by the architectural restoration of these parts of the district. One of the aims of the excavation was to locate the pasha's palace from the period of the Ottoman occupation, but medieval remains inevitably came to light as well.[57] These excavations were, however, only partially carried out: some sections of the promenade were surveyed, but the cloister's courtyard was barely touched, and therefore only fragmentary data was gained on the Ottoman complex and its architectural predecessors. Some of the remains discovered were totally reburied, while the ruins of the pasha's palace (No 2 on the map) below the Baroque palace wings were left unearthed, which means that its cellar level was more or less kept in its original state. However, the latter is spatially inaccessible and thus cannot be opened to the public.

Excavations on the eastern side of present-day Hess András Square, organized to explore the former Dominican friary (marked as No 9) in the late 1960s and early 1970s, produced more spectacular results. Almost the whole surface was explored.[58] However, research could be carried out here relatively

---

56 László Zolnay, "Középkori zsinagógák a budai várban," [Medieval synagogues in Buda Castle] *Budapest Régiségei* 22 (1971), pp. 271–284; idem, *Buda középkori zsidósága és zsinagógáik* [The medieval Jewry of Buda and their synagogues] (Budapest: Statisztikai Kiadó Vállalat, 1987). Cf. András Végh, *Buda*, i, pp. 71, 301–302 and 306–307.

57 Anon., "A Budapesti Történeti Múzeum leletmentései és ásatásai 1960–61-ben," [The archaeological rescue works and excavations of the Budapest History Museum in 1960–1961] *Budapest Régiségei* 21 (1964), pp. 295–336, here pp. 321–322; Anon., "A Budapesti Történeti Múzeum leletmentései és ásatásai 1962–1965. években," [The archaeological rescue works and excavations of the Budapest History Museum in 1962–1965] *Budapest Régiségei* 22 (1971), pp. 383–410, here p. 392; Anon., "A Budapesti Történeti Múzeum leletmentései és ásatásai 1966–1970. években," [The archaeological rescue works and excavations of the Budapest History Museum in 1966–70] *Budapest Régiségei* 23 (1973), pp. 257–288, here p. 286. The excavations were led by Győző Gerő.

58 Katalin H. Gyürky, "A domonkosok középkori kolostorának feltárása Budán," [The excavation of the medieval Dominican friary at Buda] *Budapest Régiségei* 24, no 1 (1976), pp. 371–379, here pp. 371–376 and no 2 (1976), pp. 92–93 (pics 95 and 96); eadem, *Das mittelalterliche Dominikanerkloster* (Fontes Archeologici Hungariae) (Budapest: Akadémiai, 1981).

easily as some of the remains, such as the northern church wall and the church tower, still stood to a considerable height. These standing monuments, as well as the remains excavated, were incorporated in the newly-built Hotel Hilton. The restoration and presentation of these remains is still considered exemplary today.[59]

Agenda Set by New Building Projects: Buda's Archaeology from the 1970s

The western side of the so-called northern forecourt, known today as the Hunyadi Courtyard [marked as No 1a on Fig. 1.3], was where the next large-scale archaeological survey was conducted in the royal palace. This survey contributed to our knowledge of the city's history. Research was initiated as a rescue excavation in 1972, as landscaping with machines had been commenced here without a preliminary archaeological survey, and architectural and other remains started to surface during the earthworks. Unfortunately, these were first simply destroyed either by dismantlement or explosives. It was only later that archaeological rescue and regular excavations could be organized (1974–1986). Nevertheless, the construction works at the site posed limitations and thus archaeological excavation was inevitably neither comprehensive nor systematic. Large areas accordingly remained unexplored. Nevertheless, significant results were achieved. It was thus clarified that this palace courtyard had originally belonged to the area of the city and was attached to the royal palace only later, after the houses that stood here had been gradually demolished. The remains of these houses were, however, filled up with detritus from the royal palace.[60] Among the enormous amount of finds unearthed here were the world famous remains of Gothic statuary.[61] The ruins of medieval buildings were partially conserved in 1987 and presented to the public as a park of ruins.

---

59 On the excavations that took place between 1985 and 2005, see: András Végh, "Buda város régészeti emlékeinek kutatása 1985–2005. között," [Archaeological research on the town of Buda between 1985 and 2005] in *A középkor és a koraújkor régészete Magyarországon*, i [Archaeology of the Middle Ages and the Early Modern period in Hungary], eds Elek Benkő and Gyöngyi Kovács (Budapest: MTA Régészeti Intézete, 2010), pp. 173–188.
60 László Zolnay, "Előzetes jelentés a budai Vár déli részén végzett 1975–1981. évi feltárásokról," [Preliminary report on the excavations carried out at the southern part of the Buda Castle between 1975 and 1981] *Budapest Régiségei* 26 (1984), pp. 203–216.
61 László Zolnay, "Az 1967–1975. évi budavári ásatásokról s az itt talált gótikus szoborcsoportról," [On the excavations at Buda Castle between 1967 and 1975 and the Gothic statue

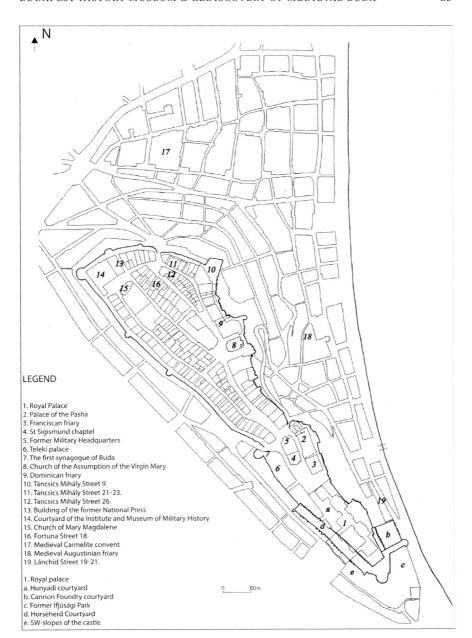

FIGURE 1.3 *Archaeological excavations in the Castle District up to 2013*

Archaeological excavations associated with landscaping in the Hunyadi Courtyard involved areas beyond the courtyard itself: the western end of the so-called Dry Ditch (*Szárazárok*), and further to the west the forecourt of the Lion's Gate. Surveys were also conducted in Szent György Square and in the forecourt of the Beggars' Gate north of the Hunyadi Courtyard. The original townscape was partially reconstructed in both places after the excavation. The western end of the Dry Ditch, its reconstructed bridge, as well as the remains of the gatehouse were opened to the public in the southern area. On the northern side of the courtyard, ruins of the Beggars' Gate, its gatehouse and the paved road that led to it, were similarly put on display.[62]

Smaller archaeological surveys were organized in the so-called Horseherd Courtyard (*Csikós udvar*, marked as No 1d), situated west of and somewhat below the level of the Hunyadi Courtyard. After small-scale exploratory surveys done in the 1980s and 1990s,[63] most of this area was properly excavated in 2005–2007 within the context of the construction of an underground garage.[64] However, the work carried out here and finished in 2012 was unfortunately not entirely successful. This was because parts of the construction area were excavated by machines, and this method, even though it was made under an archaeologist's supervision, was not the most appropriate. Also, the original medieval wall parts were simply dismantled for financial reasons.

Excavations were also conducted in other parts of the royal castle. Remnants of a medieval storage house or farm building were brought to light between 1998 and 2000 in the eastern section of the area between the two castle

---

ensemble found there] *Budapest Régiségei* 24, no 3 (1977), pp. 3–164; and 24, no 4 (1977), pp. 1–239; idem and Ernő Marosi, *A budavári szoborlelet* [Buda statue finds] (Budapest: Corvina, 1989). For further details, see the study of Szilárd Papp in this volume.

62 Károly Magyar, "Ásatások a Budavári Palota területén és annak északi előterében 1982– 1991. között," [Excavations in the territory of the royal palace of Buda and its northern esplanade between 1982 and 1991] *Budapest Régiségei* 29 (1992), pp. 109–115; idem, "A Budavári Palota Északi, ún. Koldus kapujának tornya az újabb kutatások tükrében," [The tower of the northern, so-called Beggar's gate of the royal palace of Buda in light of recent research] *Budapest Régiségei* 29 (1992), pp. 57–92.

63 Magyar, "Ásatások," pp. 112–114.

64 *Régészeti kutatások Magyarországon 2006* [Archaeological researches in Hungary in 2006], ed. Júlia Kisfaludi (Budapest: Kulturális Örökségvédelmi Hivatal – Magyar Nemzeti Múzeum, 2007), pp. 162–163 (Cat. no 40, the work of Károly Magyar); *Régészeti kutatások Magyarországon 2007* [Archaeological researches in Hungary in 2007], ed. Júlia Kisfaludi (Budapest: Kulturális Örökségvédelmi Hivatal – Magyar Nemzeti Múzeum, 2008), pp. 171–172 (Cat. no 41, the work of Anikó Tóth).

walls, in the so-called Cannon Foundry (*Öntőház*) Courtyard (No 1b).[65] The remains of three buildings were recovered in the medieval royal garden on the southwestern slopes of the castle hill in 2000 when plans were made to build an underground storage site for the National Széchényi Library. The walls of one of these have been partly preserved, and fragments of the jamb of its Renaissance window were also discovered.[66]

Remains of fifteenth-century waterworks came to light in 2004, north of the eastern Zwinger.[67] Small-scale excavations were conducted in the eastern and southern gardens of the royal palace in 2012–2013, where the construction of stairs and elevators was planned to make possible direct pedestrian traffic between the Danube bank and the castle.[68] In the same years preliminary excavations were made in the eastern Zwinger in connection with the restoration of Várkert Bazár.[69] However, only short archaeological observations were possible in the area of the former Ifjúsági Park (north of the eastern Zwinger, No 1c on the map), where an underground garage will be built.[70]

Archaeological excavations in the past decades have been associated with construction and restoration projects in the Castle District as well. The Church of Our Lady (or as it is usually called, the Matthias Church, No 8 on the map) has been a research area of the utmost importance in the last few years. This building gained its final form during the period of its transformation in

---

65 *Régészeti kutatások Magyarországon 1999* [Archaeological researches in Hungary in 1999], ed. Júlia Kisfaludi (Budapest: Kulturális Örökségvédelmi Hivatal – Magyar Nemzeti Múzeum, 2002), pp. 174–175 (Cat. no 33, by Károly Magyar); *Kincsek a város alatt. Budapest régészeti örökségének feltárása/Treasures Under the City. Survey of the Archaeological Heritage of Budapest*, ed. Paula Zsidi (Budapest: BTM, 2005), p. 173 (by Károly Magyar). Excavations were carried out in 2012 and 2013 in connection with the reconstruction of the Cannon Foundry courtyard of the Várkert Bazár. In the former, the head archaeologist was Dorottya B. Nyékhelyi; in the latter Károly Magyar.

66 *Régészeti kutatások 2000*, pp. 102–103 (Cat. no 39, by Károly Magyar); *Kincsek a város alatt*, p. 174 (by Károly Magyar).

67 Gabriella Fényes, "Középkori vízmű maradványai Budapest Lánchíd utca 19–21. alól. 1/A lelőhely," [Remains of a medieval waterwork from plot 19–21 Lánchíd Street, Budapest. Find spot 1/a] *Budapest Régiségei* 41 (2007), pp. 193–227; Károly Magyar, "A középkori budai vízművekről," [On the medieval waterworks of Buda] in *A középkor és a koraújkor régészete*, i, pp. 189–206.

68 Led by Károly Magyar and Anikó Tóth.

69 Led by Károly Magyar.

70 On the hillside five Ottoman-Period building fragments were unearthed. These were torn down after documentation was complete but at least there was a chance to make a 3D-scan of the remains. The "observing" archaeologist was Dorottya B. Nyékhelyi.

1874–1896, supervised by Frigyes Schulek.[71] It was also Schulek who unearthed and partly restored the remains of the chapel formerly identified as that of St Michael but recently as that of St Ladislas, which had been turned into a cannon chamber in the southern bastion of the Fishermen's Bastion.[72] A cemetery used in different periods was discovered south of the church in 1963,[73] and in 1968 the foundations of the northern Béla's Bastion were brought to light by archaeological investigations.[74] Nevertheless, properly planned archaeological excavations could only first be conducted here between 2005 and 2012;[75] but unfortunately they were not fully successful. A proper archaeological excavation should have been carried out before the restoration works started, but the two had to run parallel and schedules were often changed. Excavations revealed that there were graves on the northern side of the church as well; moreover, a cemetery section with multiple layers, arranged in rows and used during various periods was discovered on the eastern side, between the church's sanctuary and the Fishermen's Bastion. Graves were situated immediately below the block pavement and the concrete layer. Data was collected on the medieval buildings in the immediate surroundings of the Church of Our Lady when a 70 meter-long gas-pipeline trench was being dug.[76]

Archaeological and cultural-heritage research intermingled in some fortunate cases when the houses of medieval burghers in the Castle District were surveyed. Research started in the 1960s at 18 Fortuna Street (marked as No 16),[77] and continued in 1990–1992. A thirteenth-century dwelling house was found in the southern part of the plot situated on the corner of Fortuna and Kard Streets. It constituted a gateway and a row of rooms that lay perpendicular to Fortuna Street. An upper storey was added to the building in the fourteenth century and a new gateway was constructed on the northern side. A shop or workshop was built on the other side of the plot, closer to Kard Street, in the

---

71   József Csemegi, *A budavári főtemplom középkori építéstörténete* [The medieval construction history of the main church of the Buda Castle] (Budapest: Képzőművészeti Alap Kiadóvállalata, 1955).

72   Győző Gerő, "Adatok a budavári Szent Mihály kápolna topográfiájához," [The topography of the St Michael Chapel in Buda], *Budapest Régiségei* 21 (1964), pp. 389–393; Végh, *Buda*, i, pp. 64–65.

73   *Leletmentés 1962–1965*, p. 390 (by László Zolnay).

74   *Leletmentés 1966–1970*, p. 277 (by Katalin H. Gyürky).

75   The excavation was led by Dorottya B. Nyékhelyi. Short excavation reports were published between 2005 and 2009 in the series entitled *Régészeti kutatások Magyarországon* [Archaeological research in Hungary].

76   *Aquincumi Füzetek* 17 (2011), pp. 155–157 (Cat. no 14, by Dorottya B. Nyékhelyi).

77   *Leletmentés 1966–1970*, p. 274 (by Júlia Altmann).

late fourteenth or early fifteenth century.[78] *Sedilia* of the original medieval gateway were discovered at 14 Táncsis Mihály Street in 2003.[79]

In 1987–1990 excavations were conducted in the courtyard of the Institute and Museum of Military History, in the northeastern part of the Castle District. These brought to light not only the thirteenth-century city walls but also a whole plot on its inner side, where the ruins of medieval and Ottoman period buildings were unearthed.[80] These were, however, reburied. A storage house was intended to have been built on this location for the museum's purposes, but because of these remains the construction was not permitted by the authorities in charge of heritage preservation. This was in fact the very first case in the Castle District when a construction was canceled on archaeological grounds. When this particular storage house was planned, it was not expected that archaeological finds might surface and thus no preliminary survey had been made. This was an unfortunate mistake; this part of the northern Castle District had not been built upon since 1686. Today, of the findings discovered

---

78   Júlia Altmann, "Budapest, Fortunastraße 18. Erforschung mittelalterlicher Häuser," in *Mittelalterliche Häuser und Strassen in Mitteleuropa* (Varia Archaeologica Hungarica, 9), eds Márta Font and Mária Sándor (Budapest–Pécs: Archäologisches Institut der UAW, 2000), pp. 43–48; *Kincsek a város alatt*, p. 172 (by Judit Zádor). The original facade overlooking Fortuna Street disintegrated following reconstruction.

79   *Régészeti kutatások Magyarországon 2003* [Archaeological researches in Hungary in 2003], ed. Júlia Kisfaludi (Budapest: Kulturális Örökségvédelmi Hivatal – Magyar Nemzeti Múzeum, 2004), p. 175–176 (Cat. no 68, by Eszter Kovács).

80   Zoltán Bencze, "Előzetes jelentés a Hadtörténelmi Intézet és Múzeum udvarán folyó ásatásról," [Preliminary report on the excavations in the courtyard of the Institute and Museum of Military History] *Hadtörténelmi Közlemények* 34 (1987), pp. 370–385; idem, "Újabb beszámoló a Hadtörténelmi Intézet és Múzeum udvarán folyó ásatásról," [New report on the excavation at the courtyard of the Institute and Museum of Military History] *Hadtörténelmi Közlemények* 34 (1987), pp. 791–809; idem, "Jelentés a Hadtörténelmi Intézet és Múzeum udvarán 1987. végéig folyt ásatásokról," [Report on the excavations in the courtyard of the Institute and Museum of Military History up to the end of 1987] *Hadtörténelmi Közlemények* 35 (1988), pp. 178–195; idem, "Beszámoló a Hadtörténeti Intézet és Múzeum udvarán 1988-ban folytatott feltárási munkákról," [Report on the excavations in the courtyard of the Institute and Museum of Military History in 1988] *Hadtörténelmi Közlemények* 102 (1989), pp. 131–143; idem, "Jelentés a Hadtörténeti Intézet és Múzeum udvarán 1989-ben és 1990-ben folytatott feltárási munkáról," [Report on the excavations in the courtyard of the Institute and Museum of Military History in 1989 and 1990] *Hadtörténelmi Közlemények* 103 (1990), pp. 194–198; idem, "Archäologische Forschungen am nördlichen Seite des Burgviertels in Buda," in *Mittelalterliche Häuser und Strassen in Mitteleuropa* (Varia Archaeologica Hungarica, 9), eds Márta Font and Mária Sándor (Budapest–Pécs: Archäologisches Institut der UAW, 2000), pp. 49–56.

in the Military History Museum's courtyard only the reconstructed thirteenth-century tower (marked as No 14) is visible to visitors passing the Angevin Bastion. Fortunately, the State Printing House in the vicinity (No 13 on the map) was more professionally handled: when the printing house moved out of the building it became possible to carry out a thorough preliminary archaeological survey before new construction started. Research conducted here not only revealed a new segment of the northern city wall but also brought to light remains of the town houses encircled by the wall.[81] Thus the reconstructed city wall was able to be incorporated into the Angevin residence that was to be erected there.[82] A tower excavated at 33 Országház Street can now be seen in the courtyard of this new building. Another tower is located at the present-day 34 Országház Street; these remains are situated in the ground-floor living room of a house, not much to the delight of its present-day owner.

Among significant archaeological results of the past years, excavations[83] conducted in the lower castle area (*Váralja*)[84] must be mentioned, although there is no room here for a comprehensive discussion. The church and cemetery of the St Stephen's friary of the order of St Augustine were discovered here.[85] The Carmelite friary named after the Mother of Mercy was identified during excavations in Kapás Street.[86]

---

81   *Régészeti kutatások Magyarországon 2002* [Archaeological researches in Hungary in 2002], ed. Júlia Kisfaludi (Budapest: Kulturális Örökségvédelmi Hivatal – Magyar Nemzeti Múzeum, 2004), p. 188 (Cat. no 41, by Zoltán Bencze).

82   Zoltán Bencze, "Előzetes jelentés a volt Állami Nyomda épületeinek területén folytatott régészeti kutatásokról," [Preliminary excavations on the territory of the former National Press (Állami Nyomda)] *Budapest Régiségei* 37 (2003), pp. 113–136.

83   Most of the archaeological excavations from the 1980s were led by András Végh. Idem, "Buda város régészeti emlékeinek," pp. 178–181.

84   Végh, *Buda*, i, pp. 88–96. The territories belonged to Buda from its foundation. The suburbs of Tótfalu, Taschenthal, Szentpétermártír and Szent István had also been protected by walls along the Széna Square – Margit Boulevard – Bem József Street line.

85   *Régészeti füzetek* [Ser. I.] 49 (1997), pp. 103–104 (by András Végh); András Végh, "A középkori ágostonos kolostor felfedezése a Vízivárosban," [The discovery of the medieval Augustinian friary in the Víziváros] *Magyar Múzeumok* no 3 (1998), pp. 15–17; *Régészeti füzetek* [Ser. I.] 51 (2001), pp. 176–177 (by András Végh); *Kincsek a város alatt*, p. 185 (by András Végh).

86   Judit Benda, "Előzetes jelentés a budai középkori karmelita kolostor feltárásáról," [Preliminary report on the excavation of the medieval Augustinian friary of Buda] *Budapest Régiségei* 37 (2003), pp. 137–149; eadem, "Középkori karmelita kolostor feltárása Budán," [The excavation of a medieval Carmelite friary in Buda] in *Régészeti kutatások 2002*, pp. 117–130.

Recent Research on the Medieval Town Walls and in the Foreground of the Royal Palace

Most of the medieval city walls came to light during archaeological excavations. Some western segments of the thirteenth-century city walls (from the period of the Árpádian kings) had already been identified in the late nineteenth century below the present-day Tóth Árpád Promenade.[87] Smaller parts of the wall and its adjoining towers were saved by rescue excavations in the 1960s.[88] A shorter section of the Árpádian-period city wall and its horseshoe-shaped towers were unearthed when excavations were organized in the palace area.[89] The wall's external side was explored later.[90] A rectangular tower was found north of this, in the Hunyadi Courtyard.[91] Parts of the thirteenth-century city wall were found further to the north, in the area of the former Royal Stable and the Riding Hall (*Lovarda*) Passage;[92] however, at the point where the Teleki Palace was later erected (marked as No 6 on the map), the city wall had been completely destroyed. Between the Teleki Palace and the Fehérvári Gate the Árpádian-period city walls were brought to light to a length of 60 m.[93] The horseshoe-shaped tower at the Dry Ditch, the city wall segment and the rectangular tower in the Hunyadi Courtyard as well as the tower found south of the Fehérvári Gate were restored as historical monuments.

Interestingly, the thirteenth-century city walls have better been explored than the late medieval ones, and not much has been added to our knowledge here in the past years. The reason is that this late, external city wall is situated below the remaining walls constructed in the Ottoman, early modern and modern eras, and so the medieval remains are fully concealed. This

---

[87] Sándor Havas, "A budai Vár falai és bástyáinak leásatása," [The excavation of the walls and bastions of Buda Castle] *Archaeologiai Értesítő* 7 (1887), pp. 285–288. The description itself is not very telling, but the sketches of Frigyes Schulek are good starting points.

[88] Katalin H. Gyürky, "Városfalak a középkori Buda nyugati oldalán," [City walls on the western side of medieval Buda] *Archaeologiai Értesítő* 105 (1978), pp. 30–50.

[89] Gerevich, *A budai vár*, pp. 29–39.

[90] Zolnay, "Előzetes jelentés a budai Vár," p. 205. This became possible after the pulling down of the building of the Court Guard. Later on, it was possible to identify the timber blocking in the wall of the semi-circular tower. See Magyar, "Ásatások," p. 112.

[91] Zolnay, "Előzetes jelentés a budai Vár," p. 205; Magyar, "Ásatások," pp. 110–112.

[92] The excavations of Károly Magyar and Dorottya B. Nyékhelyi. Cf. B. Nyékhelyi, *Középkori kútlelet*, pp. 14–15 and 19–20.

[93] Zolnay, "Előzetes jelentés a budai Vár," p. 205; András Végh, "A Szent György utca 4–10. számú telkek régészeti ásatása," [Archaeological excavation of plots 4 to 10 Szent György Street] *Tanulmányok Budapest Múltjából* 31 (2003), pp. 167–190, here pp. 182–183.

area was mostly unaffected by public utility constructions or other building activities. A longer segment of this part of the city wall was first identified archaeologically and at least partly documented first in the Hunyadi Courtyard, on the western, external side of the Árpádian-period city wall.[94] However, a comprehensive excavation or thorough documentation was impossible, because the inner side of the present walls had been reinforced with concrete in order to stabilize it. These observations were, however, sufficient to clarify the relation of the earlier thirteenth-century inner wall and the late fourteenth-century external walls. While the Árpádian-period walls followed the contour of the hill plateau, the later wall was situated 6 to 10 m further out, below the plateau's margin, on the relatively gentle slope which continued more steeply or even vertically down behind this wall. The inner side of the wall was strengthened by a strongly weathered row of arches that rested on pillars.

The longest surviving section of the late medieval city wall was brought to light in the 1990s, when the western part of Szent György Square was explored by archaeologists.[95] This segment was preserved in reasonably good condition, with intact flying buttresses behind the Teleki Palace.[96] However, it has not yet been properly conserved and it is still exposed to weathering. A section of the second defense circuit was identified adjoining a thirteenth-century tower on the western side of plots 4–10 Szent György Street. A denarius coin from the time of Queen Mary (d. 1395) was deposited in its lowermost construction layer.[97] Longer sections of the second wall have also been excavated on the northern side of the Castle District, in the area of the former State Printing House. Here the wall was probably supported by buttresses on the external side to counterbalance the effects of the hill slope.[98] External buttresses are still visible on the southern side of the Transylvanian Bastion and the Fishermen's Bastion. East of the State Printing House, in the area of the electric distribution station, another short section of the second city wall was explored by

---

94 Zolnay, *Buda középkori zsidósága*, pp. 27–28; idem, "Előzetes jelentés a budai Vár," pp. 207–209; Magyar, "Ásatások," p. 111–114.
95 It was found by Károly Magyar in the territory of the Royal Stables. See Károly Magyar, "A budavári Szent György tér és környékének kiépülése: történeti vázlat 1526-tól napjainkig," [The formation of Szent György Square in Buda and its changing face (from 1526 to nowadays)] *Tanulmányok Budapest Múltjából* 31 (2003), pp. 43–126, here pp. 48–49.
96 B. Nyékhelyi, *Középkori kútlelet*, pp. 14–16.
97 Végh, "A Szent György utca," pp. 183–184. This dating is also supported by the researches of László Zolnay: idem, "Előzetes jelentés a budai Vár," p. 208.
98 Bencze, "Előzetes jelentés a volt Állami Nyomda," p. 115.

archaeologists.[99] In general, the least information on the medieval city walls relates to the eastern side, although small segments have been unearthed here as well,[100] for example behind the Dominican friary, at the early modern Carmelite friary to the south, and in the terrace of the Alexander Palace; however, poor preservation and excavation circumstances made it challenging to identify these.

Szent György Square and its vicinity, that is the area ranging from the northern facade of the palace to the southern side of Dísz Square, played a special role in the archaeological research of Buda Castle. A plan that would have appointed this area for the purpose of governmental and state displays in the early 1990s opened up new perspectives for archaeological investigation of the square and its surroundings, and even of the whole castle. After thorough preparations on a governmental level,[101] a comprehensive archaeological investigation was initiated in 1994 that aimed at exploring the whole area nearby. The project would have included the preservation of architectural remains, their presentation to the public as historic monuments, and their integration into newly erected buildings. Even though this mission was only partially accomplished from an archaeological point of view, the results are still extraordinary.

Remains of the church and the building of the medieval Franciscan friary (marked as No 3 on the map) had been explored before restoration began on the Castle Theater and Sándor Palace.[102] A small-scale archaeological survey was organized in the middle of the square in 1988, when there was a plan to build a hotel there. As a result, the ruins of a church that had belonged to

---

99 Katalin H. Gyürky, "Buda középkori városfalai" [The medieval walls of Buda] *Budapest Régiségei* 24, no 1 (1976), pp. 381–389, here pp. 382–383 and no 2 (1976), pics 94, 97, 96 and 99 a–b.

100 Katalin H. Gyürky, "Buda településének kezdetei a régészeti adatok alapján," [The beginnings of the settlement of Buda in light of archaeological data] *Archaeologiai Értesítő* 99 (1972), pp. 33–46; eadem, *Das mittelalterliche Dominikanerkloster* (Budapest: Akadémiai, 1981), pp. 49–51.

101 Based on the resolution of the Hungarian Government of 1993: No 1053/1993 (8 July).

102 Júlia Altmann, "Előzetes jelentés a budavári ferences templom kutatásáról," [Preliminary report of the excavation of the Franciscan friary at Buda Castle] *Archaeologiai Értesítő* 100 (1973), pp. 82–87; eadem, "Az óbudai és budavári ferences kolostor kutatásai," [Investigations at the Franciscan friary of Óbuda and the Buda Castle] in *Koldulórendi építészet a középkori Magyarországon* [Mendicant architecture in medieval Hungary] (Művészettörténet – Műemlékvédelem, 7), ed. Andrea Haris (Budapest: Országos Műemlékvédelmi Hivatal, 1994), pp. 143–150; Júlia Altmann, "A budavári ferences kolostor," [The Franciscan friary at Buda Castle] *Műemlékvédelem* 46 (2002), pp. 345–350.

the St Sigismund provostry (marked as No 4) were identified.[103] Excavations continued in 1994–1995. A new, unique statue of historical importance came to light in these years from a deep garbage pit on the southern side of the church.[104] Several wells and cisterns were identified in the northern part of the square, next to the former Military Headquarters (No 5 on the map). Finds of organic material were also preserved in these.[105]

The western side of the square, that is, the area where the western row of houses in the thirteenth–fourteenth-century *Platea Iudeorum* (Jew's Street) was situated, was almost fully excavated. Its northern part yielded the remains of a Jewish ritual bath, the *mikveh*. Most recently, remains of the early synagogue of Buda (marked as No 7 on the map) have also been partially recovered, even if only due to the construction of public utilities.[106] The importance of the discovery of cistern (well) No 8, in the area of the Teleki Palace, should be emphasized: here the muddy, anaerobic environment preserved organic finds, including wooden and leather objects or textiles, among them a silk tapestry decorated with the coat of arms of the Hungarian Angevin Dynasty.[107]

Unfortunately, the problem of the proper conservation and presentation of most architectural remains of historical value still awaits a solution. While in

---

103 *Régészeti Füzetek* [ser I.] 42 (1991), pp. 67–68; Anon., "A Középkori Osztály munkatársainak ásatásai és leletmentései 1981–1991. között," [The archaeological rescue work and the excavations of the Medieval Department between 1981 and 1991] *Budapest Régiségei* 29 (1992), pp. 237–251, here pp. 242–244 (Cat. no 17). The excavations were led by István Feld, Anna Gyuricza, Erzsébet Hanny, Andrea Pölös and András Végh.

104 István Feld, "Beszámoló az egykori budai Szent Zsigmond templom és környéke feltárásáról," [Report on the excavation of the former St Sigismund's Church and its surroundings at Buda] *Budapest Régiségei* 33 (1999), pp. 35–50; Gergely Buzás, "A budai Szent Zsigmond templom kőfaragványai," [Stone carvings of the St Sigismund's Church in Buda] *Budapest Régiségei* 33 (1999), pp. 51–65; István Feld and Zoltán Kárpáti, "Häuser und Parzellen der mittelalterlichen Stadt Buda in der Umgebung der Hl. Sigismund-Kirche," in *Mittelalterliche Häuser und Strassen in Mitteleuropa* (Varia Archaeologica Hungarica, 9), eds Márta Font and Mária Sándor (Budapest–Pécs: Archäologisches Institut der UAW, 2000), pp. 57–66.

105 Zoltán Bencze, "Régészeti kutatások a Dísz tér 17. sz. alatt. (Előzetes jelentés)," [Archaeological excavations at plot 17 Dísz Square (preliminary report)] *Tanulmányok Budapest Múltjából* 31 (2003), pp. 191–203.

106 András Végh, "Buda város első zsidónegyedének emlékei az újabb ásatások fényében," [The remains of the first Jewish quarter of Buda in the light of recent excavations] in *Régészeti kutatások 2005*, pp. 125–148.

107 The investigation of the soil after the excavation of well No 8 at the Teleki palace led to the identification of millions of seeds which has significantly contributed to our knowledge of the diet of the period. Cf. B. Nyékhelyi, *Középkori kútlelet*.

the northern part the ruins were not only preserved and restored as historic monuments and there were also attempts to use these structures for present-day purposes, in the southern castle area only the stable's walls have been conserved so far. It is, nevertheless, the exposed wall remains that were unearthed in the Teleki Palace, among them the so-called Angevin city walls, which pose the greatest problem: these ruins are in serious danger, as they may be permanently damaged by weathering.[108]

Perspectives on the Evaluation of Archaeological Research

A few paragraphs cannot do justice to the richness of the sites and materials excavated over eight and a half decades. But the preceding overview has probably made clear how much more we now know about the topography and everyday life of the one-time residents of the city than we did before. Let me offer instead an overview and a few examples on possible ways of evaluating the evidence, arranged by order of complexity.[109]

First of all, in many cases it has been possible to acquire data through the excavation of features which were totally unknown before. For instance, research after the Second World War has revealed the extent to which the houses standing on the Castle Hill still retain their medieval structure. In most cases only the walls on the ground floor have survived, although the medieval houses of Buda usually had more than one floor, as testified by the rare survival of a building with an upper storey at 31 Úri Street. Another example is Buda's water supply, about which a great deal of new information has been provided by the digs conducted at 19–21 Lánchíd Street in 2004, which brought to light the remains of waterworks from the Sigismund period. These did not use water from the Danube but from a spring which came to the surface here. Judging from their topographical position, the waterworks were intended to provision the royal palace.[110] Another water pipeline system led water from the Buda Hills,

---

108 The archaeological excavations in the area were completed in 2000.
109 A similar approach (with other examples) is provided by Katalin Szende, "Geschichte und Archäologie bei der Erforschung der mittelalterlichen Stadtentwicklung in Ungarn – Die Ebenen der Zusammenarbeit," in *Geschichte und Archäologie. Disziplinäre Interferenzen*, eds Armand Baeriswyl, Martina Stercken and Dölf Wild (Zurich: Chronos, 2009), pp. 193–202.
110 Magyar, "A középkori budai vízművekről," pp. 189–206. It may be the waterworks that are depicted on the Schön woodcut of 1541, north of the eastern *Zwinger* of the royal palace.

from the so-called City Well (*Városkút*) and perhaps other sources to present-day Szentháromság Square.[111]

Secondly, archaeological excavations can verify and clarify topographical data mentioned in the few surviving written sources or in the equally scarce pictorial evidence. The excavations have made it possible for the medieval town walls, mentioned and depicted in an otherwise general fashion, to be exactly located. A good example is the stretch of city wall north of the royal palace. The 1541 engraving made by Erhard Schön, which depicts the palace and the town from the west during its siege by the Ottomans,[112] shows a temporary wooden palisade on this spot, and it is noted on the picture that the palisade served to replace a stretch of the stone wall that had been destroyed by cannon fire. The excavations conducted here verified what the note states.[113] Sometime it is even possible to connect the finds with individuals. North of the site mentioned above, a late medieval cannon foundry was found at 8 Szent György Street,[114] which enabled us to identify the houses owned by the foundry masters, James and Martin, as well as of their neighbors, who are mentioned in documentary evidence. On the opposite side of Szent György Street the exact location of the Franciscan friary was determined.[115]

The next, more complex level is the common evaluation and contextualization of documentary and archaeological evidence, which can lead to new conclusions – for instance, concerning settlement structure – that extend beyond the evidence on individual sites. This approach has been applied to the medieval topography of Buda as a whole, which has allowed its reconstruction by means of a reassessment of all available written evidence in a form that allows for the integration of archaeological data.[116] Another case in point is

111 Sándor Garády, "Buda középkori és újkori vízművei, különös tekintettel a Svábhegy-Városkút kutatására," [The medieval and modern waterworks of Buda with special regard to the investigation of Svábhegy-Városkút] *Budapest Régiségei* 33 (1998), pp. 245–265; László Zolnay, "Buda középkori vízművei," [Medieval waterworks of Buda] *Történelmi Szemle* 4 (1961), pp. 16–55; *Leletmentés 1966–1970*, pp. 276–277 (excavation of László Zolnay); András Kubinyi, "Städtische Wasserversorgungsprobleme im mittelalterlichen Ungarn," in *Städtische Versorgung und Entsorgung im Wandel der Geschichte* (Stadt in der Geschichte, 8), ed. Jürgen Sydow (Sigmaringen: J. Thorbecke, 1981), pp. 180–190.

112 György Rózsa, *Budapest régi látképei* [Old views of Budapest] (Monumenta Historica Budapestinensia, 2) (Budapest: Akadémiai, 1963), Cat. 1.

113 Magyar, "A budavári Szent György tér," pp. 48–49.

114 Végh, "A Szent György utca," pp. 185–186; idem, *Buda*, i, p. 152.

115 Altmann, "A budavári ferences," pp. 345–350.

116 Végh, *Buda*, i–ii. See also the studies by András Végh, Károly Magyar and Judit Benda in the present volume.

the settlement of *Minor Pest*, which according to written evidence had existed since the eleventh century on the right bank of the Danube opposite Pest. The first archaeological traces of this settlement at the foot of the Castle Hill came to light recently in connection with the renovation of the Várkert Bazár.[117] This new discovery, once published in detail, may enable us to draw a more nuanced picture of the early history of the settlement agglomeration preceding the establishment of the city on the hilltop.

Finally, the integrated evaluation of archaeological and written evidence may encourage researchers to pose questions of more general relevance concerning settlement history and royal policy. This might be the case concerning the moving of the royal residence to the southern tip of the Castle Hill and its extension through the expropriation and demolition of burghers' houses and the moving of the Jewish quarter to the northern part of the hilltop – two actions that have parallels, *mutatis mutandis*, in many different parts of Europe. It would be too much to follow up these and similar questions here, but many other articles in this volume furnish examples of how the rich material brought to light by the work of at least four generations of archaeologists at the Budapest History Museum has been able to generate new questions and provide new answers.

---

117 The thirteenth-century finds were unearthed by György Terei.

CHAPTER 2

The Fate of the Medieval Archives of Buda and Pest

István Kenyeres

There is not a single item that survives from the medieval archives of Buda, Pest and Óbuda. The archives of Buda were lost during the course of the successive sieges and occupations of the city that took place after 1526. The documentary remains for the history of Buda thus largely consist of charters and letters that found their way into private collections. A significant quantity has, however, remained. The published volume of charters, dating from the mid-twelfth century up to 1301, thus contains more than 300 items directly relevant to the history of the city.[1] For the period from 1382 to 1439 we have a further 1200 charters in Latin and a smaller but significant number in German.[2] In addition, the city's early-fifteenth-century *Stadtrecht* survives together with a later code known as the *Laws and Customs of the Seven Towns*, as well as heterogeneous material relating to the operation of the German Butchers' Guild in the last decades of the medieval city. The very few archival documents from the Middle Ages currently held by the Budapest City Archives (*Budapest Főváros Levéltára* – BFL) derive from elsewhere and were never part of an earlier municipal archive. Investigations aimed at reconstructing the archives of the several urban units that later coalesced to form Budapest started in the late nineteenth century, and they have been in progress, with some breaks, ever since. This study reviews the current state of knowledge on the medieval archives, particularly of Buda, and discusses their reconstruction.

The Medieval Archives of Buda

Charters of privilege mark only a stage in the development of medieval towns, and not their beginning. Municipal archives, however, began only when the first charters affording the privileges of self-governance and municipal administration were granted. It was in the towns' interests to preserve the documents and charters which furnished their rights, i.e. for each to set up, maintain and

Translated by Alan Campbell
1   BTOE, i.
2   BTOE, ii. This series only publishes the documents issued in Latin.

operate an archive (*archivum civitatis*).[3] Buda's archives were also influenced by the special circumstances of the city's foundation – the resettlement of the community of Pest, on the left bank of the Danube, in the middle of the thirteenth century. The people of Pest brought the name of their former town with them (hence, *castrum novi montis Pestiensis*), and probably brought with them too their existing archives and any other documents produced in the wake of the Mongol invasion of 1241–1242.[4] Having become the *de facto* capital by the end of the thirteenth or the beginning of the fourteenth centuries, Buda became the judicial and administrative model for other Hungarian free royal towns, which thus adopted similar municipal chancelleries and the related practice of keeping municipal archives.[5] We thus have good reason to assume that the archives of late medieval Buda were very similar to the surviving medieval archives of Pressburg, Sopron, Košice and Bardejov, except that Buda, owing to its size, economic power and significance within the kingdom, probably produced rather more written documents than these other towns. Another factor contributing to the archival record was the reliance on places of authentication as institutions rather than on public notaries in Hungary, and the way that the urban magistracies fulfilled this role in much the same way as ecclesiastical institutions. Official documents (of sale, agreements, contracts and the deposit of wills) were thus made before the councillors of privileged towns

---

3   Ilona Pálffy, "A városi levéltárak kezdetei," [The beginnings of town archives] *Levéltári Közlemények* 18–19 (1940–1941), pp. 351–379, here pp. 352–358; Judit Majorossy and Katalin Szende, "Libri civitatum. Városkönyvek a középkori Magyar Királyság közigazgatásában," [Libri civitatum. Town books in the administration of medieval Hungary] in *Tiszteletkör. Történeti tanulmányok Draskóczy István egyetemi tanár 60. születésnapjára* [Circle of honor. Studies in honor of the 60th birthday of István Draskóczy], eds Gábor Mikó, Bence Péterfi and András Vadas (Budapest: ELTE Eötvös Kiadó, 2012), pp. 319–330, here pp. 320–322; Katalin Szende, "The Uses of Archives in Medieval Hungary," in *The Development of Literate Mentalities in East Central Europe* (Utrecht Studies in Medieval Literacy, 9), eds Anna Adamska and Marco Mostert (Turnhout: Brepols, 2004), pp. 107–142, here pp. 118–120; Károly Goda and Judit Majorossy, "Städtische Selbstverwaltung und Schriftproduktion im spätmittelalterlichen Königreich Ungarn. Ein Quellenkunde für Ödenburg und Pressburg," *Pro Civitate Austriae. Information zur Stadtgeschichtsforschung in Österreich* [NS] 13 (2008), pp. 62–100; Jenő Házi, "A városi kancellária kialakulása Sopronban," [The formation of the urban chancellery in Sopron] *Soproni Szemle* 10 (1956), pp. 202–215.
4   Kubinyi, *Anfänge Ofens*, pp. 32–33; György Györffy, *Pest–Buda kialakulása. Budapest története a honfoglalástól az Árpád-kor végi székvárossá alakulásáig* [The formation of Pest-Buda. The history of Budapest from the Hungarian conquest to its late Árpádian-period development as capital] (Budapest, Akadémiai, 1997), pp. 135–140.
5   Majorossy and Szende, "Libri civitatum," pp. 319–320.

in much the same way as they were made before the places of authentication maintained by orders of monks, church bodies, convents and chapters.[6] Óbuda also accommodated the most authoritative place of authentication in the realm, the Óbuda chapter, whose practice of issuing and storing documents is likely to have influenced the arrangement of the municipal chancellery and archives.[7] The city's administrative system and its publication of documents was probably also moulded by the extensive network of personal and business contacts with the Holy Roman Empire, as maintained by Buda's wealthy German-speaking merchant citizens.[8]

The predominant categories of documents in the medieval municipal archives were: (1) municipal charters and related documents, (2) letters addressed to the city and (3) town or city books (*actionale protocollum*).

For Buda, we only have indirect information regarding the first category. We do not know exactly how many charters of privilege Buda had. There are several surviving transcriptions, including the Golden Bull of 1244 (See *Appendix 2*).[9] The original *Ofner Stadtrecht*,[10] written in the early fifteenth century, almost certainly incorporated the text of some of the main charters of privilege. An addition to its text, made in 1421, refers to these charters. The *Stadtrecht*

---

[6] Ferenc Eckhart, "Die glaubwürdigen Orte Ungarns im Mittelalter," *Mitteilungen des Instituts für Österreichische Geschichtsforschung* [Ergänzungsband] 9 (1914), pp. 395–558, here pp. 429–430; Rady, *Buda*, pp. 54–68; Szende, "The Uses of Archives," p. 118; András Kubinyi, "Buda város pecséthasználatának kialakulása," [Development of seal-use in the town of Buda] in Kubinyi, *Tanulmányok*, i, pp. 271–298, here pp. 281–290.

[7] On the collegiate chapter of Buda, see András Kubinyi, "A budai káptalan késő középkori jegyzőkönyve," [The late medieval protocollum of the chapter of Buda] in Kubinyi, *Tanulmányok*, ii, pp. 671–693.

[8] András Kubinyi, "A budai német patriciátus társadalmi helyzete családi összeköttetései tükrében a 13. századtól a 15. század második feléig," [The social position of the German patriciate of Buda in the light of their family ties from the thirteenth to the second half of the fifteenth century] in Kubinyi, *Tanulmányok*, ii, pp. 457–511; idem, "Budai és pesti polgárok családi összeköttetései a Jagelló-korban," [Family ties of the burghers of Buda and Pest in the Jagiellonian period] in Kubinyi, *Tanulmányok*, ii, pp. 513–570.

[9] Albert Gárdonyi, "Buda legrégibb kiváltságlevele," [The earliest privilege of Buda] *Turul* 28 (1910), pp. 75–84 and 117–127. On its content, with reference to earlier literature, see Györffy, *Pest–Buda*, pp. 136–138. Its modern editions: BTOE, i, pp. 41–43 (no 27). Most recent edition: EFHU, iii/2, pp. 39–41 (no 34). See the charter in a bilingual form in the appendix of the present volume.

[10] László Blazovich, "Bevezetés / Einführung," in *Buda város jogkönyve*, 2 vols [The law code of Buda], eds idem and József Schmidt (Szegedi Középkortörténeti Könyvtár, 17) (Szeged: Szegedi Középkorász Műhely, 2001), i, p. 24 and 140. The surviving known copies of the *Ofner Stadtrecht* do not include the texts of royal grants in letters patent issued to Buda.

also tells us that in the legal action against Pest in 1502–1503, the people of Buda first presented eighteen privileges, and subsequently one more, a total of nineteen.[11]

Only two of the privileges granted to Buda survived the destruction of the city's medieval archives in their original form. The first was granted by John I Szapolyai on 27 March 1538. This unfortunately disappeared from the modern archives in the chaos of 1919.[12] There remains a record, however, of its content and to some extent of its form.[13] It is a key document for the late medieval history of Buda, containing complete transcriptions and texts of confirmation of eleven previous charters. The "Diploma of King John" starts by confirming the principal privileges granted by three previous Hungarian kings. It repeats the content of the Golden Bull of 1244 issued by Béla IV, which is Buda's oldest charter (although actually given to Pest),[14] and of the charter issued by Ladislas IV (the Cuman) in 1276,[15] and it includes a full transcription of a charter conferring customs exemption on Buda issued by King Sigismund in 1437.[16] The charter continues with the full transcription and confirmation of the privileges that John issued to Buda after 1530.[17]

The other privilege surviving in its original form, currently held in the BFL, was issued on 1 November 1540 by Ferdinand I and it confirmed all of the privileges which King John had conferred on Buda.[18] Neither in the year it was issued, nor at any time before the Ottoman capture of Buda on 29 August 1541,

---

11   OSt, pp. 203–204 (cap. 444). See also Szende, "The Uses of Archives," pp. 107–108.

12   The letter of privilege may have been stolen from the Budapest City Archives during the Hungarian Soviet Republic, supposedly in July 1919. See István Kenyeres, "Buda és Pest útja az 1703. évi kiváltságlevélig," [The development of Buda and Pest up to its letter of privilege in 1703] *Urbs. Magyar Várostörténeti Évkönyv* 1 (2006), pp. 159–201, here p. 168, note 40.

13   See thus *Cuspinianus János Beszéde, Budának's véle Magyar országnak ezer öt száz negyven egyedik esztendőben lett romlása emlékezetére, és harmad századára*, ed. József Podhradczky (Buda: Gyurián és Bagó, 1841) pp. 57–90. On its manuscript copies, see Kenyeres, "Buda és Pest," p. 168, note 41.

14   See note 7.

15   In the charter issued by John I Szapolyai there is a short reference, according to which Ladislas IV strengthened and broadened the terms of the privilege of 1244. Cf. Gárdonyi, "Buda legrégibb," p. 75; RA, ii/2–3, p. 161 (no 2706).

16   Edition: BTOE, iii/2, p. 291 (no 1173).

17   On the content of the charters, see Kubinyi, *Budapest*, pp. 210–212; Kenyeres, "Buda és Pest," pp. 168–170.

18   For the original copy, see BFL, IV. 1018; Buda Város Titkos Levéltára, no 3; given in *Cuspinianus*, pp. 91–93.

was the charter placed in the city's archives, and so it was presumably never formally presented. According to an eighteenth-century *elenchus* in the BFL, custody of the charter only passed from the Révay family to the city of Buda in the late eighteenth century. The charter was almost certainly carried by Ferdinand I's envoy, Ferenc Révay, the *locumtenens personalis presentiae regiae* or senior court judge (1527–1542) and later protonotary to the palatine (1542–1553), when he went to Buda in the winter of 1540–1541, remaining there during the Roggendorf siege of 1541. His attempts to negotiate with Queen Isabella, widow of John Szapolyai (who died in 1540), the city's handover were unsuccessful. Presumably, therefore, the charter was never formally bestowed but remained in Révay's keeping, thus explaining its presence in the Révay family archives. It was ultimately presented to the city on the occasion of the diet of 1790, through János Révay, bishop of Szepes (1788–1806).[19]

All that we know of documents in the second category, namely letters addressed to the city, come from reconstructions. Orders sent to Buda from the monarch or from courts survive in many cases in later transcriptions. Other towns that sent documents to Buda sometimes kept copies in their own records.[20]

We have more knowledge of the municipal records in the third category. The practice of keeping town books in German-speaking towns in Hungary was almost certainly borrowed from the cities of the Holy Roman Empire. Research in Hungary, however, suggests that places of authentication may also have influenced the way town books were kept.[21] The earliest surviving town books are mainly from the north of the kingdom, in Upper Hungary (now Slovakia), and date from the late fourteenth century.[22] Older scholarship on town books divided them into five categories: (1) books containing the rights conferred on the town and copies of documents concerning town offices and the town's

---

19   Kenyeres, "Buda és Pest," p. 171, note 55.
20   See thus MNL OL DL 25 034; Reichsstadt Nürnberg Rep. 61.a Briefbücher des Inneren Rats. See András Péter Szabó, "Budapest középkori történetének nürnbergi forrásairól. Rövid kutatási beszámoló," [On the sources of the history of medieval Buda in Nuremberg] *Urbs. Magyar Várostörténeti Évkönyv* 2 (2007), pp. 409–415, here p. 41. In the volumes of the Briefbücher, the earliest letter sent to Buda is from 19 November 1410 (Briefbücher des Inneren Rats vol. 3. fol. 91^r–^{v}) and the last is 11 July 1536 (ibid. vol. 113. fol. 12^v–13^v).
21   Majorossy and Szende, "Libri civitatum," pp. 321–322.
22   See further Majorossy and Szende, "Libri civitatum," p. 322, note 15; László Blazovich, "Die Stadtbücher und das Ödenburger Gerichtsbuch," in *Gerichtsbuch / Bírósági könyv 1423–1531*, eds Jenő Házi and János Németh (Quellen zur Geschichte der Stadt Ödenburg, Reihe A 2) (Sopron: Győr–Moson–Sopron Megye Soproni Levéltára, 2005), pp. 17–32, here pp. 19–22.

community, including collections of customary laws, (2) administrative and official books (e.g. council minutes), (3) judicial and court records, (4) records of the citizens' private legal affairs (e.g. cadastres and records of pledges, prohibitions, etc.), (5) account books concerning the town's financial affairs. More recent scholarship has reduced this scheme to three categories: (1) books of the town council (council minutes, pledge, cadastral, testamentary etc. books), (2) town court books and (3) municipal account books.[23]

For Buda, the main item in the first category of "town book" is the famous *Ofner Stadtrecht*. This does not, of course, survive in its original form but is known through copies made for Pressburg, Košice and presumably Cluj.[24] The *Ofner Stadtrecht* preserves much information concerning the keeping of municipal books, which it defines as the *Stadtbuch* and *Stadtgrundbuch*. The practices governing these must already have been in place before being codified in the *Ofner Stadtrecht*.[25] The city was required to have a "particularly important book" (*ein pesunderr mergklich puech*), which was the land register (*statgrundtpuch*), started afresh every year with the entry of the names of the judge and councillors. All matters of inheritance, property and other affairs involving the use of the municipal seal had to be entered into this book. A full entry was required, with the names of the parties and the date of issue of the document, so that if anyone should lose or burn a document issued by the city, or if it was alienated to Jews, it would be possible to issue a new document.[26] The city notary was responsible for keeping the book, but could only make entries with the approval of the judge and in the presence of two or three councillors appointed by the judge. To supplement this somewhat cumbersome procedure,

23 On the five categories, see: Konrad Bayerle, "Die deutschen Stadtbücher," *Deutsche Geschichtsblätter* 11 (1910), pp. 145–200, here pp. 192–200. On the three categories: Dieter Geuenich, "Was sind eigentlich Stadtbücher? Versuch einer Definition," in *Stadtbücher als namenkundliche Quellen* (Abhandlungen der Geistes – und Sozialwissenschaftlichen Klasse / Akademie der Wissenschaften und der Literatur, 7), ed. Friedhelm Debus (Stuttgart: Akademie der Wissenschaften und der Literatur, 2000), pp. 17–29, here p. 26; Blazovich, "Die Stadtbücher," pp. 33–34; Jörg Oberste and Jens Klinger, "Stadtbücher im Kontext – Stadtbuchforschung in Deutschland," in *Die drei ältesten Stadtbücher Dresdens (1404–1476)*, eds Thomas Kübler and Jörg Oberste (Leipzig: Leipziger Universitätsverlag, 2007), pp. 20–28, here pp. 20–21.
24 Katalin Gönczi, *Ungarisches Stadtrecht aus europäischer Sicht. Die Stadtrechtsentwicklung im spätmittelalterlichen Ungarn am Beispiel der Stadt Ofen* (Frankfurt am Main: Vittorio Klostermann Verlag, 1997), pp. 82–83; Majorossy and Szende, "Libri civitatum," p. 320; Blazovich, "Bevezetés / Einführung," pp. 17–18 and 132–133.
25 OSt, pp. 80–82 (cap. 52–55); Majorossy and Szende, "Libri civitatum," p. 319.
26 OSt, p. 80 (cap. 55).

the notary was required to record judicial affairs in a separate register. This contained entries of court proceedings and judgments and formed the basis for entries in the town book.[27] Only the notary sworn to this task could make entries in the book and only for as long as he remained in office. If he died during his term, another notary was contracted for the purpose, and – in the presence of two assigned councillors – entered any outstanding affairs using the notary's notes, registers and books (*aus seinen zedeln, registeren vnd quateren*). The importance of these procedures was made explicit in the *Ofner Stadtrecht*: entries in the *Stadtbuch* had the same authenticity as a document issued under the city's seal: *dem stat puech zu glauben ist als den statpriefen versigilt mit dem stat sigl.*[28] The *Ofner Stadtrecht* makes some other references to the keeping of the book. It required entries to be made of court sentences and imprisonments in the city jail. If somebody died without leaving a written will, his trustees and executors had to appear before the council and had to give a testimony of the oral disposals, and this will had to be entered into the book. Entries were also required of the oaths of repenting witches and sorcerers.[29] The *Ofner Stadtrecht*'s provisions indicate that Buda's book was of similar type to the *Stadtbuch* (*Ratsbuch*) also kept in cities of the Empire, which followed the law of Magdeburg and Lübeck, and we may presume that the arrangements described pre-date the *Stadtrecht*'s composition. The main entries in the *Stadtbuch* were the texts of documents which the city issued in various legal matters, depositions and transactions (property and pledges) made by citizens before the council, wills and testaments, and court proceedings and judgments. Books concerned with such a broad range of affairs – administrative, private and judicial – were similarly kept by cities in the Holy Roman Empire, such as Leipzig (*Ratsbuch*) and Dresden (*Stadtbuch*).[30]

The *Ofner Stadtrecht* mentions other books and registers kept by the city chancellery and notary. We have already referred to the separate register required for court cases, the content of which had to be subsequently entered into the book. There are also references to the notary's use of other registers and books. Besides the court register specified in the *Ofner Stadtrecht*, there were probably separate cadastres and pledge books,[31] and there is good reason

27   OSt, p. 81 (cap. 54).
28   OSt, p. 82 (cap. 55).
29   OSt, p. 82 (cap. 56); p. 161–162 (cap. 309) and p. 169 (cap. 331).
30   Thomas Kübler and Jörg Oberste, *Die drei ältesten Stadtbücher Dresdens*; *Die Leipziger Ratsbücher 1466–1500: Forschung und Edition*, 2 vols, ed. Henning Steinführer (Leipzig: Leipziger Universitätsverlag, 2003) [henceforth: Steinführer, *Die Leipziger Ratsbücher*].
31   See for instance, Végh, *Buda*, i, p. 310.

to assume that a separate series of municipal account books was also kept. In one place, the *Ofner Stadtrecht* refers to the keeping of an *Ächtbuch* (*echt puch*), a book of punishments.[32] The medieval town books which survive in the archives of other towns in Hungary, particularly Pressburg, Sopron and Košice, were organized according to these functions.[33] Since Buda was in many respects the model for these towns, we may presume it was also the source of this practice. Nonetheless, according to the pattern followed in the Holy Roman Empire, Buda was considered in law to have only a single town book (*stadtbuch, liber civitatis*) that was regarded as authentic. It provided the source for issuing authentic copies and its entries were accepted in the court of the Lord Chief Treasurer (*tárnokszék*), which was the court of appeal for the seven free royal towns (Buda, Košice, Pressburg, Trnava, Sopron, Prešov and Bardejov).[34] In the towns subject to the municipal law of Magdeburg and Lübeck, the *Stadtbuch*s were legally authoritative, whereas in the western and southern parts of the Empire they were regarded only as auxiliary records,[35] and this suggests that the parts of the *Ofner Stadtrecht* concerning the town book were probably based on or akin to Magdeburg law.

We also have some specific information on the keeping and use of the Buda *Stadtbuch*, all of which are related to property matters. A document of 1423 is the first to mention that depositions concerning property were entered into the town book: *quam fassionem ad tabulam seu librum civitatis conscribere fecisset...quam fassionem...in libro civitatis predicte asserentur esse facta et conscripta*.[36] In 1459, Matthias Corvinus instructed the Buda Council to issue a

32   OSt, p. 274 (cap. 151); Rady, *Buda*, p. 56.
33   On Pressburg, see Majorossy and Szende, "Libri civitatum," pp. 325–330; on Košice, see Ondrej R. Halaga, *Košické mestské knihy, 1394–1737* (Práce Archívu mesta Košic, 3) (Košíce: Archív mesta Košíc, 1956); idem, "A kassai városi könyvek (1394–1737)," [The town books of Košice (1394–1737)] *Levéltári Híradó* 7 (1957), pp. 518–549. See also the edition of the different town books: *Das Pressburger Protocollum Testamentorum 1410 (1427)–1529*, 2 vols, eds Judit Majorossy and Katalin Szende (Fontes rerum Austriacarum. Dritte Abteilung. Fontes iuris, xxi/1–2) (Vienna–Cologne–Weimar: Böhlau, 2010–2014); *Actionale Protocollum. Das älteste Stadtbuch von Bratislava / Preßburg aus den Jahren 1402–1506*, ed. Arne Ziegler (Bratislava: Muzeum kultúry karpatských Nemcov, 1999); *Acta iudiciaria civitatis Cassoviensis 1393–1405. Das älteste Kaschauer Stadtbuch*, ed. Ondrej R. Halaga (Buchreihe der Südostdeustchen Historischen Kommission, 34) (Munich: Oldenbourg, 1994); *Das älteste Stadtbuch der Königlich Freien Bergstadt Göllnitz/Gelnica in der Unterzips und seine Sprache*, ed. Helmut Protze (Frankfurt am Main–New York: Peter Lang, 2002).
34   Rady, *Buda*, p. 57. Entries in the town books of Sopron were also considered legally authoritative: see Házi, "A városi kancellária," p. 221.
35   Steinführer, *Die Leipziger Ratsbücher*, i, p. xxxv.
36   MNL OL DF 238 091; BTOE, iii/2, p. 73. (no 821). See also Végh, *Buda*, i, p. 310 note 972.

letter of record (*litterae fassionales*) of a property-transfer case for which a deposition (*fassio*) made by the parties before the city had been entered into its *registrum*. This is also evidence that an entry in the town book in itself constituted a legally authoritative record.[37] One document, produced in 1523, which records a property transaction has the words *Extractus libri civitatis anni 1523* written on the verso.[38] In 1524, King Louis II ordered the city, for the benefit of the St Stephen chapter of Esztergom, to seek out some documents which belonged to the chapter and had been left in the City Hall, or to issue authentic copies under the seal of the city on the basis of the *Stadtbuch* (*...extunc prothocolon sive librum civitatis vestre...*).[39] Not all of the entries into the book concerned property matters, however, and we know indirectly, through partial reconstruction, which documents had to be copied into it. Starting in the 1460s, on the versos of documents issued by the city chancellery were written in certain important matters, chiefly concerning property, the names of the persons to whom the document concerned (usually in the dative case) lower center, in the same hand in any one period.[40] These names are entered on documents issued to the most diverse persons and institutions, so that they could not have been written by a scribe or archivist in the service of the receiving party, but instead by an employee of the city chancellery, probably with the intention of serving as an index to the matter, as registered in the *Stadtbuch*. Evidence in support of this proposition is provided by the example of entries in the Leipzig *Ratsbuch*, which show the names of the parties in the margin.[41] The same may have been done in Buda. If so, then by studying documents which survive in their original form, we may be able to reconstruct some of the entries into the Buda *Stadtbuch*.

---

37   MNL OL DL 38 821; discussed in Rady, *Buda*, p. 57.
38   MNL OL DL 48 993; discussed in Végh, *Buda*, i, p. 310 note 972.
39   MOL DF 238 121; discussed in Végh, *Buda*, i, p. 310 note 972.
40   See thus MNL OL DL 93 303 (10 August 1460); BFL XV. 5 (Mohács előtti oklevelek gyűjteménye / Collectio Antemohácsiana), no 2 (4 October 1465); MNL OL DL 18 570 (19 November 1481), 93 548 (9 February 1482), 19 491 (21 February 1489); DF 208 575 (17 March 1490); DL 39 212 (4 October 1494); DF 274 182 (8 December 1494), 236 393 (29 August 1498); DL 46 582 (22 March 1502); DF 238 108 (6 April 1502); DL 46 663 (17 March 1504); DF 238 112 (28 September 1507), 275 871 (2 November 1517) and DL 50 566 (21 April 1524). Most of the charters are connected to property transactions, but there is also a pious donation (DL 46 582).
41   The phenomenon has also been identified by Steinführer, *Die Leipziger Ratsbücher*, i, pp. xlii–xliii. Entries of this type are mostly preserved in the Ratbuch in the period 1489 to 1500, published in the 2nd volume. Ibid., ii.

Archives of Pest and Óbuda

We have even less knowledge of the archives of Pest and Óbuda and the documents they held. Until the early or mid-fifteenth century, Pest was legally subordinate to Buda, and so its town chancellery could only have acquired significance later, even though the employment of a Pest town notary is mentioned as early as 1326.[42] Upon gaining its autonomy, however, Pest quickly adopted the practices of the Buda chancellery. The keeping of a town book in Pest is also mentioned:[43] a document issued by the town in a legal action concerning property in 1499 mentions a letter issued by the town in 1453, which had been retrieved *ex libris civitatis Pestiensis*.[44] As in Buda, the verso of Pest documents carries names that were used to index the town book.[45] The Pest town book was also legally authoritative, and documents copied from its entries were accepted at the (appeal) court of the Lord Chief Treasurer.[46]

Three landowners had jurisdiction over Óbuda: the queen, the Óbuda nuns (the Poor Clares) and the Buda chapter. Óbuda councillors are first mentioned in 1349 and municipal documents issued by the Óbuda judge and councillors in 1361. The town council itself and its document-issuing activity together with the use of its seal can probably be dated back to 1343, when the town became the possession of the queen.[47] From that time, Óbuda was mentioned as the queen's town (*civitas reginalis*), indicating in Hungarian law the rank of a market town (*oppidum*), notwithstanding the use of the word *civitas*. In such towns, the council also held legally authoritative functions.[48] We find property

---

42   Kubinyi, *Budapest*, p. 84.
43   Kubinyi, *Budapest*, p. 84
44   MNL OL DL 61 919.
45   e.g. MNL OL DL 18 799 (21 April 1483), 61 905 (19 April 1497) and DF 281 266 (3 April 1510).
46   Rady, *Buda*, p. 57.
47   Kubinyi, *Budapest*, pp. 84–85.
48   According to the *Tripartitum* of István Werbőczy compiled in 1514 and printed in 1517 the seals given by the kings and princes to market towns were credible on which account they might issue charters in their own affairs. "Habent praeterea civitates et oppida sigilla authentica, per reges et principes ipsis concessa, quae in factis et rebus coram eis et in medio eorum vertentibus ac emergendis, robur sortiuntur firmitatis" – DRMH, v, p. 243 (Part II, title 13, 3§). On the legal position of market towns: Vera Bácskai, *Magyar mezővárosok a XV. században* [Hungarian market towns in the 15th century] (Értekezések a történeti tudományok köréből [NS], 37) (Budapest: Akadémiai, 1965), p. 102; eadem, "A mezővárosi önkormányzat a 15. században és a 16. század elején," [Self-government of market towns in the 15th and early 16th century] in eadem, *Városok és polgárok Magyarországon*, 2 vols (Towns and bourgeoise in Hungary) (Várostörténeti tanulmányok) (Budapest: BFL, 2007), i, pp. 137–158, here pp. 138–140. On the charter issuing and seal use

matters, contracts of sale and registrations of possession among documents issued by the Óbuda town council under its municipal seal.[49] The proximity of the capital city must also have had an effect on the municipal chancellery, and although no information survives on its organization, the mode of issue of the surviving original documents suggests a sophisticated level of municipal literacy.

Other Medieval Archives in the Budapest Area

Some archives created by bodies other than the municipal authorities are important for the medieval history of Budapest and warrant a mention here. Among them were those of the Buda chapter, the nunneries of Óbuda and Margaret Island, and the convent of Felhévíz. Some fragments of these archives, particularly from the Buda chapter, survived the destruction.[50] Also of interest are the guilds. The majority of the very small number of medieval documents held in the Budapest City Archives originate from the German Butchers' Guild, which played a dominant role in Buda's economic life. The surviving documents comprise eight guild charters and one other document, the guild book, which is a uniquely valuable source for the medieval history

---

of market towns, see Erzsébet Ladányi, "Az oppidum fogalom használata a középkori Magyarországon: az oppidumok jogélete," [The use of the term oppidum in medieval Hungary: the legal life of the oppida] *Levéltári Szemle* 42 (1992), pp. 3–12; Péter Bálint Lakatos, *Hivatali írásbeliség és ügyintézés a késő középkori magyarországi mezővárosokban, okleveleik tükrében*, unpublished PhD dissertation, 2 vols [Official local written culture and administration in late medieval Hungarian market towns as reflected in their charters] (Budapest: Eötvös Loránd Tudományegyetem, 2013).

49   See for instance the original charters issued by the town of Óbuda: MNL OL DL 42 363 (7 April 1378); DL 42 363 (29 April 1387), 10 124 (4 October 1413), 10 325 (10 March 1415), 11 890 (6 January 1427), 12 626 (24 September 1434), 14 583 (21 October 1452), 14 641 (15 February 1453), 17 822 (6 July 1476), 19 620 (15 January 1490), 21 466 (21 August 1505), 21 546 (1 April 1506), 21 549 (3 April 1506), 21 584 (10 July 1506) and DF 241 117 (4 December 1513).

50   A small fragment of the material of the chapter of Buda was removed to the chapter of Pressburg. See Albert Gárdonyi, "Az óbudai káptalan magánlevéltára," [The private archives of the chapter of Óbuda] *Levéltári Közlemények* 20–23 (1942–1945), pp. 130–140. 110 charters from the period before 1526 and the protocollum kept between 1510 and 1522 were acquired by the Hungarian National Archives as part of a document exchange in 1968. István Bakács, "Az Országos Levéltár III. osztályának 1969. évi gyarapodásáról," [On the new acquisitions of the 3rd department of the National Archives in 1969] *Levéltári Szemle* 20 (1970), pp. 440–442.

of Buda, mostly containing accounts. Their survival is testimony to the importance which guild members attached to their privileges. When the Germans were expelled from Buda in 1529, they took these documents into exile with them and preserved them almost completely intact during the hundred and fifty years of Ottoman occupation. They also safeguarded their last guild book, a record to their highly sophisticated administration, containing references to three other guild books.[51]

The Destruction of the Medieval City Archives

Historians generally ascribe the destruction of the medieval archives of Buda and Pest to the Ottoman occupation following the capture of the city by subterfuge, without a fight, in 1541. The Ottomans had already occupied the capital city temporarily, however, in 1526 and 1529, causing severe destruction on both occasions. In the 1526 invasion, they burned the city down, almost certainly causing the loss of Béla IV's Golden Bull of 1244. It is known that John I Szapolyai was obliged to reissue the charter in 1526 or early 1527.[52] When Buda came into the possession of Ferdinand I Habsburg in 1527, its leaders had the lost Golden Bull confirmed by their new lord in early 1528.[53] John Szapolyai's charter of 1531 (transcribed in 1538) mentions that his own confirmation of the 1244 Golden Bull had itself been lost during the Ottoman siege of 1529, and that he was thus obliged to re-issue it.[54] The records show, therefore, that there were losses from municipal archives of Buda even before 1541 (in 1526 and 1529). The extent of the damage done on these occasions is unknown, but the administration of the Hungarian capital city certainly ceased after it fell to the Ottomans in 1541.

One important piece of information remains regarding the possible survival of some documents from the Buda archives connected with the Habsburg

---

51   Majorossy and Szende, "Libri civitatum," p. 325. For the edition of the archives of the craft of butchers, see *A budai mészárosok középkori céhkönyve és kiváltságlevelei – Zunftbuch und Privilegien der Fleischer zu Ofen aus dem Mittelalter.* (Források Budapest közép – és kora újkori történetéhez, 1 / Quellen zur Budapester Geschichte im Mittelalter und in der frühen Neuzeit, 1), ed. István Kenyeres (Budapest: BFL – BTM, 2008).
52   *Cuspinianus*, pp. 15, 58 and 72–73.
53   Ferdinand I in his charter issued to Buda transcribed the Golden Bull of 1244. Its copy is preserved in the Libri Regii: MNL OL A 57 (Archive of the Hungarian Chancellery) Libri regii vol. 1, pp. 97–100.
54   See the text of the Szapolyai-diploma from 1538 in *Cuspinianus*, pp. 58 and 72–73.

siege and Ottoman capture of the city in 1541. The Szapolyai-party judge of Buda, Péter Pálczán, who dominated the history of Buda in the 1530s,[55] wanted to surrender the city to the Habsburgs during the Roggendorf siege of 1541. The plan failed,[56] and Pálczán was obliged to flee without his family, taking with him only a couple of treasured possessions. He later settled in Pressburg, where he died in 1558. Since he had no heirs, officials of the Hungarian Chamber took an inventory of his estate. The inventory includes an item which suggests that the former judge of Buda had safeguarded some of the charters of Buda and Pest, as well as the city's copper seal. It is perhaps not unreasonable to speculate that John Szapolyai's Golden Bull of 1538 may have been among these documents, and that charters and other documents from the Buda archives may still be hidden somewhere.[57]

Archive Reconstruction Work

Since the archives of the capital city perished in the post-Mohács period, the only way of substituting for their loss is systematically to collect related charters held in other archives. The first to start this work was József Podhradczky (1795–1870) in the mid-nineteenth century. Podhraczky worked in the Urban Department of the Hungarian Chamber, where he had the opportunity to study its archives, which were otherwise hard to access. He discovered

---

55 Péter Pálczán was from Valkó County in southern Hungary. He lived in Buda from his adolescence, supposedly worked as a tailor and became one of the wealthiest merchants. By this time he worked in cattle trade. In 1527 he is mentioned as a councillor of Buda (*iuratus*). See Rady, *Buda*, p. 176. He was judge of Buda in 1530/31, 1532/33 and 1537/38. See Albert Gárdonyi, "Buda középkori levéltáráról," [On the medieval archive of Buda] *Levéltári Közlemények* 12 (1934), pp. 159–167, here pp. 159–160; Kubinyi, A "budai német patriciátus," p. 506, note 386; idem, "Buda és Pest szerepe a távolsági kereskedelemben a 15–16. század fordulóján," [The role of Buda and Pest in the long distance trade at the turn of the 15th century] in Kubinyi, *Tanulmányok*, i, pp. 361–405, here p. 403; idem, "Die Städte Ofen und Pest und der Fernhandel am Ende des 15. und am Anfang des 16. Jahrhunderts," in *Der Außenhandel Ostmitteleuropas 1450–1650*, ed. Ingomar Bog (Cologne–Vienna: Böhlau, 1971), pp. 342–433; Kubinyi, *Budapest*, pp. 210, 218 and 220.

56 Albert Gárdonyi, "A budai városi tanács árulása 1541-ben," [The betrayal of the council of Buda in 1541] *Tanulmányok Budapest Múltjából* 7 (1939), pp. 1–10; Kubinyi, *Budapest*, pp. 228–229.

57 Gárdonyi, "Buda középkori levéltáráról," pp. 164–165. Gárdonyi suggests that the 1540 letter of privilege of Ferdinand I to the city of Buda may come from the Pálczán inheritance. Ibid., p. 165. I myself doubt this assumption. See note 19 above.

many documents concerning the medieval history of Buda and Pest, and made use of some of them in publications.[58] Then, in 1870, the city of Pest engaged the eminent historian, Ferenc Salamon (1825–1892), to write the history of the city. After unification in 1873, the new city of Budapest extended his commission to Buda and Óbuda. Salamon's work was published between 1878 and 1885, and it covers the history of the city up to 1490. He did not complete the section covering source documents, including them only in a critical appendix.[59] In 1911, Dezső Csánki (1857–1933), later Director of the Hungarian National Archives (1912–1932), launched a project to systematically collect sources concerning the medieval history of the capital city. His plan was to collect sources of national and historical importance on Budapest from foreign and other archives. This was to have formed the basis for a published collection of sources and the collected material was to have been placed in the municipal archives. The council passed the plan in 1912 and work started with great intensity. Financial problems at the end of the First World War, however, brought the project to a halt. Collection resumed in 1926, again under the direction of Dezső Csánki, and was taken over after his death by Albert Gárdonyi (1874–1946), head of the Budapest City Archives (1914–1935).[60] It was under Gárdonyi's editorship that, in 1936, the first collection of sources was published. It contained archive sources concerning the area of the capital city up to the end of the Árpádian period (1301).[61] During the Second World War, under Jusztin Budó (1884–1943), director of the Municipal Archives after Gárdonyi's retirement in 1936, preparations continued for the publication of sources for the first half of the fourteenth century. By the early 1930s, 3800 documents from 97 archives had been copied, followed by a further 500 copies up to the early 1940s, when research was in progress in 85 archives. During the siege in the winter of 1944–1945, the building containing the copies was

---

58 See thus József Podhradczky, *Buda és Pest szabad kir. városoknak volt régi állapotjokról* (Pest: Beimel, 1833). His valuable manuscript collection can be found in the Széchényi National Library: *Historia diplomatica urbis Budensis et Pesthiensis, a primordiis usque ad annum 1831. conscripta per Josephum Podhradczky* – OSZK Kézirattár (Collection of manuscripts), Fol. Lat. 1205.

59 Ferencz Salamon, *Buda–Pest története*, 3 vols [The history of Budapest] (Budapest: Kocsi S. Nyomda – Athenaeum Nyomda, 1878–1885).

60 Péter Kis and Iván Petrik, "Budapest középkori történetére vonatkozó források összegyűjtésének évszázados múltja," [Collecting sources on the history of Budapest over the last century] *Tanulmányok Budapest Múltjából* 32 (2005), pp. 235–259, here pp. 235–238.

61 BTOE, i.

hit, and about 80 percent of three decades' work of research and collection was destroyed.[62]

After the Second World War, research into the medieval history of Budapest and the publication of sources passed from the City Archives to the Budapest History Museum (BTM).[63] In 1953, the city authorities decided to publish a new series of books on Budapest's history. The actual work for this was supervised by the general secretary of the editorial committee, László Gerevich (1911–1997), Director of the BTM. The committee's first decision was on the need to research and publish the sources required for the new series. This put the project of collecting medieval sources back on the agenda. The eminent medieval historian Elemér Mályusz (1898–1989) pointed out, however, conceptual problems attending the way the earlier project had gone about the task of collecting sources and the fact that much of the material had in any case been destroyed. The decision was accordingly made to start collecting anew, from scratch. Research was broadened to cover the area of Greater Budapest, created in 1950, and connections to Budapest in documents were to be interpreted in the widest possible sense. The first phase was confined to the search for documents with any relevance to Budapest. The research was joined by the medievalists (Miklós Komjáthy, 1909–1993; István Bakács, 1908–1991; the young András Kubinyi, 1929–2007) as well as by Bernát L. Kumorovitz (1900–1992), Arisztid Oszvald (1890–1973), Dénes Jánossy (1891–1966) and Antal Fekete Nagy (1900–1969), who had been ejected from academic and university positions for political reasons, and accepted the work as their only opportunity to stay in the field. An indication of the intensity of their endeavors is that by the end of 1955 they had worked through the 100,000 items of the Diplomatic Archives of the Hungarian National Archives, producing nearly 12,000 index cards of documents relevant to Budapest. The first phase of the research came to a close in 1959, and the collection was regarded as complete. Work started on transcribing and copying the documents; a structure for the series of books publishing Budapest's medieval documents was decided upon; and the eras and tasks were divided up among the authors. No edition was, however, forthcoming. Instead, emphasis shifted to writing the history of Budapest, resulting in the publication of György Györffy's book on the age of the Árpádian kings and András Kubinyi's books on the period 1301–1541. These, particularly Kubinyi's, which are still regarded as basic works of reference, largely drew on the

---

62   Kis and Petrik, "Budapest középkori," pp. 238–244.
63   For an overview of collecting activity after the Second World War, see Kis and Petrik, "Budapest középkori," pp. 248–253.

collecting activity of the 1950s.[64] Work on publishing sources came to a complete stop in the 1970s and was only revived in 1987, on the initiative of BTM director György Székely (1924–2016). It was only then that Bernát Kumorovitz's collection of Latin documents of the Sigismund era, the only complete manuscript, was published.[65]

In the early 2000s, a third major venture was launched. Research started up in a medieval working group formed within the BFL in 2000 and joined by the BTM in 2001.[66] The revived project was primarily aimed at producing a computer database of Budapest-related documents, although there was also a proposal for continuing the series of source publications.[67] The work rested on previous collections and publications, especially the remnants of the BFL's pre-Second World War collection, the BTM's collection, the published collections of documents of *Budapest történetének okleveles emlékei* (Charters for the history of Budapest), György Györffy's 1998 monograph on the Árpádian-period historical geography of the territory of Budapest,[68] the published document collections for the Angevin Period,[69] and the *Középkori Magyarország Levéltári Forrásainak Adatbázisa* (Database of Archival Sources of Medieval Hungary, MNL OL DL-DF).[70] Further research projects involving the collection of foreign sources were also proposed.[71] The database of Budapest-related medieval archival sources was aimed at the detailed study and description of the documents. The project of reviewing material for the Árpádian period is

---

64   Györffy, *Budapest*, pp. 217–349; Kubinyi, *Budapest*.
65   BTOE, iii/1–2.
66   The members of the research group were: Péter Kis, Iván Petrik, Éva Jancsó, István Kenyeres (all BFL) and Enikő Spekner (BTM).
67   Péter Kis and Iván Petrik, "Budapest középkori történetére vonatkozó levéltári források adatbázisa," [Database of the archival sources for the history of medieval Budapest] *Levéltári Szemle* 54 (2004), pp. 14–25.
68   For the volume that discusses the county of Pest as well as Pest, Buda and Óbuda, see ÁMTF, iv.
69   AOklt. The edition with minor gaps spans now the period from 1301 to 1354.
70   See here György Rácz, "Collectio Diplomatica Hungarica. Medieval Hungary Online," *Archiv für Diplomatik. Schriftgeschichte, Siegel- und Wappenkunde* 56 (2010), pp. 423–444. The Database of the Archival Documents of Medieval Hungary is available at: http://archives.hungaricana.hu/en/charters (last accessed: 25 March 2016).
71   István Kenyeres and Péter Kis, "Budapest középkori történetének bécsi levéltári forrásai. Kutatási beszámoló és terv a munka folytatására," [Sources on the medieval history of Budapest in Vienna. Research report and plans for the future] *Urbs. Magyar Várostörténeti Évkönyv* 1 (2006), pp. 299–329; Szabó, "Budapest középkori történetének nürnbergi forrásairól."

complete, and work on sources for the Angevin and Sigismund Periods has begun, but full treatment will have to wait, as will the continuation of research to cover the period up to the 1560s and 1570s. The complete database is accessible on the BFL website, which currently contains data on 4113 documents.[72]

In parallel with building the database, the BFL has launched a series of books entitled *Források Budapest közép- és kora újkori történetéhez* (Sources for the Medieval and Early Modern History of Budapest), the first volume of which serves in the manner of continuing the collection of medieval sources on the city, covering the guild book and charters of the Buda Butchers' Guild.[73] The second volume concerns a house of Ragusan merchants operating in Buda during the Ottoman occupation, based on sources in the Dubrovnik archives.[74] It is indicative of the possibilities for research in the early modern period.

---

[72] The development of the database stopped in 2010, hopefully just temporarily. It is available online at the website of the Budapest City Archives: http://lnyr.eleveltar.hu/BFLQuery/detail.aspx?ID=1713294 (last accessed: 18 January 2016).

[73] *A budai mészárosok.*

[74] Antal Molnár, *Egy raguzai kereskedőtársaság a hódolt Budán / Eine Handelsgesellschaft aus Ragusa im osmanischen Ofen* (Források Budapest közép – és kora újkori történetéhez, 2 / Quellen zur Budapester Geschichte im Mittelalter und in der frühen Neuzeit, 2) (Budapest: BFL, 2009).

PART 2

Buda before Buda

∴

CHAPTER 3

Buda before Buda: Óbuda and Pest as Early Centers

Enikő Spekner

The area of medieval Buda played a central role in the kingdom of Hungary even before King Béla IV founded the castle and town in or after 1242 on the hill above the narrowest fordable stretch of the River Danube that connected the country with Western Europe on the one hand and the Northern Balkans and the Pontic Steppe on the other.[1] The medieval kingdom of Hungary comprised the entire Carpathian Basin, virtually the whole catchment of the middle Danube, and was divided by it into two – albeit unequal – parts. The left bank, Western Hungary, is a hilly region, rich in waterways and forested low mountains, while on the right bank a wide flood land stretches into the Great Hungarian Plain. The turn of the river from west-east to the south around Visegrád defined the middle of the country.[2] The meeting of the upland and plain and the easy transit across the river were defining features of the location. Here the Danube is not only at its narrowest, but its islands also facilitate fording, while the thermal wells on its bank reduce the chance of it freezing over.[3] This is where the earliest settlements that came to be Buda on the right bank and Pest on the left emerged together with their environs. Along with the royal foundations of Esztergom, some 50 km upstream, and of Székesfehérvár, 60 km to the southeast, this region was seen as the *medium regni* throughout the Middle Ages.

Translated by János M. Bak

1 See Kubinyi, *Anfänge Ofens*, pp. 9–10; Sándor Frisnyák, "Das Karpatenbecken," in *Europas Mitte um 1000. Beiträge zur Geschichte, Kunst und Archäologie*, i, eds Alfried Wieczorek and Hans-Martin Hinz (Stuttgart: Theiss, 2000), pp. 81–84.
2 On the importance of the Danube, see László Gerevich, "The rise of Hungarian Towns along the Danube," in *Towns in Medieval Hungary*, ed. idem (Budapest: Akadémiai, 1990), pp. 26–50; Katalin Szende, "Stadt und Naturlandschaft im ungarischen Donauraum des Mittelalters," in *Europäische Städte im Mittelalter* (Forschungen und Beiträge zur Wiener Stadtgeschichte, 52), eds Ferdinand Opll and Christoph Sonnlechner (Innsbruck–Vienna–Bozen: Studien Verlag, 2010), pp. 365–397.
3 See Tibor Nagy, "Budapest története az őskortól a honfoglalásig," [History of Budapest from ancient times to the conquest] in *Bp. tört.*, i, pp. 39–216, here pp. 43–82; *Kincsek a város alatt. Budapest régészeti örökségének feltárása/Treasures Under the City. Survey of the Archaeological Heritage of Budapest*, ed. Paula Zsidi (Budapest: BTM, 2005).

Beginnings

The first urban-like settlement was that of the Celtic Eravisci, on the slopes of the present-day Gellért Hill, in the first century BC.[4] A true city was, however, built only by the Romans who expanded their empire as far as the River Danube that served as the Empire's *limes* towards the *Barbaricum*. West of it, the province of Pannonia was established in the mid-first century AD. One of its capitals at the northeastern corner of the province was Aquincum, on the territory of present-day Óbuda (the northern part of the right-bank), a settlement with a name that reaches back before the Roman conquest and means "a place where water appears."[5] Two cities were founded here: a civil one across from the northern end of Óbudai Island and a military town, which lay opposite its southern end, where the Árpád Bridge now stands. The military settlement was rebuilt and expanded in the fourth century. It was within the walls of this fortification that the first core of Óbuda developed (Fig. 3.1). Two small Roman fortifications were also built on the right bank of the river, beyond the *limes*: Transaquincum across from the military town, near the mouth of the Rivulet Rákos, and Contra Aquincum further downstream, across from the castle hill, as a place of ferry. The latter became the core of the city of Pest.[6]

During the five centuries between the retreat of the Roman Empire from Pannonia and the arrival of the Magyars several people (Huns, Gepids, Avars, Slavs and others) settled in the Carpathian Basin, but none of them established centers that have left any trace.[7] After the fall of the Avar Khaganate in the

---

4 Gyula Nováki and Mária Pető, "Neuere Forschungen in spätkeltischen Oppidum auf dem Gellértberg in Budapest," *Acta Archaeologica Academiae Scientiarum Hungaricae* 47 (1988), pp. 83–99.

5 "Ort mit Wasservorkommen" – see Peter Anreiter, *Die vorrömischen Namen Pannoniens* (Budapest: Archaeolingua, 2001), pp. 32–34.

6 From the extensive literature on the Roman period, see Klára Póczy, *Aquincum, Budapest római kori történelmi városmagja* [Aquincum, the Roman-age core of Budapest] (Budapest: Enciklopédia, 2004); *Aquincum. Ancient Landscape – Ancient Town* (Theory, Method, Practice, 69), eds Katalin H. Kérdő and Ferenc Schweitzer (Budapest: Geographical Institute Research Centre for Astronomy and Earth Sciences Hungarian Academy of Sciences, 2014); *Forschungen in Aquincum 1969–2002, zu Ehren von Klára Póczy* (Aquincum Nostrum, ii/2), ed. Paula Zsidi (Budapest: BTM, 2003); Paula Zsidi, "Ergebnisse der topographischen und siedlungshistorischen Forschungen in den Jahren 1969–1999," in *The Autonomous Towns of Noricum and Pannonia* (Pannonia ii, Situla, 42), eds Marjeta Šašel Kos and Peter Scherrer (Ljubljana: Narodni muzej Slovenije, 2004), pp. 209–230.

7 Gyula László, *Études archéologiques sur l'histoire de la société des Avars* (Archaeologia Hungarica, Series nova, 34) (Budapest: Akadémiai, 1955); Nagy, "Budapest története az őskortól," pp. 185–216; István Bóna, *Der Anbruch des Mittelalters. Gepiden und Langobarden im Karpatenbecken* (Budapest: Corvina, 1976); idem, *Germanen, Hunnen, Awaren. Schätze der Völkerwanderungszeit. Ausstellungskataloge* (Nuremberg: Verlag Germanisches Nationalmuseum, 1988),

BUDA BEFORE BUDA: ÓBUDA & PEST AS EARLY CENTERS 73

FIGURE 3.1   *The most important elements of the topography of Óbuda*
AFTER L. GEREVICH

early eighth century the region became the borderland of the neighboring Frankish, Moravian and Bulgarian-Slav polities until the arrival of the Hungarians around 896, who over the next century occupied virtually the entire Carpathian Basin.

pp. 116–129; Margit Nagy, "Die Zeit der Völkerwanderung," in *Budapest im Mittelalter*, pp. 95–101 and 439–444; eadem, *Awarenzeitliche Gräberfelder im Stadtgebiet von Budapest* (Monumenta Avarorum Archaeologica, 2), eds Éva Garam and Tibor Vida (Budapest: Magyar Nemzeti Múzeum, 1998).

The only detailed narrative relating to the early Hungarian settlement in the center of the kingdom comes from the thirteenth-century *Gesta* of Anonymus.[8] Several historians have followed his novelistic description of a princely residence in the area of Buda.[9] According to Anonymus, Árpád first settled on the island of Csepel, gave a castle to a certain Kurszán in Óbuda, and died and was buried there, where a church called Fehéregyháza was later built.[10] This narrative appears by now more than dubious.[11] Archaeological finds do not support the idea of a princely residence on the Danube. No significant finds were unearthed in the excavations on the territory of the capital. Although there is evidence of elite burials in the form of interments with horses and rich harness, silver sabre-tache plates, double pendants, and so on, there is nothing to suggest intensive settlement.[12] The available evidence suggests that the

---

8 Anonymus, *Gesta Hungarorum – The Deeds of the Hungarians* (Central European Medieval Texts, 5), eds Martyn Rady and László Veszprémy (Budapest–New York: Central European University Press, 2010).

9 Györffy, *Budapest*, pp. 251–262; György Györffy, *Pest–Buda kialakulása. Budapest története a honfoglalástól az Árpád-kor végi székvárossá alakulásáig* [The formation of Pest-Buda. The history of Budapest from the Hungarian conquest to its late Árpádian-period formation as capital] (Budapest, Akadémiai, 1997), pp. 65–73; Gyula Kristó, *A magyar állam megszületése* [The birth of the Hungarian nation] (Szegedi Középkortörténeti Könyvtár, 8) (Szeged: Szegedi Középkorász Műhely, 1995), pp. 255–275; idem, *Honfoglalás és társadalom* [Hungarian Conquest and society] (Társadalom- és művelődéstörténeti tanulmányok, 16) (Budapest: MTA Történettudományi Intézete, 1996), pp. 89–109.

10 Anonymus, *Gesta Hungarorum*, pp. 92–95 (cap. 44), and 114–115 (cap. 52).

11 See also György Györffy, "Formation d'états au IXe siècle suivant les 'Gesta Hungarorum' du Notaire Anonyme," in *Nouvelles études historiques publiées à l'occasion du XIIe Congrès International des Sciences Historiques par la Commission Nationale des Historiens Hongrois* (Budapest: Akadémiai, 1965), pp. 27–53; István Bóna, "Die Archäologie in Ungarn und die ungarische Landnahme," *Acta Archaeologica Academiae Scientiarum Hungaricae* 49 (1997), pp. 345–362; András Róna Tas, *Hungarians and Europe in the Early Middle Ages: an Introduction to Early Hungarian History* (Budapest: Central European University Press, 1999), pp. 339–372; Miklós Takács, "Wirtschafts- und Siedlungswesen in Ungarn zur Zeit Stttatsgründung," in *Europas Mitte um 1000*, i, pp. 121–125; *Research on the Prehistory of the Hungarians: a Review. Papers Presented at the Meeting of the Institute of Archaeology of the HAS, 2003–2004* (Varia Archaeologica Hungarica, 18), ed. Balázs Gusztáv Mende (Budapest: Institute of Archaeology of the HAS, 2005).

12 László Révész in consideration of the lack of direct archaeological evidence challenged György Györffy's localization of the princely living area in the Danube valley and located the power center of the Magyar princes in the Upper Tisza Valley in the first half of the tenth century. László Révész, "Vezéri sírok a Felső-Tisza vidékén," [Princely burials in the region of the Upper Tisza Valley] in *Honfoglalás és régészet* [Hungarian

development of a princely court began some time in the mid-tenth century and was connected to the construction by Grand Duke Géza (972–997) of a palace in Esztergom, and not in Buda.

Beginnings of Óbuda and Pest

During the organization of the Christian kingdom, King Stephen I founded, besides the royal residence in Esztergom – which he raised to the status of an archbishopric – an additional royal center in the marshland, along the pilgrimage route to Jerusalem (opened in 1018) at Székesfehérvár. The collegiate church of Székesfehérvár in the basilica of the Holy Virgin came to be the coronation and burial site of the dynasty. In the central part of the kingdom, he did not set up administrative (comital) or ecclesiastical centers, but retained it as royal domain for the service of his armed retinue and the servile populations subject to royal courts (*curtes*). Because of the lack of sources, the exact location and size of these courts can only be partially reconstructed on the basis of later settlement patterns, but we know that medieval Óbuda emerged from one of them.[13]

Conquest and archaeology], ed. László Kovács (Budapest: Balassi, 1994), pp. 139–150, here p. 147; László Révész, *A karosi honfoglalás kori temetők* [The Conquest-Age cemeteries of Karos] (Budapest: Herman Ottó Múzeum – Magyar Nemzeti Múzeum, 1996), pp. 202–203; on the overview of the finds from Budapest, see Csanád Bálint, "Der landnahmezeitliche Grabfund von Pestlőrinc," *Acta Archaeologica Academiae Scientiarum Hungaricae* 32 (1980), pp. 341–350; Katalin Irásné-Melis, "Die Zeit der ungarischen Landnahme 895 bis Ende des 10. Jahrhunderts," in *Budapest im Mittelalter*, pp. 102–112 and 445–450; Sarolta Tettamanti, "A honfoglalás kora és a kora Árpád-kor," [The age of the Hungarian Conquest and the early Árpádian period] in *Pest megye monográfiája, i/2. A honfoglalástól 1686-ig* [A monograph on Pest county from the Conquest until 1686], ed. Attila Zsoldos (Budapest: Pest Megye Monográfia Közalapítvány, 2001), pp. 9–30, here pp. 9–20.

13 György Györffy, *König Stephan der Heilige* (Budapest: Corvina, 1988); Nora Berend, József Laszlovszky and Béla Zsolt Szakács, "The Kingdom of Hungary," in *Christianization and the Rise of Christian Monarchy*, ed. Nora Berend (Cambridge: Cambridge University Press, 2007), pp. 319–368; András Kubinyi, "Buda város pecséthasználatának kialakulása," [Development of seal-use of the city of Buda] in Kubinyi, *Tanulmányok*, i, pp. 271–299, here pp. 290–294; ÁMTF, iv, p. 617; Attila Zsoldos, "Pest megye az Árpád-korban," [Pest county in the Árpádian period] in *Pest megye monográfiája*, i/2, pp. 31–73, here p. 46; Végh, *Buda*, i, pp. 31 and 148–149.

As before, the main function of the court on the territory of Roman Aquincum was control of the river and its crossing points. Its role was enhanced by its connection to the royal centers in Esztergom and Székesfehérvár, for the roads (following the old Roman patterns) crossing the Danube at the fords of Pest and Jenő bifurcated at Óbuda and Budafelhévíz, with branches going in two directions towards these residences.[14] Of the Roman towns only ruins survived: walls, roads, remnants of the aqueduct and water channels, but they subsequently served to define the topography of the later Óbuda settlement.[15]

While there is no known 'foundation myth' of Buda, such as for Prague or Cracow and many other towns, the place has been sometimes identified with the Etzelburg of the *Nibelungenlied*[16] and with some mythical Frankish location of Sicambria.[17]

The name "Buda" may have been derived from a personal name (even if not necessarily of that of Attila's brother). People with this name are known from the eleventh century, but there are also suggestions of an origin in Gothic,

---

14   Lajos Glaser, "Dunántúl középkori úthálózata," [The medieval road network of Transdanubia] *Századok* 63 (1929), pp. 138–167 and 257–285; Erik Fügedi, "Topográfia és városi fejlődés a középkori Óbudán," [Topography and urban development in medieval Óbuda] *Tanulmányok Budapest Múltjából* 13 (1959), pp. 7–57, here pp. 7–12; András Kubinyi, "Budafelhévíz topográfiája és gazdasági fejlődése," [The topography and economic development of Budafelhévíz] in Kubinyi, *Tanulmányok*, i, pp. 115–182, here p. 115.

15   György Székely, "A pannóniai települések kontinuitásának kérdése és a hazai városfejlődés kezdetei," [The question of the continuity of the settlements of Pannonia and the beginnings of urban development in Hungary] *Tanulmányok Budapest Múltjából* 12 (1957), pp. 7–23, here p. 11, 14, and 16; Klára Póczy, "Mit használhatott fel Aquincum településszerkezetéből a középkori Óbuda?" [What could medieval Óbuda use of the settlement structure of Aquincum] *Építés-, Építészettudomány* 15 (1983), pp. 335–352; Paula Zsidi, "The Question of Continuity in Aquincum, the Capital of Pannonia Inferior," *Antaeus* 24 (1997–1998), pp. 585–592, here pp. 589–591.

16   *Nibelungenlied. Mittelhochdeutsch/Neuhochdeutsch* (Universal-Bibliothek, 644), eds Karl Bartsch, Helmut de Boor and Siegfried Grosse (Stuttgart: P. Reclam, 1997), pp. 416–417, 452–453, 866, and 876.

17   Alexandre Eckhardt, *De Sicambria a Sans-Souci: histoire et légendes franco-hongroises* (Paris: Les Presses Universitaires de France, 1943). The Hun, the Trojan and the Hungarian myths of origin were united in the *Gesta* of Simon of Kéza, written in the late thirteenth century. See Simon of Kéza, *Gesta Hungarorum. The Deeds of the Hungarians* (Central European Medieval Texts, 1), eds László Veszprémy and Frank Schaer (Budapest–New York: Central European University Press, 1999), pp. 34–69 (cap. 9–20). See also the article of József Laszlovszky and James Plumtree in the present volume.

German, Slavic, Latin or Turkic.[18] The settlement named Buda initially covered a large territory, running from today's Békásmegyer (some 10 km north of the city center) to a good part (or the whole) of Castle Hill. From this there emerged gradually, in the course of the eleventh to thirteenth centuries, the individual settlements of Óbuda, Budafelhévíz, Szentjakabfalva, and finally the new Buda on the hilltop.[19]

The position of the Óbuda royal court was greatly enhanced when in the mid-eleventh century an important royal collegiate church (or provostship) was founded there. The ascription of the foundation to St Stephen in the chronicles is clearly a thirteenth-century invention based on the story of Székesfehérvár's foundation. Nevertheless, it is not impossible that it was initiated in the last years of King Stephen. The present consensus is that it was founded by King Peter in honor of his patron saint.[20] The church and its accompanying buildings have been located by excavations in the area of the Roman military town on the present-day Fő Square of Óbuda.[21] The extensive building complex must have housed not only the collegiate church but also the royal *curtis*.[22]

The first settlement in this administrative and ecclesiastical center was in the beginning called Budavár, that is, Buda castle. In 1154 the Arab geographer Al-Idrīsī called the place thus[23] and listed it among the significant towns,

18   Lajos Kiss, *Földrajzi nevek etimológiai szótára*, 2 vols [An etymological dictionary of geographical names] (Budapest: Akadémiai, 1988), i, p. 261, and ii, p. 267; Györffy, *Pest-Buda*, pp. 88–89; Béla Lekli, *Buda neve* [The Name of Buda] (Budapest: Éghajlat, 2012).
19   Györffy, *Pest-Buda*, pp. 103–106.
20   Alexander Domanovszky, ed., *Chronici Hungarici compositio saeculi XIV*, in SRH, i, pp. 217–505, here, pp. 316–318 (cap. 67); László Bártfai Szabó, *Óbuda egyházi intézményei a középkorban* [Ecclesiastical institutions of Óbuda in the Middle Ages] (Budapest: [n. p.], 1935), pp. 8–14; Sándor Garády, "A budai (óbudai) káptalan alapítása," [The foundation of the Buda (Óbuda) Chapter] *Tanulmányok Budapest Múltjából* 7 (1940), pp. 3–24; Fügedi, "Topográfia," pp. 16–20; Györffy, *Pest-Buda*, pp. 94–96.
21   Júlia Altmann and Herta Bertalan, "Óbuda vom 11. bis 13. Jahrhundert," in *Budapest im Mittelalter*, pp. 113–131; László Gerevich, *The Art of Buda and Pest in the Middle Ages* (Budapest: Akadémiai, 1971), pp. 11–12.
22   Györffy, *König Stephan*, pp. 142–149.
23   B.z.wār.h/B.d.wār.h = Budavára (the place of the vowels are marked with points; at the end of the word h = a): Al-Idrīsī, *Opus geographicum sive "Liber ad eorum delectationem, qui terras peregrare studeat"*, 9 vols (Clima 6. sectio, 2–3), eds A. Bombaci *et al.* (Naples–Rome: Brill, 1978), viii, pp. 878 and 882–883. I acknowledge the help of Kinga Dévényi in deciphering of the text and obtaining the exact numbers of the pages. István Elter, "Magyarország Idrīsī földrajzi művében (1154)," [Hungary in the geographic work of Idrīsī

emphasizing its importance along the Danube. Moreover, he measured from it the distances to Pressburg, Titel, and Nitra, respectively. Remarkably, he regarded these locations, together with Székesfehérvár and Siklós, as belonging to the Venetian commercial sphere of interest in the Danube-Drava region. Around 1210, Anonymus also recorded that the Hungarians call the settlement "Budavára".[24] The late thirteenth-century redaction of the *Chronicle of the Deeds of the Hungarians*, ascribed to Master Ákos, also used this expression, probably from an earlier version of the chronicle.[25] The origin of the name is unknown. The ruins of the Roman wall may have been seen as a 'castle' or else the building complex of the court and the collegiate church were fortified at some point. The limited possibilities of excavations do not allow us to reconstruct the stages in their construction. To be sure, after the beginning of the thirteenth century, there is no further reference to a castle.[26]

The building complex of Budavára seems to have been complete by the time of King St Ladislas I, for he supported the chapter by granting it the significant income of the fishing rights on the river, running from the ford of Megyer to the *Insula Magna* (Csepel Island). This was confirmed and augmented in 1148 by King Géza II. He granted the church the tolls collected on the ships transporting wine and salt upriver that were collected at the ford of Pest and at Budafelhévíz, and probably also at the port called Géza's market.[27] While this appellation is debated, it is not unlikely that it refers to the early market of Óbuda where the toll of the port was collected.[28] The name may refer to a

---

(1154)] *Acta Universitatis Szegediensis de Attila József nominatae. Acta Historica* 82 (1985), pp. 53–63.

24 Buduuar: Anonymus, *Gesta Hungarorum*, pp. 8–9 (cap. 6).

25 Budawara. Gesta magistri Akus prepositi Veteri Budensis circa 1272 (*Chronicon Pictum*, fourteenth century). See *Chronici Hungarici*, pp. 268–269 (cap. 13).

26 István Bóna, *Az Árpádok korai várai* [The castles of the Árpádian period] (Debrecen: Ethnica, 1998), pp. 24–25. Bóna does not accept Anonymus's hypothesis of the Kurszán-castle and the princely center of the Conquest period. He considers the name "Budavár" a projection of the Etzelburg of the German settlers. He believes that "Ó-Budavár" was only a ruined town in the age of Anonymus.

27 "…tributum fori Geysa et tributum portus Pest et Kerepes navium etiam cum vino sive cum salibus ascendentium, sive cum aliis venalibus descendentium eidem ecclesie regie maiestatis auctoritate condonare curavi." – MNL OL DL 105 992. Edited in BTOE, i, pp. 3–4 (no 1).

28 There are different identifications of Gézavására. See Fügedi, "Topográfia," pp. 11–12; Kubinyi, "Budafelhévíz," pp. 115–119; Végh, *Buda*, i, pp. 23–24; Katalin Szende, "Towns along the Way. Changing Patterns of Long-Distance Trade and the Urban Network of Medieval Hungary," in *Towns and Communication*, ii. *Communication between Towns*, eds Hubert Houben and Kristjan Toomaspoeg (Lecce: Mario Congedo, 2011), pp. 161–225, here

market privilege ceded by King Géza I or to the grant by Géza II. If the market was indeed granted to Óbuda, it would have been an important step in the urban development of the town. This hypothesis is supported by the likelihood that the royal court and the church generated sufficient interest in goods, even imported ones, which engendered an early, eleventh- and twelfth-century market for the unloading and selling of merchandise at the port. Finds suggesting this have been unearthed in Óbuda, outside the Roman wall (the 'castle') in the southeastern corner of the town, near the later market place. The Moravian and Austrian import ware of graphite-ceramics (storage vessels, cooking pots, plates, and pans), pointing to the Danube trade mentioned by Idrisi; the salt and wine indicate the type of domestic traffic involved; and the swiveled scales also found here further relate to a local trade in goods.[29] The royal estate and the collegiate church thus brought into being an early port and market for merchants that facilitated the early urbanization of the settlement. The collegiate church had a significant impact on this development on account of the income of the tolls. Whether Óbuda profited from the long-distance trade on

---

p. 180; for the charters that could be used in the identification, see MNL OL DL 5631, 14 211 and 106 009.

29   On the formation of towns, see Erik Fügedi, "Die Entwicklung des Städtewesens in Ungarn," *Alba Regia. Annales Musei Stephani Regis* 10 (1969), pp. 101–118; András Kubinyi, "A magyar várostörténet első fejezete," [The first phase of the urban history in Hungarian] in *Társadalomtörténeti tanulmányok* [Studies in social history] (Studia Miskolciensia, 2), ed. Csaba Fazekas (Miskolc: Bíbor, 1996), pp. 36–46; on market holding, see Boglárka Weisz, "Vásártartás az Árpád-korban," [Fair holding in the Árpádian period] *Századok* 141 (2007), pp. 879–942, here p. 932; eadem, "Vásárok a középkorban," [Fairs and markets in the Middle Ages] *Századok* 144 (2010), pp. 1397–1454, here p. 1439; on the imported ceramics, see Altmann and Bertalan, "Óbuda," pp. 113–131 and 456–459; Imre Holl, "Angaben zur mittelalterlichen Schwarzhafnerkeramik mit Werkstattmarken," *Mitteilungen des Archäologischen Instituts der Ungarischen Akademie der Wissenschaften* 5 (1974–1975), pp. 135–150; György Duma and Csaba Ravasz, "Graphithaltige Gefäße aus Österreichs Mittelalter," *Archaeologia Austriaca* 59–60 (1976), pp. 225–242; Carl von Carnap-Bornheim, "Graphit und Graphittonkeramik," in *Reallexikon der Germanischen Altertumskunde. Zwölfter Band* (*Getränke – Greiftierstil*), eds Heinrich Beck, Heiko Steuer and Dieter Timpe (Berlin–New York: De Gruyter, 1998), pp. 593–598. On the scales, see István Méri, "Árpád-kori pénzváltó mérleg," [Árpádian-period money exchange scales] *Folia Archaeologica* 6 (1954), pp. 106–115; Herta Bertalan, "XIII. századi csuklós bronzmérlegek Óbudán," [Thirteenth-century bronze chain scales at Óbuda] *Budapest Régiségei* (1998), pp. 171–180. The finds have been analyzed by Bence Péterfi (idem, *Árpád-kori grafitos kerámia a Kárpát-medencében. Az óbudai Lajos utca 163–165. sz. telkek korai kerámiaanyaga*, unpublished MA thesis [Árpádian-period ceramics with graphite from the Carpathian Basin. The early ceramics finds of plots 163–165 Lajos Street in Óbuda] [Budapest: ELTE, 2013]). I am grateful to Bence Péterfi for his suggestions as to the relevant literature and for sharing his data with me.

the Danube up to Regensburg and beyond, and down towards Byzantium, we do not know. A sizable hoard of Byzantine copper coins from the twelfth century, thought to be from Óbuda but now lost, may point in this direction.[30]

The beginnings of Pest are not much clearer than those of Óbuda, due to the very scant source material. The date at which this originally (Bulgaro-)Slavic place name became incorporated into Hungarian cannot be established. It is not impossible that the Hungarians were already acquainted with the term meaning "cave" or "oven" before their settlement in the Carpathian Basin and applied it accordingly. Its meaning is not problematic, for its literal translation was used by the Muslim settlers in the form of Bécs and by the Germans as Ofen. However, it is not at all clear why it was applied here. One explanation is that lime-burning ovens utilizing the Roman ruins gave the place its name. Another possibility is a reference to a cave on the southern slope of Pest Hill (now Gellért Hill), resembling a lime kiln, or the steep rocks of the hill.[31]

---

30   Unfortunately the Byzantine bronze finds consisting of 500 coins supposedly unearthed in Óbuda disappeared after the Second World War. Most of the bronze coins, which were not suitable for hoarding, are from the Byzantine Empire during the reign of Manuel I Komnenos (1143–1180). See András Kerényi, "Egy XII. századi óbudai bizánci pénzlelet (1143–1195)," [A twelfth-century Byzantine coin-hoard from Óbuda (1143–1195)] *Budapest Régiségei* 15 (1950), pp. 541–547; Lajos Glaser, "Der Levantehandel über Ungarn im 11. und 12. Jahrhundert," *Ungarische Jahrbücher* 13 (1933), pp. 356–363; István Gedai, "Fremde Münzen im Karpatenbecken aus den 11–13. Jahrhunderten," *Acta Archaeologica Academiae Scientiarum Hungaricae* 21 (1969), pp. 105–148; András Kubinyi, "Regensburg – Passau – Ungarn im Mittelalter," in *Bayern und Ungarn: Tausend Jahre enge Beziehungen* (Schriftenreihe des Osteuropainstituts Regensburg–Passau, Südosteuropa-Studien xii, Heft, 39), ed. Ekkehard Völkl (Regensburg: Lassleben, 1988), pp. 29–39, here pp. 31–33; Ferenc Makk, *The Árpáds and the Comneni. Political Relations between Hungary and Byzantium in the 12th century* (Budapest: Akadémiai, 1989), pp. 21–22; Károly Mesterházy, "Régészeti adatok Magyarország 10–11. századi kereskedelméhez," [Archaeological information for the 10th–11th -century trade of Hungary] *Századok* 127 (1993), pp. 450–468; András Kubinyi, "A korai Árpád-kor gazdasági fejlődésének kérdőjelei," [Questions on the economic development of the early Árpádian period] *Valóság* 39, no 3 (1996), pp. 60–65. For the most recent overview of the question, with recent literature, see Szende, "Towns along the Way," p. 181.

31   Katalin Irásné-Melis, *Adatok a Pesti-síkság Árpád-kori településtörténetéhez* [Information on the Árpádian-period settlement network of the Plain of Pest] (Monumenta Historica Budapestinensia, 4) (Budapest: Budapesti Történeti Múzeum, 1983), p. 35; Katalin Irás-Melis, "Die Herausbildung und Entwicklung der Stadt Pest bis 1241," in *Budapest im Mittelalter*, pp. 132–143, here p. 132; Kiss, *Földrajzi nevek*, i, p. 261 and ii, pp. 328–329 and 338; Györffy, *Pest-Buda*, pp. 75–76; ÁMTF, iv, pp. 543–544; Bóna, *Az Árpádok korai várai*, p. 24; Végh, *Buda*, i, p. 20.

The first mention of Pest occurs in the mid-eleventh century in relation to its ford. The ferry on both banks of the Danube was called Pest, but early settlement started only on the left bank. Its first inhabitants may have been the ferrymen in royal service. There must also have been some buildings at the ferry port on the right bank, but a more elaborate settlement only began there later. The ferry (on the right bank) was the place where Bishop Gerard was murdered by pagan rebels in 1046. According to his legend, he was first buried in the church of the Holy Virgin in Pest.[32] This church has not been located so far, but it is most likely that it stood where the later parish church of Pest, likewise dedicated to St Mary (now Március 15. Square) was built, in the southeastern corner of the ruins of the former Roman fort of Contra Aquincum. This is suggested by the excavated eleventh- or twelfth-century cemetery of commoners in the northeastern corner.[33] The settlement of the ferrymen around the church included the ferry, the port, and, probably, a market. The royal fishermen may have lived here, too, but we do not know whether they had a separate settlement. The income of the tolls and customs of the port, ferry, and fishing were collected by royal officials, but whether they had their separate organization here or belonged to the Óbuda court is not known.

Not much later, in 1061, a donation refers to an agrarian-type settlement on "Pest Island." A private landowner granted there land, a vineyard with vintners, a mill with a miller, and two households of fishermen. The location of the island is debated, but most probably relates to an oxbow island on the Danube, where the king had granted land to a secular owner.[34] Thus, the royal domain may also have contained agrarian areas.

---

32 *Chronici Hungarici*, pp. 339–342 (cap. 83–84), Emericus Madzsar, ed., *Legenda Sancti Gerhardi episcopi*, in SRH, ii, pp. 461–506, here pp. 477–478 and 501–505; Gerevich, *The Art of Buda*, pp. 13–14.

33 Katalin Irásné-Melis, "A pesti városalaprajz kialakulása és változásai a középkorban," [The formation and the changes of the ground plan of Pest in the Middle Ages] in *Társadalomtörténeti tanulmányok a közeli és a régmúltból. Emlékkönyv Székely György 70. születésnapjára* [Studies in social history from the recent past and the bygone. Studies in honor of György Székely on his 70th birthday], ed. Ilona Sz. Jónás (Budapest: Eötvös Loránd Tudományegyetem Bölcsészettudományi Kara, Egyetemes Történeti Tanszék, 1994), pp. 88–107, here p. 90; Irásné-Melis, "Die Herausbildung," pp. 132–133; eadem, "Archaeological traces of the last medieval town planning in Pest," in *"Quasi liber et pictura". Tanulmányok Kubinyi András hetvenedik születésnapjára* [Studies in honor of András Kubinyi on his 70th birthday] (Budapest: ELTE Régészettudományi Intézet, 2004), pp. 235–243, here p. 235.

34 Bernát L. Kumorovitz, "A zselicszentjakabi alapítólevél 1061-ből ('Pest' legkorábbi említése)," [The foundation charter of Zselicszentjakab from 1061 (the first mention of 'Pest')] *Tanulmányok Budapest Múltjából* 16 (1964), pp. 43–81; ÁMTF, iv, p. 538 and 544.

Another important settlement core was the emporium of Muslim traders. Little is known of its beginnings, but from later evidence its establishment can be dated to the late eleventh century. Anonymus speculated that Prince Taksony (955–c. 972) granted the "castle of Pest" to some Muslims. The castle would here again mean the Roman ruins, as we have no other indication of a fortification in that area. While Anonymus thought that these were Bulgarian "Ishmaelites," the sources suggest that they were Chorezmians, called *káliz*.[35] Their name (in their own language *khwālisz*) survives in place names such as Kálóz, Kalóc and Kalász and, in our region, Budakalász, which is north of Óbuda on the right bank. Their merchants played an important role in the commerce from Prague to the Danube Delta and to Kiev in the east. Anonymus was misled by the fact that many of them came via the Upper Volga, where Volga-Bulgaria was situated and where there was a sizable Chvorezmian merchant colony. He may, nevertheless, have known the Muslim traders of Pest from his own experience. They also stood in royal service and were employed as financial experts in the tasks of the treasure (toll collection, minting, coinage exchange, farm of the chamber). The conversion of the "Ishmaelites" (as the records called them) was instructed by the laws of the eleventh century with more or less success.[36] They may also have been active in the transport and sale of salt.[37] Pest became, besides its place in long-distance trade, one of the centers of the transportation of salt. They also gave their name to the "káliz-road", which ran from Transylvania along the River Maros to Szeged, thence overland to Dunaszekcső, where it crossed the Danube, although some trade

---

35 Anonymus, *Gesta Hungarorum*, pp. 126–127 (cap. 57); Györffy, *Pest-Buda*, pp. 74–75; with regard to the problem of Pest castle and an opposing view, see Bóna, *Az Árpádok korai várai*, pp. 56–58.

36 The laws of King Ladislas I, Book Two, art. 15–16, 18, in DRMH, i, p. 15; The laws of King Coloman, ibid., p. 30 (art. 76–77).

37 Oszkár Paulinyi, "A sóregálé kialakulása Magyarországon," [The formation of the salt regale in Hungary] *Századok* 58 (1924), pp. 627–647; András Kubinyi, "Königliches Salzmonopol und die Städte des Königreichs Ungarn im Mittelalter," in *Stadt und Salz* (Beiträge zur Geschichte der Städte Mitteleuropas, 10), ed. Wilhelm Rausch (Linz: Österreichischer Arbeitskreis für Stadtgeschichtsforschung, 1988), pp. 213–294; Boglárka Weisz, "Megjegyzések az Árpád-kori sóvámolás és -kereskedelem történetéhez," [Contributions to the history of the salt tax and trade in the Árpádian period] *Acta Universitatis Szegediensis de Attila József nominatae. Acta Historica* 125 (2007), pp. 43–57; István Draskóczy, "Salt Mining and the Salt Trade in Medieval Hungary," (in preparation).

plainly continued on the river.[38] It has been understood from Anonymus's use of the word castle that the Muslim settlement was within the Roman *castrum*, but if we presume that the eleventh-century church stood there, then it is unlikely. No finds in the cemetery there point to an oriental, Muslim population. It is more likely that they lived further north in a settlement called Újbécs in the thirteenth century. If we presume that the Muslims called Pest Bécs, then the appellation New Bécs (*Újbécs*) makes sense, and is supported by a thirteenth-century reference to a "former cemetery of pagans." In this separate settlement, the Muslims would have been able to practice their own laws and religion. The name of their leader, Billa, given by Anonymus, may have come from a place name and vineyard in Óbuda.[39]

In summary then: early Pest consisted of several separate but functionally related settlements on the royal domain. The site of the ferrymen and the royal officers as well as the Muslim emporium together supplied the basis for the urban development of the area. This may have been augmented by agrarian areas on their edge.

Óbuda as Royal Residence – Pest as German Settlement

In the last third of the twelfth century significant changes occurred in Óbuda. The provosts of the collegiate church came into closer contact with the royal

---

38   Anonymus, *Gesta Hungarorum*, pp. 126–127 (cap. 57); Ivan Hrbek, "Ein arabischer Bericht über die Ungarn. Abu-Hamid al-Andalusi al-Garnati, 1080–1170," *Acta Orientalia Academiae Scientiarum Hungaricae* 5 (1955), pp. 205–230; Károly Czeglédy, "Az Árpád kori mohamedánokról és neveikről," [On the Árpádian-period Muslims and their names] in *Nyelvtudományi előadások* [Lectures in linguistics] (Nyelvtudományi Értesítő, 70), eds Miklós Kázmér and József Végh (Budapest: Akadémiai, 1970), pp. 254–259; György Székely, "Les contacts entre Hongrois et Musulmans aux IXe–XIIe siècles," in *The Muslim East: Studies in Honour of Julius Germanus*, ed. Gyula Káldy-Nagy (Budapest: Loránd Eötvös University, 1974), pp. 53–74; Jenő Szűcs, "The Peoples of Medieval Hungary," in *Ethnicity and Society in Hungary* (*Études Historiques Hongroises 1990 publiées à l'occasion du XVIIe Congrés International des Sciences Historiques par le Comité National des Historiens Hongrois*) 7 vols, ed. Ferenc Glatz (Budapest: Institute of History of the Hungarian Academy of Sciences, 1990), i, pp. 11–20, here p. 14; Jenő Szűcs, "Két történelmi példa az etnikai csoportok életképességéről," [Two historical examples of the viability of ethnic groups] *Holmi* 20, no 11 (2008), pp. 1399–1406; Ferenc Makk, "Les relations Hungaro-byzantines aux Xe–XIe siècles," in *Études Historiques Hongroises*, iv, pp. 11–25; Szende, "Towns along the Way," pp. 167–169.

39   "...Cursus autem dicte terre Wybeech...et antiquitus fuerunt sepulchra paganorum..." – MNL OL DL 1102, given in BTOE, i, pp. 199–200 (no 185); Györffy, *Pest-Buda*, pp. 74–78.

court. During the organization of the royal chancellery, in 1186, Hadrian, the provost of the Buda chapter became its head. At this time, the chapter began to be a place of authentication (*locus credibilis*) for the entire country.[40] It was in these years that the king (Béla III) was repeatedly recorded as resident in Óbuda. In an age of itinerant kingship, kings only occasionally visited even such established centers of royal residence as Esztergom and Székesfehérvár, in which respect the royal presence in Óbuda is significant. Ansbert recorded that after Frederick Barbarossa passed through Hungary on his way to the Holy Land, he sent his envoys back from Adrianopolis, who met King Béla III at Christmas 1189 in Óbuda.[41] Previously, the king and his queen, Margaret Capet, received the Emperor in Esztergom and thereafter – according to Arnold of Lübeck – they went on a four-day hunt to Óbuda and Csepel Island.[42] This information fits well with Attila's imaginary festivities in Óbuda, as reported in Anonymus's *Gesta*, and the early thirteenth-century text of the *Nibelungenlied's* image of Etzelburg, which may have meant Óbuda (although more probably Esztergom). All told, it would seem likely that in King Béla's time Óbuda joined the two earlier royal centers of Esztergom and Székesfehérvár and that it became generally known as one of the king's residences.[43] This may have

40   1186: MNL OL DL 40 065 and 40 532; DF 208 291; ÁMTF, iv, pp. 662–663.
41   Ansbertus, Gesta Friderici 1189: "…nuntii [imperatoris] prospero itinere circa nativitatem Domini apud civitatem Ungarie, que Teutonice Czilnburg dicitur, ad regem Ungarie pervenerunt…" – *Catalogus fontium historiae Hungariae aevo ducum et regum ex stirpe Arpad descendentium*, i, ed. Albinus Franciscus Gombos (Budapest: Szent István Akadémia, 1937, repr. Budapest: Nap, 2005), p. 296 [henceforth: CFH]; Bernát L. Kumorovitz, "Buda (és Pest) 'fővárossá' alakulásának kezdetei," [The formation of Buda (and Pest) as 'capital' of Hungary] *Tanulmányok Budapest Múltjából* 18 (1971), pp. 7–57, here pp. 38–39.
42   Arnoldus Lubecensis, Cronica 1189: "…imperator a rege deductus est in urbem Adtile [!] dictam, ubi dominus imperator quatuor diebus venationi operam dedit. …" – CFH, i, p. 305.
43   Anonymus, *Gesta Hungarorum*, pp. 100–103, 106–107, 108–109 and 114–115 (cap. 46, 49, 50 and 52); Bernát L. Kumorovitz, "Adatok Budapest főváros Árpád-kori történetéhez," [Information on the Árpádian-period history of Budapest] *Tanulmányok Budapest Múltjából* 19 (1972), pp. 7–37, here pp. 21–23; Györffy, *Pest-Buda*, pp. 82–84; Péter Simon V., "A Nibelungének magyar vonatkozásai," [The Hungarian references of the Nibelungenlied] *Századok* 112 (1978), pp. 271–325; *Nibelungenlied*, pp. 416–417, 452–453, 866, and 876; Otfrid Ehrismann, "Nibelungenlied," in *Enzyklopädie des Märchens. Handwörterbuch zur historischen und vergleichenden Erzählforschung*, x, ed. Rolf Wilhelm Brednich (Berlin–New York: De Gruyter, 2002), pp. 1–16; *"Uns ist in alten Mären…" Das Nibelungenlied und seine Welt. Ausstellung in Badischen Landesmuseum, Schloss Karlsruhe, 13. 12. 2003–14. 03. 2004. Katalog*, ed. Jürgen Krüger (Karlsruhe: Primus Verlag, 2003), pp. 36–37 (the map does not show Óbuda).

been partially caused by the redirection of trade routes preferring Óbuda to Esztergom. Even though this change became significant only after the fall of Constantinople in 1204 and the decline of Rus', the consolidated internal conditions in the kingdom may have contributed further to its relevance as a royal center. The 'defendable' Esztergom was thus gradually replaced by another central location more accessible from east and west alike (*locus communior*).[44]

Another development impacted on the urbanization of the settlement, even though less positively. King Emeric and then his brother Andrew II, in 1212, granted Óbuda in perpetuity to the collegiate church, together with its market toll, wine levy, and the jurisdiction over its people.[45] The donation included a wide range of woodlands, vineyards, meadows, pastures, marshland and plow land. These agrarian parts were cultivated by the people of the church. The built-up part that was now given to the chapter was called a *civitas*, where, besides the members and staff of the collegiate church, royal guards and occasional guests had their residences. The port and market was referred to as *villa* (or *wik*), which expanded with the constant arrival of new settlers, but we know little of them.[46] German settlers may have arrived as early as the reign of King Géza II but probably *Latini*, Romance-speaking Walloons, Italians and Frenchmen, also settled in the developing royal center.[47] Adjacent

---

44 Kumorovitz, "Buda (és Pest)," pp. 7–57; Erzsébet Ladányi, "Adatok a 'locus communis – locus communior' hazai alkalmazásához," [The use of the terms 'locus communis – locus communior' in Hungary] in *Változatok a történelemre. Tanulmányok Székely György tiszteletére* [Versions of history. Studies in honor of György Székely] (Monumenta Historica Budapestinensia, 14), eds Gyöngyi Erdei and Balázs Nagy (Budapest: BTM – ELTE BTK Középkori és Kora Újkori Egyetemes Történeti Tanszék, 2004), pp. 235–236.

45 MNL OL DF 230 035, given in BTOE, i, pp. 6–11 (no 4); a sharp debate unfolded between György Györffy and Bernát L. Kumorovitz on the value of this possibly forged charter. See Györffy, *Pest-Buda*, pp. 107–108; Kumorovitz, "Adatok Budapest," pp. 8–19.

46 MNL OL DL 106 090, edited in BTOE, i, p. 12 (no 6); Györffy, *Pest-Buda,* pp. 103–108; Kumorovitz, "Adatok Budapest," pp. 19–24.

47 We do not have information on German settlers from this period; however the contemporary name of Óbuda – Etzilburg – testifies to their presence. There is only one reference, from 1231, to a Latin merchant, who accepted deposits with interest, which means he was involved in banking business. See MNL OL DL 164, edited in BTOE, i, p. 20 (no 15); Kubinyi, *Anfänge Ofens*, pp. 11–14; György Székely, "Wallons et italiens en Europe Centrale aux XIe–XVIe siècles," *Annales Universitatis Scientiarum Budapestinensis de Rolando Eötvös Nominatae, Sectio Historica* 6 (1964), pp. 3–71; Erik Fügedi, "Das mittelalterliche Königreich Ungarn als Gastland," in *Die deutsche Ostsiedlung des mittelalters als Problem der europäischen Geschichte* (Vorträge und Forschungen, 18), ed. Walter Schlesinger (Sigmaringen: Jan Thorbecke, 1975), pp. 480–498; Szende, "Towns along the Way," pp. 174–178.

to the settlement of traders and craftsmen was the seat of the royal servants and the *vicus* of the smiths. On the market place, the Church of St Margaret, the later parish church of Óbuda, was built. The market toll and the wine levy granted to the chapter suggest that the market was lucrative.

A charter dated 1217, but forged some ten years later, suggests that the settlers enjoyed the rights of the Latins of Székesfehérvár and the Germans of Pest. This indicates that they held the privilege of *hospites*. However, in the case of the Óbuda *hospites* the development of this privilege into complete urban liberties was limited by the jurisdiction of the chapter.[48] The loss of the market tolls also hindered Óbuda's economic development. The rights belonging to the church in the administration of justice, and over property transactions and vineyards came to be even more serious obstacles to the growth of urban autonomy and self-government.

Under Andrew II, around 1210–1220, a not very large but fairly representative royal palace was built near the chapter. It was not located directly on the chapter's land, but rather southeast of it, above the market place.[49] After its

---

48 MNL OL DF 236 987, edited in *Codex diplomaticus et epistolaris Slovaciae*, i (*Inde ab a. DCCCV usque ad a. MCCXXXV.*), ed. Richard Marsina (Bratislava: Academia Scientiarum Slovacae, 1971), pp. 178–179 (no 227); Györffy, *Pest-Buda*, p. 113; András Kubinyi, "Zur Frage der deutschen Siedlungen im mittleren Teil des Königreichs Ungarn (1200–1541)," in *Die deutsche Ostsiedlung des mittelalters als Problem der europäischen Geschichte* (Vorträge und Forschungen hrg. vom Konstanzer Arbeitskreis für mittelalterliche Geschichte, 18), ed. Walter Schlesinger (Sigmaringen: Jan Thorbecke, 1975), pp. 529–544; László Solymosi, *A földesúri járadékok új rendszere a 13. századi Magyarországon* [The new system of seigneurial rights in thirteenth-century Hungary] (Budapest: Argumentum, 1998), pp. 7–18; Attila Zsoldos, "A fehérváriak szabadságai," [The liberties of he burghers of Székesfehérvár] in *Székesfehérvár középkori kiváltságai* [The medieval privileges of Székesfehérvár], eds idem and Tibor Neumann (Székesfehérvár: Székesfehérvár Megyei Jogú Város Levéltára, 2010), pp. 9–42, here pp. 38–41; Katalin Szende, "Power and Inditity. Royal Privileges to the Towns of Medieval Hungary in the Thirteenth Century," in *Urban Liberties and Civic Participation from the Middle Ages to Modern Times*, eds Michel Pauly and Alexander Lee (Trier: Porta Alba, 2015), 27–67.

49 Altmann and Bertalan, "Óbuda," pp. 124–128; István Feld, "Ecilbug und Ofen – Zur Problematik der Stadtburgen in Ungarn," *Castrum Bene* 6 (1999), pp. 73–88; Krisztina Havasi, "Az óbudai királyi, utóbb királynéi vár kőemlékei," [The stone fragments of the royal, later queenly castle at Óbuda] *Budapest Régiségei* 40 (2006), pp. 221–252; eadem, "Az óbudai királyi, utóbb királynéi palota Szent Erzsébet kápolnája. A magyar királyi 'udvar' építészeti emléke(i) a 13. század első évtizedeiből," [The St Elisabeth chapel of the royal, later queenly castle of Óbuda. The architectural remain(s) of the Hungarian royal 'court' from the first decade of the Thirteenth century] in *Árpád-házi Szent Erzsébet kultusza a 13–16. században* [The cult of St Elizabeth of Hungary in the thirteenth to sixteenth centuries]

construction, the number of administrative and jurisdictional court sessions during Lent and Easter increased in Óbuda, which bolstered the consumer trade. Óbuda came to have sessions as frequently as the two older centers. Béla IV even gave preference to Óbuda.[50] The impetus towards urban development was, however, cut short by the Mongol invasion in 1241–1242, when the army of Batu Khan crossed the frozen Danube and burnt Óbuda down.[51]

At the turn of the eleventh to twelfth centuries, German settlers (*hospites*) came to Pest, establishing themselves on both banks of the Danube. On the left bank, traders and craftsmen, called *Theutonici*, settled. They built, probably at the place of a royal chapel, the fine Romanesque Parish Church of the Virgin Mary. Their settlement developed near to it, expanding beyond the limits of the mainly destroyed Roman fort. Their leader was most likely a nobleman from Lower Austria, the *Ritterburger* Werner, by whom a systematic *locatio*, under royal command began.[52] Werner had earned his wealth by long-distance trade and he invested it in landed property.

On the opposite bank, Kispest ("Little Pest", *Pest Minor*, also called *Kreinfeld, Kelenföld*), Saxon vintners settled in the originally royal vineyards. Their own church, likewise a former royal chapel, now St Gerard's parish, suggests a separate settlement.[53] The settlers from the left bank also acquired vineyards here; by 1232 burghers of both Pests were involved in growing wine. Not much later,

---

(Studia Franciscana Hungarica/Magyar Ferences Tanulmányok, 2), ed. Dávid Falvay (Budapest: Magyarok Nagyasszonya Ferences Rendtartomány, 2009), pp. 163–192.

50   Master Roger, *Epistle to the Sorrowful Lament upon the Destruction of the Kingdom of Hungary by the Tatars* (Central European Medieval Texts, 5), eds János M. Bak and Martyn Rady (Budapest–New York: Central European University Press, 2010), pp. 158–159 (cap. 15); Kumorovitz, "Adatok Budapest," pp. 7–57; Enikő Spekner, "Buda királyi székhellyé alakulásának kezdetei a 13. század első felében," [The beginning of the formation of Buda as a royal center in the first half of the thirteenth century] *Urbs. Magyar Várostörténeti Évkönyv* 7 (2012), pp. 97–132. A monograph on this issue was published in 2015: eadem, *Hogyan lett Buda a középkori Magyarország fővárosa? A budai királyi székhely története a 12. század végétől a 14. század közepéig* [How did Buda become the capital of medieval Hungary? The History of the royal seat in Buda from the end of the twelfth to the mid-fourteenth century] (Monumenta Historica Budapestinensia, 17) (Budapest: BTM, 2015).

51   Master Roger, *Epistle*, pp. 214–215 (cap. 38); Thomas of Split, *History of the Bishops of Salona and Split* (Central European Medieval Texts, 4), eds Damir Karbić, Mirjana Matijević Sokol and James Ross Sweeney (Budapest–New York: Central European University Press, 2006), pp. 288–289 (cap. 38); Szende, "Towns Along the Way," pp. 190–192 (with an overview of the relevant literature).

52   BTOE, i, pp. 23–34 (no 20); Györffy, *Pest-Buda,* p. 116; Kubinyi, *Anfänge Ofens,* p. 16.

53   MNL OL DF 200 005, given in BTOE, i, p. 18 (no 12); Végh, *Buda,* i, p. 21.

a group of five Germans from Pest rented 200 *hold*s (ca. 280 acres) land for planting wine in Kispest.[54] The size of the land that they rented suggests that they had sufficient capital to develop their investment in the long term; one of them was a bell-founder.[55]

Muslim traders remained in business next to the Germans. In 1217, when leaving for the Holy Land, King Andrew secured the dower of 8000 silver marks of Queen Jolanta with the income of the salt shipped on the Maros and the income of the Saracens of Pest.[56] The Muslims of Pest seem to have still played a major role in the transport on the "káliz road." In the early thirteenth century the king enjoyed a sizable income from the market toll of Pest, but we do not know how the traffic was divided between Muslims and Germans. In 1217, the king assigned his part of the toll to the upkeep of his court on Csepel Island. The annual income of the market amounted to 180 marks, which is some 45 kg silver.[57]

Following the prohibitions laid down by the 1217 Council of Toledo, the office-holding of Jews and Muslims was restricted in Hungary and was supposed to stop altogether according to the agreement of Bereg, made in 1233 between the king and the papal legate.[58] By that time, however, many of them had become Christians and merged into the larger society or left their settlements. This is how Újbécs may have been abandoned and taken over by the expanding German merchant colony. The *Ritterbürger* Werner had his palace there.[59]

Meanwhile, the German settlement developed rapidly. A sure sign of this was the appearance of the Dominicans, soon after the order's foundation, in the mid-1220s.[60] St Anthony's convent was built at some place on the southern border of Pest, near the later Szenterzsébetfalva. Soon it had such a reputation that in 1233 King Andrew designated it as the place where certain reparation

---

54   MNL OL DF 230 056, given in BTOE, i, pp. 20–21 (No 16); MNL OL DF 200 008, given in BTOE, i, pp. 37–38 (no 23).

55   Györffy, *Pest-Buda*, p. 116.

56   BTOE, i, p. 16 (no 10); Györffy, *Pest-Buda,* p. 112; Kubinyi, *Anfänge Ofens,* pp. 14–17; Fügedi, "Das mittelalterliche Königreich," p. 488.

57   MNL OL DL 63, edited in BTOE, i, pp. 14–15 (no 8); Györffy, *Pest-Buda,* pp. 101–102.

58   EFHU, iii/2, pp. 28 (no 25).

59   1268: MNL OL DL 651 and 667, given in BTOE, i, pp. 98–99 (no 84); MNL OL DL 942, given in BTOE, i, pp. 152–156 (no 138); MNL OL DL 1102, given in BTOE, i, pp. 199–200 (no 185); the palace is mentioned for the first time in 1268, but by this time Újbécs was considered abandoned. See ÁMTF, iv, p. 552.

60   Erik Fügedi, "Koldulórendek és a városfejlődés Magyarországon," [Mendicant orders and urban development in Hungary] *Századok* 106 (1972), pp. 69–95.

payments to the church were to be rendered. The size and the quality of its stone structure must have been impressive, for this was the only place where the inhabitants, who did not manage to flee across the river and others who had fled to the city, found refuge from the attack of the Mongols in 1241.[61]

The increase of German settlers was enhanced by the privileges granted them, which probably took place no later than 1231. The charter was lost in the Mongol devastation, thus we do not know what kind of rights it contained. Master Roger, eyewitness of the events called Pest a large and very rich German town.[62] As to the rights and duties of the settlers, we know only the privilege of 1244. King Béla IV issued his charter sealed with a golden bull in order to restore the population, lure back the people that had left, and attract new *hospites*. The privilege contains the usual prerequisites of urban self-government: free election of judge and priest, complete jurisdictional liberty and several economic advantages. These included exemption from customs and the wine levy, staple right, and free testamentary and property transfer rights. Burghers, who wished to enjoy these liberties and purchase a plot in the town, were obliged to pay the taxes for the plot and fulfill military obligations. The inhabitants of Kispest received only a staple right and exemption from the wine levy.[63] The gradual development of the settlers' civic rights allowed the emergence of a unified structure on the left bank where only the ferrymen's quarters remained part of the royal domain. However, we do not know the exact extent of the city in the thirteenth century. We can only say that the streets beyond the church and the near-by market were defined by their connection to the north-south and east-west highways. Archaeologists once believed they had found evidence for a thirteenth-century town wall surrounding an area smaller than the later one, but the written sources do not support this interpretation.[64] Only a large

---

61   MOL DF 248 770, ed. BTOE, i, pp. 21–22 (no 17); Györffy, *Pest-Buda*, pp. 118–119; Thomas of Split, *History*, pp. 276–279.

62   "...magna et ditissima Theutonica villa, que Pesth dicitur..." – Master Roger, *Epistle*, pp. 160–161 (cap. 16); "...versus Pestium, que erat maxima villa. ..." – Thomas of Split, *History*, pp. 258–259 and 272–273.

63   MNL OL DF 240 797, given in BTOE, i, pp. 41–43 (no 27) and more recently EFHU, iii/2, pp. 39–41 (no 34). See the charter and its English translation in the appendix of the present volume. Györffy, *Pest-Buda*, pp. 136–138; Kubinyi, *Anfänge Ofens*, pp. 16–20; Kubinyi, "Zur Frage der deutschen Siedlungen," pp. 538–539 and 544–546.

64   Irásné-Melis, "A pesti városalaprajz," pp. 88–91; eadem, "Die Herausbildung," pp. 132–143; eadem, "Archaeological," pp. 235–236; The existence of a thirteenth-century wall may be challenged in light of the complete destruction of Pest in 1241 by the Mongols, which has been confirmed by archaeological evidence. On the defensive capacity of Pest, see Master Roger's, *Epistle*, pp. 184–185 (cap. 28); Thomas of Split, *History*, pp. 274–279.

ditch around the town, more or less along the fifteenth-century wall (where now the Kiskörút, "Inner Ring" runs) or maybe a little further out is mentioned in the literary evidence.[65] The direction of the further development of the city was, however, radically changed when Béla IV, fearing a new Mongol attack, embarked upon an entirely new urban strategy.[66]

Óbuda and Pest after the Foundation of Buda

The urban strategy, which was aimed at enhancing the defensive value of the kingdom's towns, brought about one of the most lasting achievements of King Béla IV: the foundation of the fortified city of Buda on the Castle Hill on the right bank of the Danube. The settlement (in the thirteenth century still called a *castrum*) alternated between the names of Pest and Buda. This can be understood from the fact that the castle actually stood between Buda (Felhévíz) and Pest (Kispest). But there was more to it. The new town belonged to the Buda royal estate complex and thus it was obvious to call it Buda. The other name is more interesting. By the 1260s the town was built up with its fortifications, churches, squares and planned street network. Its burghers received the recently renewed urban privileges of Pest instead of obtaining a new privilege. This must have been the reason that it was occasionally called Pest even though we do not know the process of settlement and the identity of the first settlers. It has been assumed that the German inhabitants of left-bank Pest were moved to Buda together with their privileges, but this is contradicted by the reconstruction of Pest and the continued presence of the richest burghers, Werner's descendants, in the old town. The explanation is rather that the urban core was transferred by the king's will to the right bank of the Danube. The new settlers preferred the fast developing center and for the next two centuries Pest assumed the character of a suburb.[67]

---

65   1281: MNL OL DL 1102, edited in BTOE, i, pp. 199–200 (no 185).
66   Bálint Hóman, *A magyar városok az Árpádok korában* [The towns of Hungary in the age of the Árpádians] (Budapest: Franklin, 1908), pp. 11–32; Pál Engel, *The Realm of St. Stephen. A History of Medieval Hungary, 895–1526* (London–New York: I.B. Tauris, 2001), pp. 111–113; Jenő Szűcs, *Az utolsó Árpádok* [The last Árpádians] (Budapest: Osiris, 2002), pp. 75–90 and 311–384.
67   Györffy, *Pest-Buda,* pp. 135–220; Kubinyi, *Anfänge Ofens,* pp. 27–111; Végh, *Buda,* i, pp. 27–34; András Végh, "Buda város középkori helyrajza," [The medieval topography of Buda] *Urbs. Magyar Várostörténeti Évkönyv* 4 (2009), pp. 35–49; idem, "Urban Development and Royal Initiative in the Central Part of the Kingdom of Hungary in the 13th–14th centuries: Comparative Analysis of the Development of the Towns of Buda and Visegrád," in

The fate of the Óbuda residence was similar. In the thirteenth century it could still keep up with Buda, but it is debated which of the two was the royal residence after the mid-thirteenth century. By the next century the question was resolved in favor of the latter. Without the magnet of the royal residence, Óbuda lost the chance of becoming a fully developed town and remained subject to ecclesiastical ownership with limited autonomy.[68]

In the shadow of Buda, neither the former royal Óbuda nor the German town of Pest managed to develop into an independent city. Nevertheless, the administrative importance of the former and the commercial significance of the latter contributed to Buda's rapid urban development. Béla IV recognized the mutual significance of the settlements of the region and established the agglomeration the head of which was Buda and from the fifteenth century onwards the capital of the kingdom of Hungary.[69]

Stadtgründung und Stadtwerdung. Beiträge von Archäologie und Stadtgeschichtsforschung (Beiträge zur Geschichte der Städte Mitteleuropas, 22), ed. Ferdinand Opll (Linz: Österreichischer Arbeitskreis für Stadtgeschichtsforschung, 2011), pp. 431–446; Enikő Spekner, "'Egy és ugyanazon szabadság alatt'. Két város egy kiváltságlevél: a pesti kiváltságlevél szövevényes története," [Under one and the same freedom. Two towns, one letter of privilege. The labyrinthine history of the letter of privilege of Pest] in *Tiszteletkör. Történeti tanulmányok Draskóczy István egyetemi tanár 60. születésnapjára* [Circle of honor. Studies in honor of the 60th birthday of István Draskóczy], eds Gábor Mikó, Bence Péterfi and András Vadas (Budapest: ELTE Eötvös Kiadó, 2012), pp. 261–270.

68 1243: MNL OL DL 106 086, given in BTOE, i, pp. 39–40 (no 25).

69 Kubinyi, *Anfänge Ofens*, pp. 27–111; Végh, *Buda*; Rady, *Buda*; Szende, "Towns along the Way," pp. 192–194.

CHAPTER 4

'A castle once stood, now a heap of stones...' the Site and Remains of Óbuda in Medieval Chronicles, National Epics, and Modern Fringe Theories

József Laszlovszky and James Plumtree

It is a truth universally acknowledged that a medievalist in possession of his facilities must be in want of the Holy Grail. However little known the actual research interests of such a scholar, this truth is so well fixed in the minds of a popular audience that he or she will at some time receive questions concerning the location of Camelot, the adventures of knights, or the era in which Arthur ruled. Given the influence of medieval romance, propagated by the press, retold by Victorians to accommodate their values and concerns, and the imagery associated with cinematic portrayals, it is at times difficult to deal with the elephant(–riding knight) in the room: the imagined greatness is in stark contrast to the surviving remnants of the period.[1]

The Hungarian equivalent to such questions concerns the medieval location of Óbuda (Hungarian: *Old Buda*). Modern visitors, after making their way through the Socialist era tower blocks of present-day Óbuda, find a picturesque center straight out of a nineteenth century postcard. A recent statue commemorates one of the most famous fictional creations of one of its residents: the late-nineteenth- and early-twentieth-century author Gyula Krúdy's womanizing, wine-addled character Szindbád, who observes his way through the final decades of the Austro-Hungarian Monarchy.[2] The thought that this was once an important medieval site probably escapes their

---

Translation of "Vár állott, most kőhalom", from "Himnusz" (*Hymn*) – the Hungarian national anthem, by Ferenc Kölcsey.

1   Comparable to this study is the Victorian recasting of medieval literary and material culture to address contemporary concerns, and the influence this has held on later generations. See Charles Jay Dellheim, *The Face of the Past: The Preservation of the Medieval Inheritance in Victorian England* (New York: Cambridge University Press, 1983); Stephanie L. Barczewski, *Myth and National Identity in Nineteenth-Century Britain: The Legends of King Arthur and Robin Hood* (Oxford: Oxford University Press, 2000), and Inga Bryden, *Reinventing King Arthur: The Arthurian Legends in Victorian Culture* (Aldershot: Ashgate, 2005).

2   Gyula Krúdy, *The Adventures of Sindbad*, trans. George Szirtes (New York: New York Review of Books, 2011). Turn-of-the-century Óbuda is neatly described in John Lukacs, *Budapest 1900* (New York: Grove Press, 1988), pp. 38–39.

© KONINKLIJKE BRILL NV, LEIDEN, 2016 | DOI 10.1163/9789004307674_006

attention, unless they wander around and spot some old ruins now part of a school playground.[3] Twentieth-century archaeological research and careful scholarship has charted the growth and decline of the medieval settlement, located its buildings – including its ecclesiastical and monarchical foundations – and created a clearer picture of the historical record of the site.[4] However, unlike Buda, which is firmly lodged in the popular imagination as a medieval site (despite of – or perhaps because of – its heavily reconstructed appearance),[5] Óbuda has been subjected to a fringe argument that denies its very existence.

Rather than merely dismissing these claims as being historically erroneous, this study examines how they arose in order to comprehend how such unhistorical viewpoints persist. The case of Óbuda, while being unique, is a suitable example how use of the medieval past has resulted in misunderstanding the evidence. The modern belief that Óbuda is of minor importance in comparison to another settlement – the undiscovered Ősbuda (Hungarian: *Ancient Buda*), is built upon previous historical constructions. The confusion of the medieval nomenclature for Óbuda is additionally linked to modern Hungarian nationalism. This derives its content from nineteenth-century romantic literature, which misread medieval chronicles, particularly in respect of the early history of Hungarian settlement. The result is an imagined Óbuda, which exists in stark contrast to the medieval remains.

Location, Nomenclature, and a Site of Forgetting

The earliest phase of the medieval settlement was greatly shaped by its location. It used, for materials and, originally, for organization, the ruins of the Roman military camp and surrounding settlement of Aquincum. These ruins also shaped the medieval perception of the history of the settlement. Regardless of whether they were ever inhabited by the Huns,[6] like other Roman sites

---

3   This is the cloister of the Poor Clares; see Herta Bertalan, "Das Klarissenkloster von Óbuda aus dem 14. Jahrhundert," *Acta Archaeologica Academiae Scientiarum Hungaricae* 34 (1982), pp. 151–175.

4   For an overview, see Júlia Altmann and Herta Bertalan's two chapters, "Óbuda vom 11. bis 13. Jahrhundert," and "Óbuda im Spätmittelalter," in *Budapest im Mittelalter*, pp. 113–131 and 185–199 respectively.

5   A prime example of the period is the 'restoration' work of Frigyes Schulek, the Hungarian Eugène Viollet-le-Duc. A study of the different types of conservation on visible medieval heritage of Budapest – such as Schulek's destructive restorations, and the Hilton Hotel that incorporates a ruined Dominican church and friary – is still awaited.

6   For a Hun-Age burial discovered in the 14th district – across the river from Óbuda, see Margit Nagy, "A Hun-Age Burial with Male Skeleton and Horse Bones Found in Budapest," and for

in Central Europe, the ruins were associated with the increasingly legendary figure of Attila.

The settlement that emerged was originally called 'Buda'. The name probably comes from a Slavic personal name, but employed in the Hungarian place name fashion.[7] There is no suggestion – or early source – connecting it to the Hunnish name Bleda, the brother of Attila. After this and the other early settlement of Pest on the left bank of the river were burnt down during the Mongol Invasion (1241–1242), King Béla IV founded a new settlement on Buda Hill, utilizing its geography for defensive purposes. The new settlement had a flurry of names: "Novus Mons Budensis" (1247–1248), "Mons Pestiensis" and "Castrum Pestiense" (from 1259), "Civitas Budensis" (from 1263), and "Mons Budensis".[8] To add to the confusion, German settlers even called the site "Ofen", the German translation of the Slavic word "Pest". The confusion must have been heightened by the fact that some of the settlers originated from the earlier settlements of Pest and Buda. To distinguish between the two Budas, the former began to be called "Vetus Buda" (1261: "old Buda"), though some establishments in the former Buda continued to use "Buda" as if no change had occurred.[9] For reasons of clarity, this study uses the term "Óbuda" for the site under examination.

After the Mongol Invasion, the importance of Óbuda dwindled. During the Ottoman period, being neither a site of administration nor a military center, the settlement fell into neglect. The medieval fabric of the settlement deteriorated, reaching its nadir with the burial of noticeable landmarks (including the Roman ruins) by the Zichy family in the eighteenth century so they could assert ownership of more property.[10] Excavation of the ruins started in the nineteenth century, and still continues. As a consequence, Óbuda lacked

---

one in Óbuda, see Ágnes B. Tóth, "A Fifth-Century Burial from Old Buda (Budapest)," in *Neglected Barbarians*, ed. Florin Curta (Turnhout: Brepols, 2010), pp. 137–175 and 177–208 respectively.

7   The Hungarian fashion up to the twelfth century was to use the personal name without a suffix. This etymology of Buda is now prevalent; a more popular version has Buda as the Slavic translation (вода, *water*) of the name Aquincum. Lajos Kiss, *Földrajzi nevek etimológiai szótára* [Etymological dictionary of geographic names] (Budapest: Akadémiai 1980), pp. 131–132.

8   See the chapter by Enikő Spekner in this volume.

9   The prime example being the St Peter collegiate chapter of Buda, an eleventh-century royal foundation, which was always called the chapter of Buda, even in the late Middle Ages when the location was known as Óbuda.

10 The Zichy mansion, built near the end of the eighteenth century, uses stones from the medieval and Roman ruins.

THE SITE & REMAINS OF ÓBUDA

FIGURE 4.1   *The view of Óbuda in the* Epistolae itinerariae *of Jakob Tollius, Amsterdam, 1700.*

a significant site of memory.[11] Before archaeological study revealed such evidence, nineteenth-century Hungarian authors had turned to the medieval chronicles to connect themselves with their past: the 'narrated localities' would become the site of memory to the detriment of the physical remains (Fig. 4.1).

Óbuda in the Medieval Chronicles

Óbuda plays a significant role in medieval chronicles, one that is detached from the archaeological evidence. Since this role has influenced later perceptions of the place, they are worth elucidating. There are two medieval traditions concerned with the origins of Óbuda, neither of which originates from a native Hungarian source. German sources of the High Middle Ages attributed the ruins to the Huns, conflating the Huns with the Hungarians,[12] Óbuda was occasionally made the supposed site of Etzelburg ("Attila's town", as presented in the *Nibelungenlied*).[13] In the Frankish accounts, Óbuda was connected with Sicambria, a territory that was associated with a Germanic people said to have fled from Troy (and who were conflated in the Middle Ages with the Scythians).[14] As elsewhere in medieval Europe, where there was continuous interest in origins, classical culture and prehistoric pasts,[15] the Hungarians

---

11 The definition by Pierre Nora is taken from his *Realms of Memory: Rethinking the French Past* (New York: Columbia University Press, 1996), p. xvii.

12 For a compendium and analysis of early sources connecting Huns with Hungarians, see Péter Kulcsár, "A magyar ősmonda Anonymus előtt," *Irodalomtörténeti Közlemények* 91–92 (1987–1988), pp. 523–545.

13 For the figure of Etzel, see *The Nibelungen Tradition: An Encyclopedia*, eds Francis G. Gentry, Winder McConnell, Ulrich Müller and Werner Wunderlich (New York: Routledge, 2002), pp. 67–68; see also Franz H. Bäuml, "Attila in Medieval German Literature," in *Attila: The Man and his Image*, eds Franz H. Bäuml and Marianna D. Birnbaum (Budapest: Corvina, 1993), pp. 57–64.

14 The main study of this tradition remains Alexandre [Sándor] Eckhardt, *De Sicambria a Sans-Souci: histoires et legends Franco-Hongroises* (Paris: Presses universitaires de France, 1943), pp. 11–51.

15 For the general context, see Giles Constable, "Past and Present in the Eleventh and Twelfth Centuries: Perceptions of Time and Change," in *L'Europa dei secoli XI e XII fra novità e tradizione* (Milan: Vita e Pensiero, 1989), pp. 135–170, reprinted in his *Culture and Spirituality in Medieval Europe* (Aldershot: Ashgate, 1996); for the Hungarian context, see László Veszprémy, "Historical Past and Political Present in the Latin Chronicles of Hungary (12th–13th Centuries)," *Medieval Chronicle* 1 (1999), pp. 260–68.

used these foreign traditions to mould their own supposed antique history for social, political, polemical, and religious purposes.[16]

Among the Roman ruins of Aquincum, a collegiate church founded by the Hungarian kings was later followed by a royal manor and castle.[17] Although the Hungarians had converted to Christianity and founded a medieval Christian monarchy,[18] their reputation and their supposed association with the Huns continued unabated. Reference is made to a sword of Attila, given by the Hungarian King Salamon's mother to Otto of Nordheim, the duke of Bavaria (1063–1070), but it is noticeably a German source that attributed it to the Hunnish ruler.[19] In a similar manner, Óbuda, having visible Roman ruins that were regarded as Hunnish in origin,[20] provided circular evidence for the Attila connection: they confirmed the perception of the chronicles, which, in turn,

16 For contextualization see Björn Weiler, "Tales of First Kings and the Culture of Kingship in the West, ca. 1050-ca. 1200," *Viator* 46 (2015), pp. 101–128, and Lars Boje Mortensen, "Sanctified Beginnings and Mythopoietic Moments: The First Wave of Writing on the Past in Norway, Denmark and Hungary, c. 1000–1230," in *The Making of Christian Myths in the Periphery of Latin Christendom (c. 1000–1300)*, ed. Lars Boje Mortensen (Copenhagen: Museum Tusculanum Press – University of Copenhagen, 2006), pp. 247–273.

17 Júlia Altmann and Herta Bertalan, "Óbuda vom 11. bis 13. Jahrhundert," in *Budapest im Mittelalter*, pp. 113–131; László Gerevich, *The Art of Buda and Pest in the Middle Ages* (Budapest: Akadémiai, 1971), pp. 11–12.

18 Nora Berend, József Laszlovszky, and Béla Zsolt Szakács, "The Kingdom of Hungary," in *Christianization and the Rise of Christian Monarchy: Scandinavia, Central Europe and Rus' c. 900–1200*, ed. Nora Berend (Cambridge: Cambridge University Press, 2007), pp. 319–368.

19 Lamberti Hersfeldensis, *Annales* in *Monumenta Germaniae Historica, Scriptores*, v, ed. Georgius Heinricus Pertz (Hannover: Hahn, 1844), p. 185: [henceforth: MGH SS] "Notatum autem est, hunc ipsum gladium fuisse, quo famosissimus quondam rex Hunorum Attila in necem christianorum atque in excidium Galliarum hostiliter debacchatus fuerat. Hunc siquidem regina Ungariorum, mater Salomonis regis, duci Baioariorum Ottoni dono dederat, cum eo suggerente atque annitente rex filium eius in regnum paternum restituisset." *The Annals of Lampert of Hersfeld*, tr. I.S. Robinson (Manchester: Manchester University Press, 2015), p. 149, translates this text as "It should be noted that this was the very sword with which that most famous Attila, the king of the Huns in olden times, had raged with wild fury, slaughtering Christians and bringing ruin to Gaul. This sword had in fact been given by the Queen of the Hungarians, the mother of King Salomon, to Duke Otto of the Bavarians as a gift when, on Otto's advice and with his support, King Henry had restored her son to the throne of his father." György Györffy, *Krónikáink és a magyar őstörténet* Chronicles and Hungarian prehistory] (Budapest: Néptudományi Intézet, 1948), pp. 128–129 argues this was an invention of the chronicler.

20 Other Roman ruins were misidentified as Hunnish. A notable example is Comagena, a fortified camp on the Danube, the site of the modern town of Tulln in present-day Austria. According to the Nibelungenlied, this is where Attila met Kriemhild and, subsequently, married her. In 2005, the modern city commemorated this fictional event with the

confirmed the perception of the ruins. The earlier view maintained by German chroniclers of the Hungarians' savagery[21] may have resulted in the conviction that the Roman ruins were constructed by the Hungarians' supposed predecessor, Attila. Attila does not appear in official documents of the Hungarian kingdom of the time;[22] the first recorded reference is negative: in the dedication of Tihany Abbey to St Agnan, who had defended it from Attila.[23] In contrast to the Germans, the Hungarians were less willing to associate their settlements with Attila and his legacy.[24]

The connection between Óbuda and Attila appears to have emerged around the time of the crusades.[25] Since the overland route through Hungary was a cheaper option than the sea route, the kingdom was observed through foreign eyes unfamiliar with the history of the settlement. It is known that in accounts of the First Crusade, the kingdom of Hungary is both described incorrectly,[26] and used by the chroniclers to make polemical points independent of the events that occurred.[27] The *Kaiserchronik* (c. 1140), a popular work in the

---

unveiling of the Nibelungenbrunnen, a fountain designed by the Austrian Hans Muhr with a large ensemble of bronze statues by the Russian sculptor Mihail Nogin.

21 Alexander Sager, "Hungarians as *vremde* in Medieval Germany," in *Meeting the Foreign in the Middle Ages*, ed. Albrecht Classen (New York: Routledge, 2002), pp. 27–44.

22 Notably, the sole references to Attila in *Diplomata Hungariae Antiquissima*, i, *1000–1131*, ed. Georgius [György] Györffy (Budapest: Hungarian Academy of Sciences, 1992), p. 435, are forged documents dating from after 1526. For the Hungarian Renaissance view of Attila, see Marianna D. Birnbaum, "Attila's Renaissance in the Fifteenth and Sixteenth Centuries," in *Attila: The Man and his Image*, pp. 82–96.

23 Györffy, *Diplomata*, pp. 145–146; Lajos Csóka, *Geschichte des benediktinischen Mönchtums in Ungarn* (St. Ottilien: EOS Verlag, 1980), p. 77.

24 "Indeed, by around 1200 the Hunnish origin of the Magyars was taken for granted in the West. Not so, with the Magyars themselves." Jenő Szűcs, "Theoretical Elements in Master Simon of Kéza's *Gesta Hungarorum* (1282–1285)," reprinted in Simon of Kéza, *Gesta Hungarorum. The Deeds of the Hungarians* (Central European Medieval Texts, 1), eds László Veszprémy and Frank Schaer (Budapest–New York: Central European University Press, 1999), pp. xxix–cii, here p. xlvi.

25 The best English-language introduction to the role of Hungary in the crusades remains James Ross Sweeney, "Hungary in the Crusades, 1169–1218," *International History Review* 3 (1981), pp. 467–481; the historiography of the early crusaders is examined in Zsolt Hunyadi, "Hungary and the Second Crusade," *Chronica* 9–10 (2009–2010), pp. 55–65.

26 Nicholas Morton, "Encountering the Turks: The First Crusaders' Foreknowledge of their Enemy: Some Preliminary Findings," in *Crusading and Warfare in the Middle Ages: Realities and Representations, Essays in Honour of John France*, eds Simon John and Nicholas Morton (Farnham: Ashgate, 2014), pp. 47–68.

27 James Plumtree, "'The Threshing-Floor Sifts out the Chaff in the Breeze that Blows': Comprehending the Role of Hungary in the First Crusade," (forthcoming).

Middle Ages,[28] likewise uses the belief that Attila was buried in Óbuda to cast doubt on other authors who claimed that Theoderic had met Attila.[29] Given that a recent study of this text argues that the chronicler arranged his material to stress the success of Christianity over earlier error, this may be a way of asserting the triumph of the faith over paganism, and, also, a pointed quip at the liberties taken in contemporary popular poetry.[30] Likewise, a variant spelling of Attila's town, "Czilnburg", occurs in Ansbert's *Historia de expeditione Frederici imperatoris* (1187) describing the hosting of a crusading envoy there,[31] and the mention of Attila's town in Arnold of Lübeck's *Chronica Slavorum* (c. 1210),[32] may also have connotations not connected to concerns over accuracy.

Associating Óbuda with Etzelburg in Hungarian medieval historiography occurs in the "most famous, the most obscure, the most exasperating and most

28   Christian Gellinek, *Die deutsche Kaiserchronik. Erzähltechnik und Kritik* (Frankfurt: Athenäum-Verlag, 1971), p. 18.
29   *Deutsche Kaiserchronik* in MGH *Deutsche Chroniken*, I, ed. Edward Schröder (Hannover: Hahn, 1895), pp. 337–338: "Swer nû welle bewæren,/daz Dieterîch Ezzelen sæhe,/der haize daz buoch vur tragen./do der chunic Ezzel ze Ovene wart begraben,/dar nâch stuont iz vur wâr/driu unde fierzech jâr,/daz Dieterîch wart geborn./ze Chriechen wart er erzogen,/dâ er daz swert umbe bant,/ze Rôme wart er gesant,/ze Vulkân wart er begraben./ hie meget ir der luge wol ain ende haben." (lines 14176–87). In translation, in *The Book of Emperors: A Translation of the Middle High German Kaiserchronik*, ed. and tr. Henry A. Myers ([Morgantown]: West Virginia University Press, 2013), p. 315, this reads: "If there is anyone who insists that Theoderic ever saw Attila, let him have the Book brought out. It was forty-three years after King Attila was buried at Buda that Theoderic was born. He was raised in Greece, when he first buckled on his sword he was sent to Rome, and he was buried in Mount Aetna. And so you can see that lie put to rest."
30   Graeme Dunphy, "On the Function of the Disputations in the *Kaiserchronik*," *Medieval Chronicle* 5 (2009), pp. 77–86. See also, in a discussion of the source, Meinhard, master of Bamberg's cathedral school, criticism of Bishop Gunther for listening to stories about Attila instead of studying Christian works, Alastair Matthews, *The Kaiserchronik: A Medieval Narrative* (Oxford: Oxford University Press, 2012), p. 12.
31   Ansbertus, *Historia de Expeditione Friderici Imperatoris*, in MGH *Scriptores rerum Germanicarum, Nova series*, v, ed. A. Chroust (Berlin: Weidmann, 1928), p. 53 [henceforth: SS rer. G]: "Qui nuntii prospero itinere circa nativitatem domini apud civitatem Ungarie que teutonice Czilnburg dicitur, ad regem Ungarie pervenerunt." *The Crusade of Frederick Barbarossa: The History of the Expedition of the Emperor Frederick and Related Texts*, tr. G.A. Loud (Farnham – Burlington: Ashgate, 2010), p. 80, translates this as "The envoys had an easy journey and around Christmas time they met the King of Hungary at a town of his, called in the German language Czilnburg."
32   Arnoldus, *Chronica Slavorum*, MGH SS rer. G., xiv, ed. Georgius Heinricus Pertz (Hannover: Hahn, 1868), p. 130: "Inde domnus inperator a rege deductus est in urbem Adtile dictam, ubi domnus imperator quatuor diebus venationi operam dedit." Other variants of the German name included Eczelpurg, Zelburg, and Etzilburg.

misleading of all the early Hungarian texts",[33] the *Gesta Hungarorum* (c.1200). In the relevant passage, the author (known, elusively, as "Anonymus") includes foreign – and erroneous – traditions concerning the origin of the Hungarians. The passage that follows shows Anonymus combining literary and oral traditions on the pre-written past for the benefit of a contemporary audience.[34]

> The first king of Scythia was Magog, son of Japhet, and this people were called after him Magyar, from whose royal line the most renowned and mighty king Attila descended, who, in the year of Our Lord's incarnation 451, coming down from Scythia, entered Pannonia with a mighty force and, putting the Romans to flight, took the realm and made a royal residence for himself beside the Danube above the hot springs, and he ordered all the old buildings that he found there to be restored and he built a circular and very strong wall, and in the Hungarian language it is now called Budavár and by the Germans Etzelburg.[35]

We must ask why an author writing for a Hungarian King Béla – most likely to be Béla III – would include such a mythology. The obvious answer is that the mythological elements, created for the elite,[36] were concerned with contemporary political ambitions and self-fashioning rather than with historical accuracy: by proclaiming the increasingly familiar – if not popular – connection to Attila.[37] The chronicler Anonymus claimed the Hungarians

---

33   Carlile A. Macartney, *The Medieval Hungarian Historians: A Critical and Analytical Guide* (London: Cambridge University Press, 1953), p. 59.
34   As Veszprémy notes, "in Hungary *Vorgeschichte* actually represented *Zeitgeschichte*". Idem, "Historical Past and Political Present," p. 261.
35   Anonymus, *Gesta Hungarorum – The Deeds of the Hungarians* (Central European Medieval Texts, 5), eds Martyn Rady and László Veszprémy (Budapest–New York: Central European University Press, 2010), pp. 6–9: "Et primus rex Scithie fuit Magog filius Iaphet et gens illa a Magog rege vocata est Moger, a cuius etiam progenie regis descendit nominatissimus atque potentissimus rex Athila, qui anno dominice incarnationis CCCCLI de terra Scithica descendens cum valida manu in terram Pannonie venit et fugatis Romanis regnum obtinuit et regalem sibi locum constituit iuxta Danubium super Calidas Aquas et omnia antiqua opera, qui ibi invenit, renovari precepit et in circuitu muro fortissimo edificavit, que per linguam Hungaricam dicitur nunc Buduvar et a Teothonicis Ecilburgu vocatur."
36   On the issue of codification of myths, see Mortensen, "Mythopoiesis in Norway, Denmark and Hungary," p. 269.
37   For the increasingly sympathetic view of the medieval Hungarians to their pagan past, see Nora Berend, *At the Gate of Christendom: Jews, Muslims and 'Pagans' in Medieval Hungary, c. 1000–1300* (Cambridge: Cambridge University Press, 2001), pp. 204–205. For the popularity of variant spellings of Attila as a Hungarian name in the twelfth century, see

"chose to seek for themselves the land of Pannonia that they had heard from rumor had been the land of King Attila, from whose line Prince Álmos, father of Árpád, descended".[38] Thus, by presenting the Hun–Hungarian association as a dynastic Attila–Árpád connection – including the claim that Árpád was buried at the city of King Attila (where, Anonymus notes, a church was later founded)[39] – Anonymus asserts the territorial claims of the ruling Hungarian monarch.[40] As the *Gesta*'s recent editors noted, "it hardly needs to be emphasized that the *Gesta* is in no ways a source of information for the events that it pretends to narrate, but rather for the ideas about them current in the Hungary of the notary's times and for the literary skills of its author."[41]

Sándor Eckhardt, "Attila a mondában," [Attila in mythology] in *Attila és hunjai* [Attila and his Huns], ed. Gyula Németh (Budapest: Magyar Szemle Társaság, 1940), pp. 143–216, here p. 191.

38   Anonymus, *Gesta Hungarorum*, pp. 16–17: "Tunc elegerunt sibi querere terram Pannonie, quam audiverant fama volante terram Athile regis esse, de cuius progenie dux Almus pater Arpad descenderat." Note also the issue of tribute (pp. 22–23) and territory (pp. 26–27 and 40–41) along with descent.

39   Anonymus, *Gesta Hungarorum*, pp. 114–115: "Post hec anno dominice incarnationis DCCCCVII dux Arpad migravit de hoc seculo, qui honorifice sepultus est supra caput unius parvi fluminis, qui descendit per alveum lapideum in civitatem Atthile regis, ubi etiam post conversionem Hungarorum edificata est ecclesia, que vocatur Alba, sub honore beate Marie virginis." "After this, in the year of Our Lord's incarnation 907, Árpád left this world and was buried with honour at the head of a small river that flows through a stone culvert to the city of King Attila where, after the conversion of the Hungarians, was built the church that is called Fehéregyháza in honour of the Blessed Virgin Mary." This detail, alongside Anonymus's conception of the pagan past, is examined in László Veszprémy, "'*More Paganismo*': Reflections on the Pagan and Christian Past in the *Gesta Hungarorum* of the Hungarian Anonymous Notary," in *Historical Narratives and Christian Identity on a European Periphery: Early Historical Writing in Northern, East-Central, and Eastern Europe (c. 1070–1200)*, ed. Ildar H. Garipzanov (Turnhout: Brepols, 2011), pp. 183–201, here p. 192.

40   For the dynastic claims in context of contemporaneous historiography, see János M. Bak, "Legitimization of Rulership in Three Narratives from Twelfth-Century Europe," *Majestas* 12 (2004), pp. 43–60, reprinted in his *Studying Medieval Rulers and Their Subjects: Central Europe and Beyond* (Variorum Collected Studies, 956), eds Balázs Nagy and Gábor Klaniczay (Farnham – Burlington: Ashgate, 2010).

41   Anonymus, *Gesta Hungarorum*, p. xxxi. To their comments, we may add that Anonymus may reveal more about contemporary naming. The editors note that "Budavar" is a "problematic form, as the castle on Buda Hill was not built before the Mongol invasion in 1241", and suggest the – burg ending in the German name Etzilburg led Anonymus to describe it as "Buda Castle". The chapter house at Óbuda, that acted as the royal chancery, was built in the confines of the Roman ruins; the king did not have a castle there, but had a *curia* there as there was no need for a separate castle. This situation changed in the

Another myth concerned with Buda's historical lineage appeared in France. This foreign idea is likely to have been brought back into Hungary by Hungarians who had studied in France, particularly Paris, from the mid-twelfth century onwards. It concerned the belief that the Franks were descendants of the Trojans. Gregory of Tours reported that it was commonly believed that the Franks had come out of Pannonia, settled on the Rhine, and then moved to France.[42] The eighth-century *Liber historiae Francorum* clarified this by claiming they previously originated from Troy.[43] The tenth-century chronicler Aimoin added to this account by claiming victories for these followers of Francio, a colleague of Aeneas, against the Romans and the Germans. While "flattering the pride of the Franks", Aimoin was also using his writing (and his library) to provide them

---

early thirteenth century when a castle was constructed at Óbuda that was not within the walls of the Roman fortification. Anonymus is likely to be referring to either of these two structures.

42　Gregorius Turonensis, *Libri historiarum* in *MGH Scriptores rerum Merovingicarum* [SS rev. M], i/1, ed. Bruno Krusch and Wilhelmus Levison (Hannover: Hahn, 1951), p. 57: "Hanc nobis notitiam de Francis memorati historici reliquere regibus non nominatis. Tradunt enim multi, eosdem de Pannonia fuisse degressus, et primum quidem litora Rheni amnes incoluisse dehinc, transacto Rheno, Thoringiam transmeasse, ibique iuxta pagus vel civitates regis crinitos super se creavisse de prima et, ut ita dicam, nobiliore suorum familia. Quod postea probatum Chlodovechi victuriae tradiderunt, itaque in sequenti digerimus." Gregory of Tours, *The History of the Franks*, tr. Lewis Thorpe (Harmondsworth: Penguin, 1983), p. 125, renders this: "It is commonly said that the Franks came originally from Pannonia and first colonized the banks of the Rhine. Then they crossed the river, marched through Thuringia, and set up in each country district and each city long-haired kings chosen from the foremost and most noble family of their race. As I shall show you later, this is proved by the victories won by Clovis."

43　*Liber historiae Francorum* in MGH SS rev. M. ii, ed. Bruno Krusch (Hannover: Hahn, 1888), pp. 241–242: "Alii quoque ex principibus, Priamus videlicet et Antenor, cum reliquo exercitu Troianorum duodecim milia intrantes in navibus, abscesserunt et venerunt usque ripas Tanais fluminis. Ingressi Meotidas paludes navigantes, pervenerunt intra terminos Pannoniarum iuxta Meotidas paludes et coeperunt aedificare civitatem ob memoriale eorum appellaveruntque eam Sicambriam; habitaveruntque illic annis multis creveruntque in gentem magnam." *Liber Historiae Francorum*, tr. Bernard S. Bachrach (Lawrence: Coronado Press, 1973), p. 23 renders this "Priam and Antenor, two of the other Trojan princes, embarked on ships with twelve thousand of the men remaining from the Trojan army. They departed and came to the banks of the Tanais [Don] river. They sailed into the Maeotian swamps [of the Sea of Azov], penetrated the frontiers of the Pannonias which were near the Maeotian swamps and began to build a city as their memorial. They called it Sicambria and lived there many years growing into a great people."

with a "collective memory".[44] The thirteenth century saw a reiterating of this story with the detail that Sicambria was a city in Hungary.[45]

As with the use of foreign tradition of Attila's town being used by Anonymus, the foreign view that Sicambria existed in Hungary was similarly used by a Hungarian chronicler, Simon of Kéza for a new purpose. His *Gesta Hungarorum* (c. 1280s) combined the Frankish tradition of Sicambria with the German one of Attila, using a story from Jordanes to explain the name of Óbuda.

> [...] Attila left Eisenach and went to Sicambria, where he murdered his brother Buda with his own hands and had his body thrown in the Danube. Attila's reason was that while he was away fighting in the West his brother had overstepped the boundaries of authority he had established between the two of them and had had Sicambria renamed after himself. Although Attila issued an order to his Huns and his other followers that the city was to be referred to as the City of Attila, and the Germans out of fear respected the order and called the city Etzelburg, the Huns paid scant heed to it and continued to call it Óbuda, as they still do to this day.[46]

This account, with its quip at the expense of the German settlers, resolves the issue of having a major settlement named after the brother murdered by the ruler. This connection made by Simon of Kéza requires explanation. It was "a learned creation of identity",[47] attempting to nullify the negative western images of the kingdom to establish a notable ancestry. While appearing to present history, it explained the social and ethnic origins of the people, thereby addressing contemporary social concerns and legitimizing

---

44   Bernard Guenée, "Chanceries and Monasteries," in *Rethinking France* (Les lieux de mémoire, 4), eds Pierre Nora and David P. Jordan (Chicago: University of Chicago Press, 2010), pp. 1–25, here p. 14.

45   Eckhardt, *De Sicambria à Sans-Souci*, pp. 29–31; see also the comment "Sicambre qui est cieuetaine cites de Hongrie," cited in György Györffy, "Les débuts de l'évolution urbaine en Hongrie (suite en fin)," *Cahiers de civilisation médiévale* 47 (1969), pp. 253–264, here p. 255.

46   Simon of Kéza, *Gesta Hungarorum*, pp. 50–54: "Ab Isnaco autem curia celebrata egrediens Sicambriam introivit, ubi Budam fratrem suum manibus propriis interfecit, proiici faciens corpus eius in Danubium, eo quod ipso Ethela in partibus occidentis praeliante inter eum et fratrem eius metas stabilitas transgressus fuerat dominando. Fecerat etiam Sicambriam suo nomine appellari. Et quamvis Hunis et caeteris suis gentibus interdictum rex Ethela posuisset, ut urbs Ethelae vocaretur, Teutonici interdictum formidantes, eam Echulbuer vocaverunt, Hunni vero, curam parvam illud reputantes interdictum, usque hodie eandem vocant Oubudam sicut prius."

47   Berend, *At the Gates of Christendom*, p. 206.

rulership. Given that the convergence of the myths of Attila's town with Sicambria also occurred in the later *Chronicon Pictum* (c. 1358), it is clear that the idea of connecting the two was both popular, and retained political currency.[48]

The medieval chroniclers provided Óbuda with two foundation myths that gave the settlement an early history which was both historically incorrect and increasingly removed from the city itself. The Hungarian elites used these narratives to legitimize their authority and to vest themselves with a notable ancestry. Óbuda was the prism through which these mythical stories were first attached, and then absorbed. After the decline and neglect of Óbuda in the Ottoman and post-Ottoman period, its role as a site of history survived in these manuscripts, and in the stories that they presented.

The Medieval Myth of Óbuda in Nineteenth Century Hungarian Literature

With the historical remains of Óbuda neglected or obscured, it was the image of Óbuda as presented in the chronicles that influenced one of the canonical figures of Hungarian literature: János Arany (1817–1882). To understand how Arany depicted Óbuda, and the influence that the depiction had, we must examine the context in which Arany wrote.

The past was material which Hungarian intellectuals and artists could use to shape the present. Since the end of the eighteenth century, antiquarian objects, interpreted through the myths included in the medieval chronicles, were objects that could hold ideological value in contemporary debates about nationhood.[49] The foundation of the Hungarian National Museum in 1802 by Count Ferenc Széchényi created a new national interest in the past that would

---

48 For a facsimile of the *Chronicon Pictum* manuscript, see *Képes Krónika*, 2 vols [Hungarian illuminated chronicle] (Budapest: Helikon 1987).

49 A prime example is a carved – and, importantly, cracked – ivory horn, at Jászberény, connected by Ferenc Molnár in 1788 to a medieval myth that the captured pagan chieftain Lehel killed his captor, the German king, with a horn. The parallels to the contemporary dispute between Hungarian nobles and the Austrian Emperor Joseph II are readily apparent. Etele Kiss, "Lehel kürtje," [The horn of Lehel] in *Történelem – kép. Szemelvények múlt és művészet kapcsolatából Magyarországon* [History – image. Excerpts from the connections of past and art in Hungary] eds Árpád Mikó and Katalin Sinkó (Budapest: Magyar Nemzeti Galéria, 2000), pp. 520–526, and László Selmeczi, *Nemzeti ereklyénk, a Jászkürt* [Our national relic, the Jazygian horn] (Jászberény: Jász Múzeumért Alapítvány, 2008).

counter the legitimacy of the ruling Austrian Emperor,[50] and inspire a national reform movement.[51]

Missing, however, was a great medieval epic from Hungary that was comparable to the *Nibelungenlied*, *La Chanson de Roland*, and Arthurian romances.[52] One poet who attempted to correct this omission was Mihály Vörösmarty (1800–1855). After writing about the Scythian association (*A szittya gyermekek*), Vörösmarty wrote the epic *Zalán futása* ("The Flight of Zalán") (1825), "a founding text of Hungarian identity in the nineteenth century",[53] using the chronicle of Anonymus as a source. The popularity of the work was in part due to Vörösmarty's own poetic talents, and in part to his selection of a theme that would be highly regarded by his contemporaries. The poem, while vividly depicting one of the few successful conquests in Hungarian history (the *honfoglalás* – the occupation of the homeland), was also a broadside in the contemporary dispute with the Slovaks and the Pan-Slavic movement, both of which touched upon the issue of the historical ownership of the territory.[54]

The interest in creating a Hungarian national epic continued in the middle of the nineteenth century. The contemporary situation of the nation greatly influenced this desire: the failure of the 1848 revolution and the War of Independence (1848–1849) was followed by dictatorial rule and tighter censorship

---

50 The context is examined in *The Nineteenth-Century Process of "Musealization" in Hungary and Europe,* eds Ernő Marosi, Gábor Klaniczay and Ottó Gecser (Budapest: Collegium Budapest, 2006).

51 "Phase A", to use the terminology of Miroslav Hroch, *Social Preconditions of a National Revival in Europe: A Comparative Analysis of the Social Composition of Patriotic Groups among the Smaller European Nations* (Cambridge: Cambridge University Press, 1985), p. 23.

52 Whether they are 'missing' in the sense that they have not survived, or missing in that they never existed, is a debate that is unlikely to be resolved. For the politicizing of medieval texts, see Helmut Brackert, "Nibelungenlied und Nationalgedanke. Zur Geschichte einer deutschen Ideologie," in *Mediaevalia litteraria: Festschrift für Helmut de Boor zum 80. Geburtstag,* eds Helmut Kolb and Ursula Henning (Munich: Beck, 1971), pp. 343–364; Barczewski, *Myth and National Identity* and Isabel N. DiVanna, "Politicizing National Literature: the Scholarly Debate around *La chanson de Roland* in the Nineteenth Century," *Historical Research* 84, No 233 (2011), pp. 109–134.

53 Gábor Klaniczay, "The Myth of Scythian Origin and the Cult of Attila in the Nineteenth Century," in *Multiple Antiquities – Multiple Modernities: Ancient Histories in Nineteenth Century European Cultures,* eds Gábor Klaniczay, Michael Werner, and Ottó Gecser (Frankfurt: Campus Verlag, 2001), pp. 185–212, here p. 204.

54 János M. Bak, "From the Anonymous *Gesta* to the *Flight of Zalán* by Vörösmarty," in *Manufacturing a Past for the Present: Forgery and Authenticity in Medievalist Texts and Objects in Nineteenth Century Europe,* eds János M. Bak, Patrick J. Geary and Gábor Klaniczay (Leiden: Brill, 2015), pp. 96–106, here p. 103.

by the Austrian authorities in the 1850s. It resulted in the past, once again, being viewed through the prism of the present. One of the key figures in this movement of passive resistance was the epic poet János Arany, who had previously lamented the absence of a "naïve epic" and strove to correct this by devising his own.[55] He was aware of the political sensitivities. Responding to a call from the Austrian authorities for Hungarian poets to produce eulogies for the Austrian Emperor, Arany composed *A walesi bárdok* ("The Bards of Wales") (1857), depicting a legendary mass burning of Welsh bards at the command of Edward I for refusing to sing the monarch's praises, as a sly comment on Habsburg policies.

That same year, responding to a competition to produce a verse epic based on Hungarian history, Arany used Hungarian medieval chronicles as a source for his *Buda halála* ("The Death of Buda") (1863).[56] Though he used contemporary studies,[57] Arany's epic was indebted, as the epigraph taken from *Gesta Hungarorum* implies, to the work of Simon of Kéza.[58] In Arany's epic, the feuding brothers Attila and Bleda (called Buda in Arany's work) are turned into a foundation myth reminiscent of Romulus and Remus. Buda opts to create a city from stone in contrast to the more nomadic structures that his brother favors.[59] Arany accepted the view of Thuróczy and placed Attila's settlement

---

55   János Arany, "Naiv eposzunk," in *Arany János összes művei*, x, ed. Dezső Keresztury (Budapest: Akadémiai 1962), pp. 265–274; Pál S. Varga, "'Népies-nemzeti', 'nemzeti klasszicizmus' – a nemzeti irodalom hagyományközösségi szemlélete: 1860, Arany János, *Naiv eposzunk*," ['Folk-national', 'national classicism' – the view of common tradition in national literature: 1860, János Arany, Our naïve epic poem] in *A magyar irodalom történetei, 1800–1919* [Stories of Hungarian literature, 1800–1919], eds Mihály Szegedy-Maszák and András Veres (Budapest: Gondolat, 2007), pp. 445–460. Péter Dávidházi, "A nemzet mint *res ficta et picta* keletkezéséhez: 'Párducos Árpád' és 'eleink' útja a költészettől a történetírásig," [The formation of nation as *res ficta et picta*. 'Panther Árpád' and the road of 'our ancestors' from poetry to history] in *Vörösmarty és a romantika* [Vörösmarty and romanticism], ed. József Takáts (Pécs–Budapest: Művészetek Háza - Országos Színháztörténeti Múzeum és Intézet, 2001), pp. 95–110.

56   The text appears in *Arany János összes művei*, iv, ed. Géza Voinovich (Budapest: Akadémiai 1953), henceforth cited as Arany, *Buda halála*, followed by page, book, and line numbers.

57   For his use of secondary sources, see László Szörényi, "János Arany's *Csaba Trilogy* and Arnold Ipolyi's *Hungarian Mythology*," in *Manufacturing a Past for the Present*, pp. 81–95.

58   Arany, *Buda halála*, p. 18: '(Ethela) Budam fratrem suum manibus propriis interfecit...eo quod...metas inter fratres stabilitas transgressus fuerit dominando. Sim. de Keza Chron. Hung.'

59   Arany, *Buda halála*, p. 116 (XI. 393–396): "Budaszállás – mondák – nyilt, mezei tábor,/ Nincsen is ez helyben maradásunk bátor:/Nosza rakjunk várost, kőre követ szintén,/Valamint sok más nép teszi Naplementén." Arany János, *The Death of King Buda*, tr. Watson

somewhere in the Hungarian Great Plain (a view modern scholars predominantly agree with), and he followed the Germanic tradition of connecting Buda with Óbuda,[60] while noting that Buda built his town in the ruins of an earlier settlement.[61]

Wishing to write the missing Hungarian epic, Arany also included other pertinent Hungarian myths and motifs in *Buda halála*. One of these was the unhistorical sword of Attila. Another tale, told within the Buda story, was the legend of the miraculous stag (*Rege a csoda-szarvasról*). It concerns two brothers, Hunor and Magor, who chase a many-horned stag until they found a new land in which to settle. This tale, an explanation of the Hungarian migrations, cemented the connection between the Scythians, Huns and Hungarians.

Arany's *Buda halála* was popular and influential. The painter, Mór Than, commissioned to contribute to an exhibition asserting national values and history, depicted Attila feasting in his *Attila lakomája* ("Feast of Attila") (1870). Having desired to create the missing Hungarian epic, Arany aimed to rework the old motifs and myths from medieval Latin chronicles into a touchstone for contemporary medievalism. While it must be stressed that Arany and his fellow artists in the Hungarian Reform Movement did not set out to hoodwink their readers with an incorrect image of the past (as, by contrast, a forger would),[62] the craftsmanship of *Buda halála* has led to generations of

---

Kirkconnell and Lulu Payerle (Cleveland: Benjamin Franklin Bibliophile Society, 1936), p. 108 renders this: "'This camp,' said they, 'defenceless and alone/Has stood upon the prairie hitherto:/Then let us build a city, stone on stone,/As many nations to the westward do.'"

60   Arany, *Buda halála*, p. 21 (I. 9–14): "Tisza-Duna síkján, Zagyva folyó mellett,/Sátora egy dombon kék égre szökellett;/Ez vala a város, ez Buda királyi/Lakhelye, famüvü sátorpalotái.//Nem szorul e város tetemes falakra/Nagy henye kövekből nincs együvé rakva." *The Death of King Buda*, p. 1: "By Zagyva stream, on Tisza-Duna's plain,/On a low hill beneath the azure sky/Rose Buda's tent, the palace of his reign,/A bright pavilion rear'd on timbers high.//No need of lofty ramparts had that town,/No idle battlements of massy stone."

61   Arany, *Buda halála*, p. 116 (XI. 401–408): "Város vala régi, Duna jobbik partján,/Megtörve had által, Keve, Béla kardján;/Tornyai, bástyái, mellvédei most rom:/Húnok idejöttén alázta meg ostrom.//Teteje hamvvá lőn; még falai állnak,/Lassu enyészettel ott hagyva halálnak,/Ügyefogyott aljnép csarnokait éli,/Szél benne bitangol: az északi, déli." *The Death of King Buda*, p. 108, omitting the detail that the ruined city is on the right side of the Danube, translates the section as: "An ancient city on the Danube's bank/Had fall'n to Béla's onset long ago;/Its towers and bulwarks into ruin sank/When the besieging Hun-host laid it low.//Its roofs are ashes, but its lofty walls/Are left to moulder into slow decay;/A rude slum-folk inhabits now those halls,/And there the wandering night-winds take their way."

62   For the absence of 'spectacular forgeries (or confabulations)' in early nineteenth-century Hungary, see Bak, "From the Anonymous *Gesta*". As Bak notes, this is not to say Hungarian forgers did not exist (see in the same volume, Benedek Láng, "Invented Middle

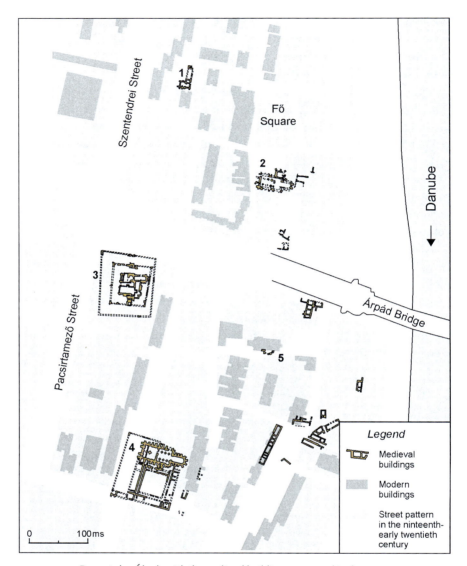

FIGURE 4.2 *Present-day Óbuda with the medieval buildings excavated in the area*

Ages in the 19th Century: the forgeries of Samuel Literati Nemes," pp. 129–143). Like the medieval chronicle writers, these users of falsities had their own reasons. Some, like the *Csíki Székely Krónika* forged by an aristocrat to promote his family, were self-interested; others, like the ethnographic researches of Gergely Nagylaki Jaksics, who claimed to have found Hungarian-speaking Scythian Huns in the Caucasian mountains, was reformist in spirit: the 'found' Hungarians lamented the condition of their European counterparts.

Hungarian schoolchildren memorizing the poem. As a consequence, once prevalent historical judgments that have long been discarded by scholars (such as the Hunnish–Hungarian connection) have continued to reside in the popular imagination to this day.

The Nineteenth-century Medieval Myth of Óbuda and Modern-day Ősbuda

Nineteenth-century romantic imaginings of Attila's town and Old Buda would seem to be relevant only as historiographical and literary curiosities, and not germane to contemporary archaeological and historical discussions. However, during the last three decades, a revival of these depictions has occurred: different, often contradictory, interpretations have emerged regarding the mythical Ősbuda ("ancient Buda"), a royal center of the kingdom of Hungary before the foundation of Buda Castle on Castle Hill.[63]

It should be noted that the location of the late medieval royal palace and royal town of Buda is rarely questioned. Excavations in the twentieth century, particularly those occurring after the devastation of World War II, revealed sections from the reign of Louis the Great, King Sigismund, and King Matthias. These remains, either reconstructed or left as ruins, can be seen today below the baroque buildings of the royal palace. The Budapest History Museum incorporates a number of medieval rooms, halls, and architectural elements in their original position. Medieval features (such as town walls, Gothic vaults, door and window frames, and, sometimes, even whole buildings and cellars) are likewise visible behind the baroque and classical facades of the houses in the Castle District. Archaeological and historical research, combined with restoration and reconstruction, manages to convince locals and tourists that they have traveled back in time to Buda in the Late Middle Ages when visiting Castle Hill with its palace and urban district. Despite sizable losses over the centuries,

---

63   Ferenc Kanyó, "Óbudátol 'Ősbudáig': Egy mítosz historiográfiája," [From 'Óbuda' to 'Ősbuda': the historiography of a myth] in *Micae Mediaevales II. Fiatal történészek dolgozatai a középkori Magyarországról és Európáról* [Studies of young historians of medieval Hungary and Europe] eds Bence Péterfi, András Vadas, Gábor Mikó, and Péter Jakab (Budapest: ELTE BTK Történelemtudományok Doktori Iskola, 2012), pp. 77–95; József Laszlovszky, "Ősbuda, Ős-Budavár, i–iii," [Ősbuda, Ős-Budavár]*Várak, kastélyok, templomok*, (2008/1), pp. 8–11, (2008/2), pp. 8–11 and (2008/3), pp. 12–15.

these features and significant discoveries (such as the hoard of Gothic statues found in 1974) have kept the medieval heritage in view.[64]

Óbuda is seen differently. Tourists and locals visiting this area, the third district of modern Budapest, often only notice the presence of Roman heritage in the present-day urban landscape. Aquincum, the important military center and governor's seat of Roman Pannonia contains a well-known museumwith vast picturesque ruins. In other parts of present-day Óbuda, original (or reconstructed) remains are visible among the nineteenth- and late-twentieth-century residential areas: a Roman military camp, a bath complex, remains of a large communal settlement, and rebuilt parts of the aqueduct. This is to say nothing of the two major landmarks: two large amphitheatres (one military, one civic). As a consequence, the general public agrees with the specialist on the notable presence of the Roman past in Óbuda.[65]

By contrast, a seismic split has emerged regarding the medieval remains of Óbuda between the consensus of historians and archaeologists (often labelled 'official' scholars) and amateur researchers who are focused on a mythical Ősbuda. Archaeological investigations, and historical studies predominantly utilizing charters, concerned with the topography and built heritage of Óbuda started much later than research into the Roman monuments, which goes back to the eighteenth century. Despite this slow beginning, important urban archaeological investigations that took place in the 1960s and 1970s revealed significant medieval remains of buildings of early Buda and the later urban settlement of Vetus Buda. Despite the only partial excavation of sites (owing to the imposition of later buildings), topographical analysis of contemporary medieval sources and careful excavation resulted in all the important settlement parts mentioned in charters being identified. These included the medieval remains of the Buda collegiate chapter, the royal castle that was used by the queen, the huge monastic complex of the Poor Clares, the parish church, and another ecclesiastical building (likely to have been the town's Franciscan friary) (Fig. 4.2). Consequently, there is agreement among historians and archaeologists that the early urban center of Buda and the later medieval market town called Vetus Buda are situated in present-day Óbuda, with the major medieval ruins laying beneath the modern urban landscape and overshadowed by the Roman remains (See Fig. 3.1). Parallel with these developments, however, a different interpretation emerged: the Ősbuda theory, developing in the 1930s,

---

64 See Károly Magyar's and Szilárd Papp's chapters in the present volume.
65 Paula Zsidi, *Archaeological Monuments from the Roman Period in Budapest* (Budapest: Archaeolingua, 2010).

of interest in the 1960s and 1970s, and, owing to the ease of publication on the internet, increasingly popular in the last two decades.

If not the originator of the theory, Sándor Sashegyi (1900–1958), an amateur archaeologist, was the first to use the term Ősbuda. The term was employed to distinguish an "ancient Buda" from the Óbuda and the site mentioned as Vetus Buda in medieval documents. A great archaeology enthusiast, Sashegyi played a significant – and positive – role in finding, identifying, and documenting a large number of sites around his home village of Pomáz (today a small town situated between Budapest and Szentendre). His site visit reports remain valuable archaeological sources. Despite this, Sashegyi's main idea concerning the role of Óbuda, Pomáz, and the whole of the Pilis region in the medieval era has been detrimental: his theories have misled and contributed to the present problematic situation. His identification of Vetus Buda with different monuments in and around Pomáz was based upon two key ideas. One concerned the amateur, and, later, professional, excavation at Pomáz-Klisza that featured a medieval site consisting of a residential building and a church.[66] Sashegyi identified this as the royal castle of Óbuda as used by the queen from the mid-fourteenth century. He was driven to this interpretation by his other idea: the location of the grave of Árpád, the successful tenth-century leader of the marauding Hungarians and eponymous ancestor of the first ruling dynasty. Nineteenth-century research on this question was characterized by heated debates over romanticized ideas. Later historians, using late medieval documents, recorded the ruler's burial place at Fehéregyháza (meaning "White church"), near Óbuda. Identification of the church was based on a water-course running in a stone channel, a detail mentioned in a charter, since the church itself was erected centuries after the burial of Árpád. Historians interpreted this feature as a medieval description of a Roman aqueduct, which modern scholars agree with. Sashegyi, however, desiring a Pomáz location for the grave, claimed as the site a point where a natural stream cutting into the rock formation, creates a spectacular narrow valley, at the nearby Holdvilág-árok. This place also features signs of past human activity. Subsequently, Sashegyi turned to romantic nineteenth-century ideas concerning Árpád's grave. These hypothetical identifications formed a coherent system in Sashegyi's view, and consequently for him it was impossible that Óbuda, or rather Ősbuda, could have existed in

---

66 József Laszlovszky, "Régészeti emlékek Pomázról," [Archaeological remains from Pomáz] and "Pomáz a középkorban" [Pomáz in the Middle Ages] in *Pomáz: természeti kincseink, történelmünk, kulturális örökségünk* [Pomáz: natural treasures, history, cultural heritage], eds József Laszlovszky, Ibolya Borbélyné Radics and Dánielné Könczöl (Pomáz: Pomáz Város Önkormányzata, 2001), pp. 27–33 and 33–51 respectively.

modern Óbuda but lay instead in the Pilis forest, particularly at Pomáz. Despite significant remains of notable medieval buildings (such as traces of the royal castle) having been already identified in Óbuda, Sashegyi stuck to his own interpretation to the end of his life, becoming increasingly depressed at the "official" opinions of archaeologists and historians. In the dark period of Stalinist rule in the 1950s, he lived more and more in the mythical Ősbuda of his own creation.[67] By the late 1970s and 1980s, historians and archaeologists were near unanimous that Árpád's grave would not be found in Holdvilág-árok (it being, rather, the location of Roman quarrying and stone-carving; with no traces of the Hungarian Conquest period being identified), and that Pomáz-Klisza's medieval ruins were not the royal castle of Óbuda (it being, rather, the village church and cemetery of Pomáz, and the residential complex being the manor house or *curia* of local nobility with the name Cikó).[68] The ideas of Sashegyi and the concept of Ősbuda would, in most circumstances, remain a curious historiographical detail, particularly following the publication of the relevant volume of the *Magyarország Régészeti Topográfiája* (*The Archaeological Topography of Hungary*),[69] the thorough and standard reference work on the archaeological sites using excavation reports and the pertinent medieval documents. This, however, was not to be the case.

From the 1970s onwards, more medieval details of Óbuda came to light from archaeological excavations. However, with the exception of the Poor Clares nunnery (mentioned in the introduction as being part of a school playground), these newly-discovered features were not transformed into picturesque ruin gardens or urban museums. Subsequently, the heritage of medieval Óbuda is predominantly invisible. Concurrent with this development was the particular character of the Kádár-era of Hungarian "Goulash Communism". There emerged a strange kind of intellectual life with relative freedom with regards to non-political issues. One such field of emerging interest was the medieval past of Hungary. Suspicions about so-called 'official' interpretations, and the homespun nature of the research, led to a variety of alternative histories appearing. This process connected with, and has been influenced by, an increasingly nationalistic (and ethnocentric) conspiracy theory. This theory can be

---

67   Laszlovszky, "Pomáz a középkorban," p. 38.
68   Gábor Virágos, *The Social Archaeology of Residential Sites: Hungarian noble residences and their social context from the thirteenth through to the sixteenth century: an outline for methodology* (Oxford: Archaeopress, 2006).
69   *Pest megye régészeti topográfiája* [Archaeological topography of Pest County] (Magyarország Régészeti Topográfiája 7), ed. István Torma (Budapest: Akadémiai, 1986), pp. 180–209.

summarized thus: 'official scholars' always serve the ruling power, who in turn want to obscure the truth about Hungarian history. This, the claim continues, results in the medieval remains of the splendid town and castle of Ősbuda, which is linked to the town of Attila, being deliberately kept hidden to remove the Hungarians from their glorious past. In this view of history, the Habsburgs refused to publish the truth because it interfered with their own debased view of the past and because they wanted to keep the Hungarians subjugated. Later, the Soviet Empire took on the mantle of hiders of the truth: their ideologically Pan-Slavic ideas did not fit with the real importance of the Árpáds and Attila.

This distorted interpretation of history continued even after the changes of 1989. The internet offers ever-increasing opportunities for publishing Ősbuda-related materials, free from scholarly checks and balances. The ease of accessing such material means that such sites are more frequently used by those curious about Hungary's past. With their romantic depictions of the semi-historical figures, these bloggers and "alternative" researchers have like their predecessors given life to creative imaginings of the past.

It is worthwhile mentioning a few of the ideas characteristic of Sashegyi's heirs. Many amateur researchers follow in his footsteps, looking for traces of Ősbuda at Csillaghegy, Budakalász or Pilismarót, settlements north of Budapest and close to the Pilis. Particular sites, with traces of Roman fortifications, stone quarries (of any era), or even scattered remains of stone buildings are identified as the ancient castle of Buda. Evidence taken from place names, combined with medieval charters and early modern depictions, create new claims and assertions. One popular idea combines the previously mentioned Fehéregyháza with the important royal center named Fehérvár ("White Castle"). Fehérvár is located in modern day Székesfehérvár, but the once important Árpádian age castle and basilica, one of the most notable ecclesiastical buildings of the Kingdom of Hungary, survives either as ruins or are invisible. Traces of the basilica, the coronation church and resting place of many medieval kings can be visited in the modern town center, but the late medieval and early modern urban fortifications are unrecognizable in the present day urban landscape. Subsequently, it is not surprising that many Ősbuda theories use early modern prints of Székesfehérvár to support their claims that particular landscape features (either seen from the air or noticeable due to carved stone materials) document the lost Ősbuda, without noting the actual location of the long-gone historic buildings. Likewise, any other particular element of medieval Hungarian history can be shoehorned in to support such claims. The only medieval monastic order founded in Hungary, the Pauline order, becomes for the adherents of Ősbuda a collection of armed monks (like a religious military order) capable of defending the huge castle. These anomalous details fuel the impression that Ősbuda was an immense construction, atypical of any medieval castle in Europe in that it occupied according to some claims the whole Pilis Mountain, a "fact" which in turn leads to the idea that it must have been built by Attila on the basis that a great monument must be the work of a great man.

Though it is easy to distinguish the conclusions from such researches from scholarly investigations, separating the romanticized view of the past from the historically accurate is not always as simple. The more recent excavations at Holdvilág-árok are an example of this. A professional archaeologist published some of the documentation produced by Sándor Sashegyi.[70] Although scholarly, the edition was initiated, and partially sponsored, by Levente Szörényi, a notable figure of modern Hungarian rock music. In addition to being the leader of the popular and prominent Illés-együttes (*Illés pop group*) and a pioneer in combining Hungarian folk music with pop and rock, Szörényi was the co-creator of the first, and most important, Hungarian rock opera *István, a király* ("Stephen, the King"). Like the historical poems of János Arany, the opera, first staged in 1983, depicted a legendary figure in a manner that addressed contemporary concerns (becoming symbolically important during the political changes in 1989). Just as the artists of the nineteenth century looked for inspiration to the Huns and ancient Hungarians, present-day authors, musicians, and filmmakers are heavily pre-occupied with depictions of the past. As a consequence, the Árpáds, are not only members of a medieval dynasty, but important touchstones for contemporary political issues. It is therefore perhaps an impossible ambition to formulate clear scholarly ideas on the interpretation of Buda, Óbuda (and even Ősbuda) without being involved in heated present-day debates. In this respect, the nineteenth-century tradition, an inheritor of the medieval traditions, is still a living presence in Hungary: the created castles of the imagination are often more influential than the castles that "once stood, now a heap of stones".

---

70 *Legendák és valóság a Pilisben* [Legends and realities in the Pilis], eds Tamás Repiszky and Levente Szörényi (Budapest: Heti Válasz 2011).

CHAPTER 5

A Royal Forest in the *Medium Regni*

Péter Szabó

Introduction

Buda in the Middle Ages formed part of the so-called "center of the kingdom" (*medium regni*), which was generated by the proximity of the four most important towns of Hungary: Esztergom, early royal center and seat of the archbishop; Visegrád, royal center in the fourteenth century; Buda, royal center and capital since the fifteenth century; and (somewhat further to the south) Székesfehérvár, burial and coronation place of the medieval rulers. The first three towns enclose a hilly and forested area, which has been called Pilis since the Middle Ages, when it was a royal forest. The word "pilis" is of Slavic origin, left behind by the same settlers who also gave its name to Visegrád ("high castle").[1] A version of *pleš* can be found in most Slavic languages; it refers to a "barren, treeless area" – and later to the tonsure of monks. The Pilis Mountains were named after their highest peak (756 m). Pilis peak is treeless nowadays, and was apparently already so when the Slavic settlers first saw it. It has probably been treeless even longer, since the end of the latest Ice Age (ca. 12,000 years ago), because on top of it grows the rare plant *Ferula sadleriana*, which cannot survive in shade and has practically no ability to colonize new territories in search of sunlight.[2]

No major city can be fully understood without considering its hinterlands. These areas had to satisfy the needs of the city but also provided opportunities. As far as needs are concerned, city dwellers required food and raw materials, many of which could not be transported very far. Probably the best known example of this is firewood, and the local supply systems of medieval London, early modern Prague and modern Paris are well-researched.[3] Opportunities

---

1 Lajos Kiss, *Földrajzi nevek etimológiai szótára*, ii [An etymological dictionary of geographical names] (Budapest: Akadémiai, 1988), pp. 346–347 and 768.
2 Tibor Kalapos, "A magyarföldi husáng (Ferula sadleriana Ledeb.) Pilis-tetői populációjának dinamikája," [The population dynamics of Ferula sadleriana Ledeb. on Pilis peak] in *Sziklagyepek szünbotanikai kutatása, Zólyomi Bálint professzor emlékének* [Ecological studies on rocky grasslands in memory of Prof. Bálint Zólyomi], ed. Péter Csontos (Budapest: Scientia, 1998), pp. 41–54.
3 James A. Galloway, Derek Keene and Margaret Murphy, "Fuelling the City: Production and Distribution of Firewood and Fuel in London's Region, 1290–1401," *Economic History Review*

were provided by the presence of rivers, which enabled long-distance transport, or by lucrative land-use types, for example vineyards. Medieval Buda was also strongly connected to its hinterland. It had a special geographical position, lying at the intersection of lowlands and more hilly terrain. The plains on the Pest side of the Danube provided arable lands and cattle pasture, the latter of which was an important type of business in the Late Middle Ages.[4] The Buda side was, as we will see, well-wooded and most probably covered the firewood needs of the city, even though due to the lack of sources we cannot map supply networks. The burghers of Buda had strong business interests in wine production, which took place in the neighboring hills.[5] The Pilis royal forest was a somewhat more distant, less intensively used part of the Buda hinterlands. In this paper, I will examine both the physical and the institutional and symbolic aspects of the history of Pilis. I will describe its functioning as a royal forest, followed by a reconstruction of settlement structure and woodland cover.

The Royal Forest of Pilis

The discussion concerning Pilis has mostly revolved around the concept of 'forest county' (*erdőispánság* in Hungarian).[6] This term was created by

---

49 (1996), pp. 447–472; František Holec, "Obchod s dřívím v Praze ve 14.–17. století," [Wood trade in Prague in the fourteenth–seventeenth centuries] *Pražský sborník historický* 6 (1971), pp. 5–100; Eunhye Kim and Sabine Barles, "The Energy Consumption of Paris and its Supply Areas from the Eighteenth Century to the Present," *Regional Environmental Change* 12 (2012), pp. 295–310.

4   See Judit Benda's chapter in the present volume.

5   András Kubinyi, "Weinbau und Weinhandel in den ungarischen Städten im Spätmittelalter und in der frühe Neuzeit," in *Stadt und Wein* (Beiträge zur Geschichte der Städte Mitteleuropas, 14), eds Ferdinand Opll and Susanne Claudine Pils (Linz: Österreichisches Arbeitskreis für Stadtgeschichtsforschung, 1996), pp. 67–84; *Budai bortizedjegyzékek a 16. század első harmadából* [Wine-tithe lists from Buda from the first third of the sixteenth century], eds Ferenc Szakály and Jenő Szűcs (Budapest: MTA Történettudományi Intézete, 2005).

6   The most important works on medieval Pilis are: ÁMTF, iv, pp. 583–714; Frigyes Pesty, *Az eltünt régi vármegyék*, 2 vols [Old counties that have disappeared] (Budapest: MTA Könyvkiadó-hivatala, 1880), i, pp. 59–67; Attila Zsoldos, "Visegrád vármegye és utódai," [Visegrád county and its successors] *Történelmi Szemle* 40 (1998), pp. 1–32; István Tringli, "Pest megye a késő középkorban," [Pest County in the Late Middle Ages] in *Pest megye monográfiája, i/2. A honfoglalástól 1686-ig* [A monograph on Pest County from the Conquest until 1686], ed. Attila Zsoldos (Budapest: Pest Megye Monográfia Közalapítvány, 2001), pp. 75–194; Gyula Kristó, *A vármegyék kialakulása Magyarországon* [The formation of counties in Hungary] (Budapest: Magvető, 1988), pp. 252–254; Péter Szabó, *Woodland and Forests in Medieval Hungary*

nineteenth-century historians who realized that in some regions of Hungary (including Pilis) administrative units were created in the twelfth–thirteenth centuries that were called counties (*comitatus*), but which were nonetheless different in a number of important ways. Because the common feature of these areas seemed to be their woodland cover, historians called them 'forest counties.'[7] This is, however, a modern term. In the Middle Ages, if scribes wanted to emphasize what made these counties special, they called them *silve regales*, royal forests.

The concept of royal forests was created some time in the Early Middle Ages in the Merovingian Frankish territories. The Latin word *forestum* was first recorded around AD 648 in a charter of the Benedictine abbey of Stavelot-Malmedy (today in Belgium).[8] Although the precise etymology of *forestum* is not clear, in the Middle Ages it was thought to have come from the expression *foris est*, referring to what is "outside something."[9] In other words, the original meaning of *forestum* had nothing to do with trees: it referred to a territory outside of common law. Medieval forests were territories set aside from the common law for keeping wild animals for the king and other magnates. Some were covered with trees, but others were not. In Hungary, the Latin term *forestum*

(Archaeolingua – Central European Series, 2 = BAR International Series, 1348) (Oxford: Archaeopress, 2005), pp. 93–118; Zsuzsa Eszter Pető, *The Medieval Landscape of the Pauline Monasteries in the Pilis Forest*, unpublished MA thesis (Budapest: Central European University, 2014).

7 Pesty, *Az eltünt régi vármegyék*, passim; Elemér Mályusz, *Turóc megye kialakulása* [The formation of Turóc county] (Budapest: Budavári Tudományos Társaság, 1922); ÁMTF, i, pp. 45–47.

8 Ellen F. Arnold, *Negotiating the Landscape: Environment and Monastic Identity in the Medieval Ardennes* (Philadelphia: University of Pennsylvania Press, 2013), pp. 46–56. In general, the word was used either as as neuter – *forestum* – or as feminine – *foresta*.

9 On the development of the concept of Royal Forests, see Heinrich Rubner, "Vom römischen Saltus zum fränkischen Forst," *Historisches Jahrbuch* 83 (1964), pp. 271–277; Jörg Jarnut, "Die frühmittelalterliche Jagd unter rechts- und sozialgeschichtlichen Aspekten," *Settimane di Studio* 31 (1985), pp. 765–808; Régine Hennebicque, "Espaces sauvages et chasses royales dans le Nord de la Francie, VIIe–IXe siècles," *Revue du Nord* 62 (1980), pp. 35–57; Chris Wickham, "European Forests in the Early Middle Ages: Landscape and Land Clearance," in idem, *Land and Power: Studies in Italian and European Social History, 400–1200* (London: British School at Rome, 1994), pp. 155–199; Clemens Dasler, *Forst und Wildbann im frühen deutschen Reich* (Cologne: Böhlau, 2001); Oliver Rackham, *The Last Forest: The Story of Hatfield Forest* (London: Dent, 1989); Charles R. Young, *The Royal Forests of Medieval England* (Philadelphia: University of Pennsylvania Press, 1979).

occurs in medieval sources only four times.[10] The concept of royal forests was adapted to local conditions creating a specific form, of which Pilis Forest is a good example.

Beginnings and the Thirteenth Century

According to the modern theory of 'forest counties', when the kingdom of Hungary was formed around AD 1000 larger uninhabited areas – including what were later to become 'forest counties' – became royal property.[11] In the sources these are described as *predia*, and their administrative heads as *procuratores* (keepers). Around 1200 these persons started to be called *comites*, and the territories *comitatus* (county). The early history of Pilis can be comfortably described along these lines. In the eleventh–twelfth centuries its territory was in royal ownership. We can see this for example when the provostry of Dömös, in the north, was founded in ca. 1107 by Prince Álmos, brother of King Coloman. Why the territory was Álmos's is not known, except that it probably had something to do with him being part of the royal family.[12] The first written source to mention Pilis, using this name and in a geographical sense, was issued by Pope Urban III to the hospitallers of Esztergom. In this document the pope referred to a charter of King Géza II of Hungary that spoke of Pilis as "his very own forest" (*propria silva sua*).[13] Pilis was transformed into a county by the thirteenth century. The first appearance of a *comes* of Pilis County is from 1225.[14]

Perhaps the most important feature of Pilis in this early period was its dense network of hunting lodges.[15] The *Chronicon Pictum* informs us that there was

---

10   *Lexicon Latinitatis Medii Aevi Hungariae*, iv, ed. János Harmatta (Budapest: Akadémiai, 1993), p. 123.

11   Eszter Magyar, "Erdőispánság," [Forest county] in *Korai magyar történeti lexikon (9–14. század)* [Early Hungarian historical lexicon, ninth–fourteenth centuries], ed. Gyula Kristó *et al.*, (Budapest: Akadémiai, 1994), pp. 194–195.

12   According ÁMTF, iv, p. 630 Dömös was donated to Álmos by King Coloman around 1100 AD; however, the evidence given is only circumstantial. See also Gábor Thoroczkay, "A dömösi prépostság története alapításától I. Károly uralkodásának végéig," [History of the provostry of Dömös from its foundation to the end of the reign of King Charles I] *Fons* 19 (2012), pp. 409–433.

13   Nándor Knauz, "Az esztergomi érsekség okmányai," [The documents of the archbishopric of Esztergom] *Magyar Sion* 1 (1863), pp. 129–136, here p. 131.

14   ÁÚO, xi, p. 182–184 (no 121). For a list of all *comites* of Pilis County, see Pesty, *Az eltünt régi vármegyék*, i, pp. 65–67.

15   Hunting lodges and forests were also connected in other parts of Europe. See Karl Bosl, "Pfalzen und Forsten," in *Deutsche Königspfalzen. Beitrage zu ihrer historischen und*

a *regale allodium* in Dömös, where King Béla I died when his throne collapsed on him.[16] Further hunting lodges lay near Pilisszentkereszt, Kesztölc, Pilisszentlászló and Pilisszentlélek.[17] The memory of these buildings survived in a written form because they were transformed into monasteries. Before 1200, wherever the king and his retinue stayed in Pilis, they had a lodge within a few hours' ride, and the archbishop, the queen, St Stephen's tomb, and their own residence within one day's journey. Such hunting lodges were known in other Hungarian forests as well, for example in Patak Forest to the north.[18] One should not suppose that they all served the personal needs of the king, although in this early period the royal court was constantly on the move. They were rather centers of venison production with a specialized personnel dedicated to hunting.

Another special feature of Hungarian forests, the presence of forest-guards (*custodes silvarum*), is first mentioned in Pilis in the year 1285.[19] These forest-guards were responsible for hunting and the administration of the forests, including the protection of physical boundaries and the regulation of wood extraction. In respect of the management of early royal estates in Hungary, there were several kinds of servants' villages whose inhabitants had to perform specific duties by way of provisioning.[20] Because early Forests were royal property, they had their own special servant settlements. Their memory has been preserved mostly in the form of place names. In our region, Kovácsi, the smiths' settlement, stood just north of Pilis peak. Peszérd, a village situated a few kilometres south-east of Esztergom, was the home of the royal dog keepers. Fedémes, at the south-eastern end of Pilis, was named after the bee keepers there. Solymár, somewhat further to the south-east, was where the falconers lived.

---

archäologischen Erforschung (Göttingen: Vandenhoeck & Ruprecht, 1963), pp. 1–29; John Steane, *The Archaeology of the Medieval English Monarchy* (London: Routledge, 1993), pp. 79–93.

16 Alexander Domanovszky, ed., *Chronici Hungarici compositio saeculi XIV*, in SRH, i, pp. 217–505, here p. 360 (cap 96).

17 See notes 19 and 20.

18 Jenő Szűcs, "Sárospatak kezdetei és a pataki erdőuralom," [The beginnings of Sárospatak and the forest estate of Patak] *Történelmi Szemle* 35 (1993), pp. 1–58, here pp. 13–16.

19 *Monumenta Ecclesiae Strigoniensis*, ii, ed. Ferdinánd Knauz (Esztergom: Typis descripsit Aegydius Horák, 1882), pp. 192–193 (no 174) and 207–208 (no 186).

20 Gusztáv Heckenast, *A fejedelmi (királyi) szolgálónépek a korai Árpád-korban* [Princely (royal) servitor populations in the early Árpádian period] (Értekezések a történeti tudományok köréből, 53) (Budapest: Akadémiai, 1970).

Changes

The most important changes to the existing system came with the transformation of the hunting lodges into monasteries and the construction of the castle of Visegrád. These changes happened more or less at the same time. In 1184, King Béla III founded a Cistercian abbey near Pilisszentkereszt,[21] which was followed in the second half of the thirteenth century by the foundation of three Pauline monasteries (in today's Pilisszentlászló, Kesztölc and Pilisszentlélek).[22] This undoubtedly meant the kings no longer wished to maintain the network of hunting lodges in its earlier form.

The Cistercians and the Paulines were in many respects very different from each other. The Cistercian Order was an international venture, which was for a long time credited with the cultivation of wilderness areas and the introduction of new agricultural and industrial techniques. Although some of these assumptions were based on the wording of the *Regula* of the Cistercians rather than their actual activities, the pioneering nature of the White Monks is undeniable.[23] The Paulines, on the other hand, were the only Hungarian monastic order which, according to its own tradition, originated actually in Pilis,

---

21 Remig Békefi, *A pilisi apátság története 1184–1814*, 2 vols [A history of the Pilis monastery 1184–1814] (Pécs: Pfeifer, 1891–1892); László Gerevich, *A pilisi ciszterci apátság* [The Pilis Cistercian abbey] (Szentendre: Pest Megyei Múzeumok Igazgatósága, 1984); Imre Holl, *Funde aus dem Zisterzienserkloster von Pilis* (Varia archaeologica Hungarica, 11) (Budapest: Archäologisches Institut der UAW, 2000).

22 Júlia Kovalovszki, "A pálos remeték Szent Kereszt-kolostora (Méri István ásatása Klastrompusztán)," [The Holy Cross monastery of the Pauline hermits (István Méri's excavations at Klastrompuszta)], *Communicationes archaeologicae Hungariae* 1992, pp. 173–207; Sarolta Lázár, "A pilisszentléleki volt pálos kolostortemplom kutatása 1985–86," [Excavations in the former Pauline monastery at Pilisszentlélek, 1985–86] *Komárom-Esztergom Megyei Múzeumok Közleményei* 5 (1992), pp. 493–518; György Györffy, "Adatok a Pilis megyei monostorok középkori történetéhez," [On the medieval history of monasteries in Pilis County], *Művészettörténeti Értesítő* 4 (1956), pp. 280–285; Pető, *The Medieval Landscape*; Beatrix F. Romhányi, "Pálos kolostorok a Pilisben," [Pauline monasteries in the Pilis] in *Laudator temporis acti: Tanulmányok Horváth István 70 éves születésnapjára* [Essays is honor of István Horváth on his 70th birthday], eds Edit Tari and Endre Tóth (Esztergom–Budapest: Balassa Bálint Múzeumért Alapítvány – Martin Opitz, 2010), pp. 223–227.

23 Louis J. Lekai, *The Cistercians: Ideals and Reality* (Kent, OH.: Kent State University Press, 1977); Giles Constable, *The Reformation of the Twelfth Century* (Cambridge: Cambridge University Press, 1996), p. 120; Michael Aston, *Monasteries* (London: Batsford, 1993), p. 74.

following the example of local hermits.[24] The Pauline brethren seem to have lived a relatively simple life.[25] But the role of the special geographical position of Pilis is clearly identifiable in both cases. Paulines as well as Cistercians were required to settle in uninhabited places (although such rules were often not taken seriously). The Pilis Mountains were an ideal location for the monks to be far from the mundane world but close to it at the same time. This is most obvious in the case of the Cistercian abbey: it was one of five monasteries established by King Béla III as part of his general westwards-oriented policy. It is perhaps not accidental that the Pilis monastery, which was among the most significant Cistercian monasteries in Hungary, was situated next to the seat of the archbishop of Esztergom.[26] The abbot of the monastery often acted on behalf of the king or the pope in important political missions. The construction of the monasteries appears to have altered the communication network of Pilis as well, whereby the main road was moved north to pass near the Cistercian abbey and the Szentkereszt Pauline monastery.[27]

Another event of the highest significance was the construction of the castle of Visegrád in the mid-thirteenth century. There had been a castle in Visegrád before, built upon the ruins of a Roman fortress on Sibrik Hill, the focal place of the ancient county of Visegrád. This had fallen into disuse by the early 1200s, when the county center moved to Esztergom.[28] As the hunting residences gradually became out-of-date and the function of the Forest was in need of some new definition, Queen Mary (wife of King Béla IV), apparently acting on her own initiative, started to build a castle above the old fortress, which she financed by selling her jewels. The new castle was at least partly ready by

---

24 Beatrix F. Romhányi, "A pálos rendi hagyomány az oklevelek tükrében," [The Pauline tradition in the light of charters] *Történelmi Szemle* 50 (2008), pp. 289–312.

25 Elemér Mályusz, *Egyházi társadalom a középkori Magyarországon* [Ecclesiastical society in medieval Hungary] (Budapest: Akadémiai, 1971), pp. 257–274; Beatrix F. Romhányi, "Die Pauliner im mittelalterlichen Ungarn," in *Beiträge zur Geschichte des Paulinerordens*, ed. Kaspar Elm (Berlin: Duncker & Humblot, 2000), pp. 143–156.

26 József Laszlovszky, "Hungarian University Peregrination to Western Europe in the Second Half of the Twelfth Century," in *Universitas Budensis 1395–1995*, eds László Szögi and Júlia Varga (Budapest: ELTE Levéltára, 1997), pp. 51–60.

27 Pető, *The Medieval Landscape*, pp. 58–64. See also Elek Benkő, "Via regis – via gregis. Középkori utak a Pilisben," [Medieval roads in the Pilis] in *Fél évszázad terepen. Tanulmánykötet Torma István tiszteletére 70. születésnapja alkalmából* [Half a century of fieldwork. Studies in honor of István Torma on his 70th birthday], eds Klára Kővári and Zsuzsa Miklós (Budapest: Magyar Tudományos Akadémia Régészeti Intézete, 2011), pp. 115–119.

28 Zsoldos, "Visegrád vármegye," pp. 14–17.

1251.[29] Eight years later Béla IV donated "the castle with the county and district of Pilis" to the queen.[30] The new castle originally had a well-defined function. It was built to protect the Dominican nuns at the Margaret Island (at that time, Hares' Island) in the event of another Mongol invasion. Margaret, one of the nuns, was the daughter of the royal couple, which undoubtedly explains why the queen was willing to sacrifice her jewels.

The transformation of the administrative structure of the royal forest of Pilis was completed by the unification of the functions of the *comes* of Pilis and the castellan of Visegrád. This merger is usually thought to have taken place immediately, but there was a notable time-gap. The first to hold the two positions at the same time was Eyza 'the Saracen' in 1285.[31] Before that, and after 1251, we know of five *comites* of Pilis.[32] Two of them are known only by their names (Philip and Oliver). As for the rest, we find one bishop (Thomas, bishop of Vác) and one archbishop (Nicholas), both chancellors of the royal court; and Joachim was master of the treasury and also *comes* of Pozsony County. This clearly shows that the county of Pilis was no longer comprehended as an economic unit but that it had a symbolic significance only. Its *comites*, very far from their previous role as keepers, received their office and title as a sign of royal honor and cared little about the woods. Pilis was managed, in ways that are unknown to us, by lesser officers appointed by the *comites*. But by the end of the thirteenth century the castellan of Visegrád and the *comes* of Pilis were indeed the same person.

The Late Middle Ages

The death of the last Árpádian, Andrew III, in 1301, marked the beginning of a new era in the life of Visegrád and the surrounding Pilis Forest. In 1323 Charles I, the new king, moved his court from faraway Timişoara to Visegrád. Why he did not choose Buda (or Óbuda) we shall never know for certain, but most probably he valued Visegrád for its geographical position and its strong fortress.[33] Signifying the growing importance of Visegrád, the Szentlászló

---

29   She issued a charter "in Wisegrad" that year – ÁÚO, vii, pp. 325–326 (no 225).
30   "castrum cum comitatu et districtu de Pelys" – ÁÚO, vii, pp. 501–503 (no 354).
31   ÁMTF, iv, p. 710.
32   ÁMTF, iv, p. 692; Pesty, *Az eltünt régi vármegyék*, i, pp. 65–66.
33   It has often been argued that King Charles I was not fond of Buda, which had supported his rivals to the throne. This theory was rejected by Tringli, "Pest megye," p. 76. The suggestion that the king may have especially valued the fortifications of Visegrád has been put

Pauline monastery was built halfway between this town and Buda.[34] The office of castellan of Visegrád (by this time merged fully with the position of the *comes* of Pilis) increased greatly in importance. For example, in the 1340s Töttös of Becse was castellan for a decade, while simultaneously filling the office of castellan of Óbuda and the household office of *magister ianitorum*; while Benedict Himfy, the next castellan (and *comes*), was later promoted to be ban of Bulgaria.[35] The union of the two offices, however, did not last long. The castellans of Visegrád used the title of *comes* of Pilis only until 1366.[36] After this time, the castellans gradually lost control over the county, or, what is equally likely, showed gradually less and less interest in the affairs of the county. There was most probably no need to make a point of demonstrating royal power in a county where it was already so overwhelmingly present. At any rate, what we do know is that the castellans ceased to call themselves *comites*, although King Sigismund continued to address letters to this apparently non-existent officer as late as 1411.[37] Parallel with this, the regular institutions of the county began to develop. In 1333, we first hear of 'noble magistrates', members of the four-man judicial committee that was the most important institution of the new 'noble' counties (although for one reason or another there were only two magistrates in Pilis County).[38] By the fifteenth century there was little difference between Pilis and any other county as far as its administration was concerned. What made Pilis County special is that it had no *comes*. Yet another

forward by Gergely Buzás, "The Remains of the Royal Palace of Visegrád from the Angevin Period," in *Medieval Visegrad. Royal Castle, Palace, Town and Franciscan Friary* (Dissertationes Pannonicae Ser. iii. 4), ed. József Laszlovszky (Budapest: Eötvös Loránd University, 1995), pp. 9–18 here p. 9.

34 Pető, *The Medieval Landscape*, pp. 58–64.
35 Pál Engel, *Magyarország világi archontológiája 1301–1457*, i [Secular archontology of Hungary 1301–1457] (História könyvtár. Kronológiák, adattárak, 5) (Budapest: História – MTA Történettudományi Intézete, 1996), p. 34. The *banatus Bulgariae* was a shortlived (1365–1369) initiative of King Louis I. However, while it existed, the ban counted among the barons, the highest officials of the kingdom.
36 With the exception of Leusták of Jolsva in the late 1380s and early 1390s. The following description of the development of Pilis County is based mostly on Tringli, "Pest megye,"
37 BTOE, iii/1, p. 295 (no 569).
38 Conventionally, we speak of two basic types of county organization in medieval Hungary. First, there was the so-called 'royal' county headed by a *comes* appointed by the king. Then, along with the emergence of the nobility and the larger changes in the thirteenth century, counties attained a form of self-governing independence (the best indicators of this are the presence of the noble magistrates and the regular assemblies of the nobles). They are accordingly known as 'noble' counties, although they were still headed by a royally-appointed *comes*.

inexplicable fact in the late medieval history of Pilis County is that it started to expand in the fourteenth century, acquiring extensive territories south of its core area at the expense of neighboring counties. This is not quite as unusual as the missing *comes*, but it is still puzzling. The resulting *comitatus Pilisiensis* was then united with Pest County some time in the fifteenth century.

One can detect a double structure that influenced the late medieval history of Pilis. On the one hand, there was the newly emerging 'noble' county, with its magistrates and territorial expansion. This line of development was entirely independent of the Royal Forest of the thirteenth century. On the other hand, the county was dominated by the castle of Visegrád. The castellan controlled the royal lands in Pilis, in other words what territory was left of Pilis Forest. The Forest, whatever the word meant in physical reality, was treated as still in existence by King Charles I, who issued a charter in 1324 in which he gave the *hospites* of (Nagy)Maros town the right to cut wood from Pilis to build houses or for firewood without any taxes or seal; however, if they wanted to sell the wood, they could only do so with the consent of the *comes* of Pilis County.[39] This charter reveals the legal system of woodland management in Pilis. The *comes* controlled woodcutting. It was most probably his seal that gave permission for this, and it was also the *comes* who collected the taxes on timber and wood. The restriction on *hospites* cutting wood for sale is a commonplace, for most privileges concerning woodland rights contained it. Few other such charters survive. In 1388, Sigismund ordered the *comes* to let the nuns of Óbuda cut wood if they needed it for building or fire. The expression *silva nostra Pilissiensis* in this charter still reflects thirteenth-century royal attitudes.[40] A century later in 1468, a mandate was directed to the castellan of Visegrád. The woodland in question was no longer called Pilis; instead we read of the woods of Visegrád. It was from these woods that the nuns acquired the right to take wood "for their kitchen" for a year.[41]

Woodland Cover in the Middle Ages

Royal forests in Europe were not necessarily wooded. However, we have no reason to doubt that the royal forest of Pilis was mostly wooded in the Middle

---

39   AOklt, viii, p. 139–140 (no 269), edited in CD, viii/2, 514–517 (no 241). Maros (today Nagymaros) is close to Visegrád but on the opposite side of the Danube. It had rights in Pilis (but not in Börzsöny) because Eyza (*comes* of Pilis and castellan of Visegrád in 1285) acquired the rights to settle *hospites* on its territory. ÁMTF, iv, p. 710.

40   BTOE, iii, p. 18 (no 43).

41   MNL OL DL 16 631.

Ages (and has remained so ever since). In this section I will analyze the issue of woodland cover in more detail. I will try to establish how wooded Pilis was in different periods, and whether woodland cover went through significant changes in the Middle Ages. There are two basic kinds of direct sources that provide information: archival and bio-scientific. The latter includes for example malacology, anthracology and pollen analysis. Unfortunately there is only one pollen sample available from Pilis, taken from the dried-out pond of the Cistercian abbey. Although the results are hard to interpret due to difficulties in dating and presentation, it is clear that in the Middle Ages there were open areas in the neighborhood of today's Szentkereszt. This, however, says little about Pilis as a whole. Medieval archival sources could in principle be of more help. In particular, the *estimationes*, a special kind of Hungarian source typical for the fifteenth century, record precise acreages of various land-use types, including woodland.[42] But unfortunately not a single *estimatio* is available for Pilis.

For want of direct sources, one needs to turn to settlement history, making the assumption that where there were no settlements in Pilis there was woodland. Such an approach can give us only a very general idea of woodland cover and its changes, but this being the only option, it is worth investigating. In contrast to natural scientific and written sources, settlement historical data is excellent for the territory. The entire area of Pilis was included in the fifth and seventh volumes of the *Archaeological Topography of Hungary* (*Magyarország Régészeti Topográfiája* – MRT).[43] The MRT was originally designed to gather all known archaeological sites and finds of a particular territory from prehistory to the early modern times, but its authors did more than that. They consulted the written sources referring to individual settlements and they also took advantage of extensive field surveys to establish the locations of as many settlements as possible.[44] These surveys were restricted to visible finds on the surface (in reality almost exclusively potsherds). Although the methodology of dating of potsherds was not very precise when the pertinent volumes of the MRT were prepared, establishing dates within individual centuries proved

---

42 Szabó, *Woodland and Forests*, pp. 47–79.
43 *Komárom megye régészeti topográfiája. Esztergom és a Dorogi járás* [The archaeological topography of Komárom County. The region of Esztergom and Dorog] (Magyarország Régészeti Topográfiája, 5), eds István Horváth, Márta H. Kelemen and István Torma (Budapest: Akadémiai, 1979); *Pest megye régészeti topográfiája. A budai és szentendrei járás* [The archaeological topography of Pest county. The region of Buda and Szentendre] (Magyarország Régészeti Topográfiája, 7), ed. István Torma (Budapest: Akadémiai, 1986).
44 Dénes B. Jankovich, *A felszíni leletgyűjtés módszerei és szerepe a régészeti kutatásban* [The methods of surface find collecting and its role in archaeological research] (Budapest: Magyar Nemzeti Múzeum – MTA Régészeti Intézet, 1993).

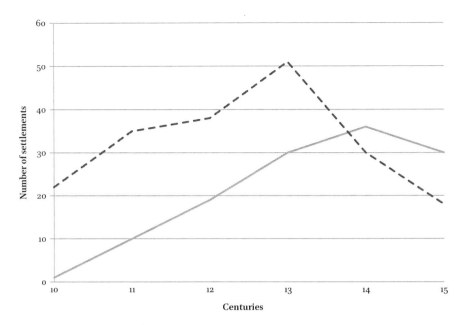

FIGURE 5.1 *The number of settlements in Pilis by century (Full line: settlements mentioned in written documents. Dashed line: settlements located through field surveys, not mentioned in written sources.)*

possible. Combining the different sources of information, the MRT volumes compiled brief descriptions of all settlements in the given region, including those that were mentioned in written sources and those that are known from archaeological finds only. One methodological drawback should perhaps be mentioned: field surveys cannot be conducted in woodland, where the ground vegetation makes finds invisible. Whether this may have affected the soundness of the results of settlement historical research in Pilis will be discussed later on.

Medieval documents mention thirty-seven settlements in Pilis. With one exception,[45] they were all connected to archaeological sites. Archaeological research established that eighteen settlements had been established at least one century earlier than their first mention in charters. The full line in Fig 5.1 illustrates the number of settlements by century based on the combined evidence of charters and archaeological research. In addition to settlements that we know of from documents, there were many others never mentioned in writing and only discovered in field surveys. The dashed line in Fig 5.1 shows

---

45   *A budai és szentendrei járás*, p. 205.

the number of these settlements by century. There were approximately twice as many such settlements as those known from written sources. Such a proportion was not a peculiarity of Pilis; similar settlements, typically from the eleventh–thirteenth centuries, were located in large numbers in other parts of Hungary as well. It is remarkable that while the number of settlements steadily grew for both types until the thirteenth century, after that settlements recorded in written sources remained stable but settlements recorded only through archaeological fieldwork sharply declined. All this is line with the generally accepted theory of medieval Hungarian settlement history, which put down the disappearance of these usually small settlements to wars, epidemics and agrarian crises.[46] Recent research has emphasized the fundamental role of the changes in agrarian production structures, namely that estates based on work performed by serfs were gradually replaced by nucleated villages where peasants worked their individual plots.[47]

Fig. 5.2 shows the location of all settlements. Along the Danube, their distribution was even, and they appear not to have penetrated the depths of Pilis Forest. This may be the result of field survey techniques, but that would not affect the settlements that have written documentation. Nevertheless, the settlements that have charter evidence basically surround the forest. It appears that the people living in more stable settlements preferred to stay outside of the woodland or, vice versa, that those settlements that managed to survive longer were the ones that were not within the woods.

There were two areas where the 'purely-archaeological' settlements largely outnumbered the documented ones. One of them is the region of today's Pomáz; the other is the valley between the middle part of the Pilis Mountains (Hosszúhegy) and the south-eastern end of it (Kevélyek), together with the northern part of the valley of Pilisvörösvár, which is the south-western side of Hosszúhegy. This is partly explained by the geography of the region. The longish limestone Pilis Mountains rise steeply from the neighboring flat areas. Around here, the dividing line between habitable and non-habitable places is sharp. Many smaller settlements were established here in the eleventh–thirteenth centuries, in accordance with general Hungarian trends. Early settlers inhabited all possible places, but did not venture the impossible. The northern part of the region offered more scope for settlement expansion towards woodland. The gently rolling slopes would have been manageable for medieval settlers, as some sites within the hills amply demonstrate. However,

---

46 István Szabó, *A falurendszer kialakulása Magyarországon* [The formation of the village network in Hungary] (Budapest: Akadémiai, 1966).

47 Tringli, "Pest megye," pp. 102–104.

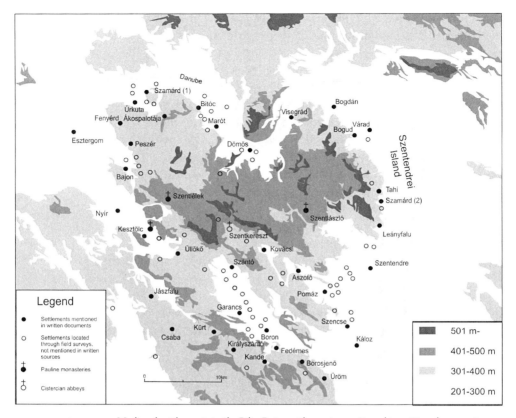

FIGURE 5.2 *Medieval settlements in the Pilis. Dots: settlements mentioned in written documents. Circles: settlements located through field surveys, not mentioned in written sources. Crosses: monasteries.*

very few sites have been found in these places. Providing that all this is not the result of survey techniques, it seems probable that whoever owned the woods preferred them uninhabited. The overall impression that settlement research provides is that woodland cover was by and large stable in Pilis throughout the Middle Ages.

Conclusions

In an administrative sense, Pilis in the Middle Ages was a royal forest (*silva regalis*), the Hungarian version of the west European *forestum*. In its early history, its specific features included hunting lodges and servant populations specific to the forest. In the thirteenth century, and in a manner akin to other private royal estates, Pilis was transformed into a county, but it kept its physical boundaries. As part of a deliberate process, the newly-built castle of Visegrád took over the functions of the hunting lodges, which were transformed into monasteries. In other words, the royal house completed the modernization of the region without losing control over it. This system functioned until the Late Middle Ages, when Pilis became one of the regular 'noble' counties with certain anomalies that remind us of its origins as a royal forest.

Due to the lack of written sources and palaeoecological research, little is known of the historical ecology of the forest. The analysis of the settlement structure shows that the area around Pilis was settled early, and apart from the desertion of smaller settlements characteristic of the entire kingdom, the settlement structure was stable until the Ottoman occupation in the sixteenth century, when the whole area was depopulated. The territory surrounded by settlements was most probably covered by woodland.

Once there were royal forests all over Europe. With few exceptions, however, little remains nowadays of their former social and physical structure. A peculiarity of Pilis is that several elements that made up the royal forest are still there: the royal castle of Visegrád, the woodlands with the most important wild animals (red deer, roe deer and wild boar), and – though only in ruins – some of the monasteries. On the other hand, the settlement structure has been completely transformed. It is nonetheless important to appreciate the connection between the history of the forest and the existence of the many rare plant species and associations that are now part of the Duna-Ipoly National Park. Elements of continuity in the special status of Pilis certainly contributed to the survival of this unique landscape right next to the most important centers of medieval Hungary.

PART 3

The Topography of Buda

∴

CHAPTER 6

Royal Residences in Buda in Hungarian and European Context

Károly Magyar

Early Royal Seats

From the early eleventh century to the middle of the thirteenth, three locations alternated in the role of royal seat: Esztergom, Székesfehérvár and Óbuda. All three were in the area where the Danube turns south, in the *medium regni,* the center of the kingdom.[1] The principal trading routes also intersected in this region, and it was also where the ruling Árpád dynasty held large domains and forests.[2] The proportion and structure of crown lands went through many subsequent changes, but they retained their dominance in the region throughout the Middle Ages. As in many other states of Europe, no permanent royal seat emerged during this period, because monarchs and their courts were in constant movement among their domains and court centers. Even within the *medium regni* region, it is possible to identify more than a dozen administrative and estate centers, mansions and hunting lodges capable of accommodating the king and his court. One was Visegrád, which started as a county center and steadily grew in importance.

Esztergom became a center in the 970s under Prince Géza. It was there that his son Stephen was baptized and, in 1000, crowned as the first king of Hungary. Later canonized, Stephen founded an archiepiscopal center there, and its archbishops headed the Hungarian Church throughout and beyond the medieval period. The princely, later royal and archiepiscopal seat was located in a castle on a hill overlooking the Danube.

Translated by Alan Campbell
1 Bernát L. Kumorovitz, "Buda (és Pest) 'fővárossá' alakulásának kezdetei," [The beginnings of the formation of Buda (and Pest) as capital] *Tanulmányok Budapest Múltjából* 18 (1971), pp. 7–57.
2 László Gerevich, "The Rise of the Hungarian Towns along the Danube," in *Towns in Medieval Hungary*, ed. idem (Budapest: Akadémiai, 1990), pp. 26–50; Katalin Szende, "Towns Along the Way: Changing Patterns of Long-Distance Trade and the Urban Network of Medieval Hungary," in *Towns and Communication*, ii. *Communication between Towns*, eds Hubert Houben and Kristjan Toomaspoeg (Lecce: Mario Congedo Editore, 2011), pp. 161–225, esp. pp. 169–183.

The princely palace[3] in Esztergom and the first church there, dedicated to St Stephen the Protomartyr and serving as both palace chapel and baptismal church, lay at the highest, northern point of a broad plateau. Later, the archbishop's palace was built as part of the same complex. The Cathedral of St Adalbert was built to the south, in the middle of the plateau. (What remained of the building after the Ottoman occupation was obliterated by construction work in the eighteenth and nineteenth centuries, so that its three-aisle basilica form – altered several times during the Middle Ages – is known only from contemporary floor plans and views.)[4] Beside it, to the south, was the *monasterium Sancti Adalberti*, the house of the clerics who served the cathedral. There is disagreement regarding the role of the triangular area further south, at the end of plateau. Excavations have revealed scattered remains of buildings from the eleventh and twelfth centuries: a small square tower, a round building (probably a rotunda), and some other buildings that seem to have been dwellings.[5] Some archaeologists and historians consider these to have constituted the royal palace, set up when the king moved south from the archbishop's palace. Others suppose them to have belonged to the dwelling place of the *comes* i.e. head of Esztergom County, founded around the middle of the eleventh century.

The site of these early buildings seems to have become a *tabula rasa* in the late twelfth or early thirteenth centuries, when a complex emerged which was completely different in layout and architecture. Some elements of this have survived to the present-day in relatively good condition.[6] At the southern tip of the hill there was a large residential tower in the form of an irregular pentagon,

---

3   Here and hereafter I use the term 'palace' in the wider sense as it is used in the modern literature, see e.g. James or Keevill in note 53; i.e. it covers all kinds of royal residences.
4   *Komárom megye régészeti topográfiája. Esztergom és a Dorogi járás* [The archaeological topography of Komárom County. The region of Esztergom and Dorog] (Magyarország Régészeti Topográfiája, 5), eds István Horváth, Márta H. Kelemen and István Torma (Budapest: Akadémiai, 1979), pp. 84–87, 91–95 (by István Horváth) and 95–96 (by Emese Nagy); István Horváth, "Esztergom," in *Medium regni*, pp. 9–42, here pp. 23–27; idem, "Gran (Esztergom) zur Zeit Stephans des Heiligen," in *Europas Mitte um 1000. Beiträge zur Geschichte, Kunst und Archäologie. Handbuch zur Ausstellung*, 2 vols, eds Alfred Wieczorek and Hans-Martin Hinz (Stuttgart: Theiss 2000), ii, pp. 576–580, here pp. 576–578.
5   Emese Nagy, "Rapport préliminaire des fouilles d'Esztergom 1964–1969," *Acta Archaeologica Academiae Scientiarum Hungaricae* 23 (1971), pp. 181–198; *Komárom megye*, pp. 96–97 (by Emese Nagy).
6   Horváth, "Esztergom," pp. 16–21; idem, "Gran"; Konstantin Vukov, *A középkori esztergomi palota épületei* [The buildings of the Medieval Palace of Esztergom] (Budapest: Építésügyi Tájékoztatási Központ Kft., 2004).

connected to two tapering quadrangular courtyards, situated in tandem. The tower and the buildings around the smaller courtyard connecting to the north may have been the private apartments of the royal family; the high status of the site is indicated by surviving ornamental doorways and elegant vaulted interior spaces. The palace chapel stood on the east side, a masterpiece of Hungarian Late Romanesque–Early Gothic architecture.[7] Lining the larger northern courtyard on the western and northern sides was a large L-shaped building. On the upper floor of its long west range, overlooking the Danube, was the great hall (approximately 45 × 10 m, connecting to the kitchen at the south end). This configuration is usually likened to the German *Pfalz* arrangement. The southern palace was thus a separate, castle-like complex within the castle. Its construction was formerly credited to Béla III, but more recent research has shifted responsibility to his son Emeric. In 1256, Béla IV donated the entire castle to the archbishop.

Esztergom was to some extent similar in outline to Prague and Cracow, the seats of two nearby duchies (later kingdoms).

Prague became the seat of a ruler long before Esztergom or Cracow. The Hradčany/Hradschin promontory on the left bank of the Vltava first assumed a special place in the Czech lands in the final third of the ninth century, and particularly the turn of the ninth and tenth centuries,[8] a place it retained – except for a period in the eleventh and twelfth centuries – from then onwards.

The second Christian church in the Czech lands, dedicated to the Virgin Mary, was built on the west side of the spur. It was a small single-nave church, and its remains have been excavated.[9] Somewhat later, two considerably larger ecclesiastical buildings were built on the east part of the ridge, surrounded by ramparts. At the highest point of the area in the east, Duke Vratislas I (915–921) started construction of the St George's Church of longitudinal – probably

---

7 Imre Takács, "A gótika műhelyei a Dunántúlon a 13–14. században," [Gothic workshops in Transdanubia in the thirteenth and fourteenth centuries] in *Pannonia Regia. Művészet a Dunántúlon 1000–1541* [Art in Transdanubia, 1000 to 1541], eds Árpád Mikó and Imre Takács (Budapest: Magyar Nemzeti Galéria, 1994), pp. 22–33, here p. 22–24; Ernő Marosi, "Esztergom stílusrétegei 1200 körül," [The stylistic layers of Esztergom around 1200] in *Pannonia Regia*, pp. 154–158; Imre Takács, "Transregional Artistic Cooperation in the 13th Century in Accordance with Some Hungarian Court Art Examples," *Acta Historiae Artium Academiae Scientiarum Hungaricae* 49 (2008), pp. 63–76.

8 Jozef Žemlička, "Herrschaftszentren und Herrschaftsorganisation," in *Europas Mitte um 1000*, i, pp. 367–372, here pp. 368–371; Ladislav Hrdlička, "Prag," ibid., i, pp. 373–375.

9 Ivan Borkovský, *Pražský hrad v době přemyslovských knížat* [The Castle of Prague in the Age of the Přemyslids] (Prague: Academia, 1969), pp. 90–102, 150 and 152; *The Story of Prague Castle* (Prague: Prague Castle Administration, 2003), pp. 52–59 (by Jan Frolík).

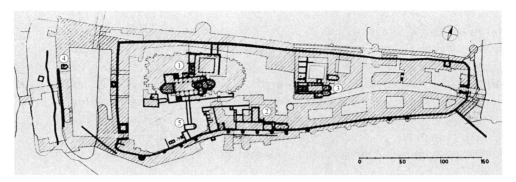

FIGURE 6.1 *Ground plan of the buildings of Prague Castle around 1180 (1: St Vitus's Cathedral; 2: royal palace; 3: St George's Basilica; 4: Church of the Virgin Mary; 5: St Bartholomew's Church)*
AFTER D. MENCLOVÁ

basilica – plan in 920. It was consecrated under the rule of his son Wenceslas (921–935) in 925, and became the place of interment of later kings and members of the ruling family.[10] The other, rotunda-shaped church on the ridge was built to the west somewhat later, also by Wenceslas and dedicated to St Vitus. Wenceslas's remains were interred there after 938, a fact which may lie behind the choice of this church as the cathedral of the Prague diocese upon its foundation in 972–973. St Vitus's Cathedral – later rebuilt on a basilica plan – became the last resting place of many other prominent figures, and St Adalbert's relics were also reburied there.[11] Directly to the southwest was the bishop's palace.[12] The earliest ducal palace is thought to have lain in the area between these two later churches, but no traces of it have yet been identified.[13]

A completely new ducal residence was built in the twelfth century.[14] Work on this started after 1135 under the rule of Soběslav (1125–1140) and came to completion around 1180 (Fig. 6.1). The new palace was built alongside, and resting on, the inner side of the already-standing south castle wall. This

10 Borkovský, *Pražský hrad*, pp. 102–120 and 152; *The Prague Castle*, pp. 60–63 (by Jan Frolík).
11 Borkovský, *Pražský hrad*, pp. 120–132; *The Prague Castle*, pp. 64–67 (by Jan Frolík), 89–92 (by Klára Benešovská) and pp. 93–102 (by Milena Bravermanová); Jana Mařiková-Kubková and Iva Herichová, *Archeologický atlas Pražského hradu. Díl I. Katedrála sv. Víta – Vikařská ulice* [Archaeological Atlas of Prague Castle. St Vitus's Cathedral – Vikařská Street] (Castrum Pragense, 10), pp. 63, 67–68 and 86.
12 Borkovský, *Pražský hrad*, pp. 82–83; *The Prague Castle*, pp. 103–107 (by Jan Frolík); Mařiková-Kubková and Herichová, *Archeologický atlas*, pp. 63 and 69–70.
13 Mařiková-Kubková and Herichová, *Archeologický atlas*, pp. 62–63 and 86–87.
14 Borkovský, *Pražský hrad*, pp. 57–58 and 151; *The Prague Castle*, pp. 122–127 (by Jan Frolík and Petr Chotěbor).

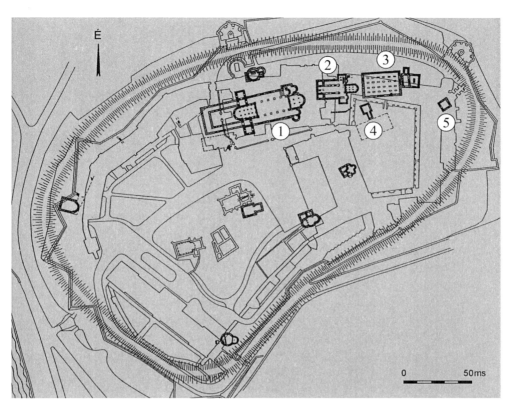

FIGURE 6.2 *Ground plan of the pre-Romanesque and Romanesque buildings of Cracow's Wawel (1: Romanesque cathedral; 2: Church of Mary of Egypt; 3: "24-pillar building"; 4: Cellarium; 5: The Stołp)*
AFTER Z. PIANOWKSI

elongated building on an east–west axis, with the palace chapel of All Saints at its east end, formed the basis for all further extensions. The area of the palace was at all times only separated from the rest of the castle by a perimeter wall.

In *Cracow*, among wet, marshy land on a meander of the Vistula, the ducal center was built on the Wawel Hill, which rises 25 m above its surroundings (Fig. 6.2). The earliest pre-Romanesque remains of stone buildings are grouped in the highest northern and north-eastern area of the ridge. Only one of these was definitely of secular function: a structure sunk into the rock and identified as a *cellarium* or outbuilding of the ducal palace. The residential section of the palace has not yet been identified.[15] The remains of three sacred buildings

15 Zbigniew Pianowski, "Krakau (Kraków)," in *Europas Mitte um 1000*, i, pp. 479–482 and Zbigniew Pianowski, "Monumental Architecture of Early Medieval Kraków. /Architektura monumentalna wczesnośredniowiecznego Krakowa," in *Kraków w chrześcijańskiej*

have been found to the northwest of the cellar, and a further three to the southwest. The nearest of the three to the northwest may have belonged to the palace, the middle may have been the early cathedral, and the third the baptismal chapel. The nearest of the three to the southwest may also have belonged to the palace, but the affiliation of the other two is unknown. The ground plans of these six buildings are very diverse: three were rotundas (with one apse, two apses and four lobes respectively), two had a longitudinal, and one may have had a cruciform layout.[16] Some of them may also have been burial places.[17] In the initial period, the ducal palace may have been directly adjacent to the cathedral complex, but there is as yet no evidence of there having been any major structure, such as a defensive wall, separating the two.

On the area of the ducal residence, there are large-scale buildings identifiable from the Romanesque era (mid-eleventh to early twelfth centuries). To the north of the early building identified as a *cellarium* (next to the north range of today's palace) was a rectangular building on an east–west axis. The large building (28.5 × 19.5 m), is known as the "24-pillar building" on the basis of the foundations of four rows of six pillars on its ground floor. This kind of multi-pillar design is unknown in any other royal architecture of the time or later. It most closely resembles the *horreum* of the Romanesque era. The thickness of the walls suggests that it was a two- or three-storey palace building. The lower, vaulted level may have served as a store, but perhaps also as accommodation in periods of extreme weather. The second storey may have housed the great hall, and the third, the duke's residential apartments. The ground in front of the palace was surfaced with lime mortar, and may have been the site of the ducal throne.[18] To the east, the palace building connected to a smaller, but thick-walled, trapezoidal building. It was previously thought to have been a

---

Europie X–XIII w. / Krakow in Christian Europe 10th–13th c. Katalog wystawy / Catalogue of the Exhibition (Cracow: Muzeum Historyczne Miasta Krakowa, 2006), pp. 162–219, here pp. 168–169.

16 Klementyna Żurowska, "Sakralarchitektur in Polen," in *Europas Mitte um 1000*, i, pp. 502–506, here pp. 504–505.

17 Michał Kara and Zofia Kurnatowska, "Christliche Bestattungen," in *Europas Mitte um 1000*, i, pp. 527–530, here pp. 529–530. The identification of the churches known by their patron saints from the written sources with the physical evidence remains problematic. Opinions continue to change.

18 Kazimierz Radwański, *Kraków przedlokacyjny. Rozwój przestrzenny* [Cracow before the Granting of its Foundation Charter] (Cracow: Polskie Tow. Archeologiczne i Numizmatyczne Oddzial w Nowej Hucie, 1975), pp. 52–53 and p. 47 Fig. 18; Zbigniew Pianowski, "L'architecture préromane et romane au château royal de Cracovie," *Cahiers de civilisation médiéval* 38 (1995), pp. 141–163, here p. 153; idem, *Monumental Architecture*, pp. 176–177.

dwelling, but a recent proposal identifies it as the palace chapel. To the southeast of this complex, the remains of an architecturally separate, square floor-plan tower (the *Stołp*) have survived. This was functionally connected with the palace, although it was built later and was not aligned on the same east–west axis. An interesting contrast with Prague and Esztergom is that the large-scale, multi-phase Romanesque building on the castle area was not followed by reconstruction of the defensive works in stone. This seems to have taken place only much later, around the turn of the thirteenth century.

The topography of these three early ducal/royal centers was thus in many ways similar. All three were in dominant situations above a major river, giving control of land and water routes and river crossings, and of the settlements which grew up beneath them. Even more importantly, all three were both centers of secular power and the Church.[19] This is not surprising, because unlike some southern and western areas of Europe, Christianity did not become established through the survival of early church centers, but through direct adoption by the ruler and his court. The symbiosis of secular and ecclesiastical authority in the three locations, however, took different forms and lasted for different periods. In Esztergom, sections dedicated respectively to royal and ecclesiastical functions may have initially been in direct physical proximity, but they gradually separated out, as shown by the two or more phases of the south palace. The king subsequently abandoned his residence there altogether. The original arrangement in Prague and Cracow may have been similar. In Prague, the ruler moved out of the castle temporarily and later the bishop moved out permanently, although the cathedral and the chapter stayed in place. Nor was there a permanent coexistence of 'church and state' in Cracow: the royal palace there moved into a completely separate castle-like complex of its own, much as in Esztergom, and the bishop, at the end of the medieval period, moved his residence to the town.

Although Esztergom was the chief center of the Hungarian Church, it never attained the cultic significance of Prague or Cracow. We have seen that the churches in Prague were from the beginning the places of interment of dukes and persons revered as saints. Later, the Bohemian kings were laid to rest in St Vitus's Cathedral, some being reburied from elsewhere. Some members of ducal families – so far unnamed – may probably have been buried in some of the early churches of Wawel. The cathedral held the relics of Stanislas of Szczepanów, revered as a saint and ultimately canonized, giving it a special significance.[20] It is therefore not surprising that Polish kings were also buried

---

19 On the importance of cohabitation, see Gerevich, "The Rise," pp. 33–34.
20 Kara and Kurnatowska, "Christliche Bestattungen," p. 529.

there after 1333 and, from 1320 onwards, the church became the place of coronations as well. By contrast, only one Hungarian ruler and no saintly figures were ever buried in the Esztergom Cathedral.[21] Although St Stephen was invested as prince and later crowned king there, and the archbishop had the 'canonical' right to crown Hungarian kings, Esztergom did not become the place of coronation, again unlike Prague and Cracow. In Hungary, coronations and royal burials mostly took place in Székesfehérvár.

Székesfehérvár (originally *Fehérvár*, meaning 'white castle') was another ecclesiastical and judicial center, but bore no similarity to these other royal and ecclesiastical seats. It lay on the plain, on islands in marshland, and although scattered Romanesque remains have been found in the area, they seem to have had no significance for the medieval settlement. Although some scholars see the place as having been significant from the time of Prince Géza,[22] it seems to have acquired true importance only after 1018, from which time a section of the land route to the Holy Land via the Balkans passed through it.

Earlier research envisaged a ducal and royal center on the large central island, surrounded by earthen ramparts. The picture which has emerged more recently, however, is of an inner and outer castle surrounded by stone walls.[23] A fairly well excavated church complex lying in the east of the main island, outside the 'castle', has details that are definitely linked to St Stephen.[24] The Virgin Mary Collegiate Church was in all probability regarded as the 'official' place of coronation of Hungarian kings after Stephen onwards, because it hosted all except one of the coronations known to have taken place in Székesfehérvár. It also served as the burial place of a number of Hungarian kings and their families.[25]

---

21 Stephen III (died in 1172). The other king buried in Esztergom was Béla IV. However, he and his wife were buried not in the basilica, but in the Franciscan friary, situated at the foot of the Castle Hill.

22 E.g. Alán Kralovánszky, "The Settlement History of Veszprém and Székesfehérvár in the Middle Ages," in *Towns in Medieval Hungary*, ed. László Gerevich (Budapest: Akadémiai, 1990), pp. 51–95, here p. 52–53.

23 Gyula Siklósi, "Székesfehérvár," in *Medium regni*, pp. 43–64 and idem, *Die mittelalterlichen Wehranlagen, Burg- und Stadtmauern von Székesfehérvár* (Varia Archaeologica Hungarica, 12) (Budapest: Archäol. Inst. der UAW, 1999).

24 Kralovánszky, "The Settlement History," pp. 81–89; Piroska Biczó, "The Church of the St Mary Provostry at Székesfehérvár (the Royal Basilica)," in *Medium regni*, pp. 65–76, and eadem, "Das königliche Marienstift zu Székesfehérvár im Lichte der neueren Grabungen," *Acta Historiae Artium Academiae Scientiarum Hungaricae* 52 (2011), pp. 5–29.

25 Pál Engel, "Temetkezések a székesfehérvári bazilikában. (Függelék: A székesfehérvári koronázások)," [Funerals at the royal basilica in Székesfehérvár. Appendix: the coronations

The separate but nearby configuration of the early palace and basilica in Székesfehérvár in many respects resembles the disposition of the royal and ecclesiastical complex of Westminster. Overall, they also seem to have been functionally similar, with the difference that Székesfehérvár never became the permanent royal residence or seat of government. In the French lands, the functions of coronation and burial which in Hungary were held by the Church of the Virgin Mary in Székesfehérvár and in England by St Peter's abbey in Westminster (neither of them cathedrals! – and neither were used as the only royal burial places), were divided between Reims Cathedral and the abbey of St Denis near Paris.

After the Mongol invasion, the site of the early Székesfehérvár Castle was divided among the newly-settled population. No traces of it remain, unlike the basilica which stood outside its precincts, which survived and was regularly extended up until the end of the medieval period. Archaeologists have established that the old castle was replaced by a completely new castle with a regular floor plan in the north-east corner of the re-established and reconfigured town.[26]

The third royal center, *Buda* (the later *Óbuda* i.e. Old Buda) only rose to prominence in the late twelfth and early thirteenth centuries. Judging from the Church of St Peter and the collegiate chapter which the king founded there, Óbuda must have been a favored place of sojourn for kings from the middle of the eleventh century at the latest.[27] The exact location of the royal residence is as yet unknown, but may be guessed as having stood within the town beside St Peter's Church, of which a very few archaeological remains have been found. The Church and with it the early core of the town were built within the walls of the Late Roman fort, which was to some degree restored.

A completely new royal residence was built outside the Roman walls, to the southwest, probably as a consequence – and certainly an indicator – of Óbuda's rising significance. The architecture of this building, some remains of which have been excavated, appears to have been a transition between castle and palace.[28] Its core was a rectangular building measuring approximately

---

at Székesfehérvár] *Századok* 121 (1987), pp. 613–637. 15 of the 37 medieval kings were interred there.

26   Siklósi, "Székesfehérvár."
27   Gerevich, "The Rise," pp. 38–40.
28   László Gerevich, *The Art of Buda and Pest in the Middle Ages* (Budapest: Akadémiai, 1971), pp. 20–23. On the more recent excavations, see: Júlia Altmann, "Neue Forschungen über die Burg der Königin in Óbuda," *Acta Archaeologica Academiae Scientiarum Hungaricae* 34 (1982), pp. 221–233 and eadem, "Óbuda," in *Medium regni*, pp. 89–114. On the typology of

30 × 35 m with four ranges enclosing a small courtyard. The castle wall around it had an irregular quadrilateral plan, 55/60 × 65/68 m, and beyond that was a 13–17 m wide ditch shored with masonry on both sides. The outer perimeter of the area thus measured 85/100 × 95/108 m. Research on castle architecture calls this regular form a 'Kastell type' ground plan, i.e. a quadrangular castle enclosing a central courtyard.[29]

The entrance to the complex was on the north side, as evidenced by the remains of a bridge and gate structure. The palace core was entered through the ground floor of a massive 9 × 11 meter tower in the middle of the north range. This gatehouse also served as the vestibule of the chapel situated in the east half of the range and as a passageway to the south, leading to the courtyard. The chapel's original chancel only slightly projected from the east frontage, having an apse shaped as six sides of an octagon on the outside with a semicircular interior. It was later demolished and replaced by a longer and wider Gothic chancel supported by buttresses. At the southern end of the east frontage was a polygonal projection of the same scale and shape as the original chapel, connected on the inside to a room with hypocaust heating.

The portal in the north wall of the tower projected from the frontage and had a series of jambs narrowing towards the door. In the four corners of the vestibule on the ground floor of the tower, perpendicular to the diagonals, were compound piers supporting the vaulting. The space had an irregular octagonal floor plan (when the piers are included) and a floor of red marble slabs. On the east side was the elaborate doorway to the chapel, with highly ornate, molded polychromatic jambs of white limestone and red marble. Excavations have also discovered the remains of portals on the east and west ranges, with elaborately ornamented jambs. (The 7.6 m wide, 11.2 m long ground floor room on the east side also had a red marble floor.) These architectural details also serve to date the complex: the latest art historical analysis places them in the first quarter of the thirteenth century. If this dating is correct, the Óbuda building is one of the earliest Kastell-type palaces in Central Europe. Emperor Frederick II Hohenstaufen (1220–1250) started construction of the 'model' regular ground-plan 'castels' in southern Italy and Sicily in the 1220s,[30] while those

the building as an urban or 'town castle', see István Feld, "Ecilburg und Ofen – Zur Problematik der Stadtburgen in Ungarn," *Castrum Bene* 6 (1999), pp. 73–88, here pp. 75–77.

29 *Wörterbuch der Burgen, Schlösser und Festungen*, eds Horst Wolfgang Böhme, Bernhard Friedrich and Barbara Schock-Werner (Stuttgart: Reclam, 2004), pp. 166–167.

30 On the castle and palace building activity of Frederick II, see e.g. Gary M. Radke, "The Palaces of Frederick II," in *Intellectual Life at the Court of Frederick II Hohenstaufen* (Center for Advanced Study in the Visual Arts. Studies in the History of Art, 44 = Symposium Papers, 24), ed. W. Tronzo (Washington, D.C.: National Gallery of Arts, 1994), pp. 179–186, and Dankwart Lestikow, "Castra et Domus. Burgen und Schlösser Friedrichs II. im

recently attributed to Ottokar Přemysl (1253–1278) in Central Europe date only from the 1250s.[31]

Originally the king's residence, and later the queen's, the thirteenth-century castle of Óbuda has some special points of interest. First of all, despite having a very small floor area compared to earlier royal palaces, the aesthetic program of its architecture is highly sophisticated, and clearly designed as a display of royal grandeur. The outer castle wall of elegant ashlar blocks was unique in Hungarian secular architecture of the time – except for Esztergom. And unusual even beyond Hungary was the ornate north portal of the gatehouse, whose dimensions suggest that it also served as a great tower or *Bergfried*. Added to this was the imposing space behind the portal at the base of the tower, essentially a simple passage to the inner courtyard, but also serving as an elegant vestibule for the chapel, with a red marble floor and a ribbed vault. The ranges surrounding the courtyard also display remarkable features. The thickness of the excavated walls (1.30–1.40 m) shows that there must have been at least one upper storey. Contemporary practice (perhaps less common in the Anglo-Norman lands) of putting the royal apartments, the great hall and other important rooms on the first floor, or at least on a raised level, with subordinate functions being accommodated on the ground floor, was certainly not implemented here. Evidence for this comes from the ornate portal leading into ground-floor spaces in each of the east and west ranges, as well as the red marble floor and the south-east apse-like corner room with its underfloor heating.

Overall, it seems that Óbuda Castle has a special place in the castle and palace architecture of Hungary, and indeed of Central Europe. The architecture of the crusader knights is often suggested as the origin of its design. This is because the king possibly responsible for its construction, Andrew II, enjoyed good relations with the knights and indeed went on a crusade himself in 1216–1217, but there is as yet no direct evidence for this connection.

The Rise of Buda – and Visegrád

Óbuda underwent a major change in function at the turn of the thirteenth and fourteenth centuries. Béla IV's foundation of the "new Buda" after the Mongol

---

Königreich Sizilien," in *Kunst im Reich Kaiser Friedrich II. von Hohenstaufen. Akten des internationalen Kolloquiums (Rheinisches Landesmuseum Bonn, 2. bis 4. Dezember 1994)*, ii, eds Kai Kappel, Dorothee Kemper and Alexander Knaak (Munich–Berlin: Klinkhardt & Biermann, 1996), pp. 21–34. Both contributions give useful bibliographies.

31   Tomáš Durdík, *Kastellburgen des 13. Jahrhunderts in Mitteleuropa* (Prague: Academia, 1994).

invasion completely altered the urban hierarchy both in the area and throughout the kingdom, as well as affecting the role played by royal centers. As we have seen, the king finally donated Esztergom to the archbishop in 1256, and the site of the former royal castle of Székesfehérvár was divided up among the new burghers of the town. Although Székesfehérvár retained its position as the place of coronation and – mostly – of royal burial, it had lost its special significance. Óbuda seems to have shared with the new foundation of Buda the honor of being a royal center for a while in the second half of the thirteenth century.

By the turn of the century, however, the new city clearly had the advantage. It was within the walls of Buda that the last king of the Árpád dynasty, Andrew III, died; alone among Hungarian kings, he was also buried there, in the Franciscan friary of St John. In the interregnum which followed, seizing and holding Buda became a central objective for the contenders.[32] It is telling, for example, that the new king elected in 1301, Wenceslas of the Bohemian house of Přemysl (king of Hungary until 1305 and king of Bohemia 1305–1306) made his entrance to Buda before setting off for his coronation in Székesfehérvár, from which he returned to his Buda residence. His immediate successor, Otto Wittelsbach of Bavaria (1305–1307), followed his example. A foreign source of 1308 unambiguously refers to Buda as the *civitas principalis*. The question remains as to where, in this new walled town, the royal residence stood, and what did it look like?

One view is that a royal palace in the north-northeast corner of Buda was in use from the foundation of the town until the 1380s. The court then moved to a new palace at the south end, following construction work which started in the 1340s or 1350s.[33] The source describing the above event of 1301 gives clear support for this view, because the *Kammerhof* mentioned as the royal house is referred to in later documents as *antiqua domus regis*, and its topographical location is given quite accurately.[34]

We know relatively little, however, about the building complex itself. The Schön drawing of 1541 is the earliest to identify it, and shows its core to have consisted of one or more large towers. The sources certainly indicate that it consisted of several buildings, one of which was the St Martin's Chapel. It was also presumably the location of the mint, which had been moved from Esztergom and most probably gave the building its name. On later ground plans,

---

32 On the chaotic period of the shift in power, see Enikő Spekner, "Sedi reali nell'Ungheria dell'età angioina," in *L'Ungheria angioina* (Bibliotheca Academiae Hungariae – Roma. Studia, 3), ed. Enikő Csukovits (Rome: Viella, 2013), pp. 237–263.
33 As consistently argued by László Zolnay.
34 For a thorough analysis of the relevant sources, see Végh, *Buda*, i, pp. 269–272.

only its outlines can be identified. These, together with some exploratory excavations of the site, show it to have been an urban palace complex with no fortifications of its own.[35] In this respect it resembled, for example, the Palace of Westminster, but with the difference that the latter did not lie within city walls. Much closer to it in time, space and function is the Italian Court (*Vlašský Dvůr*), which still stands in Kutná Hora in Bohemia. It also housed a mint and later accommodated the king, at first on an occasional basis and later for sustained periods. It stood within the boundary of the town, but from the beginning was defended like a castle with its own wall and later a ditch. Entrance to the irregular oval, walled area was through a gate opening to the north-east. The buildings which gradually went up along the walls – those in the south and southwest with workshops underneath and residential and ceremonial spaces above – encompassed a completely closed courtyard in the center.[36] There is no evidence as yet that the *Kammerhof* in Buda had a separate curtain wall, ditch and closed-courtyard layout, although the complex abutted the town wall and had its own gate into the suburb. It is possible that the gatehouse, some ruins of which have been found, connected to the interior tower or towers, forming thereby a continuous complex.

A contrasting view is that in the second half of the thirteenth century, the royal palace of Buda already stood at the south end of Castle Hill, being the lowest part of the elongated triangular plateau.[37] Although joined to the town to form a common defensive unit, it stood apart as a separate castle from the beginning, so that the town lay before it as a kind of *Vorburgstadt*[38] i.e. "outer

---

35 László Zolnay, "Ásatások a budai I., Táncsics Mihály u. 9. területén. A XIII–XIV. századi budai királyi rezidencia kérdéséhez," [Excavations in Buda, 9 Táncsics Mihály Street. The question of the royal residence in Buda in the thirteenth–fourteenth centuries] *Archaeologiai Értesítő* 94 (1967), pp. 39–47.

36 The complex that housed the royal mint may have stood around 1300 and may be connected to King Wenceslas' II monetary reform of the same year. It was almost continuously renewed and expanded. During the reign of Wenceslas IV (1363/1378–1419) it was made comfortable enough for royal visits. Unfortunately a number of original medieval architectural details fell victim to nineteenth-century renovation works. For the latest account, see František Záruba, "Der Welsche Hof in Kuttenberg (Kutná Hora)," *Burgen und Schlösser* 3 (2010), pp. 168–176.

37 László Gerevich, *A budai vár feltárása* [Excavation of the castle of Buda] (Budapest: Akadémiai, 1966); Gerevich, *The Art of Buda*, pp. 46–48. Gerevich considers the *Kammerhof* as a royal mint house that might have replaced an early royal manorial complex on the same site.

38 On this morphological type, see András Kubinyi, "Burgstadt, Vorburgstadt und Stadtburg. Zur Morphologie des Mittelalterlichen Buda," *Acta Archaeologica Academiae Scientiarum Hungaricae* 33 (1981), pp. 161–178, more recently Feld, "Ecilburg and Ofen," pp. 81–83.

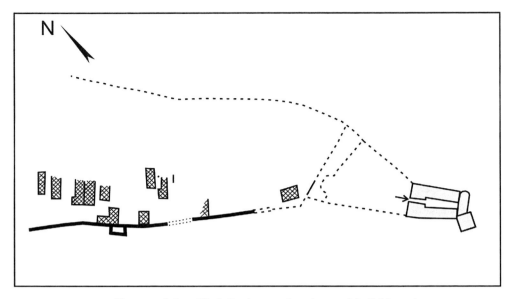

FIGURE 6.3 *The ground plan of Buda Castle around 1350 (research by K. Magyar)*

castle". This of course would presume that the castle was built before, or at the latest at the same time as, the town was laid out. There is as yet no evidence for this having happened in Buda. The earliest written source that makes a definite topographical reference to the south palace/castle is from 1390,[39] although archaeological excavations and indirect historical information date its origin with confidence to no later than the 1340s or 1350s (Fig. 6.3).[40] This complex consisted of a great tower on the southernmost tip of Castle Hill and a trapezoidal-plan block (approximately 48 × 18/22 m) connecting to the northeast of the tower, in the center of which was a narrow closed courtyard (the Small Court, approximately 25 × 5/8 m). At the south end, there may have been a chapel, of which later reconstructions left only the polygonal chancel, butting out from the wall like an oriel. Opposite was the north range, with the great hall on its upper floor. The orientation of the rectangular great tower to the

---

39 Végh, *Buda*, i, pp. 269–272.
40 In fact, some earlier, thirteenth century architectural remains have also came to light which László Gerevich, the leader of the excavations thought to have belonged to the earliest palace. However, they are few in number, while their scattered location and their heavily disturbed state hinder their correct identification. The first remnants forming a coherent architectural ensemble on the site have been dated as *terminus ante quem non* by a coin of 1332 of King Charles I. It was found in one of its foundation trenches.

south (11.9 × 11.1 m) deviated by a significant angle from the long axis of the palace block to the north, whose west wall connected to the corner of the tower.[41] The eponym of the tower, referred to in the sources as Stephen's Tower: *turris condam ducis Stephani* is identified by most researchers as Prince Stephen of Anjou (1332–1354), younger brother of Louis I, although an earlier origin cannot be ruled out.[42] To the north of these, a forecourt spread out into a trapezium, and was divided from the civilian city by a transverse ditch (Dry Moat I) dug into the rock. We currently know nothing about the role of the forecourt or the buildings which lay on it.

Visegrád was a royal residence with many remarkable features. Historians have proposed that around the time the kingdom of Hungary was established, it was the center of the county of the same name (later divided into other counties). The walls and towers of the fourth-century Roman fort on Sibrik Hill, laid out on an irregular plan, were re-used between the tenth and thirteenth centuries. The large gatehouse on the west side, for example, was a residential tower. New construction on the site of the old fort included a large secular building and a church. These could clearly have accommodated the king, on an occasional basis, as well as the head of the county, the *ispán* (*comes*).[43] The whole complex may have been finally abandoned due to the Mongol invasion of 1241–1242.

The new castle of Visegrád is first mentioned in 1255. A source from 1259 states that it was built by the wife of Béla IV, Mary Laskaris, at her own expense, to provide a refuge for widows and orphans in times of need. These two

---

41   Gerevich, *A budai vár*, pp. 121–138, 155–159 (on the tower) and 185–186. For the oriel that can be identified as the chancel of the former chapel and an evaluation of the whole complex, see Károly Magyar, *A budai középkori királyi palota építészeti együttesének változásai (1340–1440) európai kitekintésben*, [The changing architectural face of the medieval Royal Palace at Buda, 1340–1437, in European context] unpublished PhD dissertation (Budapest: ELTE BTK, 2008), pp. 47–51.

42   The identity of Stephen is elusive and might even refer to the later King Stephen V, son of Béla IV. See Enikő Spekner, "Adalékok a budavári István torony névadójának kérdéséhez," [Notes on the eponym of the Stephen Tower at the Buda Castle] *Budapest Régiségei* 35 (2002), pp. 403–425. See also Károly Magyar, "Adatok a budai István-torony kérdésköréhez," [Some data on the question of the Stephen Tower at Buda] in *"Es tu scholaris." Ünnepi tanulmányok Kubinyi András 75. születésnapjára* [Studies in honor of András Kubinyi on the occasion of his 75th birthday] (Monumenta Historica Budapestinensia, 13), eds Beatrix F. Romhányi *et al.* (Budapest: BTM, 2004), pp. 13–36.

43   "…dominus Rex ad Castrum suum de Wysegrad…". See *Monumenta Ecclesiae Strigoniensis*, i, ed. Nándor Knauz (Esztergom: Typis descripsit Aegydius Horák, 1874), pp. 429–430 (no 560).

sources obviously refer to the castle situated on the hilltop, the *Upper Castle*. However, there was another castle located on the slope of the hill, the *Lower Castle*, the origin of which is not revealed in any extant source. Nevertheless, this could not be much younger than the Upper Castle, and the twin castles formed a single defensive system during the Middle Ages. Entrance to the Upper Castle was via a gatehouse at the southern tip. On the north-east side of the courtyard, at the highest point of the rock, was a five-sided great tower with its edge pointing east. It may have had a chapel on the third storey. Immediately beside it was a cistern dug out of the rock. The original residential range may have been on the inner side of the north castle wall; no other buildings are known.[44] The simplicity of the whole structure reflects its function as a place of refuge.

A castle wall reinforced with two towers and a gatehouse opening to the north led west from the castle all the way down to a tower beside the Danube, from where it wound its way back up the hill to close the loop. This shorter stretch also had a gate to the south, but without a gatehouse. On the raised, gently-sloping terrace-like area enclosed by the castle wall, and reaching down to the river, was a large detached tower of 'classical' residential type. This was the area of the Lower Castle, which did not have the closed, compact character of the Upper Castle. To the south of the two new castles, on the strip of land widening out at the foot of the hill, a completely new settlement for *hospites* was laid out by no later than the 1280s. It later grew into a town.[45]

When Charles I first took up residence in Visegrád, he thus had two castles and a settlement to serve his needs. Although the security offered by the two castles was no doubt the decisive factor in choosing the location,[46] this was the period when the residential significance of the civilian settlement first became

---

44 Lajos Bozóki, *A visegrádi vár és kőfaragványai. (Burg Visegrad)* [Visegrád Castle and its stone carvings] (Lapidarium Hungaricum, viii. Pest megye, 2: Visegrád, Alsó- és Felsővár), ed. Pál Lővei (Budapest: Magyarország Építészeti Töredékeinek Gyűteménye, 2012), p. 17. At ibid., pp. 13, 18 and 21–22; Bozóki pays special attention to the east tower and its typological classification.

45 Orsolya Mészáros, "The Town: Administration, Inhabitants, Institutions," and "Topography and Urban Property Transactions" in *The Medieval Royal Town at Visegrád: Royal Center, Urban Settlement, Churches* (Archaeolingua – Main Series, 32), eds József Laszlovszky, Gergely Buzás and Orsolya Mészáros (Budapest: Archaeolingua, 2014), pp. 90–92, 160–170. As early as 1285 the king granted the settlement at Maros (today Nagymaros) situated on the other side of the Danube to the *hospites* of Visegrád. Later Maros became a town.

46 This has been emphasized e.g. by András Végh, "Urban Development and Royal Initiative in the Central Part of the Kingdom of Hungary in the 13th–14th centuries: Comparative Analysis of the Development of the Towns of Buda and Visegrád," in *Stadtgründung und Stadtwerdung. Beiträge von Archäologie und Stadtgeschichtsforschung* (Beiträge zur

manifest. The king had some kind of town house there which was suitable for long periods of residence. He and his family were the targets of an assassination attempt there 1330.[47] The Charles-period royal house was a complex which ranged up the gentle slope at the foot of the hill about 500 m to the south of the two castles, in a scattered layout of buildings of various kinds, one of which was a 28 × 14 m stone house with an upper storey.[48]

Visegrád therefore had three places providing royal accommodation during the reign of Charles I: the two castles were better defended, but cramped and enclosed, while the house in the town was more vulnerable, but freer and more spacious. Whether the king used one of these as his actual residence and the others for ceremonial or other purposes, and at what times, are questions that remain unanswered for lack of detailed sources. It seems that the royal residence comprised all three of them in combination. This no doubt made it possible to provide fitting accommodation for the two principal guests at the Visegrád royal summit of 1335: King John Luxemburg of Bohemia and King Casimir III Piast (the Great) of Poland.[49]

This heterogeneous but highly concentrated system of residences almost certainly made Visegrád unique in Europe at the time. Although it was not rare for there to be two or more royal residences in or around one town (such as in London, Paris, Naples, Prague or indeed Buda), they did not lie so closely together. It was only later that Visegrád came to its zenith as a royal residence. Apart from a very short period during the reign of Louis I (the Great) when the status of principal royal seat passed back to Buda (1346/47–1355),[50] Visegrád

Geschichte der Städte Mitteleuropas, 22), ed. Ferdinand Opll (Linz: Österreichischer Arbeitskreis für Stadtgeschichtsforschung, 2011), pp. 431–446.

47 "in suburbio castri Wysegrad in *domo suo*" (italics mine KM). For a brief account of the Angevin-Period palace, see Gergely Buzás, "The remains of the royal palace of Visegrád from the Angevin period," in *Medieval Visegrad. Royal Castle, Palace, Town and Franciscan Friary* (Dissertationes Pannonicae, Ser. iii. 4), ed. József Laszlovszky (Budapest: Eötvös Loránd University, 1995), pp. 9–18 here pp. 9–10; recently Gergely Buzás, "History of the Visegrád Royal Palace," in *The Medieval Royal Palace at Visegrád* (Archaeolingua. Main Series, 27), eds idem and József Laszlovszky (Budapest: Archeolingua, Budapest, 2013), pp. 17–140, here pp. 20–26.

48 On their location, see Buzás, "Visegrád Royal Palace."

49 The king of Bohemia was accompanied by his son, Charles, the Margrave of Moravia, the later Emperor Charles IV. Prince Rudolf I of Saxony, Prince Boleslav III of Legnica (Silesia) and the envoys of the Teutonic Knights were also present. See György Rácz, "The Congress of Visegrád," in *Visegrád 1335*, ed. idem (Budapest: International Visegrad Fund – State Archives of Hungary – Pázmány Péter Catholic University, 2009), pp. 17–29.

50 Earlier Visegrád was thought to have been left by the royal court in January 1347 (see e.g. *Magyarország történeti kronológiája*, i, *A kezdetektől 1526-ig* [The historical chronology of Hungary. From the beginnings to 1526], ed. Kálmán Benda [Budapest: Akadémiai, 1983],

remained the unrivalled residence of the king until about 1410. This entailed enormous construction projects, primarily concentrated within the area of the royal house in the town.

To serve this function, the former scattered complex of buildings gradually gave way – at least in the north of the area – to a palace of interconnecting ranges in a more or less regular layout, which extended further up the slope to the east, constrained by the local relief.[51] The chapel for the palace complex was built immediately to the south of the south-east corner of the so called Northeast Palace, on the slope opposite the west main gate, in the 1360s. It was a longitudinal, single-nave building, oriented north–south (!). To the south and south-west of it there was an irregular arrangement of smaller buildings of completely different types. Some of these were survivors from the previous period of construction, the reign of Charles I.[52] This part of the palace complex, which included the mint and a goldsmith's workshop, retained its 'poetic disorder' until the end of the medieval period.

The relief of the area, which had hitherto been managed by the use of existing and ad hoc terracing, started to be exploited more purposefully. In modern terminology, architecture was combined with landscape architecture. The key visual component was clearly the new, quadrangular block of the Northeast Palace with the apartments of the king and queen and the chapel in its central axis. The Northeast Palace also offered a splendid view across the Reception Court to the Danube and the hills on the opposite side of the river. The complex also provided for the satisfactory separation of the communal, semi-private and private spheres of court life, and an efficient arrangement of accommodation, administration, ceremonial and service functions.

There seem to be very few examples of stately complexes of similar character to Visegrád Palace. The initial configuration bears some similarity to the architectural complex at Clarendon in Wiltshire, England, around 1270. Clarendon 'grew into' a spectacular residence from a 'simple' royal hunting lodge,

---

p. 209). Most recently August or September 1346 seems to be more likely. See László Iván, *A visegrádi vár története a kezdetektől 1685-ig* [History of the castle of Visegrád from the beginnings to 1685] (Visegrád: Magyar Nemzeti Múzeum Mátyás Király Múzeuma, 2004), p. 34, note 43.

51 Buzás, "Visegrád Royal Palace." In this study the building phases of Louis I and Sigismund Era have been completely reconsidered as compared with Buzás's earlier works, cf e.g. idem, "The Remains."

52 Some of these buildings have been thoroughly described in Buzás, "The remains," pp. 11–18; for the remainder, see idem, "Visegrád Royal Palace."

and so was connected to an enormous game park, but no settlement formed around it.[53]

The Hôtel Saint-Pol in Paris was also partly contemporary to the Visegrád complex, and perhaps bears greater similarity than Clarendon. This residence was laid out by Charles V (1364–1380) in the outskirts of the Marais in the 1360s on an area created by purchasing and merging four large private properties. The complex, enclosed by a simple perimeter wall, was intrinsically and fundamentally civilian in its architecture. It included at least one tower, however, which may have had a residential function and also held some of the royal treasury. The properties already included enormous gardens, and these were further developed. These pleasant surroundings in themselves predestined the complex to serve as the royal family's private residence. (Indeed, it was the birthplace of many royal princes and princesses.) However, there were also some state offices operating within its walls.[54]

The Growth of the Royal Palaces at Buda, Cracow and Prague

Buda remained a favored center, especially for royal receptions. It seems that large events of extended duration and many participants, requiring grand royal display and substantial logistical support were increasingly held in Buda. The construction of the Angevin-Period palace after 1350 on the southern part of Castle Hill seem to have spanned the period 1355–1382, considering that work probably started only after the death in 1354 of Prince Stephen of Anjou, who (presumably) lived there, and must have been finished before 1381/1382.[55] That was when the *Kammerhof* was given away, so that a palace of similar specification must already have been available.

---

53 Thomas Beaumont James, *The Palaces of Medieval England c. 1050–1550: Royalty, Nobility, the Episcopate and their residences from Edward the Confessor to Henry VIII* (London: Seaby, 1990), pp. 11, 16 and 17 Fig. 4; Graham D Keevill, *Medieval Palaces: An Archaeology* (Stroud: Tempus, 2000), pp. 105–107, with a ground plan on p. 106.

54 Mary Whiteley, "Deux vues de l'hôtel royal de Saint-Pol," *Revue de l'Art* 128, no 2 (2000), pp. 49–53; Philippe Lorentz and Dany Sandron, *Atlas de Paris au moyen âge. Espace urbain, habitat, société, religion, lieux de pouvoir* (Paris: Parigramme, 2006), pp. 90–91 and see further http://histoiredumarais.canalblog.com/archives/2009/09/28/15235702.html (last accessed 9 March 2015), with more details on the acquisition of the properties.

55 Gerevich, *The Art of Buda*, pp. 63–74, where all the Angevin-period construction works are discussed together and thought to have been completed by 1366. However, the later date that was identified by Gerevich and others as the consecration date of the new chapel has recently proved to refer to the chapel of Visegrád.

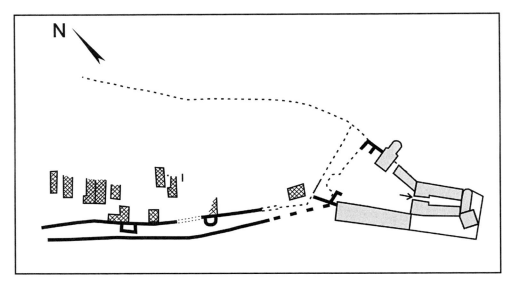

FIGURE 6.4 *The ground plan of Buda Castle around 1390 (research by K. Magyar)*

Construction at that time was probably concentrated on the trapezoidal-shaped forecourt in front of the existing palace core, the later Grand or Inner or State Court (Fig. 6.4). Here a large new rectangular range (approximately 58 × 15 m) was built on the western side, oriented north–south. Only the east wall of this building stood on the rock plateau, marking the original edge of the forecourt, and its entire west section extended down the slope.[56] The west wall of the western range seems to have served as an outer castle wall for some time, and perhaps continued to the south as a 'real' castle wall.[57] The new chapel was built opposite this palace range, on the east side. It was oriented, unlike its counterpart in Visegrád, in the customary east–west direction. Part of the nave and the polygonal apse extended, like the west range, on to the slope beyond the edge of rock plateau. This may have to some extent been responsible for the building's two-storey design. The upper chapel was aligned with the courtyard on the plateau (of internal length 21.4 m, and width 8 m at the nave and 5.8 m at the chancel). Its substructure on the slope constituted a lower chapel, partly cut out of the rock on its west side. This is the only surviving part of the complex today. Sufficient details of its vaulting and two tracery windows have survived to enable reconstruction. These fragments provide almost the

---

56 Gerevich, *A budai vár*, pp. 97–111. Here the range has been dated to the Sigismund-period; Magyar, *A budai*, pp. 68–74.
57 Magyar, *A budai*, p. 74.

only basis for dating the chapel.[58] The late Angevin-period buildings seem to have been constructed in response to an increased need for residential and ceremonial spaces. They marked a considerable increase in usable space over the previous buildings, achieved partly by making use of the slopes. This enabled a much more open court to be laid out, giving better expression to the new frontages.

The south palace of Buda then underwent a truly large-scale phase of building during the reign of Sigismund of Luxemburg, i.e. subsequent to the developments in Visegrád. Although his intense interest in Buda lasted only the first thirty or thirty-five years of his fifty-year rule, after which his attention turned to Pressburg, it resulted in a palace complex which in terms of floor area and architecture was in the European front rank. The motivation for this was undoubtedly Sigismund's ambition to become King of the Germans and ultimately Holy Roman Emperor, which demanded a display of royal grandeur in which architecture played an essential part.

The ever-increasing demands for space are demonstrated in the expansion of the palace site (Fig. 6.5). The new palace ranges – one incorporating

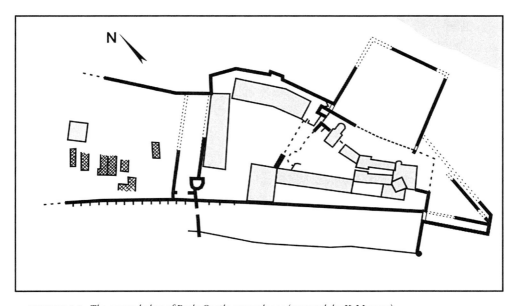

FIGURE 6.5 *The ground plan of Buda Castle around 1440 (research by K. Magyar)*

58 Gerevich, *A budai vár*, pp. 207–216; Magyar, *A budai*, p. 62–65. The shape of the windows and the profile of their jamb moldings are similar to those at Visegrád. See Buzás, "Visegrád Royal Palace."

a magnificent great hall – and service buildings[59] were located mainly on the rocky plateau or directly beneath its perimeter (on the south side). The project required a large and completely new ceremonial court, the Sigismund Court, to the north, divided from the city by a newly-dug ditch in the rock (Dry Moat II). The work of laying the land to the north as another forecourt may have started at the same time, but was completed only much later. Expansion to the north was at the expense of the town, which thereby lost some of its land. Sigismund's project did not betray aspirations to a grand, coherent architectural concept of the kind that was apparent in Visegrád. The complex thus remained, until the end of the medieval period, an assorted assemblage of palace ranges and other buildings which grew up 'organically' at different times.

The same does not entirely apply to the fortifications. By the end of the period, these extended beyond the new, so-called Sigismund's Courtyard and down the slopes – all the way to the line of the Danube in the east. The defensive system involved multiple parallel castle walls (many of them retaining walls), and the wards between them were sometimes used as palace courts, but mostly they had a defensive function. Although they seem to have been built in phases that followed the changes to the core of the palace complex, the end result was a visually-unified system. Adjoining the palace to the west was an enormous new garden (approximately 200/220 m × 80/100 m).

The architecture of Prague and Cracow mentioned in connection with Esztergom also bears comparison with the southern palace of Buda in its Angevin-period version. Although it involved buildings of different types from those in Buda, where construction did not follow local antecedents, there was some artistic and architectural 'diffusion' and occasionally even direct influence, owing to the political, dynastic and personal links between the ruling families. For example, Charles IV came to Buda at least twice (in 1337 and 1365) and before that, as Margrave of Moravia, he visited Visegrád three times (in 1335, 1338 and 1342). Louis I visited Prague once (in 1343), Cracow four times (in 1351, for the betrothal of Charles IV in 1363, for his coronation in 1370, and in 1373), and Casimir III came to Visegrád three times (in 1335, 1339 and 1342) and to Buda once (in 1368). These contemporary rulers, therefore, all had direct experiences of each others' courts, and saw for themselves the standards exemplified in ceremonial display and court life, as well as the physical setting for royal palaces.

---

59   With its dimensions (ca. 70/75 × 18/20 m) the new Great Hall was among the largest in contemporary Europe, and bears comparison with Westminster Hall (ca. 73 × 20 m), the Grand Salle of the Palais de la Cité at Paris (ca. 70 × 27 m) and the Sala della Ragione (80 × 27 m) at Padua.

After a long break, construction of the royal seat of *Prague* restarted in 1333, upon the arrival of Charles, heir to the throne (Margrave of Moravia 1334, King of Bohemia 1346–1378). Charles built his new palace on the French pattern.[60] The lower level of the ruined Romanesque palace was retained, but only as a kind of foundation for the new building. The new storey above it was extended to the north and west. The old gatehouse was later completely enclosed by other buildings and assumed the role of a *Bergfried*. Also connected with the work on the castle during Charles' reign was the beginning of a full reconstruction of the Romanesque St Vitus's Cathedral. The project took its primary importance from the need to provide a fitting seat for what had just been upgraded from an episcopate to an archiepiscopate. The new cathedral – which took a very long time to build – naturally had a place in the display of royal grandeur and legitimacy. It was the place of coronation and the repository of the coronation insignia, and also held a pantheon of royal ancestors: In 1373–1374, Charles brought the earthly remains of some of his predecessors into the newly-completed chapels of the chancel, and had them interred in new stone sarcophagi decorated with carved likenesses.

The work on the royal palace ordered by Charles IV was hardly complete when his son Wenceslas IV (1378–1419) started an entirely new project.[61] Wenceslas left the castle altogether in 1383 and moved into a new palace in the Old Town. Despite the major building work this entailed, the royal palace in Prague was relegated to secondary status among Bohemian royal residences for the next hundred years and regained its importance only in 1484, during the rule of Wladislas Jagiello (1471–1516). This was accompanied by reconstructions and extensions in the Late Gothic and Renaissance styles, of which the finest example, combining the two, is the Wladislas Hall (62 × 16 m), completed in 1502. Construction work in Prague continued even after Wladislas was elected king of Hungary in 1490 and moved his main seat to Buda. By the time of its completion in 1509, the exterior of the palace was thoroughly transformed, and only in its outline did it resemble the palace of Charles and Wenceslas.

---

60 "Et in brevi tempore domum regiam construxit nunquam prius in hoc regno talem visam, ad instar domus regis Francie cum maximis sumptibus edificavit…" – František of Prague, quoted by Jiří Fajt, "Charles IV: Toward a New Imperial Style," in *Prague, The Crown of Bohemia 1347–1437*, eds Barbara Drake Boehm and Jiří Fajt (New York–New Haven: The Metropolitan Museum of Art – Yale University Press, 2005), pp. 3–21, here p. 17, note 23.

61 Petr Chotěbor, "Mladší lucemburská přestavba Starého královského paláce na Pražském hradě," [The late Luxemburg-era rebuilding of the Royal Palace at Prague Castle] *Castellologica Bohemica* 10 (2006), pp. 55–70.

In *Cracow*, the Mongol invasion of 1241 did not set off a wave of building fortifications in stone as it did in Buda and Visegrád. Nevertheless, that was when Conrad of Masovia, after seizing the Wawel, first separated the ducal palace in the north-east from the rest of the castle, creating the Upper Castle and the Lower Castle (*Zamek górny – Zamek dolny*). Although no stone castle walls can be traced to the second half of the thirteenth century, palace buildings were certainly built of stone at that time. The Early Gothic *palatium* lay on the north side of the Upper Castle, oriented east–west, and was built on the site of earlier structures.[62] The erection of new castle walls in stone has been usually dated to around 1300, and attributed to King Wenceslas II of Bohemia, who between 1291 and 1305 also sat on the Polish throne. Subsequent construction by the Piasts in the fourteenth century, under the reign of Wladislas I Łokietek (1320–1333) and Casimir III, gradually built up the strip all round the inside of the castle walls, with an enclosed court in the center. The chronicles make particular mention of the building works ordered by Casimir.[63]

There was major construction both in the actual royal residence, the Upper Castle (*Zamek królewski*) and the Lower Castle. Between 1320 and 1364, the Romanesque cathedral was renovated in the Gothic style as a place befitting coronations and royal burials. South of the cathedral, the Churches of St Michael and St George were also rebuilt in the Gothic style, and chapters were accommodated beside them.[64] The Lower Castle was not the sole province of church bodies, however, because it was also the place – probably from the beginning – where members of the higher nobility with influence at court built their residences.[65]

---

62   Zbigniew Pianowski, *Wawel obronny: zarys przemian fortyfikacji grodu i zamku krakowskiego w. IX–XIX* [Wawel fortifications: an outline of changes in the defensive system of Wawel Hill from the ninth to the nineteenth century] (Biblioteka Waweliana, 8) (Cracow: Państwowe Zbiory Sztuki na Wawelu, 1991), pp. 161–162 and the appendix ground plan, no iv.

63   "Imprimis castrum Cracoviensis mirificis domibus, turris (!), sculpturis, tectis nimium decoris ornavit" as related by Jan z Czarnkowa; quoted by Antoni Franaszek, *Budowle gotyckie zamku królewskiego na Wawelu. Na tle dziejów w czasach nowożytnych* [The topography of the Gothic buildings at the Wawel] (Biblioteka Waweliana, 6) (Cracow: Ministerstwo Kultury i Sztuki – Zarząd Muzeów i Ochrony Zabytków, 1989), p. 62; Pianowski, *Wawel obronny*, p. 140, note 15.

64   Pianowski, *Wawel obronny*, p. 162.

65   *Wawel 1000–2000. Jubilee Exhibition: Artistic Culture of the Royal Court and the Cathedral. Wawel Royal Castle May – July 2000. Cracow Cathedral – The Episcopal, Royal and National Shrine. May – September 2000. Catalogue*, i, eds Magdalena Piwocka and Dariusz Nowacki (Cracow: Zamek Królewski na Wawelu, 2000), p. 16.

No major construction in the castle is known from the reign of Louis I (the Great) of Hungary (king of Poland: 1370–1382), but the work gained new momentum under Wladislas II Jagiello (1386–1434). The work done then put the Wawel, and the royal castle within it, into the form it was to retain until the turn of the fifteenth and sixteenth centuries. A completely new era of building started in 1506. Work carried out in several phases up to the middle of the sixteenth century radically transformed the whole complex, changing even the ground plan.[66] As in Buda and Prague, the new architecture was a combination of Gothic and Renaissance styles.

The Palace in Sigismund's Time and Alterations by Matthias[67]

Notwithstanding the uncertainties, an attempt to find out what the Buda palace looked like during the reign of King Matthias[68] must start with the situation at the end of the Sigismundian period. It seems that Matthias's buildings followed the layout and architectural framework which his predecessor

---

66 For the latest account of works of the Renaissance period, see Andrzej Fischinger and Marcin Fabiański, *The Renaissance Wawel. Building the Royal Residence* (Cracow: Wawel Royal Castle, 2013).

67 The following part of the study is based on my former work: Károly Magyar, "Towards a Reconstruction of Matthias-Era Residences," in *Matthias Corvinus, the King*, pp. 89–99, with bibliography. In what follows, I refer only to the most important works and to the most recent publications. For a rich bibliography, see Péter Farbaky, "Florence and/or Rome? The Origins of Early Renaissance Architecture in Hungary," in *Italy & Hungary*, pp. 345–367. For the various historical sources referring to Buda Palace, see Balogh, *A művészet Mátyás király udvarában*, 2 vols[Art in the Court of King Matthias] (Budapest: Akadémiai, 1966), i, pp. 23–101. On the humanist background of Matthias' building project, see Rózsa Feuer-Tóth, *Art and Humanism in Hungary in the Age of Matthias Corvinus*, ed. Péter Farbaky (Budapest: Akadémiai, 1990); Farbaky, "Florence," pp. 345–347.

68 The first visual reconstruction by Kálmán Lux, *A budai vár Mátyás király korában* [Buda Castle in the age of King Matthias] (Budapest: Author's edition, 1920) was followed by Jolán Balogh, "A budai királyi várpalota rekonstruálása a történeti források alapján," [A reconstruction of the Royal Palace at Buda based on historical sources] *Művészettörténeti Értesítő* 1 (1952), pp. 29–40, and by the relevant section of Jolán Balogh, *Mátyás király és a művészet* [King Matthias and the Arts] (Budapest: Magvető, 1986). See further, Rózsa Feuerné Tóth, "A budai királyi palota 1478–1500 között épült reneszánsz homlokzatai. Egy eszmei rekonstrukció lehetőségei," [Renaissance façades built between 1478–1500 in the Royal Palace of Buda. Opportunities for a theoretical reconstruction] [edited, complemented with reconstructions, and annotated by Péter Farbaky] *Ars Hungarica* 14 (1986), pp. 17–50 and Farbaky, "Florence," pp. 360–365.

had put in place, i.e. the castle walls, courtyards and palace buildings, and that he only renovated and partly extended these. Bonfini also highlighted Sigismund's status as a predecessor.[69]

The core of the palace, the residential and public buildings, were arranged around three main courtyards and a forecourt (being *in statu nascendi*) aligned in order of ascending size from south to north, on the plateau of Castle Hill, which broadens out in a trapezoidal shape. These are surrounded one level below by closed or 'internal' courtyards arranged in a U shape on the slopes of the hill. Further down were similar but much larger areas, i.e. wards enclosed by the castle walls (Fig. 6.6).[70]

The Main Courtyards of the Palace

The most southerly and earliest of the main courtyards, the so-called Little Court, was completely enclosed by buildings of various ages.[71] These most likely accommodated the private quarters of the king and queen, and the west range (probably the ground floor) may have included the storehouse (*domus tavernicalis*) for the treasury and archive.[72] On the west side of this, but one level lower than the plateau, was an enormous basement-like space which is usually identified as the remains of the *cisterna regia* and supposed to have had a hanging garden on its roof. By inference from the palace of Urbino, this little garden between the ranges of the palace is supposed to have joined the private apartments of the king and queen.[73] The king's quarters, however, could have had some connection with the next, central courtyard, known as the Great or Internal or State Court.[74] According to some – much later – sources (Omichius

---

69 Bonfini, *Decades* III-III-343–347 (p. 75).

70 For the ensemble up to the age of King Sigismund, see Magyar, *A budai*, and for the later period see idem, "'Et…introivit ad Hungariam sola germanica ancilla nomine Maria…' – Mary of Hungary and Buda," in *Mary of Hungary*, pp. 97–119.

71 Gerevich, *A budai vár*, pp. 121–133; Balogh, *A művészet*, i, pp. 68–72, where it is called the "Harmadik udvar" i.e. "Third Courtyard".

72 Gerevich, *A budai vár*, p. 182–183; others, however, like László Zolnay, identify the Storehouse with another, Sigismund-period range built later, beside the west range of the Small Courtyard, but on a lower level than the plateau. On the sources for this, see Balogh, *A művészet*, i, pp. 73–76.

73 Feuerné Tóth, "A budai királyi palota," p. 22. On the origins of Renaissance hanging gardens, see Feuer-Tóth, *Art and Humanism*, pp. 92–93, and Farbaky, "Florence," pp. 358–360.

74 Gerevich, *A budai vár*, pp. 112–120 (sources) and 292–298 (Renaissance building); Balogh, *A művészet*, i, pp. 56–68., where it is mentioned as the "Második udvar," i.e. "Second

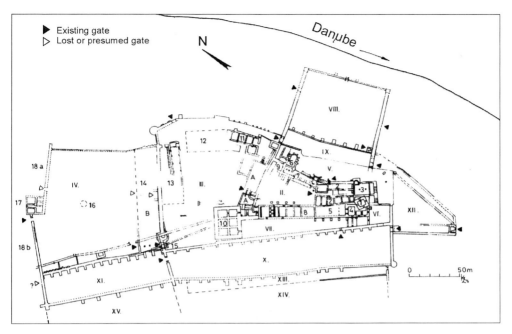

FIGURE 6.6 *The royal palace of Buda in the late fifteenth century (research: Károly Magyar) A: Dry Moat I (Inner dry ditch); B: Dry Moat II (Outer dry ditch); I: Small Courtyard; II: Inner, Great, or State Courtyard; III: Sigismund Courtyard; IV: North Forecourt; V–VII: Enclosed courtyards on the lower terraces surrounding the plateau; VIII– XIII: Wards flanked by walls on the slope of the hill; XIV–XV: Royal gardens on the western slope; 1: The Stephen Tower at the southernmost point of the plateau; 2: The east and west ranges of the Angevin-era palace core; 3: The southeast range of the palace (age of Sigismund), with remains of a bay window of an earlier building, presumably a chapel; 4: The southwest range of the palace (age of Sigismund); 5: Cisterna Regia; 6: Chapel, presumably on Angevin-era foundations, rebuilt later; 7: Southeast range of the Great Courtyard; 8: West range of the Great Courtyard; 9: Northeast building of the Great Courtyard; 10: Incomplete Tower (age of Sigismund); 11: Southeast building of the Sigismund Courtyard: kitchen; 12: Northeast building of the Sigismund Courtyard: 'Matthias's unfinished palace' (on Sigismund-era foundations?); 13: Sigismund's palace with a great hall; 14: The site of the original bridge leading to the Sigismund Courtyard; 15: A later bridge with a gate tower (converted from a tower belonging to the Arpadian-era town wall) leading to the Sigismund Courtyard; 16: The likely site of the Hercules sculpture (age of Matthias); 17: Remains of the so-called 'Friss palota' (age of Sigismund), later used as a gate tower; 18a-b: The eastern and western sections of the North Curtain Wall (c. 1470–1541) (research by K. Magyar)*

Courtyard"; Gerevich, *The Art of Buda*, pp. 103–107; Péter Farbaky, "A budai középkori királyi palota díszudvara," [The Great Court of the medieval royal palace at Buda] *Ars Hungarica* 16 (1988), pp. 143–171.

1572, Vratislav Vencel of Mitrovica, 1591), the "King's (bed) chamber" was somewhere close to the library.[75] Since the latter is known to have been on an upper floor[76] beside the chapel[77] situated near the middle of the east side of the State Court, the library must have been in the short, south-east range of that courtyard and thus the 'King's chamber' was to the south of that, probably in the north range of the Little Court, on the first floor.[78] This transverse range also formed the south range of the State Court, and the doorway and passage in the center on the ground floor linked the two courtyards together. The location of the chapel corresponds with Bonfini's description: "On the Danube side, [Matthias] built a small chapel with a water organ, and decorated the double font with marble and silver."[79] The first part of this sentence is usually interpreted as meaning that Matthias did not build a new chapel, but converted the upper church space of the two-floor chapel built in the late Angevin or early Sigismund Periods. This is supported by the large number of late Gothic vault rib fragments found in the east enclosed courtyard to the east of the chapel, which may be supposed to date from the Matthias period and to be linked to the chapel.[80] The location of the library in the south-east range of the State Court, between the chapel and the 'King's chamber', itself demonstrates the significance it was assigned as a statement of royal grandeur.[81]

---

75 Balogh, *A művészet*, i, p. 66. The extent to which two travelers to Buda 80–100 years after Matthias's death could have received from the Ottomans reliable information on what the room had been used for is, of course, questionable. It cannot be likely that the king's or queen's apartment, either then or in the time of Matthias's predecessors, consisted of a single "bedchamber". In the Urbino Palace, regarded by some as a possible model for the reconstruction of the Buda palace (e.g. Feuer-Tóth, *Art and Humanism*, p. 93), the ducal couple had residential quarters consisting of three rooms each (plus small service areas). See Janez Höfler, *Der Palazzo ducale in Urbino unter den Montefeltro (1376–1508). Neue Forschungen zur Bau- und Ausstattungsgeschichte* (Regensburg: Schnell – Steiner, 2004), pp. 132–135, 197 (Fig. 31) and 198–199. The room in question was probably a kind of audience hall.

76 Balogh, *A művészet*, i, pp. 62–65. On its situation, see Balogh, "A budai királyi várpalota," p. 33, who places in this short range the throne room or council hall and the queen's room, which is physically impossible. See also Gerevich, *A budai vár*, pp. 113–114.

77 Gerevich, *A budai vár*, pp. 207–216; Balogh, *A művészet*, i, pp. 59–62.

78 Károly Magyar, "'Et...introivit ad Hungariam'," in *Mary of Hungary*, pp. 97–119, here pp. 97–99.

79 Balogh, *A művészet*, i, p. 38; Bonfini, *Decades*, IV-VII-92 (p. 136).

80 "Fragments of a late Gothic net-vaulting from the Royal Palace of Buda" – *Matthias Corvinus, the King*, p. 336 (by András Végh).

81 In Urbino, the library occupied a room on the ground floor of the north range of the palace beside the Court of State, immediately adjacent to the north main door. Höfler, *Der Palazzo ducale*, p. 185, Fig. 27.

The long and wide building diagonally opposite the south-east range takes up the entire west side of the State Court. It provided much more space than the part of the palace we have discussed so far. Matthias substantially rebuilt it and probably added a new, second floor. The work was most likely completed only during the time of his successor, Wladislas II, as evidenced by a door frame marked with the year 1502, mentioned by later travelers. The approach to the new floor may have been linked to the construction of a system of open passages, probably three floors high, in front of the ranges lining three sides of the courtyard – south-east, south and west. It may be inferred from Bonfini that the arcaded passage on the ground floor was probably older, but the double ambulatory above it was built by Matthias.[82] Archaeological remains also confirm the existence of the arcaded passage.[83] Descriptions from the Ottoman period also mention the passages and their associated red marble columns,[84] and one states that the plinths and capitals of the columns were decorated by animal figures, including the raven of the Hunyadi family. Most researchers accept that the upper passages or *loggia*s were designed in Renaissance style. In support of this are the twelve signs of the zodiac which decorated the panelled ceiling above the top passage, mentioned by Bonfini and known from other sources to have been carved from wood.[85] The actual form of the loggia and the number of levels is not conveyed by the descriptions and is disputed, as is the question of when it was built.[86] Although not mentioned specifically by any source, it is usually supposed that the pillared loggias were lined by balustrades. A large number of balustrade fragments have been found, although

---

82 "In medio area veteri porticu circumventa, quam duplicia coronant ambulacra, quorum supremum novoque palatio prepositum, qua ad summa triclinia conscenditur, duodecim signiferi orbis sideribus insignie non sine admiratione suscipitur…" Given in Bonfini, *Decades*, IV-VII-95 (p. 136).

83 Balogh, *A művészet*, i, p. 39 and 56. Balogh does not rule out the possibility that Matthias also built the ground floor arcade, and Bonfini's reference to a "vetus porticus" only applies to its old Gothic style. She also favors the single-upper-storey version of the passages. Balogh, *Mátyás király*, pp. 122–123 and 140. In front of the west range of the courtyard, four large pillar footings were found, but no archaeological material which could date them. See Gerevich, *A budai vár*, p. 97.

84 Balogh, *A művészet*, i, pp. 56–57.

85 Balogh, *A művészet*, i, p. 57, with reference to Bonfini, Gerlach, Schweigger and Lubenau.

86 Feuerné Tóth, "A budai királyi palota," pp. 24–26, with Farbaky's drawing reconstructing the loggias along the west side of the courtyard: Fig. 8. On dating to Matthias period: p. 47 note 23. Another reconstruction to the same side, see Péter Farbaky, "Der Königspalast von Buda im Zeitalter der Renaissance," in *Budapest im Mittelalter*, pp. 259–273, here p. 262 (drawn by György Szekér).

they are of various materials and different types.[87] Some are definitely from the time of Wladislas II, because they bear the Polish eagle and the W monogram, but it is difficult to decide which of them come from the State Court. Another important issue is the relationship between the columns and the balustrades, which suggests that the arcade had a fundamental role in starting off what became a very popular arrangement of columned passages decorated with balustrades, both in Buda and also in Visegrád.[88]

A separate issue is what the outer walls of the palace ranges surrounding the courtyard looked like after the work carried out during the Matthias period. Attempts at reconstruction so far only extend to the west frontage of the west range.[89]

Several sources mention a fountain supplied by pipes, and Bonfini described it as being decorated by a statue of Pallas Athene. This must have stood at the southern side of the State Court, probably in front of the south-east range.[90] Fragments of several fountains have been found on the palace site and the Castle District, but their original locations have not been identified.[91] In addition, the *in situ* rim of a traditional draw-well, decorated with coats of arms of Matthias

---

87 The several balustrade versions have been pointed out by Balogh, *Mátyás király*, pp. 132–133. On one possible form of the balustrade: Feuerné Tóth, "A budai királyi palota," p. 27 Fig. 11 (drawing by Péter Farbaky). For a short, but important summary, see "Balustrade from the Royal Palace of Buda" in *Matthias Corvinus, the King*, p. 336 (by András Végh). See further Farbaky, "Florence,"pp. 365–367.

88 Taking into account the two-upper-floor (?) passages on all three (?) sides of the courtyard, it is reasonable to ask some questions: Were these built in a single phase, to a coherent plan? Were there balustrades throughout the system of passages, or only on prominent sections? And were these all of the same type? Some indication may come from a statistical study of the stone finds of the kind done on the balustrades of the Court of State in Visegrád where, however, only one type of balustrade was applied and – it seems – only on one level. See Gergely Buzás, "The Royal Palace in Visegrád and the Beginnings of Renaissance Architecture in Hungary," in *Italy & Hungary*, pp. 369–407, esp. pp. 394–403.

89 Feuerné Tóth, "A budai királyi palota," p. 21 , figs 4–5 (two versions drawn by Péter Farbaky); a third version of the west elevation by György Szekér is given in Farbaky, "Der Königspalast," p. 262.

90 Bonfini, *Decades*, IV-VII-97 (p. 136); Balogh, "A budai királyi várpalota," p. 33; eadem, *A művészet*, i, pp. 38–39 and 145–146; Gerevich, *The Art of Buda*, pp. 111–112.

91 Gerevich, *A budai vár*, plate xxii; Balogh, *A művészet*,i, p. 121, and ii, p. 162–165, fig. 158; Balogh, *Mátyás király*, p. 229; on some important white marble fountain fragments, see Dániel Pócs, "White Marble Sculptures from the Castle of Buda: Reconsidering Some Facts about an Antique Statue and a Fountain by Verocchio," in *Italy & Hungary*, pp. 553–608, here p. 555–591.

Corvinus and Beatrice of Aragon, has been found in the south internal courtyard,[92] and there may have been something similar on the roof of the *cisterna regia*. The courtyard was also decorated – probably on the level of an upper floor – by a sculpture of three armed Hunyadi figures, with Matthias in the center, his father John on one side, and his brother Ladislas on the other.[93]

The building along the fourth, north side of the State Court is shrouded in even greater mystery than the other three ranges, because although a thick-walled building has been found on the north-east corner, its western end has not. The courtyard itself was divided from the next courtyard, Sigismund's Court, by a ditch cut out of the rock (Dry Moat 1). The two were linked by a bridge with a gatehouse on its internal side. On the far side of the bridge, to the west (left), was the enormous Csonka (i.e. "Incomplete") Tower, which King Sigismund started to build and left unfinished.[94] Although situated in the southwest corner of the adjoining Sigismund's Court, this tower functionally belonged to the State Court and formed its boundary and northern defense. It was directly connected to the west range of the courtyard. By this time, it was already in use as a prison, first occasionally, and later on a more regular basis.[95]

Old and New Buildings of Sigismund's Court

The building on the east side of Sigismund's Court, and those on its south-east and north-east, probably presented an almost unbroken façade in an angular reverse-C shape. The " ⌐"-shaped block in the south-east corner, whose basement remains have been found, was the kitchen; its distinctive chimneys are

---

92 Gerevich, *A budai vár*, p. 154, and plate xxii/1.
93 Bonfini, *Decades*, IV-VII-96 (p. 136); Balogh, "A budai királyi várpalota," p. 32; Balogh, *A művészet*, i, p. 39, 138. Balogh, *Mátyás király*, p. 101 imagines the statues to have stood in a niche above the main door of the "Matthias Palace" on the east side, but the sources provide no actual evidence for this.
94 "In media fere arce turrim amplissimam fundavit ex quadrato veluti cetera omnia lapide, que ad duo subdialia pertinet, sed morte initum opus non absolvit," – Bonfini, *Decades*, III-III-346–347 (p. 75).
95 Gerevich, *A budai vár*, pp. 77–86 and 95–96; Balogh, *A művészet*, i, pp. 53–55. Matthias first held Hussite and Polish prisoners here, see thus Bonfini, *Decades*, IV-I-92 (p. 7), and later those who interfered with the work of the law courts (1486). Concluding from the dimensions of its partly revealed ground-walls, we may suppose that this could be the largest (ca. 35 m x 26 m) defensive tower in medieval Hungary.

clearly identifiable from the image in the Schedel Chronicle [see Fig. 0.4].[96] To the north, this connected to a straight building on an area which has still not been excavated, and so its form can only be inferred from the depiction. This is particularly unfortunate, because it is perhaps this building which is the subject of most questions concerning constructions during Matthias's reign. It is the most likely candidate for what Bonfini and – a good thirty years later – Velius describe as the "incomplete palace" in Sigismund's Court.[97] From Bonfini's description, all that appears certain is that the west façade facing the courtyard connected to two red marble grand stairways, and its bronze door was decorated by the deeds of Hercules and inscribed at the top with an inscription by Bonfini. Crucial among the questions surrounding the Northeast Palace is the date of the original picture (or pictures) of the Schedel woodcut, i.e. whether the building it features dates from before or after reconstruction (or even, according to some hypotheses from the time of its foundation). Since this is not known, any interpretation of the details in the picture (mullion-and-transom windows, arched doors, arcaded basement) as characteristically Renaissance[98] or from the Sigismund-period[99] belongs to the realms of imagination. Progress in this area could in principle be expected from excavation in the area.

To the northwest of that building, perpendicular to it, was a much longer palace range, which may be identified as the building which appears in the sources as Sigismund's palace.[100] Although a small part of its basement has

96 By determining the shape of the roof to be a chimney stack, Lux, "A budai vár," pp. 11–12 was the first to identify the building as a kitchen. See Magyar, "'Et…introivit ad Hungariam,'" p. 93; Sándor Tóth, "Die Gebäude des Budaer Königspalastes zur Zeit Sigismunds von Luxemburg," in *Sigismundus Rex et Imperator*, pp. 200–218, here p. 205.

97 "In hac igitur quadrata area ante Sigismundi atria vetus a latere palatium instaurare ceperat, quod si prestare potuisset, plurimum de superba vetustate referebat." See Bonfini, *Decades*, IV-VII-98 (p. 136). See also, Gerevich, *A budai vár*, pp. 63–64; Balogh, *A művészet*, i, pp. 48–51 quotes relevant sources, but merges the 'Friss Palota' into Matthias's incomplete palace, and interprets Velius's important description as being of the Court of State. Lux, "A budai vár," pp. 14–15. mistakenly identifies this building as the Friss Palace.

98 Feuerné Tóth, "A budai királyi palota," pp. 28–31; Farbaky, "Florence," pp. 360–365.

99 According to some opinions the arcaded basement here can be traced to the blind arcade on the façades of the papal palace of Avignon. It should be pointed out, however, that although Sigismund did visit Avignon and even obtained some kind of picture of the palace, the Buda arcade-arches are of a different kind and served a completely different purpose, since they were buttresses supporting a terrace-like structure and probably also constituted the basement section of the building behind them.

100 The older literature unanimously identified this as the "Friss Palace" mentioned in the sources. See thus Balogh, *A művészet*, i, pp. 47–53; Gerevich, *A budai vár*, pp. 62 and 64–69.

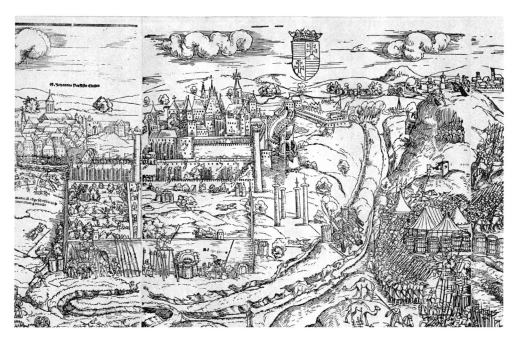

FIGURE 6.7 *The royal palace of Buda from the west on Erhard Schön's engraving. The siege of Buda (1541)*

been excavated, and two of its walls appear on both the Schedel (see the front cover and Fig. 0.4) and Schön illustrations (Fig. 6.7), its actual shape is the subject of debate.[101] Matthias's rebuilding hardly seems to have affected this edifice, if at all. Nonetheless, its enormous great hall was the venue of several ceremonial events involving large numbers of people during Matthias's reign and later, such as Matthias's and Beatrice's wedding in 1476.[102] North of the palace range, a new ditch (Dry Moat II) was cut across the rock plateau, dividing the palace from the city district to its north.

The houses which originally occupied this approximately 90/100 × 110/120 m area were gradually demolished and gave way to a 'transitional zone' in front

 However, an analysis of the sources suggests that the "Friss Palace" may be identified with another building which lay a little to the north, originally in what was part of the city. See Károly Magyar, "A Budavári Palota északi, ún. Koldus-kapujának tornya az újabb kutatások tükrében," [The gatehouse of the northern, so-called Beggar's Gate of the Royal Palace of Buda in light of recent research] *Budapest Régiségei* 29 (1992), pp. 57–92.

101   For the first visual reconstruction of the north palace range, see Gerevich, *A budai vár*, fig. 17 (drawing by Gy. Kollár) which provides the basis for the further reconstructions of György Szekér and Gergely Buzás.

102   Balogh, *A művészet*, i, p. 52.

of the palace, towards the city. At the end, the area was finally divided from the city by an enormous transverse wall and attached to the palace as a forecourt. No precise dates can be given for the process, but it probably started during Sigismund's reign and reached completion by 1541 at the latest. It is significant here on two counts.

First, as is known from the sources, it was on this area, on the forecourt of the palace, that Matthias's brother Ladislas was beheaded, in full view of the city's inhabitants, in March 1457.[103] This means that there must have been some kind of open area there at the time. Secondly, it is known that Matthias, in commemoration, raised a statue of Hercules cast in bronze and set on a red marble plinth on the site of his brother's execution.[104] It is probably not far from the truth to imagine this area as the venue for large-scale events. Certainly, the area which Bonfini mentions in some places as the *hippodrom* and elsewhere as the *propyleum* was later used for equestrian tournaments and also as an arsenal.[105]

Some thought should also be given to the royal gardens, which spread over the western approaches to the castle, under the palace defenses. Bonfini discussed them in detail.[106] The first and last 'authentic' picture of them is on the Schön (Fig. 6.7) engraving and its variants, because during the Ottoman period all but a few sections of the garden walls were destroyed. Schön shows them to have consisted of two or three parts divided by walls, which probably mark the phases of their construction.[107] Small garden sheds also feature on the picture, on the south side. These probably include the part of three small garden buildings which have recently been discovered in archaeological excavations, thus identifying the route of the south enclosure wall. One of the three buildings has retained, on its original site, a Renaissance plinth ledge which is the only *in situ* architectural detail from this era. In front of it, the stone frame of one of the windows, fallen from the upper floor, has also been found.[108]

---

103   Bonfini, *Decades*, III-VIII-249–263 (p. 197–198); Balogh, *A művészet*, i, pp. 39 and 44.
104   Balogh, *A művészet*, i, pp. 138–143; Árpád Mikó, "Imago Historiae," in *Történelem-kép. Szemelvények múlt és művészet kapcsolatából Magyarországon* [History – image. Selected examples of the relationship between art and history in Hungary], eds idem and Katalin Sinkó (Budapest: Magyar Nemzeti Galéria, 2000), pp. 34–47, esp. p. 42–47 which builds on a red marble carving with an inscription found on the recent Szent György Square, probably from the plinth of the statue. See ibid. Cat. no III-6 (by Árpád Mikó and Károly Magyar).
105   Balogh, *A művészet*, i, pp. 44–45; Gerevich, *A budai vár*, pp. 18–21.
106   Balogh, *A művészet*, i, pp. 38–39; Bonfini, *Decades*, IV-VII-92–108 (pp. 136–37).
107   The drawing shows a narrow, elongated triangular part of garden between two large garden sections. Its role is difficult to interpret.
108   *Kincsek a város alatt. Budapest régészeti örökségének feltárása / Treasures under the City. Survey of the Archaeological Heritage of Budapest*, ed. Paula Zsidi (Budapest: BTM,2005), p. 174 (by Károly Magyar).

Having described the royal palace in Buda during the Matthias Era, we again face the question of how 'Renaissance' were the buildings used as residences by King Matthias. The architectural remains provide enough evidence to state that the new style brought from Italy was applied to different degrees at different sites. But the surviving fragments we have may present a highly misleading picture, because many of the component parts of the building, such as the roofs and the panelled ceilings, and most of the fittings (except for the stove-tiles) have completely disappeared. The same is true of the gardens. Without these, any picture of the palaces we produce, be it Gothic or Renaissance, cannot truly be complete.

Closing Remarks

A general remark applying to the three royal seats of Buda, Prague and Cracow as they developed in the fourteenth and fifteenth centuries is that they underwent almost continuous construction and expansion. This was of course a general phenomenon among royal palaces adapted and developed from existing buildings rather than being built from scratch. The work was driven by the rising demands of functionality, comfort, display and defense, increasing numbers of courtiers and officials, and changing architectural fashions. Differences between them consist mainly in the spatial extent and the form of the buildings, as dictated by their location.

In Buda, heightened demands led to a major expansion of the whole area of the palace. This required its extension onto the hillside and considerable incursion into land previously occupied by the city.[109] The situation was different in Prague and Cracow, where the area of the royal residence (palace and castle) marked off within the existing castle was never significantly expanded, perhaps because there was no opportunity to do so.[110] Instead, the existing building was extended with side wings (Prague), or the court was enclosed by new buildings, partly by the demolition of older ones (Cracow). In Prague and Cracow, however, involvement in non-secular building outside the royal

---

109   One may mention here the works of Philip le Bel at Paris aiming at expanding the area of the Palais de la Cité. In advance, all properties surrounding it were bought up by the king. In the case of Buda we do not have any written sources which could throw light on the legal background to the annexation of the city area. However, in the case of the urban palace at Visegrád, we may suppose a similar situation to Paris.

110   The expansion of the palaces may have been limited by the existing ecclesiastical buildings. In Prague it was St Vitus's Cathedral on the north and the St George's Church on the northwest, while in Cracow St Stanislas's Cathedral on the west proved the main obstacles to growth.

residence in the strict sense also contributed to the display of royal grandeur, particularly the reconstruction of the two cathedrals. In Buda, this occurred to a somewhat lesser extent with the building of the newly-founded St Sigismund's Church in the area of the city.

Finally while the architectural development of palace ensembles at Prague and Cracow was almost continuous during the entire sixteenth century, it was in the case of the Buda Palace essentially 'frozen' by the 1520s at the latest. In the 1530s, under King John Szapolyai, however, much building was done to the fortifications of the palace and the city, aiming to adapt them to warfare fought more intensively with artillery than in the previous hundred years. This building work was continued after the Ottoman occupation in 1541, but the use of the medieval palace as a high status dwelling for prominent persons came to end. Some Western European travelers who visited the complex in the next 145 years could only record the palace's fading glory. The decay was accelerated by a gunpowder explosion in 1578 which entirely destroyed the North and Northeast Palace ranges of the Sigismund's Courtyard. Subsequent sieges caused further damage. However, even after the final siege of 1686, when the whole ensemble fell in ruins, there remained some ranges – such as the western one on the State Court – which could have been saved. It was only in the 1730s that the last remains of the medieval royal palace were pulled down to give way to the new Baroque palace of the Habsburg rulers.

CHAPTER 7

Buda-Pest 1300 – Buda-Pest 1400. Two Topographical Snapshots

András Végh

Why Buda-Pest?

"Budapest, Capital of Medieval Hungary" – to have chosen such a title for this study would surely have raised a few eyebrows.[1] After all, Budapest has only existed since 1873, when the independent but neighboring centers of Buda, Pest and Óbuda were, after a long series of developments, fully united as the capital of Hungary. The 'capital city' of medieval Hungary was of course Buda on its own, which became the permanent seat of the royal court in the early fifteenth century and remained so until the fall of the independent Hungarian kingdom. Buda also held a leading position among Hungarian towns from the time of its foundation in the middle of the thirteenth century, and was officially the senior free royal town from the middle of the fifteenth.[2] This view, however, is slightly distorted. The royal seat of Buda was not a singular, discrete entity, nor even a large city surrounded by villages and farms, but only part of an agglomeration of different centers of population.[3] On the opposite bank of the Danube was Pest, another free royal town, with Szenterzsébetfalva, a lower-ranking *oppidum* or market town to the south, and several small villages to the north. Buda itself was bounded only by the village of Kelenföld to the south, but by a whole series of settlements to the north: Felhévíz – another market town – and Szentjakabfalva were the direct neighbors, and then came Óbuda, which was itself divided into the 'queen's town' and the 'chapter's town'. Such a group of population centers around the royal seat was not unique in the Central and Eastern European region. The medieval capitals of both the Bohemian and Polish kingdoms were similar assortments of settlements arranged around

---

Translated by Alan Campbell
1   András Kubinyi, "Buda – Die mittelalterliche Haupstadt Ungarns. Ein deutsch-ungarische Stadt in Ostmitteleuropa," in *Budapest im Mittelalter*, pp. 15–41; See also András Kubinyi's article in the present volume.
2   András Kubinyi, *Anfänge Ofens*; Rady, *Buda*; András Végh, "Buda," in *Medium regni*, pp. 165–199.
3   Kubinyi, *Budapest*.

the royal seat.[4] Unification of the administratively-independent districts that made up Prague and Cracow only started in the late eighteenth century.[5] An important difference, however, is that the expressions 'medieval Prague' and 'medieval Cracow' cover the whole agglomerations, while medieval Buda refers only to the city itself and not the other centers surrounding it. The clearly-delineated areas of Buda, Pest and Óbuda are always referred to by their specific names.

So what are we to do if we are embarking on a comparative urban history study and want to refer to the whole agglomeration? First of all, we must recognize that the names of some districts became intermingled even in the Middle Ages. Buda took its Latin and Hungarian name from the older Buda, a town to its north (later Óbuda, i.e. "Old Buda" in Hungarian). In German, however, the "new" Buda was called Ofen, a literal translation of the Slavic place name Pest. Throughout the medieval era, the council of Buda referred to the city in all of its documents as *castrum novi montis Pestiensis*, even though Buda was the name in general use at the time. The interrelationship of the towns is thus apparent even in the medieval nomenclature, but in a way that causes more confusion than clarity for our present purpose. For a discussion of the late medieval Hungarian capital as a whole, we therefore seem to have little choice but to create an artificial collective name for its component towns and villages. 'Capital city' is a modern-age concept in any case, and the Hungarian word for it, *főváros*, did not have the same sense or legal definition in the medieval language.[6] In this chapter, we would like to extend the term 'capital city' to refer to the whole group of urban centers of varying legal status which lay around the royal seat. All of them played a part in sustaining the royal court, and all owed their outstanding rate of development to its presence. In the two centuries preceding unification, when Pest had overtaken Buda in importance, the idea of a single 'capital city' was expressed by the term "Pest-Buda". For the medieval period, when the location of the royal residence held primacy, it is more appropriate to turn this round and refer to the 'capital' as Buda-Pest. The use of two

---

4 György Székely, "Städtische Agglomeration im Osten Mitteleuropas (13.–15. Jh.): Berlin, Buda, Prag, Krakau," in *Mittelalterliche Häuser und Strassen in Mitteleuropa* (Varia archaeologica Hungarica, 9), eds Márta Font and Mária Sándor (Budapest – Pécs: Archäologisches Institut der UAW, 2000), pp. 9–16.

5 The autonomous parts of Prague (Staré Mesto, Nové Mesto, Malá Straná and Hradčany) were united in 1784; in Cracow (Stare Miasto, Wawel, Kazimierz, Kleparz and Stradom) the same process took place in the 1790s.

6 Bernát Kumorovitz L., "Buda (és Pest) 'fővárossá' alakulásának kezdetei," [The beginnings of the formation of the 'capital' of Hungary, Buda (and Pest)] *Tanulmányok Budapest Múltjából* 18 (1971), pp. 7–57. See also the article of András Kubinyi in the present volume.

BUDA-PEST 1300 – BUDA-PEST 1400. TWO TOPOGRAPHICAL SNAPSHOTS   171

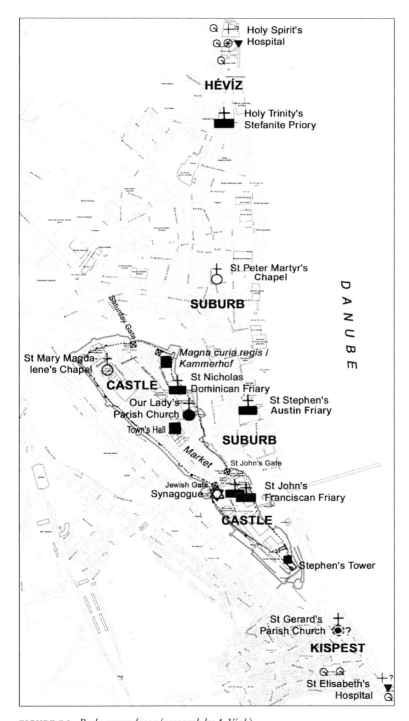

FIGURE 7.1 *Buda around 1300 (research by A. Végh)*

names is also an allusion to the city's double origins, and the hyphen indicates the independence of the centers and clearly distinguishes the medieval capital from modern Budapest.

To introduce the general character of the medieval city, we will look at its state of development at two dates a century apart. One is the year 1300, by which time Buda was past the initial uncertainties of the period of foundation, and Pest and Óbuda had adapted to the new situation caused by its growth. The other, 1400, came after a period of sustained economic development which prepared the way for the permanent presence of the royal seat. Subsequently, the group of urban centers that constituted Buda-Pest operated collectively as the capital city of the kingdom of Hungary for another hundred and twenty years.[7]

It is usual to precede a historical topographical analysis with a few words about the geographical attributes that determined the development of the city, but since Enikő Spekner has covered this in her chapter on an earlier period, we will avoid repetition and merely refer to the main literature in the footnotes.[8]

Buda-Pest around 1300

The Political Situation

Around 1300, Buda-Pest was undoubtedly the principal city in the central region of the kingdom (*medium regni*).[9] The last king of the Árpáds, Andrew III, was often resident in Buda, as witnessed by the place of issue of his

---

[7] This study is mainly based on the following works: Kubinyi, *Anfänge Ofens*; idem, *Budapest*; idem, "Topographic Growth of Buda up to 1541," in *Nouvelles études historiques publiées l'occasion du XIIe Congres International des Sciences Historiques par la Commission Nationale des Historiens Hongrois*, i, eds Dániel Csatári, László Katus and Ágnes Rozsnyói (Budapest: MTA, 1965), pp. 132–157; Rady, *Buda*; Végh, *Buda*.

[8] Katalin Szende, "Stadt und Naturlandschaft im ungarischen Donauraum des Mittelalters," in *Europäische Städte im Mittelalter* (Forschungen und Beiträge zur Wiener Stadtgeschichte, 52), eds Ferdinand Opll and Christoph Sonnlechner (Innsbruck – Vienna – Bozen: Studien Verlag, 2010), pp. 365–397; *Aquincum. Ancient Landscape – Ancient Town* (Theory, Method, Practice, 69), eds Katalin H. Kérdő and Ferenc Schweitzer (Budapest: Geographical Institute Research Center for Astronomy and Earth Sciences Hungarian Academy of Sciences, 2014); Katalin Szende, "Towns Along the Way. Changing Patterns of Long-Distance Trade and the Urban Network of Medieval Hungary," in *Towns and Communication*, ii. *Communication between Towns*, eds Hubert Houben and Kristjan Toomaspoeg (Lecce: Mario Congedo Editore, 2011), pp. 161–225.

[9] Györffy, *Budapest*; Rady, *Buda*; ÁMTF, iv, pp. 596–626.

charters.[10] It is not easy to interpret which town this meant, because the use of the name Buda was not yet completely fixed and could have referred to either the king's house in Buda (the *Kammerhof*) or his Óbuda palace. What is definite, however, is that King Andrew III chose in 1301 to be buried in the church of the Franciscan friary in Buda. In the wars to secure the throne fought for a quarter of a century after his death, possession of Buda-Pest was of more than military importance; it symbolized control over the kingdom. This shows up in the royal entrances to the city (Wenceslas 1301, Otto 1305), in which the parish church of Buda played a central role; a royal coronation in Buda (Charles 1309); the diets held in Pest and Rákos Field beside it, including diets to elect the king (1307, 1308, 1310, 1314); and a synod held in Buda by the Papal legate (1308). This is not to downplay the military significance of Buda. The part defended by a wall, i.e. Buda Castle (*castrum Budense*),[11] was one of the most important fortresses in the realm and had a large garrison. It was besieged unsuccessfully in 1301 (Charles I) and in 1311 (Máté Csák), and taken by assault in 1307 (Charles' followers). Charles I wrote of it in 1308: "after we took governance of our kingdom (i.e. at the Diet of Rákos), we went to our principal city of Buda with the prelates, barons and nobles of the realm."[12] A succession of monarchs (Wenceslas, Otto and Charles) spent long periods within the walls of the fortress city between 1301 and 1315. The castle of Óbuda was of much less military significance, and was often granted to barons (Wenceslas to the sons of Henrik of the Héder clan: Charles I to Máté Csák, and later to the Drugets).

The Legal Status of the Urban Agglomeration and the Individual Towns

Around 1300, the Buda-Pest agglomeration stretched over a length of about seven kilometres on each side of the Danube. The northernmost settlement on the right bank was Óbuda, occupied a plan at the mouth of a broad valley. It was an early royal center built on the place of the old Roman legion camp. The collegiate chapter of Óbuda controlled the town at the time, although its jurisdiction did not extend to the royal castle of Óbuda within its bounds.[13]

---

10   RA, ii/4.
11   One of the many examples: "in occupatione castri nostri Budensis" (1307; MNL OL DL 40 308, edited in AOklt, ii, pp. 81–82 [no 173]).
12   "cum...suscepto regni nostri gubernaculo in Budensem civitatem nostram principalem una cum prelatis, baronibus regnique nostri nobilibus...venissemus" (22 September 1308/31 March 1332; MNL OL DF 229 866, edited in AOklt, ii, p. 199 [no 459]).
13   Júlia Altmann and Herta Bertalan, "Óbuda von 11. bis 13. Jahrhundert," in *Budapest im Mittelalter*, pp. 113–131.

Beside Óbuda, separated by a narrow branch of the Danube, was Köncöl Island (now Óbudai Island), also the property of the chapter, with a small estate center on its southern area. On the left bank opposite Óbuda, at the outflow of the Rákos Stream, was the village of Besenyő.[14] To the south of Óbuda, where the hills come right down to the riverbank, the habitable area was squeezed to a narrow strip. First came Szentjakabfalva, followed by an area of hot and cold springs later known as Felhévíz, on which lay the village of Szentháromságfalva owned by the Hospitallers of St Stephen, and minor estates, mills and baths owned by the Order of the Holy Spirit, the Dominican nuns of Margaret Island (in the Middle Ages: Hares' Island), the royal castle of Óbuda, and private landowners.[15] Between Óbuda and the area of the hot springs, Margaret Island divided the river into two branches. On it lay the Dominican nunnery of the Virgin Mary, founded by King Béla IV. On its estate was a small settlement of *hospites* ('guests', i.e. people who had settled from elsewhere with special rights) and two friaries, one Franciscan and one Premonstratensian. There were also small castles at each tip of the island, by that time probably already in ruins – one belonging to the archbishop of Esztergom in the north, and one belonging to the Knights Hospitallers of St Stephen in the south.[16] At the southern end of the island, a ferry connected the area of hot springs near Buda with the village of Jenő on the left bank, the estate of the Dominican nuns, where the ferrymen lived.[17] Immediately after the springs came the town of Buda, which was divided into two parts: the *castrum,* the castle on the plateau of today's *Vár-hegy* (i.e. Castle Hill); and the *suburbium* beneath it, stretching down to the Danube and not surrounded by a wall.[18] Finally, in the narrow valley entrance between the outstretched end of the Castle Hill and neighboring Pest Hill (Gellért Hill), another area of hot springs, lay the *hospes* village of Kispest (in German: Kreinfeld) at the right-bank side of the Pest ferry, the most important of the Danube crossings.[19] The ferry on the other side lay in the town of Pest, which had perhaps suffered greater destruction than the others during the Mongol invasion

---

14   ÁMTF, iv, p. 510.
15   András Kubinyi, "Budafelhévíz topográfiája és gazdasági fejlődése," [The topography and economic development of Budafelhévíz] in Kubinyi, *Tanulmányok*, i, pp. 115–182; idem, *Anfänge Ofens*, pp. 23–25.
16   Katalin Irás-Melis, "Die Margareteninsel und ihre Klöster im Mittelalter," in *Budapest im Mittelalter*, pp. 409–414; ÁMTF, iv, pp. 644–657.
17   ÁMTF, iv, pp. 523–525.
18   Kubinyi, *Anfänge Ofens*, pp. 33–69; Végh, *Buda*, i, pp. 53–122.
19   Kubinyi, *Anfänge Ofens*, pp. 20–23; ÁMTF, iv, pp. 571–574; Végh, *Buda*, i, pp. 88–89.

of 1241.[20] To the north, the greater part of Bécs/Újbécs was in the possession of the Dominican nuns of Margaret Island, while a smaller part of neighboring Pest passed to the Drugets, the family of the palatine and close followers of King Charles I, in the early 1300s.[21] To the south, Szenterzsébetfalva was a royal settlement of *hospites* independent of Pest. At about the same time, it passed to a Buda councillor called Wulving or Ulving who had good connections with the king.[22]

Overall, land ownership in Buda-Pest was as follows. The king held Buda and Pest. He also owned the royal castle of Óbuda, although he transferred it into the possession of barons (usually the palatine) several times after 1301. The village of Bécs was similarly granted to the palatine. Szenterzsébetfalva, a neighbor of Pest to the south, was owned by one of the Buda councillors who acquired estates around Buda-Pest. The rest of the land was the property of ecclesiastical establishments founded by the kings, all autonomous local institutions with a special legal status. The Óbuda collegiate chapter, which operated as a national place of authentication, was not subject to the jurisdiction of the bishop, and the Dominican nuns on Margaret Island and the Knights Hospitallers of Felhévíz enjoyed papal exemption. Neither did the diocesan episcopal jurisdiction extend to Buda and Pest. Although the right bank of the Danube lay within the diocese of Veszprém and the left bank in the diocese of Vác, the parish churches in Buda and Pest had been founded by the king and were directly subordinate to the archbishop of Esztergom rather than the dioceses.[23] Secular administration followed a similar arrangement. Buda and Pest lay under the authority of the master of the royal treasury (*magister tavernicorum*)

---

20   Kubinyi, *Anfänge Ofens*, pp. 14–20; Katalin Irásné-Melis, "A pesti városalaprajz kialakulása és változásai a középkorban," [The formation and the changes of the ground plan of Pest in the Middle Ages] in *Társadalomtörténeti tanulmányok a közeli és a régmúltból. Emlékkönyv Székely György 70. születésnapjára* [Studies in social history from the recent past and the bygone. Studies in honor of György Székely on his 70th birthday], ed. Ilona Sz. Jónás (Budapest: Eötvös Loránd Tudományegyetem Bölcsészettudományi Kara, Egyetemes Történeti Tanszék, 1994), pp. 88–107; Katalin Irás-Melis, "Der Wiederaufbau der Stadt Pest und ihre Blüte im Spätmittelalter," in *Budapest im Mittelalter*, pp. 366–380, here pp. 366–369; AMTF, iv, pp. 538–550.

21   ÁMTF, iv, pp. 552–553.

22   ÁMTF, iv, p. 557.

23   Miklós Jankovich, "Buda-környék plébániáinak kialakulása és a királyi kápolnák intézménye," [The origins of the parishes surrounding Buda and the institution of the royal chapels] *Budapest Régiségei* 19 (1959), pp. 57–98; Marie-Madeleine de Cevins, *Az egyház a késő-középkori magyar városokban* [The church in Hungarian towns in the late Middle Ages] (Budapest: Szent István Társulat, 2003).

and not the counties of Pilis (right bank) or Pest (left). Another peculiar legacy affected the relations between Buda and Pest. The legal status of both was defined by a charter issued prior to the Mongol invasion of 1241–1242. Rather than issue a new charter when he founded Buda, Béla IV extended the old privileges of Pest to the new foundation.[24] These rights were enjoyed by the burghers of both towns. Pest was considered as part of the territory of Buda Castle.[25] The broad river separating the two, however, was a serious barrier to everyday communication. Consequently, Pest retained a level of self-government despite being subordinate to Buda. The council governing Buda consisted of a *rector* appointed by the king and twelve jurymen or councillors, while local affairs in Pest were controlled by a judge and four jurymen delegated by the Buda councillors.[26] In terms of privileges and administration, Buda-Pest was more united around 1300 than in later centuries.

The Boundaries and Ground Plans of the Constituent Settlements

Óbuda enclosed quite a large area, within boundaries that are well recorded.[27] It extended over the flat land at the valley entrance and up to the ridges and peaks of the surrounding hills, beginning and ending at the Danube. The boundary started in the north across the semi-marsh pastures above the ruins of the completely abandoned Roman town (*colonia Aquincum*), continued beside the neighboring vine-growing villages of Megyer, Üröm, Örs and Gercse in the hills, then passed through more wooded areas and turned to the south before reaching the Danube at Szentjakabfalva. The outskirts of the town included forests, extensive vineyards, plow land and great expanses of meadows that were periodically flooded. The town itself was built beside the bank of the Danube on the ruins of the Roman legionary camp. The major roads (such as the *limes* road on the bank of the Danube) and the walls of the late Roman (fourth century) fort made their effects felt in the medieval town, and to some extent were actually put to use. The seat of the chapter (the church and the houses of the canons) lay on the area of the late Roman fort. To the south was

---

24 EFHU, iii/2, pp. 39–41 (no 34); Kubinyi, *Anfänge Ofens*, pp. 69–70; Végh, *Buda*, i, pp. 28–34.
25 "quod ubique in districtu castri Pestiensi siue in suburbio siue in antiqua Pesth tributum solui debeat dominabus antedictis" (2 December 1313; MNL OL DL 1837, edited in AOklt, iii, pp. 285–286 [no 635]).
26 Kubinyi, *Anfänge Ofens*, pp. 71–77; András Kubinyi, "Die Zusammensetzung des städtischen Rates im mittelalterlichen Königreich Ungarn," *Südostdeutsches Archiv* 34–35 (1991–1992), pp. 23–42.
27 Bernát L. Kumorovitz, "Adatok Budapest főváros Árpád-kori történetéhez," [Data on the history of Budapest in the Árpádian period] *Tanulmányok Budapest Múltjából* 19 (1972), pp. 7–37.

a *hospes* settlement of merchants and tradesmen, near the harbor. Because the medieval town cannot be properly mapped to modern Óbuda, we do not know its overall structure or street plan, although archaeological excavations have uncovered some details.[28]

Szentjakabfalva and Szentháromságfalva have been even less researched than Óbuda. The geographical setting – a narrow strip of land between the hills and the riverbank – effectively dictated a linear layout along the Danube. The land owned by the Knights Hospitallers of Felhévíz, however, was not restricted to the riverside. It extended over many of the adjoining hills (today *Rózsadomb, Szemlő-hegy, Rókus-hegy*), with their intensively-cultivated vineyards.[29]

The boundaries of Buda at this time are not known exactly, but could not have embraced a very wide area. To the north, at the hot springs, the city came up against the estate of the Dominican nuns of Margaret Island, and at the south end, the Castle District stretched almost down to the river and directly adjoined Kispest. The only opportunities for Buda to own external land lay in the valley (today *Ördög-árok*) and the vine-growing hills to the west, but its actual possessions there are unknown. It did make efforts to expand, however, and acquired the vine-growing village of Nándor on the slopes of Nándor Hill (now *Svábhegy*) before 1323. The separate *hospes* settlement of Kispest also merged with Buda in the early fourteenth century, thus bringing within the city boundaries the vine-covered hills of Madár Hill (today *Nap-hegy*) and Pest Hill (or Gellért Hill) which directly neighbored Castle Hill to the south. Even with these additions, however, Buda's landholdings remained somewhat modest.[30]

The city itself was of quite sizable proportions. The fortress of the Castle District (*castrum*) ran parallel with the Danube for about a kilometre and a half on a plateau about 50–80 metres above the water level. Nature constrained it to an elongated triangular ground plan, varying between 150 and 400 metres in width. Its streets were laid out to a deliberate – if not geometrically-regular – plan that has largely remained intact up to the present day.[31] Plots of uniform size were laid out on the inside of the castle walls around the irregular perimeter of

---

28   László Gerevich, "The Rise of Hungarian Towns along the Danube," in *Towns in Medieval Hungary*, ed. idem (Budapest: Akadémiai, 1990), pp. 26–50, here p. 35 fig. 7; Altmann and Bertalan, "Óbuda," pp. 113–131; Júlia Altmann, "Óbuda," in *Medium regni*, pp. 89–109.
29   Kubinyi, *Anfänge Ofens*, pp. 23–25.
30   Végh, *Buda*, i, pp. 35–38.
31   András Végh, "Plot and System of Plots in a 13th Century Founded Hungarian Royal Town – the Example of Buda," in *Trnava a počiatky stredovekých miest* [Trnava and the beginnings of medieval towns] (Pamiatky Trnavy a Trnavského kraja, 12), ed. Jaroslava Žuffová (Trnava: Mesto Trnava and Krajský pamiatkový úrad Trnava, 2009), pp. 79–86.

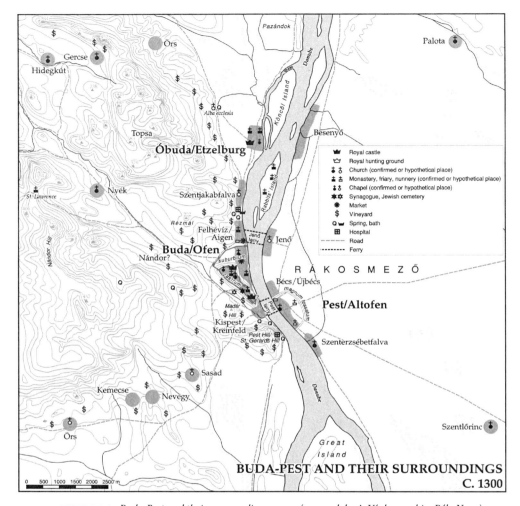

FIGURE 7.2 *Buda-Pest and their surroundings c. 1300 (research by A. Végh, graphics Béla Nagy)*

the hill, and these determined the route of the streets.[32] The tapering southern end could accommodate only the plots along the castle walls and one central block. Two market places, one in the north and one in the middle, occupied the area between the plots along the castle wall. Between the two market places, the plateau was wide enough for two blocks to be marked out for building. These were also made up of uniform plots and aligned with the castle wall on

32   The original plots measured out on the Castle Hill at the time of the foundation were more or less quadrangular, with their longer sides being twice as long as the shorter ones, i.e. the façades, that were c. 19–20 meters long.

the west side. The two elongated blocks thus formed between the four streets connecting the market places conformed to the line of the west castle wall on one side and were forced into an irregular form on the other, to take account of the east wall. On the east side, the area between and around the parish church, the Dominican friary and the royal house deviated somewhat from this regular system, probably because the sites of these buildings were allocated prior to the parceling of the land.[33]

On the hillside to the north of the castle, and on the longer hillside and flat land to the east down to the Danube, the *suburbium* stretched along a distance of 1.8 kilometres and occupied approximately twice as much area as the Castle District. It was not, however, uniformly built over. Plots containing residential buildings were built more densely in the south, extending up the hill all the way to the castle wall at some points. Beside the Danube, the edge of the built-up area hardly reached the boundary with the hot springs, and there were only a few houses on the farms and gardens on the north slopes of the hill. The streets of the suburb were laid out around the Roman road running alongside the Danube. Streets and roads ran perpendicularly towards the Castle District in the south and to the highway to Székesfehérvár under Castle Hill. On the little plain that enters a valley in the north, at some distance from Castle Hill, a system of streets formed a rectangular grid, possibly influenced by the remains of an old Roman settlement.[34]

The settlement of Kispest, lying in a very narrow valley entrance, was confined to the surroundings of the ferry on the north side of the stream flowing into the Danube (now *Ördög-árok*). It lay on the road beside the Danube, and there was another main route running perpendicularly from the ferry towards the highway to Székesfehérvár. The scattered excavations carried out in this area have not revealed the structure of Kispest. Its outskirts, as we have seen,

---

33   The street system of Sopron inside the Roman walls followed the same pattern as that of Buda. See Katalin Szende, "Settlement structure and topography in Sopron between the Hungarian Conquest and late seventeenth century," in Ferenc Jankó, József Kücsán and Katalin Szende, *Sopron* (Hungarian Atlas of Historic Towns, 1) (Sopron: Győr-Moson-Sopron Megye Soproni Levéltára – Győr-Moson-Sopron Megyei Múzeumok Igazgatósága Soproni Múzeum, 2010), pp. 16–17.

34   Végh, *Buda*, i, pp. 88–96; Katalin H. Kérdő, "Die Anfänge von Aquincum und die Änderungen in der Siedlungsstruktur in Víziváros in den Jahrhunderten der Römerzeit. Archäologischen Angaben zur Geschichte von Aquincum-Víziváros," in *Die norisch-pannonischen Städte und das römische Heer im Lichte der neuesten archäologischen Forschungen* (Budapest: Pro Aquinco Stiftung – Budapest Historisches Museum, 2005), pp. 83–99.

extended to the hills of Madár Hill (today *Nap-hegy*) and Gellért Hill, and were almost entirely planted with vines.[35]

On the opposite bank of the Danube, our topographical knowledge is somewhat less definite. The village of Besenyő has been located by archaeological research, but its layout remains unknown.[36] Not even the archaeologists have discovered the village of Jenő, and Bécs/Újbécs is almost equally obscure. We know that there was a large ditch dividing the part of Újbécs granted to the Dominican nuns of Margaret Island from the part acquired by the burghers of Pest, and the same ditch ran right round the town of Pest.[37] Its route, however, has so far eluded archaeological investigation. Pest occupied an island surrounded by a former backwater of the Danube, a marshy stream called the Rákos-árok, but this was some distance away, and the ditch around the town is usually thought to have been artificial, running along the semicircular course of the later town walls (today's Kiskörút). Around 1300, however, the town of Pest does not seem to have reached the ditch. The topographical references to the Franciscan and Dominican friaries in Pest suggest that they were built within the ditch but outside the town of the time, or at its edge.[38] Upon being resettled after the Mongol invasion, Pest presumably did not reach its former dimensions. There is a clear inner area of the city ground plan which is separated from the outer part by a semicircle, approximately concentric with the ditch.[39] The rebuilt town must only have extended across this area. The skeleton of its street plan was dictated by the road along the bank of the Danube and the roads perpendicular to it running up to the ferry harbors. Several minor perpendicular streets and squares connected the riverside road with the Danube. The square shaped market place in the middle of the town formed up on the site of a late Roman fort.[40]

As far as we know, the territory of Pest was confined to the inhabited land. To the north, it directly adjoined Újbécs, and to the north-east it was bounded by the land of the Premonstratensian provostry of St Michael on Margaret

---

35 Végh, *Buda*, i, pp. 88–89.
36 Eszter Kovács, "Budapest, XIII. Cserhalom utca – Rákos patak – Váci út – Csavargyár utca," [Budapest, 13th district, Cserhalom Street – Rákos Stream – Csavargyár Street] in *Archaeological investigations in Hungary, 2007*, ed. Júlia Kisfaludi (Budapest: KÖH, 2008), pp. 197–198.
37 ÁMTF, iv, p. 552.
38 "apud ecclesiam beati Petri in Rakus" (10 October 1307: MNL OL DL 39 259, AOklt, ii, pp. 110–111 (no 243), edited in CD, viii/1, pp. 221–223 [no 105]); "in loco fratrum predicatorum iuxta flumen ipsum sito…in dicto loco predicatorum prope civitatem Pestensem ultra ipsum Danubium ex opposito dicti castri…" (1308: Mon. Vat. i/2, p. 116 and 118).
39 It runs along Régiposta Street, Városház Street, Cukor Street and Nyári Pál Street.
40 Irás-Melis, "Die Wiederaufbau," pp. 366–369.

Island. We do not know its neighbors to the east and south-east, but Rákos Field, which accommodated the Hungarian diets, is unlikely to have belonged to the town. Finally, the direct neighbor on the bank of the Danube to the south was the village of Szenterzsébet.[41] Pest was not, however, left entirely without outlying land. The charter granted by Béla IV gave the town the Kövérföld area (presumably where Kőbánya is today, the 10th District of Budapest) for purposes of cultivation. It is unlikely, however, that Kövérföld actually adjoined the land of the town itself.[42]

The Royal Seat

When the king was in the Buda-Pest area in the period around 1300, he usually resided in the royal house in Buda (the *Kammerhof*).[43] This was a complex at the north-eastern tip of the fortified town and not separated from it. Its frontage directly faced the street between the Dominican friary and the Saturday Gate.[44] Contemporary views show that it must have had several towers, but the few and scattered archaeological excavations carried out so far have only identified one.[45] Various parts of buildings have come to light, but cannot yet be connected into a system, although some have been identified

---

41 The exact location of Szenterzsébet has not been clarified. Katalin Irás-Melis locates its center by the former nunnery of the Poor Clares that stood in Szerb Street; according to other opinions the settlement occupied the site where the ruins of the so-called Pusztatemplom (Desolate church) of Ferencváros were to be found. Knowing the location of the Dominican friary of Pest would greatly facilitate the identification: "directam et equalem medietatem cuiusdam possessionis Zenthfalua vocate in fine civitatis Pestiensis, ubi esset claustrum fratrum predicatorum, existentis" (12 September 1403: BTOE, iii/1, pp. 178–179 [no 363]).

42 EFHU, iii/2, pp. 39–41 (no 34).

43 László Zolnay, "A XIII–XIV. századi királyi palotáról. A budai várostörténet néhány kritikus kérdése," [On the thirteenth–fourteenth century royal palace. Some critical questions of the urban history of Buda] *A Művészettörténeti Dokumentációs Központ Évkönyve* (1959–1960), pp. 7–64; László Zolnay, "Opus Castri Budensis. A XIII. századi budai vár kialakulása," [The formation of Buda Castle in the thirteenth century] *Tanulmányok Budapest Múltjából* 15 (1963), pp. 43–107; Kubinyi, *Anfänge Ofens*, pp. 56–61; Végh, *Buda*, i, pp. 269–272.

44 Its location is comparable to that of the so-called Královský dvůr in the Old Town of Prague.

45 László Zolnay, "Ásatások a budai I., Táncsics Mihály u. 9. területén. A XIII–XIV. századi budai királyi rezidencia kérdéséhez," [Excavations in Buda, 9 Táncsics Mihály Street. On the question of the royal residence in Buda in thirteenth–fourteenth centuries] *Archaeologiai Értesítő* 94 (1967), pp. 39–47; László Zolnay, "Ásatások a budai I., Táncsics Mihály u. 9. területén," [Excavations in Buda, 9 Táncsics Mihály Street] *Archeologiai Értesítő* 95 (1968), pp. 40–60.

as the foundations of the royal chapel consecrated to St Martin.[46] A written source mentions that the *Kammerhof* lay beside a gate in the city wall. The charters which mention the royal residence use the expressions "house" and "royal court", which do not properly convey the fortified character of the complex in this strategically important corner of the town, but they do give its location. It did not have a very large floor plan. It was about 70 metres long, covering the area of only four average plots, and could only have expanded along the street within the strip about 40–50 metres wide between the street and the castle wall. Since kings spent so much of their time in Buda, the dignitaries who frequented the court and the courtiers themselves had to have appropriate accommodation there. They were required to become citizens before acquiring property, which they usually sought near the royal residence.[47]

The tapering south end of the town may also have been royal property. The earliest building there was Stephen's Tower, but whether it was already standing at that time or was erected only in the 1340s is still disputed.[48] It certainly could not yet have been connected to a building complex capable of accommodating the royal court.[49]

The other royal residence in Buda-Pest, the palace of Óbuda, had been in frequent use during the century up to 1300. King Andrew III preferred his Buda residence during the second part of his reign, and, after he died, his successors usually granted their Óbuda castle to one of their powerful followers.[50] Historians now unanimously identify the royal palace of Óbuda with the building excavated beside the southwest corner of the late Roman fort, outside the fort walls.[51] It was a square palace of small floor area (about 30 × 30 metres)

---

46   Katalin H. Gyürky, "A Szent Márton kápolna régészeti maradványai Budán," [Archaeological remains of the St Martin Chapel in Buda] *Archeologiai Értesítő* 111 (1984), pp. 29–42.

47   Végh, *Buda*, i, pp. 320–321.

48   Enikő Spekner, "Adalékok a budavári István torony névadójának kérdéséhez," [Contributions to the question of the origin of the name of the Stephen's Tower of Buda Castle] *Budapest Régiségei* 35 (2002), pp. 403–426.

49   Károly Magyar, "Adatok a budai István-torony kérdésköréhez," [Information on the question of the Stephen Tower at Buda] in *"Es tu scholaris." Ünnepi tanulmányok Kubinyi András 75. születésnapjára* [Studies in honor of András Kubinyi on the occasion of his 75th birthday] (Monumenta Historica Budapestinensia, 13), eds Beatrix F. Romhányi *et al.* (Budapest: BTM, 2004), pp. 13–36.

50   During the fight over the dynastic succession, first the Kőszegi family and then Máté Csák were owners of the castle; during Charles I's reign it was granted to the Drugeths: ÁMTF, iv, pp. 685–686.

51   Altmann and Bertalan, "Óbuda," pp. 124–128; Júlia Altmann, "Neue Forschungen über die Burg der Königin in Óbuda," *Acta Archaeologica Academiae Scientiarum Hungaricae* 34 (1982), pp. 221–233.

standing in a courtyard enclosed by a walled moat and a regular trapezium-shaped castle wall, and had a 10 × 10 metre courtyard in the center. A tower rose up in the center of the north range, connected to a chapel on the east side. The excavated remains date the building to the first quarter of the thirteenth century, and it was clearly aligned with the walls of the late Roman fort, as its location demanded. The name *civitas Athile regis/Budavár/Etzilburg* which appears in the twelfth century must have referred to the walls of the Roman fort in some repaired condition.[52] The question remains as to how the two castles were related, and when the Roman fort lost its function. At present, this seems to have been precipitated by the Mongol invasion, but nothing certain can be said.

Some historians have claimed that there was also a royal house in Pest.[53] Our present knowledge does not support this proposition, which is based on some documents concerning Werner's palace, a record mentioning a fifteenth-century "Bécs Castle" and some archaeological findings (tower remains, stove tiles decorated with the royal arms). These, however, should be seen as items of separate provenance.

In the second half of the thirteenth century, kings also frequently spent time beside the nunnery on Margaret Island. The palace building with a rectangular floor-plan excavated to the north of the convent has been archaeologically identified as the house of the royal court.[54] After the Árpád dynasty died out, however, kings rarely made personal visits to the convent.

A favorite hunting ground for kings around 1300, as it had been for many centuries, was the so-called *Magna Insula* (today Csepel Island). Unfortunately the remains of the royal lodge at the north end of the island have yet to be found; nor are there written records as to when it was built.[55] The dates of charters issued by kings hunting on the island cannot be relied on, because they may have spent many nights in a tent.

Tents were also the accommodation for the assembled nobility of the kingdom when they held diets at that time on Rákos Field, near Pest.[56] Rákos Field was also called "the center of the realm" (*medium regni*), indicating its

---

52   ÁMTF, iv, pp. 661–663.
53   Irás-Melis, "Die Wiederaufbau," pp. 371–372; Irásné Melis, "A pesti városalaprajz," pp. 99–101.
54   Katalin Irásné Melis, "Régészeti adatok a budapesti 11–13. századi királyi udvarhelyek kutatásához," [Archaeological information on the research of royal manors in Budapest in the eleventh–thirteenth centuries] *Budapest Régiségei* 33 (1999), pp. 297–308.
55   Irásné Melis, "Régészeti adatok," pp. 291–292.
56   ÁTMF, iv, pp. 550–551.

symbolic significance.[57] The absence of villages on what was an area of rich pastureland seems to have been deliberate. The nearest villages in the Pest area lay at a distance of 7–9 kilometres (Palota, Párdi, Szentmihály, Szentlőrinc and Gubacs) except along the bank of the Danube.

Defensive Function

In the period of war after 1301, the castle of Óbuda played no part in the hostilities, unlike the city of Buda, whose Castle District (*castrum*) was a major fortress, and a very modern one by Hungarian standards.[58] The top of Castle Hill was surrounded by a single wall which followed the irregular lines of the edge of the plateau. Two metres wide at the foundations, the stone wall was reinforced by semicircular and square towers at regular intervals along the north and west sides. Many of these have been uncovered by archaeological excavations. No towers are known of on the east side, but the royal palace and the Dominican and Franciscan friaries were built into the wall. The wall had a total length of about three kilometres and enclosed an area of about 27 hectares, a much larger fortified area than the royal castles at the centers of the counties and larger even than any other walled town in Hungary.[59]

There were major gates at four places in the wall. At the north, the Saturday Gate (today's *Bécsi kapu*, i.e. Vienna Gate) opened onto one of the town's market-places. Two mutually-opposite gates opened directly on to the other market place, which lay where the plateau narrows: St John's Gate (today *Vízi kapu* i.e. Water Gate) on the east side towards the Danube and Jewish Gate to the west towards the vine hills and the Székesfehérvár highway (today Fehérvári kapu). At the south, the Kreinfeld Gate led to Kispest (*Kreinfeld*), but its exact location is not known.

---

57   6 July 1299/1299 – ÁMTF, iv, p. 551.
58   Károly Magyar, "Buda im 13. Jahrhundert" in *Budapest im Mittelalter*, pp. 153–184, here pp. 160–162; András Végh, "A középkori várostól a török erődig. A budai vár erődítéseinek változásai az alapítástól a tizenötéves háborúig," [From the medieval town to the Ottoman fortress. The changing of the fortifications of Buda Castle from the foundation to the Fifteen Years War] *Budapest Régiségei* 31 (1997), pp. 295–312, here pp. 295–296.
59   In medieval Hungary, only the walls of Trnava had a comparable length of 3 km. The walls of Košice, Levoča and Sibiu were also significant, but somewhat shorter in their perimeter. The walls of the Old Town of Prague were c. 3.5 km long; those of Cracow's Old Town measured a little more than 3 km. See Zdeněk Dragoun, "Schema der Entwicklung von selbständigen befestigten Anlagen in Prag bis Mitte des 13. Jahrhunderts," in *Burg und Stadt* (Castrum Bene, 6) ed. Thomáš Durdík (Prague: Archeologický Ústav AV ČR, 1999), pp. 33–40.

The other part of Buda-Pest were not surrounded by fortifications. Pest had no walls in 1300. It was surrounded only by a ditch, whose defensive function is debatable. In Óbuda, the Roman town walls did not, as far as is presently known, fulfill any defensive function. Archaeological research has demonstrated the continued use of some towers, but probably with different functions.

Churches and Graveyards

Buda-Pest was not an episcopal seat. In the *medium regni*, St Stephen founded an archiepiscopal seat in Esztergom, and collegiate chapters were established in Székesfehérvár and Óbuda.[60] The chapter was outside the jurisdiction of the bishop of Veszprém, whose diocese was otherwise territorially the most competent, and was directly subject to the archbishop of Esztergom. The ecclesiastical jurisdiction of the Óbuda chapter, however, only extended to the area of Óbuda, which belonged to it, and not to the whole of Buda-Pest. It constituted a place of authentication, i.e. an office authorized to issue authenticated documents, recognized throughout the realm, and its provosts in this period held several times the offices of chancellor or vice-chancellor in the royal court.[61] The church of the chapter, consecrated to St Peter, lay within the area of the late Roman fort (on the east side of today's Fő Square in Óbuda). Archaeological excavations have so far found only details of some walls and fragments of stone-carvings, and its full ground plan is still uncertain.[62] The church suffered severe damage during the Mongol invasion, and although it was eventually repaired, it may still have been partially in ruins around 1300. In the church graveyard there stood a chapel to the Virgin Mary which accommodated a small chapter with a staff of six. The canons' houses lay in a row beside the church and thus also within the area of the former Roman fort. The civilian community to the south of the chapter had a chapel consecrated to St Margaret.[63] The little church which held the parish rights in Óbuda around 1300 was in the peculiar position of lying outside the town, at the foot of the vine slopes, in an area which was uninhabited at that time.[64] St Mary's Church was also known as the White Church (*Alba ecclesia*), and may have been the earliest

---

60   Medieval tradition connects the foundation of the Óbuda chapter to St Stephen, but the chapter was most probably established under his successor, King Peter.
61   László Bártfai Szabó, *Óbuda egyházi intézményei a középkorban* [The ecclesiastical institutions of Óbuda in the Middle Ages] (Budapest: [n. p.], 1935), pp. 8–14.
62   Júlia Altmann, Vilmosné Bertalan and Zoltán Kárpáti, "A budai (óbudai) társaskáptalan Péter temploma [The St Peter Church of the Buda (Óbuda) Chapter]," *Budapest Régiségei* 37 (2003), pp. 39–62.
63   Bártfai Szabó, *Óbuda*, p. 46.
64   Bártfai Szabó, *Óbuda*, pp. 14–27.

medieval Christian church in Óbuda (the Christian past of Roman Aquincum having been lost to memory). Local tradition of the fifteenth century attributed its foundation to Charlemagne.[65] In the period around 1300, the chapter exercised parish rights through one of its canons.

Besides the Óbuda chapter, there were another two church entities which possessed substantial lands in the area: the Knights Hospitallers of St Stephen, based in the area of the hot springs, and the Dominican nuns of Margaret Island. The Hungarian-founded Stephanites of Esztergom were granted the Holy Trinity Church among the hot springs in 1187, and set up a priory there. The Stephanites enjoyed a papal exemption. We do not know the form of their early church among the Buda springs, but archaeological excavation has discovered a fourteenth- or fifteenth-century church which was presumably built on the same site. It lies to the south of the springs on the west side of the road beside the Danube (on the site of the building which now stands on the corner of Török Street and Margit Boulevard).[66]

King Béla IV founded the Dominican nunnery dedicated to the Virgin Mary on Margaret Island at the same time as the town of Buda. The nuns received spiritual guidance from the Dominican friars, and their convent was under the direct jurisdiction of the pope. They also received a large part of the island as an estate, together with the village of Jenő at the ferry on the left bank, opposite the southern tip of the island, part of the estate of Újbécs, and a minor estate among the hot springs on the right bank. The convent itself lay on the east side of the island towards the north, and its ruins have been the subject of several excavations. At the center of a complex of several courtyards stood a single-nave church with a nuns' gallery, on the south side was the convent house around a cloister, and to the north was a palace where the king took residence. The small monastery of the Premonstratensian Order on the island

---

65 Bonfini, *Decades*, I-IX-239–240 (p. 193); Gregorius Gyöngyösi, *Vitae fratrum eremitarum Ordinis Sancti Pauli primi eremitae*, ed. Ferenc Hervay (Budapest: Akadémiai, 1988), p. 124. This tradition can be neither confirmed nor disproved. Anonymus considers this church the oldest one, being built by Árpád's grave. See Anonymus, *Gesta Hungarorum – The Deeds of the Hungarians* (Central European Medieval Texts, 5), eds Martyn Rady and László Veszprémy (Budapest – New York: Central European University Press, 2010), pp. 114–115 (cap. 52).

66 Géza Supka, "A budafelhévizi Szentháromság-templom," [The Holy Trinity Church of Budafelhévíz] *Archaeologiai Értesítő* 27 (1907), pp. 97–119; Károly-György Boroviczényi, "Cruciferi sancti regis Stephani. Tanulmányok a stefaniták, egy középkori magyar ispotályos rend történetéről," [Studies on the history of the medieval Hungarian Order of Hospitallers, the Stephanites] *Orvostörténeti Közlemények* 37–38 (1991–1992), pp. 7–48.

lay not far to the north of the convent, with a church dedicated to St Michael.[67] We will later describe the Franciscan friary on the island.

Finally, there was a tiny hermit's cell dedicated to St Lawrence in the forest of Nándor Hill above Buda (today *Szép Juhászné*, in the saddle between the hills of *János-hegy* and *Hárs-hegy*). Hermits of the Hungarian-founded Pauline Order began to build their first friary here around 1300, and later extended it through donations by King Charles I, the *rector* of Buda Hans (*Johannes*), son of Heinz (*Hench*) and other Buda citizens. It soon grew into the center of the Hungarian-founded order of friars.[68]

These were the ecclesiastical institutions which owned land in Buda-Pest, but there were also church entities within them. It should be pointed out that towns in Hungary typically had a single parish church covering the whole community, the only exceptions being where the population was divided along ethnic, geographical or even historical lines.[69] All of these exceptions are to be found in the ecclesiastical history of Buda-Pest. There were three autonomous parish churches operating in Buda-Pest around 1300, every one of them excluded from the jurisdiction of the diocesan episcopates by virtue of their royal foundation.[70] The oldest among them was the parish church of Pest, whose origins can be traced to the eleventh century. The parish church dedicated to the Virgin Mary was built in the south-eastern corner of the Roman fort. In the early fourteenth century, the walls of the Roman fort were no longer standing, and the church was situated to the south of a square market-place in the center of the town, beside the Danube. Some details of that building have been found: parts of the three-nave church's foundations and a stretch of wall from a tower on the west frontage.[71] The parish church of Kispest was dedicated to St Gerard, the bishop who was martyred there. It is first mentioned in the first half of the thirteenth century, before the Mongol invasion, but we do not know when it was built or exactly where. It cannot be definitely identified with the church ruins found on the south side of *Erzsébet-híd* (i.e. Elizabeth Bridge), and no archaeological excavation has yet been carried out on what is

---

67　Irás-Melis, "Die Margareteninsel," pp. 409–414.

68　Zoltán Bencze, "Die Paulinerorden im mittelalterlichen Ungarn. Das Hauptkloster von Budaszentlőrinc im Spiegel geschichtlicher und archäologischer Daten," in *Budapest im Mittelalter*, pp. 415–425.

69　de Cevins, *Az egyház*, pp. 20–26.

70　Jankovich, "Buda-környék," pp. 57–98.

71　Lajos Némethy, *A pesti főtemplom története* [The history of the main parish church in Pest] (Budapest: Rudyánszky, 1890); Katalin Irás-Melis, "Die Herausbildung und Entwicklung der Stadt Pest bis 1241," in *Budapest im Mittelalter*, pp. 132–143, here pp. 138–139.

today the site of Tabán parish church.[72] The parish church of Buda, like that of Pest, was dedicated to the Virgin Mary. The Parish Church of Our Lady lay in the middle of the Castle District directly adjacent to the east castle wall. Its location was unusual in the sense of not being positioned in the center of the newly-founded city's market-place, even though a suitable site was available, but was connected to the north end of the market place via a narrow lane. The church was a three-nave basilica with an elongated polygonal apse. It completely filled the space between the street and the castle wall, and was surrounded by a graveyard.[73] There were also two chapels which belonged to the parish from the time of its inception. The Chapel of St Mary Magdalene lay on the north part of the Castle District, in the middle of the square where markets were held on Saturdays. An excavation of its ruins, under the former Garrison Church, has revealed it to have been a single-nave building reminiscent of a simple village church, with a short straight apse.[74] On the site of the former Roman settlement in the flat northern part of the suburb, two streets away from the bank of the Danube, at what is now the corner of Csalogány Street and Medve Street, archaeological excavations have uncovered some details of another small single-nave building with an elongated polygonal apse, the St Peter Martyr Church.[75]

Besides the parish churches, there were seven mendicant-order friaries and two Beguine convents in Buda-Pest. The Franciscans had four friaries, the Dominicans two, and the Austin Hermits one. The Dominican friary of St Anthony in Pest was built before the Mongol invasion, and the same may be presumed

---

72   Jankovich, "Buda-környék," pp. 81–82; Sándor Garády, "Budapest székesfőváros területén végzett középkori ásatások összefoglaló ismertetése 1931–1941. I. Egyházi célú maradványok és temetők feltárása," [On the excavations carried out in the territory of Budapest, 1931–1941, I. Church remains and cemeteries] *Budapest Régiségei* 13 (1943), pp. 167–254, here pp. 184–193.

73   Lajos Némethy, *Nagyboldogasszonyról nevezett budapestvári főtemplom történelme* [History of the main parish church of Our Lady in Buda] (Esztergom: Horák Egyed, 1876); József Csemegi, *A budavári főtemplom középkori építéstörténete* [The architectural history of the main parish church of Buda in the Middle Ages] (Budapest: Képzőművészeti Alap, 1955); Magyar, "Buda im 13. Jahrhundert," pp. 166–168; Enikő Spekner, "A budavári Boldogasszony-egyház alapítástörténete," [The foundation of the Church of Our Lady of Buda Castle] *Budapest Régiségei* 37 (2003), pp. 91–112.

74   Vilmosné Bertalan, "Mittelalterliche Baugeschichte der Maria-Magdalena-Pfarrkirche (später Garnisons-kirche) in der Budaer (Ofner) Burg," *Acta Technica* 67 (1970), pp. 229–231.

75   Katalin H. Gyürky, "Adatok a budai Szent Péter külváros topográfiájához," [Information on the topography of the Szent Péter suburb] *Budapest Régiségei* 22 (1971), pp. 223–243.

of the Franciscan friary of St Peter in Pest. The location of both is unknown, but under the rules of the mendicant orders, they must have been far from the town center, somewhere in the outskirts. The Dominican friary must have lain on the bank of the Danube in the south of Pest, and the Franciscan on the east side on the highway leading eastwards from the town (today Kossuth Lajos Street).[76] Things were different in Buda, where the Dominican and Franciscan friaries stood in the Castle District and the Austin friary in the suburb. There have been archaeological excavations on all three sites. The Dominican friary of St Nicholas occupied a key position on the east castle wall (now the Hilton Hotel) between the Church of Our Lady and the royal house.[77] The Franciscan friary of St John the Evangelist also stood beside the east wall, but in an out-of-the-way southern part of the Castle District (today the Várszínház, i.e. Castle Theater and the Sándor Palace).[78] The Austin friary of St Stephen Protomartyr stood on the hillside in the south of the suburb, at some distance from the St Peter Martyr Church, and had a graveyard on its northern side (the site is now 17–19 Szalag Street).[79] The Franciscans also had friaries in Óbuda and on Margaret Island. Church ruins excavated in front of the west gate of the late Roman fort in Óbuda have been identified as the Franciscan friary of St Francis.[80] The ruins of the convent of St Clare still stand in the middle of the west side of the island.[81] The Beguine house of the Franciscan third-order nuns stood opposite the Buda friary. Sources also mention a Dominican Beguine house in Buda, but its location is not known.[82]

In addition to the Christian churches, there was a synagogue in Buda, and in quite an unusual place, built directly on to one of the town gates (Jewish Gate).

76 ÁMTF, iv, pp. 538–543.
77 Katalin H. Gyürky, *Das mittelalterliche Dominikanerkloster in Buda* (Fontes Archaeologici Hungariae) (Budapest: Akadémiai, 1981).
78 Júlia Altmann, "Az óbudai és a budavári ferences templom és kolostor kutatásai," [The Franciscan churches and friaries of Óbuda and Buda Castle] in *Koldulórendi építészet a középkori Magyarországon* [Mendicant architecture in medieval Hungary] (Művészettörténet – Műemlékvédelem, 7), ed. Andrea Haris (Budapest: Országos Műemlékvédelmi Hivatal, 1994), pp. 143–148.
79 András Végh, "Medieval archaeology in urban site. Investigations in Budapest, I–II. Víziváros, the medieval suburb of the town of Buda," in *Vindobona – Aquincum. Probleme und Lösungen in der Stadtarchäologie* (Aquincum nostrum, ii/5), eds Paula Zsidi, Orsolya Láng and Annamária Szu (Budapest: Historisches Museum der Stadt Budapest, 2009), pp. 37–44, here p. 38.
80 Altmann, "Az óbudai," pp. 137–142.
81 Irás-Melis, "Die Margareteninsel," pp. 412–413.
82 Végh, *Buda*, i, pp. 61–62, 260 and 264–266.

It was a two-nave hall, of the larger type of Ashkenazy synagogues, and its dimensions match those of the synagogues of Prague and Vienna. The excavations have also discovered remains of a ritual bath on the south side of the synagogue.[83]

Plots, Dwellings, and their Occupants

Nowhere in the area of Buda-Pest has a single dwelling house from the period around 1300 survived in a form that could be described as intact. Archaeological excavations have yielded some knowledge of houses in Buda, and to a lesser extent of those in Óbuda and Pest.[84] There was a standardized system for building on the uniform-size plots of the Buda Castle District.[85] (In time, of course, plots were divided or merged, and this changed the pattern of building.) Each plot had an entrance in the middle, wide enough to admit a cart, and houses could be built on each side, aligned perpendicular to the street. The north side was usually built on first (the direction of the prevailing wind is north in Buda), but there were quite frequently houses on both sides of the gate. We know almost nothing about how many floors the houses had, but certain sources suggest that some buildings with upper floors existed even at that time.[86] There were also buildings in the interior of the plots: an outbuilding for storage was often built about half way along the boundary, and some plots also had a house at the end.[87] Cellars were cut out of the rock under most houses, and were almost a necessity for most citizens, because they owned vineyards, and made and stored their wine at home.[88] The main building materials were wood and stone. Even the cellars were often built of wood. Similar building methods have been found in the south of the suburb, while

---

83   András Végh, "Les synagogues de Buda (XIVᵉ et XVᵉ siècles): fouilles récentes," in *Archéologie du judaïsme en France et en Europe. Colloque international, Paris, 14 et 15 janvier 2010*, eds Paul Salmona and Laurence Sigal (Paris: La Découverte, 2011), pp. 215–224.

84   László Gerevich, "Gótikus házak Budán," [Gothic houses in Buda] *Budapest Régiségei* 15 (1950), pp. 123–238; András Végh and Judit Zádor, "Topographie und Architektur der Stadt Buda im Spätmittelalter," in *Budapest im Mittelalter*, pp. 292–314.

85   Végh, "Plot".

86   Examples include 3 and 4 Dísz Square, and 1 Hess András Square.

87   András Végh, "A Szent György utca 4–10. számú telkek régészeti ásatása. Előzetes jelentés," [Archaeological excavation of 4–10 Szent György Street. Preliminary report] *Tanulmányok Budapest Múltjából* 31 (2003), pp. 187–188.

88   András Kubinyi, "Weinbau und Weinhandel in den ungarischen Städten im Spätmittelalter und in der frühe Neuzeit." in *Stadt und Wein* (Beiträge zur Geschichte der Städte Mitteleuropas, 14), eds Ferdinand Opll and Susanne Claudine Pils (Linz: Österreichisches Arbeitskreis für Stadtgeschichtsforschung, 1996), pp. 67–84.

in the north, around the Parish Church of St Peter Martyr, wooden buildings predominated.[89]

Information on housing conditions in Buda-Pest, the identity of landowners and house owners, and the distribution of social classes in each settlement can only be gleaned in tiny fragments from a very small number of sources.[90] Most of the inhabitants of Buda and Pest belonged to the families of house-owning citizens (*cives*). Certainly, they are the only people mentioned in the surviving documents, which are silent on the poorer tenants and labourers. Most inhabitants were German, but there were also Hungarian and Jewish communities. In Óbuda, Szentháromságfalva, Kispest, Szenterzsébet and the villages owned by the Dominican nuns of Margaret Island, inhabitants with various rights as citizens are referred to in the sources as settlers or *hospites*. These were mainly Hungarians, but there were also many Germans in Kispest and Óbuda. Wedged among the citizens' properties were scattered families and communities serving the royal court of Buda. The Pest ferrymen lived within Pest, but separately from the town community, and were led by their own judge. There were royal fishermen in the suburb of Buda, and scattered royal vintners among the Buda springs. Most of the peoples who had formerly been in royal service, however, by then bore allegiance to ecclesiastical landlords (the Óbuda chapter, the Knights Hospitallers of Felhévíz, the Dominican nuns of Margaret Island). Examples are the ferrymen of Jenő and the vintners among the hot springs, both of whom were in the service of the Dominican nuns.

Buda is the only town for which we have anything more than a rough picture of the population.[91] Its local government was controlled by a group of property-owning citizens who also possessed land in the countryside and usually bore the title of *comes*. They built their houses at points scattered throughout the Castle District, but with a slight concentration in the north around the Dominican friary and the royal residence. They also had properties, gardens and farms in the suburb. The bulk of the citizenry was made up of merchants and craftsmen, but information concerning where they lived is sparse. There were also nobles who owned houses in Buda (as there were to a lesser extent in Óbuda), a condition for which was entry into the community of citizens. Houses belonging to noblemen are known of at many points of the Castle

---

89   Végh, "Medieval archaeology," pp. 38–42.
90   Kubinyi, *Anfänge Ofens*, pp. 91–99; Kubinyi, *Budapest*, pp. 60–67.
91   András Kubinyi, "Soziale Stellung und Familienverbindungen des deutschen Patriziat von Ofen in der ersten Hälfte des 14. Jahrhunderts," *Archiv für Sippenforschung* 36 (1970), pp. 446–454; Végh, *Buda*, i, pp. 329–333.

District, although they too tended to concentrate around the royal residence in the north.[92]

Buda-Pest around 1400

The Political Situation

Hungary's sovereign around 1400 was King Sigismund of Luxemburg. Sigismund faced severe troubles at the time. Indeed, he was taken captive for a while in 1401, and had to face a rebellion in 1403 aimed at inviting King Ladislas of Naples (1386–1414) to rule the country. He came through these tribulations successfully, however, and finally consolidated his power in the realm,[93] partly through an alliance with the Garai-Cillei league of barons, which he cemented by marrying Barbara of Cilli in 1405. Sigismund continued and completed the palace begun by his predecessor King Louis I and at the same time, over a period of a few years starting in 1408, transferred the administration and judiciary of the royal court from Visegrád to Buda.[94] This re-established the city as the royal seat, which it remained until the time of the Ottoman conquest.

The Legal Status of the Urban Agglomeration and the Towns

Buda-Pest comprised essentially the same settlements around 1400 as it had a hundred years previously, the only additions being a few villages around Buda.[95] Logod (first mentioned in 1390), a village belonging to the Buda parish priest, grew up on the west slope of Castle Hill, directly beneath the Castle District. The queen's village of Kelenföld (first mentioned in 1380) lay at the south foot of Gellért Hill. Kispest was by this time a suburb of Buda, and its name changed to Alhévíz ("lower, i.e. southern hot springs"). The name Felhévíz (i.e. "upper hot springs") came to be used for the settlement among the springs to the north of Buda. Together with Alhévíz, the suburb of Buda stretched for about two and a half kilometres along the bank of the Danube.

92 Végh, *Buda*, i, pp. 318–321.
93 Kubinyi, *Budapest*; Rady, *Buda*.
94 Márta Kondor, "Hof, Residenz und Verwaltung: Ofen und Blindenburg in der Regierungszeit König Sigismunds – unter besonderer Berücksichtigung der Jahre 1410–1419," in *Kaiser Sigismund (1368–1437) – Urkunden und Herrschaftspraxis eines europäischen Monarchen*, eds Karel Hruza and Alexandra Kaar (Vienna – Cologne – Weimar: Böhlau, 2012), pp. 215–233.
95 Kubinyi, "Topographic," pp. 132–157; Végh, *Buda*, i, pp. 39–40 and 88–89.

There were important changes in property ownership in Óbuda.[96] By that time, the town had been divided into two districts, one belonging to the chapter and the other to the queen. The majority of property in the latter was held by a new ecclesiastical institution, the Poor Clares convent of the Virgin Mary. This all started in 1343, when King Louis I, at the commencement of his reign, provided a residence for the queen mother, Elizabeth Piast, by granting her the royal castle of Óbuda. In 1355, he marked out the area of Óbuda that should remain with the chapter, and granted the rest to the queen mother. She acquired the town's market-place and harbor, and from that time, the 'queen's town' had its own government, with a council of four councillors under a judge, like the Pest council. Queen Elizabeth had already founded a Poor Clares' convent in Óbuda with papal approval, and it was ready for the nuns to take up occupation by 1346.[97] The convent received many donations of property from the queen during her long life, and others from citizens of Óbuda. These comprised more than thirty houses, many of them mutually adjacent, a butcher's shop and a trading house (*domus apotecariorum*) and baths built by the queen. The Poor Clares thus accumulated substantial land within the queen's town, land which did not fall within the powers of the town authorities.

The relations between Buda and Pest started to change after 1400. Pest's judge was no longer delegated by the Buda council, and its municipal government (the judge and four councillors) became independent of Buda.[98] Pest was able to extend its area to the north by annexing the southern part of Bécs/Újbécs. The village of Szenterzsébetfalva directly to the south, however, continued as a *hospes* settlement with an independent council of judge and councillors, and its property was divided among several landowners.[99]

The Boundaries and Ground Plans of the Constituent Settlements

The changes in internal structure and layout around 1400 are easiest to trace in Buda. The minimal information on Pest hardly warrants the term

---

96   Bernát L. Kumorovitz, "Óbuda 1355. évi felosztása," [The division of Óbuda in 1355] *Budapest Régiségei* 24, no 1 (1977), pp. 279–302.

97   Herta Bertalan, "Das Klarissinenkloster von Óbuda aus dem 14. Jahrhundert," *Acta Archaeologica Academiae Scientiarum Hungaricae* 34 (1982) pp. 151–176; eadem, "Corrardus 'procurator operum domine regine...senioris'," *Budapest Régiségei* 40 (2007), pp. 71–94.

98   Kubinyi, *Budapest*, p. 84.

99   18 July 1394 – BTOE, iii/1, pp. 87–88 (no 176); 12 September 1403 – BTOE, ii/1, pp. 178–179 (no 363).

'scattered'. There was a major change in property ownership in Óbuda, but the available archaeological and historical information is too meager to permit any topographical interpretation.[100] The inhabited area of the 'chapter's town' was divided from that of the 'queen's town' by a line running east–west from the queen's castle to the Danube. The convent of the Poor Clares stood in the southern part of the inhabited area. In the outskirts, the chapter only retained the northern stretch of the riverbank and the northern half of the vine slopes, the rest of the area being assigned to the queen's town.

In Buda, the system of streets and plots established in the years around 1300 was consolidated and expanded, particularly in the suburb.[101] The district of Tótfalu grew up on the north slope of Castle Hill (first mention 1390), along the routes from the Saturday Gate of the Castle District to the gates of the suburb. Tótfalu had a very loose layout, with large gardens between the house plots. Also to the north, but in the valley, was a settlement known only by the German name of Taschental (first referred to as such in the *Ofner Stadtrecht* of the early fifteenth century). It may be regarded as the western extension of the settlement around the Church of St Peter Martyr. The Carmelite friary formed here the center of the district.

Changes in the Castle District followed the relocation of the royal residence and the large-scale construction of the royal palace to the south (see next chapter). After the royal house (*Kammerhof*) in the north was granted away in 1382, the area greatly depreciated in value. The changes caused by transfers of ownership, however, started to make their effects felt in the fifteenth century. Several citizens' plots were taken over for the construction of the new royal palace, and social effects here included the clearing of the Jewish quarter and the appreciation in value of the land.[102]

The Royal Seat

By 1400, the royal court of Buda was no longer where it had been a century before. King Louis I embarked on a major expansion of a small complex around Stephen's Tower at the southern end of the town in the 1360s. To the north of the existing buildings, on a triangular courtyard separated from the town by

---

100 Júlia Altmann and Herta Bertalan, "Óbuda im Spätmittelalter," in *Budapest im Mittelalter*, pp. 185–199.

101 Kubinyi, "Topographic," p. 147; Végh, *Buda*, i, pp. 92–96.

102 András Végh, "Középkori városnegyed a királyi palota előterében. A budavári Szent György tér és környezetének története a középkorban," [The medieval town quarter in the foreground of the royal palace. The history of the Szent György Square and its surroundings in the Middle Ages] *Tanulmányok Budapest Múltjából* 31 (2003), pp. 7–42; Végh, *Buda*, i, p. 321.

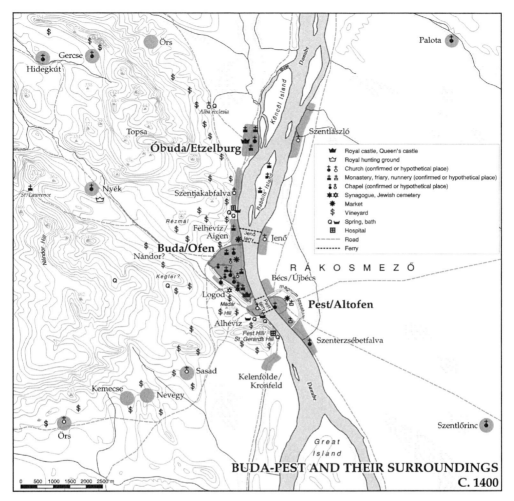

FIGURE 7.3 *Buda-Pest and their surroundings c. 1400 (research by A. Végh, graphics Béla Nagy)*

a ditch, he erected new palace buildings and a two-storey royal chapel, and renovated the old buildings.[103] In 1382, the king granted away the palace in the north of the town to his favorite religious order, the Paulines, and in particular their friary of St Lawrence, near Buda.[104] This grant is a sign that the new

103 Károly Magyar, "Der Königspalast in Buda," in *Budapest im Mittelalter*, pp. 201–235; Károly Magyar, "A középkori budai királyi palota fő építési korszakainak alaprajzi rekonstrukciója I.," [The reconstructed groundplans of the main architectural periods of the medieval royal palace of Buda] *Budapest Régiségei* 31 (1997), pp. 101–120.

104 Gyöngyösi, *Vitae fratrum*, pp. 77 and 185.

palace was capable by this time of accommodating the court. After the king died, construction continued under his daughter Queen Mary and took on new momentum under her husband, Sigismund of Luxemburg. As we have noted, Sigismund started to move the governing bodies and judiciary of the court from Visegrád to Buda in 1408, and he regarded this new principal residence as his capital city.[105] Gaining the titles of King of the Germans in 1410 and King of Bohemia in 1419 (ultimately becoming Holy Roman Emperor in 1433), he strove to build up the royal palace of Buda into a place of grandeur that befitted his new power.[106] He added further ranges to the south of the palace built by Louis, and to the northwest, at the end of the ditch, he raised the enormous Csonka (i.e. "Incomplete") Tower reminiscent of the towers of Karlštejn built by his father Emperor Charles IV. Encroaching onto the land of the city for a new north court, he cleared some 8–10 plots to erect several buildings, notably a hall – probably of two storeys – to accommodate large-scale receptions. A ditch was dug to divide the new court from the town. The royal palace was defended by new fortifications, which will be covered in the next section. The building resulted in a new royal residence within the boundaries of the city, although clearly delineated from it.[107] As well as being directly connected to the city of Buda in the north, the palace had a connection with Pest via the Danube ferry which landed right under its walls. As a consequence of its location, the palace dominated the city.

There was no major reconstruction of the queen's castle in Óbuda, but there were perceptible conversions in the palace building, involving the addition of a new and larger chancel to the palace chapel and the extension of the east range.[108]

Defensive Function

The fortifications of Buda developed considerably during the fourteenth century.[109] An outer wall was built in front of the inner wall, right at the perimeter of the plateau, in some places carved into the hillside like a retaining wall.

---

105 First mentioned as such in 1390; after this date, the term *castrum* was used for the royal palace instead of the city.

106 Magyar, "Der Königspalast"; Imre Holl, "A budai palota középkori építéstörténetének kérdései," [The questions of the architectural history of the medieval palace of Buda] *Budapest Régiségei* 31 (1997), pp. 79–99; Sándor Tóth, "Die Gebäude des Budaer Königspalastes zur Zeit Sigismunds von Luxemburg," in *Sigismundus Rex et Imperator*, pp. 200–218.

107 The location of the royal palace in Buda is very similar to that of the palace on the Hradčany within Prague.

108 Altmann, "Neue Forschungen," pp. 222 and 228.

109 Végh, "A középkori várostól," pp. 296–297; idem, *Buda*, i, pp. 104–107.

It had no towers, but was reinforced by relatively closely-spaced pillars. The wall was thinner than the inner town wall and its battlements were lower.[110] The suburb had also been fortified by then.[111] Because the suburb was bounded by the walls of the Castle District in the west, those of the royal palace in the south and the unfortified Danube in the east, it only needed a city wall in the north.[112] The new wall was a kilometre and a half in length. Starting from the northwest tip of the Castle District, it ran north to the foot of Castle Hill, where it turned east and gently curved along the boundary with Felhévíz (today's Vérmező Street, Margit Boulevard, Bem József Street) and down to the Danube. It was not reinforced by towers. It had four gates: the Tótfalu Gate (at what is now Várfok Street) towards the Székesfehérvár highway, shortly after that the Taschental Gate (at today's Széna Square), a little door (at Horvát Street), and finally the Felhévíz Gate at the riverside road (today Fő Street). What lay at the end of the wall on the bank of the Danube at this time is not known. The gun tower discovered by excavation is from a later period.[113]

From the south, the suburb was defended by the fortifications of the new royal palace.[114] These included two parallel walls, 80–100 metres apart, reaching down from the top of the hill to the road beside the Danube. Beside the riverbank, they were linked by another wall. The royal palace was completely surrounded by new walls. Although these connected to the outer town wall, they stood even lower down the hillside, and inner courtyards were laid out in the area between them and the palace. Connecting to the walls on the south side were outer curtain walls reaching down the gentle slope to Alhévíz and meeting at a point where there was a gate. To the west, there was another wall parallel with the main walls enclosing another outer courtyard lower down on the hillside.

Churches and Graveyards

The number of ecclesiastical institutions and churches in Buda-Pest increased remarkably in the period up to 1400. The most prominent patrons of the new foundations and building projects were King Louis I and his mother

---

110   The double circle of walls is typical of the fortification of Hungarian towns.
111   The dating of the walls of the suburbs is uncertain, and there have not been any excavations conducted in respect of these. The first piece of documentary evidence refers to a new gate in 1390.
112   Similar to the New Town of Prague, where the bank of the Vltava was encircled by walls – although they were much longer than in Buda – but the riverbank itself was not fortified.
113   Végh, *Buda*, i, pp. 104–108.
114   László Gerevich, *A budai vár feltárása* [The excavation of Buda Castle] (Budapest: Akadémiai 1966), pp. 227–238.

Queen Elizabeth, who were active in the middle of the fourteenth century.[115] Of particular note were two large building projects in Óbuda, the convent for the Poor Clares and a new church for the chapter, both attributable to Queen Elizabeth. These proceeded in parallel, the Poor Clares convent being finished by 1346 and the chapter's new church by 1348. The buildings have since completely decayed, but remains of their foundations have been uncovered by archaeological excavation.[116] The Poor Clares convent was in the south of Óbuda (at what is now the corner of Fényes Adolf Street and Perc Street), in the part of the town granted to the queen in 1355. It had three aisles divided into eight vault sections, and the western half was taken up by an enormous nuns' gallery supported by a single central pillar. Polygonal side chapels protruded from the walls on each side of the elongated chancel. The scattered surviving remains are enough to trace the floor plan, and tell of a 'modern' church constructed to high standards. Louis the Great referred to it in his charters as being "wonderfully crafted". The queen was buried in the Corpus Christi chapel beside the church in 1380. The convent, built around a large cloister, stood to the south. For two centuries, it accommodated a community of noble-born nuns and was well endowed with estates. The Óbuda Poor Clares convent was the last religious community to be richly endowed by royalty upon its establishment. The chapter's new church was built on the south side of the old St Peter's Church, already said to be partly in ruins (on what is the Fő Square of Óbuda). It was simpler and shorter than the Poor Clares' church, but had a similar floor plan. Apart from some stone carvings and fresco fragments, nothing remains of its famed beauty, the subject of several complimentary descriptions.

We also know of other constructions in Óbuda. After the queen's town was marked out in 1355, the parish rights passed from St Mary's Church (*Alba ecclesia*) to St Margaret's Chapel, which thus became due for a major extension. The remains of St Margaret's Church await archaeological excavation under today's Óbuda Parish Church, and so far only the remains of one side chapel have come to light.[117] A charter mentions a chapel dedicated

---

115 Bernát Kumorovitz L., "Idősb Erzsébet királyné építkezéseinek történetéhez," [On the history of the building activity of the Elder Queen Elizabeth] *Tanulmányok Budapest Múltjából* 17 (1966), pp. 9–26; Altmann and Bertalan, "Óbuda im Spätmittelalter," pp. 185–199.

116 Bertalan, "Das Klarissinenkloster."

117 Csaba Csorba, "Az óbudai Szt. Margit egyház és környékének kutatása," [Research on the St Margaret's Church of Óbuda and its surroundings] *Budapest Régiségei* 24, no 1 (1976), pp. 257–268.

to St Ladislas beside the queen's castle (1413), but its precise location is yet unknown.[118]

The activities of King Louis and his mother, Queen Elizabeth, in founding and building churches also extended to Buda. In the *Kammerhof*, the royal residence of the time, the royal chapel dedicated to St Martin was renovated at the turn of the 1340s and 1350s. Parts of its foundations have been excavated under 7 Táncsics Mihály Street.[119] Later, in the royal palace being built in the south of the town, Louis started building a new two-storey chapel dedicated to the Virgin Mary. Its lower chapel has been restored and is open to visitors.[120] The king built a chapel dedicated to St George in the most important market place of the town around 1370, and it was raised to the rank of rectorate, independent of the parish churches. It stood at the north end of what is now Dísz Square, and was completely demolished in 1688.[121] The king and queen founded a Carmelite friary in Taschental, a relatively sparsely populated district in the north of the suburb of Buda, in 1372, and it was occupied mainly by German-born monks. Excavations have uncovered the foundations of the east and south wings of the friary, which was completely demolished during the period of Ottoman rule. The building was surrounded by a graveyard and garden enclosed by a stone wall.[122]

The citizens of Buda were also involved in founding churches. The councillor, Wulving *comes*, founded a chapel dedicated to the Holy Kings of Hungary, subsequently more commonly known as St Ladislas's Chapel, in the graveyard of the Parish Church of Our Lady. We have no information on the origins of St Michael's Chapel, which also stood in the graveyard, but on the hillside. Neither do we know the founder of All Saints' chapel, which gave its name to the street in front, but it stood on the plot of a private house. The Corpus Christi Chapel, also of unknown origin, stood on the north hillside in the suburb. Not even its location is known exactly.[123] The parish priest's village,

---

118 18 May 1413: BTOE, iii/1, pp. 327–328 (no 630).
119 Katalin H. Gyürky, "A Szent Márton kápolna régészeti maradványai Budán," [The archaeological remains of the St Martin's Chapel in Buda] *Archaeológiai Értesítő* 111 (1984), pp. 29–42.
120 Gerevich, *A budai vár*, pp. 207–216.
121 Végh, *Buda*, i, p. 63.
122 Kund Miklós Regényi, *Die ungarischen Konvente der Oberdeutschen Karmelitenprovinz im Mittelalter* (METEM, 31) (Budapest – Heidelberg: METEM, 2001); Judit Benda, "The excavation of a medieval Carmelite monastery in Buda," in *Archaeological investigations in Hungary 2002*, ed. Júlia Kisfaludi (Budapest: KÖH, 2004), pp. 117–130.
123 Végh, *Buda*, i, pp. 64–65 (St Ladislas), pp. 68–69 (All Saints), pp. 101–102 (Corpus Christi) and pp. 102–103 (St Michael).

Logod on the west side of Castle Hill, also built a church (today Bugát lépcső, Logodi Street).[124] In addition to these, nearly all previously-existing churches were extended. The nave of the Parish Church of Our Lady was rebuilt as a hall church, and new side-chapels were extended up to the chancel. When the Church of St Mary Magdalene became a parish church in its own right, the existing little church building was demolished and replaced on the same site by a three-aisle church with an elongated chancel. The Church of St Peter Martyr had also become an independent parish church and was extended into a three-aisle building. The chancels of the Franciscan and Dominican friaries were enlarged.[125] There were probably parallel developments in Pest, but apart from the major expansion of the Parish Church of Our Lady, we do not know any details. Given the unfortunate loss of Buda's censuses, the increases in the size of the churches are important indications of population expansion, and in some cases mark changes in the demands of liturgy and church art (chancel extensions).

Finally, the sovereign reigning in 1400, King Sigismund, built in the first quarter of the fifteenth century the lesser Church of the Virgin Mary, also known as St Sigismund's Church, between two streets at the highest point of the hill in front of the royal palace. Originally intended as the king's chapel in the town, the building in many respects copied the Liebfrauenkirche in Nuremberg, founded by Sigismund's father, Emperor Charles IV. Excavations have revealed the foundations of the demolished building, and found remains of its furnishings buried in pits. It had an elongated chancel connected to a square nave which was divided by two rows of columns. Written sources praise the beauty of the church, an opinion confirmed by the recovered fragments.[126]

Plots, Dwellings, and their Occupants

The construction of the new royal palace and the arrival and permanent presence of the court (after 1408) brought far-reaching changes to the city of Buda, notably in the composition of its population. The prelates and barons of the

---

124 Garády, "Budapest székesfőváros," pp. 214–218; László Gerevich, *The Art of Buda and Pest in the Middle Ages* (Budapest: Akadémiai, 1971), pp. 41–42.

125 Gerevich, *The Art of Buda*, pp. 37–38; Végh and Zádor, "Topographie," pp. 295–303.

126 András Végh, "Beiträge zur Geschichte des Neueren Kollegiat-Stiftes zu Unserer Lieben Frau oder St. Sigismund von Buda (Ofen)," *Acta Archaeologica Academiae Scientiarum Hungaricae* 50 (1998), pp. 215–231; István Feld, "Beszámoló az egykori budai Szent Zsigmond templom és környéke feltárásáról," [Preliminary report on the archaeological excavation of the St Sigismund's Church and its surroundings] *Budapest Régiségei* 33 (1999), pp. 35–50.

king's council were obliged to acquire dwelling houses in Buda so that they could attend council meetings. Courtiers of high and low rank also needed properties in Buda. The process only started around 1400, but as it gathered momentum, a large proportion of the houses in the Castle District soon passed out of civil ownership, although the nobles who acquired houses in Buda – even barons and prelates – were until 1498 formally required to enter the community of Buda citizens.[127] A secondary consequence of the purchase of houses by barons and prelates was an increase in the number of houses donated to religious communities. The most prominent beneficiaries of this were the chapter of St Stephen Protomartyr in Esztergom and various friaries of the Pauline Order, and they also included some large monasteries of the Benedictine Order.[128]

The composition of the citizenry had also undergone considerable changes by 1400.[129] The sources, although they are quite scarce, indicate that the Hungarian population had caught up with the German and had gained economic strength. Some developments serve as indicators of these trends: the Hungarian parish in the Castle District became independent, an independent parish was created in the suburb, and parish boundaries separating communities of burghers of different ethnic affinity became permanent. From that time, the north of the Castle District belonged to the Hungarians and the central third to the Germans. In front of the royal palace, there was a concentration of noble properties (although these were also scattered throughout the town).

The Jews still lived in their old street around 1400, but this area appreciated in value owing to its proximity to the new royal palace, and became increasingly unsuitable as a Jewish quarter. The Jews were soon moved out (an event whose date and circumstances remain unknown) and a new Jewish quarter was established directly to the east of the old palace (*Kammerhof*) abandoned by the king (today Táncsics Mihály Street). The Italian merchants still owned houses in the area of the street named after them.

---

127   Végh, *Buda*, i, pp. 318–327.
128   Végh, *Buda*, i, pp. 323 and 326–327.
129   András Kubinyi, "Deutsche und Nicht-Deutsche in den Städten des mittelalterlichen ungarischen Königreiches," in *Verfestigung und Änderung der ethnischen Strukturen im pannonischen Raum im Spätmittelalter* (Internationales kulturhistorisches Symposion Mogersdorf, 25), ed. Reinhard Härtel (Eisenstadt: Amt der Burgenländischen Landesregierung, 1996), pp. 159–175; András Végh, "Buda: The Multi-Ethnic Capital of Medieval Hungary," in *Segregation – Integration – Assimilation. Religious and Ethnic Groups in the Medieval Towns of Central and Eastern Europe* (Historical Urban Studies), eds Derek Keene, Balázs Nagy and Katalin Szende (Farnham: Ashgate, 2009), pp. 89–99.

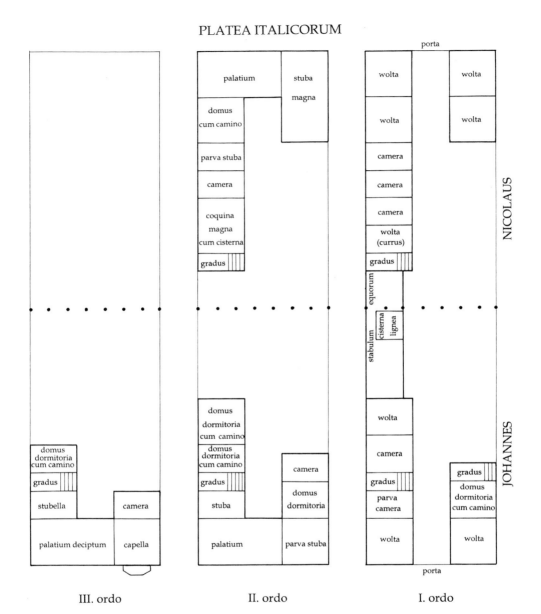

FIGURE 7.4 *Division of the house of János Garai and Miklós Garai in the medieval St George Street (today Dísz tér), 1412 (research by A. Végh, graphics Zs. Kuczogi)*

All of these changes led to more intensive use of available land in the Castle District. The market-places were built on, as was the vicinity of the Parish Church of Our Lady. The civilian population, which was growing, was forced into the suburb, building on previously empty land on the bank of the Danube and the hillsides.

The burghers' houses of the Castle District spread out and expanded within the configuration described above, by means of more intensive building on the existing plots and sometimes by merging plots. A surviving description from 1412 gives a clear account of a typical house in Buda – one owned by barons, but acquired from wealthy merchants (Fig. 7.4).[130] An ensemble of buildings occupying two merged plots opened on to different streets, one street front having two storeys and the other three. The buildings were arranged in a U-shape behind both streets, and there was a courtyard in the space between the two houses with a stable on one side. There were vaulted rooms (*wolta*) and stores (*camera*) on the ground floor of the houses, and bedrooms (*domus dormitoria*), heated rooms (*stuba, domus cum camino*), halls (termed *palatium* in the sources) and the kitchen (*coquina magna*) on the upper storeys. A house chapel was also mentioned.

Conclusion

By 1400, Buda-Pest had developed further than any other city in the kingdom of Hungary, and had established itself so firmly as the permanent royal seat and 'capital city' that it would be unchallenged in this role for a long time to come. This topographical survey has hopefully conveyed the essence of a medieval town and royal seat which has now largely disappeared, but which was at the time a worthy peer of Prague and Cracow.

---

130   25 August 1412: BTOE, iii/1, pp. 314–315 (no 607).

CHAPTER 8

The Monastic Topography of Medieval Buda

Beatrix F. Romhányi

Buda, the late medieval capital of the Hungarian kingdom, was not the ecclesiastical center of the country, and no archbishopric or bishopric had its seat there. Nevertheless, the shaping of its ecclesiastical topography began a considerable time before its foundation, and the institutions present on its territory prior to the city's establishment influenced the history and the topography of Buda in the long term. When discussing the monastic topography of Buda one cannot avoid taking into consideration the institutions of Óbuda, Felhévíz, the Margaret Island (Hares' Island in the Middle Ages) and Pest as well as of some other sites surrounding the city, since these settlements – although legally separate – formed an economic unit long before the birth of modern Budapest.

Before the Foundation of Buda

The political center of the medieval Hungarian kingdom, called *medium regni* by contemporaries – to which later the territory of the capital and the royal residence belonged – was marked from the first half of the eleventh century by ecclesiastical foundations (see Fig. 8.1). The earliest foundations bordered the royal forest of the Pilis, the southernmost edges of which reached as far as Buda. I will not deal with the whole *medium regni* area in this study, but only with the part which belonged to the territory of the future capital. One of these foundations – the first in this region, in fact – was St Peter's collegiate chapter of Buda (later Óbuda), founded by King Peter in the 1040s.[1] The chapter was

---

[1] On the history of the town see László Bártfai Szabó, *Óbuda egyházi intézményei a középkorban* [The ecclesiastical institutions of Óbuda in the Middle Ages] (Budapest: [n. p.], 1935), as well as the relevant parts of *Bp. tört.*, i–ii. The German volume *Budapest im Mittelalter* gives an overview of the whole territory of today's Budapest (especially important for the present topic are the articles of Júlia Altmann, Zoltán Bencze, Katalin Írásné Melis, Enikő Spekner and András Végh). For the most important information on ecclesiastical institutions (with further literature) see Beatrix F. Romhányi, *Kolostorok és társaskáptalanok a középkori Magyarországon* [Monasteries and collegiate chapters in medieval Hungary] (Budapest: Pytheas, 2000; revised and enlarged CD-ROM version: Budapest: Arcanum, 2008). A fundamental work on the medieval topography of Buda has been published by András Végh, *Buda*.

always styled "of Buda", although it did not in fact move into the new city on the Castle Hill. Its estates extended over parts of the later capital. St Peter's chapter was the most important ecclesiastical institution on the territory of Buda before the foundation of the new city on the Castle Hill.

Despite the fact that the territory was part of the *medium regni* – but possibly because of the presence of the chapter – monastic foundations can be attested to only relatively late. South of the later capital, *banus Apa* of the Becsegergely kindred founded his family monastery in the middle of the twelfth century, transforming the earlier parish church of the village of Kána into an abbey. Characteristically for medieval Hungary, the foundation can be dated only by the fact that the founder is mentioned in charters between 1150 and 1158. The abbey itself is first mentioned only in 1236 as having common estates with the nearby Benedictine abbey of Telki, thus implying that Kána abbey was also Benedictine. The two abbeys leased their fields in *Pest minor* (i.e. the part of Pest on the right bank of the Danube) to the burghers of Pest in 1240.[2] In 1258 the patroness of the abbey, Petronella, mentioned the abbey in her testament.[3] The estates of the monastery are mentioned in 1325,[4] but the abbey itself disappears for more than a century, although its continued existence has been proven by archaeological investigations.[5] Finally, Paul, the priest of Buda and governor of the abbey, is mentioned in 1495.[6]

Shortly before the official foundation of the new capital, the presence of the royal court intensified in the area. Many of the charters of King Béla IV were issued in Óbuda, even before 1241. Further expressions of royal interest were the foundation of new ecclesiastical institutions like the Premonstratensian provostry on the Margaret Island and the donation of a large landed property to the newly founded Cistercian abbey at Petrovaradin (now in Serbia).

The small Premonstratensian provostry on Margaret Island was founded before 1225 by King Andrew II and existed until the end of the fifteenth century,

---

2 BTOE, i, pp. 37–38 (no 23): "pro supradictis ducentis iugeribus terrarum, in quibus plantaverunt vel plantabunt vineas, a festo sancti Michaelis proxime venturo in tertia revolutione eiusdem...solvent decem marcas bonorum frisaticorum ad pondus, vel si frisatici defecerint, solvent in argento decime conbustionis ad pondus...". See also László Bártfai Szabó, *Pest megye történetének okleveles emlékei 1002–1599-ig* [Charters on the history of Pest County, 1002–1599] (Budapest: Ablaka, 1938), no 24.
3 Bártfai Szabó, *Pest megye*, no 39.
4 Bártfai Szabó, *Pest megye*, no 203.
5 Katalin H. Gyürky, *A Buda melletti kánai apátság feltárása* [Archaeological research on Kána abbey near Buda] (Budapest: Akadémiai, 1996).
6 MNL OL DL 32 522 (15 June 1495).

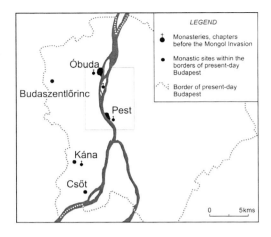

FIGURE 8.1
Monasteries and monastic estates on the territory of Buda before 1241

and at least in name up to the Ottoman occupation of Buda. Its importance was very limited, and so were its estates.[7] After the foundation of the Dominican nunnery on the island (see below) the role of the provostry retreated even further into the background.

The Cistercian abbey of Petrovaradin, founded by King Béla IV in 1234 on the estates of *banus Petur*, the possible murderer of Béla's mother, received the tithes of the vineyards in Krenfeld (Kelenföld), in the Buda area. This right remained in the hands of the Cistercians until the end of the Middle Ages and represented a significant part of their income. The urban house of the abbey (see further below) was probably where its wine was stored and sold – although we do not have written evidence for this.

On the Other Side of the Danube: Pest

There is no trace of any early (i.e. eleventh- or twelfth-century) monastic presence in the town of Pest, but its central position and urban development in the area of the later capital is reflected in the fact that one of the first Dominican friaries was founded in Pest before the Mongol invasion, on the southern

---

7 The provostry had parcels of land in Borosjenő near Buda and in Pazand, where it also had a mill. See BTOE, i, pp. 18–19 (no 13–14) and 305–306 (no 286); *A Podmaniczky család oklevéltára*, ii [The archive of the Podmaniczky family], ed. Imre Lukinich (Budapest: MTA, 1939), no 128 (MNL OL DL 24 089), no 164 and 169; ZsO, vi, pp. 140 and 206 (nos 349 and 636).

edge of the town.[8] Although the town suffered much in 1241 – the friary itself, along with the people who found refuge in the buildings, was burnt down by the Mongols – its economic and especially commercial importance continued almost uninterrupted. The Dominicans likewise rebuilt their convent soon after the disaster. The Dominican church and the convent buildings stood in Szenterzsébetfalva, south of the town itself. Their precise location has been the subject of debate, since there are no archaeological remains. It was most likely located somewhere in the area of the later Pauline monastery of Pest (today the Faculty of Theology of the Péter Pázmány Catholic University).

After the Foundation of Buda

King Béla IV's selection of Buda as his royal residence shaped the city's monastic topography. Apart from the earlier institutions mentioned above, most of the monastic landscape of the area was marked by his foundations: the Dominican and the Franciscan friaries of the castle, the Austin friary on the Danube side of the hill, and the Dominican nunnery on Margaret Island. A further three Franciscan friaries – in Pest, on Margaret Island and in Óbuda – can be connected to him. The only institutions to emerge later in this area were the monastery of the Poor Clares of Óbuda, the Carmelite friary in the suburb of Taschental, and two Pauline monasteries.

Mendicant Friaries

After the Dominican friary of Pest, a second convent of the Dominicans was founded in Buda (see Fig. 8.2). The Dominicans settled in the castle shortly after the foundation of the town, and certainly before 1252, since in that year the general chapter of the order decided to hold their next chapter in the new friary of Buda. In the event, the general chapter of 1254 of the Dominican Order took place in this building, where the new prior general, Humbertus de Romanis was elected. This building was the first religious house built in the Castle District in the years immediately after the foundation of the new capital. The intimate relationship between the king and the order was reflected in the site of the friary, which stood in the closest proximity to the early royal palace,

---

8 The friary dedicated to St Antony the Abbot in Szenterzsébetfalva, south of the town, is first mentioned in 1233, in the so-called oath of Bereg (MNL OL DF 248 770).

between the *Kammerhof* and the parish church. The legal status of the latter has been debated, and in the early period it may also have served as a royal chapel. Thus the Dominican friary made its appearance in the political center of the city and of the kingdom. This changed to some extent later, by the mid-fourteenth century, when the royal palace moved to the southern part of the castle hill, and the *Kammerhof* building became first the house of the Pauline Order, and later a private property.

Of the four Franciscan friaries, the Pest friary was probably the earliest.[9] It was built between 1253 and 1260, and stood close to the eastern gate of the town, on the same site as it occupies today. This first friary was followed by the second one in the Buda castle before 1270. It was built on the southern edge of the town, in the vicinity of the *Platea Iudeorum* (Jews' Street). Major parts of the church were reused in the seventeenth century when the Carmelites were given the ruined building (which today houses the Várszínház), while the remains of the cloister were discovered in the 1990s under the Sándor Palace (today the seat of the President of the Republic).[10]

Despite its apparently unfavorable location, the friary did not lack royal support. King Béla IV had already left Buda when the Franciscan friary was built. The church and the cloister were finished under the reign of his successors, especially King Ladislas IV, his mother, and the last Árpádian king, Andrew III. King Andrew was also buried in its church. Between 1313 and 1437 the Hungarian province of the Franciscans held its chapters seven times in this convent. A major change occurred in the life of the friars when in 1444 the papal legate Giuliano Cesarini gave several friaries, including the Buda friary, to the

---

9   In John R.H. Moorman's book (idem, *Medieval Franciscan Houses* [Franciscan Institute Publications, History Series, 4] [New York: Franciscan Institute – St Bonaventure University, 1983]) the details given for the medieval Hungarian friaries are outdated. The Hares' (correctly Háros) Island was the site of the Premonstratensian provostry of Csőt founded in 1264 by King Béla IV. This monastery was given to the Paulines in 1475–1477, who held it till the Ottoman period. It was never possessed by the Franciscans. The Buda and the Pest friaries were taken over by the Observant branch of the Franciscans in 1444, although the decision was made in the year before.

10 See also Júlia Altmann, "Az óbudai és a budavári ferences templom és kolostor kutatásai," [Research on the Franciscan friaries of Óbuda and Buda] in *Koldulórendi építészet a középkori Magyarországon* [Mendicant architecture in medieval Hungary] (Művészettörténet – Műemlékvédelem, 7), ed. Andrea Haris (Budapest: Országos Műemlékvédelmi Hivatal, 1994), pp. 143–148; József Laszlovszky, "Crown, Gown and Town: Zones of Royal, Ecclesiastical and Civic Interaction in Medieval Buda and Visegrád," in *Segregation – Integration – Assimilation. Religious and Ethnic Groups in the Medieval Towns of Central and Eastern Europe* (Historical Urban Studies), eds Derek Keene, Balázs Nagy and Katalin Szende (Farnham: Ashgate, 2009), pp. 179–203.

observant branch of the order. From then on, it became one of the most important convents of the Observant Vicariate, which often held its chapter meetings in this building.

From the second half of the fourteenth century, after the royal palace moved to the southern edge of the Castle Hill, the Franciscan friary in Buda became part of a transitional zone separating the royal residence from the city. From this time on, different types of lay convention, including diets, were regularly held in the monastery. The friars left the buildings in or shortly before 1541, the year when Buda came under Ottoman rule.

The foundation dates of the remaining two Franciscan friaries, on Margaret Island and in Óbuda, are both mentioned as being in the last third of the thirteenth century, around 1270 and 1280 respectively.[11] Their founder must have been one of the kings. Despite their relatively late dating, this was most probably King Béla IV. Unlike the friaries of Pest and Buda, they remained until the mid-sixteenth century (i.e. the Ottoman occupation) in the hands of the Conventual Franciscans, and the friary of Óbuda became the center of the province after 1444.

The other mendicant communities, namely the Austin Hermits and the Carmelites, had just one friary each in the area. The former settled not in the castle but in the suburb on the eastern side of the castle hill. Their convent is first mentioned in 1276, but it was probably founded before 1270. There is a *Platea Armenorum* (Armenians' Street) mentioned in connection with this part of the city, and the choice of friars may have been influenced by missionary ideals. It should be noted that the Esztergom friary of the order stood similarly in the part of the city most likely to have been connected with the Armenians.[12] The precise place of the Buda Austin friary was for decades the subject of debate. Earlier it was identified with the Toigun pasha mosque (today the Capuchin church), but the archaeological investigations led by András

---

11   For the Óbuda friary, see also Vilmosné Bertalan, "A középkori ásatások – kutatások története Óbudán 1850–1975," [The history of the excavations and of research in Óbuda 1875–1950] *Budapest Régiségei* 24 (1976), pp. 31–42, here p. 34. For the Island, see Rózsa Feuerné Tóth, *Margitsziget* [Margaret Island] (Budapest: Képzőművészeti Alap, 1955).

12   The Esztergom friary is first mentioned in 1272. The order itself was present in Hungary from the 1250s at the latest; most of their houses belonged originally to the Order of St William. After the Great Union (1256) this order tried to re-establish its autonomy, and in this it was partially successful. Nevertheless, the Hungarian friaries remained within the Order of the Austin Hermits. There is no evidence as to whether the Buda friary belonged to the Order of Saint William.

Végh identified the remains of its church somewhat closer to the castle, in Szalag Street.[13]

The last mendicant friary of Buda was founded by King Louis I in 1372 for the Carmelites in the suburb called Taschental. This part of the town was sparsely inhabited in the late Middle Ages and the friary stood among orchards. The building was rediscovered in 2002. The remains of the convent building were found on plot 4, Csapláros Street, while those of the church are partly under the street and partly under the houses on the opposite side (see Fig. 8.3).[14]

Nunneries, Beguine Houses

There were no nunneries in Buda itself, but two powerful female communities, both founded and supported by the rulers and their relatives, existed in its very close vicinity: the Dominican nunnery on the Island and the Poor Clares convent at Óbuda. The first was founded by King Béla IV and his wife in 1252 for their daughter Margaret.[15] Thanks to royal donations, the nunnery developed into one of the wealthiest and most influential religious houses in medieval Hungary. Soon after the death of Princess Margaret her tomb on Margaret Island became a place of pilgrimage. In 1272, when her tomb was first recorded as part of the process of her canonization, most of the pilgrims came from the Buda area. The existence of the nunnery directly influenced the development of Buda, since King Béla IV granted them many rights on the territory of the new capital. Among others, the Island nunnery had possession of the tolls of the Buda market, and the official scale used by the town was also in their possession.[16]

---

13   András Végh, "New Excavations in the Area of Szentpétermártír – a Medieval Suburb of Buda," in *Mittelalterliche Häuser und Straßen in in Mitteleuropa* (Varia Archaeologica Hungarica, 9), eds Márta Font and Mária Sándor (Budapest – Pécs: Archäologisches Inst. der UAW, 2000), pp. 67–74; Végh, *Buda*, i, pp. 100–101.

14   Judit Benda, "Előzetes jelentés a budai középkori karmelita kolostor feltárásáról," [Preliminary report of the archaeological excavation of the medieval Carmelite friary of Buda] *Budapest Régiségei* 37 (2003), pp. 137–149; Végh, *Buda*, i, pp. 99–100.

15   For archaeological research, see Rózsa Feuerné Tóth, "A margitszigeti domonkos kolostor," [The Dominican nunnery on the Margaret Island] *Budapest Régiségei* 22 (1971), pp. 245–269 and Katalin Irásné Melis, "A Budapest Margit-szigeti domonkos apácakolostor pusztulása a 16–17. században," [The destruction of the Dominican nunnery on Margaret Island in the sixteenth and seventeenth centuries] *Budapest Régiségei* 38 (2004), pp. 107–120.

16   Judit Benda, "A kereskedelem épületei a középkori Budán, ii. Mészárszékek háza, zsemleszékek háza, árucsarnok," [Commercial buildings in medieval Buda. The house of

The Poor Clares convent was established almost a century later, thanks to the donation of Queen Elizabeth Piast, the wife of the Angevin king, Charles I. Papal permission was given in 1334 and building operations were carried out in the 1340s.[17] The nunnery received large estates, but due to its relatively late foundation (i.e. long after the foundation of Buda), it was unable to make such a deep impact on the city as its Dominican counterpart.

The urban character of Buda and Pest is also demonstrated by the presence of beguine houses. Beguines are first mentioned in Pest in 1272 – one of them was a witness in the process of St Margaret's beatification in that year – and they were probably under the spiritual leadership of the Dominican friars. There is no further evidence on this beguine house. A reference from 1520, when a Franciscan confessor was appointed for them by the provincial chapter, probably relates to another beguine community. None of the houses can be located, partly due to the insufficiency of written evidence.

In Buda, there were two separate beguine houses, the first of which appears in charters at the end of the thirteenth century. It was an urban house opposite the Franciscan friary and its inhabitants were supervised by the friars. This beguine house – for an unknown reason also called Sybilla monastery – was founded in 1290 by the widow of Master Moys. From the first, its inhabitants were consistently called nuns (*moniales*). The existence of this institution can be traced through the late Middle Ages, almost until the Ottoman occupation. Archaeological research has allowed its exact location to be identified: on the northern side of the Church of St Sigismund, separated from the church by a lane. The original building opened onto *Platea Sancti Johannis* (St John's Street), but in the sixteenth century it was enlarged to occupy a double plot, with a further exit into *Platea Sancti Sigismundi regis* (St Sigismund's Street).[18]

The other beguine house in *Platea Sancti Pauli* (St Paul's Street) was under the spiritual leadership of the Dominicans, and it is mentioned in the 1390s in connection with the house of the palatine, Nicolas Kont. The community itself was already present at the beginning of the century, in 1308, but it cannot be proven that they owned the same house then. The location of the house remains uncertain; it is possible that it lies under No 5 Fortuna Street.[19]

---

butcheries, bakeries, market hall] *Tanulmányok Budapest Múltjából* 37 (2012), pp. 23–58, here p. 46. I am grateful to Judit Benda for drawing my attention to this evidence.

17   Vilmosné H. Bertalan, "Das Klarissenkloster von Óbuda aus dem 14. Jh.," *Acta Archaeologica Academiae Scientiarum Hungaricae* 34 (1982), pp. 151–176; Brian McEntee, "The Burial Site Selection of a Hungarian Queen: Elizabeth, Queen of Hungary(1320–1380), and the Óbuda Clares' Church," *Annual of Medieval Studies at CEU* 12 (2006), pp. 69–82.

18   Végh, *Buda*, i, pp. 61–63.

19   Végh, *Buda*, i, p. 125 and 265.

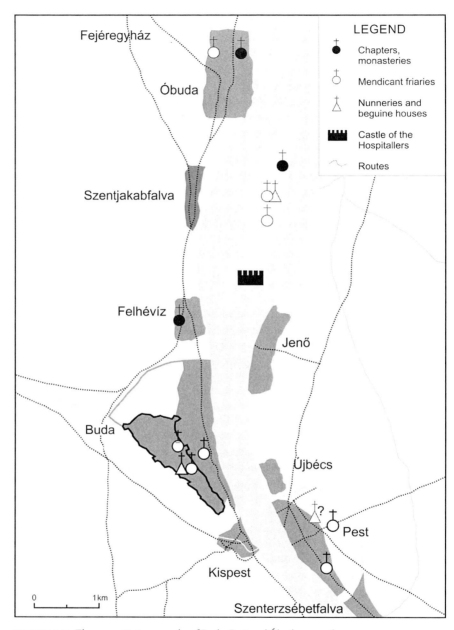

FIGURE 8.2 *The monastic topography of Buda, Pest and Óbuda around 1300*

THE MONASTIC TOPOGRAPHY OF MEDIEVAL BUDA 213

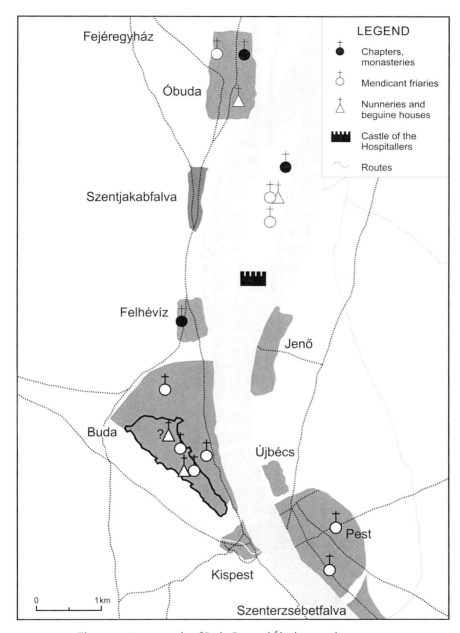

FIGURE 8.3 *The monastic topography of Buda, Pest and Óbuda around 1400*

The Paulines

The first Pauline monastery on the territory of Buda was on account of the eremitic origin of the order situated outside the castle on the slopes of the Buda Hills, and it had been founded by the end of the thirteenth century. The monastery of St Lawrence became the center of the emerging order from the beginning of the fourteenth century, after papal approval was given the order by the legate Cardinal Gentilis in 1308. The monks' connection to Buda was formalized in 1381 when King Louis I donated to them the *Kammerhof* building (the earlier royal palace in the northern part of the castle). Since this building did not fit the purposes of the order, the monks exchanged it some time before 1412 for the house of Hermann of Cilli. This house, also called the "Great House of the Paulines," remained in their hands until the mid-sixteenth century. Notwithstanding the danger, the most precious treasure of the order, the relics of St Paul the Hermit, were kept there until a new chapel was built in the monastery.

The order's second monastery in the Buda area was founded by King Matthias in 1480. The monks received an earlier church which was erected over what was held at the time to be the tomb of Grand Prince Árpád. The new monastery seems to be part of a 'holy circle' around Buda, the third member of which was the monastery of Csőt, originally founded in 1264 by King Béla IV for the Premonstratensians,[20] and given by King Matthias to the Paulines sometime between 1475 and 1477 (see Fig. 8.4).

The Knights Hospitaller Castle on Margaret Island, and the Stephanite Priory, and the Hospital of the Holy Spirit at Felhévíz

The Knights Hospitaller played a substantial role in the shaping of the landscape of Buda, since they had a castle on the southern end of Margaret Island, which was built after the Mongol invasion (probably before 1253) and which was a part of the defensive system initiated by King Béla IV. Reference to the castle continues to occur in the sources until the fourteenth century, and its ruins were still visible in the nineteenth century.

The convent of the Stephanite Order in Felhévíz, dedicated to the Holy Trinity, was founded after the Mongol invasion,[21] and is often mentioned in

---

20   Bártfai Szabó, *Pest megye*, no 50. The provostry had significant estates on Csepel Island, in Esztergom and elsewhere.
21   András Kubinyi, "Budafelhévíz topográfiája és gazdasági fejlődése," [The topography and economic development of Budafelhévíz] in Kubinyi, *Tanulmányok*, i, pp. 115–182, here

charters before the mid-fifteenth century. Thereafter the order lost its property and the earlier priory was transformed into a collegiate chapter by the pope. The priory stood under the jurisdiction of the Esztergom house of the Order, to which the kings had given the earlier parish church of the Felhévíz settlement in the mid-twelfth century.[22]

At the beginning of the fourteenth century, the monastic topography of the region was enriched by the appearance of the hospital of the Order of the Holy Spirit. The institution is first mentioned in 1330 when Ortolfus, the master of the hospital and the *generalis praeceptor* of Hungary, sold the inhabited estate of the hospital in Nandur (Nándor) for 100 marks of silver to a member of the Buda council. The sum was used for the building of the hospital's church.[23] The hospital is often mentioned in charters, especially in connection with the mills of Felhévíz (in the area of today's Lukács and Császár baths). This suggests that the hospital stood at the upper edge of the *Malomtó* (i.e. "mill lake"), in the royal part of the settlement (in fact it was probably of royal foundation, too). The hospital remained in the hands of the order until the end of the Middle Ages.[24]

Monastic Estates in and around the Town

Another form of monastic presence also characterized Buda's topography: the houses and manors owned by different abbeys and other religious houses in and around the town (see Fig. 8.6). Unfortunately, the records relating to these possessions are scarce and very fragmentary. Most of them are mentioned just once, so we do not usually know how they came to be acquired, how long they were owned or what their exact purpose was. Another problem is that we cannot give any accurate figures or even estimates concerning the proportion of

---

pp. 140–144. The convent was probably established around 1245; its prior, Peter, is mentioned in the canonization process of St Margaret. The convent had earlier been misassigned to the Knights Hospitaller; the correct identification is thanks to Károly György Boroviczény (idem, "Cruciferi Sancti Regis Stephani. Tanulmányok a stefaniták, egy középkori magyar ispotályos rend történetéből," [Cruciferi Sancti Regis Stephani: Studies on the history of the Stefanites, a medieval Hungarian Hospitaller Order] *Orvostörténeti Közlemények* 37–38 [1991–1992], pp. 7–48 and 155–170.).

22 Kubinyi, "Budafelhévíz," pp. 119–121. After the foundation of Buda the changed situation led to a protracted suit between the convent and the bishop of Veszprém over the right to tithe there.
23 Kubinyi, "Budafelhévíz," p. 147.
24 Kubinyi, "Budafelhévíz," p. 148.

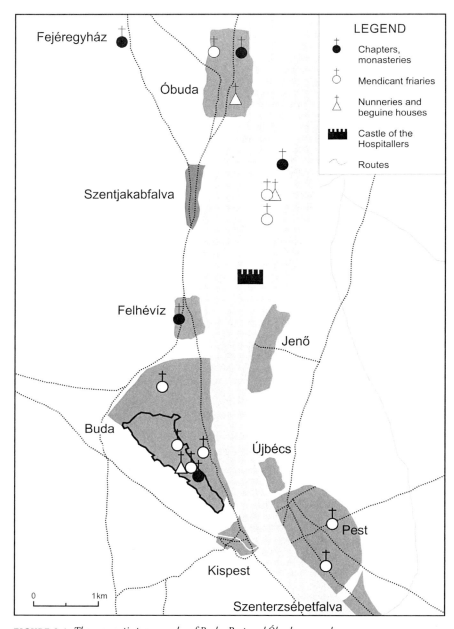

FIGURE 8.4 *The monastic topography of Buda, Pest and Óbuda around 1500*

THE MONASTIC TOPOGRAPHY OF MEDIEVAL BUDA 217

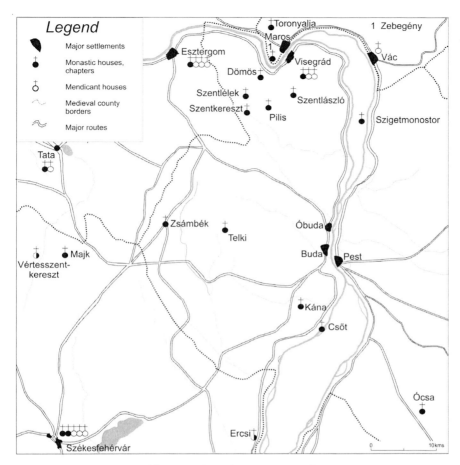

FIGURE 8.5 *Monasteries and friaries in the* medium regni *around 1500*

ecclesiastical possessions within the town. The reason for this is that most of our sources come from ecclesiastical archives, the documents of the city itself and of other institutions having perished during the sixteenth and seventeenth centuries.

Urban Houses

Benedictine Abbeys

A number of Benedictine abbeys possessed urban houses and plots in the castle and the suburb of Buda. The earliest to be mentioned is a house in the castle belonging to Tihany abbey, donated by George, canon of Veszprém, before

1394.[25] The abbey acquired a second house in 1458 in the *Platea Carnificium* (Butcher's Street) in the suburb, in exchange for one of its estates in Somogy County.[26] Szekszárd abbey acquired its house in the castle, located near one of the houses of St Stephen's chapter of Esztergom, before 1400 in exchange for one of its estates in Tolna County.[27] In the same period the abbey of Bakonybél owned two houses in the city. One of them – bought by Abbot Martin with the money of his abbey – first appears in an action at law in 1411, and it is also mentioned in 1425. It stood opposite St Peter the Martyr's Parish Church in the suburb. The other house, mentioned in 1451 and 1452, stood in the castle, on Szombatpiac (*in foro Sabbati*).[28] We do not know whether these houses were at the times they are mentioned owned by the abbeys.

Like Abbot Martin, Peter, the abbot of Szenttrinitás (Holy Trinity) abbey in Baranya County, invested the money of his monastery in 1432 when he bought a house in the suburb near to the Danube for 70 florins; its further history is unknown.[29] The inhabitants of the house of the abbey of Szék are mentioned once in 1442; its location cannot be identified, but we may suppose it was also in the suburb.[30]

There is evidence for houses belonging between 1510 and 1524 to the abbey of Pannonhalma. The first is mentioned in 1510 when it was already in the possession of the abbey.[31] The other was bought by the abbot, Máté Tolnai, in 1516 and the relevant extant charter relates to this transaction.[32] The houses neighbored one another and stood in the *Platea Sancti Johannis*, near the Franciscan friary.[33] As already mentioned, the abbeys of Kána and Telki also had some possessions on the territory of the city, but they did not own any houses there – at least there is no evidence of any.

The only Cistercian abbey possessing a house in Buda is – not surprisingly – the Petrovaradin (in Hungarian Pétervárad) abbey, which had large vineyards on the territory of the town. It acquired a house in *Platea Sancti Pauli* in around 1457 from a former judge of the town, Imre of Buda, for the rather high sum

---

25   Végh, *Buda*, ii, nos 106–107.
26   Végh, *Buda*, ii, no 301. It is noteworthy that in this case the abbey exchanged a closer estate for the faraway house in Buda.
27   Végh, *Buda*, ii, no 134.
28   Végh, *Buda*, ii, nos 164, 198 and nos 269, 275.
29   Végh, *Buda*, ii, no 218.
30   Végh, *Buda*, ii, no 244.
31   Végh, *Buda*, ii, no 532.
32   Végh, *Buda*, ii, no 592.
33   Végh, *Buda*, i, pp. 145–147 and 149.

of 600 florins.[34] But the monastery's possession of the house was not undisturbed: in 1483 it had to sell the rear part of it for 232 florins, because it had already been taken by other occupants.[35]

The Pauline Monasteries and the Carthusians

The urban houses of the Pauline monasteries represent a special case, at least as far as their large number is concerned (see Fig. 8.6). The first house of the order was most probably the *Kammerhof* building (see above). This was followed by the acquisition of a series of houses and plots, many of them fairly close to or even neighboring the Great House. The monasteries of Örményes and Csatka owned houses in *Platea Sancti Pauli* (obtained in 1382 and 1396, respectively). Other houses belonging to different monasteries of the Order stood in *Platea Omnium Sanctorum* (All Saints' Street) (Örményes – 1392; Lád – 1394; Szentkereszt and Szentlélek – 1425) in the *Platea Italicorum* (Italians' Street) (Szentlőrinc – 1402; Kékes – 1495, 1515) and in *Platea Sancti Nicolai* (St Nicolas' Street) (Örményes – 1392). There were some more houses in *Platea Sancti Johannis* (Veresmart – 1440s), in Keddhely (Örményes – 1390) and in the *Platea Magna* (Large Street) (Örményes – 1392). As can be seen, the monastery of Örményes possessed the largest number of houses, but one has to add that it had sold most of these by the mid-fifteenth century. The only house retained by the monastery until the end of the Middle Ages was the one in the *Platea Sancti Pauli*. The monastery of Fehéregyháza received a house in Óbuda in 1517.[36] The central monastery of the order, of St Lawrence in Buda, was given a house in Pest around 1480[37] and a further house, belonging to an unidentified monastery, was also located in Pest in the sixteenth century.[38]

The urban houses were usually given to the Paulines by their patrons in order to ensure regular cash income for their monasteries, i.e. to be rented out. But the long distances (e.g. in the case of Örményes or Veresmart) made it in practice impossible to manage them directly and the central administration of the Order – which acted for the faraway monasteries – did not always respect the interests of the owners. Thus the monasteries were driven to sell their

---

34   Végh, *Buda*, ii, no 316.
35   Végh, *Buda*, ii, nos 376–378, 381 and 383.
36   *Documenta Artis Paulinorum*, 3 vols, eds Béla Gyéressy, Ferenc L. Hervay and Melinda Tóth (Budapest: MTA Művészettörténeti Kutató Csoportja, 1975–1978), i, p. 147 [hereafter: DAP].
37   Gregorii Gyöngyösi, *Vitae fratrum Eremitarum Ordinis Sancti Pauli Primi Eremitae*, ed. Ferenc Hervay (Budapest: Akadémiai, 1988), c. 64.
38   *Formularium maius Ordinis S. Pauli primi Heremitae*, eds Beatrix F. Romhányi and Gábor Sarbak (Budapest: Szent István Társulat, 2013), no 83 (f. 39ᵛ). The manuscript is in Budapest, ELTE Egyetemi Könyvtár Kézirattár, Cod. Lat. 131.

houses. The monasteries in the Pilis, on the other hand, were purchasers of houses in the city. Szentkereszt and Szentlélek possessed a house in common in *Platea Omnium Sanctorum* from 1425, while the monastery of Kékes had one in the *Platea Italicorum* by the end of the fifteenth century.[39] All in all, by the end of the Middle Ages different Pauline monasteries owned at least five houses in Buda, as well as one in Óbuda and two in Pest.

Although the number of sources is restricted, the evidence suggests that most of these houses were purely sources of rent. However, those which were owned by the Pauline monasteries on the long term served also as accommodation and as stores for the goods traded by the Paulines. In one case we have evidence for the cellar of one of these houses that had to be enlarged in order to store a larger quantity of wine than before.[40]

The house of the wealthiest Carthusian priory of Hungary, the Lövöld Charterhouse, stood between the parish church and the Dominican friary (1441), in the *Platea Teutonicorum* (Germans' Street), among the houses of the leading cloth merchants of Buda (1503–1505).[41] In the early sixteenth century another Charterhouse, that of *Vallis Auxilii* (today Felsőtárkány) near Eger, also had a house in the *Platea Italicorum*, since the prior let it for 20 florins in 1507.[42]

The Mendicant Orders

There are two indications that Franciscan friaries possessed houses in Buda. In 1433, a charter mentions the house of the Segesd friary as neighboring the house of the Pauline monastery of Lád. Since none of the houses mentioned in the charter can be identified exactly and there is no further evidence for this house belonging to the Franciscans, the history of the house remains shadowy. It is most likely that the house was a *pro anima* donation and that they sold it either because of the prescriptions of the order or because of the distance. Similarly there is but a single record of the house of the Buda friary, in 1442, in the same charter which mentions the house of Szék abbey.[43] Neither the location nor the fate of this house can be traced, but given that two years later the

---

39   Beatrix F. Romhányi, "Die Wirtschaftstätigkeit der ungarischen Pauliner im Spätmittelalter (15.–16. Jahrhundert)," in *Die Pauliner. Geschichte – Geist – Kultur* (Művelődéstörténeti műhely = Tagungen zur Ordensgeschichte, iv/2), ed. Gábor Sarbak (Budapest: Szent István Társulat, 2010), pp. 129–199, here p. 188.
40   F. Romhányi, *Die Wirtschaftstätigkeit*, p. 141. Further data on the management of urban houses – also in other towns – see ibid., pp. 137–146.
41   Végh, *Buda*, i, p. 198.
42   Végh, *Buda*, i, p. 240.
43   Végh, *Buda*, ii, no 244.

friary was taken over by the Observant branch of the order, it was presumably sold.

We do not have any evidence that any Dominican friary possessed a house in Buda. There is a single case in 1514 when the local friary was given a rent of 12 florins per year for 25 years by a burgher of Buda who wished to be buried in the Dominican church.[44] At much the same time, in 1512, the Pest friary inherited half of a house, donated to it by a widow, but her granddaughter immediately protested; the outcome of the case is unknown.

The Carmelite friary also received a house at the end of the Middle Ages, although not in the city itself. A devout nobleman, burgher of Buda and notary of the royal chancellery, Peter Söptei, left to the friars his house in the quarter Újváros (i.e. "new town"), which was probably a new part of the settlement outside the walls, west of what is today's Széna Square.[45] Predictably, the further history of this house, as well as its exact location, is unknown.

Nunneries

The two important female institutions of the region, the nunneries of Óbuda and of Margaret Island, also played a significant role in the life of Buda and Pest as landholders. From this point of view the more important was the Dominican nunnery which owned a part of Fehéregyáza with rights connected to the market, and it was also the patron of the Parish Church of St Mary in Buda. In Buda itself the Dominican nuns – as patrons of the parish church – had several houses in its cemetery. These houses were demolished by the priest in the 1340s in order to build a "palace", probably a representative hall, in its place. In 1346 the parties agreed that the priest would pay 20 marks rent per year to the nuns for this building (which presumably became the priest's domicile).[46] The nuns had a further house opposite the parish church from no later than the 1380s,[47] and in 1506 they received another on the Szombathely market place from Helena Cobor, who drew up her will in the nunnery on the island.[48]

The other nunnery, belonging to the Poor Clares of Óbuda, came into the possession of a house in *Platea Sancti Nicolai* close to the parish church, relatively early, in 1374, thanks to the bequest of a widow whose daughter was a nun in their monastery. Further information on the house dates from the first

---

44   Végh, *Buda*, ii, no 574. The same testator also left a sum of 100 florins to the convent.
45   MNL OL DL 93 640. (1494).
46   Végh, *Buda*, i, p. 211.
47   Végh, *Buda*, i, p. 249.
48   Végh, *Buda*, i, p. 296.

third of the fifteenth century and from 1475.[49] The nunnery received another house before 1506 from a burgher of the town and sold it soon after for 300 florins to the judge of Székesfehérvár; thus they were in this case but temporary owners.[50]

The Hospital of the Holy Spirit in Felhévíz

The Hospital of the Holy Spirit does not appear in the charters as a house owner; apparently it merely had the right to rents in the city in the fifteenth century, some of which were sold in the 1470s.[51] However, we learn from a charter dated between 1526–1529 that it received from King John Szapolyai the house of the late Imre Szerencsés (a converted Jew and the treasurer of Louis II), in Szent György Street. Later, the order exchanged this house for the house of John Podmaniczky in the *Platea Italicorum*.[52]

Manors, Vineyards and Other Properties

There is little evidence concerning the manors belonging to religious institutions in the area of Buda and Pest. We do know that the Pest Dominican friary received in 1465 from a certain nobleman, Balázs Kenderesi, a manor and other possessions somewhere in the area of the city,[53] and another one in 1478 in Soroksár (south of the town), but the friary relinquished the latter almost immediately in return for money.[54] According to the *lucrum camerae* register of 1494 and 1495, the Dominican friary of Buda received money from the royal court to buy a manor in Gubacs,[55] but there is no further evidence referring to this, so we cannot know what really happened. There is also evidence of another manor of the Dominican friary, in Örs (today Budaörs), from the early sixteenth century, when two unknown persons wanted to sell or to pledge a part of it.[56]

---

49 Végh, *Buda*, i, p. 250.
50 Végh, *Buda*, i, p. 221.
51 Végh, *Buda*, ii, nos 343, 361 (1475, 1479).
52 Végh, *Buda*, i, p. 204 and 244; Végh, *Buda*, ii, no 732.
53 MNL OL DL 16 159 (1465).
54 MNL OL DL 59 651 (1478).
55 Johann Christian von Engel, *Geschichte des ungrischen Reichs und seiner Nebenländer*, i (Halle: Johann Jacob Gebauer, 1797), p. 40.
56 Martinus Georgius Kovachich, *Formulae solennes styli in cancellaria…* (Pest: Typis Matthiae Trattner, 1799), no 146 [236].

The Pauline monastery of Fehéregyháza had significant holdings in the Buda region. In the sixteenth century it possessed two manor houses in Buda itself,[57] and two noble houses in the nearby village of Gercse.[58] It also purchased a shambles in Óbuda in 1506.[59] These possessions suggest that the monastery – or the two Pauline monasteries of St Lawrence and Fehéregyháza together – were involved in agriculture and in animal husbandry. The above-mentioned cases have a common feature: our records of them merely allude to their religious ownership, without providing any insight into their history, their exact location or their function. There is an isolated case when a friary was given vineyards. The Austin Hermits of Buda received three vineyards from Peter Söptei, notary of the royal chancellery, in 1481.[60] Some items in the accounts of Prince Sigismund would lead us to believe that the friars in fact possessed the vineyards over the long term.[61]

Smaller vineyards belonged to the abbey of Kána south of Buda, and larger estates in Felhévíz to the Dominican nunnery, which was also in possession of a part of the settlement. There are references also to the nunnery having mills and a bath.[62]

The Spiritual Impact of the Monasteries

The monasteries influenced not only the social, ecclesiastical and economic life of the region, but their presence also contributed to the spiritual wealth of the medieval capital. The Dominican nunnery was the gathering place of aristocratic women in the second half of the thirteenth century. The other nunnery, belonging to the Poor Clares, played a similar role in attracting girls of aristocratic families from the fourteenth century onwards. Although the Dominican nunnery ceased to be an aristocratic magnet in the later Middle Ages,

---

57   Végh, *Buda*, ii, no 756. Although the evidence dates from 1544, it undoubtedly reflects the medieval situation.
58   DAP, i, p. 147. The two noble houses were given to the monastery as pious donations in 1517, but the hermits sold one of them two years later.
59   DAP, i, p. 147.
60   MOL DL 93 590 (the relevant charter was issued in 1488).
61   Between 1500 and 1502 the Austin Hermits regularly gave grapes to Prince Sigismund and they received alms in return. See Adorján Divéky, *Zsigmond lengyel herczeg budai számadásai, 1500–1502, 1505* [The accounts of Sigismund, Polish prince at Buda, 1500–1502, 1505] (Magyar Történelmi Tár, 26) (Budapest: MTA, 1914), p. 28, 48, 94, 123 and 171.
62   AO, vi, pp. 288–289 (no 188). The bath was the subject of a legal action of the nuns with the Stefanite convent.

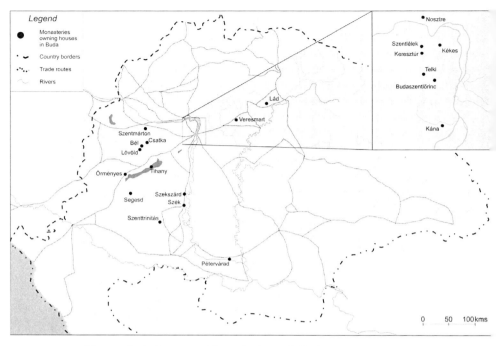

FIGURE 8.6 *Monasteries in the countryside owning houses in Buda*

a Hungarian nun, Lea Ráskai, composed the Hungarian legend of St Margaret within its walls in the early sixteenth century.[63]

As far as the friaries are concerned, the Dominicans and the Franciscans played the most conspicuous role in this regard. The Buda Dominican friary was the seat of the provincial prior until the end of the Middle Ages (1541) and it was also used for the *studium provinciale*, which received from the end of the fourteenth century the rank of a *studium generale*, although it failed to achieve any international reputation: not a single foreign student was sent to study there. Nevertheless, its prestige grew. By the end of the fifteenth century Petrus Niger and Franciscus Nardus de Neritono were among its professors, and in 1507 eight teachers of the Paris *studium generale* came to teach in Buda.[64] The building complex reflected the double function of provincial

---

63 On such early Hungarian literature see *Látjátok feleim… Magyar nyelvemlékek a kezdetektől a XVI. század elejéig* [Can you see, my brothers… Monuments of the Hungarian language from the beginnings to the early sixteenth century], ed. Edit Madas (Budapest: OSZK, 2009).

64 András Harsányi, *A domonkosrend Magyarországon a reformáció előtt* [The Dominican Order in Hungary before the Reformation] (Debrecen: Nagy Károly, 1938), pp. 145–154.

center and *studium generale* of the order, and it was one of the largest buildings on the Castle Hill.

The Franciscan friary was also one of the largest and most important friaries within the province. After 1444, when it was taken over by the Observant branch of the order, it became the seat of the Observant vicar. Two prominent preachers and sermon writers of the order, Pelbart of Temesvár (Timişoara) and Osvald of Laskó, resided there.[65] Their sermon collections were published many times and disseminated all over Europe. As vicar, Osvald of Laskó also played a prominent role in the organization of the observant province, which was formally constituted in 1517.

We know little about the Carmelites, but it may be noteworthy that Andreas, the son of the sculptor Veit Stoss, was prior of the Buda friary (1513–1519) and later became the provincial of the South German province. The years between 1490 and 1520 were a flourishing period for the convent, when its importance grew within the province and several learned members of the order spent a number of years there (beside Stoss, one can name Johannes Carpentarius who also later became provincial prior).[66]

Among the Pauline monks we find several prominent personalities of late medieval ecclesiastical literature: the preacher and poet Albert Csanádi, Gregorius Gyöngyösi, author of a history of the order entitled *Vitae fratrum*, and Bálint Hadnagy, the author of the Miracles of St Paul the Hermit – Gyöngyösi and Hadnagy even became general priors of the order.[67] Apart from these, there were also renowned organists and artists, and especially sculptors, in the monastery of St Lawrence.

There were also pilgrimage places associated with the monasteries: the tomb of St Margaret on the Hares' Island, later renamed after the holy princess, and the tomb of St Paul the Hermit in the monastery of St Lawrence, attracted thousands of pilgrims. Although there is no direct evidence, the reliquary of St Gerhard preserved in the Franciscan friary of Buda may also have become an object of devotion. The Paulines were perhaps the most popular religious

---

65 Zoltán J. Kosztolnyik, "Pelbartus of Temesvar: A Franciscan Preacher and Writer of the Late Middle Ages in Hungary," *Vivarium* 5 (1967), pp. 100–110; idem, "Some Hungarian Theologians in the Late Renaissance," *Church History* 57, no 1 (1988), pp. 5–18.

66 Kund Miklós Regényi, *Die ungarischen Konvente der oberdeutschen Karmelitenprovinz im Mittelalter* (Budapest – Heidelberg: METEM, 2001), p. 98; idem, "Karmeliták a középkori Magyarországon," *Capitulum* 1 (1998), pp. 67–83, here p. 77.

67 Gábor Sarbak, "Der Paulinerorden an der Schwelle der Neuzeit," in *Bettelorden in Mitteleuropa. Geschichte, Kunst, Spiritualität. Referate der gleichnamigen Tagung vom 19. bis 22. März in St. Pölten*, eds Heidemarie Specht and Ralph Andraschek-Holzer (St. Pölten: Diözesanarchiv St. Pölten, 2008), pp. 316–325.

community in the region, at least in the second half of the fifteenth century, and their reputation had its impact on religiosity as well. According to one of Gyöngyösi's stories, for instance, they – and not the friars living in the town – were asked in 1480 to pray for rain, and in fact, it did start raining after their procession.

Conclusions

Having arrived at the end of this short overview of monastic institutions and possessions we have to admit that the picture presented is rather fragmentary. Nevertheless, it is clear that the monastic landscape of the Buda area – comprising the city and the surrounding settlements – was complex. Monastic institutions appeared in the region in the twelfth century at the latest, although they were not among the most important ecclesiastical institutions of the time. Unlike many West European towns and cities, there were no monastic enclosures in Óbuda or in Pest. Urban development was already underway in the area before the setback of the Mongol invasion, and this was reflected among other things in the foundation of the Dominican friary of Pest.

The second half of the thirteenth century saw not only the foundation of a new capital in Buda, but also a spectacular enrichment of the monastic landscape. In this period a series of mendicant convents emerged in the region. All the mendicant communities in the country at that time (i.e. the Dominicans, the Franciscans and the Austin Hermits) settled in the new city. The hierarchy between them is, indeed, reflected in the pattern of settlement, the Dominican friary being situated at the heart of the new political center, between the early royal palace and the parish church, while the Franciscans and the Austin Hermits built their churches in more conventional locations, at the edge of the city and in the suburb respectively. This urban network of friaries was completed a century later when the Carmelite friary was founded in 1372. All of these religious houses were established thanks to royal generosity, but early ties with the burghers can be demonstrated in the case of the Dominicans (tombstones), and supposed in the case of the other convents as well.

The monastic landscape of Buda would be incomplete without the inclusion of the institutions of the broader region (see Fig. 8.5), especially Óbuda, Felhévíz, Margaret Island and Pest. The three settlements together with the island were at the end of the thirteenth century home to four Franciscan convents, two Dominican convents, and one convent of the Austin Hermits, as well as a convent of the Stefanite Order. Beside these new foundations the only other monastic institution in this area was the Premonstratensian provostry on Margaret Island. Thus all three, Buda, Pest and Óbuda, were marked mainly by the presence of the new mendicant orders. The castle of the Knights Hospitaller on Margaret Island can be regarded as a 'semi-monastic' building. This ecclesiastical landscape was completed in the thirteenth century by the two beguine houses in Buda and Pest and the nunnery on the island, as well as by a Carmelite friary and the hospital of the Order of the Holy Spirit in Felhévíz and the Poor Clares monastery of Óbuda in the following century.

Beside the physical presence of religious institutions themselves, the monastic landscape of Buda was also shaped by the monastic holdings (mainly houses, but also some landed property) in and around the city. The main ecclesiastical owners of houses in Buda were the Benedictine abbeys (from the end of the fourteenth century six abbeys held altogether ten houses in the castle and in the suburb) and the Pauline monasteries (between the end of the fourteenth and the beginning of the sixteenth century nine Pauline monasteries owned fourteen houses). Unfortunately the sparse documents rarely allow any insight into the history of these holdings. For example we do not always know whether a religious institution was in possession of a given house in the long term or not. In some cases, houses mentioned in connection with the Pauline monasteries were not in their possession, or they only enjoyed rents from them. Besides these orders, the nunneries of the island and of Óbuda, the Cistercians, the Carthusians, the Hospital of the Holy Spirit and the Franciscans appear as house owners or receivers of rent, while the Dominicans received only a rent for a certain period of time. The urban houses of the religious orders often appear in the neighborhood of other ecclesiastical properties (e.g. the archbishop of Esztergom, the St Stephen's collegiate chapter of Esztergom and the houses of other religious orders). Urban houses were held by some of the orders in the other parts of the settlement as well: the Paulines had houses in Óbuda and Pest, the Carmelites in Felhévíz, and the Dominicans perhaps in Pest. There are two periods of concentration – or at least of better documentation: the period between the 1370s and the 1420s, and the early sixteenth century.

Some of the religious communities of Buda and Pest had small landed properties in the immediate countryside. Both Dominican friaries as well as the Pauline monasteries acquired manors (and the latter ones received noble houses as well), while the Austin Hermits and the nunneries owned vineyards. The possession of mills can only be proven in the case of the two nunneries, although it cannot be excluded that the Pauline monasteries also had – perhaps temporarily – mills in the Buda area. As an exception in this region – but rather commonly elsewhere in the country – the Pauline monastery of Fehéregyháza bought a butchery in Óbuda, and the Dominican nunnery ran a bath on the territory of Felhévíz, near the Danube.

In conclusion, the image we gain from our source material, despite its inadequacy, is a colorful one, reflecting the complexity of the monastic presence in and around Buda. Decisive changes happened in the monastic landscape of the region in the second half of the thirteenth century in connexion with the foundation of Buda itself, and the main characteristics of this landscape were imposed in that period, with the coming of new religious institutions. While there was no major change in the monastic network as regards the actual institutions involved, the monastic presence became more striking because of the different properties which contributed to the economy of the owners. The estates of the religious communities appear in larger number from the turn of the fourteenth and fifteenth centuries. After a busy first period reaching to the mid-fifteenth century, the monastic presence receded to a certain extent (for instance, when a number of urban houses were sold), but it remained prominent until the end of the Middle Ages. The most important holders remained, as ever, the various abbeys, the Pauline monasteries and the nunneries.

Last but not least we need to recall the spiritual impact of the monastic communities. The Paulines and the nunneries played an important role in the formation of Hungarian literature, the preachers of the different orders influenced public opinion, the foreign professors of the Dominican *studium generale* as well as the Carmelite friars coming from abroad transmitted new ideas, and the friars who were artists and artisans contributed to the artistic quality of the medieval Hungarian capital.

CHAPTER 9

Sacred Sites in Medieval Buda

Gábor Klaniczay

"For religious man, space is not homogeneous; he experiences interruptions, breaks in it; some parts of space are qualitatively different from others. 'Draw not nigh hither', says the Lord to Moses; 'put off thy shoes from off your feet, for the place whereon thou standest is holy ground' (Exodus, 3, 5). There is, then, a sacred space, and hence a strong, significant space; there are other spaces that are not sacred and so are without structure or consistency, amorphous. Nor is this all. For religious man, this spatial nonhomogeneity finds expression in the experience of an opposition between space that is sacred – the only *real* and *real-ly* existing space – and all other space, the formless expanse surrounding it."[1]

Mircea Eliade, addressing the "sacralisation of the world", first of all shows that the forms of sacred space reproduce and symbolize the various views the different religions have about the universe and the cosmos.[2] In this respect it might be important to add that the natural environment of human settlements did not only serve as an object for the projection of certain views about the cosmos but also offered privileged spaces for this role. The contrast between sacred and profane, which structured space, is often articulated with cultural boundaries that separate human civilization from nature; cosmological ideas are mixed with symbolic landscapes and concepts about the sacrality of nature.[3] In this sense, religious ideas about sacred mountains and sacred islands present a combination of the sacrality of space and that of nature.

While thinking about the spatial distribution of the sacred sites at medieval Buda, I was struck by the phenomenon that the present inhabitants of

---

Translated by Ildikó Csepregi

[1] Mircea Eliade, *The Sacred and the Profane. The Nature of Religion* (London: Harcourt Brace Jovanovich, 1959), p. 20.

[2] For more recent overviews of this topic see Carsten Colpe, "Sacred and Profane," and Joel P. Brereton, "Sacred Space," in *The Encyclopaedia of Religion*, xi, ed. Mircea Eliade (New York: Simon & Schuster Macmillan, 1995), pp. 511–525 and 526–535; *Defining the Holy: Sacred Space in Medieval and Early Modern Europe*, eds Andrew Spicer and Sarah Hamilton (Hants: Ashgate, 2005); *Sacred Sites and Holy Places: Exploring the Sacralization of Landscape through Time and Space*, eds Sæbjørg Walaker Nordeide and Stefan Brink (Turnhout: Brepols, 2013).

[3] John Howe, "Creating Symbolic Landscapes: Medieval development of Sacred Space," in *Inventing Medieval Landscapes. Senses of Place in Western Europe*, eds John Howe and Michael Wolfe (Gainesville: University Press of Florida, 2002), pp. 208–223.

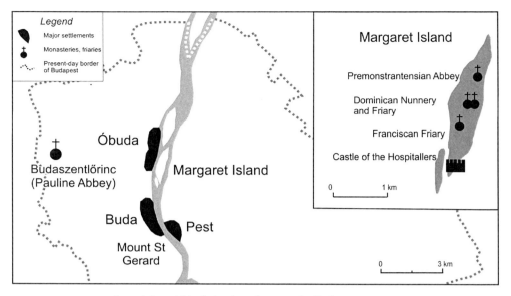

FIGURE 9.1   *Sacred sites within the borders of present-day Budapest*

Budapest – without being conscious about it – live in a space harmoniously structured around two sacred centers that are in salient contrast with each other: a sacred mountain and a sacred island. To complete the picture, the Gellért Hill (called *Gellért-hegy*, i.e. "Mount Gerard" – even though its height is only 235 meters above sea level, it does look like a mountain from the Danube) and the Margaret Island have an interesting opposition that recalls archetypes: the sacredness of the mountain has a male aspect while the sacredness of an island is a female one. Towards the end of the Middle Ages a third type of nature-bound sacrality complemented this picture: the wilderness and the caves of the Pauline hermits (Fig. 9.1). In my essay I will provide a historical overview, indicating how the cult of the respective saints was articulated within this spatially defined sacrality.[4]

---

4   My essay incorporates the materials of two studies of mine: "Il monte di San Gherardo e l'isola di Santa Margherita: gli spazi della santità a Buda nel Medioevo," in *Luoghi sacri e spazi della santità*, eds Sofia Boesch Gajano and Lucetta Scaraffia (Turin: Rosenberg & Sellier, 1990), pp. 267–284, and "Domenicani, eremiti paolini e francescani. Osservanti ungheresi e i loro santuari alla periferia," in *Ordini religiosi e santuari in età moderna*, ed. Lucia M.M. Olivieri (Bari: Edipuglia, 2013), pp. 19–34.

The Sacred Mountain of St Gerard

In respect of sacred mountains and sacred islands, starting points in the Mediterranean are obvious. There are hardly any more suggestive images of the holiness of mountains, reaching to heavenly heights, than the biblical imagery of Mount Sinai, Mount Carmel, Mount Tabor and Mount Golgotha[5] or the references to the heights of the Olympus and other Zeus-bound heights in Greece; likewise it would be difficult to speak of the sacredness of island without mentioning Homeric examples.[6] In the northern parts of Europe, Celtic civilization created a similar point of departure: for example the visions of the netherworld characteristic of Celtic and Nordic mythology that make references to islands that survived in several medieval cults, legends and mythical tales (the travels of St Brendan, the island of Avalon in the Arthurian legends etc.).[7]

My introduction to the two natural, sacred sites of medieval Buda can also be viewed from the perspective of local Celtic traditions. One of the first groups that settled in Pannonia in the fourth century BC consisted of the Celtic Eravisci who made settlements on the territory of the future Budapest. According to the testimonies of archaeological excavations, they selected two places to inhabit: the island and the mountain of which I shall speak below. The most important reason was probably that these were the most favorable spots for crossing the Danube, which is narrowest at the foot of Mount Gerard and at the side branches of Margaret Island; as a result commercial routes also passed here. At the same time, another factor could also have influenced the selection of these sites: the Celts' regard for the sacral dimension, attested by the sanctuaries excavated on the slopes of the mountain as well as on the island. On the

---

5 On holy mountains, see the good general overview in Ichiro Hori, "Mountains and Their Importance for the Idea of the Other World in Japanese Folk Religion," *History of Religions* 6 (1966), pp. 1–23; on Sinai, see Jaš Elsner and Gerhard Wolf, "The Transfigured Mountain: Icons and Transformations of Pilgrimage at the Monastery of St Catherine at Mount Sinai," in *Approaching the Holy Mountain: Art and Liturgy at St Catherine's Monastery in the Sinai*, eds Sharon E.J. Gerstel and Robert S. Nelson (Turhout: Brepols, 2010), pp. 37–72.

6 Erwin Rohde, *Seelenkult und Unsterblichkeitsglaube der Griechen* (Freiburg – Leipzig: Mohr, 1894), pp. 63–137; Gullög Nordquist, "The Ancient and Sacred Greek Landscape," in *Sacred Sites*, pp. 142–185.

7 János Honti, "A sziget kelta mítoszáról," [On the Celtic myth of the island] *Argonauták* 1 (1937), pp. 3–13; Eldar Heide, "Holy Islands and the Otherworld: Places beyond Water," in *Isolated Islands in Medieval Nature, Culture and Mind* (CEU Medievalia, 14) eds Gerhard Jaritz and Torstein Jørgensen (Budapest: CEU Press, 2011), pp. 57–80.

side of Mount Gerard the Celts created a kind of sacred zone honoring their most important divinity called Tuath.[8]

After the Celts, the inhabitants of the region constructed settlements in various places over the next millennium. The Romans used the island again, both for its thermal springs and for its strategic importance on the *limes* that followed the line of the Danube. Yet, the religion of the Romans saw more sacrality in the river itself than the island. We have, for example, a surviving votive altar bearing the inscription: *Danuvio Sacrum Vetulenus Apronianus Legionus*.[9]

Mount Gerard obtained a renewed importance only in the Middle Ages, again within a sacred context. The site was linked to the death of St Gerard, a martyr bishop from the time of the conversion of the Hungarians. Gerard, of Venetian origin, came to the territory of the kingdom of Hungary as a pilgrim, around the year 1020. Following the invitation of the Hungarian king, St Stephen, he remained in the country, first as a tutor of the royal prince, Emeric, and from 1030 as bishop of Csanád (today Cenad). In these decades he became a prominent figure in the formation of the Christian Church in Hungary. One event illustrates well this aspect of his character. After the death of St Stephen (in 1038) Gerard, according to his legends, was brave enough to enter into an open conflict with Stephen's second successor to the throne, Samuel Aba, by refusing to give him the Easter benediction, because he found that the king tolerated pagan customs.[10]

A few years later, in 1046, a devastating pagan revolt broke out, which led to the murder of several Christian clerics; Bishop Gerard was also among the victims. Gerard was on his journey from Székesfehérvár (*Alba Regia*), an important center of the Hungarian kingdom, to the camp of Andrew, the new aspirant for the throne, who was encamped at Pest. When Gerard arrived at the Danube, the pagan rebels attacked his entourage and murdered the bishop, just when he was about to cross the river. Of Gerard's martyrdom there are two different accounts in his two legends. The *Legenda minor*, known also by the

---

8   Éva B. Bónis, *Die spätkeltische Siedlung Gellérthegy-Tabán in Budapest* (Budapest: Akadémiai, 1969).

9   Bálint Kuzsinszky, "Aquincum római feliratai. III. közlemény," [Roman inscriptions of Aquincum, Part 3] *Budapest Régiségei* 6 (1899), pp. 109–150, here p. 122.

10 László Szegfű, "La missione politica ed ideologica di San Gerardo in Ungheria," in *Venezia e Ungheria nel Rinascimento*, ed. Vittore Branca (Florence: Olschki, 1973), pp. 23–36; József Gerics, "Die Kirchenpolitik des Königs Peter und deren Folgen," *Annales Universitatis Scientiarum Budapestinensis de Rolando Eötvös nominatae. Sectio Historica* 24 (1985), pp. 269–276; idem, "Auslegung der Nacherzählung mittelalterlicher Quellen in unserer Zeit (Bischof Sankt Gerhard von Tschanad über König Aba)," *Acta Historica Academiae Scientiarum Hungaricae* 32 (1986), pp. 335–348.

title *Passio beatissimi Gerardi*, and regarded by a great number of scholars as the more authentic version, was written after 1083, the year of the canonization of the first group of Hungarian saints (Andrew-Zoerard, Benedict, Stephen, Emeric and Gerard); its final form was given probably in the middle of the twelfth century. Here the text says:

> When he arrived at the river Danube, behold, a wicked mob of people surrounded him and hurled stones at our father, who was seated in his cart, but these did not touch him then, since God was protecting him. From his side, our father opposed [them] with a blessing and the sign of the holy cross. But at last, grabbing and turning backwards the heads of the horses, they topple the cart, throw down our father, and start stoning him furiously. Then, like the Protomartyr, the first martyr of Pannonia *falling on his knees* on the ground *cried out with a loud voice*: "Lord Jesus Christ, *lay not this sin to their charge*, for they know not what they do!" *And when he had said this*, stabbed in the chest by a spear, *he fell asleep in the Lord*.[11]

Other documents also speak of stoning, such as the *Legenda maior* of St Stephen, written before 1083 as well as the Legend of St Stephen written by Bishop Hartvik,[12] which at this point follows the earlier legend. This account of Gerard's murder by stoning was prominent until the end of the thirteenth century. Even in the oldest legend of St Margaret (written around 1273) we can read about Gerard as *tunc paganis lapidibus obrutus martirium pertulerat*.[13]

There is, however, a new version of the story in the so-called *Legenda maior* of Gerard, entitled *De S. Gerhardo episcopo Morosensi et martyre regni Ungarie* [BHL 3424] where the mountain is transformed from a simple place of death

---

11   Emericus Madzsar, ed., *Legenda Sancti Gerhardi episcopi*, in SRH, ii, pp. 461–506, here pp. 477–478; a new edition is forthcoming in *Sanctitas Principum: Sancti Reges, Duces, Episcopi et Abbates Europae Centralis (Saec. XI–XIII) – The Sanctity of the Leaders: Holy Kings, Princes, Bishops, and Abbots from Central Europe (Eleventh to Thirteenth Centuries)* (Central European Medieval Texts, 7), ed. Gábor Klaniczay (Budapest: CEU Press [in press]). I cite from this edition the translation by Cristian Gaşpar.

12   Emma Bartoniek, ed., *Legendae Sancti Regis Stephani*, in SRH, ii, pp. 401–440, here p. 388 and 422; for an English version see Nora Berend, transl., Hartvic, *Life of King Stephen of Hungary* in *Medieval Hagiography. An Anthology*, ed. Thomas Head (New York – London: Garland, 2000), pp. 379–396, here p. 388.

13   Kornél Bőle, ed., *Legenda Beatae Margaritae de Hungaria*, in SRH, ii, pp. 685–709, here p. 699.

into the instrument of his martyrdom. According to this description, the pagans first attacked Gerard with stones but

> thereupon they became even crueler, rushed upon him and turned over his carriage on the shores of the Danube. Then they dragged him off his carriage, put him into a cart (*biga*) and pushed him down from Mount Kreenfeld.[14] As he was still breathing, they thrust a lance into his chest, finally dragged him to a rock and crushed his skull... The Danube swept it for seven years, but could not wash off the blood from the stone on which St Gerard's head was smashed, until the priests took away the stone and the blood.[15]

Numerous doubts have been raised about the historical authenticity of the *Legenda maior* of Gerard, which survived in a version transcribed around the mid-fourteenth century, and which seems to be a largely reworked and interpolated text of an archaic legend of Gerard, different from the *Legenda minor*.[16] I have the suspicion that the more colorful second version of Gerard's martyrdom was probably such a later insertion.

It might also be worthwhile to draw attention to a hagiographic parallel. The motif of the martyr's blood which could not be washed away was also present in the tenth–eleventh-century legends of the martyred duke of Bohemia, St Wenceslas.[17] The graphic scene of the martyr bishop hauled down the rocks in a cart, on the other hand, must have been a local invention.

When did this account appear in the sources? Disregarding the *Legenda maior* because of the difficulties of its dating, the first references to Gerard being hauled down from the mountain appear in the second half of the thirteenth century. The oldest description is that of the *Chronicon pontificum et imperatorum*, written by Martinus Oppaviensis (d. 1278), according to whose account: "In those times St Gerard, a bishop in Hungary was tied to a cart

---

14 i.e. the mountain which was to be named after him.
15 *Legenda Sancti Gerhardi*, p. 502.
16 For an overview of the debates, see Gábor Klaniczay and Edit Madas, "La Hongrie," in *Hagiographies. Histoire internationale de la littérature hagiographique latine et vernaculaire en Occident des origines à 1550*, ii (Corpus Christianorum), ed. Guy Philippart (Turnhout: Brepols, 1996), pp. 138–140.
17 Marina Miladinov, transl., *Passion of Saint Wenceslas by Gumpold of Mantua*, in *Vitae Sanctorum Aetatis Conversionis Europae Centralis (Saec. X–XI). Saints of the Christianization Age of Central Europe (Tenth–Eleventh Centuries)* (Central European Medieval Texts, 6), ed. Gábor Klaniczay (Budapest: CEU Press, 2013), pp. 62–63.

which was hauled down to the precipice from the highest mountain, and he won the crown of martyrdom."[18] In the *Gesta Hungarorum*, written by Simon of Kéza between 1282 and 1285, we can read: "Bishop Gerard of Csanád won the crown of martyrdom in Pest when he was pushed off the mountain in a cart by Hungarians."[19] We find the same description, somewhat enlarged, in the *Hungarian Chronicle-compilation* preserved from the fourteenth century, which subsequently became the basis of the representative *Chronicon pictum* (c. 1360) prepared in the court of Louis I (the Great). The description contains here precisely the same wording and sequence as the passage from the *Legenda maior*, ending with the skull of Gerard crushed on a rock.[20] Whether the *Chronicle* was the source of the *Legenda maior* here, or vice versa, is hard to ascertain.[21]

Supposing that the story of the cart emerged only in the first half of the thirteenth century, it might be illuminating that we encounter for the first time precisely in these decades, in the year 1236, the privileges of the *ecclesia B. Gerardi martyris de parvo Pest seu Cremfeld*, erected on the place where the saint's skull had been crushed.[22] This church (or chapel) surely did not have its own relics; according to the *Legenda minor*, Gerard's body had been carried, shortly after his death to the seat of his bishopric, Marosvár (today part of Cenad). The fourteenth-century *Hungarian Chronicle-compilation* and the *Legenda maior* both claim that this transfer took place seven years after his death, and the former also mentions that even the blood-covered rock had been transported there.[23] My hypothesis is that it could have been the need to compensate for the lack of the relics of the martyr bishop, which gave rise to the idea that the rocky hill behind the church had a prominent role in the martyrdom, which

---

18 "Huius tempore sanctus Gerardus episcopus in Ungaria super bigam ligatus de altissimo monte cursu precipiti martirio coronatur" – *Catalogus fontium historiae Hungariae aevo ducum et regum ex stirpe Arpad descendentium*, 3 vols, ed. Albinus Franciscus Gombos (Budapest: Szent István Akadémia, 1937, repr. Budapest: Nap, 2005), ii, p. 1575 [henceforth: CFH].

19 "Gerardus...de monte submissus in biga martyrio coronatur," – Simon of Kéza, *Gesta Hungarorum. The Deeds of the Hungarians* (Central European Medieval Texts, 1), eds László Veszprémy and Frank Schaer (Budapest – New York: Central European University Press, 1999), pp. 124–126.

20 Alexander Domanovszky, ed., *Chronici Hungarici compositio saeculi XIV*, in SRH, i, pp. 217–505, here p. 341 (cap. 83–84).

21 László Szegfű, "Gellért püspök halála," [The death of Bishop Gerard] *Acta Universitatis Szegediensis de Attila József nominatae. Acta Historica* 66 (1979), pp. 19–28, here pp. 22–24.

22 CD, iv/1, pp. 60–61.

23 *Chronici Hungarici*, p. 341 (cap. 83–84); *Legenda Sancti Gerhardi*, p. 502.

should be honored in the cult of the saint. The wording *mons sancti Gerardi* appears for the first time in 1273.[24]

The thirteenth century, when a cult around this sacred mountain emerged, was also the century when a noteworthy urban development started in this area. On the other side of the Danube, the city of Pest became a fast developing commercial center. A telling indicator of its development is that the Dominicans founded there one of their first of their convents in Hungary.[25] At the same time, other settlements emerged in the neighborhood: Kreenfeld (Kreinfeld, Kelenföld) on the side of Mount St Gerard; Felhévíz more to the north, in the vicinity of the thermal springs on the right bank of the Danube; and even further to north, near the former Roman colony of Aquincum, Óbuda that became the Queen's residence.[26] The settlements of the future urban agglomeration established increasingly stronger relationships to one another.[27]

One of the aspects of the link between urbanization and religious life could be a heightened sensibility for some sacred aspects of the natural environment, from which the city started to discern itself. It could have been the result of such an attitude that the most important new saint cult of the thirteenth century, that of St Margaret, also emerged in a place of special natural characteristics, that is on one of the islands on the Danube.

The Margaret Island as a Sacred Center

Among the miracles of St Margaret of Hungary, who lived between 1242 and 1270, we can find the following account:

> A certain honest man called Ponsa…made frequent devout visits to the virgin Margaret's tomb. One day this man said to his companions, "let's go make our pilgrimage and greet St Margaret." When certain religious overheard this, they argued fatuously against his devotion. Because he was a layman and easily deceived, they were successful in swaying him from his purpose. When two days had passed, the same man said to his friends: "Let's go and take a trip to the island of Our Lady the Virgin Mary," completely

---

24   *Legenda Beatae Margaritae*, p. 699.
25   Nikolaus Pfeiffer, *Die ungarische Dominikanerprovinz von ihrer Gründung bis zur Tatarenwüstung 1241–1242* (Zurich: Leemann, 1913), pp. 29–30.
26   Györffy, *Budapest*, pp. 249–295.
27   On this, see the study by Enikő Spekner in this volume.

forgetful of his earlier devotion. When they took the boat, his right hand was seized by a violent pain, which spread to his shoulder before they had crossed the Danube. His right hand became totally numb and stiff, so that he did not have the strength to lift it up or move it down even a little way below his chest. He at once realized that he had been punished for letting himself be led astray. Fearful and trembling he approached the tomb of the aforesaid virgin Margaret, but he received no mercy or blessing from the creator because his mind had not yet been purified as it ought to have been from the fault of hesitation. Then contrite of heart and humbled, persevering in his laments, he prayed in these words for the virgin's pardon: "O blessed Margaret, consecrated to God, people coming from various parts of the kingdom who are sick and suffer from afflictions of all kinds joyfully return home cured. I, on the other hand, left home healthy, but because of my unbelief I shall return half dried up, to the everlasting shame of me and my family." Meanwhile the pain grew much worse, and the repentant man shed his tears all the more profusely at the base of the tomb, and kept begging for the blessing of a cure all the more insistently. When his petitions had increased in fervour, a cure was not long in coming. For before the Vespers had been completed, he recovered perfect health, and proclaimed to everyone in loud voice the miraculous deeds of God, the merits of the virgin Sister Margaret and the plaintive insistence of his own prayers.[28]

This complex miracle allows us to formulate various hypotheses. I stumbled upon it during my research on royal and dynastic sanctity,[29] and I also relied upon it in illustrating the structure of an archaic and ambivalent type of miracle, the 'punishment miracle' or 'miracle of vengeance'.[30] Now I would like to use this story to show how the 'dynamics of the miracle'[31] are inscribed into a natural space that contributes to the symbolic efficacy[32] of the relics. The healing power that emanated from the relics became manifest here through the effects produced by its proximity. Margaret punished the man who forgot his

28   *Legenda Beatae Margaritae*, pp. 703–704.
29   Gábor Klaniczay, *Holy Rulers and Blessed Princesses. Dynastic Cults in Medieval Central Europe* (Cambridge: Cambridge University Press, 2002), pp. 275–276.
30   Gábor Klaniczay, "Miracoli di punizione e *malefizia*," in *Miracoli. Dai segni alla storia*, eds Sofia Boesch Gajano and Marilena Modica (Rome: Viella, 1999), pp. 109–137.
31   Pierre-André Sigal, *L'homme et le miracle dans la France médiévale (XIe–XIIe siècle)* (Paris: Cerf, 1985), pp. 165–225.
32   Claude Lévi-Strauss, "L'efficacité symbolique," *Revue de l'histoire des religions* 135 (1949), pp. 5–27.

vow with a harsh physical pain that manifested itself exactly on the border of the saint's territory. As he got closer to the sacred place, the pain became stronger. In order to get relief, the man had to supplicate the saint next to her relics.

The river that protects the island has a special role in this narrative: it was during the passage through the river, in a boat, that the miracle-working capacity of the saint started to manifest itself. This boat-transfer to the island recalls associations from ancient mythology, such as journeys to the netherworld,[33] and it can be considered as a prominently 'liminal' stage of a 'rite of passage', as analyzed by Victor Turner.[34] The island, called at the time the Island of Hares, had a truly religious character during the Middle Ages. Besides the Dominican convent, built between 1244 and 1252 to accommodate the royal princess and a large group of nuns from the highest aristocratic circles of Hungary, there was an adjacent small Dominican house for friars who secured the spiritual supervision of the convent. There was also a chapel belonging to the Premonstratensian Order, a small fortress owned by the Hospitallers of the Order of St John, a small convent of the Poor Clares, another one for the Order of St Augustine, and some other houses that hosted Beguine sisters.[35] This group of buildings can be seen on the etching made by Enea Vico in 1542 (Fig. 9.2).

The foundation of the Dominican convent was due to a tragic event: the Mongol invasion in 1241 that resulted in the almost total devastation of the country. King Béla IV was forced to flee as far as Dalmatia and he made a vow to dedicate his future child to the service of God if the country was saved. When King Béla IV took back his territories, he practically founded the country anew and this also had a great impact on Buda, the future capital of the kingdom, where he made several new foundations. Next to Óbuda, the town that had developed within and around the remnants of the Roman Aquincum and facing Pest, the town of merchants, King Béla ordered the construction of a fortified city, on the hills on the right bank of the Danube, which, with its rocky walls would be able to resist any future Mongol attack. The royally-founded Dominican female convent had been constructed on the point of intersection of the borders of these three important towns, a multiple periphery that had

---

33　Claude Carozzi, *Le voyage dans l'au-delà d'après la littérature latine, V^e–XIIIe siècle* (Rome: École française de Rome, 1994).

34　Victor Turner, "Liminality and Communitas," in idem, *The Ritual Process: Structure and Anti-Structure* (Ithaca – London: Cornell University Press, 1977), pp. 94–130; idem and Edith Turner, *Image and Pilgrimage in Christian Culture* (New York: Columbia University Press, 2013), pp. 1–39.

35　These religious institutions are described in Ilona Király, *Árpádházi Szent Margit és a sziget* [St Margaret of Hungary and the Island] (Budapest: Panoráma, 1979), pp. 29–40 and 207–230.

FIGURE 9.2   *The Margaret Island in 1542 (Enea Vico's etching)*

the potential to develop into a symbolic center, a 'celestial' point in the future metropolis. An etching from the early seventeenth century (Fig. 9.3) shows the three: Pest, Buda and Óbuda, together with the Margaret Island. In the background one can also see the Mount St Gerard, the sacred pole on the other periphery. King Béla IV must have had a sensibility for these sacred dimensions. In the freshly-founded town of Buda he laid the foundation of several religious institutions, among them the male Dominican convent dedicated to St Nicholas, where the Order of the Preachers held its general chapter in 1254.[36] He also founded a house for the Franciscans, who towards the end of his life became dearer to him and more influential than the Dominicans.[37]

---

36   Pfeiffer, *Die ungarische Dominikanerordensprovinz*, p. 31; András Harsányi, *A domonkosrend Magyarországon a reformáció előtt* [The Dominican Order in Hungary before the Reformation] (Debrecen: Nagy Károly Grafikai Műintézete, 1938, repr. Budapest: [n. p.], 1999), pp. 24–26; Beatrix F. Romhányi, *Kolostorok és társaskáptalanok a középkori Magyarországon* [Monasteries and collegiate chapters in medieval Hungary] (Budapest: Pytheas, 2000; revised and enlarged CD-ROM version: Budapest: Arcanum, 2008), p. 16.

37   Erik Fügedi, "La formation des villes et les ordres mendiants en Hongrie," *Annales ESC* 25 (1970), pp. 966–987.

FIGURE 9.3 *View of Óbuda in the early seventeenth century*
BTM, GRAPHICS COLLECTION

For the emergence of the cult-place of St Margaret of Hungary we have an exceptionally rich source: the acts of her canonization process. The daughter of King Béla IV, offered to God's service by her parents, spent the major part of her life in this Dominican convent, on the Island of Hares, where she died in the fame of sainthood in 1270. To have her sanctity recognized, an ecclesiastical procedure was initiated in 1272 at the request of King Stephen V (Margaret's brother) to Pope Gregory X, who issued the papal authorization for a first investigation.[38] This resulted in the questioning of forty witnesses and recorded ten miracles during Margaret's lifetime, four visions in connection with her death,

---

38   We know of the petition of Stephen V from the bull of Innocent V in 1276. Cf. the introduction of Vilmos Fraknói, in *Inquisitio super vita, conversatione et miraculis beatae Margarethae virginis,* in *Monumenta Romana episcopatus Vesprimiensis,* I, ed. idem (Budapest: Franklin 1896), p. cix. Recently a copy of the bull of Gregory X has been discovered by Bence Péterfi, "Újabb adalékok Árpád-házi Margit középkori csodáinak sorához," [New additions to the medieval miracles of St Margaret of Hungary] in *Micae mediaevales. Tanulmányok a középkori Magyarországról és Európáról* [Studies in the history of medieval Hungary and Europe], eds Zsófia Kádár, Gábor Mikó, Bence Péterfi and András Vadas (Budapest: ELTE BTK Történelemtudományi Doktori Iskola, 2011), pp. 83–106, here p. 86; cf. Gábor Klaniczay, "Efforts at the Canonization of Margaret of Hungary in the Angevin Period," *Hungarian Historical Review* 2 (2013), pp. 313–340, here pp. 316–317.

and twenty-eight posthumous miracles. A list of these miracles (among them the one of Ponsa, quoted above) were added to her first legend, the *Legenda vetus*, most likely written by her spiritual director, Marcellus, prior provincial of the Dominicans in Hungary.[39] Relying upon this first documentation and renewed requests from the new king, Ladislas IV (the Cuman) a new inquest was ordered by Pope Innocent V in 1276. The papal committee, including two Italian legates, recorded more than one hundred and ten depositions between July and October 1276. Eleven new lifetime miracles, three miraculous signs connected to her death and thirty-eight new posthumous miracles were added to the miracle list of Margaret, resulting in a total of ninety-five miracles.[40] Despite these efforts, her canonization did not take place during the Middle Ages. After several failed attempts on the part of the Angevin kings, Charles I and Louis I and also on the part of King Matthias Corvinus in the Renaissance as well as of the Habsburgs in the early modern period, she was eventually canonized only in 1943.[41] Margaret's grave on the Hares' Island, nevertheless, became a popular cult-place throughout the last centuries of the Middle Ages.

When analysing the accounts of the witnesses during the canonization process, one can observe a striking phenomenon: the territory of the convent is described as a space imbued with the miracle-working power of the saintly princess. The epicenter of this thaumaturgic space is, of course, her sarcophagus in the center of the sanctuary. In the depositions we have a colorful description about how the Dominican nuns respected this sacred center: they could not go into the 'public' part of the church, but they watched the beneficiaries of miracles with great curiosity, peeping through the small window behind the altar, from the nuns' choir. We have the record of a miracle, where a sister teased Margaret, even maliciously tested her: "Virgin Margaret, if you want me to believe that you're a saint, show me some miracle."[42] And the paralyzed woman suddenly got up and walked around the tomb.

During the fourteenth and the fifteenth centuries, in the numerous accounts of miracles recorded in the European canonization processes, long-distance miracles gradually surpass in number those happening near the tomb of the

---

39 *Legenda Beatae Margaritae*; as regards the attribution to Marcellus, see Klaniczay, *Holy Rulers*, pp. 423–424.

40 *Inquisitio super vita*, pp. 162–383; for the most recent analysis of this text, also providing an estimate of how much of the original investigation documents have been lost, see Viktória Hedvig Deák, *La légende de sainte Marguerite de Hongrie et l'hagiographie dominicaine* (Paris: Cerf, 2013), pp. 286–323.

41 Klaniczay, "Efforts at the Canonization".

42 "Virgo Margaretha, si vis quod ego credam, quod tu sis sancta, ostende mihi aliquod miraculum." See *Inquisitio super vita*, p. 187 and 193.

saints.[43] The late thirteenth-century miracles of Margaret, however, still show a more archaic pattern: more than 70 percent of the miracles occur near the tomb of the saint. This allows us to observe how proximity to the relics made the miracles possible, and how a kind of concentric miraculous power was thought to be radiating from the sanctuary. In view of this, some devout found it worthwhile sleeping on the Island on the first night of pilgrimage, being hosted by some other religious institutions there.[44]

On certain occasions, similar to the 'incubation-miracle,' i.e. the 'temple sleep' best described in the cults of Byzantine saints (like Sts Cosmas and Damian or St Artemios),[45] Margaret came in night-time apparitions to the pilgrims who were sleeping nearby and invited the sick to come to her tomb to obtain a complete miracle cure.[46] Such was the case of "a nobleman named Petrucius from the Kata kindred," paralyzed for more than three years. In the *Legenda vetus* of Margaret the story is told in the following way:

> the virgin Sister Margaret, with certain venerable persons accompanying her, appeared to him in a dream. Filled with piety as she was, she touched with her virgin hands the part worst affected by the paralysis and said, "In the name of Our Lord Jesus Christ, in accord with your faith, may you receive the health you hoped for." Then she disappeared at once.

---

43   André Vauchez, *La sainteté en Occident aux derniers siècles du moyen âge. D'après les procès de canonisation et les documents hagiographiques* (Rome: École française de Rome, 1981), pp. 495–559; Christian Krötzl, "Miracles au tombeau – miracles à distance. Approches typologiques," in *Miracle et karāma. Hagiograhies médiévales comparées,* ed. Denise Aigle (Turnhout: Brepols, 2000), pp. 557–576; Thomas Wetzstein, "'Virtus morum et virtus signorum?' Zur Bedeutung der Mirakel in den Kanonisationsprozessen des 15. Jahrhunderts," in *Mirakel im Mittelalter. Konzeptionen, Erscheinungsformen, Deutungen,* eds Klaus Herbers, Martin Heinzelmann, and Dieter R. Bauer (Stuttgart: Steiner, 2002), pp. 351–376.

44   This was the case of Petric of Kata, who found accommodation in the convent of the Augustinian nuns, where a relative of his lived. Cf. *Inquisitio super vita,* p. 304, witness 54.

45   Mary Hamilton, *Incubation and the Cure of Diseases in Pagan Temples and Christian Churches* (London: W.C. Henderson & Son, 1906); Hippolyte Delehaye, "Les recueils antiques de Miracles de saints," *Analecta Bollandiana* 43 (1925), pp. 1–85 and 305–325; A.-J. Festugière, *Sainte Thècle, Saints Côme et Damien, Saints Cyr et Jean (extraits), Saint Georges* (Paris: A. et J. Picard, 1971); Ildikó Csepregi, "The Miracles of St Cosmas and Damian: Characteristics of Dream Healing," *Annual of Medieval Studies at CEU* 7 (2002), pp. 89–122.

46   Gábor Klaniczay, "Dreams and Visions in Medieval Miracle Accounts," in *Ritual Healing. Magic, Ritual and Medical Therapy from Antiquity until the Early Modern Period* (Micrologus Library, 48), eds Ildikó Csepregi and Charles Burnett (Florence: SISMEL, 2012), pp. 147–170.

He awoke and cast off his illness, feeling himself completely well. At the tomb of the virgin Margaret, accompanied by a large train (for he was a nobleman), he publicly proclaimed to all the grace of healing received through the merits of his benefactress, and he has not stopped proclaiming it even to this day.[47]

Among the witnesses of the second investigation in 1276 we do not find Petrucius, but his case is presented by his father-in-law, Nicolaus, and also by other relatives. According to Nicolaus's account there were two apparitions of St Margaret, on two subsequent nights. The description of the unexpected cure allows us to get a realistic picture of the family's feelings in such a shocking experience: "when his children saw this, some laughed, others cried."

> When asked who were present when the said Petrucius, as he stood beside the aforesaid tomb, recounted everything that had happened to him, as he said, he replied, "Three thousand people, and a lot more." When asked the names of some of that three thousand, he replied, "How can I enumerate the whole kingdom?"[48]

This context is important if we want to understand the psychological mechanisms of miracles: the crowd at the solemn proclamation of the healing included the family, the relatives, the friends, and all other unknown people and the investigating authorities. The explosion of the emotions and then the repeated narrations, were embellished and articulated in front of these people each time.[49]

There is yet another miracle relating to the convent of Margaret on the island, the miracle of the flooding Danube. This shows us Margaret as a living saint, who has the capacity to dominate the elements and make an impact on the forces of nature. Her confessor Marcellus narrates the event in the following way:

> I had come from Esztergom to this monastery and this blessed Margaret said to me, 'We were in danger of being submerged because of the flooding of the Danube [...] and the water came up to here on me,' showing a

---

47 *Legenda Beatae Margaritae*, p. 704.
48 *Inquisitio super vita*, pp. 334–335.
49 For insightful analyses of these mechanisms, see Sigal, *L'homme*, pp. 182–196; Michael Goodich, "Filiation and Form in Late Medieval Miracle Story," *Hagiographica* 3 (1996), pp. 306–322; repr. in idem, *Lives and Miracles of the Saints. Studies in Medieval Latin Hagiography* (Variorum) (Aldershot: Ashgate, 2004).

certain place, and I answered, 'Come, come, I don't believe this', and then she said, 'Lord Jesus Christ, show to the prior who is here the truth of what happened, so that he may believe my words'; and the water backed up so fast that I had to flee from it and get up on a beam on the wall in which there are pillars that support the porch of this cloister, and the water was quite a bit higher than it had been before, and until early morning it ebbed away, so that hardly a trace of it was seen.[50]

This same 'flood-miracle' is transformed in the fourteenth-century *Legenda maior* of Margaret, written by Garinus,[51] into an epic, almost Baroque, narrative:

> The Danube broke in like a furious river moved by the Lord's spirit. Most powerful waves rose from the river and inundating everything the water broke into the abode of the sisters, streaming into the territory of the cloister, the buildings, the cells… The sisters were terrified that the flood would destroy their entire convent, and in their fear they climbed to the roofs…[52]

Knowing the frequent floods of the Danube, this story is actually quite believable.[53] And it is understandable that such situations can give rise to a reliance on the supernatural power of a saintly person, such as Margaret.

The canonization investigations, and all these miracle-stories, which they recorded and proclaimed, must have contributed to the sacral standing of the Island. Although the canonization of Margaret did not follow, there are several indices, which testify to the saintly aura of the Island in the fourteenth and fifteenth centuries. During the reign of the Angevin Dynasty new efforts were invested to promote the cult of the pious Dominican princess. In 1306 the Dominicans around King Charles I sent a friar named Andreas to Avignon in an endeavor to restart the canonization process of Margaret (with no success).[54]

---

50   *Inquisitio super vita*, pp. 280–281; the same event is told by other witnesses: pp. 183, 186, 191–192, 223 and 242–243.

51   On this see Viktória Deák, "The Birth of a Legend: the so-called 'Legenda Maior' of St Margaret of Hungary and Dominican Hagiography," *Revue Mabillon* [NS] 20 [81] (2009), pp. 87–112; and eadem, *La légende de sainte Marguerite*, pp. 169–323.

52   CFH, iii, pp. 2507–2508.

53   András Vadas, "Long-Term Perspectives on River Floods. The Dominican Nunnery on Margaret Island (Budapest) and the Danube River," *Interdisciplinaria Archaeologica* 4, no 1 (2013), pp. 73–82.

54   Klaniczay, *Holy Rulers*, p. 324.

Beatrice of Luxemburg, the second wife of Charles, gave new privileges to the convent, exempting it from royal taxes, "for the reverence of the blessed Margaret, trusting in her protection in the skies and here on earth."[55] The third wife of Charles, Elizabeth Piast, invited, after her visit to Naples in 1331, the renowned Italian sculptor Tino di Camaino to Buda, to prepare a sepulchral monument for Margaret on the Island.[56] The inauguration of this sculpted funeral monument, which must have been similar to the one he prepared for the niece of Margaret, Mary of Hungary, in Naples, in the Donnaregina church,[57] gave the opportunity to offer new indulgences to the sanctuary on the Island of Hares which must have assumed in these decades the new name *Isola Sanctae Margaritae*.

The renewed pilgrimages of the Hungarian queen, Elizabeth Piast, in Italy made a spectacular display of the riches of the Hungarian Angevins in Milan, Bologna, Rome, Naples and Bari. According to her Franciscan chronicler, János Küküllei, she was received as "the Queen of Sheba" in Rome in 1344.[58] Among others, these propagandistic acts had the aim of motivating the Dominican Order to take up again the case of the canonization of Margaret. Indeed, it was around 1340 that Garinus (Garin Gy l'Évêque), the future General Master of the Order undertook the writing of the already mentioned *Legenda maior* in Avignon.[59] The joint initiative of the queen and the Dominican Order finally succeeded in 1379 in obtaining a bull from Urban VI to recommence the canonization process, but the Great Schism, which exploded immediately after this, again prevented it.[60] Nevertheless, the prestige of the cult-place of the saintly princess continued to be recognized by the papacy. Cardinal Giovanni

---

55 Király, *Árpádházi*, p. 142 note 19.
56 Pál Lővei, "The Sepulchral Monument of St Margaret of the Árpád Dynasty," *Acta Historiae Artium* 27 (1980), pp. 175–222.
57 Tania Michalski, "Die Repräsentation einer *Beata Stirps*. Darstellung und Ausdruck an den Grabmonumenten der Anjous," in *Die Repräsentation der Gruppen*, eds Otto-Gerhard Oexle and Andrea von Hülsen-Esch (Göttingen: Vandenhoeck & Ruprecht, 1998), pp. 187–224; *The Church of Santa Maria Donna Regina: Art, Iconography, and Patronage in Fourteenth Century Naples*, eds Janis Elliott and Cordelia Warr (Aldershot: Ashgate, 2004).
58 Johannes de Thurocz, *Chronica Hungarorum*, i, eds Elisabeth Galántai and Julius Kristó (Budapest: Akadémiai, 1985), pp. 163 (cap. 134).
59 Tibor Klaniczay, "La fortuna di Santa Margherita d'Ungheria in Italia," in *Spiritualità e lettere nella cultura italiana e ungherese del basso medioevo* (Civiltà veneziana, Studi, 46), eds Sante Graciotti and Cesare Vasoli (Florence: Olschki, 1995), pp. 3–27; Deák, "The Birth."
60 Otfried Krafft, "Árpád-házi Szt. Margit szentté avatási perének 1379-es újrafelvétele," [The reopening of the canonization process of St Margaret of Hungary] *Századok* 140 (2006), pp. 455–464; Klaniczay, "Efforts at the Canonization."

Dominici gave new indulgences to the sanctuary of Margaret on the occasion of his visit to Buda in 1409.[61]

This sacral prestige was not limited to ecclesiastical circles, for the royal court took an active part in its propagation. A fourteenth-century Italian short story collection, entitled *Il paradiso degli Alberti*, written by Giovanni Gherardi da Prato, contains an account of the trip to Buda of two Florentine travelers who wanted to meet King Louis I.[62] Once in Buda, housed by a distant relative of theirs, and trying to approach the king, the Italians were told that the king was not to be reached, because he was "not in Buda but on the Island." The anecdote narrates, how the Italians hired a boat to cross the river; once on the Island they entered there a garden surrounded by a stonewalls, and found there the king but they did not recognize him. Because of his simple dress, they took him for a priest. The king enjoyed the conversation with them in such anonymity, and was amused to see the Italians amazed and embarrassed when his identity was revealed by other courtiers who arrived and paid him due homage. The Island described here must have been the Margaret Island, where Louis was apparently withdrawing "in private," without royal splendor, finding a space to meditate. His attitude was probably similar to that of his contemporary, Emperor Charles IV, who had the castle of Karlštejn constructed for himself as a separate space for his private devotions.[63]

In the fifteenth century, in 1462, there emerged a renewed attempt to reopen the canonization procedures of Margaret. King Matthias Corvinus wrote a petition in this matter to Pope Pius II (once more, without result).[64] There was also a local initiative behind this royal request. The energetic prioress of the convent, Anne, had organized the notarial registration of almost a dozen

---

61 Király, *Árpádházi*, p. 142.
62 Giovanni Gherardi da Prato, *Il paradiso degli Alberti*, ed. Antonio Lanza (Rome: Zauli, 1975), pp. 231–235; Tibor Kardos, *Studi e ricerche umanistiche italo-ungheresi* (Debrecen: Kossuth Lajos Tudományegyetem 1967), pp. 23–30.
63 Jiri Fajt and Jan Royt, *Magister Theodoricus: Court Painter of Emperor Charles IV. Decorations of the Sacred Places at Castle Karlstejn* (Prague: Národní galerie v Praze, 1997); Iva Rosario, *Art and Propaganda: Charles IV of Bohemia, 1346–1378* (London: Boydell & Brewer, 2001).
64 *Mátyás király levelei*, i [Letters of King Matthias], ed. Vilmos Fraknói (Budapest: A M.T. Akadémia Történelmi Bizottsága, 1893), pp. 10–13; Gábor Klaniczay, "Matthias and the Saints," in *Matthias Rex 1458–1490: Hungary at the Dawn of the Renaissance,* eds Iván Horváth et al. (Budapest: Eötvös Loránd University Faculty of Humanities, Centre des hautes études de la Renaissance, 2013), pp. 1–18, here pp. 8–10. Published as e-book: http://Renaissance.elte.hu/wp-content/uploads/2013/10/Gabor-Klaniczay-Matthias-and-the-Saints.pdf (last accessed: 25 February 2015).

new miracles that occurred at the grave of the blessed Margaret. One could discover in these documents the persistence of the habits of the miracle-seeking pilgrims around the shrine: "they lamentably prostrated themselves in orations around the sepulcher." Prioress Anne also had other goals. By promoting the cult of Margaret, she could thus obtain that her convent be placed under special pontifical supervision, and be exempted from the tutelage of the local Dominican friars. This triumph of the sisters, however, was short-lived: in 1489 the friars took back control, and exiled Prioress Anne to another cloister.[65]

In sum, the Dominican convent on the Margaret Island remained one of the most prominent religious institutions in medieval Hungary. This was also reflected in its cultural contribution. In the late fifteenth and early sixteenth century it became the most prolific place for the production of codices in Hungarian vernacular. The works of two nuns stand out: those of Lea Ráskai, who copied five codices, among them the Hungarian vernacular legend of Margaret; and those by Márta Sövényházi, who wrote the major part of the most exquisite codex of the nuns at the Margaret Island, the Codex of Érsekújvár, containing a series of legends, among them the rhymed legend of St Catherine of Alexandria.[66] If there is an aura of sainthood mediated by vernacular legends, then the radiation from the Dominican convent of the Margaret Island was the strongest in medieval Hungary.

From the late fourteenth century on, however, on the peripheries of late medieval Buda yet a third sacred pole emerged, beside the holy mountain of St Gerard to the south of it and the Island of St Margaret to northeast. On the northwestern edges, in the hilly region covered by forests the Pauline Hermits established a sanctuary of St Paul in their central monastery at Budaszentlőrinc, which quickly became a popular faith-healing shrine.

Budaszentlőrinc: The Monastery of the Order of St Paul the First Hermit

The Order of St Paul the first Hermit was the only religious order founded in Hungary. Its origin goes back to the groups of hermits that settled in the Hungarian forests in the thirteenth century, living, for the most part, according to the Augustinian rule. These religious groups became a new, legitimate

---

65 Péterfi, "Újabb adalékok."
66 János Horváth, *A magyar irodalmi műveltség kezdetei* [The beginnings of Hungarian literary culture] (Budapest: Magyar Szemle, 1931), pp. 218–238.

order following the authorization given them by Cardinal Gentile Particino da Montefiore, a papal legate in 1308. With the support of the Angevin kings and of their new aristocracy, within a few decades the Order of St Paul had become one of the most significant religious orders in Central Europe, even outside the boundaries of the Hungarian kingdom. Their most renowned sanctuary was that of Jasna Góra (Czestochowa), in Poland.[67] The monastery in Budaszentlőrinc (St Lawrence at Buda), designed to become the center of the Order, was founded at the beginning of the fourteenth century.[68]

When King Louis I won a war against Venice in 1380 it gave him the occasion to obtain the precious relics of the patron saint of his favorite religious order. Hence the peace treaty with Venice in 1381 included the donation of the body relic of St Paul the first Hermit to the king of Hungary (the head relic had already been given to Emperor Charles IV, the most passionate collector of relics of his time[69]). The body of St Paul was progressed through the country, and arrived at its final destination in Budaszentlőrinc in 1389, in a solemn translation procession.[70] Afterwards, the relics became the central attraction of the new, much-visited sanctuary in Budaszentlőrinc, a place of pilgrimage and of miraculous cures. Gregorius Gyöngyösi, the early sixteenth-century General of the Order mentions some of these miracles in his *Vitae fratrum heremitarum Ordinis Sancti Pauli primi heremitae* (1522).[71] The Pauline brothers prepared detailed documentation of the miraculous cures and these accounts were

---

67   Emil Kisbán, *A magyar pálosrend története*, 2 vols [History of the Hungarian Pauline Order] (Budapest, 1938–1940); Beatrix Fülöpp-Romhányi, "Die Pauliner im mittelalterlichen Ungarn," in *Beiträge zur Geschichte des Paulinerordens*, ed. Kaspar Elm (Berlin: Duncker & Humblot, 2000), pp. 143–156; Levente F. Hervay, "A pálos rend eredete," [The origin of the order of the Paulines] in *Decus solitudinis. Pálos évszázadok* [Pauline centuries], eds Sándor Őze and Gábor Sarbak (Budapest: Szent István Társulat, 2007), pp. 57–65.

68   Mihály Zákonyi, "A Buda melletti Szent-Lőrincz pálos kolostor története," [The history of the Pauline convent of St Lawrence near Buda] *Századok* 45 (1911), pp. 513–530, 586–606, 686–711 and 764–780.

69   Rosario, *Art*.

70   We have a description of it from the eighteenth century, edited by P. Matthias Fuhrmann, *Anonymi hungarici historia Translationis S. Pauli I. Eremitae*. See also MNL OL Acta Paulinorum, E 153 fasc. 420, fol. 10; Cf. Éva Knapp, "Wunder des heiligen Paulus des Einsiedlers. Analyse der Mirakelaufzeichnungen bei der Reliquie in Budaszentlőrinc," in Gábor Tüskés and Éva Knapp, *Volksfrömmigkeit in Ungarn. Beiträge zur vergleichenden Literatur- und Kulturgeschichte* (Dettelbach: J.H. Röll, 1996), pp. 143–171.

71   Gregorius Gyöngyösi, *Vitae fratrum eremitarum ordinis Sancti Pauli primi eremitae*, ed. Ferenc Hervai (Budapest: Akadémiai, 1988), p. 183 (cap. 88).

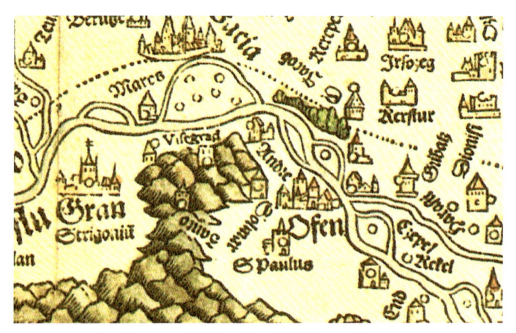

FIGURE 9.4 *The* medium regni *with Budaszentlőrinc (S. Paulus), map of Lazarus secretarius from 1528*
OSZK, MAP COLLECTION

assembled between 1507 and 1511 by brother Bálint Hadnagy, who published a miracle collection containing eighty-eight cases.[72]

Instead of trying to characterize the Pauline sanctuary of Budaszentlőrinc on the basis of these miracle cures told by the pilgrims,[73] I would like to highlight two special features of this cultic site. The first concerns the importance of its peripheral location, close to the wilderness. The monastery is located in a hilly zone near Buda (Fig. 9.4). These hills had some caves near the monastery, which – still today – bear the name of the 'Caves of the Hermits'. These caves, no doubt, also served as a place to withdraw for some brothers and also a place that illustrated well their eremitic life in the eyes of the pilgrims.

The second feature brings us to the variety of ways the city of Buda and the sanctuary functioned together. The most frequent contact between the two was making a pilgrimage. In the miracle accounts we can follow the pilgrims

---

72 *Miracula Sancti Pauli Primi Heremite. Hadnagy Bálint pálos rendi kézikönyve 1511* [The Pauline manual of Bálint Hadnagy] (Agatha, 13), ed. Gábor Sarbak (Debrecen: Kossuth Egyetemi Kiadó, 2003).
73 This aspect is discussed in detail in the works of Éva Knapp and Gábor Sarbak cited above.

in their journey from their lodgings in Buda, across the Vienna Gate, and up into the Buda Hills, before entering the sanctuary and approaching the relics.[74] Occasionally it could happen that the relics were brought out from the sanctuary, in order to cure the bedridden in their urban homes, mostly in cases when the patients were unable to move.[75] Another example of the co-existence of city and sanctuary was when the relics were carried through the city in a solemn procession, as in 1480, to invoke, successfully, the rainfall after a long period of drought (following which the brothers earned the title of *portiores pluviarum*).[76]

In the *Vitae fratrum heremitarum* of Gregorius Gyöngyösi, there is a beautiful description of the harmonious relationship between the city and the sanctuary. In 1522 the head relic of St Paul was also acquired from Prague and thus the saint's body relic was completed. Gyöngyösi describes the solemn translation:

> Accompanied by the King and Queen, the barons of the country and a huge crowd of noblemen and the people, of men and women and in a splendid ecclesiastical procession, Bishop Simon of Zagreb carried the head of the saint in his own hands. After leaving Buda through the city gate, this procession met the other procession, of the brothers who descended from their convent to the borders of the city. The bishop handed them the head of our holy father. The hermits received it on their knees, singing his hymn and then returned solemnly with the relic to their monastery.[77]

Early Modern Aftermath

The early modern times brought a tragic change in the life of Buda, which also affected its nature-bound sanctuaries. The first victim was the Pauline monastery at Budaszentlőrinc. After the fatal defeat of the Hungarian army at Mohács in 1526, the Ottoman troops penetrated the countryside as far as Buda, and they destroyed the Pauline monastery, killing twenty-five friars:

> In the church the splendid paintings, the wonderful, beautifully crafted choir, the elegant organ and everything else was consumed by fire; the

---

74 *Miracula Sancti Pauli*, pp. 106–107 (no 59).
75 *Miracula Sancti Pauli*, pp. 102–105 (no 57).
76 *Vitae fratrum*, pp. 133–134 (cap. 64).
77 *Vitae fratrum*, pp. 181–182 (cap. 87).

roof of the sanctuary collapsed. The altars were destroyed, the images horribly cut to pieces, the graves turned over, and the block covering the marble tomb of St Paul broken in three. The living quarters and the workshops of the excellent monastery were all burnt and razed to the ground. They broke all the utensils, and ate all the food. They remained ten days in the monastery; they scoured all corners, and destroyed everything. They have nowhere made such a ravaging as in this monastery. It seems this monastery will never be restored in its original status till the end of the world.[78]

Before the arrival of the Ottoman troops, the principal treasure of the sanctuary, the relics of St Paul the Hermit, were translated to the north Hungarian castle of Trenčín, but they did not survive there long, for a fire destroyed them. Other treasures of the Pauline Order were also successfully evacuated, but the sanctuary near Buda was completely annihilated.[79]

The Margaret Island had a similar fate. Fearing the imminent renewal of the Ottoman invasion, in 1540, the Dominican sisters fled to Pressburg, to be hosted there for two centuries by the Poor Clares, and they took the precious relics of Margaret with them.[80] In 1541, during the siege of Buda, the Ottoman army set the deserted monastery on fire and although Margaret's name appeared occasionally even later (the Turks used to call the island not only as Margaret Island but also as the "Island of the Girl"), its aura of sacrality had definitely come to an end.

The sacred function of Mount St Gerard, however, did not fade away completely. We have no knowledge of what happened to the sanctuary and the hospice dedicated to St Gerard, but the mountain soon acquired a new sacred function. Suleiman ordered in 1541, the year of the Ottoman siege and conquest of Buda, the construction of a wooden fortress on the top of the hill, called *palafitta*, which was destined to be both a military space and a cult place, in honor of a Bosnian-Ottoman martyr of the fifteenth century, Gerz Ilyās.

Gerz Ilyās died around 1490, as one of the Bosnian leaders of the Ottoman army, in the war against the Serbs and the Hungarians. His relics were transferred to Buda probably when this new cult, with a strong military character, had been instituted. Just as in the case of St Gerard, some later rationalizations

---

78 *Vitae fratrum*, pp. 177–178 (cap. 83).
79 Kisbán, *A magyar pálosrend*, i.
80 Lajos Némethy, *Adatok Árpádházi Boldog Margit ereklyéinek történetéhez* [Information on the history of the relics of Blessed Margaret of Hungary] (Budapest: Rudnyánszky, 1884), pp. 242–245.

tried to create a closer link between the mountain and the Ottoman martyr. According to description of İbrahim Peçevi, a Turkish chronicler living in Pécs in the seventeenth century, the head of Gerz Ilyās was, after his death, sent to Buda as war booty and the Hungarian king, appreciating his heroism, let him be buried with honors on the top of Gellért Hill. Peçevi included in his account the songs and heroic poems that commemorated the fame and preserved the cult of the Ottoman hero, but he also added the legend of St Gerard "of the infidels", stressing at the same time that the cult of the Ottoman hero was superior to that of the preceding Christian martyr.[81] The *palafitta* of Gerz Ilyās and the adjacent mosque was visited by Evlia Celebi, a well-known Turkish traveler of the seventeenth century, who regarded the place as one of the popular pilgrimage sites of his time. Evlia Celebi mentioned also that the weapons of the Ottoman hero had been nailed to the Vienna Gate at the Buda Castle. Actually, this was also a kind of syncretistic appropriation, for Hungarians claimed (according to a document from 1573) that the same weapons on the gate belonged to the legendary fourteenth-century chivalric hero Miklós Toldi.[82]

By this new Ottoman cultic use, Mount St Gerard must have acquired a negative reputation in the eyes of the local (German and Hungarian) inhabitants of Buda. This may be the explanation for a comprehensive new turn in the 'sacral' history of this mountain. In the seventeenth and eighteenth centuries Mount St Gerard was regarded as the principal place where the Hungarian witches held their nightly gatherings, the Witches' Sabbath.

An explanation for this might be that the German-speaking inhabitants of Buda called the cult-site of Gerz Ilyās "Blockhaus" because of its wooden construction. Hence the German name of Mount St Gerard became Blocksberg during the seventeenth century. This name was the same as Blocksberg (Brocken) in the Harz Mountains in Germany, the place most often mentioned as the location of the Witches' Sabbath on Walpurgis-night in the German records of witchcraft beliefs.[83] It is not impossible that it was this association that made the Mount St Gerard – Blocksberg the gathering place of witches in Hungary, even if this hypothesis is at odds with the fact that the historical accounts of witchcraft relating to this site came from the witch trials of distant

---

81   M. Köhbach, "Gellérthegy – Gerz Ilyās Tepesi. Ein Berg und sein Heiliger," *Südostforschungen* 37 (1978), pp. 130–144, here pp. 132–137.

82   *Evlia Cselebi török világutazó magyarországi utazásai 1660–1664* [The travels of Evlia Celebi in Hungary], ed. Imre Karácson (Budapest: Gondolat, 1985), pp. 272 and 288–292.

83   Edouard Jakobs, *Der Brocken in Geschichte und Sage* (Halle: Pfeffer, 1879); Julio Caro Baroja, *Les sorcières et leur monde* (Paris: Gallimard, 1972), pp. 143–144; Wolfgang Behringer, *Witches and Witch-Hunts. A Global History* (Cambridge: Polity Press, 2004), p. 80.

Debrecen and Szeged, and not from the people living in the neighborhood of the mountain.[84]

Let me conclude this overview of the ambivalent sacred history of Mount St Gerard with one quotation. It comes from a thesis written in 1656 on witches in the Protestant theological school in Debrecen, titled *Disputatio Theologica de lamiis veneficiis*, by János Mediomontanus (Czimbalmos). In this text we find the following:

> according to the beliefs of the people (*vulgus*), in a certain hour of the night the witches go on the Mount St Gerard, next to Buda…many women and men, raising flags and insignia, followed by the sound of the drums and trumpets, they go there on horseback, at incredible speed, and eat delicious meals and fine wines on tables that are laid in royal splendor and to the tune of nice music they dance in a ring; then, if they feel like, they return with the same speed to their previous dwelling place.[85]

This colorful story then shows up in more than a dozen accounts in the confessions of the tortured witches in Hungarian witch trials, for the analysis of which there is no space here.[86]

***

By way of conclusion, I cannot avoid mentioning, very briefly, the modern continuation of the function of Mount St Gerard and the Margaret Island. The topographic situation of these places changed radically during the eighteenth and nineteenth centuries. Both Buda and Pest were developing fast: in 1873 they were united to form Budapest and bridges were constructed to connect

---

[84] Sándor Dömötör, "Szent Gellért hegye és a boszorkányok," [Mount St Gerard and the witches] *Tanulmányok Budapest Múltjából* 7 (1939), pp. 92–111; idem, "A boszorkányok gyűlése a magyar néphitben," [The gathering of witches in Hungarian folk beliefs] *Ethnographia* 50 (1939), pp. 210–221.

[85] J.C. Mediomontanus, *Disputatio theologica de lamiis veneficiis…sub praesidio d. Georgii C. Comarini* (Oradea: Abrahamum Kertesz Szenciensem, 1656), p. B2.

[86] I have analyzed this information in Klaniczay, "Il monte," pp. 275–276. For the relevant sources, see Andor Komáromy, *A magyarországi boszorkányperek oklevéltára* [Documents of the witch-trials in Hungary] (Budapest: MTA, 1910), pp. 135 and 193–196; Ferenc Schram, *Magyarországi boszorkányperek 1529–1768*, 3 vols [Witch-trials in Hungary, 1529–1768] (Budapest: Akadémiai, 1970–1982), i, pp. 79–80, 253, 337, 344, 381, 525 and 533; ii, p. 344, 431, 443, 446, 478 and 486, and iii, p. 300; János Reizner, *Szeged története*, iv [History of Szeged] (Szeged: Szeged szab. kir. város közönsége, 1900), pp. 400, 410–411 and 416.

the two parts of the city. Among these bridges the Margaret Bridge connected the Margaret Island with the two riverbanks; and the Elizabeth Bridge, starting from the slopes of Mount St Gerard, reached to the riverbank of Pest. Whereas in the Middle Ages and in the early modern period these sacred places were at the peripheries of the two towns (and they were suitable for this sacred role partly on account of their topographic position), now they were at the very center of the capital city, which continued to expand around them. The island became a favorite park, with a little zoo, with well-cared paths, with hidden benches, suitable for couples in love, with sport clubs and ever increasing entertainment facilities, with a Casino and a Grand Hotel. The sacred past is recalled only by the Margaret spa, built on the thermal water springs, and archaeological remains, in the form of a ruin park of the medieval monastery. Not even Margaret's canonization in 1943 altered this new profane role of the island, and it did not reacquire its sacred dimensions.

The sacred history of Mount St Gerard, however, took yet another turn. While the cult of St Gerard had been re-established, with moderate success, by the Jesuits in the seventeenth century, twentieth-century urban planning chose the rocky slope facing the Elizabeth Bridge for an impressive romantic memorial statue of St Gerard, towering over a waterfall on the rocks where, according to legend, the martyr bishop was hauled down the rocks in a cart. The top of the mountain, towering above Buda and Pest acquired a new role after the Second World War, when it became the place of consecration of the new Communist regime. On the same site where the Turkish *palafitta* of Gerz Ilyās stood and where in 1849 an Austrian fortress called *Citadella* was constructed to fight against the Buda Castle, which had been taken by the Hungarian revolutionaries, a giant monument was erected in 1947, to commemorate the Soviet 'liberation' of the country. It remains to this day. In the middle of it there is a female figure, raising with two hands a palm, as a symbol of peace; at her foot on the right side there is St George, slayer of the dragon; while on the left, there is a Soviet soldier, with steely gaze, who holds in his hand a flag. The monument, the work of the sculptor Zsigmond Kisfaludy-Stróbl, apparently tried to amalgamate the preceding sacred traditions of the mountain: that of St Gerard, the martyr, come from abroad, carrier of a new faith; that of Gerz Ilyās, a hero who died in the rank of the conquering and victorious troops, and maybe also that of the witches, who complemented the male sacrality of the mountain with the feminine.

Times are changing. The Soviet soldier was removed after 1989. There are new plans to replace the Liberation Statue with a gargantuan Holy Crown.

CHAPTER 10

Merchants, Markets, and Shops in Late Medieval Buda, Pest and Óbuda

Judit Benda

Since the eleventh century, Buda has lain at an intersection of major transit trade routes. Its geographical position, combined with the narrowing of the Danube and the presence of several islands and nearby hot springs, has always assured it special significance. The early settlements grew up beside the Roman ruins, and their inhabitants used and renovated the existing Roman infrastructure (waterways and roads, ferries, freshwater streams and hot springs). The development of towns and villages[1] between the eleventh and thirteenth centuries came to an abrupt halt when the kingdom was invaded and devastated by the Mongol army. As he reconstituted his realm, Béla IV realized there was a need for a modern set of laws and an effective system of defense. The development of towns proved to be among his most lasting achievements. The Golden Bull of 1244 (see *Appendix 2*) provided the basis of Buda's staple right:[2] *Item naves et carine descendentes et ascendentes cum mercibus et curribus apud eos descendant et forum sicut prius habeant cottidianum*. Every merchant coming to the city by ship or wagon was obliged to stop and offer his goods for sale there. The staple right gave real momentum to the development of the city. Since Buda lay in broad terms on one of the possible routes connecting the Levant with the Hansa towns, the city soon found a place among the trading centers of the time.[3] Exports passing through the city were mainly cattle for slaughter and raw materials such as leather and wine. The finished goods which dominated imports – broadcloth, spices and craft products – met local demand.

The countless sieges and reconstructions of Buda, Pest and Óbuda over the centuries have left very few medieval buildings intact. Most fortunate in this

---

Translated by Alan Campbell
1 Kubinyi, *Anfänge Ofens*, pp. 9–27.
2 MNL OL DF 240 797. Given in German in the *Stadtrecht* as "Item Dy Scheff oben herr ab, von niden hin auf oder wägen mit kaufmanschaft kümen, süllen Ofen nider gelegt werden und sullen da hingeben, als vor alterr herr kumen ist." in OSt, pp. 86–87. (cap. 67).
3 András Kubinyi, "Die Städte Ofen und Pest und der Fernhandel am Ende des 15. und am Anfang des 16. Jahrhunderts," in *Der Aussenhandel Ostmitteleuropas 1450–1650*, ed. Ingomar Bog (Cologne – Vienna: Böhlau, 1971), pp. 342–433.

respect has been the Castle Hill, the site of the medieval *castrum*, its isolation having saved it from the urban redevelopment of later times. There, the ground floors, cellars and even upper floors of many medieval buildings have survived, although not all have been studied and restored. In the *suburbium* and in Pest and Óbuda, the medieval buildings, with one or two exceptions, were all subsequently demolished. We can obtain further information on these buildings from some written documents, particularly those generated by court cases and the sale of houses. The numerous laws relating to trade set down in the *Ofner Stadtrecht*, the core of which was written between 1405 and 1421, are also informative. Foreign trade brought with it international contacts, and Buda had several buildings corresponding to types common across Europe. As a result, research can make use of a great many analogues.[4] Much can be reconstructed even from the sparse, fragmentary data that we have. Here I attempt to sketch out the workings of markets and shops in the late medieval city (Fig. 10.1).

Annual Fairs

Annual fairs were major events in the life of late medieval Buda and Pest. They were under the supervision of the market judge, and were opened and closed by the ringing of bells and the raising of a flag.[5] Anyone convicted of debt or an unintentional crime had his sentence suspended and was freed for the period of the fair, but had to resume his punishment when it was over. We do not know how much this law was observed, but the twice-daily sittings of the court for the period of the fair and the threat of double-rate fines probably had some deterrent effect against the increase in crime normally experienced at such times.

In the *castrum*, there was a fair on the day of Our Lady (*unser lieben Frawn markt*, 8 September)[6] and another on Mary Magdalene's day (22 June).[7] In the *suburbium*, the annual fair was held on Peter and Paul's day (29 June).[8]

---

4 Because of the lack of space, discussion of the parallels to the various buildings cannot be undertaken here.
5 OSt, pp. 160–161. (cap. 306–307).
6 MNL OL DF 246 809; MNL OL DL 1286; 1221 and 1254; Karl Otto Müller, *Welthandelsbräuche. Deutsche Handelsakten des Mittelalters und der Neuzeit*, v (Stuttgart: [n. p.], 1934, repr. Wiesbaden: F. Steiner, 1962), p. 200.
7 MNL OL DL 36 498; DL 23 972.
8 MNL OL DL 36 498; DL 23 972; Martinus Georgius Kovachich, *Formulae solennes styli in cancellaria...* (Pest: Typis Matthiae Trattner, 1799), p. 539.

MERCHANTS, MARKETS & SHOPS 257

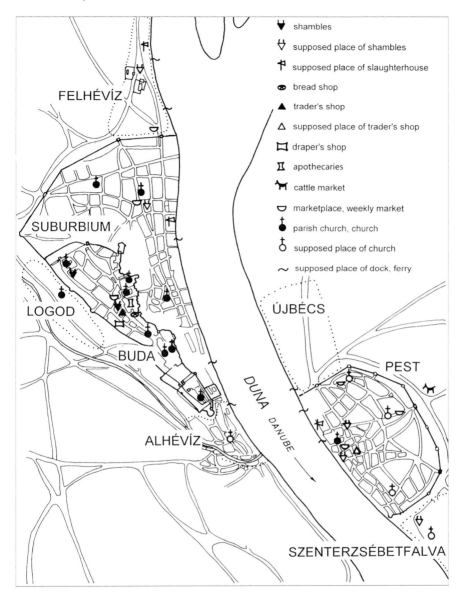

FIGURE 10.1   *The topography of Buda and Pest with commercial buildings and market places (research by J. Benda, graphics Zs. Kuczogi)*

In Felhévíz (whose medieval name was Aigen) it was held on Whitsunday,[9] and in Pest there were fairs on St Nicholas' day (6 December)[10] and on the feast of St Peter in Chains (1 August).[11] Foreign merchants described business as being much brisker at the Pest fairs than at their Buda counterparts. The Pest fairs started eight days before the holiday and finished eight days after it. The fair itself thus lasted seventeen days, and together with the preparations beforehand (erecting booths) and the clearing up afterwards, probably took up most of the month. Hans Paumgarten wrote of them in 1506.[12]

The Pest fair was also called *Anger*,[13] meaning "in the fields". This was probably the same as the fair held on St Peter's day next to the Hatvan Gate. Nearby were the famous livestock fairs, where large numbers of horses, beef cattle and sheep changed hands.[14] The animals were driven along the *via bovaria* to towns in Italy, Austria, Germany and Moravia, where there was a ready market for meat of such good quality and price. Bertrandon de la Broquière noted in 1433 that:

> Pest is inhabited by many horse-dealers; and whoever may want two thousand good horses, they can furnish the quantity. They sell them by stables full, containing ten horses, and their price for each stable is two hundred florins... They come for the most part from the mountains of Transylvania, which bound Hungary to the eastward.[15]

9   OSt, p. 132. (cap. 211.); MNL OL DL 25 311; DL 32 685; Theodor Ortvay, *Geschichte der Stadt Pressburg. Band ii. Abteilung 3: Der Haushalt der Stadt im Mittelalter, 1300–1526* (Pressburg: Carl Stampfel, 1900), p. 98.

10 Müller, *Welthandelsbräuche*, p. 93; MNL OL DL 17 539.

11 MNL OL DL 7716, 8056, 40 389, 64 747 and 18 560; Iván Petrik, "A nyulak szigeti apácamonostor vámkonfliktusai Budával és Pesttel," [The customs conflicts of the nunnery of the Hares' Island with the towns of Buda and Pest] *Urbs. Magyar Várostörténeti Évkönyv* 3 (2008), pp. 227–248, here pp. 230–232; Boglárka Weisz, "Vásárok a középkorban," [Fairs in medieval Hungary] *Századok* 144 (2010), pp. 1397–1454, here p. 1439; Kubinyi, *Budapest*, p. 13 and 106.

12 András Kubinyi, "Budai kereskedők udvari szállításai a Jagelló-korban," [The court deliveries of the merchants of Buda in the Jagiellonian period] in Kubinyi, *Tanulmányok*, i, pp. 337–359, here p. 351–352; Müller, *Welthandelsbräuche*, p. 199: Und ainer auf Sant Niclaus tag zu Pest facht an 8 tag vor und wert 8 tag nach. [...] und zu Pest auf sant Petters kirchwichin 8 tag vor und nach.[...] Und die merkt zu Pest send gewonlich besser dan die zu Offn, also das man auf denselben alle ding pfenwart mer verkouft dan zu Offen.

13 OSt, p. 198 (cap. 427); Ortvay, *Pressburg*, p. 98.

14 MNL OL DL 106 083/241. See the edition of the charter in the study of János M. Bak and András Vadas in the present volume.

15 István Szabó, "A hajdúk 1514-ben," [The heyducks in 1514] *Századok* 84 (1950), pp. 178–198, here p. 189. *The Travels of Bertrandon de la Brocquiere,* trans. Thomas Johnes (Hafod: Hafod Press, 1807), pp. 311–312.

The fair tolls at the Buda and Pest fairs were collected by the agents of the Dominican nuns living on Margaret Island, Béla IV having endowed the convent with this right in 1255. Although it was only the fair of the Our Lady's in Buda which existed at this time, the nuns also laid claim to the tolls from fairs founded later. The burghers of both Buda and Pest regularly attacked the nuns' toll collectors and smashed their scales and measuring implements. Over the centuries, this enduring conflict and its associated court cases generated many documents that shed light on the history of the city.[16]

Weekly Markets

Documentary records tell us that weekly markets were held in the castrum of Buda on Tuesdays and Saturdays, and in Pest on Tuesdays.[17] The Buda market day, for an unknown reason, was changed to Wednesday in the fifteenth century.

The Buda weekly markets were thus on Wednesdays, on the square around the Church of Our Lady, and on Fridays on the area next to the Church of Mary Magdalene. The name of the *Szombat piac* (Saturday Market) in Buda remained "from the old custom".[18] Local farmers were allowed to sell their produce until midday on market days, for the purpose of supplying the city. Professional traders could only set up their stalls after the lowering of the 'free market' flag. Their numbers, nationalities and positions on the market place[19] were decided and marked out by the City Council. Those transgressing the rules were fined and had their wares confiscated. Quarrelling stallholders were punished by shaming. Anyone convicted by the court had to carry bricks on his back all round the market place from the City Hall to St George's Gate. Traders' stalls were laid out according to their wares. There were three categories. At the prestigious end of the elongated market place (Fig. 10.2), the space bounded by the parish church, City Hall and the apothecaries, were stalls selling fruit, vegetables and cereal produce for porridge. In front of the bakers' shops, were stalls for milk, dairy products, cheese, eggs and salt; and in front of the

---

16   Petrik, "A nyulak szigeti," pp. 227–246; MNL OL DL 16 034, 12 469 and 14 712.
17   MNL OL DL 40 389, 64 747, 18 560 and 16 661; Weisz, *Vásárok*, p. 1439.
18   OSt, p. 137 (cap. 227); MNL OL DL 40 389, 16 661 and 2712.
19   The location of the market of the Germans was in the Tárnok Street (1st district); that of the Hungarians was on Kapisztrán Square. In the suburbium, in the surroundings of the Iskola Street – Medve Street – Csalogány Street in the 1st district. The market of Óbuda was located at the end of Lajos Street in the 3rd district and Pest's was at the Szabad sajtó Street in the 5th district, close to the southern side of the parish church of the town.

FIGURE 10.2 *The market of Tárnok Street on the medieval market square, end of the nineteenth century*
BTM, PHOTO COLLECTION

butchers' shops and retail shops, stalls for chicken, goose, duck, suckling pig, game and dried meat. The fishmongers were kept separate on the other side of the City Hall, on the Fishmarket.[20]

Market Hall

Under the city's staple right, long-distance merchants had to make their way, in most cases, to the warehouse *yn dy stat zu ofen, In dy nyder lag*.[21] As in other towns, the warehouse or market hall (*nyderlag, kaufhaus*) was a large hall into which several traders at a time could drive their wagons carrying bales of goods. The bales were opened and the goods were weighed with the help, and under the supervision, of middle-men (*unterkäufel*) before being purchased

20 OSt, p. 115 (cap. 155) and p. 123 (cap. 180); Kubinyi, *Budapest*, p. 16; Végh, *Buda*, i, pp. 181–185.
21 OSt, p. 190 (cap. 405).

according to the city's current price list.[22] The middle-men were officials who swore an oath before the city council and received their pay as a percentage of the transactions they made. They were experienced in trading procedures, and knowledge of several languages (Latin, German, Italian, Polish) was probably essential to their job. The clauses of the *Ofner Stadtrecht* prescribing their duties must have formed part of the rules governing the operation of the market hall, the *Kaufhausordnung*.[23] Four of these clauses give the names of goods that came into the warehouse, providing an insight into the buying and selling of commodities in medieval Buda, and the kinds and origins of imported products. Retail goods included special textiles (embroidered linen, gauze), fancy craft products (gold lace, belts with carved bone or bronze mountings), everyday objects (combs, scissors, locks, suspended food sacks, hats, paper) and exotic fruits (figs, raisins, capers, ginger, olive oil). Bales of broadcloth came to Buda from such diverse places as Florence, Bruges, Mechelen, Cologne and Frankfurt. Cheaper fabrics came from closer by: from Vienna, Cracow and Transylvania. The main export goods were raw materials and livestock. There was a high demand for Hungarian cowhide and sheepskin, and tallow and beeswax for candles. Buda's position in the center of the kingdom also brought it consignments of minerals: salt, iron, copper, tin and lead.[24]

The location of the market hall is not recorded in any document, but the floor plan can be identified from a 1686 survey by the military engineer, Nicolas Marcel de La Vigne. In 1587, Reinhard Lubenau saw a hall used as a trading house by the Ottomans, and wrote of it in his travel diary:

> Further on we came to a great palace, beside which was a stable for a hundred horses, but very ruined, and close by a heavily fortified building, with strong, stone pillars which was and still is a market hall for outsiders, but very much collapsed. But it was still strongly guarded, and the merchants of all nations were within.[25]

---

22   OSt, pp. 96–97 (cap. 95) and pp. 195–197 (cap. 423–424); Lajos Kemény, "Buda város árszabása II. Lajos korában (1522.)," [The prices of the town of Buda in the age of Louis II, 1522] *Történelmi Tár* 12 (1889), pp. 372–384.
23   OSt, pp. 96–97 (cap. 92–96) and pp. 190–201 (cap. 405–422).
24   OSt, pp. 96–97 (cap. 95) and pp. 195–197 (cap. 423–424); Kemény, "Árszabás," pp. 372–384.
25   Weitter sei wier zu einem grossen Palatio komen, daneben ein Pferdestal auf etlich hundert Pferde, aber sehr verfallen, balde daneben gahr ein starkes gemauertes Gebeude mitt lautter steiner Pfeiler, welches ein Kaufhaus vor die Fremden gewesen und noch ist, aber sehr einfeldt. Wirdt aber gleichwol wol bewachet; wahren von allerlei Nation Kaufleut drein, see Wilhelm Sahm, *Beschreibung der Reissen des Reinhold Lubenau* (Mitteilungen

FIGURE 10.3 *The medieval market hall before its demolition (late nineteenth century)*
BTM PHOTO COLLECTION

The building must originally have had an upper storey, its joists resting on two rows of carved stone pillars. It was a detached building with narrow lanes on three sides and the main road on the fourth. There were two doors on its narrow side and at least three openings on the long side. Fortunately, the warehouse building stood in a converted form until the late nineteenth century, functioning as an arsenal (Fig. 10.3). It was demolished in 1894 to make way for the Buda Redoute (subsequently the Vigadó Theater).[26] The plan drawing made before demolition shows a two-colonnade hall dating from the late Middle Ages. The building lay in the medieval *suburbium* of Buda, beside the main road, near where the harbor is thought to have been. Since this building corresponded in

ausder Stadtbibliothek zu Königsberg i. Pr. 4) (Königsberg: Kommissions Verlag von Ferdinand Beyers Buchhandlung, 1912), pp. 80–81.
26   8 Corvin tér Budapest, 1st district.

its location and architectural features to the requirements of wholesale trading functions, it most likely acted as the Buda goods market hall or warehouse.[27]

Buda Dwellings of Burghers and Traders

Plots within the city of Buda were long and narrow, with sides in proportions between 1:2 and 1:2.5.[28] They were laid out after the city was founded, and the first buildings were probably built of timber. Wills and conveyances from the turn of the thirteenth and fourteenth centuries, however, tell of stone buildings, towers, cellars and entrance passages.[29] Houses and mansions were built on the long sides of the plots, leaving enough space to drive a cart between them. During the fifteenth century, the stone buildings were extended and heightened, with the addition of vaulted entrance passages. Vaulted ceilings were added to cellars and ground and first-floor rooms in several places.[30] Most of the buildings had two upper storeys by then, as attested to by documents describing the way the buildings were divided up.[31] The descriptions listed the interior spaces of the buildings. Shops operated from out of the entrance passages, and there were cellars underneath them. The household stores and workshops were in the ground-floor courtyard, and the stables and latrines at the end of the

27 Judit Benda, "A kereskedelem épületei a középkori Budán, ii. Mészárszékek háza, zsemleszékek háza, árucsarnok," [Commercial buildings in medieval Buda. The house of butcheries, bakeries, market hall] *Tanulmányok Budapest Múltjából* 37 (2012), pp. 23–58, here pp. 44–45.

28 The sizes of the full plots in medieval Buda were between 18 to 20 meters in width and 36 to 46 meters in length. See Erzsébet Lócsy, "Középkori telekviszonyok a budai Várnegyedben, i," [Medieval plot structure in the Castle District of Buda], *Budapest Régiségei* 21 (1964), pp. 191–208, here pp. 191–205; András Végh, "Buda város középkori helyrajza," [The medieval topography of Buda] *Urbs. Magyar Várostörténeti Évkönyv* 4 (2009), pp. 35–49, here p. 39. The measuring out of the plots in the time of the foundation is likely to have been carried out with a rope, although the exact length of the Buda "rope" is unknown. See István Bogdán, *Magyarországi hossz- és földmértékek a XVI. század végéig* [Hungarian linear and land measures until the end of the sixteenth century] (A Magyar Országos Levéltár Kiadványai, iv. Levéltártan és történeti forrástudományok, 3) (Budapest: Akadémiai, 1978), pp. 71–77. For information on measuring out a plot with rope (1408), see MNL OL DL 9375.

29 MNL OL DF 208 838, 229 964, 229 865, 266 368 and DL 24 678.

30 László Gerevich, "Gótikus házak Budán," [Gothic houses in Buda] *Budapest Régiségei* 15 (1950), pp. 121–238; idem, *The Art of Buda and Pest in the Middle Ages* (Budapest: Akadémiai, 1971), pp. 41–56. Gerevich's typology, which dates from the 1950s, requires revision.

31 MNL OL DF 208 156, 238 294, 208 689, 238 102; MNL OL DL 9937 and MNL OL DF238 159.

garden. Rooms, heated bedrooms and kitchens ranged along the first floor, and several buildings had a vaulted hall decorated with frescoes (*palatium depictum*), some with a little private chapel alongside. Access to the upper floor was by stairs from the entrance passage or courtyard. In the late medieval period, residential buildings had more and more rooms and were built with access to the upper floor along decks lying on timber or stone consoles.[32]

Very few remnants of upper storeys, and perhaps one second storey, have survived the wars and sieges of previous centuries.[33] We know much more about ground floor spaces and cellars, because many have been researched and restored as historic buildings. Some of these, if they contain a modern shop or restaurant, can still be inspected today. Most ground-floor rooms have groined vaults dating from the fifteenth century. Facing the street were either small, simple stone-cased windows, or more elaborate windows, made of sculpted stone. The shop was entered either directly via the entrance passage, or up some steps. The mezzanine level rested on the vaulting of cellars which had originally had a flat ceilings supported by cantilevers.[34] The passage to the cellar opened from the street or the entrance passage or the back room, and had stone steps cut into the subsoil or a built wooden staircase. Buildings in Buda often had a three-level system of cellars. The first level lay directly beneath the ground floor and was presumably mostly used to store merchandise. Underneath were deeper cellars cut into the marl. Their cool, moist atmosphere was well suited to maturing and storing wine. The work of storing and retrieving goods in the cellars spawned a separate trade: the *korcsolyás* or cellarman, who hauled barrels up and down on wooden sleds. The vast majority of buildings had one little cellar, dug deep into the subsoil during the fourteenth and fifteenth centuries. Cellars were dug using the mining techniques of the time, employing vertical shafts and inclined tunnels, and from their dimensions we may infer they were designed as refuges for valuables and people.

The shops, butchers' shops, bakers' shops and warehouses were all built primarily for commercial purposes (although people may also sometimes have lived in them), and so we will look separately at the architectural features of each.

---

32   MNL OL DL 71 201.
33   31 Úri Street Budapest, 1st district, front façade.
34   I am grateful for this information to Judit Réti-Zádor, who is working on the medieval cellar system of Buda.

Wholesalers

Wares brought into the town by foreign merchants (*gast, frombderr kaufman*) were bought by local wholesalers. These often acted as local representatives of foreign (Viennese, Augsburg and Venetian) merchant companies or family companies. They received and despatched consignments, provided a place to receive the goods, and promoted their sale. Merchandise from abroad often arrived through several middle-men. Italian merchants brought mainly spices, silk, velvet and Mediterranean fruits via Venice, Florence and Genoa from the Levant trading routes.[35] German merchants brought raw materials from the Hansa towns, and broadcloth and manufactures from Regensburg and – later – Frankfurt, Nuremberg, Augsburg and Vienna.[36]

Merchants coming to the city from elsewhere in the country or abroad (*inlenderr, auslender kaufman*) and even settled merchants who had citizenship could only sell their wares in bulk.[37] This meant no less than one mark's worth of spices and 100 yards of linen if the merchant was from outside, i.e. not a Buda citizen. Even retailers were constrained to sell their wares on in bulk, trading no less than 10–30 pounds of spices and 6 bolts of cloth.[38] The *Ofner Stadtrecht* also stipulated how local traders were to conduct their business, stipulating that "merchants and retailers may do business in their shops or premises and nowhere else",[39] and that "shopkeepers shall not sell in an open stall, but only in a vaulted shop".[40]

There are some houses, mainly in what are now Úri Street and Országház Street, whose owners were probably involved in long-distance trade and – as was the medieval custom – carried on their business in their own houses (Fig. 10.4).

---

35 György Székely, "Magyarország és Buda városa Velence és Genova között a 14–15. század fordulóján," [Hungary and the town of Buda between Venice and Genoa at the turn of the fourteenth century] *Tanulmányok Budapest Múltjából* 23 (1991), pp. 9–18, here pp. 13–15.

36 András Kubinyi, "Buda és Pest szerepe a távolsági kereskedelemben a 15–16. század fordulóján," [The role of Buda and Pest in the long distance trade at the turn of the fifteenth century] in Kubinyi, *Tanulmányok*, i, pp. 361–405, here pp. 377–393.

37 On the merchants and their families of Buda and Pest, see the works of András Kubinyi, such as: "Buda és Pest szerepe"; idem, "Budafelhévíz topográfiája és gazdasági fejlődése," [The topography and economic development of Budafelhévíz] in Kubinyi, *Tanulmányok*, i, pp. 115–182; idem, "Die Pemfflinger in Wien und Buda," *Jahrbuch des Vereins für Geschichte der Stadt Wien* 34 (1978), pp. 67–88; idem, "Budai kereskedők."

38 OSt, p. 88 (cap. 70) and pp. 100–101 (cap. 104).

39 OSt, pp. 87–95 (cap. 68–90).

40 OSt, p. 121 (cap. 174).

FIGURE 10.4   *Úri Street 31, Budapest, 1st District. House of a wholesaler*
PICTURE: ÁGNES BAKOS AND BENCE TIHANYI

The shops on the ground floor (*gewölbe, wolta*) could only be accessed via the entrance passage. Seated booths (*sedile, Sitznische*), which had been present in the city since the late thirteenth century, took on a new function as part of the exterior space of the shop, a kind of portal which also displayed the prosperity of the business. This is manifested in the uniform mouldings carved around seated booths and shop doors dating from the fifteenth century onwards, conferring a uniform exterior to the shops behind them. There were usually two, and up to four shops in any one building. The owner either used them himself or leased them to merchants or artisans. A 'shop' at that time thus referred to a residential building owned by a merchant who lived upstairs and worked on the ground floor. It was where orders and deliveries were negotiated, and it also served as a showroom. The back courtyard wings of some buildings were formed into arcades, following the contemporary architectural fashion of Italian and south German towns. Mediterranean-style courtyard arcades may also have served to receive goods in large quantities.[41]

41   Judit Benda, "A piactól az árucsarnokig. Kereskedelmi célra készült épületek a középkori Budán," [From the market to the market hall. Commercial buildings in medieval Buda] *Történelmi Szemle* 53 (2011), pp. 259–282, here pp. 273–275.

There are surviving records of the layout of three buildings, giving details of each room.[42] One of these was the Garais' house,[43] which stood in front of St George's Chapel. It is recorded as having two shops to the right of the entrance and one to the left, and two storerooms. The *Serechen Noghaz,* i.e. János Szerecsen's mansion, was built on two merged plots[44]: on the *Platea Omnium Sanctorum* (All Saints' Street) side there was a shop on the right at ground level, and two shops and two storerooms on the left. On the *Platea Italicorum* (Italians' Street) side, four shops and four storerooms on the ground floor are mentioned. The division of a building between Demeter Chysar and Antal Garai[45] describes three shops and three storerooms on each side of the entrance passage. One of these was the workshop of the owner, the sword-grinder Demeter. All of these documents mention cellars under the shops. The Hungarian word for shop, *bolt*, derives from the Latin word meaning "vault", and many, but by no means all, of the premises described as vaulted actually contained a shop. This was certainly the case for the Buda houses of the great merchants (such as Gailsam, Forster, Bernardi, Haller, Pemfflinger, Fugger and Freiberger).[46]

Cloth Merchants

The cloth merchants from southern Germany were among the wealthiest citizens of the city in the fifteenth century. Among the merchant families who settled and operated in Buda were the Hallers, Pemfflingers, Vogelweiders and Freibergers.[47] Maintaining close family ties, these businessmen imported semi-finished or finished textiles in bulk from their former homeland and sold them in Buda for a profit. They were serving a very healthy demand, because the city's lands had no major sheep flocks or fields growing hemp or flax. An indication of this is that the weaving trades (linen weavers, fullers, dyers, carders, bleachers) appear in the *Ofner Stadtrecht* only as headings, which means

---

42   Végh, *Buda*, ii, ff. 62.a, 62.b and 63.
43   Végh, *Buda*, i, pp. 174–176; MNL OL DL 9937.
44   Végh, *Buda*, i, pp. 227–231. MNL OL DL 9937.
45   Végh, *Buda*, i, pp. 242–243; MNL OL DF 238 112.
46   Helmut Haller von Hallerstein, "Deutsche Kaufleute in Ofen zur Zeit der Jagellonen," *Mitteilungen des Vereins für Geschichte der Stadt Nürnberg* 51 (1962), pp. 467–480; Kubinyi, "Budai kereskedők"; idem, "Buda és Pest kereskedelme".
47   András Kubinyi, "Budai és pesti polgárok családi összeköttetései a Jagelló-korban," [Family connections of the burghers of Buda and Pest in the Jagiellonian period] in Kubinyi, *Tanulmányok*, ii, pp. 513–570, here pp. 528–542; Andreas Kubinyi, "Die Nürnberger Haller in Ofen," *Mitteilungen des Vereins für Geschichte der Stadt Nürnberg* 52 (1963–64), pp. 80–128, here p. 82; idem, "Die Pemfflinger," pp. 67–88; idem, "Buda és Pest kereskedelme," p. 383.

there must have been no need to set forth rules for their work. The weights-and-measures rules for tailors and clothes dealers (master tailors, jerkin makers, linen merchants, second-hand clothes dealers) and the definitions of the material they could use convey an impression of diligent tradesmen. There was a ban on "the purchase and fulling of upper or lower garments contaminated with blood."[48] Four classes of broadcloth may be identified among the foreign textiles sold in Buda in large quantities. The most expensive were from Italy, England and Flanders. Next came products made in the German towns, followed by those from the Polish and Austrian lands, and finally Viennese and Transylvanian heavy-cloth dreadnought.[49] There are sources other than the *Ofner Stadtrecht* which tell us the names of fabrics delivered to Buda. The customs tariff compiled by János Sybenlinder in 1436 and the municipal tariff issued in 1522 also give detailed lists of contemporary varieties of broadcloth, taffeta, damask, and silk.[50]

Buda had a small weaving industry, as is revealed by a regulation governing tailors, which mentions broadcloth, "made and fulled here". The semi-broadcloth known as *dirdumdey* in German and *bubó* in Hungarian was made with a warp of linen and weft of wool.[51] Semi-finished broadcloth bought either locally or imported had to be made into a saleable state, so that fulling, napping and cutting were done in Buda. The cloth was probably compacted in water mills situated on the Danube. Piling and cutting off stray threads with shears was done in city workshops. In the district of St Peter's in the *suburbium* there was a *Platea Chapowcha* (*Csapó utca*, i.e. Fullers' Street),[52] probably the place where the fullers (*csapó*) lived. Most of the fullers worked in mills they rented in Felhévíz.[53]

The workshops and wholesale shops stood on the row of buildings on the east of the main market place in the castrum. The street was named after the cloth merchants or cutters (*kamerherren oderr gewand sneiderr*), recorded in various forms (*in Platea Pannirasorum, Poztomethew wucza* [*Posztómető utca*], *Nyrew Ucza* [*Nyírő utca*]).[54] It was made up of residential buildings which also

---

48   OSt, pp. 107–109 (cap. 131–142).
49   OSt, pp. 196–197 (cap. 424). For the varieties of imported clothes, see György Székely, "Posztófajták a német és nyugati szláv területekről a középkori Magyarországon" [Cloth types from German and Western Slavic areas in medieval Hungary] *Századok* 109 (1975), pp. 765–795, here pp. 765–791.
50   Kemény, "Árszabás," pp. 375–377; MNL OL DF 239 625.
51   OSt, p. 108 (cap. 136).
52   Végh, *Buda*, i, p. 109.
53   Kubinyi, "Budafelhévíz," pp. 153–160.
54   Végh, *Buda*, i, p. 81 and 83; MNL OL DL 25 556, 38 658; DF 200 608; DL 22 331 and 25 556.

contained the cloth merchants' shops and workshops (*gvant lauben*). There were shop windows on the street front and seated booths, accessed by doors, in the entrance passages. Retail sales were thus made on the street side, while traders buying in bulk could inspect the quality of the fabric in the vaulted shops that opened from the access passages. The workshops were usually situated in the rooms facing the courtyard.[55] Nyírő/Posztómető Street was not the only place where cloth dealers operated. Their workshops (*camera lapidea pro incidendis pannis*) are also mentioned around the Church of Our Lady[56] and among the *boltae ubi panni vendi consuerint*.[57] The royal treasury also operated a broadcloth store in Buda, because it often requested towns to pay some of their annual taxes in broadcloth.[58] In the sixteenth century, this cloth was usually paid out as 'bounty' to soldiers serving on the southern frontiers.[59]

Apothecaries (spicers)

Like the cloth merchants, spicers or apothecaries occupied vaulted ground-floor shops in residential buildings, where they made and sold their medicines – tinctures, spirits, and herbal mixtures. These lay in the row of buildings along the east of the main market[60] (*in serie apothecariorum, vor den apoteken*). The apothecaries had to keep their shops open at all times, even Sundays and holidays, day and night, to serve the sick.[61] This is an indication of the backwardness of medical care, most citizens being unable to pay for the expertise of university-educated doctors. The apothecary had to be able not only to make the medicines but also to recognize diseases and give advice on treatment. The documents of the sale of property show that in many cases apothecaries owned the whole building rather than renting a shop on the ground floor.[62]

We know the location of the apothecaries partly from contracts of sale for the buildings,[63] and partly from the description of the market in the *Ofner*

---

55 The houses of the cloth merchants may have stood at the row of houses 2–28 Úri Street, Budapest, 1st district. See Benda, "A piactól," p. 271.
56 MNL OL DL 11 944.
57 Végh, *Buda*, ii, p. 77 (no 238).
58 Kubinyi, "Budai kereskedők," p. 351; MNL OL DF 238 113.
59 Kubinyi, "Buda és Pest kereskedelme," pp. 365–366.
60 Row of houses 1–13 Tárnok Street, Budapest, 1st district.
61 OSt, p. 99 (cap. 102).
62 Végh, *Buda*, i, p. 186.
63 Végh, *Buda*, i, pp. 82–83; MNL OL DL 15 766; DF 238 272; DL 17 675; DF 238 300, 238 301 and 238 303.

Stadtrecht.[64] The apothecaries' row stretched from the corner house opposite the Church of Our Lady to the bakers' shops. It may have extended further, because no less than twenty-seven stallholders should have been able to set up in front of them. The expression *offen laden*, i.e. "open shop", in the *Ofner Stadtrecht* indicates that the apothecary, like the shopkeeper, sold his wares directly to the street. Only one identifiable building remains on the former apothecaries' row and it retains all the characteristics of this type of building. There is a shop window and a narrow 'service' door on the street front.[65] In 1516, the staff of a shop belonging to an apothecary named György saved the life of Boldizsár Body by bolting the door against his attackers when he sought refuge there from a skirmish.[66] The document records that the apothecary's shop was open even on the day of the king's funeral. Several assistants worked there, and it was accessed by a door from the street.

Shopkeepers (retailers)

The wares brought into the city from far afield were sold to the public by a class of merchants called *kalmár* (*krämer, institor, kalmar*).[67] The *kalmár* selected his wares from what was on offer from the wholesalers. "Fine *kalmár* wares" (*spezerei*) were spices and medicinal herbs, and included pepper, sugar, ginger, cinnamon and saffron. "Coarse *kalmár* wares" (*grobe*) referred to chemicals, dyes and exotic fruits: sulphur, saltpetre, soap, verdigris, figs, raisins, rice and olive oil. Haberdashery merchants sold fabrics by the yard (*ellenwaren*). *Kalmár*s who sold wares "by piece" dealt in products by local and foreign craftspeople, including paper, books, mirrors, glassware, hats, belts and knives. The work of the *kalmár*s in towns was governed by the *Krämerordnungen*, and the duties of guild members in Buda are known from certain articles of the *Ofner Stadtrecht*.[68] They could only sell *kalmár* wares in their shops, which could open only with the permission of the judge and the council. *Kalmár*s had to take great care with quality, because counterfeit and degraded goods could cause losses to customers and thus damage their own reputation. Some

---

64   OSt, pp. 113–114 (cap. 154).
65   13 Tárnok Street, Budapest, 1st district; Benda, *A piactól*. pp. 270–271.
66   Végh, *Buda*, ii, pp. 164–165; MNL OL DL 37 194.
67   Eugen Nübling, *Ulm's Handel im Mittelalter* (Ulm: Nübling, 1900) pp. 448–460; Heinrich Eckert, *Die Krämer in süddeutschen Städten bis zum Ausgang des Mittelalters* (Berlin – Leipzig: Dr. Walther Rotschild, 1910), pp. 32–58.
68   OSt, p. 100 (cap. 104).

*kalmár*s worked with assistants in the shop: scribes, servants and maidservants (*schribere, knechte oder megede*).[69]

The city council must originally have assigned their shops to the center of the market place: three rows of tiny buildings in Buda and two in Pest.[70] The *Ofner Stadtrecht* referred to them by the expression *pey den stein kremen*, and the Hungarian name of the street, *Platea Kalmarwcza* (Kalmár utca, i.e. "Kalmárs' Street"), appeared in the early sixteenth century.[71] In other towns, the *kalmár*s paid rent to the council for use of shop buildings (*Kramladenzins*). No such rule is known of for Buda, because the buildings were privately owned. Archaeological research has discovered details of small buildings dated to the second half of the fourteenth century and reconstructed and extended several times during the fifteenth and sixteenth centuries.[72] Several surviving details of the walls tell much about the history of their construction and the way they were used. The fourteenth-century *kalmár* shops were usually stone-built and consisted of one or two independent shops.[73] Their cellars were used for storage, the ground floor for sales, and the upstairs floor for dwelling. The customer received his purchases through the serving window without going into the shop. The wares and the staff entered the shop via a narrow door. Their location in the city center, directly adjacent to the weekly market, must have benefited their business. Some of these buildings can still be seen today, having been restored to their medieval architectural form (Fig. 10.5).

Butchers' Shops

Much of the city's export trade was in livestock. Hungarian horses and cattle were favored commodities in north Italian, Austrian and south German towns, and a large proportion of them were supplied via the Pest livestock fairs. The work of butchers, who slaughtered the animals (mostly beef cattle) and

---

69 Eckert, *Die Krämer*, pp. 74–75.
70 The retail (*kalmár*) shops stood in the area in between Úri Street – Tárnok Street – Szentháromság Street in the present-day 1st district in Buda, and in the area Irányi Street – Molnár Street – Kéménysepro Street – Március 15. Square in Pest in the present-day 5th district.
71 Végh, *Buda*, i, p. 78; MNL OL DL 50 311; DF 243 332; OSt, p. 114 (cap. 154).
72 Architectural elements of the *kalmár* shops were identified at 10–20 Tárnok Street, 1–2 Anna Street and 9–19 Úri Street in the 1st district, Budapest.
73 Judit Benda, "A kereskedelem épületei a középkori Budán, i. Kalmárboltok," [Commercial buildings in medieval Buda. Retailers' shops] *Budapest Régiségei* 57–58 (2009–2010), pp. 93–120, here pp. 95–99.

FIGURE 10.5   Úri Street 13/Anna Street 2, Budapest, 1st District. Retailers' shops
PHOTO: ÁGNES BAKOS AND BENCE TIHANYI

prepared the meat for the kitchen, was an important aspect of late medieval food culture. The Buda city tariff records the farm animals slaughtered for meat in that period: beef cattle, cows, calves, sheep, lambs and pigs.[74] A guild charter of 1481[75] stipulating a ban on the slaughter of sick animals provides a list of the species regularly slaughtered: beef cattle, cows, sheep, lambs, and goats, and mentions the game animals whose meat was sold on the market: fawns, deer, wild goats, bears and boar.[76] The *Ofner Stadtrecht* also shows game dealers to have a wide range of wares: venison, hind calf, fallow deer, bear, wild boar, rabbit, squirrel, pheasant, hazel grouse, black grouse, wild duck, moorhen, partridge and thrush all appeared on the counter.[77] We know from documents of legal actions against fishmongers that butchers also had the right to sell large fish (sturgeon [Acipenser sturio, A. huso], carp, catfish).[78]

Cattle were slaughtered in a slaughterhouse or more correctly on a 'slaughter bridge' (*wagohyd, Schlachthaus, Schlachbrücke*) by slaughtermen and their

74   Kemény, "Árszabás," pp. 374–375.
75   MNL OL DF 286 050 (3rd article).
76   MNL OL DF DF 286 050 (6th article).
77   OSt, p. 102. (cap. 108).
78   MNL OL DF 286 056.

apprentices (*Bruckknecht*). The wooden bridge was in the suburb beside the harbor on the Danube. Cattle were slaughtered on the bridge, i.e. above the water, or if necessary in the harbor.[79] There were also dwellings near the slaughterhouse, in the *Platea Carnificum* (Butchers' Street).[80] The carcasses, flayed and cut in half, were taken from the slaughterhouse to the butchers' shops or shambles in the city market (*fleisch pengken, in ordine macellorum, sedes carnificium, mezarzek*) and cut up to order. Besides fresh meat, the butchers sold sausages (*hurka* and *kolbász*), smoked meat, tallow and animal hides. People could also eat at a public kitchen[81] (*alte küche*) beside the shambles. It was regarded as a municipal kitchen, although the butchers' guild was responsible for running it.[82] Butchers selling meat that was rotten or contained maggots or worms faced confiscation of their wares, fines, and being banned from working.[83] Butchers in Buda rented their shops from the guild, while those in Pest and Óbuda bought the freeholds in theirs; in all cases, they were heritable rights. The shambles occupied permanent sites within the building, but they were re-allocated among butchers in Buda each year on the third Sunday of Lent. Journeymen were 'allocated', which meant they were employed by the guild, although they probably received their pay from the master butcher.[84] There is a detailed study of the butchers' guild, the master butchers and their residences by András Kubinyi and András Végh included in a parallel Hungarian and German edition, which also gives the full text of the Buda German butchers' guild book.[85]

The butchers' shops were mostly in wooden huts until the fifteenth century, and often stood beside each other. The butchers cut up and sold the meat on a large table, and hung it on hooks on a rack behind. In the second half of the fifteenth or the early sixteenth century, these wooden huts gave way in Buda,

79 MNL OL DF 286 056; DF 286 050 (3rd article).
80 MNL OL DF 286 057. Végh, *Buda*, i, pp. 114–118; András Kubinyi, "A középkori budai mészároscéh," [The medieval butcher's craft of Buda] in *A budai mészárosok középkori céhkönyve és kiváltságlevelei – Zunftbuch und Privilegien der Fleischer zu Ofen aus dem Mittelalter* (Források Budapest közép – és kora újkori történetéhez, 1/Quellen zur Budapester Geschichte im Mittelalter und in der frühen Neuzeit, 1), ed. István Kenyeres (Budapest: BFL – BTM, 2008), pp. 15–55.
81 Végh, *Buda*, i, p. 72; OSt, p. 114 (cap. 154); MNL OL DF 200 608 and DL 38 658.
82 Benda, "A kereskedelem, ii," pp. 34–35.
83 OSt, pp. 101–102 (cap. 105).
84 Kubinyi, "Mészároscéh," pp. 26, 47 and 50.
85 Kubinyi, "Mészároscéh," pp. 31–36; András Végh, "A budai német mészárosok céhkönyvének helyrajzi vonatkozásai," [Topographic references in the medieval crafts book of the German butchers of Buda] in *A budai mészárosok*, pp. 57–72, here pp. 62–71.

FIGURE 10.6   Lajos Street 158, Budapest, 3rd District. Shambles
PHOTO: ÁGNES BAKOS AND BENCE TIHANYI

Pest and Óbuda to long stone-built buildings divided into small chambers. We know their locations from property sale contracts, which mention them as place markers in the row of buildings on the main market place, for example: *una domus lapidea in serie apothecariorum in vicinitatibus domorum confraternitatis carnificum.*[86]

Several passages of the section of the *Ofner Stadtrecht* governing the market prescribe where traders had to set up their stalls: "in stone-built shops, in the corner building opposite the butchers' shops" and "at the back, at the shambles, directly adjacent to the wall".[87] It is possible to reconstruct the work which went on inside them from features of buildings still standing today. The butcher worked in a chamber on the ground floor and served his wares through a window; customers did not enter the shop. The upper floors of the long buildings were used for storage (hides, tallow, tools). These had only narrow windows for lighting and ventilation. The house of the German butchers' guild in Buda still stands, as does the house of the Óbuda guild (Fig. 10.6).[88] Our only information on the house of the Buda Hungarian guild, the houses of the Pest

86   Végh, *Buda*, i, p. 79 and pp. 181–185; MNL OL DL 15 766 ands 17 675.
87   OSt, pp. 113–115 (cap. 154).
88   The one for Buda is at 18–20 Tárnok Street, 1st district; the one for Óbuda is at 158 Lajos Street, 3rd district. On the archaeological investigation of the latter, see Vilmosné Bertalan, "Budapest, III. ker. Lajos u. 158. számú ház feltárása," [Research on the house 158 Lajos Street, 3rd district Budapest] *Budapest Régiségei* 31 (1977), pp. 323–348.

Hungarian and German guilds, and the butchers' shops in the *suburbium* and Felhévíz comes from references in charters and modern maps.[89]

Bakers' Shops

Bread was also important to the town's inhabitants. The baking industry made good use of local natural features, setting up mills on the outflows of hot-water springs into the Danube, which allowed them to work throughout the year.[90] The *Ofner Stadtrecht* precisely stipulated the weight of flour that could be milled from one *gerla* (sack) of wheat, and the number of rolls and loaves which could be baked from them.[91] It distinguished 'hard' (wheat and rye) from 'soft' grains (barley and oats).[92] Other grains were sold directly on the market for porridge: spelt wheat, barley, oats and aniseed.[93] Although the *Ofner Stadtrecht* does not mention rye specifically as a bread grain, it must have been used in large quantities. Charters usually mention fields as being sown with barley and rye in equal proportions.[94] This is borne out by analyses of seeds retrieved from archaeological excavations.

The *Ofner Stadtrecht* distinguishes three kinds of baker and thus three kinds of bakery product.[95] Bakers selling black bread (*wechtler pegken*) had to sell their wares from cloths spread on the ground. Those selling ordinary bread (*müttel pegken*) had to sell from a table or rack. Master bakers (*maisterr pegken*) could only sell their white bread and other bakery goods (pretzels, rolls and *csúcsos vekni*s [small pointed loaves]), made from flour that had been sieved several times over, from bakers' shops. The master bakers had to bake their wares in the market place: *semel pachen auf dem margkt*. The ordinary and black-bread bakers must have had several bakeries that they either built themselves or rented. The names of streets in the Buda *suburbium* link them to the bakery trade (Búza utca [Wheat], Malomszer [Mill], Molnár utca [Miller], *Platea Pistorum* [Bakers' Street]).[96] Bakers, especially those owning

---

89   Benda, "A kereskedelem, ii," pp. 27–33.
90   Kubinyi, "Haller," pp. 80–128. Kubinyi, "Budafelhévíz," pp. 153–160; MNL OL DL 3110, 5289, 13 682, 18 572, 20 563 and 21 930.
91   OSt, pp. 110–111 (cap. 145) and p. 203 (cap. 443).
92   OSt, p. 112 (cap. 149).
93   OSt, p. 114 (cap. 154).
94   MNL OL DL 75 537, 55 338 and 55 606.
95   OSt, pp. 110–111 (cap. 145 and 147).
96   Végh, *Buda*, i, pp. 108 and 118–119; MNL OL DF 283 678.

a mill, became prominent citizens of the city.[97] One roll baker (*pistor semellarum*), János Kremzer, for example, supplied 700 florins' worth of bakery goods to the court of Wladislas II.[98]

Charters and the *Ofner Stadtrecht* tell us that bakers' shops in the main market of Buda (*apotheca semellarum, prot pengk, zemlyezek*) operated in the eastern row of buildings on the market place.[99] A seventeenth-century pen-and-ink drawing records the frontage of the building which stood there in the Middle Ages.[100] It had four little doors and windows, possibly acting as service hatches. The building, which was knocked down 300 years ago, seems to have accommodated the bakers' shops rather than dwellings, although this cannot be certain. Two buildings in *Theywcza* (*Tej utca*, i.e. "Milk Street")[101] beside the medieval Saturday Market appear to have been used as bakers' shops or for other retail functions.[102] The legacy of the bakers' shops in Pest includes the name of Kalácssütő Street ("milk-loaf baker"),[103] and there survives a charter about a roll baker called Osvát who lived in *Platea Sancti Petri* (St Peter's Street) beside Mátyás Boltos.[104]

Conclusions

Buda's brisk trade in the Middle Ages is testified both in the written documents and by archaeological finds and the remains of buildings built for commercial purposes that have survived to our own times. These buildings were usually located in or beside market places or fair grounds that can often be identified with the help of topographic data in the documentary record. The shops were not uniform, but diverse on account of the kind and quantity of the commodities that were sold in them. In the case of wares produced on the premises, the shops were combined with workshops befitting the needs of the craft. All this resulted in various types of shops of varying sizes and interior arrangements.

---

97 MNL OL DL 22 546 and 106 075.
98 MNL OL DL 39 227.
99 Végh, *Buda*, i, p. 86 and 184; MNL OL DL 17 675, 38 658 and DF 200 608.
100 Budapest, BFL, Budai Telekkönyvi Iratok, IV, 1009, G, II-144; Benda, "A kereskedelem, ii," pp. 35–39.
101 Végh, *Buda*, i, p. 85; MNL OL DL 18 468, 38 658 and DF 208 203.
102 The present-day name is Kard Street. The two presumed buildings are either 18 Fortuna Street or the back part of the house in front, 8 Bécsikapu Square.
103 Kubinyi, *Budapest*, p. 14.
104 Ottó B. Kelényi, "Iparosok és kereskedők Budán és Pesten a középkorban," [Artisans and merchants in medieval Buda and Pest] *Budapest Régiségei* 13 (1943), pp. 219–334, here p. 327.

The buildings in which members of the merchant guilds worked (retailers, wholesale merchants and middle-men) as well as those guild craftsmen who produced directly for the market (butchers, bakers, apothecaries) were distinguished by their architectural features. The *Ofner Stadtrecht*, compiled in the first half of the fifteenth century, contains sales-related regulations that had long been part of the guild statutes, and these statutes also refer to the characteristics of the buildings where different products were sold.

This study describes how the various shops identified and localized with the help of written evidence can be distinguished from neighboring residential buildings on the basis of their architectural features. The retailers' shops stood in the middle of the market places. These were small houses with one or two rooms, with cellars used for storage, ground floors for selling and the first-floor rooms for dwelling space. The premises, on which butchers as well as the master bakers who produced fine and white ware worked, were located in long buildings that consisted of rows of small units used both as workshops and retail stores. The apothecaries and the cloth merchants worked on the ground-floor of burgher houses, with their shops being accessible to customers from the outside; the shops of the wholesalers were also located on the ground floors of burgher houses, but customers were only able to enter these via the entrance passage in the gateway. Long-distance merchants arriving in the city had to deposit their wares in a special warehouse located in the suburb. The personnel working in this large hall unpacked the bales and middle-men arranged the business transactions.

Commercial life developed in different ways in the three main parts of the Hungarian capital during the late Middle Ages. Buda became the main market for imported wares, while Pest played the leading role in the export trade. Óbuda on the other hand never rose above the level of a market town and provided premises for traders in subsistence commodities. The processing of grains and livestock transported to the capital from all over the country brought great profit to the local millers and master butchers. In sum, Buda and its agglomeration became the commercial center of Hungary until the Ottoman occupation in the middle of the sixteenth century.

CHAPTER 11

Commercial Contacts of Buda along the Danube and beyond

István Draskóczy

King Sigismund enumerated in one of his charters issued between 1389 and 1402[1] the places from where merchants visited Buda. His list included Vienna, the Holy Roman Empire, Poland, Bohemia, Russia, Prussia, Venice and other parts of Italy. In 1550, one generation after the fateful battle of Mohács (1526), the city magistrates of Vienna remembered the Hungarian capital as a place where merchandise was exchanged between Austrians and traders from Nuremberg, Silesia, Poland, Bohemia, Moravia and Italy.[2] These two randomly selected references indicate how broad-ranging the commercial contacts of late medieval Buda were.[3]

Early Contacts with the West

Due to the economic development of Europe generally and of Hungary in particular, the importance of west-bound foreign trade began to increase in the thirteenth century. Europe's more sophisticated economic centers needed gold, silver, copper, livestock (oxen and horses), wine and other foodstuff, in exchange for which cloths of various sorts, industrial and luxury products and

---

Translated by Katalin Szende

1   The document is mentioned in OSt, p. 87 (cap. 67). See also Boglárka Weisz, *Vásárok és lerakatok a középkori Magyar Királyságban* [Markets and staples in the medieval kingdom of Hungary] (Budapest: MTA BTK Történettudományi Intézete 2012), pp. 76–77.
2   Lajos Gecsényi, "Folytonosság és megújulás Magyarország és a felnémet városok gazdasági kapcsolataiban a középkortól a kora újkorig," [Continuity and renewal in the economic connections of Hungary and the Upper German towns from the Middle Ages to the Early Modern period] in idem, *Gazdaság, társadalom, igazgatás. Tanulmányok a kora újkor történetéből* [Economy, society, administration. Studies in early modern history] (Győr: Győr-Moson-Sopron Megye Győri Levéltára, 2008), pp. 409–423, here p. 411.
3   Most of our knowledge of the economic life of medieval Buda comes from the works of the late Professor András Kubinyi (1929–2007). See his collected works of the history of Pest, Buda and Óbuda: Kubinyi, *Tanulmányok*.

spices were imported into Hungary. Trade with the West was central to Buda's economy, and remained so until the end of the Middle Ages.[4]

Buda was substantially predestined for its central role in the economy of the entire Carpathian Basin on account of its location on the Danube. Buda and Pest were also at the junction of the country's main land routes. One of these routes connected the Hungarian capital through Győr and Moson to Vienna; another route led from the Adriatic to Buda via Zagreb; and yet another connected Buda and Venice through Ptuj (Pettau), Veszprém and Székesfehérvár. From Bohemia and Moravia, Buda could be reached via Trnava and Esztergom; from Silesia, through Trenčín and Esztergom. The mining district of Kremnica, Banská Štiavnica and Banská Bystrica, which were rich in silver and copper ores, lay a mere 160–170 kilometres north of Buda. Routes from north-eastern Hungary (esp. Košice), from the Great Hungarian Plain and from Transylvania (through Oradea) converged on Pest.[5] Indeed, Buda's trade with towns west of Hungary was facilitated by the fact that many of its burghers were settlers from the Austrian provinces and Regensburg, and on account of subsequent waves of immigration about half of the population remained German-speaking until the end of the Middle Ages.[6]

One of the earliest sources that provides us with concrete details concerning Buda's trade is the list of customs tariffs for the Buda fair that was put into writing in 1255. This points to a brisk trade in a wide range of commodities, including agricultural products (grain, wine, livestock), leather, wax, salt, as well as iron, lead and silver. The main imports from the west were cloth and

---

4 Balázs Nagy, "Magyarország külkereskedelme a középkorban," [The foreign trade of Hungary in the Middle Ages], in *Gazdaság és gazdálkodás a középkori Magyarországon. Gazdaságtörténet, anyagi kultúra, régészet* [Economy and farming in medieval Hungary: Economic history, material culture, and archaeology], eds András Kubinyi, József Laszlovszky and Péter Szabó (Budapest: Martin Opitz, 2008), pp. 235–276; Franz Irsigler, "Die Bedeutung Ungarns für die europäische Wirtschaft im Spätmittelalter," in *Sigismund von Luxemburg. Ein Kaiser in Europa*, eds Michel Pauly and François Reinert (Mainz am Rhein: Philipp von Zabern, 2006), pp. 27–34.

5 Jenő Szűcs, *Az utolsó Árpádok* [The last Árpádians] (Budapest: MTA Történettudományi Intézet, 1993), pp. 225–229 and 265–274; Katalin Szende, "Towns along the Way. Changing Patterns of Long-Distance Trade and the Urban Network of Medieval Hungary," in *Towns and communication*, ii. *Communication between Towns*, eds Hubert Houben and Kristjan Toomaspoeg (Lecce: Mario Congedo Editore, 2011), pp. 161–225.

6 Kubinyi, *Anfänge Ofens*, p. 93; András Végh, "Buda: The Multi-Ethnic Capital of Medieval Hungary," in *Segregation – Integration – Assimilation: Religious and Ethnic Groups in the Medieval Towns of Central and Eastern Europe* (Historical Urban Studies), eds Derek Keene, Balázs Nagy and Katalin Szende (Farnham: Ashgate, 2009), pp. 89–99.

linen, the trade in which was mainly in the hands of merchants from the German lands. The tariff document distinguished between cheap grey cloth and the more expensive varieties, but does not give a detailed list of the latter. It only specifies that the custom dues to be paid must correspond to the value of the wares, namely 4 *pondera* (one *pondus* equalling 1/48 *marcae*) for every 5 *marcae* of value. The list does not mention copper, one of the main export articles of medieval Hungary, but by the fourteenth century Buda was beyond doubt one of the main transit markets for this metal (exported probably as black copper).[7] The next big transit market of this product was Vienna, from where it was transported either further west or to Venice.[8]

The two main trading centers, with established links to Buda even in the thirteenth century, were Vienna and Regensburg.[9] Vienna rose to prominence as an important transit point in the East–West trade in the twelfth century. The town received its staple right from Leopold VI, duke of Austria (1198–1230), in 1221, but at that time this right was not enough to monopolize the trade towards Hungary. Documents testify that merchants from Vienna traveled east along the Danube. The kings of Hungary confirmed for them in 1270 and again in 1279 the regulations issued by Béla IV in 1260 on the collection of tolls at three places along the river: at Abda, Győr, and Füzitő. In 1297 Andrew prohibited the imposition of unjust and unprecedented tolls on foreigners. The charters on these matters were kept in Vienna, and were confirmed, together with other privileges granted to the Viennese, by King Ladislas V in 1453.[10]

---

7   Martin Štefanik, "Die Anfänge der slowakischen Bergstädte," in *Stadt und Bergbau* (Städteforschung, A 64), eds Karl Heinrich Kaufhold and Wilfrid Reininghaus (Cologne–Weimar, Vienna: Böhlau, 2004), pp. 295–312, here p. 303; Wolfgang von Stromer: "Die Saigerhütte," in *Technologietransfer und Wissenschaftsaustausch zwischen Ungarn und Deutschland. Aspekte der historischen Beziehungen in Naturwissenschaft und Technik*, eds Holger Fischer and Ferenc Szadadváry (Munich: Oldenbourg, 1995), pp. 27–57, here p. 32.

8   EFHU, iii/2, pp. 44–46 (no 38); Szűcs, *Az utolsó Árpádok*, pp. 225–230; György Székely, "Niederländische und englische Tucharten im Mitteleuropa des 13.–17. Jahrhunderts," *Annales Universitatis Scientiarum Budapestinensis de Rolando Eötvös nominatae. Sectio Historica* 8 (1966), pp. 14–19; CD, viii/3, pp. 56–59 (no 1).

9   BTOE, i, pp. 247–249 (no 228); EFHU, iii/2, pp. 84–89 (no 67–68); Kubinyi, *Anfänge Ofens*, pp. 82–84.

10 EFHU, iii/2, pp. 51–52 (no 42); József Teleki, *Hunyadiak kora Magyarországon*, x [The age of the Hunyadis in Hungary] (Pest: Emich, 1853), pp. 372–379; Kubinyi, *Anfänge Ofens*, p. 83; Jan Lukačka, "Verkehrs- und Handelsbeziehungen zwischen den Städten Wien, Pressburg und Ofen bis zur Mitte des 15. Jahrhunderts," in *Städte im Donauraum, Bratislava – Pressburg 1291–1991*, ed. Richard Marsina (Bratislava: Slovenská historická spoločnosť, 1993), pp. 159–164.

It was Regensburg, however, that was the prime trading hub in Central Europe at this time, and the influence of the Bavarian city was strongly felt in Buda as well. This is attested, for instance, by the fact that the weight of the *marca* of Buda (245.53779 g) is identical with that of the standard weight in Regensburg, and not with the *marca* used in twelfth-century Hungary (233.3533 g) or in Vienna. By the mid-thirteenth century Hungarians were frequently to be found in Cologne, just as merchants from Regensburg were present in Hungary,[11] having been granted King Andrew III's special protection in 1291.[12] King Louis the Great, following the example of his predecessors, also gave Regensburg commercial franchises. Burghers from Regensburg even decided to settle in Buda during the thirteenth and fourteenth centuries; thus, for instance, the Kratzer family, who moved to Buda via Vienna.[13] Regensburg never ceased to be an important transhipment port for transport on the Danube throughout the Middle Ages, but its leading role in Danubian commerce was gradually taken over by Nuremberg.[14]

Royal economic policy continued to be an important regulatory force in commercial contacts. In the 1320s and 1330s King Charles I introduced a royal monopoly on gold and silver, which were being extracted from Hungarian sources in increasing quantities. Charles banned the export of these precious metals in any form other than minted coins. Gold florins were minted from 1325 onwards following Florentine patterns. Gold coins became standard currency throughout the Middle Ages, whereas silver denars frequently fluctuated in value due to their changing silver content. Charles's regulations, along with his support of the towns, strengthened Hungary's commercial contacts with foreign lands.[15]

---

11   Ferdinand Opll, "Studien zu frühen Wiener Handelsgeschichte," *Wiener Geschichtsblätter* 35, no 2 (1980), pp. 53–61; *Wien. Geschichte einer Stadt*, i, eds Peter Csendes and Ferdinand Opll (Vienna–Cologne–Weimar: Böhlau, 2001), pp. 221–223; Renáta Skorka, "A bécsi lerakat Magyarországra vezető kiskapui," [Legal loopholes in the staple of Vienna], *Történelmi Szemle* 54 (2012), pp. 1–16.

12   Bálint Hóman, *Magyar pénztörténet 1000–1325* [History of Hungarian coinage, 1000–1325] (Budapest: MTA, 1916), pp. 122–124.

13   András Kubinyi, "Regensburg – Passau – Ungarn im Mittelalter," in *Bayern und Ungarn. Tausende Jahre enge Beziehungen*, ed. Ekkehard Völkl (Regensburg: M. Lassleben, 1988), pp. 29–39, here pp. 33–35.

14   Kubinyi, "Regensburg," pp. 36–37; *Nürnberg, Geschichte einer europäischen Stadt*, ed. Gerhard Pfeiffer (Munich: Beck, 1971), pp. 177–179 (by Hermann Kellenbenz).

15   Pál Engel, *The Realm of St. Stephen. A History of Medieval Hungary, 895–1526* (London–New York: I.B. Tauris, 2001), pp. 153–156; Irsigler, "Die Bedeutung," pp. 27–28; Boglárka Weisz, "Entrate reali e politica economica nell 'età di Carlo I.," in *L'Ungheria angioina*

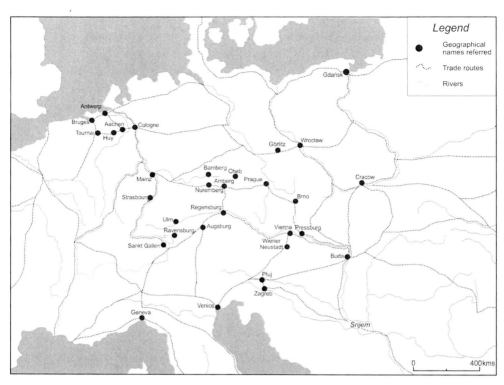

FIGURE 11.1 *The medieval communication networks of Europe with the geographic names referred to in the article*

It was not all plain sailing, however. Frederick III (the Fair), duke of Austria (1308–1330), renewed Vienna's staple right in 1312, and the new regulations set higher barriers to commercial relations between merchants from the South German territories and Hungary. The internal conflicts in Hungary following the contested succession of the Angevins, as well as military conflict in the Austrian duchies and Bavaria, posed further threats to commerce.[16] The deterioration of Austrian-Hungarian relations under Charles I after 1324 also had a negative impact on trade.[17]

    (Bibliotheca Academiae Hungariae – Roma, Studia, 3), ed. Enikő Csukovits (Rome: Viella, 2013), pp. 205–236, here pp. 210–213 and 223.
16   Skorka, "A bécsi lerakat," *passim*.
17   Ambrus Pleidell, *A nyugatra irányuló magyar külkereskedelem a középkorban* [Hungary's trade with the West in the Middle Ages] (Budapest: Budavári Tudományos Társaság, 1925), pp. 33–59.

Partners and Rivals: Vienna, Pressburg, Cologne and Nuremberg

Under the pressure of these circumstances, John of Luxemburg, king of Bohemia, and Charles I concluded a commercial agreement at Visegrád in 1335 in order to topple Vienna's dominance. In order to outmanoeuvre Vienna, a staple right was granted to Brno, and in 1336 Charles reduced the tolls to be paid by traders coming from the Czech lands across the Hungarian border via Trnava and Esztergom to Buda, thus giving more favorable access to the Hungarian capital. In 1337, merchants from Mainz, Nuremberg, Augsburg, and Prague persuaded the archbishop of Esztergom to take similar measures at the toll stations owned by his diocese in favor of traders from Swabia, the Rhine valley, Flanders, and Bohemia. This list makes clear who were the ultimate beneficiaries of the agreement. The toll reductions set down in the charter of 1336 were later reissued by King Louis the Great in the form of special grants for the merchants of Prague, Cologne, Huy, Nuremberg, Brno, Cheb (Eger), Amberg and Wrocław (Breslau).[18]

The use of the northern route is attested to by the complaints of Cologne and Huy, namely that despite their privileges their burghers were still required to pay the earlier, and higher, tolls. The two cities had their grants reissued in 1350, 1364, and 1384.[19] In 1364 Olf Pichman and his brother-in-law (*sororius*), Matthias, requested the confirmation of the same charter from the king. Matthias was most probably the head of the wealthiest Cologne textile merchant family in Vienna, the van der Bachs. A later head of this firm, Jakob van der Bach, was a burgher of Buda in 1420, and his business contacts in Hungary also extended to Pressburg.

Next to Cologne, Nuremberg took pride of place as trading partner of Buda. For a city with such well-developed cloth production and metalworking industries, Hungary was an attractive business target. Merchants from Cologne imported cloth produced in their home town and its vicinity as well as in other Upper German towns and in the Low Countries. They exchanged the cloth for golden florins and copper, obtained mainly from Hungary and Bohemia. The

---

18 Pleidell, *A nyugatra irányuló*, pp. 35–41; Balázs Nagy, "Transcontinental Trade from East–Central Europe to Western Europe (Fourteenth and Fifteenth Centuries)," in... *The Man of Many Devices, Who Wandered Full Many Ways... Festschrift in Honor of János M. Bak*, eds Balázs Nagy and Marcell Sebők (Budapest–New York: CEU Press, 1999), pp. 347–356, here pp. 347–350.

19 *Magyar diplomácziai emlékek az Anjou-korból*, 3 vols [Hungarian diplomatic records from the Anngevin period], ed. Gusztáv Wenzel (Budapest: MTA Könyvkiadó Hivatala, 1874–1876), ii, pp. 47, 63–65 and 633–634, and iii, pp. 533–535.

presence of burghers from Nuremberg in Buda is attested to in a debt case handled by the city council in 1360 regarding the purchase of oxen.[20]

The toll reductions granted by the charter of 1336 were extended conjointly to merchants of Nuremberg and Prague in 1357 (and reconfirmed in 1364 and 1383), although it is plain that they had been active in Buda well before this date. The common action of the Prague and Nuremberg merchants are easily explained in the light of the close economic links between the two cities. King Louis further extended the privileges of the Nuremberg traders in 1370 and 1371.[21] These charters fitted well into the series of toll reductions and exemptions that the city obtained for its burghers in western and central Europe in the course of the fourteenth century.[22]

The burghers who approached the king for such favors belonged to the wealthiest merchant houses of their home towns. The customs privileges for Nuremberg were obtained in 1357 by Wolfram Stromeir, whose close relative, Ulrich, traded in copper from Hungary. The business network of the Stomeirs extended to a large number of European cities, including Antwerp, Bruges, Cologne, Strasbourg, Vienna, Wrocław, Cracow and Gdańsk. The families of Perthold Holzschuher and Johannes Ebner who petitioned for privileges from Louis I in 1364 also had wide-ranging contacts. Perthold was active in Buda around 1358–1360; and Hermann Ebner and Ulrich Eysvogel sold cloth from Nuremberg and Tournai in the Hungarian capital. Leopold Schürstab also spent much time in Buda between 1363 and 1383. Other prominent Nuremberg merchants such as Vorchtel Herdegger and Bertold Kraft, remained in Buda right up to their deaths.[23]

---

20 Rainer Stahlschmidt, "Das Messinggewerbe in spätmittelalterlichen Nürnberg," *Mitteilungen des Vereins für Geschichte der Stadt Nürnberg* 57 (1970), pp. 124–130, here pp. 127–130; Wolfgang von Stromer, "Zur Organisation des transkontinentalen Ochsen– und Textilhandels im Spätmittelalter. Der Ochsenhandel des Reichserbkämmerers Konrad von Weinsberg anno 1422," in *Internationaler Ochsenhandel (1350–1750)* (Beiträge zur Wirtschaftsgeschichte, 9), ed. Ekkehard Westermann (Stuttgart: Klett–Cotta, 1979), pp. 171–195, here p. 172; Richard Perger, "Nürnberger im mittelalterlichen Wien," *Mitteilungen des Vereins für Geschichte der Stadt Nürnberg* 63 (1976), pp. 1–98, here p. 7.

21 *Magyar diplomácziai emlékek*, ii, pp. 482–486, 617–618, 667 and 686–687; ibid, iii, pp. 12, 73–74 and 511–515.

22 Hans Schenk, "Die Beziehungen zwischen Nürnberg und Prag von 1450–1500," in *Der Außenhandel Ostmitteleuropas 1450–1650*, ed. Ingomar Bog (Cologne–Vienna: Böhlau, 1971), pp. 185–203.

23 Hektor Ammann, *Die wirtschaftliche Stellung der Reichsstadt Nürnberg im Spätmittelalter* (Nuremberg: Verein f. Geschichte d. Stadt Nürnberg and Edelmann, 1970), pp. 165–166; Wolfgang von Stromer, *Oberdeutsche Hochfinanz 1350–1450*, i (Wiesbaden: Steiner, 1970),

One of the important commodities transported via the northern route was wine, which was produced in quantity and profitably in Pressburg and many other places. Hungarian wine was sought after in Bohemia and Moravia, but was not allowed to be sold in Vienna, because wine was the main local produce there as well, and the city's markets were strictly protected. Buda was also famous for its wine, but practically all of this was consumed locally. The burghers of Pest owned vineyards in faraway Srijem (Srem, *Szerémség* in Hungarian), in the southern part of medieval Hungary, where the best wine of the country came from. It was marketed in Pest (for instance to buyers from Silesia) or transported to Košice, from where local merchants exported the vintage to Poland.[24]

The route bypassing Vienna remained in use until the Hussite wars, but in the long run it did little to diminish the importance of Vienna. There was no getting round the fact that it was easier to reach Buda from the West via the Austrian ducal seat. Furthermore, one of the main commercial routes connecting Silesia and Bohemia with Italy also passed through Vienna, and the Viennese maintained strong contacts with Venice. Thus the capital of the Austrian provinces remained a prime commercial hub, from where not only western, but also Italian commodities were forwarded to Buda.[25]

For merchants from Cologne and Nuremberg, Vienna made sense as a base for their interests further afield. Buda was within easy reach not only for the Viennese, but also for those merchants who settled and acquired burgher rights in these two cities. A few examples serve to illustrate the intricate web of contacts. In 1404 Gerhard van Tyl, a burgher of Buda, undertook to repay his

---

pp. 25, 98 and 102–104; András Kubinyi, "A budai német patríciátus társadalmi helyzete családi összeköttetései tükrében a 13. századtól a 15. század második feléig," [The social position of the German patriciate in Buda as reflected in their family ties from the thirteenth to the second half of the fifteenth century], in Kubinyi, *Tanulmányok*, ii, pp. 457–512, here pp. 486–487; Rady, *Buda*, pp. 94–96.

24   Csendes and Opll, *Wien*, pp. 223–225; Katalin Szende, *Otthon a városban. Társadalom és anyagi kultúra a középkori Sopronban, Pozsonyban és Eperjesen* [At home in the town: Society and material culture in medieval Sopron, Pressburg and Prešov] (Társadalom- és Művelődéstörténeti Tanulmányok, 32) (Budapest: MTA Történettudományi Intézet, 2004), p. 38; András Kubinyi, "Die Städte Ofen und Pest und der Fernhandel am Ende des 15. und am Anfang des 16. Jahrhunderts," in *Der Außenhandel Ostmitteleuropas 1450–1650*, ed. Ingomar Bog (Cologne–Vienna: Böhlau, 1971), pp. 342–433, here pp. 412–414.

25   Peter Csendes, "Zu Wiener Handelsgeschichte des 16. Jahrhunderts," *Wiener Geschichtsblätter* 29 (1974), pp. 219–225; Herbert Hassinger, *Geschichte des Zollwesens, Handels und Verkehrs in den östlichen Alpenländern vom Spätmittelalter bis in die zweite Hälfte des 18. Jahrhunderts* (Stuttgart: Steiner, 1987), p. 552.

debts to his creditors from Cologne, Johann van Heimbach and Johann Pomel, in Vienna. The Heimbach family from Cologne also had business ties outside Vienna, in two Hungarian towns close to the western border, Pressburg and Sopron. One of the most important firms in Nuremberg was the company of Ulrich Stromeir, who received a letter of protection from Duke Rudolf IV in 1358. Leopold Schürstab, whose activity in Buda is attested from 1383, had an uncle who owned a house in Vienna in 1399. The Vorchtel family was also active in the Austrian capital.[26]

Vienna's role in the transit trade was complemented by Pressburg, a town about 60 km east of it within the borders of medieval Hungary. Pressburg's economic prosperity grew in the second half of the fourteenth and the first half of the fifteenth centuries and it became a convenient secondary center in Vienna's east-bound trade. Merchants from Pressburg visited Vienna regularly and vice versa, and family ties developed between the burghers of the two places, primarily through marriage. In 1402 Pressburg received staple right from King Sigismund (together with Sopron and Trnava). Although the ruler revoked the right in the same year, it seems to have remained in force as far as foreign merchants were concerned. Pressburg thus became the western gate of the kingdom of Hungary.[27]

In this period of Pressburg's economic boom, merchants from Cologne based in Vienna sold large quantities of cloth in the form of commodity credit to traders from Pressburg. It was more lucrative to trade with partners close-by than to visit the more distant Buda. In this way, transport costs could be minimized, and debts were easier to recover. In spite of all these advantages, around 1420 merchants from Cologne decided to quit both Vienna and Pressburg and to reduce their overheads by commissioning other German merchant networks to sell their wares. Their place was accordingly taken by merchants from Nuremberg who had been active in Vienna for some time. They sought not only golden florins from Hungary but other commodities as well, such as copper and oxen, and their primary merchandise was likewise cloth, sold as commodity credit.[28] The number of Viennese merchants doing business in

26 Gunther Hirschfelder, *Die Kölner Handelsbeziehungen im Spätmittelalter* (Cologne: Kölnisches Stadtmuseum 1994), pp. 125, 138–139 and 147–148; Perger, "Nürnberger," pp. 12–17, 24 and 47.
27 Szende, *Otthon a városban*, pp. 34–39.
28 Klaus Militzer, "Kölner Kaufleute in Pressburg und im Donauraum im 14. und 15. Jahrhundert," in *Städte im Donauraum*, pp. 121–134; Renáta Skorka, "Pozsony gazdasági szerepe a 15. század első felében a zálogszerződések tükrében," [The economic role of Pressburg in the first half of the fifteenth century as revealed in pledge contracts] *Századok* 138 (2004), pp. 433–466, here pp. 441–446 and 451–452.

Pressburg also increased from the end of the 1420s, but the loans provided by them were not on the scale of those furnished by their counterparts from Nuremberg. This points to a relative lack of capital among the Viennese trading companies.[29]

The result of all this was that in the first half of the fifteenth century Pressburg took over the leading role from Buda in the transit trade from the West. According to the customs accounts, the value of wares imported at Pressburg in 1457/58 was 166,564 florins, the dominant merchandise being cloth of different sorts, from luxury quality cloth imported from the Low Countries to the cheap types of Silesia, representing a total value of 131,155 florins. From 1440 onwards the town of Pressburg rented out the local toll station where a duty, known as the thirtieth, was collected on exports and imports. Between 1451 and 1458 the common income of Pressburg, Rusovce (on the right bank of the Danube opposite Pressburg) and Buda from the thirtieth was a gross 64,618.5 florins, of which Buda's share was a mere 4782 florins, or 7 percent.[30] This number not only indicates that merchants paid their customs dues at Pressburg, but also shows the economic significance of this town as Hungary's western gateway on the Danube. Merchants from Vienna continued, however, to visit Hungary both in the fourteenth and the fifteenth centuries, journeying both by river and overland.[31] Many of those who arrived in Hungary paid the thirtieth at Pressburg and continued their journey onwards to Buda, selling their merchandise there. Some Viennese companies even kept agents in the Hungarian capital.[32] After 1408 Sigismund gradually moved his seat from Visegrád to Buda, and the central judiciary courts and offices were also transferred there. The presence of the court and other governmental organs, as well as the nobles and burghers gathered there, obviously increased Buda's commercial potential.[33]

---

29 Ferenc Kováts, "A magyar arany világtörténeti jelentősége és kereskedelmi összeköttetéseink nyugattal a középkorban," [The role of Hungarian gold in world history and the economic ties of Hungary with the West in the Middle Ages] *Történeti Szemle* 11 (1922), pp. 104–143, here p. 136; Skorka, "Pozsony gazdasági," pp. 449–452. For the connections of Vienna with Pressburg, see Richard Perger, "Beziehungen zwischen Preßburger und Wiener Bürgerfamilien im Mittelalter," in *Städte im Donauraum*, pp. 149–158.

30 Kováts, "A magyar arany," pp. 120–125.

31 *Magyar diplomácziai emlékek*, iii, pp. 73–74; *Quellen zur Geschichte der Stadt Wien. Regesten aus dem Archive der Stadt Wien* ii/1–3 (Vienna: [n.p.], 1900–1907), ii/1, nos 663, 671, 848, 934, 979, 1003–1005, 1155 and 1161; ii/2, nos 3499, 3506, 3506a, 3507, 3748 and 3812.

32 *Quellen zur Geschichte der Stadt Wien*, ii/2, nos 2620, 2715–2716 and 3225; Kubinyi, "A budai német patríciátus," p. 486.

33 Kubinyi, "Die Städte Ofen und Pest und der Fernhandel," p. 351.

Although the merchant companies of Pressburg profited from the transit trade, it seems that they did not themselves have sufficient capital to finance independent commercial activities. Thus they had to rely on loans not only from their western business partners but also from the merchants of Buda. We certainly find plenty of evidence of burghers of Pressburg and Sopron being indebted to their counterparts in Buda. For instance, in 1447 a merchant from Pressburg took over livestock as commodity credit from a former judge of Pest and a burgher of Buda and obligated himself to repay them in cloth from Aachen and Cologne.[34] Buda burghers provided credit to noblemen and their fellow burghers alike, and gave loans to the king as well. In 1433 a merchant from Buda was robbed of his merchandise to the value of 1000 florins during a fair in Vienna.[35] Most of the cloth passing through Pressburg ended up in Buda. The *Ofner Stadtrecht* mentions 43 sorts of foreign cloth, to which the rough cloth from Transylvania, the so-called *aba*, can be added. The thirtieth customs tariffs recorded 32 sorts of fine (medium or better quality) cloth. In 1457/58, 59 sorts of cloths passed through the toll station of Pressburg.[36]

Buda's Key Position

Buda's key role in commodity exchange was reinforced by its staple right. In the fourteenth century this applied to merchants from abroad as well as to native ones (except for the burghers of Sibiu in Transylvania, who were exempted from the Buda staple by King Louis I). In 1402, however, Sigismund issued a decree that local merchants could not be forced to offer their wares for sale in the capital, and the same principle was restated in the laws of 1405.[37] This change was favorable for the Hungarian towns generally, but not for Buda. To be sure, foreigners were still compelled to sell their merchandise to traders in Buda or other Hungarian towns and in principle they were not allowed to travel further.

---

34 Andreas Kubinyi, "Die Nürnberger Haller in Ofen," *Mitteilungen des Vereins für Geschichte der Stadt Nürnberg* 52 (1963–64), pp. 80–128, here pp. 84–85.

35 Emma Lederer, *A középkori pénzüzletek története Magyarországon (1000–1458)* [The history of medieval finance in Hungary, 1000 to 1458] (Budapest: Kovács József, 1932), pp. 163–167; Kubinyi, *Budapest*, p. 50. The activity of the Pressburgers in Buda is attested to by their shops in the capital. See György Székely, "Hunyadi László kivégzése – struktúraváltozások a magyar állam és a főváros kormányzásában," [The execution of László Hunyadi: Structural changes in the government of the Hungarian state and the capital] *Tanulmányok Budapest Múltjából* 22 (1988), pp. 61–102, here p. 77.

36 OSt, pp. 195–197 (cap. 423–424); BTOE, iii/2, pp. 270–273 (no 1139).

37 DRH 1301–1457, pp. 199–200.

But Buda hoped for more. Its burghers wanted to have a monopoly on trade with Transylvania, as reflected by the *Ofner Stadtrecht* that only allowed Transylvanians to come as far as the capital with their wares and no further, while foreigners were forbidden, in accordance with the principles set up by the king, from traveling to Oradea and onto Transylvania. These strict regulations could be circumvented by foreigners acquiring burgher rights in Buda. This was indeed a common tactic adopted by agents or members of foreign merchant companies, and they also frequently established family ties with their business partners in the Hungarian capital.[38]

The Transylvanian route grew in importance because of the participation of the Saxon towns in the Levantine trade. Merchants from these towns imported mainly spices (first and foremost pepper) which they exchanged for western cloth (including varieties from Cologne, Nuremberg, and the Low Countries) and knives from the Austrian provinces. Most of the cloth in these exchanges

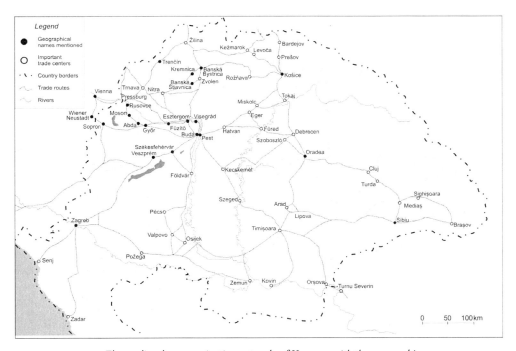

FIGURE 11.2 *The medieval communication networks of Hungary with the geographic names referred to in the article*

---

38   OSt, pp. 86–87, 190–191 and 198–200 (cap. 405–409 and 426–434); Kubinyi, *Budapest*, pp. 47–52; idem, "Die Städte Ofen und Pest und der Fernhandel," pp. 383–385.

passed through Buda; a smaller part traveled from Poland via Košice to Oradea, the main meeting point of Hungarian and Transylvanian merchants.[39]

In economic terms, Transylvania was a well-advanced region of the kingdom of Hungary. Its significance was based on mineral wealth (gold, silver, salt), and the horses of Transylvania were also renowned. Merchants arriving from Western Europe could purchase the commodities from Transylvania most easily in Buda and Pest.[40]

An important source of income for the burghers of Buda was the rental of church tithes as well as of the proceeds of the royal financial administration, such as the thirtieth customs dues and the revenues of the mining and minting chambers. Local burghers were particularly active in the Buda mint, which was in operation from the mid-thirteenth century to 1467 and again from 1521. The mining and minting business was attractive to foreigners as well, as it provided them with easy access to precious metals and copper. In order to be appointed to such an office one needed both the royal favor and good connections with Buda. Friedrich Kratzer, for instance, was a councillor in Buda in the fourteenth century, but also a count of the mining and minting chamber at Kremnica for several years.[41]

The number of Florentines doing business in Buda grew in significance from the middle of the fourteenth century. Many of them purchased houses there as well. The Italians imported luxury wares: fine cloth, silk and spices. By the

---

39 András Kubinyi, "A városi rend kialakulásának gazdasági feltételei és a főváros kereskedelme a 15. század végén," [The preconditions of the formation of the bourgeoisie and trade in the capital at the end of the fifteenth century] in Kubinyi, *Tanulmányok*, i, pp. 307–336; Zsigmond Pál Pach, "Levantine Trade and Hungary in the Middle Ages (Theses, Controversies, Arguments)," in idem, *Hungary and the European Economy in Early Modern Times* (Variorum) (Aldershot: Ashgate, 1994), vi, pp. 20–22; idem, "The Transylvanian Route of Levantine Trade at the Turn of the 15th and 16th Centuries," in idem, *Hungary and the European Economy*, vii, pp. 7–13 and 28–31.

40 *Le Voyage d'Outremer de Bertrandon de Broquière*, ed. Charles Schefer (Paris: Ernest Leroux, 1892), p. 236; András Kubinyi, "Erdély a Mohács előtti évtizedekben," [Transylvania during the Decades before the Battle of Mohács] in *Tanulmányok Erdélyről* [Studies on Transylvania], ed. István Rácz (Debrecen: Csokonai, 1988), 65–73, here pp. 69 and 73; *History of Transylvania*, i, eds Ioan-Aurel Pop and Thomas Nägler (Cluj-Napoca: Romania Cultural Institute, 2005), pp. 261–263 and 319–332 (the works of Ioan-Aurel Pop and Anton Dörner); Márton Gyöngyössy, *Pénzgazdálkodás és monetáris politika a késő középkori Magyarországon* [The money economy and monetary politics in late medieval Hungary] (Budapest: Gondolat, 2003), pp. 102–119 and István Draskóczy: "Sóbányászat és -kereskedelem Magyarországon a középkorban," [Salt mining and the salt trade in medieval Hungary] *Valóság* 57, No 4 (2014), pp. 56–67.

41 Kubinyi, "Regensburg," p. 36.

last third of the fourteenth century, the Italians settled in Buda had taken over practically all the leading financial offices from the Hungarians.[42] The Italians also competed for the mineral resources of Hungary with entrepreneurs from the southern German territories, especially from Nuremberg. During the 1403 uprising against Sigismund, most of the Italians supported Ladislas of Naples, a pretender to the Hungarian throne, which led to their goods being subsequently confiscated by the king. Earlier historiography contended that from this time onwards the Germans gained an advantage over the Italians, but this thesis can no longer be sustained. New research has uncovered ample evidence of the quick recovery of contacts and the renewed involvement of Italians in Hungary, in trade and in financial administration alike, not least due to the successful networking of Filippo Scolari (also known as Pipo of Ozora).[43]

Sigismund's two most influential German financial advisers, Ulrich Kammerer and Mark of Nuremberg, hailed from Nuremberg and became burghers of Buda at the turn of the fourteenth century. They were members of two separate trading companies in their home town, the Kammerer-Seiler-Amman-Grau and the Flextorfer-Kegler-Zenner, and they both established an extensive business network all over Central Europe. In the early fifteenth century they acquired positions at the apex of Hungary's financial administration. In 1409 Mark of Nuremberg, Hans Siebenlinder, Hans Stadler and Niklas Lebmester, all burghers of Buda, formed an alliance to rent all the thirtieth customs revenues of the country. Like Mark, Hans Stadler had also moved from Nuremberg to the Hungarian capital; Hans Siebenlinder was born in a market town in northern Hungary and besides being active in the financial administration he was also judge of Buda.[44]

---

42 Zsuzsa Teke, "Firenzei üzletemberek Magyarországon 1373–1405," [Florentine businessmen in Hungary, 1375 to 1405] *Történelmi Szemle* 37 (1995), pp. 129–150.

43 Zsuzsa Teke, "Firenzei kereskedőtársaságok, kereskedők Magyarországon Zsigmond uralmának megszilárdulása után 1404–1437," [Florentine trade companies and merchants in Hungary, after the consolidation of the reign of Sigismund, 1404 to 1437] *Századok* 129 (1995), pp. 195–214; Krisztina Arany, "Success and Failure – Two Florentine Merchant Families in Buda during the Reign of King Sigismund (1387–1437)," *Annual of Medieval Studies at CEU* 12 (2006), pp. 101–123; Katalin Prajda, "The Florentine Scolari Family at the Court of Sigismund of Luxemburg in Buda," *Journal of Early Modern History* 14 (2010), pp. 513–533.

44 Stromer, *Oberdeutsche Hochfinanz*, pp. 118–151. For the overview of their activity in Hungary, see Elemér Mályusz, *Kaiser Sigismund in Ungarn 1387–1437* (Budapest: Akadémiai, 1990), pp. 202–206. The daughter of Kammerer married a Nuremberger in Buda, and his granddaughters married burghers of Buda. One of them was Peter Reichel, a mine-owner and oft-time head of the royal minting chambers. Siebenlinder's second wife was from

Apart from precious metal and coins, another important commodity that shaped Buda's commercial profile was copper. It was mined in great quantities in the area of Banská Bystrica, which was in reach of Venice, the main south European hub of the copper trade, via either Vienna or Buda. From the Hungarian capital, it could be transported in carts through Ptuj to Venice; another option was to take the copper to one of the harbors in the Eastern Adriatic and ship it to Venice from there. Copper was also transported westwards through Pressburg, and northwards via Poland and Prussia, and thence even as far as Flanders. Thus Buda did not have such a monopoly on the distribution of Hungarian copper as Prague had with Nuremberg for Bohemian silver and copper. Unlike their counterparts in Prague, however, burghers of Buda also featured as owners of mines.[45]

Between 1440 and 1462 Hungary was in the throes of civil war, which made foreigners act with more caution.[46] Peaceful conditions were only re-established during the reign of Matthias Corvinus, who forced the warring sides to come to terms. He spent much more time in Buda than his predecessors, and it was then that Buda finally became a long-term royal seat. The output of precious metals used for minting had diminished in the first half of the fifteenth century but it increased again under Matthias' rule, making the Hungarian markets more attractive. By 1467 the king stabilized the value of the silver denar, with a hundred pieces equal to one golden florin. As the result of a treasury reform in the same year, all royal revenues (except for those that were directly set aside for the provisioning of the court) were placed under the

    Vienna, and his daughter married a burger of Buda who came originally from Basle. See Kubinyi, "A budai német patríciátus," pp. 493–497.

45   Kubinyi, "Die Städte Ofen und Pest und der Fernhandel," pp. 398–399; Martin Štefanik, "Kupfer aus dem ungarischen Königreich im Spiegel der venezianischen Senatsprotokolle in 14. Jahrhundert," in *Der Tiroler Bergbau und die Depression der europäischen Montanwirtschaft im 14. und 15. Jahrhundert*, eds Rudolf Tasser and Ekkehard Westermann (Innsbruck: Studien Verlag, 2004), pp. 210–226, here pp. 212–213; Szabolcs Varga, "Zágráb szerepe a magyarországi városhálózatban a középkorban," [The role of Zagreb in the urban network of Hungary in the Middle Ages] *Urbs. Magyar Várostörténeti Évkönyv* 3 (2008), pp. 249–273, here p. 261; *Das Kaufmannsnotizbuch des Matthäus Schwarz aus Augsburg von 1548*, eds Ekkehard Westermann and Markus A. Denzel (Stuttgart: Steiner, 2011), pp. 160–161 and 488–490; Josef Janaček, "Prag und Nürnberg im 16. Jahrhundert," in *Der Außenhandel Ostmitteleuropas 1450–1650*, ed. Ingomar Bog (Cologne–Vienna: Böhlau, 1971), pp. 204–228.

46   The Italians nevertheless stayed on and appear as holders of financial offices: István Draskóczy, "Italiener in Siebenbürgen im 15. Jahrhundert," in *The First Millennium of Hungary in Europe*, eds Klára Papp *et al.* (Debrecen: Debrecen Univerity Press, 2002), pp. 61–75.

direct authority of the treasurer. The offices of the treasury and the minting chambers were headed by noblemen or burghers of Buda and of other royal towns; in contrast to the previous period, there were now hardly any officials of foreign origin in the financial administration.[47]

The economic crisis that befell Vienna in 1459 put an effective end to commercial contacts along the western border of Hungary. In the budget year 1459/60 the thirtieth customs at Pressburg fell to a mere 479 florins compared to 1456/57 when the revenues were 8399 florins. Pressburg was never again able to enjoy the same level of income as it had before the crisis. In 1495/96 the amount of cloth cleared through the thirtieth customs was only one-seventh of that in 1457/58. Hostilities between the Austrian provinces and Hungary did nothing to foster commercial contacts either and were especially detrimental to the towns of Western Hungary.[48] Due to the depressed conditions in Pressburg a number of previously prominent local merchant families, such as the Gailsams and Kochaims, decided to move their enterprise and their capital to Buda.[49]

In the 1480s Matthias suspended the staple right of Pressburg and Sopron, a privilege they had still enjoyed in the 1460s, in order to promote the capital. The next step came in 1515 when, after lengthy negotiations, south German merchants negotiated an agreement between the king of Hungary and the duke of Austria in Vienna, according to which foreigners were allowed to trade

---

47   Pál Engel, Gyula Kristó and András Kubinyi, *Histoire de la Hongrie medievale*, ii. *Des Angevins aux Habsbourgs* (Rennes: Presses universitaires de Rennes, 2008), pp. 211–220 and 239–241 (the part in question is by András Kubinyi); András Kubinyi, "A késő középkori magyar nyugati kereskedelmi kapcsolatok történetéhez," [On the history of Hungary's western economic contacts in the late Middle Ages] in *R. Várkonyi Ágnes emlékkönyv születésének 70. évfordulója ünnepére* [Studies in honor of the 70th birthday of Ágnes R. Várkonyi], ed. Péter Tusor (Budapest: ELTE Bölcsészettudományi Kara, 1998), pp. 109–117; Gyöngyössy, *Pénzgazdálkodás*, pp. 243–310.

48   Ferenc Kováts, "Korakapitalisztikus gazdasági válság Magyarországon I. Mátyás király uralkodása alatt," [An early capitalist economic crisis in Hungary during the reign of King Matthias Corvinus] in *Emlékkönyv dr. Mahler Ede a budapesti kir. Magyar Pázmány Péter Tudományegyetem ny. nyilvános rendes tanárának nyolcvanadik születésnapjára* [Studies in honor of Ede Mahler on his 80th birthday] (Budapest: Arany János Irodalmi és nyomdai Műintézet, 1937), pp. 178–194; Radoslav Kusenda, "Dovoz textílií do Bratislavy koncom 15. a začiatkom 16. storočia," [The import of textiles to Pressburg at the end of the fifteenth and at the beginning of the sixteenth centuries] *Historický Časopis* 4 (1994), pp. 409–424, here p. 422; Szende, *Otthon a városban*, pp. 44–45.

49   András Kubinyi, "Budai és pesti polgárok családi összeköttetései a Jagelló-korban," [Family ties of the burghers of Buda and Pest in the Jagiellonian period], in Kubinyi, *Tanulmányok*, ii, pp. 513–570, here pp. 529–535.

directly among themselves, even if only in modest quantities. This measure considerably reduced Vienna's role in the transit trade and facilitated direct contacts between Hungarian merchants and the south German territories. The restoration of peaceful relations between Austria and Hungary after Matthias's death also contributed to the new commercial revival.[50]

The livestock trade stagnated in the central decades of the fifteenth century, but began to recover again after the 1460s. Burghers of Buda and Pest entered into this business on a large scale, upgrading the commercial activity of the two cities from a simple transit trade to a more pro-active one with a focus on export. The animals were brought to the markets of Buda and especially Pest, and were driven further to Vienna, Wiener Neustadt or Ptuj, their final destination being Venice or the cities of the South German region. The export of livestock became increasingly the domain of Hungarian merchants. For foreigners it was more profitable to take home Hungarian silver coins in exchange for their wares, and not some sort of return cargo, because after Matthias's monetary reform the silver content of the denars was higher than what the relative prices of the gold and silver justified. Taking home these valuable coins thus increased trade profits even further.

Old and New Trends: From the Late Fifteenth Century to the Ottoman Occupation

In the late fifteenth and early sixteenth century the offices of the thirtieth customs located in the center of the country, namely at Buda and Székesfehérvár, became more lucrative than their counterparts on the western border, at Pressburg and Sopron. This new trend was due not only to the increased volume of livestock trade but also to the fact that the merchants of Buda established direct contacts with their Viennese and south German partners, bypassing Pressburg's middle role. These merchants preferred to clear the customs for their merchandise in the center of the country, and not at the border.[51]

As in previous periods, there was a wide range of commercial and family contacts between the Hungarian capital and Vienna.[52] A case in point are the Pemfflingers, a family originally from Regensburg who later settled in Vienna

---

50 Kubinyi, *Budapest*, p. 99; Szende, *Otthon a városban*, pp. 44–45; Csendes, "Wiener Handelsgeschichte," p. 221.
51 Kubinyi, "Die Städte Ofen und Pest und der Fernhandel," *passim*.
52 *Quellen zur Geschichte der Stadt Wien*, ii/3, nos 4029 and 4975; ii/4, nos 5506, 5861 and 5903; Kubinyi, "Budai és pesti polgárok," p. 535.

and then became leading businessmen in Buda. Hans Pemfflinger, who turns up in the sources between 1477 and 1514, was judge of Buda for eight years within this period, a noteworthy achievement. His brother Mark lived in Radkersburg for a while, then moved to Buda, and was finally appointed royal judge in Sibiu by the king in 1521.[53] A new feature of the contacts between Vienna and Buda was that the movement was now no longer one-sided, for burghers from Buda also settled in Vienna and acquired real estate there. This trend was connected in the first place with King Matthias's capture of Vienna in 1485, but it is also a sign of the growing strength of Buda's bourgeoisie. To be sure, not all of them succeeded in establishing a stable presence in Austria.[54] One of the success stories involves Peter Juncker (also known as Edlasperg), a burgher of Buda born in Banská Štiavnica, who turned up in Vienna in the 1490s and acquired a house there. His son Ladislas inherited the family business in Vienna.[55] Burghers of Buda also had strong ties with other Austrian towns, including Wiener Neustadt.[56]

Buda maintained its contacts with towns in the Upper German territories in the second half of the fifteenth and the beginning of the sixteenth century, important points of reference being Ulm, Bamberg, Augsburg, Sankt Gallen, Ravensburg, and, first and foremost, Nuremberg. The significance of the Hungarian market for Nuremberg is attested to by the efforts of its merchants to revive the route bypassing Vienna during the period of Matthias's wars with

---

53 András Kubinyi, "Die Pemfflinger in Wien und Buda," *Jahrbuch des Vereins für Geschichte der Stadt Wien* 34 (1978), pp. 67–87.

54 *Quellen zur Geschichte der Stadt Wien*, ii/3, no 5025; ii/4, nos 5518 and 6142; István Kenyeres and Péter Kis, "Budapest középkori történetének bécsi levéltári forrásai. Kutatási beszámoló és terv a munka folytatására," [Sources for the medieval history of Budapest in Vienna. Research report and plans for the future] *Urbs. Magyar Várostörténeti Évkönyv* 1 (2006), pp. 299–329, p. 329; Kubinyi, "Die Pemfflinger," pp. 73–75; Richard Perger, "Die ungarische Herrschaft über Wien 1485–1490 und ihre Vorgeschichte," *Wiener Geschichtsblätter* 45 (1990), pp. 53–87, here pp. 77–78.

55 Kubinyi, "Budai és pesti polgárok," pp. 540–544; Richard Perger, *Die Wiener Ratsbürger 1396–1526 : ein Handbuch* (Vienna: Deuticke, 1988), p. 190; Lajos Gecsényi, "Az Edlaspergügy (a magyar kereskedők bécsi kapcsolatai a 16. század első felében)," [The Edlasperg-affair (the Viennese connections of Hungarian merchants in the first half of the sixteenth century)] in idem, *Gazdaság, társadalom, igazgatás*, pp. 289–309, here p. 297. Members of the Jung/Juncker family were famous mining entrepreneurs in Banská Bystrica and Baia Mare in the fifteenth and sixteenth centuries.

56 Othmar Pickl, *Das älteste Geschäftsbuch Österreichs* (Graz: Verlag der Historischen Landeskommission, 1966), pp. 41 and 381; Kubinyi, *Budapest*, p. 101.

Austria. They approached the Hungarian king several times in the 1480s with such a proposal.[57]

One of the richest burghers who moved from Nuremberg to Buda was Ruprecht Haller, scion of a prominent merchant family. He brought with him considerable capital and used it for trading in copper and cloth. He became an honored citizen of Buda. One of his sons, Hans, also had an extensive business network; his other son, Peter became the founder of the Transylvanian branch of the family. Other Nuremberg families who settled in Buda in this period include the Mairs, and a member of a wealthy Kaltenhauser company who was court purveyor in 1525. We also know of an agent of the Nuremberg merchant, Hans Meistaler, who had relatives in Buda. The Tucher family was another which imported cloth.[58] At the same time, Hungarian merchants visited Nuremberg, and they joined their counterparts from Nuremberg on visits to the Frankfurt fairs. The Buda burgher Lorenz Ebenhauser, whose brother lived in Wiener Neustadt, sent agents in the 1510s to Vienna and Nuremberg; their partners in Nuremberg accumulated a debt of 2000 florins with him. The court case over the reclaiming of this sum was still going on in 1533.[59]

Relations were not always smooth, however. At the end of the fifteenth century, the Buda council passed a resolution to prevent foreigners trading there. In retaliation, Nuremberg sent deputations to Buda in 1497 and the following years, threatening to introduce similar measures against Hungarians trading in their own city. In the end, they were successful in having the restrictions lifted.[60]

---

57 Hans Schenk, *Nürnberg und Prag, ein Beitrag zur Geschichte der Handelsbeziehungen im 14. und 15. Jahrhundert* (Wiesbaden: Harrassowitz, 1969), pp. 169–170.

58 Kubinyi, "Die Nürnberger Haller," pp. 86–103. On Nurembergers acting in Buda, see further: Helmut Frhr and Haller von Hallerstein, "Deutsche Kaufleute in Ofen zur Zeit der Jagellonen," *Mitteilungen des Vereins für Geschichte der Stadt Nürnberg* 51 (1962), pp. 467–480; Kubinyi, "Die Städte Ofen und Pest und der Fernhandel," pp. 400–406; Michael Diefenbacher, "Der Handel des Nürnberger Patriziats nach Osten – das Beispiel Tucher um 1500," *Mitteilungen des Vereins für Geschichte der Stadt Nürnberg* 94 (2007), pp. 62–72.

59 Lajos Thallóczy, "Középkori gazdaságtörténeti adatok Nürnberg levéltáraiból," [Information on medieval economic history in the archives of Nuremberg], *Magyar Gazdaságtörténeti Szemle* 7 (1900), pp. 76–81; Ammann, *Die wirtschaftliche Stellung*, p. 44; Lajos Gecsényi, "Egy budai polgár adóssági pere a birodalmi kamarai bíróság előtt (1519–1533)," [The debt-suit of a burgher of Buda before the court of law of the chamber of the Empire, 1519 to 1533] in *Tiszteletkör. Történeti tanulmányok Draskóczy István egyetemi tanár 60. születésnapjára* [Circle of honor: Studies in honor of the 60th birthday of István Draskóczy], eds Gábor Mikó, Bence Péterfi and András Vadas (Budapest: ELTE Eötvös Kiadó, 2012), pp. 189–197.

60 Kubinyi, "Die Nürnberger Haller," p. 90; Schenk, *Nürnberg und Prag*, pp. 170–172.

In 1494 Jacob Fugger from Augsburg formed an alliance with János Thurzó, a mining entrepreneur, for the exploitation of the copper mines in the valley of the Hron. The mining, processing, and trade in copper made this partnership extremely lucrative, but it went against the interests of several business companies in Hungary and Nuremberg. The Fuggers also established an agency (*factoratus*) in Buda which carried on extensive banking activity. In 1525, however, their assets were confiscated by the Hungarian authorities, whose intention was to hand over the copper business to the Fuggers' competitors, a combination of local entrepreneurs and businessmen from Nuremberg. The next year the Fuggers managed to reestablish their position, and they gave up their agency in Buda only in 1533.[61]

The business network of the south German cities also extended towards the north-east, to Wrocław, the capital of Silesia, and thence to Cracow and Lviv. Wrocław's fifteenth-century development was, like Buda's, mostly determined by her contacts with Vienna and Nuremberg, compared to which direct connections to Buda seem to have been, if not negligible, then certainly of secondary importance. We know of sixteen persons from fifteenth-century Buda who maintained contact with Wrocław, the highest number of partners from any settlement in Hungary. These included the above-mentioned Peter Edlasperg. The main import articles were cheap cloth from Poland, Silesia and Görlitz, but also finer textiles from the Low Countries. Pepper, saffron, wine and livestock were in return transported to Silesia from Hungary, and the Hungarian florin was also in widespread use there. We learn, too, of burghers from Buda who had Silesian creditors.[62]

The commercial network of Buda and Pest we have described above was destroyed by the Ottoman conquest. In 1526 the Ottoman army plundered Buda. The city was contested by the two claimants to the Hungarian throne, John

---

61 Enikő Spekner, "A budai Fugger faktorátus. Egy délnémet kereskedő- és bankház képviselete a késő középkori Budán," [The Fugger factor at Buda: The agency of a south German merchant and bank company in medieval Buda], in *Vándorutak – múzeumi örökség. Tanulmányok Bodó Sándor tiszteletére, 60. születésnapja alkalmából* [Wandering ways – museum heritage: Studies in honor of Sándor Bodó on the occasion of his 60th birthday], eds Gyula Viga, Szilvia Holló and Edit Cs. Schwalm (Budapest: Archaeolingua, 2003) pp. 429–434.

62 Kubinyi, *Budapest*, p. 101; Grzegorz Myśliwski, "Wrocław's Economic Links with the Upper German Lands in the Thirteenth to Fifteenth Century," *Acta Poloniae Historica* 102 (2010), pp. 5–42; idem, *Wrocław w przestrzeni gospodarczej Europy (XIII–XV wiek). Centrum czy pryferie?* [Wrocław in the economic space of Europe between the thirteenth and the fifteenth centuries: center or periphery?] (Wrocław: Wydawnictwo Uniwersytetu Wrocławskiego, 2009), pp. 277–279, 282, 286–287 and 350–354.

Szapolyai and Ferdinand of Habsburg. When Szapolyai gained the upper hand in 1529, most of the Germans chose to flee Buda. Soon thereafter, in 1541, both Buda and Pest were occupied by the Ottomans and for the next 145 years it formed part of their empire. The earlier business contacts, however, did not completely vanish. The Buda merchants who moved away or fled were able to continue their businesses elsewhere on the foundations they had previously built up.[63]

Conclusions

Buda was the economic center of the country and its commercial contacts westwards along the Danube are as old as the city itself. In the division of labour and resources in Europe between the thirteenth and sixteenth centuries Hungary developed strong ties first and foremost with the southern regions of the Holy Roman Empire. At the outset, contacts with Regensburg proved to be decisive; from the mid-fourteenth century Nuremberg took over the leading role. In the late Middle Ages the strongest links developed with Pressburg, Vienna, and Nuremberg, thus connecting the Buda commercial elite to the south German economic area. The balance, however, was not constant, and for a while Pressburg overshadowed Buda's importance. For instance in 1439, when a list of towns and cities to be invited to the fair of Ulm (another city on the Danube) was drawn up, Pressburg was the only place included from Hungary, although the list contained otherwise a total number of 414 localities from Bruges to Venice and from Genoa to Wrocław.[64] Buda's leading role was consolidated again in the second half of the fifteenth century, when it was not only a capital, but also a fixed royal seat. Of all the foreign merchants in Buda those from Nuremberg had the strongest influence, and the capital resources they had access to far outweighed those of their competitors from Vienna. In the late Middle Ages, Nuremberg became the undisputed commercial center of Central Europe, making Vienna and Wrocław, along with Buda, satellites in

---

63 Lajos Gecsényi, "Die Auseinandersetzungen des Wiener Stadtrats mit den aus Pest und Buda/Ofen vertriebenen Bürgern im Jahre 1534," *Wiener Geschichtsblätter* 61, no 3 (2006), pp. 54–64; József Bessenyei, *Menekültek...A kereskedelem helyzete Magyarországon 1526 után* [Refugees... The position of trade in Hungary after 1526] (Miskolc–Budapest: Miskolci Egyetemi Kiadó, 2007).

64 Michael Rothmann, "Marktnetze und Netzwerke im spätmittelalterlichen oberdeutschen Wirtschaftsraum," in *Netzwerke im europäischen Handel des Mittelalters*, ed. Gerhard Fouquet and Hans-Jörg Gilomen (Ostfildern: Thorbecke, 2010), pp. 135–188, here p. 143.

its network system. Buda became the south-eastern corner-point in the expansion of this mighty imperial city.[65] The Ottoman conquest had tragic consequences for Buda, but Hungary's ties to the south German area did not cease. The links between the two areas were too strong to be destroyed simply by the fall of a city.[66]

---

65 Csendes and Opll, *Wien*, p. 223; Myśliwski, "Wroclaw's economic links," pp. 21–29.
66 Gecsényi, "Folytonosság és megújulás," pp. 409–431.

PART 4

Buda as a Power Center

CHAPTER 12

The Government of Medieval Buda

Martyn Rady

At first sight, the government of medieval Buda resembles arrangements in most Central European cities. The city was founded in the late 1240s in what appears to be an example of *Siedlungsverlegung*, whereby the privilege of self-government previously granted to Pest was, along with Pest's seal and arms, conferred on the new city set on the Buda Hill.[1] Buda's origin in the earlier Pest settlement is reflected in its thirteenth-century name, which alternated between (*Novus*) *Mons Budensis*, *Civitas Budensis*, *Castrum Pestiense* and (*Novus*) *Mons Pestiensis*.[2] Although it is uncertain whether the city was planted by a consortium of enterprisers (*Unternehmerkonsortium*), it constituted, at least in part, a typically planned settlement.[3] Judicial, regulatory and administrative authority was vested in a council or *Rat* of twelve men, headed by a judge (*Richter, iudex*) or headman (*maior ville, villicus*), all of whom were annually elected by the citizen community. Later on, in the middle decades of the fifteenth century, the right of election was placed in the hands of an outer council of one hundred citizens. For most of the Middle Ages, the government of the city lay with an urban elite made up of prosperous German merchants, although these were later obliged to share power with representatives of the city's Hungarian population. The sense of urban solidarity underpinning the city's communal organization was played out in the civic rituals of election and of assembly. It is also celebrated in the form of an extensive *Stadtrechtsbuch*, composed in the early fifteenth century, which brought together Buda's customs, laws and privileges.[4]

1 Kubinyi, *Anfänge Ofens*, p. 70. For *Siedlungsverlegung* as involving both the physical and legal transfer of the settlement, see Herbert Fischer, *Die Siedlungsverlegung im Zeitalter der Stadtbildung* (Vienna: Verlag Herold, 1952), p. 15. For the link between *Siedlungsverlegung* and *Wappenverleihung*, see Christa Schillinger-Prassl, *Die Rechtsquellen der Stadt Leoben* (Vienna–Cologne–Weimar: Böhlau, 1997), p. 33.
2 Györffy, *Budapest*, p. 298.
3 Kubinyi, *Anfänge Ofens*, pp. 29 and 63; Katalin Szende and András Végh, "Royal Power and Urban Space in Medieval Hungary," in *Lords and Towns in Medieval Europe: Maps and Texts*, eds Anngret Simms and Howard B. Clarke (Farnham: Ashgate [in press]).
4 For the *Stadtrechtsbuch* see: OSt. This supersedes the edition of Andreas Michnay and Paul Lichner, *Ofner Stadtrecht von MCCXLIV–MCCCXXI* (Pressburg: Carl Friedrich Wigand, 1845). See also *Buda város jogkönyve*, 2 vols [The law code of Buda], eds László Blazovich and József

The impression of unexceptionalism is, however, illusory, for Buda was unlike the imperial cities that lay to its west. Buda was small and its population, including its suburbs, can scarcely have numbered more than 15,000 persons. The city was, moreover, dominated by the palace and the institutions of royal government. These subverted the jurisdictional rights belonging to the judge and council, even to the extent of overturning the principle of self-government given in the city's founding charter. Buda's customary law was, moreover, twisted as a consequence of the large number of noblemen living in the city, so that the right of the citizen to alienate his property (and thus to use it as collateral in merchant ventures) was compromised. Although Buda's liberties were regularly extended to other towns and cities in the kingdom, the city's development as a typically Central European 'mother town' was hindered by the intrusion of a royal officer into its affairs. In this respect, the history of medieval Buda's government may most profitably be conceived from the perspective of a *Residenzstadt*, wherein the jurisdictional rights of the city and its autonomy were circumscribed by proximity to the institutions of territorial lordship.[5]

Villicus and Rector

The 1244 charter (see *Appendix 2*) was granted by Béla IV in the aftermath of the destruction of the Pest settlement by the Mongols in 1241–1242.[6] The

---

Schmidt (Szegedi Középkortörténeti Könyvtár, 17) (Szeged: Szegedi Középkorász Műhely, 2001), which includes a translation of the *Stadtrechtsbuch* into Hungarian and supporting essays in German.

5 For Buda as a *Residenzstadt*, see András Kubinyi, "Királyi székhely a késő középkori Magyarországon," [Royal seat in late medieval Hungary] in Kubinyi, *Tanulmányok*, i, pp. 223–227, here 224. Also Katalin Szende, "Városkutatás és rezidencia-kutatás. Európai helyzetkép és magyar eredmények," [Urban history research and *Residenzforschung*. European overview and Hungarian state of research] *Urbs. Magyar Várostörténeti Évkönyv* 7 (2012), pp. 11–44, here pp. 27–30; József Laszlovszky and Katalin Szende, "Cities and Towns as Princely Seats: Medieval Visegrád in the Context of Royal Residences and Urban Development in Europe and Hungary," in *The Medieval Royal Town at Visegrád: Royal Center, Urban Settlement, Churches* (Archaeolingua – Main Series, 32), eds József Laszlovszky, Gergely Buzás and Orsolya Mészáros (Budapest: Archaeolingua, 2014), pp. 9–44. For the impact more generally of the *Residenz* on urban autonomy, see Frank G. Hirschmann, *Die Stadt im Mittelalter* (Munich: Oldenbourg, 2009), pp. 35–36.

6 The charter was clearly awarded to the older Pest settlement and not to the nascent community on the Buda Hill. It thus refers to *Pest minor* (Kreinfeld, Kelenföld) as lying on the 'further' bank of the Danube (*Minor Pesth ultra Danubium sita*). See Elemér Révhelyi, "Kelenföld (Tabán) helye és neve," [The location and the name of Kelenföld (Tabán)] *Tanulmányok*

original does not survive, but plainly it carried the king's pendant gold seal.[7] The privilege commences with an arenga typical of this decade, in which the king declares his wish to augment the number of his subjects.[8] Explaining that Pest's original charter had been lost at the time of the Mongol invasion, Béla confirmed its contents, most of which were concerned with the city's commercial rights. It included, however, a short provision on the city's government: "They [the citizens] may elect a mayor of the town, whomever they want and once elected they shall present him to us, and he should judge all their secular affairs. If he does not demonstrate to anyone the justice that is due, the headman and not the city shall be brought before us or to someone appointed by us."[9] The same principle of self-government was enunciated in the charter issued by Ladislas IV in 1276. On this occasion, however, reference was no longer made to Pest, but to the *castrum* of Buda, and Ladislas IV's grant is described as amplifying the terms of the 1244 charter – "We further grant to them [the citizens] that they shall not be forced to accept any judge appointed by us, but they shall have as headman whomever they wish by free election, as was laid down earlier in the text of the privilege of our grandfather [Béla IV], and the headman should annually resign his office into the hands of the citizens."[10] Although neither charter refers to an elected council, this was clearly in place by no later than 1268.[11]

Budapest Múltjából 4 (1936), pp. 34–58, here p. 36. The transfer of the population and of their legal rights to Buda must have happened in the late 1240s. See András Végh, "Buda" in *Medium regni*, pp. 163–212, here p. 207.

7   The text is given in BTOE, i, pp. 41–43 (no 27); also in EFHU, iii/2, pp. 39–41 (no 34). An English translation is given in Ágnes Ságvári, *Budapest: the History of a Capital* (Budapest: Corvina, 1973), pp. 78–79. See both the edited text of the original charter and the translation in the appendix of the present volume.

8   On the arengas of charters given to Hungarian cities in the thirteenth century, see András Kubinyi, "A királyi várospolitika tükröződése a magyar királyi oklevelek arengáiban," [Royal urban policy as reflected in the arengas of Hungarian royal charters] in *Eszmetörténeti tanulmányok a magyar középkorról* [Studies in the intellectual history of medieval Hungary], ed. György Székely (Budapest: Akadémiai, 1984), pp. 275–291.

9   EFHU, iii/2, pp. 39–41 (no 34). See *Appendix 2*.

10 "Ad hec concessimus eisdem, ut non cogantur recipere aliquem judicem per nos datum, sed ex electione sua libera assumant in villicum, quem volunt, prout in tenore privilegii avi nostri superius est expressum, qui quidem villicus in anni revolutione villicatum debeat in manus civium resignare" – BTOE, i, pp. 157–158 (no 140); EFHU, iii/2, pp. 64–65 (no 55). The 1276 privilege is given in English translation in Ságvári, *Budapest*, p. 80.

11 BTOE, i, pp. 100–101 (no 86); EFHU, iii/2, pp. 59–60 (no 50). A list of Buda's judges and councillors for the period 1259 to 1529 is given in Rady, *Buda*, pp. 169–176.

Despite the terms of the 1244 charter and its confirmation more than thirty years later, it is evident that the right of self-government was soon disregarded by the ruler. Around 1260, the city was represented in litigation by the *villicus* Peter.[12] Thereafter, however, the office of elected headman was superseded by a royal appointee, who held the title of *rector*. The first of these was the Lower Austrian knight, Henry Preussel (Preuchul), who was appointed *rector* by Béla IV during the course of his war with his son, Stephen (V). Preussel was killed in battle in 1265 and his place briefly taken by one of Stephen's supporters, the Ban Mikod.[13] With the restoration of peaceful conditions, we might have expected the office of elected headman to be re-established and there is some possibility that for a time the government of the city was returned to Peter, acting in the capacity of former (*quondam*) *villicus*.[14] In 1268, however, the office of *rector* was given to the chamberlain (count) of the treasury, Walter. The selection of Walter for this role seems part of a deliberate strategy to impose officers of the royal mint over several of the kingdom's cities – much the same happened in Zagreb, where in 1266 the chamberlain Archynus was imposed as judge.[15] The policy of combining urban and fiscal functions did not endure beyond the 1280s.[16] *Rector*s continued, nevertheless, to be appointed as judges over the city, acting explicitly in the role of the monarch's plenipotentiaries, *pro tempore constituti*.[17] It was not, indeed, until the mid-1340s that the city was able to make good the right to appoint its chief magistrate.

The office of *rector* partly survived because it was useful to a small group of the city's citizens, whose members filled the office over decades, often being

---

12   BTOE, i, pp. 70–71 (no 53) and 73–74 (no 57).
13   Kubinyi, *Anfänge Ofens*, p. 72; for Mikod, see also Attila Zsoldos, *Magyarország világi archontológiája 1000–1301* [Secular archontology of medieval Hungary] (História könyvtár. Kronológiák, adattárak, 11) (Budapest: História – MTA Történettudományi Intézete, 2011), p. 147.
14   BTOE, i, pp. 71–72 (no 54). See also Erik Fügedi, "Középkori magyar városprivilégiumok," [Medieval Hungarian urban privileges] in idem, *Kolduló barátok, polgárok, nemesek. Tanulmányok a magyar középkorról* [Mendicants, burghers and nobles. Studies on the history of medieval Hungary] (Budapest: Magvető, 1981), pp. 238–310, here p. 308.
15   Klaus-Detlev Grothusen, *Entstehung und Geschichte Zagrebs bis zum Ausgang des 14. Jahrhunderts* (Wiesbaden: Harrassowitz, 1967), pp. 279–281.
16   Possibly the Rector Hench (Heinz), who held office from the late 1270s to 1288, is identifiable with a chamberlain of the same name. See Kubinyi, *Anfänge Ofens*, p. 73; Zsoldos, *Magyarország világi archontológiája*, p. 248.
17   Hence, "Nos Carolus de Veteri Buda miles, iudex pro domino rege in Buda" – *Monumenta Romana episcopatus Vesprimiensis*, i, ed. Vilmos Fraknói (Budapest: [n.p.], 1896), p. 302 (1276); BTOE, i, pp. 230–231 (no 215) (1287).

replaced by their sons. Outsiders who were drafted in might, like the *rector* Walter, be murdered by scions of the older established families, or, like Peterman, imposed on the city in 1301 by the Bohemian king, forced after a short time to flee. All in all, we can establish two sets of families who dominated the office of *rector*.[18] The first comprised the descendants of the *villicus* Peter, whose own period in office had been cut short by the imposition of royal *rectors*. Peter was probably himself the son of the knight Werner, who had in the 1230s built a palace on the left bank of the Danube. We can speculate that Werner and Peter were both active as entrepreneurs in establishing the settlement on the Buda Hill. Peter's son and grandson, Werner and Ladislas respectively, were complicit in Walter's murder in 1276 and they in turn held the office of *rector*, with only a few short breaks, from 1288 to around 1319. Ladislas, who died without heir, was in 1319 replaced as *rector* by Johannes, and Johannes was in turn succeeded in 1337 by his son, Nicholas.[19] The *rector*s were also connected by marriage and descent to many of the families whose members served on the council. Almost a half of council places were in the 1330s held by relatives of the *rector*s Johannes and Nicholas.[20]

The institution of *rector*s also benefited the ruler. The heart of the new city lay to begin with on the north part of the Buda Hill, in the area between the Magdalene church and the Church of Our Lady, which was also the site of the Saturday (later Friday) Market.[21] Both churches were in operation by the 1250s. Overlooking the Danube were two further stone buildings – the Dominican friary and a royal palace or *Kammerhof*. The layout of the city walls suggests that these were built prior to or at the same time as the city's fortification and they may indeed be older than the 1240s. The *Kammerhof* fulfilled a double function.[22] It was a mint, which we know to have been functioning as early as

---

18 For this and much of what follows, András Kubinyi, "A budai német patriciátus társadalmi helyzete családi összeköttetései tükrében a 13. századtól a 15. század második feléig," [The social position of the German patriciate in Buda in the light of their family ties from the thirteenth to the second half of the fifteenth century] in Kubinyi, *Tanulmányok*, ii, pp. 457–511, here pp. 467–473.
19 For Ladislas, see also Végh, *Buda*, i, p. 140.
20 Kubinyi, "A budai német patriciátus," p. 473.
21 See András Végh's contribution to the present volume.
22 The extensive literature on the Kammerhof is reviewed in Végh, *Buda*, i, pp. 271–272; Károly Magyar, *A budai középkori királyi palota építészeti együttesének változásai (1340–1440) európai kitekintésben*, unpublished PhD dissertation [The history of the architectural ensemble of the medieval palace of Buda (1340–1440) in European context] (Budapest: ELTE, 2008), pp. 13–14. See also Károly Magyar's contribution to the present volume.

1255, but it was also a royal residence. The combination of mint and royal residence is not unusual – the fourteenth-century Visegrád palace, the so-called Italian Court in Kutná Hora in Bohemia, and the Brussels Prinsenhof also fulfilled both roles.[23] Plainly, the *rector*s had some sort of responsibility for the *Kammerhof*. We have already noted how the *rector* Walter was a chamberlain of the mint. Peterman was subsequently described as the prefect of Buda and of its citadel and the *rector* Johannes as the *capitaneus* of Buda, which suggests a military function, possibly in relation to the palace garrison.[24] The identification made in 1315 of the title of *rector* with the *conservator domus regiae* further indicates that the *rector*s may have acted in the capacity of castellans, with a particular responsibility for the maintenance of the *Kammerhof*.[25]

We do not know when the *Kammerhof* ceased to function as a palace and mint, but it seems to have been during the reign of Louis I.[26] It was subsequently known as the *antiqua domus regis*, the royal mint having shifted in the meantime to a site adjacent to the Church of Our Lady.[27] Doubtless, its role as a royal residence was superseded by the larger palace at the southern end of the Buda Hill, which was extensively rebuilt during King Louis's reign. As the center of political weight shifted from the north of the Buda Hill, the office of *rector* was allowed to lapse. Already by the 1330s it had become usual for one of the city's elected councillors to act in the capacity of *vice-iudex*, discharging some of the duties that otherwise belonged to the *rector*.[28] So when in either 1346 or 1347 the *rector* Nicholas died, the office of elected chief magistrate and headman might be straightforwardly restored, with the *vice-iudex*

---

23 Peter Spufford, "The Mint Buildings of Medieval Europe," in *XIII Congreso Internacional de Numismática,* ii, eds Carmen Alfaro *et al.* (Madrid: Ministerio de Cultura, 2003), pp. 1059–1065, here pp. 1061–1064 (with additional examples); Klára Benešovská, *Architecture of the Gothic* (Prague: Prague Castle Administration, 2001), p. 244; Gergely Buzás, "Visegrád," in *Medium regni*, pp. 115–161, here p. 120.

24 Gusztáv Wenzel, "Budai regeszták," *Magyar Történelmi Tár* 1 (1855), pp. 69–124, and 4 (1857), pp. 89–182, here p. 112; CD, viii/3, pp. 386–387 (no 163).

25 György Györffy, *Pest-Buda kialakulása. Budapest története a honfoglalástól az Árpád-kor végi székvárossá alakulásáig* [The formation of Pest-Buda. The history of Budapest from the Hungarian conquest to its late Árpádian-period formation as capital] (Budapest, Akadémiai, 1997), p. 194; Végh, *Buda,* i, pp. 166 and 173.

26 András Végh, "A középkori várostól a török erődig," [From the medieval town to the Ottoman fortress] *Budapest Régiségei* 31 (1997), pp. 295–312, here p. 295.

27 BTOE, iii/2, p. 8 (no 683) (1416). The Buda *Stadtrechtsbuch* likewise refers to the *alten kamerhoff peyn Iudenn* (OSt, p. 46 [Prol., D]). For the subsequent location of the mint, see Lajos Huszár, *A budai pénzverés története a középkorban* [The history of minting at Buda in the Middle Ages] (Budapest: Akadémiai, 1958), p. 21. See also, Végh, *Buda,* i, p. 267.

28 Kubinyi, *Budapest*, p. 80.

taking on the functions of chief magistrate.[29] Certainly, the surviving council lists do not indicate any great change in membership that might be taken as evidence of a putsch. Moreover, the new judge, Lorand, had served as a councillor for at least a decade. The institution of royally-appointed *rector*s thus came to an end without any attendant turmoil. Nevertheless, the history of the *rector*s, which extended for almost seventy years, in apparent defiance of the city's charters, indicates Buda's vulnerability to royal intrusions on its right of self-government.

Institutions of Government

The city's restored self-government was headed by an elected judge or *Richter* and a council or *Rat* of twelve. The judge was consistently described in the Latin documents issued by the city as a *iudex* and the councillors as *iurati* (*Geschworenen*), on account of the oaths of office that they swore on the occasion of their appointment.[30] Buda also had a *Stadtschreiber*, or city scribe, appointed by the judge and council, who was in charge of the city's chancellery.[31] Although the city's archive was destroyed during the Ottoman occupation, its scribal office was evidently large, being divided into several departments, each having its own seal.[32] Subordinate magistrates took charge of business in the suburbs and also heard commercial disputes.[33] A Judge of the Money or *Geldrichter* (*iudex pecuniarum*) was responsible for hearing litigation involving financial disputes up to the value of forty florins. The *Geldrichter* was appointed by the judge out of the ranks of the councillors and later acted as the city's deputy judge.[34] The *Geldrichter* had a deputy, whose task it was to resolve disputes involving minor debts.[35]

As was typical in the Middle Ages (and indeed later), no distinction was made between judicial and administrative competences. Nevertheless, in the

---

29 The surviving list of councillors for 1346–1347 gives the names of the judge and of only eleven councillors. Presumably, the judge had upon Rector Nicholas's death been appointed from out of the twelve and had not been replaced.
30 The title of *villicus* was not restored.
31 OSt, p. 69. (cap. 28).
32 Kubinyi, *Budapest*, pp. 167–168.
33 OSt, p. 72. (cap. 33).
34 See OSt, p. 78. (cap. 49), where the *Geldrichter* is considered a *Stadtrichter*. The vacancy left among the twelve by the appointment of the *Geldrichter* was filled at the discretion of the judge, who had the right to co-opt. OSt, pp. 69 and 199 (cap. 29 and 167).
35 OSt, p. 120 (cap. 171).

organization of business coming before it, the council gave priority to its role as a court of law, in which capacity it met as a magistracy on three days in the week. Of the remainder, one day was given over to city business and a further day to discussing matters affecting ecclesiastical institutions.[36] Besides their judicial duties, the judge and sworn men of the council were in charge of the public works of the city and responsible for composing commercial regulations affecting the quantities of goods that might be put up for sale, for maintaining order in the markets, for regulating the guilds, and for the appointment of watchmen, dung collectors, and so on. The judge and council were also empowered to notarize conveyances and to see that new owners took possession of property within the city with the necessary procedural safeguards. Most contentiously, they were in charge of allocating taxes within the city. They were assisted in this task by an advisory body of twenty-four citizens made up of appointees of the council.[37] This was intended as a safeguard against malfeasance and had been instructed by King Sigismund in 1403 following disturbances, which appear to have been caused by perceived inequities or irregularities in the collection of taxation.[38] The council also appointed a dozen or so officers to help with the assessment of taxes from vineyards.[39]

The principal source for the government of Buda is the city's *Stadtrechtsbuch*, which was composed in stages during the earliest decades of the fifteenth century.[40] Since it contains extracts from royal legislation given in 1405, this year represents the *terminus post quem* for its text. The inclusion of craft and commercial regulations drawn up by the council in 1421 and reference to a judgment of 1424 suggest that the bulk of the volume was drawn up around this time. The text only survives in later copies, and the stages of its composition are uncertain. Plainly though, a good part of the book was the work of one man, who tells us at one point that he is called Johannes. The text is long, running to 175 pages in the leading edition – 445 chapters in all, in addition to a Prologue. Its purpose is, however, less certain, for it provides no insights into the daily routines of city government. Its account of legal practices is thin and mostly concerned the presentation of plaints. It says nothing about the warrantying of property even though charters issued by the council regularly

---

36 OSt, pp. 119–120 (cap. 168).
37 OSt, p. 63. (cap. 12).
38 BTOE, iii/1, pp. 181–182 (no 370); OSt, p. 63 (cap. 15).
39 OSt, p. 140. (cap. 236/b).
40 For the manuscripts of the *Stadtrechtsbuch*, see Katalin Gönczi, *Ungarisches Stadtrecht aus europäischer Sicht. Die Stadtrechtsentwicklung im spätmittelalterlichen Ungarn am Beispiel Ofen* (Frankfurt am Main: Klostermann, 1997), pp. 82–83.

spelled out that this was an integral and ancient part of the city's customary law (*secundum usum et consuetudinem nostre civitatis ab antiquo approbatam*).[41] Other aspects of the city's allegedly customary procedures are also missing, as for instance the manner of responding to a summons.[42] The main part of the text includes no references to judgments of the council and thus to the 'living law' of the city.[43] Johannes and his continuators knew something, however, of the city's charters and they quote passages from them, including texts taken from documents that have since been lost.[44] A large part of the text is dedicated to the regulation of the crafts and to civic rituals, which are often described in lavish detail.

The principal event in Buda's civic ceremony was the election of the judge, council and Stadtschreiber. This was performed annually on St George's Day (April 24) in the main square between the City Hall and the Church of Our Lady. The outgoing judge solemnly laid down his staff of office and the citizens deliberated on his successor in the presence of the whole community, eventually arriving at a unanimous decision.[45] A similar process attended the appointment of the councillors and city scribe, although Johannes's description of their election is slender. Judge, councillors and *Stadtschreiber* delivered their oaths of office, which the *Stadtrechtsbuch* repeats in full.[46] Thereafter, Buda's principal seal was brought from the City Hall, taken out of its locked box, and shown to the crowd.[47] The judge was then formally presented to the king or, in his absence, to the burgrave of the palace, in accordance with the terms of the 1244 privilege.[48] On the Friday following the election, the judge and councillors toured the city, and householders were expected to greet them

---

41   BTOE, iii/1, pp. 8, 10, 12–13, 20, 22, 23 (nos 19, 23, 28, 49, 52, 54, etc.).

42   András Kubinyi, "A budai jogkönyvről. Ismertetés Mollay Károly monográfiájáról," [On the Law Code of Buda. Review of Károly Mollay's monograph] in Kubinyi, *Tanulmányok*, i, pp. 297–298, here p. 298.

43   The contrast with the earlier Vienna *Stadtrechtsbuch* is in these respects striking. See Heinrich Maria Schuster, *Das Wiener Stadtrechts- oder Weichbildbuch* (Vienna: Manz, 1873), pp. 37–38.

44   OSt. p. 86 (cap. 65). Discussed by András Kubinyi, "Die Fleischerzunft zu Ofen im Mittelater," in *A budai mészárosok középkori céhkönyve és kiváltságlevelei – Zunftbuch und Privilegien der Fleischer zu Ofen aus dem Mittelalter*. (Források Budapest közép- és kora újkori történetéhez, 1/Quellen zur Budapester Geschichte im Mittelalter und in der frühen Neuzeit, 1), ed. István Kenyeres (Budapest: BFL–BTM, 2008), pp. 87–138, here pp. 89–90.

45   OSt, pp. 67, 70–71 and 83 (cap. 24, 31, 32, 58 and 59).

46   OSt, pp. 75–76. (cap. 42–44).

47   OSt, p. 84. (cap. 62).

48   OSt, pp. 67 and 71 (cap. 24 and 32).

appropriately.[49] The *Stadtrechtsbuch* also describes in detail the festivities on the occasion of a royal coronation or upon the king's entry to the city.[50]

The account given in the *Stadtrechtsbuch* of elections to city offices presents authority as being vested in the community, all sections of which, rich and poor, were participants in its ritual. In fact, the right of election belonged to the small section of the population who owned property within it, thus constituting "the commons of the city, well possessed and landed, sensible people" (*Der stat gemain wol gessessen vnd geerbt, Vernunftige leüt*).[51] All others were simply spectators. Plainly, however, elections did not always proceed in the calm and sober atmosphere described in the *Stadtrechtsbuch*. We know, therefore, that in 1402 there were irregularities in the election of the judge and council, which resulted in an 'illegal' government that lasted for more than a year.[52] The names of the supposed conspirators – Andrew the Butcher and Lawrence the Furrier – suggest that the coup, if such it was, may have been engineered by guildsmen. Possibly, their actions were motivated by contemporary concerns over taxation or were aimed at breaking the power of the merchant families who dominated city government. Although Andrew and Lawrence were subsequently forbidden by Sigismund from holding office in the city, surviving council lists indicate that members of the wealthier craft guilds were from this point onwards more likely to win places in Buda's government. In 1420, the office of judge was held by a guildsman (Johannes *Rasor*).[53] The *Stadtrechtsbuch* also noted that when weighty business needed discussion sworn representatives of the guilds should attend the City Hall.[54]

For the first two centuries of its history, Buda's government was dominated by Germans – a circumstance which prevailed in most of Hungary's cities.[55] Germans held the high office of judge and the majority of places on the council. The *Stadtrechtsbuch* declared that the judge should be a German of pure descent (*derr selbig richterr von deutscher artt sey von allem geschlächt*) and

---

49   OSt, p. 82 (cap. 57).
50   OSt, pp. 61–62 (cap. 6 and 7).
51   OSt, p. 67 (cap. 24).
52   BTOE, iii/1, pp. 181–182 and 188–189 (nos 370 and 383); see also Kubinyi, *Budapest*, pp. 68–69.
53   BTOE, iii/2, pp. 47–49 (no 767).
54   OSt, p. 72 (cap. 34).
55   See more generally on this subject, András Kubinyi, "Die Zusammensetzung des städtischen Rates im mittelalterlichen Königreich Ungarn," *Südostdeutsches Archiv* 34–35 (1991–1992), pp. 23–42 (also published in idem, *König und Volk im spätmittelalterlichen Ungarn: Städteentwicklung, Alltagsleben und Regierung im mittelalterlichen Königreich Ungarn* [Herne: Tibor Schäfer, 1998], pp. 103–123).

that ten of the city councillors should be German, the remaining two Hungarian.[56] Lists of councillors included in letters issued by the city indicate that the bottom two or three places were generally held by Hungarians. Buda was a bilingual city and the oaths delivered by the incoming judge and councillors were delivered in both German and Hungarian.[57] Nevertheless, it was also a divided city, with separate guilds for Germans and Hungarians, different markets and market days, competing churches, and little evidence of inter-marriage between the two communities.[58] The Germans' mastery of the city reflected their commercial predominance and their superiority in terms of wealth, which sustained their control of the organs of government. During the late fourteenth and early fifteenth centuries, however, the fortunes of Buda's German elite experienced a downturn. Many of the leading families either died out or, having made money, left the city. They were partly replaced by poorer elements, who lacked the wealth and trading connections of their predecessors, and by guildsmen. By contrast, the Hungarian population of the city prospered, often as a consequence of their links to the royal court and palace.[59] The number of Hungarians living in Buda was swollen by noblemen and churchmen, who often bought houses in the city, and by the clerks and *litterati* who worked in the royal administration after it moved to Buda in the first decade of the fifteenth century. At its height, the royal court and central offices of the kingdom had more than a thousand staff and we must imagine that most of these were resident in the city.[60] During the period of the king's residence in the palace and when the courts were in session, the number of Hungarians in the city was further swollen by the influx of petitioners, litigants and lawyers. These thronged the inns, where a part of the kingdom's judicial business was consequently undertaken.[61]

---

56   OSt, pp. 67–69 (cap. 24 and 27).
57   On language use in medieval Hungarian cities, see Katalin Szende, "Integration through Language: the Multilingual Character of Late Medieval Towns," in *Segregation – Integration – Assimilation. Religious and Ethnic Groups in the Medieval Towns of Central and Eastern Europe* (Historical Urban Studies), eds Derek Keene, Balázs Nagy and Katalin Szende (Farnham: Ashgate, 2009), pp. 205–233.
58   Kubinyi, "A budai német patriciátus," p. 508.
59   András Végh, "Buda: the Multi-Ethnic Capital of Medieval Hungary," in *Segregation – Integration – Assimilation*, pp. 89–99, here p. 92.
60   Kubinyi, "Királyi székhely," p. 225.
61   Imre Hajnik, *A magyar bírósági szervezet és perjog az Árpád- és a vegyes-házi királyok alatt* [The judicial system and procedural law in Hungary during the Árpádian period and the reigns of kings of different houses] (Budapest: MTA, 1899), pp. 229–230.

German hegemony was manifested in the confraternity known as the Corpus Christi fellowship, attached to one of the altars in the Church of Our Lady, which counted at this time as the principal German church in the city. The confraternity was wealthy and its members well-connected. Later evidence shows that it held assets in Nuremberg alone estimated at over 2000 gulden. In 1526, on the eve of Mohács, it deposited 5000 gulden for safe-keeping in Nuremberg.[62] The confraternity and the ecclesiastical arrangement which made the Hungarian Church of Mary Magdalene subordinate to Our Lady's became the focus of resentment. In July 1436, visitors from Pressburg reported that a certain George Litteratus "has caused great unhappiness amongst the priesthood and particularly to the priest of Our Blessed Lady's. He would like Our Lady's to be the chapel and filial Church of Mary Magdalene. Along with his Hungarian supporters he wants to confiscate the luxuries which people have left to Our Lady's and especially those most valuable treasures which have been given to the Corpus Christi Brotherhood. He is plotting all sorts of incredible things."[63] The Germans were not slow to act. To pre-empt the opposition, they secured in 1437 the election as judge of a wealthy Hungarian, who by marriage and commerce had aligned himself with the city's Germans.[64] When this measure proved insufficient, some leading Germans kidnapped in May 1439 one of the city's Hungarian spokesmen and had him murdered. Upon discovery of the crime, rioting broke out, with German shops and homes destroyed and their occupants killed.[65]

The disorder could scarcely have lasted more than a few hours, but in its wake a far-reaching reform of Buda's institutions was undertaken.[66] Henceforth, parity would be observed in respect of appointments to the council, with Hungarians and Germans having six representatives each. The office of judge would alternate annually between the two national groups. The right of election was, however, now circumscribed. Plainly, the interests of the Hungarian

---

62 Martyn C. Rady, "Church, Nationality and Revolt in Late Medieval Buda," in *The Church in Pre-Reformation Society: Essays in Honour of F.R.H. Du Boulay*, eds Caroline M. Barron and Christopher Harper-Bill (Woodbridge: Boydell, 1985), pp. 189–198, here p. 194.

63 Kubinyi, *Budapest*, p. 71.

64 Kubinyi, "A budai német patriciátus," p. 493.

65 András Kubinyi, "Népmozgalmak Budapesten a feudalizmus korában," [Popular movements in Budapest in the feudal period] *Tanulmányok Budapest Múltjából* 14 (1961), pp. 7–15, here pp. 9–10.

66 The new arrangements are given in Elek Jakab, *Oklevéltár Kolozsvár története első kötetéhez*, i (Buda: A Magy. Kir. Egyetemi Könyvnyomdában, 1870) [Documentary Collection for the history of Cluj], pp. 280–285.

and German leadership coincided – neither had any interest in extending political power down the social scale, particularly to the poorer elements in the city, who seem to have been mainly responsible for the recent violence.[67] Accordingly, the right of election was taken out the hands of the *stat gemain* of the *Stadtrechtsbuch* and entrusted to a body of one hundred citizens, made up equally of Germans and Hungarians, who were co-opted by the outgoing judge and council.[68] To their number were added representatives of the guilds. The committee of twenty-four, which had supervision of tax collection, was also split equally between Hungarians and Germans. The arrangements laid down in 1439 endured until the expulsion and massacre of the Germans by the Ottomans fifty years later, and were in the early eighteenth century restored following the city's recapture.[69] Such was their reputation for the maintenance of stability that they were at the royal instruction extended in 1458 to the Transylvanian city of Cluj.[70] In respect of Buda's ecclesiastical organization, the Hungarian Church of Mary Magdalene, together with the Church of St Peter Protomartyr, were given a status equal to Our Lady's, within newly defined parish boundaries.[71] We should, however, note that the priest of Our Lady's, who should by the terms of the 1244 charter and according to the *Stadtrechtsbuch* have been elected by the citizens, was from the mid-fifteenth century onwards usually a royal appointee and often of Hungarian origin.[72]

---

67   Kubinyi, "Népmozgalmak Budapesten," p. 9.
68   The institution of an Outer Council plainly derived from practices followed elsewhere. See Eberhard Isenmann, *Die deutsche Stadt im Mittelalter 1150–1550* (2nd ed. Vienna–Cologne–Weimar: Böhlau, 2012), pp. 269 and 377.
69   István Nagy, "A választó polgárság testülete Budán a XVIII. században," [The body of burgher electors in eighteenth-century Buda] *Tanulmányok Budapest Múltjából* 13 (1959), pp. 139–166. See also, István Kenyeres, "Buda és Pest útja az 1703. évi kiváltságlevélig," [Buda and Pest until its letter of privilege in 1703] *Urbs. Magyar Várostörténeti Évkönyv* 1 (2006), pp. 159–201.
70   Mária Lupescu Makó, "Der Ausgleich von Klausenburg 1458," in *Klausenburg. Wege einer Stadt und ihrer Menschen in Europa*, eds Ulrich Burger and Rudolf Gräf (Cluj: Presa Univ. Clujeană, 2007), pp. 39–50; Ágnes Flóra, *The Matter of Honour: The Leading Urban Elites in Sixteenth Century Cluj and Sibiu*, unpublished PhD dissertation (Budapest: CEU, 2014), pp. 46–48 and 69–71.
71   Végh, "Buda: the Multi-Ethnic," p. 92; idem, *Buda város*, i, pp. 123–136.
72   Kubinyi, *Budapest*, pp. 154–155; András Kubinyi, "Polgári értelmiség és hivatalnokrétege Budán és Pesten a Hunyadi- és a Jagelló-korban," [Burgher intellectuals and bureaucrats in Buda and Pest in the Hunyadi and the Jagiellonian Periods] in Kubinyi, *Tanulmányok*, ii, pp. 598–619, here p. 609.

Urban Law, Noble Law and the Tavernicus

The central, walled part of the city was extensively settled in the fifteenth century by noblemen. The most southerly part of the city, which lay next to the royal palace, included members of some of the greatest baronial families (Somi, Perényi, Bánfi; later the Szapolyai, Kubinyi etc.).[73] The square nearest to the palace (Szent György) was occupied by a mixture of wealthy German merchants and prominent noblemen, and over the course of the fifteenth century these squeezed out the citizens.[74] Even in other areas of the city, where craftsmen and merchants predominated, we may note the presence of noble homes, including large mansions.[75] According both to the 1244 privilege and the *Stadtrechtsbuch*, all those with property in the city were expected to contribute to taxation. It seems, however, that many nobles shirked this responsibility (although some plainly paid).[76] In 1492, it was laid down by the diet that noblemen living in Buda were exempt from city taxes and the text of the law implied that this was their customary right, which the magistracy had trespassed upon.[77] Noblemen also regularly conveyed properties within the city or launched legal actions over them using the agency of ecclesiastical chapters rather than the city council.[78]

The large noble presence within the city affected Buda's laws and customs, which became increasingly influenced by the legal practices observed by the nobility. The city's charters mimicked those published for the nobility, including in their texts warranty clauses, the *per eum* and *renunciatio* formulas (which conveyed the property on the new owner's heirs and voided all the vendor's rights), and the promise to reissue upon presentation a patent recording a property transaction in the form of a privilege. The customary law of the nobility influenced not only the form of the city's charters but also Buda's substantive and procedural law. The privilege of 1244 presumed that citizens would leave properties to their heirs. It was only, therefore, when a citizen died without a successor that he might freely dispose of his goods. The *Stadtrechtsbuch* repeated this provision.[79] From the fourteenth century onwards, however, the

---

73   Végh, *Buda*, i, pp. 149 and 155.
74   Végh, *Buda*, i, p. 171.
75   Végh, *Buda*, i, pp. 209, 223 and 246.
76   Végh, *Buda*, i, p. 315; Kubinyi, *Budapest*, p. 153.
77   DRMH, iv, pp. 44–47 (1492:105).
78   BTOE, iii/1, pp. 162–163 (no 329); BTOE, iii/2, pp. 70–71, 73 and 98–99 (nos 815, 821 and 869); Végh, *Buda*, ii, nos 179, 235, 273, 277, 301, 322, 326 and 366. Cf. OSt, p. 129. (cap. 201) – "Alle kauff schullen geschen mit der stadt prieff".
79   OSt, p. 128. (cap. 200).

right of heirs to succeed to inherited property was converted in the city to a concurrent right of ownership. Thus, in order to alienate landed estate, the owner had to obtain the consent of his successors and have this formally recorded in the deed of sale or pledge.[80] In imitation of the noble custom of *aviticitas* (entailment), the property of citizens was later described as *hereditates avitae et paternae*. As among the nobility, the main exception to this rule was property that the owner had himself acquired by purchase rather than by inheritance, which remained freely disposable.[81]

The application of noble rules of inheritance to property within the city proved a constraint to mercantile endeavor, as a consequence of which bankruptcy law tended to overlook the rights of successors in favor of commercial creditors.[82] Nevertheless, the need to obtain the agreement of heirs and kinsmen prior to a sale or pledge was plainly irksome and imposed an unwelcome constraint on alienation. In order to obviate this restriction, citizens sometimes included in deeds of alienation the so-called *assumptio* clause, borrowed from noble customary practice, which conveyed a fictive consent and imposed penalties on kinsmen should they later contest an alienation.[83] Nevertheless, the city's laws in respect of property were not completely eroded by noble intrusions. The period of *praescriptio*, after which a possessor's rights became uncontested (save in cases of *malae fidei*) remained at a year, thus contributing to the security of ownership, while the rights of daughters to inherit from the paternal estate were generally acknowledged.[84]

The attenuation of the city's jurisdictional rights is particularly visible in respect of its appellate authority. From the middle of the thirteenth century, and increasingly thereafter, the liberties given to Buda in the 1244 privilege were conveyed by the ruler on other cities of Hungary, in which respect Buda functioned very much in the manner of a *Vorbildstadt*.[85] Even where they were

---

80   Wenzel, "Budai regeszták," pp. 126–128; BTOE, iii/1, pp. 6–7, 12–13, 22, 23, 300 and 344 (nos 17, 28, 52, 54, 579 and 663); BTOE, iii/2, pp. 96–97, 179–180 and 296 (nos 865, 1021, 1183, etc.).
81   Rudolf Schmidt, *Statut grada Iloka iz godine 1525* (Zagreb: Nadbiskupska tiskara, 1938), pp. 35 and 65. For the more general subversion of urban law by the noble law of the countryside, see Martyn Rady, *Customary Law in Hungary: Courts, Texts and the Tripartitum* (Oxford: Oxford University Press, 2015), p. 156.
82   Schmidt, *Statut*, p. 69.
83   BTOE, ii/1, pp. 9798 (no 197) (1395); MNL OL DL 39 213 (1494). The operation of the *assumptio* is explained in Martyn Rady, "Warranty and Surety in Medieval Hungarian Land Law," *Journal of Legal History* 23 (2002), pp. 23–36, here pp. 29–34.
84   Blazovich and Schmidt, *Buda város*, i, pp. 208–213.
85   Fügedi, "Városprivilégiumok," pp. 290–291. See also Katalin Szende, "Power and Identity. Royal Privileges to the Towns of Medieval Hungary in the Thirteenth Century," in *Urban*

not so expressly granted, it is evident that cities might unilaterally adopt as their own the rights given in the 1244 charter.[86] Out of the system of charter bestowal the practice developed of cities referring legal actions for adjudication to the place or 'mother city' from which they derived their liberties. The royal law of 1405, known as the *Decretum Minus*, which was published following an assembly of delegates of the kingdom's cities and towns, sanctioned this practice by permitting litigants "to appeal any judgment passed by their judges and citizens [...] to the judges of that city by whose laws such a city or free town lives."[87]

From an early stage, however, the development of mother-city jurisdiction came into collision with the rights pertaining to the *Tavernicus* or *Magister Tavernicorum*. The *Tavernicus* was a royal officer, who was originally in charge of a servile group of provisioners responsible for stocking the stores on which the king's itinerant court relied.[88] By the thirteenth century, the *Tavernicus* had overall responsibility for the kingdom's mints and freedom from the intrusion of the *Tavernicus*'s bailiff and moneyers is listed in the 1244 privilege as one of Pest's liberties. The connection between the kingdom's cities and the minting organization resulted in the *Tavernicus* acquiring some responsibility for urban affairs. Privileges given to cities in the thirteenth and fourteenth centuries thus occasionally referred to the *Tavernicus* as the authority to whom appeals from the judgments of the council and petitions for the impeachment of city officers should be addressed.[89] During the late fourteenth century, the court of the *Tavernicus* frequently met with assessors drawn from the council of one or more cities of the kingdom.[90] It was the function of the assessors to assist the *Tavernicus* in determining what the relevant urban law was. As one *Tavernicus* explained in 1434, when directing the citizens of Pressburg to attend his court: "On account of the ambiguity and difficult nature of the case, we are unwilling to proceed and pass judgment without your circumspect selves being in attendance."[91]

Liberties and Civic Participation from the Middle Ages to Modern Times, eds Michel Pauly and Alexander Lee (Trier: Porta Alba, 2015), 27–67. For Buda as a *Vorbildstadt*, see Gönczi, *Ungarisches Stadtrecht*, p. 75.

86   AO, vii, pp. 402–406 (no 225).
87   DRMH, ii, p. 36.
88   István Petrovics, "Tárnokmester," [Tavernicus] in *Korai magyar történeti lexikon (9–14. század)* [Early Hungarian historical lexicon, ninth–fourteenth centuries], ed. Gyula Kristó, Pál Engel and Ferenc Makk (Budapest: Akadémiai, 1994), p. 662.
89   Fügedi, "Városprivilégiumok," p. 287.
90   ZsO, i, p. 127 (no 1017); MNL OL DL 71 362 and 6998.
91   Imre Szentpétery, "A tárnoki itélőszék kialakulása," [The formation of the court of law of the tavernicus] *Századok* [Supplementum] 68 (1934), pp. 510–590, here p. 565.

Besides the relevant mother city, the *Decretum Minus* of 1405 listed the *Tavernicus*'s court as an alternative forum to which urban appeals might be brought. Seemingly, therefore, two separate appeal structures were in operation. In practice, however, the mother-city court and the Tavernicus's court combined. The merger of the two institutions took several decades to become complete and in its earliest stages was marked by haphazard arrangements. The *Stadtrechtsbuch* thus noted that "when the *Tavernicus* (*Tarnagkmaister*) wishes to judge matters, he shall summon and call the judge and sworn citizens of the city. And should there be in the city the judge and citizens of other cities he should also call them."[92] Almost certainly it is this informality of arrangements which explains why on some occasions we will find the *Tavernicus* judging in the company of just one city's magistracy and on others with representatives drawn from a number of places.[93] Nevertheless, by the 1440s the cities whose councillors attended the *Tavernicus*'s court had settled at seven (later eight) – Buda, Košice, Pressburg, Trnava, Prešov, Bardejov and Sopron (and subsequently Pest). All of these, with only one exception, had received Buda's privileges and thus belonged to its jurisdictional orbit as filial cities.[94] During the second half of the fifteenth century, the seven cities that belonged to the court of the *Tavernicus* framed their own code of law, the *Laws and Customs of the Seven Cities*, which was closely modeled on Buda's own customary arrangements. This included such institutions as an Outer Council of a hundred citizens, co-opted by the outgoing council, and a committee of twenty-four citizens to oversee taxation.[95] The primacy of Buda was further registered in the court's location in the city (and not in the palace) and in the right attaching to the city council to take charge of the court's protocols between sessions.[96]

---

92 OSt, p. 64 (cap. 16).
93 ZsO, ii/1, p. 387 (no 3270); ZsO, ii/2, pp. 183–184 (no 6423) and ZsO, viii, p. 100 (no 254).
94 The exception was Trnava – unsurprisingly since its charter (issued in 1238) predated the foundation of Buda.
95 The text of the *Laws and Customs* is reproduced in a garbled form in M.G. Kovachich, *Codex Authenticus Iuris Tavernicalis* (Buda: Typys Regiae Universitatis Pestanae, 1803). The Latin text is edited by Schmidt, *Statut*; a German version is given in Štefánia Mertanová, *Ius tavernicale: štúdie o procese formovania práva taverníckych miest v etapách vývoja taverníckeho súdu v Uhorsku (15.–17. stor.)* [Studies in the legal development of the tavernical towns in the period of the development of the tavernical court, fifteenth–seventeenth century] (Bratislava: Veda and Vydavateľstvo Slovenskej akadémie vied, 1985), pp. 155–215.
96 Ibolya Felhő, "Buda elsősége a tárnoki városok között," [The primacy of Buda among the towns of the Tavernicus] *Tanulmányok Budapest Múltjából* 19 (1972), pp. 153–178, here pp. 156–157. The court of the Tavernicus might thus be held, as in 1496, in the home of one

The development of the court of the *Tavernicus* into the Buda mother-city court, the law of which closely followed Buda's own, was never complete. As a consequence, the Buda mother-city court did not progress into a *Schöffenstuhl* in a manner analogous to the privileged families of cities further west.[97] First, it remained under the presidency of a royal officer, the *Tavernicus*, who was drawn from the ranks of upper nobility. Secondly, although citizens were present as assessors in the court, noblemen might also be in attendance, thus vitiating the cities' rights to administer their own law.[98] Moreover, since the *Tavernicus*'s court constituted a royal court, it was possible to appeal actions further and have them taken up into the structure of noble adjudication headed by royal judges and administered by protonotaries trained in the customary law of the nobility. It was only in the 1490s that attempts were undertaken to ensure that, when the suits of citizens were considered, the law followed in the principal royal appeal court should reflect urban customs. Even so, the royal enumeration of the content of the cities' customary law was slender, amounting to only seven articles.[99] Presumably, in all other regards the noble laws and customs of the kingdom were held to apply.[100]

Conclusion

In 1847, József Eötvös described Hungary's medieval cities as "alien, representing a separate element outside the collective nation. They stood like German islands in the midst of a Hungarian sea. They had their own foreign language and customs, and, as the Buda *Stadtrecht* confirms, their foreign laws as well."[101] Eötvös's stark characterization was an underlying assumption in much historical writing in the nineteenth and twentieth centuries.[102] Study of Buda's government and of the manner in which it exercised its jurisdiction

---

of Buda's citizens. See Béla Iványi, *Eperjes szabad királyi város levéltára*, i [The archive of the free royal town of Prešov] (Szeged: Szegedi Városi Ny., 1931), p. 68.

97   Discussed in Isenmann, *Die deutsche Stadt*, pp. 193–195.
98   Martinus Georgius Kovachich, *Formulae solennes styli in cancellaria...* (Pest: Typis Matthiae Trattner, 1799), p. 300.
99   Kovachich, *Codex Authenticus*, pp. 45–53.
100 On the more general relationship of *Stadtrecht* to *Landrecht*, see Gönczi, *Ungarisches Stadtrecht*, pp. 213–229.
101 József Eötvös, *Magyarország 1514-ben* [Hungary in 1514] (Pest: Hartleben, 1847), Ch. 1.
102 Discussed by Katalin Gönczi, *A városi jog és feljegyezései a középkori Magyarországon* [The urban law and its codifications in medieval Hungary] (Acta Juridica et Politica Fasc. liv, 7) (Szeged: JATE ÁJK, 1998), p. 4. See also, Szende, "Power and Identity."

must qualify this approach. The city's institutions of self-rule were from the very first disturbed by the imposition of a royally-appointed *rector* in place of an elected headman and judge. Buda's development as a *Schöffenstuhl* was likewise impeded by the city's subordination to a royal official, the *Tavernicus*. The Hungarian presence in the city, which was augmented by the proximity of the palace, forced the remodeling of its government after 1439 to accommodate the city's growing Hungarian population, while Buda's laws and customs were also influenced by aspects of the larger noble law at work in the kingdom as a whole. Buda was thus never free to develop the autonomy and legal and jurisdictional independence which were the characteristics of urban government elsewhere in Central Europe.[103] As it was, the urban estate was weak in Hungary. In the case of Buda, this situation was compounded by the city's function as a royal *Residenzstadt*, which shaped its offices, customary law and the composition of its government. In this respect, Buda's development as a capital took place at the expense of its liberties.

---

103   Isenmann, *Die deutsche Stadt*, p. 207.

CHAPTER 13

Diets and Synods in Buda and Its Environs

János M. Bak and András Vadas

Several factors influenced the choice of location for those medieval assemblies at which the ruler and a larger or smaller number of those sharing power with the monarch met and deliberated on matters of state. As far as we can see, mythical, ancient meetings (like Szer in the Hungarian and Duvno in the Dalmatian-Croatian tradition) did not define where their medieval successors met. In the earlier centuries such meetings – in a remote way precursors to diets – were styled synods, although they were also attended by laymen and were held in ecclesiastical centers, such as Split in Dalmatia or St Martin's (Pannonhalma) in Hungary. It seems that the occasion of the gathering of the army for campaigns, be it for defense or distributing booty, offered occasions for an exchange between warrior elite and king and some of them, as in the case of the Field of Rákos in Hungary,[1] came to be sites of diets, especially those which were attended by a great number of noblemen. Royal courts that then grew into parliaments and diets were also held from the beginning near the royal residence – if there was one. In turn, these meeting places often came to strengthen the gradually developing central residences or 'capitals', such as Prague, Olomouc, or Buda. In the Holy Roman Empire, but elsewhere too, royal cities had the privileges and burden of housing these assemblies, such as Frankfurt, Nuremberg, Buda or Prague.[2] Some of them were also the traditional places for election and coronation (such as Prague), but they were often held at a different place, such as Frankfurt and Aachen, Gniezno and Cracow,

---

The authors acknowledge the bibliographic and other notes of Norbert C. Tóth and Gábor Mikó (both Hungarian Research Group for Medievistics) delivered in respect of an earlier version of the present paper.

1 See below, *passim*. In the late twelfth century, Croatian troops gathered near Zadar and may have had deliberations there. For the Czech and Polish examples, see János M. Bak and Pavel Lukin, "Consensus and Assemblies in Early Medieval Central and Eastern Europe," in *Political Assemblies in the Earlier Middle Ages* (Studies in the Early Middle Ages, 7) eds P. S. Barnwell and M. Mostert (Turnhout: Brepols, 2003), pp. 95–114, here pp. 99–100.
2 On the location of diets in the Holy Roman Empire, Poland and Hungary, see Julia Dücker, *Reichsversammlungen im Spätmittelalter. Politische Willensbildung in Polen, Ungarn und Deutschland* (Ostfildern: Thorbecke, 2011), pp. 47–50, 109–111 and 187–190 and eadem [Julia Burkhardt], "Procedure, Rules and Meaning of Political Assemblies in Late Medieval Central Europe," *Parliaments, Estates and Representation* 35 (2015), pp. 153–170.

Biograd or Székesfehérvár. In Poland, the medieval diets met in a town more or less in the middle of the realm, but rarely at the royal residence. Whether these variations could or should be connected with the similar but different 'political culture' of the states of Central Europe[3] will need a discussion of its own.

In the following, we try to trace the interaction between synods and diets on the one hand and the development of Buda as *caput regni* on the other. While it would be certainly anachronistic to talk about diets or general assemblies (*congregatio generalis, dieta*) before the late thirteenth century,[4] there are records of assemblies for the first century of the Hungarian kingdom, such as the meetings (synods) of the great men of the realm, *ispán*s and bishops, at Szabolcs in 1092 or the synod of Esztergom (ca. 1100) and the "council of Tarcal" under King Coloman,[5] but no continuity from these to the later diets can be

---

[3] For this, see, e.g. Gottfried Schramm, "Polen–Böhmen–Ungarn: Übernationale Gemeinsamkeiten in der politischen Kultur des späten Mittelalters und der frühen Neuzeit," in *Ständefreiheit und Staatsgestaltung in Ostmitteleuropa. Übernationale Gemeinsamkeiten in der politischen Kultur vom 16.–18. Jahrhundert*, eds Joachim Bahlcke, Hans-Jürgen Bömelburg and Norbert Kersken (Leipzig: Universitätsverlag, 1996), pp. 13–38.

[4] On the history of these assemblies in general, see György Bónis, "The Hungarian Feudal Diet (13th to 18th Centuries)," *Recueils de la Société Jean Bodin pour l'histoire comparative des institutions* 29 (1971), pp. 725–765; János M. Bak, *Königtum und Stände in Ungarn im 14.–15. Jh.* (Wiesbaden: Steiner, 1973); Stanisław Russocky, "Les assemblés prérepresentatives en Europe centrale," *Acta Poloniae Historica* 30 (1974), pp. 33–52.

[5] See: DRMH, i, pp. 12–15, 60–65 and 23–31. On the date of the synod, see Levente Závodszky, *Szent István, Szent László és Kálmán korabeli törvények és zsinati határozatok forrásai* [The sources of the laws and synodical agreements in the period of St Stephen, St Ladislas and Coloman the Learned] (Budapest: Szent István Társulat, 1904), p. 95; also, Monika Jánosi, "Az első ún. esztergomi zsinati határozatok keletkezésének problémái," [The problems of the formation of the agreements of the so-called first synod of Esztergom] *Acta Universitatis Szegediensis de Attila József nominatae. Acta Historica* 83 (1986), pp. 23–30. On the synods of Esztergom and Tarcal, see also Szabolcs Anzelm Szuromi, "Az első három Esztergomi zsinat és a magyarországi egyházfegyelem a 12. században," [Church discipline and the first three synods of Esztergom] in *Tanulmányok a magyarországi egyházjog középkori történetéből. Kéziratos kódexek, zsinatok, középkori műfajok* [Studies in the history of medieval canon law. Codices, synods, medieval genres] (Bibliotheca Instituti Postgradualis Iuris Canonici, iii, Studia, 3), ed. Péter Erdő (Budapest: Szent István Társulat, 2002), pp. 87–127; Szabolcs Anzelm Szuromi, "Esztergomi zsinatok és kánongyűjtemények a XII. századi Magyarországon," [The synods of Esztergom and canon law collections in twelfth-century Hungary] *Iustum Aequum Salutare* 2 (2006), pp. 191–201; Gábor Thoroczkay, "Megjegyzések a Hartvik-féle Szent István legenda datálásának kérdéséhez," [Notes on the dating of the Hartvik version of the St Stephen legend] in idem, *Írások az Árpád-korról. Történeti és historiográfiai tanulmányok* [Studies in the history fo the Árpárian Period. Historic and historiographic writings] (TDI Könyvek, 9) (Budapest: L'Harmattan, 2009), pp. 67–87, here pp. 71–74.

claimed. Despite the fact that the Hungarian Chronicle mentions a *generalis congregatio* at Arad during the reign of Béla II in 1131 the event had no direct connections to the general assembly of the barons and the nobility that met regularly from the thirteenth century onwards.[6]

What seems to be more likely is that a royal court of law in Székesfehérvár (*Alba Regia*), the traditional coronation city and necropolis to many Hungarian kings, was an established tradition by the time of its first explicit mention in 1222, on the occasion of the issue of the Golden Bull on noble liberty by King Andrew II.[7] In that charter, the king or his representative promised to hold such assemblies every year on St Stephen's Day (20 August) in the coronation town of Székesfehérvár. However, when the lesser freemen, the *servientes regis* requested that the privileges granted to the *nobiles* in 1222 be extended to them, the meeting was held near the old royal residence at Esztergom.[8] The memory of assemblies at Székesfehérvár remained alive, though. In 1299, King Andrew III decreed that annual meetings should be held there, but apart from the following year when the decisions of the 1298 diet were ratified, it did not become a regular practice.[9] Coronation diets did, however, later assemble there, all the way down to the election of John I Szapolyai as king of Hungary on 11 November 1526.[10]

As far as we know, the first *generalis congregatio* in Buda was the one in 1276 when an assembly of the barons and the nobility of the country (*communis*

---

[6] "fecit congregationem generalem in regno iuxta Arad" – Alexander Domanovszky, ed., *Chronici Hungarici compositio saeculi XIV*, in SRH, i, pp. 217–505, here pp. 446–447. (cap. 160) See also Erzsébet S. Kiss, "A királyi generális kongregáció kialakulásának történetéhez," [On the history of the formation of the general assemblies in Hungary] *Acta Universitatis Szegediensis de Attila József nominatae. Acta Historica* 39 (1971), pp. 3–45, here p. 11.

[7] DRMH, i, pp. 32–35; on the Golden Bull, see Attila Zsoldos, "II. András Aranybullája," [The Golden Bull of Andrew II] *Történelmi Szemle* 53 (2011), pp. 1–38.

[8] In 1267, see DRMH, i, pp. 40–41. More recently, see Attila Zsoldos, "Az 1267. évi dekrétum és politikatörténeti háttere. (IV. Béla és ifjabb István király viszályának utolsó fejezete.)," [The decree of 1267 and its political background (the last episode of the conflict of Béla IV and Stephen V, the younger king)] *Századok* 141 (2007), pp. 803–842.

[9] On this, see Loránd Szilágyi, "III. Endre 1298. évi törvénye," [The Law of 1298 of Andrew III] *Annales Universitatis Scientiarum Budapestinensis de Rolando Eötvös Nominatae. Sectio historica* 1 (1957), pp. 135–171, here p. 141. See also on the decree itself, József Gerics, *A korai rendiség Európában és Magyarországon* [The Early Regime of Estates in Europe and Hungary] (Budapest: Akadémiai, 1987), pp. 288–309.

[10] Rezső Gaberdeen, *A rákosi országgyűlések*, unpublished dissertation [The diets at Rákos] (Budapest: [n.p.], [1916]). The copy we used is available in Budapest, Szabó Ervin Könyvtár (Szabó Ervin Metropolitan Library), Budapest Gyűjtemény (Budapest Collection). Cat. no B 328/78.

congregacio Baronum et Nobilium Regni nostri) gathered together with the king.¹¹ Beginning in 1277, royal charters were issued at Rákos – a flat land in the surroundings of Pest, named after a rivulet that may have been rich in crayfish (*rák* is Hungarian for crayfish) – which from the late thirteenth century became the regular meeting place of the assemblies.¹² The location of the Field of Rákos is the subject of controversy. Even in medieval historiography the references to the location of the Field of Rákos are somewhat contradictory. Some indications refer to Rákos as being right by the town of Pest, just outside its late medieval walls. But some references, as a charter from 1512, supports the idea that the Field of Rákos may have been more distant from the walls. This document records a plan to relocate the cattle market of Pest from the Hatvan Gate to further away, "to the Field of Rákos" (*dictum forum pecorum non ibi, scilicet in loco consueto, sed ad alium locum, videlicet ad campum Rakos*). Less than a kilometer from the line of the walls of late medieval Pest, a supposedly marshy area surrounded the town, lay the so-called Rákos ditch (Fig. 13.1). The late medieval cattle market was by far the biggest in the country, with supposedly tens of thousands of cattle being sold on the spot. The relocation of the market to an area further from the Hatvan Gate but still within the Rákos ditch would have left a very narrow space for such an amount of stock. It is, therefore, rather more likely that the Field of Rákos mentioned in the charter corresponds with the area that extended beyond the Rákos ditch.¹³

---

11   See: MNL OL DL 1153, edited in ÁÚO, ix, p. 353 (no 251) and MNL OL DL 91 127; for editions, see RA, ii/3, pp. 368–369 (no 3407). On the problem of the dating of these two charters, see S. Kiss, "A királyi," pp. 24–28.

12   The location appears in earlier sources. In both *Gesta Hungarorum*, that of Anonymus (Emil Jakubovich, ed., *Gesta Hungarorum*, in SRH, i, p. 94) and of Simon of Kéza (Alexander Domanovszky, ed., *Gesta Hungarorum*, in SRH, i, p. 164) the rivulet Rákos near Buda is mentioned and in the early part of the Hungarian Chronicle it is recorded that in 1074 King Salamon's army pitched camp at Rákos before the battle with his cousins (*Chronici Hungarici*, p. 387. [cap. 119]). For the name Rákos in respect of the diets, see Béla Iványi, *Adalékok régi országgyűléseink Rákos nevéhez* [Information on the Rákos name of our ancient diets] (Szeged: Tudományegyetem Barátainak Egyesülete, 1935). See also for the diets held at Rákos, László Szende, *A Rákos mezei országgyűlések története* [The history of diets on the field of Rákos] (Budapest: Papcsák Ügyvédi Iroda, 2010).

13   For this, see Judit Benda, "A kereskedelem épületei a középkori Budán, ii. Mészárszékek háza, zsemleszékek háza, árucsarnok," [Commercial buildings in medieval Buda. The house of butcheries, bakeries, market hall] *Tanulmányok Budapest Múltjából* 37 (2012), pp. 7–41, here p. 8, note 6 and her contribution in the present volume; István Tringli, "Vásártér és vásári jog a középkori Magyarországon," [Market places and market rights in medieval Hungary] *Századok* 144 (2010), pp. 1291–1344, here p. 1318. For the original charter, see MNL OL DL 106 083/241. For the edition of the charter, see the appendix.

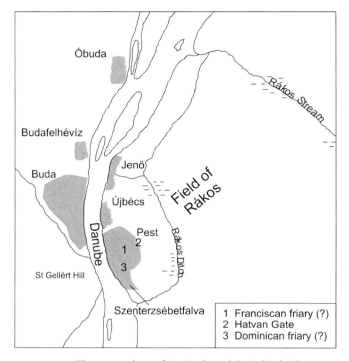

FIGURE 13.1 *The surroundings of Pest-Buda and the Field of Rákos*

The first charter issued by King Ladislas IV from Rákos dates to 1275, but the first case when the king undoubtedly met the nobility there was in May 1277.[14] The meeting may have opened at an unusual place: the king issued a charter on 23 May 1277 at the *Magna Insula* (Csepel Island, south of Budapest) close to Pest (*iuxta Pest prope magnam insulam*).[15] This is the first known gathering where issues of major importance (principally the alliance with Rudolf I) were negotiated, followed by the discussion of other issues of particular interest. A week later, on the 30 May the king issued a second charter, this time at Rákos, which suggests that the assembly took place between these two dates and locations.

14 On the political situation of the period, see Attila Zsoldos, "Tététnytől a Hód-tóig (Az 1279 és 1282 közötti évek politikatörténetének vázlata)," [From Tétény to Lake Hód (An outline of the political history of the years between 1279 and 1282)] *Történelmi Szemle* 39 (1999), pp. 69–97.
15 MNL OL DF 285 549.

Between 1277 and 1318 both the last Árpádian kings and King Charles I met the nobility and the barons on the Field of Rákos. There is no doubt that the king and the barons again met there in 1286; however, there is no indication that the nobility took part in the *congregatio*.[16] None of the charters issued there refer to the presence of other than the barons and prelates; in all likelihood the king issued the charters with the consent of what was later to become the royal council. However, if indeed only the great men were present at this meeting, it is rather puzzling why it was held in the wide Field of Rákos instead of Buda, where the king was regularly residing at this time.

There is some indication that, just as in the neighboring Croatia, Bohemia and Poland, the place of the assemblies coincided with the meeting place of the army before military campaigns. Some believe that Rákos served as a place of muster under Ladislas IV while preparing the campaign against King Ottokar I (leading to the significant battle of the Marchfeld).[17] Although there is no direct written evidence for this muster at Rákos, royal charters were issued in the summer from Buda which makes it possible that the king and the nobility gathered there to start the campaign in alliance with Rudolf I. This hypothesis may be supported by the fact that in 1299 the army was dismissed on the field of Rákos.[18] Having the army meet at Rákos on the left bank of the Danube, beyond the town of Pest, was logical since it was the closest area to Buda, where a great number of people could assemble.

The fact that several congregations met at Rákos does not mean, however, that this was the only place to witness major gathering of the king, the barons and the nobility. In July 1279 the nobility and the Cumans met the king and the barons at Tétény (*Tetum* or *Thetin* some ten kilometers southwest of Buda, today part of the 22nd district of Budapest).[19] As, despite the efforts of the legate Philip, bishop of Fermo, the decisions made at the diet were not enforced, Philip decided to call the clergy to the Dominican friary in Buda in order to excommunicate the king in the presence of the Hungarian prelates. Ladislas IV attempted to hinder the gathering by prohibiting the burghers of Buda from supplying the participants, but he did not succeed.[20] It is doubtful whether

---

16 On the assembly, see: S. Kiss, "A királyi," pp. 40–42. See also ÁMTF, iv, pp. 550–551.
17 ÁMTF, iv, p. 551.
18 ÁMTF, iv, p. 551.
19 Zoltán J. Kosztolnyik, *Hungary in the Thirteenth Century* (East European Monographs, 439) (Boulder: East European Monographs, 1996), pp. 264–265 and S. Kiss, "A királyi," pp. 36–39.
20 On the synod itself, see Kosztolnyik, *Hungary*, pp. 272–283. For the prohibition: CD, v/3, p. 28. See also: László Zolnay, "'Opus castri Budensis.' A XIII. századi budai vár kialakulása,"

the canons of excommunication were ever approved and implemented, as the sequence of manuscripts relating to the Buda synod of 1279 is difficult to reconstruct.[21] Although some major meetings are documented as taking place in more distant locations such as Oradea (1279) or Szeged (1286), it was the Buda – Esztergom – Székesfehérvár triangle of the *medium regni* where these first proto-parliaments were held, before Buda became – as discussed elsewhere in this volume – the effective capital city of the kingdom (Fig. 0.2).

The first more or less formal *parlamentum* known to us was held in Óbuda after the coronation of the last Árpádian king, Andrew III, on 1 September 1290.[22] This yielded the earliest formal *decretum* (that can be called the first piece of 'legislation' proper). A few years later, in 1298, the nobility was called to gather at the church of the Franciscans in Pest (*nos...apud ecclesiam Fratrum minorum in Pesth...cum omnibus nobilibus Hungariae, singulis Saxonibus, Comanis, in unum convenientes*) after which they held the diet at Rákos.[23] The church of the Franciscans according to the literature may have been close to the thirteenth century wall at the eastern part of Pest,[24] next to the road that led to Kerepes. The only proof is the fact that the church of the order still stands there, but no archaeological or written evidence from the thirteenth century supports this. The only remains that were discovered under

[The formation of the castle of Buda in the thirteenth century] *Tanulmányok Budapest Múltjából* 15 (1963), pp. 43–107, here p. 88.

21 See: Nora Berend, "The Manuscript Tradition of the Synod of Buda (1279)," in eadem, *At the Gate of Christendom: Jews, Muslim and 'Pagans' in Medieval Hungary, c. 1000–c. 1300* (Cambridge: Cambridge University Press, 2001), pp. 275–278. A different opinion has been expressed by Péter Langó, "Kun László kun törvényei. Megjegyzések a kunok középkori jogi státusáról," [The Cuman laws of Ladislas IV. Notes on the medieval legal position of the Cumans] in *Jászok és kunok a magyarok között. Ünnepi kötet Bánkiné Molnár Erzsébet tiszteletére* [Jazygians and Cumans amongst Hungarians. Studies in honor of Erzsébet Bánkiné Molnár], eds Edit Bathó and Zoltán Újváry (Jászberény: Jász Múzeumért Alapítvány, 2006), pp. 60–77. Berend has now published her response to Langó's essay. See Nora Berend, "Forging the Cuman Law, Forging an Identity," in *Manufacturing a Past for the Present: Forgery and Authenticity in Medievalist Texts and Objects in Nineteenth-Century Europe* (National Cultivation of Culture, 7), eds János M. Bak, Patrick J. Geary and Gábor Klaniczay (Leiden: Brill, 2014), pp. 109–128.

22 DRMH, i, pp. 42–45.

23 CD, vi/2, p. 131. For the decrees see also DRMH, i, pp. 46–51.

24 Beatrix F. Romhányi, *Kolostorok és társaskáptalanok a középkori Magyarországon* [Monasteries and collegiate chapters in medieval Hungary] (Budapest: Pytheas, 2000; revised and enlarged CD-ROM version: Budapest: Arcanum, 2008), p. 51 and ÁMTF, iv, p. 545 and Györffy, *Budapest*, pp. 283–284. For the ecclesiastical topography of Buda and Pest, see also Beatrix F. Romhányi's contribution to the present volume.

the present Baroque church building were identified as belonging to a mosque from the Ottoman Period.

Recollection of a diet held in 1299 is preserved in a number of charters. The nobility met the barons and the king in the Dominican friary of Pest (*congregatione nostra in Pest in ecclesia fratrum Praedicatorum habita per nos adherant*).[25] The exact location of the friary is still unknown despite the existence of a few charters referring to it. Earlier it was thought to have been at the same place where it was after the Ottoman occupation, but archaeological evidence proves that the present building replaced three medieval houses and not a church. It was suggested that the friary lay a little south of the late medieval town of Pest next to the Danube.[26] György Györffy, however, argued that the parish church of Szenterzsébetfalva (where the Dominican friary originally stood) was the one now in Szerb Street, and that the friary lay on the present-day Egyetem Square (within the thirteenth century wall, near the road leading to Szeged).[27] As in the case of the Franciscan church, however, this is also only a presumption based on topographical observations (i.e. the general locations of mendicant churches in towns) and on other indirect evidence. It is not clear whether the entire meeting of the diet took place there or only some negotiations. The palatine Máté Csák and King Andrew III issued charters at Rákos around the same time.[28] Several barons as well as the palatine issued charters at the field of Rákos again in 1300.[29]

During the decade following the death of Andrew III, in 1301, several meetings of the powerful men of the realm were held in Buda, but none of them deserves the title of a diet. As far as we know, only a number of great lords, some of them true petty kings ('oligarchs') were present. During his legatine mission in support of the Angevin claimant, Charles, the papal legate Nicholas Boccasini (the later Pope Benedict XI), held 'diets' both in Buda and Pressburg.[30] The latter may have been chosen for a meeting with the most powerful local warlord, Máté Csák, whose strongholds were in the northwest part of the country. (The town of Pressburg was to become the meeting place of the diet

25 MNL OL DL 38 135.
26 Albert Gárdonyi, "Középkori települések Pest határában," [Medieval settlements on the borders of Pest] *Tanulmányok Budapest Múltjából* 8 (1940), pp. 14–27, here p. 23.
27 ÁMTF, iv, pp. 544–545.
28 See for instance: MNL OL DL 7735; DL 76 182 and 76 184. For the latter ones, see Tibor Szőcs, *Az Árpád-kori nádorok és helyetteseik okleveleinek kritikai jegyzéke* [Critical calendar of the charters of the palatines and their vicars in the Árpádian period] (Budapest: MOL, 2012), pp. 245–246 (nos 298–299).
29 Szőcs, *Az Árpád-kori nádorok*, pp. 253–254 (no 314).
30 For this and the following, see Mon. Vat. i/2, p. liv.

for centuries during the Habsburg era.[31]) Little is known of Boccassini's essentially unsuccessful mission.[32] The Hungarian Chronicle mentions that the legate stayed in Buda for a number of days: *Qui Bude residendo diebus plurimis, aliquot videns se nichil posse proficere, reversus est in curiam.*[33] He arrived at Buda on the 25 October 1301[34] but the exact day of his leaving the city is unknown. The Chronicle leaves no doubt that his stay was not without difficulties, for on departing the city he excommunicated its inhabitants.[35] The first diet after the death of Andrew III took place at Rákos in 1307. On 10 October 1307, the palatine Amádé Aba along with some of the oligarchs accepted Charles of Anjou as king of Hungary. The charter was issued in St Peter's Church of the Franciscans (which indeed is the one in Pest). It is rather surprising that according to the scribe the church stood close to or at Rákos: *Actum hoc apud ecclesiam B. Petri in Rakus*, which implies a rather broad understanding of its location[36]

More is known of the diet called by the next and more successful, papal legate, Cardinal Gentile Particino da Montefiore, on 27 November 1308. The legate resided in Buda Castle, whence he issued a number of letters from 2 November 1308 to 21 April 1309.[37] Gentile held a diet, called for 18 November to Buda, but the supporters of the Angevin king came with sizable troops, thus their meeting was held in Pest, on the plains near the town (obviously Rákos) where there was sufficient space for their encampments. The great men of the realm met in the Dominican church of Pest (which this time is mentioned as lying near

31 On the symbolic meaning of the location of the diets in the early modern times, see Géza Pálffy, "A magyar országgyűlés helyszínei a 16–17. században. A szimbolikus politikai kommunikáció kora újkori történetéhez," [The locations of the Hungarian diets in the sixteenth–seventeenth centuries. On the history of symbolic politics in Early Modern Hungary] in *Rendiség és parlamentarizmus Magyarországon. A kezdetektől 1918-ig* [Estates and parliaments in Hungary from the beginnings to 1918], eds Tamás Dobszay *et al.* (Budapest: Argumentum, 2013), pp. 65–87.

32 See Géza Érszegi, "Zum Wirken des päpstlichen Legaten Nicolaus Bocassini in Ungarn," in *"swer sînen vriunt behaltet, daz ist lobelîch". Festschrift für András Vizkelety zum 70. Geburtstag*, eds Márta Nagy and László Jónácsik (Piliscsaba–Budapest: Katholische Péter-Pázmány-Universität Philosophische Fakultät, 2001), pp. 157–172.

33 *Chronici Hungarici*, pp. 483–484 (cap. 190).

34 Augustin Theiner, *Vetera monumenta historica Hungariam sacram illustrantia*, i (Rome: Typ. Vaticana, 1859), p. 391. See also *Monumenta Ecclesiae Strigoniensis*, ii, ed. Ferdinandus Knauz (Esztergom: Typis descripsit Aegydius Horák, 1882), p. 498 (no 527).

35 *Chronici Hungarici*, p. 484 (cap. 190).

36 MNL OL DL 39 259, edited in CD, viii/1, pp. 221–223 (no 105). See also Gárdonyi, "Középkori települések," p. 24.

37 Mon. Vat. i/2, pp. 60–99. For the charter issued 27 November 1308, see: CD, viii/1, pp. 264–269 (no 135) and AOklt, ii, pp. 213–214 (no 494).

the Danube) something that was not unheard of, as discussed above.[38] The records of the legate describe the scene, which was unusually staid. The king and Gentile presided; right of them were lined up the prelates, and to their left the barons; behind them stood the "nobles and burghers." On 3 December 1308 Gentile again called a meeting, this time referred to as *concilium*.[39] The record is dated from Buda, but we do not know where precisely the meeting was held. Apart from the official document issued by Gentile on the negotiations carried out between May and July that year, charter evidence also supports the presence of the prelates and the barons in Buda in the spring of 1308.[40] In the first half of the reign of Charles I diets were held every few years, for example, in May 1312 and July 1318, at Rákos.[41] A diet took place in between these two, in August 1313, with the presence of a part of the barons of the country who at that time were on the side of the king. Their gathering, unlike most of the diets of the period, was held in the castle of Buda.[42]

The only documented diet called by Louis I of Anjou in November-December 1351 met again in Buda (but was attended by a great number of nobles, so it may not have been in the castle).[43] Two diets during the reign of Queen Mary again met in Buda, the first in 1384 and the second in the

---

38   On this see: Enikő Csukovits, *Az Anjouk Magyarországon, i. 1. Károly és uralkodása (1301–1342)* [The Angevins in Hungary. Charles I and his reign] (Budapest: MTA Bölcsészettudományi Kutatóközpont Történettudományi Intézet, 2012), pp. 60–61.

39   Mon. Vat. i/2, pp. 268–297 and AOklt, ii, pp. 216–218 (no 501).

40   For instance see: MNL OL DL 2073 (AOklt, ii, p. 278 [no 634]); CD, viii/1, pp. 333–337 (no 163).

41   MNL OL DF 269 067, AOklt, iii, pp. 73–74 (no 150). For the edited charter, see Vincent Sedlák, *Regesta diplomatica nec non epistolaria Slovaciae*, i (Bratislava: Academiae Scientiarum Slovacae, 1980), pp. 391–393. For the mandate that called the "generalis congregatio" at Rákos in 1318, see: MNL OL DF 277 247 and AOklt, v, pp. 38 (no 65). For the edited charter, CD, viii/2, pp. 163–164 (no 52). On the diets during the reign of Charles I, see Csukovits, *Az Anjouk*, p. 94.

42   Pál Engel, "Az ország újraegyesítése. I. Károly küzdelmei az oligarchák ellen (1310–1323)," [Reuniting the country. The conflict of Charles I against the oligarchs (1310–1323)] in idem, *Honor, vár, ispánság. Válogatott tanulmányok* [Honor, castle, county. Collected essays], ed. Enikő Csukovits (Budapest: Osiris, 2003), pp. 320–408, here p. 334. (First published in *Századok* 122 [1988], pp. 89–147). See also: MNL OL DL 33 568 and AOklt, iii, pp. 258–259 (no 577); Attila Bárány, "Debreceni Dózsa küzdelme a bihari oligarchákkal," [The conflict of Dózsa Debreceni with the oligarchs of Bihor] in *Debrecen város 650 éves. Várostörténeti tanulmányok* [The town of Debrecen is 650 years old. Studies in urban history] (Speculum Historiae Debreceniense, 7), eds Attila Bárány, Klára Papp and Tamás Szálkai (Debrecen: Debreceni Egyetem Történelmi Intézet, 2011), pp. 75–126, here p. 82.

43   DRMH, ii, pp. 14–17. See also DRH 1301–1457, pp. 141–148.

following year.[44] In 1384, two speakers of the diet presented the nobility's requests (to confirm the noble privileges as her father had done) to the queen residing in Buda. It is thus likely that the nobles met elsewhere, a practice that was to become ever more usual. The diet of 1385 is significant in that it is the first time on which explicitly elected delegates of the counties were invited and thus, being a smaller number, it may have assembled in or near the royal palace at Buda.[45] The diet held in Buda was followed by the coronation of Charles the Short of Durazzo as king of Hungary at Székesfehérvár with at least part of those present in Buda attending.[46]

During the interregnum following the murder of Charles the Short and the captivity of the queens, the lords of Sigismund of Luxemburg's party gathered in the coronation city of Székesfehérvár on 27 August 1386, where they acted "in the name of the Holy Crown" and prepared Sigismund's formal election and coronation.[47] The first diet called by Sigismund, met in 1397 at Timişoara in the southeast of the kingdom.[48] This time the location was chosen for military reasons, since Timişoara served as a headquarters for the defense of the kingdom against the ever growing Ottoman threat. (A similar southern location was then chosen half a century later for the diet that met at Szeged, called by Wladislas I in 1444 before he embarked on the campaign that led to the defeat

---

44   On their date, see Pál Engel and Norbert C. Tóth, *Itineraria regum et reginarum (1382–1438)* (Subsidia ad historiam medii aevi Hungariae inquirendam, 1) (Budapest: MTA Támogatott Kutatóhelyek Irodája, 2005), pp. 36–37; Szilárd Süttő, *Anjou-Magyarország alkonya. Magyarország politikai története Nagy Lajostól Zsigmondig, az 1384–1387. évi belviszályok okmánytárával*, 2 vols [The twilight of Angevins in Hungary. The political history of Hungary from Louis I the Great to Sigismund of Luxemburg with documents on the inner struggles of 1384–1387] (Szeged: Belvedere Meridionale, 2003), i, p. 52.

45   MNL OL DL 38 885. See also: DRMH, ii, pp. 14–17 and DRH 1301–1457, pp. 141–148. Only the decree issued at the second one is explicit about the location, but charters suggest that the first one also met in the capital. For the date of the diet, see: Engel and C. Tóth, *Itineraria*, p. 37. See also Süttő, *Anjou-Magyarország*, i, pp. 107.

46   Johannes de Thurocz, *Chronica Hungarorum*, i, eds Elisabeth Galántai, Julius Kristó (Bibliotheca Scriptorum Medii Recentisque Aevorum. Series Nova, 7) (Budapest: Akadémiai, 1985), pp. 195–196 (cap. 190).

47   István R. Kiss, "Az 1386. évi országgyűlések," [The diets of 1386] *Századok* 47 (1913), pp. 721–735. For the decrees accepted at the diet, see DRMH, ii, pp. 18–20; DRH 1301–1457, pp. 149–153. The meeting was called to the traditional location and included an oath on the head reliquary of King St Stephen I, so as to give the kingless assembly a kind of "sacred" legitimization. See also Bak, *Königtum*, p. 28.

48   On the diet of Timişoara and its context, see József Gerics, "Az 1397. évi országgyűlés helye az országgyűlések történetében," [The place of the diet of 1397 in the history of the diets of Hungary] *Hadtörténelmi Közlemények* 111 (1998), pp. 618–622.

at Varna; for the diet called by King Matthias in 1459, when he returned from a Bosnian campaign;[49] and the diet in 1463 when Matthias gathered his army for a military campaign at Tolna.[50]) In Timişoara King Sigismund, who had barely escaped from the disaster at Nicopolis, combined the confirmation of most of the articles of the Golden Bull with a plan for the reform of the country's armed forces.[51] Two further diets during the reign of Sigismund were held in Pressburg (1402 and 1435) when he, returning from his German realms, met the estates.[52] Diets were also held in April 1390 and November 1392 somewhere in Buda, but their exact locations are unknown[53] and the same is true for the gathering of the barons of the country in 1405.[54] It is rather difficult to assess the diets of Sigismund's reign, since from the early 1400s most of the diets were

49 See: Pál Engel, "A szegedi eskü és a váradi béke. Adalék az 1444. év eseménytörténetéhez," [The oath of Szeged and the treaty of Oradea. On the history of the year 1444] in *Mályusz Elemér emlékköny. Társadalom- és művelődéstörténeti tanulmányok* [Studies in honor of Elemér Mályusz. Studies in social and intellectual history], eds Éva H. Balázs, Erik Fügedi and Ferenc Maksay (Budapest: Akadémiai, 1984), pp. 77–96 and DRMH, iii, pp. 9–14.

50 On these, see Richárd Horváth, *Itineraria regis Matthiae Corvini et reginae Beatricis de Aragonia* (História könyvtár. Kronológiák, adattárak, 12 = Subsidia ad historiam medii aevi Hungarie inquirendam, 2) (Budapest: História – MTA Történettudományi Intézete, 2011), p. 73.

51 DRMH, ii, pp. 21–28; DRH 1301–1457, pp. 157–174.

52 The first diet of Pressburg in 1402 decided the right of Albert of Habsburg to inherit the Hungarian throne if Sigismund did not have a child. See MNL OL DF 287 045. For the edited text of the charter, see CD, x/4, pp. 132–134 (no 46). On the diet, see Norbert C. Tóth, "Nádorváltások a Zsigmond-korban (1386–1437). Az 1439. évi 2. tc. nyomában," [Changes of the palatines in the Sigimundian era (1386–1437). In pursuit of the 2nd decree of 1439] in *Tiszteletkör. Történeti tanulmányok Draskóczy István egyetemi tanár 60. születésnapjára* [Circle of honor. Studies in honor of the 60th birthday of István Draskóczy], eds Gábor Mikó, Bence Péterfi and András Vadas (Budapest: ELTE Eötvös Kiadó, 2012), pp. 53–65, esp. pp. 59–60. It was from the diet of 1435 that Sigismund's so-called *Decretum maius*, the first attempt at systematic legislation was issued. See DRMH, ii, pp. 63–76; DRH 1301–1457, pp. 258–276. For the places Sigismund visited around the time of the diets, see Engel and C. Tóth, *Itineraria*, p. 79 and 129.

53 Norbert C. Tóth, "Szász vajda utódainak felemelkedése és bukása. A család vázlatos története 1365–1424 között," [The rise and fall of the heirs of Szász voivode. A sketch of the family between 1365 and 1424] in *A Szilágyság és a Wesselényi család (14–17. sz.)* [The Sălaj region and the Wesselényi family: 14th–17th c.] (Erdélyi Tudományos Füzetek, 277), eds Géza Hegyi and András W. Kovács (Cluj: Erdélyi Múzeum Egyesület, 2012,), pp. 135–166, pp. here pp. 140–141 and C. Tóth, "Nádorváltások," p. 55.

54 MNL OL DF 256 783. For the decrees of the diet of Buda in 1405, see: DRMH, ii, pp. 35–45; DRH 1301–1457, pp. 189–213.

held in the absence of the king and in most cases no formal decrees survived. However, it is likely that the barons met regularly – supposedly on a yearly basis – in Buda. A study of the itinerary of the barons governing the realm may shed light on these assemblies; they might have taken place in Buda without the presence of the wider strata of the nobility.

The first Habsburg king of Hungary, Albert, met the estates in Buda in 1439. However, two years later in 1441 the diet called by Wladislas I gathered in the town of Pest.[55] From 1442, a charter is preserved inviting the nobles of Szabolcs County to a diet at Buda. The delegates of some 35 counties gathered there in June,[56] but the king decided to move the diet – for reasons unknown – to Hatvan (some 50 km northeast of Pest) later that year.[57] The diet indeed took place in Hatvan with the presence of the barons of the country, which is well reflected in the charters issued by barons there (e.g. 27 August).[58] The charter which contains the decrees of the diet issued in Hatvan is dated 28 August.[59] In the subsequent years we know only that the royal council met regularly in Buda and that a diet was held there in 1444 when, after the so-called Winter Campaign, the nobility and the barons met the king in Buda.[60]

Wladislas I called a diet for the first days of August to Szeged which duly met.[61] After the battle of Varna and the disappearance of Wladislas, a small circle of barons acted in the name of the realm and held several gatherings both in Pest and Buda.[62] In 1445 the prelates of the country along with the barons called the nobility to gather in Pest, which indeed happened.[63] In the spring

55 MNL OL DL 92 932. Elemér Mályusz, "A magyar rendi állam Hunyadi korában, i," [The Hungarian Ständestaat in the age of Hunyadi] *Századok* 91 (1957), pp. 46–123, here p. 80.
56 Mályusz, "A magyar rendi," p. 82.
57 MNL OL DL 44 332. See in details, Mályusz, "A magyar rendi," p. 65 and 85.
58 MNL OL DL 103 596.
59 MNL OL DL 80 768, edited in *A zichi és vásonkeői gróf Zichy-család idősb ágának okmánytára* 12 vols [Documentary collection of the Zichy family and of the older branch of the Zichys of Vásonkeő], eds Imre Nagy, Iván Nagy and Dezső Véghely (Budapest: Magyar Történelmi Társulat, 1871–1931), ix, pp. 44–45 (no 42).
60 Mályusz, "A magyar rendi," p. 84.
61 On the events around the diet, see Pál Engel, "A szegedi eskü és a váradi béke," pp. 77–96.
62 On these gatherings, see Nándor Knauz, *Az országos tanács és országgyűlések története 1445–1452* [The history of national councils and diets, 1445–1452] (Budapest: Emich Nyomda, 1859).
63 MNL OL DL 50 583 and DL 80 828. The former is edited in *Zala vármegye története. Oklevéltár* ii [The history of Zala County. Cartulary], eds Imre Nagy, Dezső Véghely and Gyula Nagy (Budapest: Zala vármegye közönsége, 1890), p. 524; the latter in *A zichi és vásonkeői*, ix, pp. 91–93 (no 92). For the diet, see: Mályusz, "A magyar rendi," pp. 84–85.

of 1446, an assembly of the nobility and the barons was held in Székesfehérvár. The location was chosen to show that the purpose was to elect a new king after the death of Wladislas.[64] In the summer of 1446 another diet was held to elect John Hunyadi as regent in the absence of the under-age king, Ladislas V, but its location is not clear.[65] The limitations of the regent's authority were approved on 13 June 1446 "on the Field of Pest" (*in campo Pestiensi*). At this time, the nobility was invited to attend personally,[66] thus there was such a number of people present that they had to encamp outside the city walls.[67]

In the next year the estates also met. This time the nobility and the towns were invited to gather, although no mention of the city is preserved in the mandate to the diet.[68] The diet should have started at Pentecost but in fact the great men gathered only in autumn. As the nobility was represented by delegates, there was enough space in the castle of Buda for the diet. In 1448 the estates were called again to gather in Buda.[69] There is a charter issued on 12 April 1448 by Regent Hunyadi who, returning from campaign, called the nobles to gather in the town of Pest by St George's Day,[70] which suggests that the choice of venue, either the field of Pest or the castle of Buda, depended on the numbers that turned up. The diet may have taken place on the Field of Pest as the barons issued charters together and the chief justice individually in Pest; moreover, the archbishop of Esztergom also issued a charter *in Pest in generali regnicolarum convencione*.[71]

---

64   On the diet, see the account of two German burghers of Buda, István Renes and Péter Jungetl. Given in MNL OL DL 107 539.

65   MNL OL DL 13 938. The same term occurs in a charter issued on 6 November 1446 (MNL OL DL 13 990).

66   "non unus aut duo, sed singuli singulariter et universi universaliter in presenti congregatione interfuerunt" – MNL OL DL 55 329. See also Mályusz, "A magyar rendi," p. 87.

67   On the larger circumstances, see Knauz, *Az országos tanács*, pp. 41–42; for the decrees, see MNL OL DF 278 310.

68   For the mandate sent to Mihály Ország Guthi, see Knauz, *Az országos tanács*, pp. 57–58.

69   "Sed quia iam domino duce Hys diebus unacum universis dominis prelatis, Baronibus et proceribus huius Regni in Congregacione generali in Festo beati Georgy martiris et diebus subsequentibus ad Id deputatis celebranda Bude constituemur" – Knauz, *Az országos tanács*, p. 80.

70   MNL OL DL 80 908, edited in *A zichi és vásonkeői*, ix, pp. 184–185 (no 145).

71   MNL OL DL 93 095. For the charters of the barons, see for instance, MNL OL DL 100 585, MNL OL DL 13 444 and DL 14 163. For the charter of László Pálóczi, chief justice of Hungary, see MNL OL DF 222 330.

In the next year the barons of the country met again at Buda, where both the barons and the palatine issued charters from the *congregatio* held in the city of Buda (*in civitate Budae*).[72] In spring 1450, the barons and some members of the nobility met in Buda where they agreed to meet the whole of the nobility on the Field of Pest. Accordingly the estates met in the summer of 1450 in Pest.[73] The next year the diet again met in Buda as the nobility had been invited to attend only through delegates.[74] At the beginning of 1452 a diet was held in Pressburg for the first time since Sigismund's reign. In this instance, the place was chosen so that the delegates elected by the diet could easily reach Vienna to negotiate with the Austrian estates.[75] After the unsuccessful negotiations another diet was called to Buda. The political situation changed rapidly as, during the first days of the diet, Emperor Frederick III handed over Ladislas V to Ulrich of Cilli and the Hungarian barons. After long negotiations on the location of a diet, the estates finally gathered for the first time in years in the presence of the king, Ladislas V, in January 1453 in Pressburg.[76]

At the beginning of 1454 the diet was called to meet in Buda, but there were problems with the arrival of the estates because of the flood of the Danube.[77] Despite the belated arrival of some of the deputies and the king's absence, the diet went ahead in Buda. The decrees of the diet were issued in late January, which was soon followed by another diet in March. At the beginning of 1455, the diet met again in Buda where Ladislas V was also present.[78] Later that year another diet exceptionally met in Győr.[79] In 1456 the prelates and the barons of the country were again called to gather in the capital city. Peculiarly, the invitations to the diet sent to the towns of Bardejov and Pressburg referred to Pest

---

72   MNL OL DL 14 273 and DL 14 274.
73   MNL OL DL 89 985 and Knauz, *Az országos tanács*, pp. 95–97; further, Mályusz, "A magyar rendi," p. 91.
74   Mályusz, "A magyar rendi," p. 92.
75   MNL OL DL 44 615 and DL 14 518. See further, Mályusz, "A magyar rendi," pp. 93–94.
76   Antal Áldásy, "A magyar országgyűlés követsége V. Lászlóhoz 1452 október havában," [The legation of the Hungarian diet to Ladislas V in October 1452] *Századok* 44 (1910), pp. 554–562.
77   MNL OL DL 44 718. See also Andrea Kiss, *Floods and Long-Term Water-Level Changes in Medieval Hungary*, unpublished PhD dissertation (Budapest: CEU, 2011), pp. 308–309.
78   "Bude, in congregatione eorundem praelatorum et baronorum nostrorum" – MNL OL DL 14 921.
79   MNL OL DL 81 209; 81 210; DL 81 212. For the text of the latter, see *A zichi és vásonkeői*, ix, p. 501 (no 367). See also: MNL OL DL 106 542.

as the place of the diet[80] while those sent to the counties named Buda.[81] The diet in fact may have gathered in Buda (*praelatis ac magnatibus baronibus hic Budae*).[82] The last diet called by Ladislas V was in spring 1457 when according to one mandate the nobility should have met in Pest and Rákos. This diet was then postponed and there were attempts by the king to hold a meeting of the estates in Pressburg.[83] The diet was again postponed and then the situation changed radically with the sudden death of Ladislas on 27 November 1457.

After the death of Ladislas Posthumus, the diet for the election of a new king met in Pest in January 1458: *in hac presenti congregatione generali eorundem in Civitate Pestiensi celebrata.*[84] It was from here that in the oft-described way the enthusiastic lesser nobility and the citizenry marched on to the frozen Danube – so to say in the middle between the twin cities – and "acclaimed" the son of the hero of the Ottoman wars, Matthias Hunyadi, as king. (We know that the deals leading to this were worked out in many other places between the leading families, and finally the lords decided in the castle of Buda to call home the young Matthias from Prague.) The legendary scene on the Danube, so frequently depicted by painters and described by poets appeared quite early in historical writing. The humanist archbishop of Esztergom, Miklós Oláh, already mentions it in his mid-sixteenth-century *Hungaria*.[85]

In the spring of 1458 the nobility was called to a diet in Pest and the decree of the diet was also issued there.[86] Matthias, however, stayed in Buda during its course, which make it possible that the diet indeed took place again on both sides of the Danube, the lesser nobility being encamped on the Field of Rákos,

---

80   Knauz, *Az országos tanács*, p. 148.
81   MNL OL DL 55 587 and 55 588. See also Knauz, *Az országos tanács*, p. 102.
82   MNL OL DL 15 008.
83   MNL OL DL 44 838; see Mályusz, "A magyar rendi," pp. 102–104.
84   MNL OL DF 270 347 edited in József Teleki, *Hunyadiak kora Magyarországon*, x [The age of the Hunyadis in Hungary] (Pest: Emich, 1853), pp. 570–571 (no 277). For the decrees accepted here, see DRMH, iii, pp. 1–3, which is the decree issued by the uncle of King Matthias, Mihály Szilágyi, as regent.
85   Nicolaus Olahus, *Hungaria – Athila*, eds Colomannus Eperjessy and Ladislaus Juhász (Budapest: Egyetemi Nyomda, 1938), cap. 10.
86   On the political situation and the diets of the period, see Tamás Pálosfalvi, "Szegedtől Újvárig. Az 1458–1459. esztendők krónikájához," [From Szeged to Újvár. On the history of 1458 and 1459] *Századok* 147 (2013), pp. 347–380. The diet met between 25 July and 5 August. See Norbert C. Tóth, "Nádorváltás 1458-ban. Mátyás király első országgyűlésének időpontja," [The change of the palatine in 1458. The date of the first diet of King Matthias] *Turul* 84 (2011), pp. 98–101.

and the barons and prelates along with the king in the Buda Castle.[87] In 1459 the diet met elsewhere than the capital, in Szeged, where the king was also present.[88] In 1460 a diet was held again far from the capital of the country, at Eger, where Matthias, the governor Mihály Szilágyi, and the voivode of Transylvania were all present, which suggests a meeting of national importance.[89] In June 1462 a diet met in Buda.[90] The mandate of Matthias for this diet sent to László Töttös includes an exceptional reference to the location of the diet. The king invited Töttös either to Pest or to Buda (*in civitate nostra Budensi vel Pestiensi*) for the diet which implies that by this time the exact location of the diet was again decided only according to the number of participants.[91] As mentioned above, the diet of 1463 was held further away from the capital, in Tolna, where the nobility was called for a campaign against the Ottomans.[92] In 1464 the coronation diet was held, as usual, in Székesfehérvár.[93] The 1465 diet was called to Buda.[94] At the beginning of 1466, the prelates and the barons of the country (*prelatis et baronibus nostris in opido Tolnavar*) again gathered at Tolnavár after a campaign towards the southern borderlands against the Ottomans.[95] In 1467 a diet was again held in Buda.[96] The diet of 1468 in Pressburg met immediately after the king returned from his campaign to Bohemia.[97] At the beginning of December 1470 a diet met in Buda[98] as well as in the two succeeding years in late spring.[99] The diet of 1471 is worth noting, for it was

---

87 DRMH, iii, pp. 4–8 and DRH 1458–1490, pp. 88–106. See also Horváth, *Itineraria*, p. 63.
88 See MOL DF 213 742 and DL 81 324. For the decrees of the diet: DRMH, iii, pp. 9–14 and DRH 1458–1490, pp. 107–118.
89 Horváth, *Itineraria*, p.66.
90 For the decrees of the diet: DRMH, iii, pp. 15–17 and DRH 1458–1490, pp. 123–127. See also Horváth, *Itineraria*, p. 70.
91 MNL OL DL81 495; edited in *A zichi és vásonkeői*, x, pp. 221–222 (no 170). See also András Kubinyi, "A magyar országgyűlések tárgyalási rendje 1445–1526," [The order of discussions at the Hungarian diet, 1445–1526] *Jogtörténeti Szemle* 8, no 2 (2006), pp. 3–11, here p. 5.
92 Horváth, *Itineraria*, p. 73. For the decrees of the diet, see DRH 1458–1490, pp. 134–139.
93 DRH 1458–1490, pp. 142–150 and DRMH, iii, pp. 18–23. See as also Bonfini's account of the coronation in Bonfini, *Decades*, IV-I-1.
94 Martinus Georgius Kovacich, *Supplementum ad Vestigia Comitiorum*, ii (Buda: Typis ac Sumptibus Typographiae Regiae Universitatis Pestiensis, 1800), p. 175.
95 DRH 1458–1490, p. 158.
96 DRH 1458–1490, pp. 162–168 and DRMH, iii, pp. 71–72.
97 DRH 1458–1490, pp. 174–178. See also Mór Wertner, "Magyar hadjáratok a xv. században," [Hungarian military campaigns in the fifteenth century] *Hadtörténeti Közlemények* 12 (1912), pp. 201–231, here p. 208.
98 DRH 1458–1490, pp. 184–189.
99 For 1472, see DRH 1458–1490, pp. 205–209.

one of the two occasions after the coronation in 1464 when the nobility was called to be present personally and not represented by envoys. It was obviously intended to demonstrate the power of Matthias after the conspiracy of János Vitéz.[100] The fact that the whole of the nobility was present makes it clear that Buda was only the place where the decrees were issued and that it was not the place where the lesser nobles gathered. We should note here that meetings of the diet at this time excluded representatives of the kingdom's townsfolk. An important exception was in 1475 when the towns (and the nobles personally) were invited to the diet at Buda.[101]

A diet gathered in Buda in April 1472.[102] In 1474 a diet was held in Buda, but the king did not attend. His call for the diet was issued in Opava, and his role in this case was simply one of approving the decisions of the estates.[103] The next year the estates again gathered in Buda, this time with the king present.[104]

In the spring of 1476[105] and in March 1478 and again in 1481 diets were held in Buda.[106] The decree given in 1481 was issued there and a charter of István Bátori, chief justice of Hungary, mentions the prelates and barons being gathered "here in Buda" (*hic Bude*).[107] The next year the diet met again in Buda,[108] and since the towns were not invited and the nobility were represented by deputies, the castle and city seem to have provided enough space for the gathering. The *Decretum maius* of Matthias Corvinus was issued after a diet again held in Buda at the end of 1485 (the decree was issued 25 January 1486).[109] In 1488 three diets were held within a relatively short period of time. These diets

---

100   András Kubinyi, "A Mátyás-kori államszervezet," [The administrative system during Matthias's reign] in *Emlékkönyv Mátyás király halálának 500. évfordulójára* [Memorial volume for the 500th anniversary of the death of King Matthias Corvinus], eds Gyula Rázsó and László V. Molnár (Budapest: Zrínyi, 1990), pp. 53–145, here pp. 79–80, and Kubinyi, "Tárgyalási rend," p. 4. For the decrees of 1471, see DRH 1458–1490, pp. 190–202 and DRMH, iii, pp. 24–28.
101   DRH 1458–1490, pp. 223–226.
102   Kovacich, *Supplementum ad Vestigia Comitiorum*, ii, p. 213.
103   For the decrees: DRMH, iii, pp. 29–31 and 98.
104   DRH 1458–1490, pp. 223–226. For the diet that took place in Buda, see MNL OL DL 17 677.
105   DRH 1458–1490, pp. 229–230, and Horváth, *Itineraria*, pp. 104–105. For the decrees, see DRH 1458–1490, pp. 231–234.
106   DRH 1458–1490, pp. 235–243, and DRMH, iii, pp. 32–35.
107   MNL OL DL 30 903. For the decrees, see: DRH 1458–1490, pp. 246–251 and DRMH, iii, pp. 36–40.
108   DRH 1458–1490, pp. 255–257.
109   For the diet, see MNL OL DL 39 323. For the decree: DRH 1458–1490, pp. 265–321 and DRMH, iii, pp. 41–69.

were meant to come to an agreement regarding the tax levy and Matthias was present at none of these.[110] The last diet of Matthias' reign took place in 1489 when the prelates and barons met again in Buda.[111]

After the death of King Matthias, the political situation became unstable. The election of a new king was a key issue from the very first moment. In these years, the Field of Rákos became the central scene of political events as the general assemblies during the last turbulent decades of the Jagiellonian age were usually held there.[112] The summons of the diet took place immediately after the death of King Matthias. The nobility met for the election diet in the spring of 1490, at Rákos, while the lords and prelates held council in Buda Castle. (This was to be, and perhaps had been for some time earlier, the typical procedure, thus foreshadowing the upper and lower house of the Hungarian diet, formalized only in the seventeenth century.) The two 'estates' in 1490 then met in Pest to hear the representations of the foreign emissaries.[113] Since Buda Castle was in the hands of Matthias's natural son, John Corvin, and his adherents were encamped at Rákos, the opposing party, supporting Wladislas Jagiello the later Wladislas II, planned to attack the castle. They finally agreed to move the diet "to Pest," but no more precise information is known to us on the location chosen.[114] The three adjacent locations – Buda, Pest, and the Field of Rákos – were to be the 'battle grounds' over the subsequent decades, representing respectively the aristocracy (the royal council, the *prelati et barones*) on the one hand and the lesser nobility (often armed in great numbers) on the other.[115] In the Jagiellonian period the diets took place around these three locations, which became so self-evident that the call for the diet in 1505 ordered

---

110   See András Kubinyi, *Matthias Rex* (Budapest: Balassi, 2008), pp. 125–126.

111   DRH 1458–1490, pp. 327–328.

112   On the diets between 1490 and 1496, see Tibor Neumann, "Királyi hatalom és országgyűlés a Jagelló-kor elején," [Royal power and the diet at the beginning of the Jagiellonian period] in *Rendiség és parlamentarizmus*, pp. 46–54. On the problem of the diets held in the second half of the reign of Wladislas II, see Gábor Mikó, "Ismeretlen országgyűlési emlék a Jagelló-korból" [An unknown parliamentary record from the Jagiellonian period] *Történelmi Szemle* 56 (2014), pp. 455–480.

113   *Magyar diplomacziai emlékek Mátyás király korából, 1458–1490*, iv [Hungarian diplomatic records from age of King Matthias], eds Iván Nagy and Albert Nyáry (Budapest: MTA, 1878), p. 221 (no 154) and p. 227 (no 157).

114   Dezső Szabó, *Küzdelmeink a nemzeti királyságért 1505–1526* [Struggles for a national monarchy 1505–1526] (Budapest: Franklin, 1917), p. 89, based on a manuscript copy of reports from Poland.

115   For an overview, see Szabó, *Küzdelmeink*, and idem, *A magyar országgyűlések története II. Lajos korában* [History of the diets in the age of Louis II] (Budapest: Hornyánszky, 1909).

the nobility to gather simply "here".[116] By the early sixteenth century the two 'chambers' communicated in writing with each other, as was proven recently by Gábor Mikó.[117]

Considering that from many meetings of the diet only the royal charters containing the decrees survived – and these are usually dated from the king's chancellery in Buda – we do not always know where the assembly actually took place. Nonetheless, it is not inappropriate to state that most of the diets, once they were more or less regularly held, met in Buda or its surroundings.

This is not the place to discuss the history of the tumultuous diets of the early sixteenth century. In the 36 years following the death of Matthias, the nobility was called to a diet 43 times at least, and these were mostly held simultaneously in Buda and the field beyond the walls of Pest. The conflicts between the factions of the nobility[118] occasionally reached the point of armed confrontation. In May 1519, the nobles demanded that the lords come down to them to Rákos, which they refused. Thereupon, they tried to take the castle by a surprise attack, which, of course, failed. (We know that in 1525 the castellan of Buda kept 300 soldiers in arms for its defense; hardly any fewer would have been present before.[119]) After their failure, most of the nobles left and the king's candidate for count palatine, the highest officer of the realm, for whose election the diet had been called, was elected by a mere 55 votes.[120] There were a few other instances, too, when the nobles appeared at the gates of Buda, but were refused entry. For instance in 1516 John Szapolyai (the future King John I) and his men chased them away.

During the last years of the independent Hungarian kingdom, the already noted elements of the future bicameral diet became more evident, now connected with the two locations on both sides of the Danube.[121] In May 1525,

---

116 "tu eiuscemodi diaetae et congregationi regnicolarum nostrorum ad praefatum diem festi L. omnino interesse et huc ad nos absque armis venire velis nec aliqua ratione te excuses" – Bódog Schiller, *Az örökös főrendiség eredete Magyarországon* [The origin of the hereditary aristocracy in medieval Hungary] (Budapest: Kilián, 1900), pp. 317–318 (no 3).

117 Gábor Mikó, "Ismeretlen országgyűlési emlék".

118 See Martyn Rady, "Jagello Hungary," in, DRMH, iv, pp. xi–xlvii, here pp. xxiv–xliv. See also Bak, *Königtum*, pp. 62–70.

119 Vilmos Fraknói, "II. Lajos király számadási könyve, 1525. január 12–július 16," [The account book of Louis II, 12 January to 16 June 1525] *Magyar Történelmi Tár* 6 (1876), pp. 47–236, here p. 150.

120 Marino Sanuto, *I Diarii*, xxviii (Venice: Visentini, 1890), pp. 386, quoted in Szabó, *Küzdelmeink*, p. 171.

121 For the events of these years, see András Kubinyi, "Országgyűlési küzdelmek Magyarországon 1523–1525-ben," [Parliamentary struggles in Hungary in 1523–1525] in

the king sent a prelate and a baron to the nobles at Rákos to present the royal propositions, which mainly concerned the defense of the realm from the ever growing Ottoman threat. (Belgrade, the linchpin of the southern defense had fallen in 1521 and Hungary was virtually open to invasion.) The nobles promised to reply within a day. On the Saturday, a delegation of sixty noblemen went up to Buda, but instead of responding to the king's agenda, they presented their complaints (*gravamina*). (This procedure then became typical until the nineteenth century.) The nobles protested the 'foreign counselors' of the king and demanded a reform of the royal council in favor of the lesser nobles. King Louis II replied that he needed time to reply and he promised to deliver his response the following week. The nobles were dissatisfied with the king's procrastination and failure to promise any reform. They shouted that they would not be cheated. The next day the nobles requested, unusually, that Louis come to them on the field, otherwise they would make decisions without him. A delegation of 120 went up to Buda to invite the king. Even though his counselors and the papal legate opposed the move, on the Wednesday the king appeared at 5'o clock a.m. (our only reference to the beginning of meetings of the diet!) in Rákos.[122] While honorably received, he was asked why the decisions of the previous diet (about the foreigners) had not been implemented, to which he replied that, "It was not me!", and left. Next day, the lords accused the nobles of leaving them out of negotiations, whereupon they were told to come to Rákos themselves. Finally, the nobles decided to call a new diet at Hatvan, planning to gather there armed in great numbers on an open field. The decrees of that diet were not, however, approved by the king. The diet of the independent kingdom of medieval Hungary met for the last time – just four months before the disaster at Mohács – in Buda and on the Field of Rákos.

Alas, the urban records of Buda and Pest did not survive the Ottoman centuries, thus we have no such records as there are in the Holy Roman Empire or the British Isles, recording the 'mundane' circumstances of diets and parliaments. We know nothing about the 'logistics' of all this, such as the housing of the delegates (or the masses of those present), their supplies, their relationship to the townsmen, and so on. Neither have images of the diet in session, like those of the Polish sejm (from the early sixteenth century) or from other countries, come down to us.

Honoris causa: tanulmányok Engel Pál tiszteletére [Honoris causa. Studies in honor of Pál Engel], eds Tibor Neumann and György Rácz (Budapest and Piliscsaba: MTA Történettudományi Intézet – PPKE BTK, 2009), pp. 125–148.

122 See Szabó, *Küzdelmeink*, p. 81 and idem, *A magyar országgyűlések*, p. 203.

The only document, in any way comparable to those records, is a house conscription ordered by Sigismund of Luxemburg in 1437, which he prepared for the Council of Basle. In this, the emperor listed the facilities of Buda, proposing that the city would be able to accommodate the participants should the Council be relocated for political reasons from the Swiss town.[123] The figures suggest that a diet in Buda could have been held even with a sizable number of participants. According to the survey, the castle itself and the suburbs had 1235 rooms and there was enough stable space for almost 4000 horses. These numbers suggest that there were sufficient facilities to accommodate a diet if the members of the nobility were present only through delegates, even taking into account the entourages of the prelates and barons. However, Buda including its suburbs would not have been able to host the thousands of nobles who appeared at some of the assemblies, especially in the later Middle Ages – hence, we suppose, the move to the open fields well beyond the walls of Pest.

In summary, then, we have seen that in spite of the occasional gathering of members of the 'political nation' at another location (mostly for military reasons) diets and synods between the 1290s and 1526 were held in the center of the realm, either in Buda, Pest or the fields around the latter.[124] The only important exceptions were the coronation diets held in Székesfehérvár.[125] There was no competition, like that between Frankfurt and Nuremberg, and holding a diet elsewhere in protest or opposition to a part of the assembly (usually the aristocracy) was, just as in Poland, a rarity (e.g. the diets in Pressburg during Sigismund's reign or the Hatvan diet in 1442 and 1525). In this way, the meeting of the estates in or around Buda enhanced its development as the capital city of the kingdom.

---

[123] For the text of the conscription, see František Palacký, *Urkundliche Beiträge zur Geschichte des Hussitenkrieges vom Jahre 1419 an*, ii. *Von den Jahren 1429–1436* (Prague: Tempsky, 1873), pp. 473–475. For the political background of the planned transfer of the council see Antal Áldásy, "A baseli zsinat áthelyezése Budára," [The relocation of the Council of Basle to Buda] *Budapest Régiségei* 7 (1900), pp. 99–114.

[124] András Kubinyi, "Buda, Magyarország középkori fővárosa," [Buda, the capital of medieval Hungary] *Tanulmányok Budapest Múltjából* 29 (2001), pp. 11–22. See the English version of the article in the present volume.

[125] On the coronation diet of 1440 in Székesfehérvár, see also János M. Bak, "'Good king Polish Ladislas…' History and memory of the short reign of Władysław Warneńczyk in Hungary," in *Central and Eastern Europe in the Middle Ages. A Cultural History* (*Essays in Honour of Paul W. Knoll*), eds Piotr Górecki and Nancy van Deusen (London–New York: I.B. Tauris, 2009), pp. 176–183 and 278–281. It may be worth noting that the burghers of Buda held the privilege of guarding the gates of the coronation church in Székesfehérvár. For this, see the fifteenth century OSt, p. 61 (cap. 6) and p. 119 (cap. 166).

Appendix

Protocollum Budense No 3^{tium} Ab Anno 1510 usque 1522 conscriptum (MNL OL DL 106 083. *No 241;* [*p. 145*] *18 April 1512*)

Item nobilis Gallus de Mÿskolcz provisor curie religiosarum dominarum sanctimonialium de insula leporum nominibus et in personis earundem dominarum sanctimonialium nostram personaliter veniens in presentiam per modum protestationis et inhibitionis nobis significare curavit in hunc modum, quod licet forum pecorum ab olim, cuius initium memoria hominis non comprehendit, in civitate Pesthiensi prope scilicet portam Hathwan kapw celebrari solitum fuerit et consuetum, theloniumque seu tributum exinde provenire debentia prefatis dominabus sanctimonialibus solvere debuerunt, tamen nunc circumspecti iudex et iurati cives dicti civitatis Pesthiensis, nescitur quo ducti spiritu aut quo freti consilio, dictum forum pecorum non ibi, scilicet in loco consueto, sed ad alium locum, videlicet ad campum Rakos, ubi utputa eedem domine sanctimoniales nihil penitus thelonii aut aliquid emolumenti habere possunt, transtulerunt ac fieri et celebrari facere curaverunt in preiudicium et dampnum iurisque derogamen ipsarum dominarum sanctimonialium protestantium valde magnum, unde facta huiusmodi protestatione idem Gallus Mÿskolczÿ nominibus et in personis quarum supra memoratos iudicem et iuratos cives dicti civittatis [sic!] Pesthiensis ab alienatione et quavis translatione dicti fori a loco pretacto, quolibet iam factis vel fiendis prohibuit contradicendo et contradixit inhibendo publice et manifeste coram nobis harum nostrarum vigore et testimonio literarum mediante. Datum in dominica quasi modo Anno domini 1512.

CHAPTER 14

Royal Summits in and around Medieval Buda

Balázs Nagy

The Context of Medieval Royal Meetings

Royal summits as international meetings of rulers were not typical instruments of medieval diplomacy. Although historiography has explored many details of the typology of royal meetings and compiled lists of them, these works usually concentrate on the diplomatic and political factors, rituals and ceremonies, but do not always explore the interactions of a summit and the place where it happened.[1] This is especially true in the case of political meetings held in East Central Europe. The royal centers around and in Buda were locations of royal meetings in Hungary throughout the Middle Ages, but their roles are underrepresented in the historical literature.

The ceremonies followed at the medieval royal meetings had a prevailing custom and traditionally fixed way of representation. The parity of the participants' status at the meeting was demonstrated by the reception of the visiting ruler. At monarchic summits the first and last moments of the rulers' encounter had a special importance, emphasized also by rituals. The first meeting might be marked by the ritual kiss of the rulers and the celebration of the reception of the arriving party and the departure by the transmission of gifts.[2] Dining and taking part together at church ceremonies are also typical elements of medieval royal meetings.[3]

Some of the well-known political meetings in the Middle Ages have had an extensive discussion in the historical literature. The well-known meetings of

---

1 Ingrid Voss, *Herrschertreffen im frühen und hohen Mittelalter: Untersuchungen zu den Begegnungen der ostfränkischen und westfränkischen Herrscher im 9. und 10. Jahrhundert sowie der deutschen und französischen Könige vom 11. bis 13. Jahrhundert* (Beihefte zum Archiv für Kulturgeschichte; 26) (Köln: Böhlau 1987); John B. Gillingham, "The Meetings of the Kings of France and England, 1066–1204," in *Normandy and its Neighbours, 900 – 1250*, eds David Crouch and Kathleen Thompson (Turnhout: Brepols, 2011), pp. 17–42; Gerald Schwedler, *Herrschertreffen des Spätmittelalters: Formen, Rituale, Wirkungen* (Mittelalter-Forschungen; 21) (Ostfildern: Thorbecke 2008).

2 On the ritual and symbolism of kissing in the Middle Ages, see: Kiril Petkov, *The Kiss of Peace: Ritual, Self, and Society in the High and Late Medieval West* (Leiden: Brill, 2003).

3 Schwedler, *Herrschertreffen*, pp. 331–403.

Charlemagne and Leo III in Paderborn and in Rome, for example, had long-term consequences for the relationship of the papacy and the Carolingian Empire.[4] The early history of the Holy Roman Empire is also connected with a well-known political meeting at the imperial diet of Quedlinburg in 973. Here Otto I welcomed the rulers and representatives of various European countries just a few weeks before his death.[5] He intended to present his imperial power before his German vassals, his previously enthroned son, Otto II, and various foreign dignitaries. The location of Quedlinburg represented the dynastic power of the Ottonians, thus this summit was particularly significant for all the participants.

Not much later, another political meeting shaped the formation and Christianisation of East Central Europe. In the year 1000, Otto III visited Gniezno, one of the emerging centers of the early Polish state, and met Bolesław I Chrobry at the tomb of St Adalbert of Prague.[6] Since the historical literature has widely discussed the political consequences of this meeting, here it is enough to refer to some other aspects of the event. Gniezno lay in the center of the heartland of the early Polish state, an eminent place for the emergence of the Piast dynasty in tenth- and eleventh-century Poland. The participants, Emperor Otto III, Bolesław I Chrobry, with the symbolic presence of the relics of St Adalbert, made this meeting one of the most significant events in early medieval Poland.

Early Royal Meetings in Hungary

Turning to the history of the royal meetings in medieval Hungary, one should remember that Buda as a royal residence and the site of several royal meetings cannot be examined only in itself, without its broader environs. Buda

---

4   *799: Kunst und Kultur der Karolingerzeit: Karl der Große und Papst Leo III. in Paderborn; Katalog der Ausstellung Paderborn 1999*, 3 vols, eds Christoph Stiegemann and Matthias Wemhoff (Mainz: Philipp von Zabern, 1999); Johannes Fried, "Papst Leo III. besucht Karl den Großen in Paderborn oder Einhards Schweigen," *Historische Zeitschrift* 272 (2001), pp. 281–326.
5   *Der Hoftag in Quedlinburg 973. Von den historischen Wurzeln zum Neuen Europa*, ed. Andreas Ranft (Berlin: Akademie-Verlag, 2006).
6   Out of the vast literature on the Gniezno meeting see among others: Johannes Fried, *Otto III. und Boleslaw Chrobry. Das Widmungsbild des Aachener Evangeliars, der "Akt von Gnesen" und das frühe polnische und ungarische Königtum* (Stuttgart: Steiner, 2001); Zofia Kurnatowska, "The Stronghold in Gniezno in the Light of Older and more Recent Studies," in *Polish Lands at the Turn of the First and the Second Millenia*, ed. Przemyslaw Urbańczyk (Warsaw: Instytut Archeologii i Etnologii Polskiej Akademii Nauk, 2004) pp. 185–206.

became a permanent royal residence only in the early fifteenth century, but its wider hinterland already played a role in the administration of the country in an earlier period. The concept of the *medium regni* has been discussed in the scholarly literature from the 1960s as well as in several studies in the present volume, and the conclusions were that the center of the realm played a special role in the organization of the country from as early as the period of state foundation.[7] Esztergom, Székesfehérvár, and Óbuda are located in the central region of the county, and the furthest distance between them was no more than 80 km. Two of these three centers, Esztergom and Óbuda lay on the Danube, both at convenient crossing points on the river. Besides the three main points at the *medium regni* a good number of other settlements offered residences and hunting places for the royal court, Dömös and Visegrád being the most important of these.[8]

Both Conrad III (1138–1152), the king of the Germans, and Louis VII (1137–1180), the king of France, crossed Hungary in 1147 on their way to the second crusade.[9] Their journeys through Hungary were recorded by Otto of Freising and Odo of Deuil (Diogilo), respectively.[10] The French king met King Géza II of Hungary, and we may assume that this meeting happened in Esztergom, the royal residence at the time. Odo Deuil recorded some details of the talks between these two monarchs, e.g., the intervention of Louis VII on behalf of Boris, pretender to the throne, even mutual friendly royal gestures, but the place where they met is not mentioned in any of the sources.[11] One generation later, in 1172, Henry the Lion (1156–1180), duke of Bavaria, and Henry II (1141–1177), duke of Austria, called Jasomirgott, went on a pilgrimage to Jerusalem and on their way to the Holy Land they also stopped in Esztergom, hoping to meet

---

[7] Besides the volume *Medium regni* see also the comments of several authors of this volume on the concept of *medium regni*. E.g. the chapters of Péter Szabó, Károly Magyar, András Végh, Beatrix Romhányi, János M. Bak and András Vadas, András Kubinyi and Katalin Szende.

[8] *The Medieval Royal Palace at Visegrád* (Archaeolingua. Main Series, 27), eds Gergely Buzás and József Laszlovszky (Budapest: Archaeolingua, 2013).

[9] Zsolt Hunyadi, "Hungary and the Second Crusade," *Chronica* 9–10 (2009–2010), pp. 55–65.

[10] On Odo Deuil see: Beate Schuster, "The Strange Pilgrimage of Odo of Deuil," in *Medieval Concepts of Past: Ritual, Memory, Historiography*, eds Gerd Althoff, Johannes Fried and Patrick Geary (New York: Cambridge University Press, 2002), pp. 253–278; Jonathan Phillips, "Odo of Deuil's *De profectione Ludovici VII in orientem* as a source for the Second Crusade," in *The Experience of Crusading. vol. 1: Western Approaches*, eds Norman Housley and Marcus Bull (Cambridge: Cambridge University Press, 2003), pp. 80–95.

[11] *Monumenta Germaniae Historica, Scriptores*, xxvi, ed. Georg Waitz (Hannover: Hahn, 1882), p. 63.

the king of Hungary, Stephen III, who unfortunately died right before their arrival.[12]

Frederick I Barbarossa (1152–1190) passed through Hungary on the third crusade and met Béla III in 1189.[13] At that time, the formal reception of the emperor was held in Esztergom; all the representation and political talks, a meeting with the queen of Hungary, happened there, but the two monarchs also visited Óbuda, the supposed seat of Attila, and spent two days hunting there.[14] Óbuda by that time was a settlement of special interest because of a royal mansion built there and the St Peter's chapter, which originated in the first half of the eleventh century. Ansbert, who (besides Arnold of Lübeck) gives an account of the stay of Frederick I Barbarossa in Hungary similarly describes the events in his work on the emperor's crusade.[15] He also confirms that the main meeting of Frederick I and the king of Hungary happened in Esztergom, but also touches upon their hunting together. According to Ansbert, Béla III "entertained the emperor for two days on a broad island on the Danube with hospitality and hunting."[16] Ansbert refers certainly refers to Csepel Island,

---

12 Gyula Pauler, A *magyar nemzet története* az *Árpádházi királyok alatt*, 2 vols [The History of the Hungarian Nation under the Árpádian kings] (2nd ed. Athenaeum: Budapest, 1899) i, p. 320.

13 On the stay of Frederick I Barbarossa in Hungary, see the study by Enikő Spekner in the present volume. See also: Balázs Nagy, "The Towns of Medieval Hungary in the Reports of Contemporary Travellers," in *Segregation – Integration – Assimilation. Religious and Ethnic Groups in the Medieval Towns of Central and Eastern Europe* (Historical Urban Studies), eds Derek Keene, Balázs Nagy and Katalin Szende (Farnham: Ashgate, 2009), pp. 169–178.

14 "Inde domnus inperator a rege deductus est in urbem Adtile dictam, ubi domnus imperator quatuor diebus venationi operam dedit." Arnoldi Chronica Slavorum – *Monumenta Germaniae Historica, Scriptores Rerum Germanicarum in usum Scholarum*, xiv, ed. Georgius Henricus Pertz (Hannover: Hahn, 1868), iv. 8. (De peregrinatione imperatoris) pp. 130.

15 On Ansbert, see: Marie Bláhová, "Ansbert," in *The Encyclopedia of the Medieval Chronicle*, ed. Graeme Dunphy (Leiden–Boston: Brill, 2010), pp. 104; Graham A. Loud, "Introduction," in idem, *The Crusade of Frederick Barbarossa* (Farnham: Ashgate, 2010), pp. 1–31, here pp. 2–3.

16 "Preterea in *insula sua familiari et uenatica*, que Danubio cingente satis late extenditur, per duos dies imperatorem detinuit" – Hippolyt Tauschinski and Matthias Pangerl, eds, *Ystoria de expeditione Friderici I imperatoris*, in *Codex Strahoviensis. Enthält den Bericht des sogenannten Ansbert über den Kreuzzug Kaiser Friedrich's I. und die Chroniken des Domherrn Vincentius von Prag und des Abtes Gerlach von Mühlhausen* (Fontes rerum Austriacarum, i, Abteilung, Scriptores, 5) (Vienna: Kaiserlich-Königliche Hof- und Staatsdruckerei, 1863), pp. 1–90, here p. 19; English translation: "The History of the Expedition of the Emperor Frederick," in Loud, *The Crusade of Frederick Barbarossa*, pp. 33–134, here p. 58.

48 km long, with the northern end in the territory of modern Budapest, about 6 km south of medieval Buda. From the earliest times Csepel Island, known as *Magna Insula* in the Middle Ages, had a strong connection to the royal court as a hunting ground, summer residence, and place of the royal stud-stable.[17] Thus, it was a plausible decision to invite Frederick I Barbarossa and his entourage to Óbuda and the nearby Csepel Island for hunting.

The royal estate on Csepel Island was used not much later again for a diplomatic meeting. In 1203, King Emeric met here the representatives of the Bogumils from Bosnia, who vowed to abandon their earlier denomination and accept the Catholic hierarchy.[18]

The intensification of the foreign policy and activity of King Andrew II towards the Balkans and towards the Latin Empire in the 1210s is seen in the marriage of the king and Yolanda de Courtenay, the daughter of Peter II of Courtenay, the Latin emperor. Thus, Andrew II was the brother-in-law of Robert Courtenay (1221–1228), the next Latin emperor. Robert traveled through Hungary on his way to his imperial coronation on 25 March 1221. During his journey, he spent some months in Hungary in the winter of 1220–1221 and was accompanied by Andrew II and his first-born son, Béla, to Constantinople in early 1221. Unfortunately not much is known about the activity of the future Latin emperor in Hungary, but his prolonged stay certainly reflected the importance of the connections between him and Andrew II.[19] All the examples

17   ÁMTF, iv, pp. 189–193.
18   Pauler, A *magyar nemzet története*, ii, p. 30; ÁMTF, iv, p. 198. "Actum in insula regia" – Augustin Theiner, *Vetera monumenta Slavorum meridionalium historiam (sacram) illustrantia maximam partem nondum edita ex tabulariis Vaticanis deprompta, collecta ac serie chronologiia disposita*, i (Rome: Typis Vaticanis, 1863), p. 20.
19   Attila Bárány, "Courtenay Róbert latin császár Magyarországon," [Robert Courtenay, Emperor of the Latin Empire in Hungary] in *Francia-magyar kapcsolatok a középkorban* [French-Hungarian Contacts in the Middle Ages] (Speculum Historiae Debreceniense, 13), eds Attila Györkös and Gergely Kiss (Debrecen: Debrecen University Press, 2013), pp. 153–180; Pauler, *A magyar nemzet története*, ii, pp. 75–76. Some hypotheses in the historical literature assume that a tombstone excavated in Pilisszentkereszt after 1967 might mark the burial place of the Latin emperor, Robert Courtenay, who died in Morea in 1228. Irrespective of whether this hypotheses can be proved or not, the significance of the Pilisszentkereszt Cistercian abbey is unquestionable. The Pilisszentkereszt abbey, located in the Pilis Mountains, was founded by King Béla III in 1184 and had a special importance and an exceptional connection to the royal court. Queen Gertrudis, assassinated in 1213 was also buried there. Ferenc Hervay, *Repertorium historicum ordinis Cisterciensis in Hungaria* (Bibliotheca cisterciensis, 7) (Rome: Editiones Cistercienses, 1984) pp. 141–153. For recent research on Queen Gertudis, see: *Egy történelmi gyilkosság margójára. Merániai Gertrúd emlékezete, 1213–2013*. [On the margin of a historical murder. The memory of

listed here demonstrate that there were several places in the central region of the country which might have offered a favorable location for a royal summit before the later emergence of Buda as a fully-fledged permanent royal residence.

After the Árpáds: New Contacts of the Angevin Rulers

The next period brought a significant change in the foreign policy of Hungary and consequently interrupted the visits of foreign rulers to the country. With the decline of the crusades in the Holy Land there was a decrease in the series of the military campaigns which had earlier taken some European monarchs to Hungary. The Mongol invasions in 1241 and 1242 also had a similar effect. The extinction of the Árpád dynasty in 1301 and the arrival of the Angevins as the ruling dynasty brought a new start, but of course in a very different political context. The Angevins had close family and political links with the Luxemburgs of Bohemia and the Piasts of Poland and thus the fourteenth century was characterized by meetings of different members of these dynasties.

King Charles I of the new ruling dynasty faced some difficulties at the beginning of his rule; he could not establish a stable permanent royal residence in the central region of the country. This was partly due to local hostilities in Buda and also because large territories of the country were ruled by oligarchs.[20] Under these circumstances, Charles decided to locate his residence in Timișoara, in the remote southeastern region of the country. It was quite an unusual decision, since all the significant royal residences before and after were located in the central part of the kingdom. Even so, Charles only kept temporary residence in Timișoara between 1315 and 1323, and there is no information that he held any diplomatic meeting there.[21] After the death of his chief opponent, Máté Csák, and after defeating the remaining major oligarchs, he decided to move his residence back to the central region of the country, but not to Buda, by that time the most significant town, but to Visegrád, 45 km north of Buda. In 1323 Charles I visited Visegrád and found that it would be a suitable location

Gertrudis of Meran, 1213–2013] (Ferenczy Múzeum kiadványai, A. Monográfiák, 2), eds Judit Majorossy (Szentendre: Ferenczy Múzeum, 2014).

20 István Petrovics, "The Fading Glory of a Former Royal Seat: the Case of Medieval Temesvár," in ...*the Man of Many Devices, Who Wandered Full Many Ways...: Festschrift in Honor of János M. Bak*, eds Balázs Nagy and Marcell Sebők (Budapest: CEU Press, 1999) pp. 527–538; Kubinyi, *Budapest*, pp. 43–44; Rady, *Buda*, pp. 35–37.

21 Petrovics "The Fading Glory," p. 530.

for a royal residence.[22] This decision was followed by an intensive period of building, in both the upper fortress and the royal palace, which made Visegrád a suitable place for meetings of diplomatic and political importance.[23]

The active foreign policy of Charles I towards his Central European partners in the 1330s resulted in several diplomatic meetings with John of Luxemburg of Bohemia (1310–1346) and Casimir III (the Great) of Poland (1333–1370). The main meeting in Visegrád in November 1335 was preceded by discussions in Sandomierz, in Lesser Poland, with representatives of John of Luxemburg and Casimir III of Poland in May 1335 and later, in August, in Trenčín between the envoys of the Hungarian, Polish and Bohemian rulers. One can see from these events that the preparatory meetings before the summit of the monarchs were used to outline the main points of the proceedings.

For the meeting in November 1335 Charles invited his Polish and Bohemian counterparts, Casimir III and John, and also the son of the latter, Charles, Margrave of Bohemia (the later Emperor Charles IV).[24] In addition, representatives of the Teutonic order, Duke Rudolf I of Saxe-Wittenberg, and Duke Bolesław III the Generous (Rozrzutny) of Legnica were present. Several political questions were discussed in Visegrád; John of Luxemburg finally withdrew his pretensions to the crown of Poland and in return Casimir III surrendered Silesia and agreed to pay him 20 thousand silver marks. Mediation between Poland and the Teutonic knights was also on the political agenda of the conference.[25]

Besides the talks and discussions the Hungarian monarch also intended to impress his guests and he succeeded in that; the memory of the meeting was

22 Pál Engel, "Az ország újraegyesítése. I. Károly küzdelmei az oligarchák ellen (1310–1323)," [Reuniting the country. The conflict of Charles I against the oligarchs (1310–1323)] in idem, *Honor, vár, ispánság. Válogatott tanulmányok* [Honor, castle, county. Collected essays], ed. Enikő Csukovits (Budapest: Osiris, 2003), pp. 320–408. here p. 351–354. (First published in *Századok* 122 [1988], pp. 89–147). pp. 128–132. Attila Zsoldos, "Kings and Oligarchs in Hungary at the Turn of the Thirteenth and Fourteenth Centuries," *The Hungarian Historical Review* 2 (2013), pp. 211–242.

23 On Visegrád in the period of Charles I see: Gergely Buzás, "History of the Visegrád Royal Palace," in *The Medieval Royal Palace at Visegrád*, pp. 17–140, here pp. 20–26.

24 On the context of the Visegrád meeting see: Balázs Nagy, "Transcontinental Trade from East-Central Europe to Western-Europe (Fourteenth and Fifteenth Centuries)," in *...The Man of Many Devices, Who Wandered Full Many Ways...*, pp. 347–356.

25 On the Visegrád conference in general, see: *Visegrád 1335: tudományos tanácskozás a visegrádi királytalálkozó 650. évfordulóján* [Visegrád 1335: Scholarly Conference on the 650th Anniversary of the Visegrád Royal Meeting], ed. József Köblös (Budapest: Egyetemi Nyomda, 1988); Stanisław Szczur, "Az 1335. évi visegrádi királyi találkozó," [The 1335 Royal Meeting at Visegrád] *Aetas* 1 (1993) pp. 26–42.

recorded in the medieval historiography of all the participating countries.[26] Alongside Francis of Prague, the fifteenth-century Polish historiographer Jan Długosz, Charles IV of Bohemia in his autobiography and John Thuróczy also included details of the meeting in their work.

The main documents of the meeting were issued on 19 November 1335, the feast of St Elizabeth, the patron saint of the queen of Hungary, wife of Charles I, sister of Casimir III of Poland. Thus, the date of the approval of the documents certainly also had a symbolic connotation.[27]

The meeting itself lasted for more than three weeks;[28] John Thuróczy gave the most precise information on the events of the meeting, commenting on the allowances given to the participants and their entourages. According to this text, 2500 loaves of bread were given to the delegation of the king of Bohemia and 1500 loaves of bread to the king of Poland. Besides these, other foodstuffs, sufficient amounts of wine, and fodder for the horses of the delegations were offered as well. John Thuróczy gave an overview of the royal gifts, especially jewellery, given to the king of Bohemia. It included 50 silver jars, two quivers, two belts, a magnificent chess board, two valuable saddles, a knife with a belt worth 200 silver marks, and an elaborate pearl-oyster.[29] This description shows that the gifts were usual requisites of a royal summit.

On the basis of the bread and wine consumption mentioned by Thuróczy, György Rácz attempted a reconstruction of the number of participants of the various delegations and calculated the total number of the participants of the congress around 10,000 people.[30] This mass must have been a major challenge for housing and provisioning all the delegates, particularly since the upper castle, the lower castle, and the royal house in Visegrád were in an underdeveloped form at the time of the royal conference, before the next building period under the reign of Louis I. After the departure of the participants from

---

26   György Rácz, "The Congress of Visegrád," in *Visegrád 1335*, ed. idem (Budapest: International Visegrad Fund – State Archives of Hungary – Pázmány Péter Catholic University, 2009), pp. 17–29, here p. 23; György Rácz, "The Congress of Visegrád in 1335: Diplomacy and Representation," *The Hungarian Historical Review* 2 2 (2013), pp. 261–287, here pp. 266–270.

27   Rácz, "The Congress of Visegrád in 1335," p. 271.

28   Rácz, "The Congress of Visegrád in 1335," p. 274.

29   Johannes de Thurocz, *Chronica Hungarorum* (Bibliotheca Scriptorum Medii Recentisque Aevorum. Series Nova, 7), eds Elisabeth Galántai and Julius Kristó (Budapest: Akadémiai, 1985), pp. 152–153 (cap. 124). For the English translation of the text, see: Rácz, "The Congress of Visegrád in 1335," p. 270.

30   Rácz, "The Congress of Visegrád in 1335," p. 282. For the English translations of the documents of the Visegrád meeting see: *Visegrád 1335*, pp. 140–141, p. 156, pp. 167–168.

the Visegrád meeting some further royal decisions were made based on the agreements reached during the talks. One example is the decree of Charles I determining a route running from Hungary to Bohemia with the fixing of the taxes payable *en route*.[31]

The congress of Visegrád was soon followed by other meetings of the Polish and Hungarian rulers. Only a few months later, the next meeting was held at Marchegg, on the Morava River, where they united their forces against the duke of Austria.[32] In the summers of 1338 and 1339, Casimir III again visited Visegrád with his entourage, met Charles I, and agreed that the son of Charles I would succeed Casimir III on the Polish throne if he died without a male heir.[33]

Other purposes served as occasions for royal meetings as well. One month after the death of Charles I of Hungary, on 16 June 1342, Casimir III of Poland and Margrave Charles of Moravia, the later Charles IV (1346–1378), visited the burial place of the late king in Székesfehérvár, paid a visit also to Visegrád, and took part in a memorial ceremony.[34] Additionally, the monarchs met Elizabeth Piast, the widow of Charles I, and the new ruler of Hungary, Louis I.

Louis I, son and successor of Charles I, continued the dynamic diplomatic activity of his father with regular visits abroad. In the winter of 1344–1345 he met John of Bohemia in Wrocław,[35] and they departed together for a joint campaign against the Lithuanians and, in 1351, Louis visited Casimir at his residence in Cracow before the two monarchs embarked on a military operation against the Lithuanians and Ruthenians.[36]

---

31 *Magyar diplomacziai emlékek az Anjou-korból*, i [Hungarian Diplomatic Records from the Angevin-period], ed. Gusztáv Wenzel (Budapest: MTA Könyvkiadó Hivatala, 1874–1876), pp. 343–345.

32 Paul W. Knoll, *The Rise of the Polish Monarchy: Piast Poland in East Central Europe, 1320–1370* (Chicago: University of Chicago Press, 1972), p. 86.

33 "Anno domini millesimo tricentesimo tricesimo nono Kazmyrus rex Polonie in mense lulii venit in Wyssegrad ad Karolum regem [cum episcopis] Hungarie cum episcopis et baronibus regni sui, et de consensu et voluntate omnium illorum regnum Polonie libere resignavit domino Lodowico filio regis Karoli, filio sororis sue eo, quod non haberet filium, et ad hoc confecerunt evidens instrumentum" – Johannes de Thurocz, *Chronica Hungarorum*, i, p. 153 (cap. 124).

34 "Deinde vero potentissimi regis obitum famosissimum rex Kazmyrus Polonie proximus eiusdem et marchio Morauie in Wyssegrad venientes condolenti animo celebrauerunt" – Johannes de Thurocz, *Chronica Hungarorum*, i, 159 (cap. 128); László Szende, *Piast Erzsébet és udvara (1320–1380)*, unpublished PhD dissertation [Elisabeth Piast and her Court (1320–1380)] (Budapest: Eötvös Loránd Tudományegyetem, 2007), pp. 23–24.

35 Schwedler, *Herrschertreffen des Spätmittelalters*, p. 439.

36 *Chronicon Dubnicense: Cum codicibus Sambuci Acephalo et Vaticano, cronicisque Vindobonensi picto et Budensi accurate collatum; Accesserunt II. Adnotationes chronologicae seculi XII et XIII-i; III. Chronicon Monacense; IV. Chronicon Zagrabiense et Varadiense; V. Joannis

The first real royal summit was held in Buda in 1353, when Charles IV visited Hungary. After the death of his second wife, Anne of the Palatinate, earlier that year, the king decided to re-marry. Soon thereafter, in mid-March, there was a meeting of Charles IV, Louis of Hungary, and the margraves of Moravia and Brandenburg in Vienna, in the court of Albert II, duke of Austria, where the participants agreed that Charles would marry Anna of Schweidnitz (Świdnica).[37] Charles left for Hungary in May 1353 and the royal marriage was celebrated in a special way in Buda. Probably on 27 May, Charles married Anna of Schweidnitz and on the same day Louis I of Hungary also married Elizabeth of Bosnia (Kotromanić).[38] The double marriage ceremonies were followed by a confirmation of the political alliance of the parties.[39]

The next meeting of monarchs took place only two years later. In January 1355, Casimir III of Poland visited his nephew and Hungarian counterpart in Buda to discuss the succession to the Polish throne. As a result of these talks, Casimir agreed to accept Louis of Hungary as his heir and successor in Poland.[40]

de Vtino brevis narratio de regibus Hungariae (Historiae Hungaricae fontes domestici. Pars prima. Scriptores, 3), ed. M. Florianus (Pécs: [n. p.], 1884), pp. 162–163; Paul W. Knoll, "Louis the Great and Casimir of Poland," in *Louis the Great, King of Hungary and Poland* (East European Monographs, 194), eds S.B. Vardy, G. Grosschmid and L.S. Domonkos (New York: Boulder: East European Monographs, 1986) pp. 105–127, here p. 111 and Schwedler, *Herrschertreffen des Spätmittelalters*, p. 440.

37 Antal Pór "Anjouk és Wittelsbachok (Nagy Lajos szövetkezése IV. Károly császár ellen.)," [Anjous and Wittelsbachs (The alliance of Louis I Great against Emperor Charles IV)] *Századok* 41 (1907), pp. 681–705, 777–792 and 887–911, here pp. 684–685.

38 "De nupciis Karoli et regis Ungarie el cum quibus dominabus. Item mense iunii anni liii. rex Romanorum Karolus quartus el Ludwicus rex Ungarie convenerunt in civitate dicta Boffen (i.e. Ofen, Buda) in Ungaria, et ibi utrique simul nupcias celebrarunt. Et rex Karolus duxit filiam ducis de Swednitz heredem ducatus, rex vero Ungarie filiam ducis de Boffen (i.e. Bosnien), et ambe de Polonia" – Heinrich von Diessenhofen [Heinricus Dapifer de Diessenhoven], *Historia ecclesiastica* in *Fontes rerum Germanicarum*, iv, ed. J.F. Böhmer (Stuttgart: J.G. Cotta'scher Verlag, 1868), pp. 16–126, here pp. 87–88. (The different meanings of 'Boffen' are discussed by the editor of the text.)

39 Schwedler, *Herrschertreffen des Spätmittelalters*, p. 441; Karl Nehring, "Ungarn," in *Kaiser Karl IV. Staatsmann und Mäzen. Katalog der Ausstellungen Nürnberg und Köln 1978–1979*, ed. Ferdinand Seibt (Munich: Prestel, 1978), pp. 183–185, 455, here p. 184; István Petrovics, "A középkori pécsi egyetem és alapítója," [The Medieval University of Pécs and its Founder] *Aetas* 20/4 (2005), pp. 29–40, here p. 31. See also: *Regesta Imperii*, viii, no 1559d. See the online version at: http://www.regesta-imperii.de/id/1353-06-00_1_0_8_0_0_1769_1559d (last accessed 14 February 2015).

40 Knoll, "Louis the Great and Casimir of Poland," pp. 111–112; *Codex diplomaticus Regni Poloniae*, i, ed. Maciej Dogiel (Vilnius: Typ. Regia, et Reipublicae, Collegii Scholarum Piarum, 1758), pp. 37–38.

Unfortunately, neither the precise events nor the special arrangements for the royal meetings can be reconstructed from the sources.

Talks over royal marriage were the usual subjects of discussion at meetings of medieval monarchs. It was so in 1365, when Emperor Charles IV of Luxemburg visited Louis of Hungary, again to discuss a possible marriage of his son, Wenceslas, to Elizabeth, the daughter of Louis' younger brother, Stephan.[41]

Just some months after Charles IV's visit to Buda, the Hungarian court became central to the evolution of a wider political constellation. When John V Palaiologos (1341–1391), the Byzantine emperor, experienced the strengthening danger of the Ottoman expansion and the threat of the Bulgarians, he decided to journey to Buda in the hope of forging a political alliance. The last years before the emperor's journey to Hungary Byzantium were marked by the Ottoman conquest of Gallipoli in 1354, the first stronghold to be captured in Europe by them, and the arrival of the first Ottomans outside the walls of Constantinople itself in 1359. Adrianopolis and Philippopolis were taken by the Ottomans in 1362 and 1363. John V, in a letter sent to Pope Urban V, proposed the unification of the Greek and Latin churches, but since his suggestion remained unanswered, he turned his attention to Hungary. This was the first time that a Byzantine emperor traveled out of his empire not in a military campaign but on a diplomatic mission. John departed for this journey in the winter of 1365–1366, traveled on the Black Sea to the estuary of the Danube, and from there he sailed upstream on the river with his entourage, among them his two sons. One of the chief functionaries of region, the voivode of Transylvania, Dénes Lackfi, accompanied the emperor on his journey to Buda. Giovanni Conversini da Ravenna described the details of the meeting of the emperor and the Hungarian king there.[42]

---

41   Schwedler, *Herrschertreffen des Spätmittelalters*, p. 451; Samuel Steinherz, "Die Beziehungen Ludwigs I. von Ungarn zu Karl IV. Zweiter Theil: Die Jahre 1358–1378," *Mitteilungen des Instituts für Österreichische Geschichtsforschung* 9 (1888), pp. 529–637, here p. 563; Ulrike Hohensee, "Herrschertreffen und Heiratspoltik. Karl IV., Ungarn und Polen," in *Die Goldene Bulle. Politik – Wahrnehmung – Rezeption*, ii, eds Ulrike Hohensee et al. (Berlin: Akademie, 2009), pp. 639–664, here p. 656.

42   "Rex munificentissimus amplissima procerum pompa regalique magnificencia Caloianni ultro se obvium obtulit. Comspectoque caput aperuit, equo descendit regiaque honorificencia salutavit. Contra Caloiannes non acclinavit, non caput nudavit, verum equo sedere perstitit et augustissimam Ludovici maiestatem fastu pertinax excepit." – Tibor Kardos, "Ricordi ungheresi nel Rerum Memorandarum Liber di Giovanni Conversino da Ravenna," in idem, *Studi e ricerche umanistiche italo–ungheresi* (Debrecen: Studia Romanica Debreceniensia, 1967), pp. 31–44, here p. 44; Tibor Kardos, "Magyar tárgyú fejezetek Giovanni

In the spring of 1366 the two rulers sent two envoys to Pope Urban V, who, returning to Hungary, carried letters from the pope addressed to Louis I and John V. From the letters of the pope it turned out that the Byzantine emperor had offered to reunite the Greek and Latin churches if he received military support against the Ottoman threat.[43]

On his departure from Buda, John V left his son, Manuel, as a guarantor in the Hungarian royal court. Louis I accompanied his guest to Vidin, the border of his realm. The negotiations in Buda finally turned out to be unsuccessful as the Byzantine emperor did not accept all the conditions dictated by his counterparts. The stay of the Byzantine emperor in Buda was lengthy, for he and his entourage stayed for almost a whole year, which is even more remarkable since the formal royal residence was still in Visegrád.[44] While the political and ecclesiastical context of the meeting has been extensively discussed in the literature, the sources do not give many details on the stay of the Byzantine ruler in Buda.[45] It is only known from the remark of Demetrios Kydones that John V was accompanied by a small number of people.[46] The known members of the emperor's entourage were Manuel (II) Palaiologos and Michael, the sons of John V, and *cancellarius* George Manichaites.[47]

---

da Ravenna emlékiratában," [Chapters about Hungary in the Memoirs of Giovanni da Ravenna] *Archivum Philologicum* 60 (1936), pp. 284–297, here pp. 295–296.

43   CD, IX/III, pp. 594–600 (no 319).

44   Oskar Halecki, *Un empereur de Byzance à Buda,*" in idem, *Un empereur de Byzance à Rome. Vingt ans de travail pour l'union des eglises et pour la defense de l'empire d'Orient* (Warsaw: Naktadem Towarzystwa Naukowego Warszawskiego, 1930, repr. London: Variorum Reprints, 1972), pp. 111–137; Gyula Moravcsik, "Bizánci császárok és követeik Budán," [Byzantine Emperors and their Envoys in Buda] *Századok* 95 (1961), pp. 832–847, here pp. 842–843.

45   Joseph Gill, "John V Palaeologus at the Court of Louis I of Hungary (1366)," *Byzantinoslavica* 38 (1977) pp. 31–38, reprinted in idem, *Church Union: Rome and Byzantium, 1204–1453* (London: Variorum Reprints, 1979), IX; Peter Wirth, "Die Haltung Kaiser Johannes V. bei den Verhandlugen mit König Ludwig I. von Ungarn zu Buda im Jahre 1366," *Byzantinische Zeitschrift* 56 (1963), pp. 271–272; Attila Bárány: "Magyarország és a kései keresztes hadjáratok," [Hungary and the Late Crudades] in *Magyarország és a keresztes háborúk: lovagrendek és emlékeik* [Hungary and the Crusades: the knightly orders and their legacy], eds József Laszlovszky, Judit Majorossy and József Zsengellér (Máriabesnyő: Attraktor, 2006), pp. 139–165, here pp. 142–146.

46   Stavroula Andriopoulou, *Diplomatic Communication between Byzantium and the West under the Late Palaiologoi (1354–1453)*, unpublished PhD Dissertation (Birmingham: University of Birmingham, 2010), p. 109. Available online: http://etheses.bham.ac.uk/1515/1/Andriopoulou_11_PhD.pdf (last accessed 14 February 2015).

47   Andriopoulou, *Diplomatic Communication*, pp. 139–140.

The diplomatic activity of King Louis I did not cease in the later years of his reign. Casimir III of Poland traveled to Hungary in 1369, and entered into an alliance with the king of Hungary against Emperor Charles IV.[48] The meeting was held in Buda in February 1369; the treaty was accepted on 14 February.[49] Thus, the Polish king would have crossed the Carpathians in the winter. The February treaty was extended and confirmed in September of same year in Pressburg when Rupert and Albert of Wittelsbach also joined this alliance of Hungarian and Polish rulers.[50]

In the case of the royal meetings in 1369 memory of the summits has been preserved in the sources; however, neither the progress of the events, nor any influence on the urban setting of Buda was recorded.

The Reign of Sigismund: Buda as Permanent Royal Residence in International Diplomacy

The long reign of Sigismund of Luxemburg was marked by his exceptional activities in diplomacy. Sigismund himself traveled a great deal, as far as Constantinople in 1396 and London in 1416.[51] His travels and international political meetings were, of course, partly connected not only to his position as king of Hungary (from 1387), but also to his roles as king of the Romans (from 1411), king of Bohemia (from 1419) and as Holy Roman Emperor (from 1433). The list of his meetings with other monarchs demonstrates that his diplomatic activity was intensive from the beginning of his reign, not only after his coronation as king of Bohemia and Holy Roman Emperor. He was very active in international diplomacy throughout the whole of his reign, and because of that activity many of his meetings were held not in his main royal residence in Buda, but in different locations in Europe during his extensive travels.[52]

48 MNL OL DL 288 981 published in CD ix/4, p. 157 (no 83); Schwedler, *Herrschertreffen des Spätmittelalters*, p. 452; Knoll, *Rise of the Polish Monarchy*, p. 230.

49 Steinherz, "Die Beziehungen Ludwigs I. von Ungarn zu Karl IV.," p. 573.

50 Steinherz, "Die Beziehungen Ludwigs I. von Ungarn zu Karl IV.," p. 575.

51 Attila Bárány, "Zsigmond király angliai látogatása," [The Visit of King Sigismund to England] *Századok* 143 (2009), pp. 319–356.

52 On the contacts of Sigismund with other rulers of the period see: Gerald Schwedler, "Rituelle Diplomatie. Die persönlichen Beziehungen Sigismunds von Luxemburg zu benachbarten Königen und den Herrschern des Balkans," in *Kaiser Sigismund (1368–1437) – Urkunden und Herrschaftspraxis eines europäischen Monarchen*, eds Karel Hruza and Alexandra Kaar (Vienna–Cologne–Weimar: Böhlau, 2012), pp. 411–427. On the transformation of Buda as a main royal residence under the rule of Sigismund see: Márta Kondor,

In the first two decades of his reign, Sigismund held several meetings with other rulers, but in most cases these involved family matters since many times Sigismund met his older brother, Wenceslas of Luxemburg, king of Bohemia and ruler of Germany. Most of these meetings were held outside Hungary.

The first royal meeting Sigismund held in Buda was one of the most spectacular and significant in the history of such events in medieval Hungary.[53] Sigismund had been elected as king of the Romans in 1410 and this certainly strengthened his international influence. In a conflict between the Teutonic order and Poland, Sigismund first supported the German knights and only changed his orientation after the battle of Tannenberg/Grünwald (15 July 1410) when he embraced a more conciliatory policy towards Poland. In February 1412, Sigismund and Wladislas II (1386–1434) began peace negotiations, first through intermediaries and in mid-March in personal meetings at Stará Ľubovňa, close to the Polish–Hungarian border; they agreed to keep peaceful contacts between the two countries.[54] After successful negotiations, Sigismund invited his Polish counterpart to visit Hungary. They traveled together through the northeastern part of Hungary, visiting Oradea, Debrecen, and Diósgyőr, also taking part in a major hunting party organized in their honor. The two monarchs finally arrived at Buda in late May 1412, just some days before Pentecost. Jan Długosz reports in detail about the program of the two monarchs in Buda.[55] They also went hunting on Csepel Island, south of Buda, and the two kings joined a major celebration of several rulers and illustrious guests who were visiting Buda at the same time. This occasion was certainly the first event when several foreign monarchs took part at the same meeting in Buda.

"Hof, Residenz und Verwaltung. Ofen und Blindenburg in der Regierungszeit König Sigismunds – unter besonderer Berücksichtigung der Jahre 1410–1419," in ibid., pp. 215–233.

[53] On the urban policy of Sigismund and especially on the significance of the royal meetings in this context see: Katalin Szende, "Between Hatred and Affection. Towns and Sigismund in Hungary and the Empire," in *Sigismund von Luxemburg. Ein Kaiser in Europa. Tagungsband des internationalen historischen und kunsthistorischen Kongresses in Luxemburg, 8–10 Juni, 2005.*, eds Michel Pauly and François Reinert (Mainz: Philipp von Zabern, 2006), pp. 199–210, esp. p. 208.

[54] Norbert C. Tóth, "Zsigmond magyar és II. Ulászló lengyel király személyes találkozói a lublói béke után (1412–1424)," [The Personal Meetings of King Sigismund of Hungary and Wladislas II of Poland after the Peace Treaty of Stará Ľubovňa (1412–1424)] *Történelmi Szemle* 56 (2014), pp. 339–356, here p. 342.

[55] Joannis Dlugossii [Jan Długosz], *Annales seu Cronicae incliti regni Poloniae. Liber Decimus et Undecimus, 1406–1412*, ed. Danuta Turkowska (Warsaw: Wydawnictwo Naukowe PWN, 1997) p. 202.

The importance of the event is emphasized by the fact that various written accounts have survived of the meeting. Besides the work of Jan Długosz, a list of the participating notables has also come down to us.[56] The festivities were connected to Pentecost, followed by the feast of Corpus Christi, which was celebrated by the two rulers together, taking part in the procession as well.[57]

An undated letter by a member of the Teutonic order also gives a detailed report on the meeting of numerous foreign guests. According to this account, the participants came from seventeen different countries and included kings, princes, archbishops, and bishops. The meeting was accompanied by tournaments, where a knight from Silesia and another from Austria received steeds with gold and silver horseshoes as gifts.[58] Besides the Hungarian and Polish kings, the papal legates, Albert and Ernest, dukes of Austria, the dukes of Bavaria and Silesia, Tvrtko II of Bosnia, Hervoja of Spalato, Stefan Lazarević of Serbia and many other dignitaries were present.[59] The royal company was entertained by 86 musicians and the list gives an apparently overestimated number (40,000) for the horses used by the participants during the royal festivities. The organization of a royal meeting of this size required early

---

56   *Sigismundus Rex et Imperator*, pp. 454–455. cat. 5.21; ZsO, iii, p. 527 (no 2224), for the manuscript, see: MNL OL DL 39 277; Eberhard Windecke also relates some events of the visit of Wladislas II in Hungary, but mistakenly gives 1416 as the year of the happenings. *Eberhart Windeckes Denkwürdigkeiten zur Geschichte des Zeitalters Kaiser Sigmunds*, ed. Wilhelm Altmann (Berlin: K. Gaertners Verlagsbuchhandlung, 1893) p. 90 (cap. 102).

57   "Feria tercia post Sancte Trinitatis Budam reversi maximo cultu maximaque veneratione circa honorandum festum Corporis Christi fuere versati" – Dlugossii, *Annales seu Cronicae incliti regni Poloniae*, p. 202; See also: Károly Goda, "Buda Festiva: Urban Society and Processional Culture in a Medieval Capital City," *Czech and Slovak Journal of Humanities* 2 (2011), pp. 58–79, here p. 70.

58   "Item ist gar vil fursten Heren Ritter und Knechte gewesen zu dem hoffe zu Oven inn Ungern, mit namen III konige, III heuptlude drier lande, Dispot der Servoy, Item XIII Herzogen, XXI graven, XXVI Herren on die ungerischen Herren und XVc Ritter, IIIm knecht geschetzt, ein kardenal, ein legat, III Erzbischof, XI ander bischoffe, LXXXVI pfiffer und Bosimer, XVII Heroolt und uf XLm pferde geschetzt an allen Arten. Item von XVII landen sprache und lute alz Ungern, Beheymer, Bolander, Prusen, Rusen, Litauwen, Krichen, Dattaren, Durken, Walachien, Bosen, Sirfien, Winden, Walhen, Dutschen, Franzosen, Engelsche, Albanesen, Abrahemsche lute vom heiligen grabe und sust vil heslicher Heiden mit langen Berten, grosen Bruchen (Bauchen?), hohen Huten und langen goltern. Auch wart der hoff VIII Tage virtzogen als er sollte gewesen sin und ein Ritter uß der Slesien genannt Her Nemsche hat das beste gethann und ein knecht us Osterrich, dem sin zwey virdeckte Ros worden mit guldenen und silbernen Huvysen" – CD, x/5, pp. 246–248 (no 110).

59   Elemér Mályusz, *Kaiser Sigismund in Ungarn 1387–1437* (Budapest: Akadémiai, 1990), pp. 106–108.

preparations and arrangements. Sigismund sent out letters of invitation to the bishop of Passau and other invitees in early April, about one month in advance.[60]

This was certainly one of the largest and most magnificent royal meetings held in medieval Buda. According to one estimate the participants of the retinues of the monarchs and notables may have numbered more than four thousand persons.[61] The organization of this unprecedented meeting certainly exceeded the capacity of the Buda court in the early fifteenth century. The former royal residence in Buda, the *Kammerhof* was donated to the Pauline monks in 1381 and the building of the new royal palace was still in progress.[62] Provisional dwellings must have been also used to accommodate the guests and visitors in Buda, with many of them camping on the outskirts of Buda.[63] The hunting party and the attendance at the liturgical procession undoubtedly contributed to the settlement of the former disputes between Sigismund and Wladislas of Poland.[64]

The next series of royal meetings in Buda followed in 1424, which was again an active year in the foreign policy of Sigismund. On his European travels Eric VII of Pomerania, king of Denmark, Norway and Sweden, visited Sigismund in Hungary. According to Eberhard Windecke, Sigismund greeted Eric VII with Cardinal Branda da Castiglione, who was a special councillor to the king. Sigismund entertained Eric in Buda Castle and Visegrád in March 1424.[65] This demonstrates that in spite of the fact that the permanent royal residence had

60 CD, x/5, pp. 242–246 (nos 107–109).
61 ZsO, iii, pp. 527 (no 2224). In 1437 Sigismund planned to relocate the synod of Basle to Buda and in preparation he ordered the listing of the available accommodation for the delegates in Buda and its suburbs. This document proves that Sigismund was aware of the logistical problems of major international meetings with numerous participants. See the essay by János M. Bak and András Vadas in this volume, esp. n. 123.
62 On the Kammerhof see: Végh, *Buda,* i, pp. 269–272.
63 Albert Gárdonyi, "Magyarország középkori fővárosa," [The medieval capital of Hungary] *Századok* 78 (1944), pp. 219–231, here p. 226.
64 On the presence of the Bosnian envoys at the Buda royal meeting and also in general on the meeting see: Emir O. Filipović, "Viteške svečanosti u Budimu 1412. godine i učešće bosanskih predstavnika," [Chivalrous festivities held in Buda in 1412 and the participation of Bosnian magnates] in *Spomenica Marka Šunjića (1927–1998)*, ed. Dubravko Lovrenović (Sarajevo: Filozofski fakultet u Sarajevu, 2010), pp. 285–306.
65 "...also reit konig Sigemont und Placentinus der cardinale gein dem konige von Denemarg mit vil fürsten und herrn und wart herlich zu Ofen und zu Blindenburge empfangen und gon Ofen in das sloβ gefurt" – *Eberhard Windeckes Denkwürdigkeiten*, p. 173 (cap. 198).

been transferred by that time from Visegrád to Buda, Visegrád still kept a special position and served as a secondary residence.

After the meeting in Buda, the two kings traveled together to Cracow to attend the marriage ceremony of Wladislas II of Poland and Sophia of Halshany (Sonka Olshanskaya).[66] After the festivities in Poland, Sigismund and Eric both returned to Hungary, first to Visegrád and from there to the Pauline monastery of Saint Lawrence (Budaszentlőrinc) in the outskirts of Buda.[67] Sigismund, at that time already king of the Romans, convened a meeting with the envoys of the prince-electors, whom he met together with King Eric after Easter.[68]

Later the same year, in the summer of 1424, John VIII Palaiologos also arrived in Buda to seek military support against the Ottomans. This was the second visit of a Byzantine emperor to Buda. After John V, his grandson, John VIII, was also forced to appeal to Latin Christian rulers for help. The Ottomans besieged Constantinople in 1424 which forced the Byzantine emperor into action. According to George Sphrantzes, the historiographer of the Palaiologian court, John VIII left Constantinople on 15 November 1423, and according to Windecke he arrived in Buda only in mid-June 1424. Two anonymous authors confirm that before arriving in Hungary John VIII also visited Italy and France. When the news of the arrival of the Byzantine emperor reached Sigismund, he left Buda and went to meet John VIII about half a mile from the city. Both of them dismounted their horses and greeted each other. Thus, the first meeting happened outside of Buda and Sigismund accompanied his high-ranking guest to his Buda residence, where he was entertained with great respect and special care. For eight weeks the Byzantine emperor and his entourage enjoyed the hospitality of Sigismund, who paid all the costs of the visit.[69]

---

66 Joannis Dlugossii (Jan Długosz), *Annales seu Cronicae incliti regni Poloniae. Liber Undecimus, 1413–1430*, ed. Danuta Turkowska (Warsaw: Wydawnictwo Naukowe PWN, 2000) pp. 194–197.

67 Zoltán Bencze and György Szekér, *A budaszentlőrinci pálos kolostor. Das Paulinerkloster von Budaszentlőrinc* [The Pauline monastery of Budaszentlőrinc] (Monumenta Historica Budapestinensia, 8) (Budapest: Budapesti Történeti Múzeum, 1993).

68 *Eberhard Windeckes Denkwürdigkeiten*, p. 172 (cap. 197).

69 "also kam dem Romschen konig botschaft, wie daz der keiser von Kriechen und von Constantinopeln komen solt, als er ouch det also bereit sich der Romsch konig Sigmont und reit im gar köstlich hingegen ein halbe mile under Ofen. do sie züsamen komen, do drat der Römsche konig ab und der keiser ouch ab von den pferden und empfingen sich gar lieplich under einander; und fürt in also gon Ofen und erboit im zucht und ere. der keiser waz ouch bi dem Romschen konige zu Ungern wol 8 wochen lang; und waz der keiser mit alle sim volg verzert, das bezalt der Romsche konig alleß sampt" – *Eberhard Windeckes Denkwürdigkeiten*, p. 177 (cap. 205).

Only sporadic information has survived about the issues discussed during John VIII's visit to Buda. Gyula Moravcsik refers to two anonymous eulogies of John VIII and his father Manuel II in which the author specifies the objective of this imperial visit. According to these reports, the emperor explained the endangered situation of Byzantium because of the siege of the city by the Ottomans and asked Sigismund for help. There are strong reasons to believe that the question of the Church union was also discussed.[70] Sigismund seemed ready to help, but in the end Byzantium did not receive any effective military support from Sigismund, who directed his attention thereafter to affairs in the Holy Roman Empire and the Hussite problem.[71] There is an astonishing difference between the descriptions of the 1366 visit of John V and the stay of John VIII in 1424. In the latter case the Byzantine emperor was much friendlier with the Hungarian king, certainly in part because of his title of king of the Romans and also because of the growing Ottoman threat to Byzantium. At the same time, Despot Stefan Lazarević of Serbia also came to Buda and presented Sigismund with special gifts, silk shawls, Turkish drums and other items of Turkish character.[72] Besides the mutual presentation of gifts, the other typical element of these royal summits was that the participants took part together in a procession. In this case as well, John VIII, Sigismund and his wife, Barbara, and Cardinal Branda da Castiglione participated together in the Corpus Christi procession on 21 June 1424. When they departed from Buda, Sigismund gave his guests magnificent gifts. The Byzantine emperor received eight gilded chalices, 1000 Hungarian golden florins, various textiles, including velvet, cloth and six excellent horses. The gifts for the despot of Serbia were proportionally smaller, according to his position. He was given roughly as many gifts as the Byzantine emperor.[73]

---

70 Andriopoulou, *Diplomatic Communication*, p. 214.
71 Moravcsik, "Bizánci császárok és követeik Budán," pp. 842–843.
72 "In der selben zit kam herzog Dischpot von Sirfie und wart von dem konige schone empfangen. und er brocht dem konige gar schone erunge, (das der Sirfen trügent 26 mannen) guldin und sidin tucher, Durkische dromen colben schosseln und satteldeck und ander Dorcschis geret und gefert und schankt das dem Romschen konige" –*Eberhard Windeckes Denkwürdigkeiten*, p. 177 (cap. 206).
73 "In der selben zit do schiet Dischbot der herzog von Sirfie und der keiser von Kriechen und von Constantinopel von dem Romschen konige wider heimzüziehen. do schankte der konig dem keiser von Constantinopel 8 vergulte köpfe, tusent Ungerscher guldin 6 samet 3 rot 3 swarz, 3 plauw Mechelsche tiücher, 6 hubsche pferde. und schankt der konig dem Dischbot vier verguldeter köpf, 500 Ungerscher guldin, 3 samet, 6 Mechelsche tücher, 4 pfert. also schieden die herrn hinweg." – *Eberhard Windeckes Denkwürdigkeiten*, p. 186–187 (cap. 220).

After Sigismund: Buda without Royal Summits

According to the surviving records, no other foreign ruler visited Buda or attended a royal meeting in the environs of Buda in the central region of medieval Hungary, the so-called *medium regni* between 1424 and 1541, when the Ottomans conquered Buda. In the last period of Sigismund's reign there were no further royal meetings in Buda, partly because of the fact that the overall number of international meetings decreased significantly. After his death, the rulers of Hungary from the Habsburg and Jagiellonian dynasties were usually rulers of other countries as well, and thus their diplomatic activities were not concentrated only in Hungary. Matthias Corvinus met several times his counterparts and rivals, like George of Poděbrady, Wladislas II of Bohemia and Emperor Frederick III, but not in Buda or its environs.[74] By the period of Matthias the methods and formats of medieval diplomacy had also changed. Regular missions and royal envoys now dominated diplomacy, mediating political issues and collecting information for their home country. The court of Matthias Corvinus was in regular diplomatic contacts with various Italian cities (Venice and Florence first of all) and other European courts.[75]

The last foreign visitor of the Buda royal court from a ruling family was Prince Sigismund, the later king of Poland (1506–1548). Sigismund as younger brother of King Wladislas II of Hungary (1490–1516) spent some years in the Hungarian royal court after 1498. Although his stay in Buda was not because of a political mission, paradoxically his account books on the daily expenditures of his household are one of the most detailed source on the daily life in the royal seat of Buda.[76]

---

[74] Antonín Kalous, "Rituály a ceremonie při setkávání panovníků: případ Matyáše Hunyadiho (Korvína)," [Rituals and Ceremonies at the Royal meetings. The case of Matthias Corvinus] in *Rituály, ceremonie a festivity ve střední Evropě 14. a 15. století* [Rituals, Ceremonies and Festivities in fourteenth- and fifteenth-century Central Europe] (Colloquia mediaevalia Pragensia, 12), eds František Šmahel and Martin Nodl (Prague: CMS, 2009), pp. 121–136.

[75] Attila Bárány, "Matthias' European Diplomacy in the 1480s," in *Matthias and His Legacy: Cultural and Political Encounters between East and West* (Speculum Historiae Debreceniense, 1), eds Attila Bárány and Attila Györkös (Debrecen: A Debreceni Egyetem Történelmi Intézetének Kiadványai, 2009), pp. 365–392; Zsuzsa Teke, "Mátyás és Firenze," [King Matthias I and Florence] in *Tiszteletkör. Történeti tanulmányok Draskóczy István egyetemi tanár 60. születésnapjára* [Circle of honor. Studies in honor of the 60th birthday of István Draskóczy], eds Gábor Mikó, Bence Péterfi and András Vadas (Budapest: ELTE Eötvös Kiadó, 2012), pp. 85–95.

[76] Adorján Divéky, *Zsigmond lengyel herczeg budai számadásai, 1500–1502, 1505* [The accounts of Sigismund, Polish prince at Buda, 1500–1502, 1505] (Magyar Történelmi Tár, 26)

Conclusions

Summarizing the history of royal summits in medieval Buda and its surroundings, one can establish that visits of foreign rulers to a different country might have various effects. Royal meetings had several ceremonial characteristics, and the available sources usually do not include many details on the specifics of the events. In several cases, gift giving and participating in public events were characteristic elements of the meeting.

In the Árpádian period, until the turn of the thirteenth century, rulers who traveled through Hungary on their way to the Holy Land usually attended meetings with the monarchs of Hungary. In these cases little information has survived about the factual issues discussed. These early travelers usually visited Esztergom, the main royal residence in that period, and occasionally stopped at Óbuda or at Csepel Island in the territory of modern Budapest. In the next period, Visegrád was the dominating royal residence in the central region of the country. This role is reflected in its significance as a location for royal meetings. During the Angevin period, the rulers of Bohemia and Poland visited the Hungarian royal court several times. The frequency of the meetings and the issues discussed and agreed upon reflect the importance of the dynastic links and political connections of the Hungarian, Bohemian, and Polish rulers of that period. Although most of the royal meetings of King Sigismund were not held in Buda or other locations in the *medium regni* of Hungary, his active role in the international politics of the late fourteenth and especially the early fifteenth century is demonstrated by a couple of sumptuous royal meetings held in Buda in his period. At both the 1412 and 1424 summits he brought together monarchs who happened to visit Buda at the same time. By that time the buildings of the Hungarian royal court, especially the ceremonial hall that was one of the largest in Europe, and the ceremonies held there made the Buda court a convenient and suitable place for international meetings.[77] Two Byzantine emperors visited the royal court of Buda, John V in 1366 and his grandson, John VIII, in 1424. Since the visits of Byzantine emperors to Western countries

---

(Budapest: MTA, 1914); *Jagelló Zsigmond herceg udvarának számadáskönyve (1504–1507). The Court Account Book of Sigismund Jagiellon (1504–1507)*, ed. Krisztina Rábai (Szeged: Quintus Kiadó, 2014); *Účty dvora prince Zikmunda Jagellonského, vévody hlohovského a opavského, nejvyššího hejtmana Slezska a Lužic, z let (1493) 1500–1507: Kritická edice pramene. Rationes curiae Sigismundi Iagellonici, ducis Glogoviensis et Opaviensis, Silesiae et Lusatiarum summi capitanei, de annis (1493) 1500–1507*, ed. Petr Kozák (Prague: Scriptorium 2014).

77 See the study by Károly Magyar in the present volume.

were quite exceptional in the Middle Ages, these meetings had great importance. The sojourn of John v in 1366 and John viii in Buda had also exceptional reasons. The two emperors visited the kings of Hungary to get support and even military help against the Ottoman threat against Constantinople, but their gestures remained unanswered for various reasons.

The sporadic information on the proceedings of royal meetings usually do not include information on the practical aspects of the summits, like accommodation for the ruler and his entourage or pastimes during the stay of a foreign monarch, although it seems clear that meetings which were attended by numerous rulers might easily exceed the capacity of the hospitality available both in Buda and in Visegrád. After the grand royal meetings of King Louis or Sigismund, Buda had to wait several centuries to welcome the next foreign rulers visiting with a peaceful purpose the former capital of the medieval kingdom of Hungary.

CHAPTER 15

Buda, Medieval Capital of Hungary

*András Kubinyi**

There is an enormous literature on the 'capital city question'. The distinct but overlapping concept of the 'royal seat' or residence has also attracted much attention in the last decade and a half.[1] Hungarian historians have recently shown capital-city characteristics to have been concentrated in an area known as the "center of the realm" (*medium regni*) in the period following the foundation of the state. These characteristics were shared among the three towns at the edge of that area: Esztergom, Székesfehérvár and Óbuda. The center subsequently transferred from Óbuda to Buda, but some capital functions remained in the other two cities: the archbishop of Esztergom was Hungary's primate and *legatus natus* in the late medieval period, and Székesfehérvár remained the city of coronation and royal burial.[2]

International historians have also recognized the significance of the Hungarian *medium regni*.[3] Buda finally became the residence of the king only

---

Translated by Alan Campbell
* András Kubinyi (1929–2007) was and will always remain one of the most influential researchers of medieval Buda (see the introductory chapter of the present volume). This article is a translation of one of his last studies dedicated to this city's past: "Buda, Magyarország középkori fővárosa," *Tanulmányok Budapest Múltjából* 29 (2001) 11–22 [reprinted in Kubinyi, *Tanulmányok*, ii, pp. 538–549].
1 A considerable part of the previous scholarship is referred to, and the problem is well presented in Evamaria Engel and Karen Lambrecht, "Hauptstadt – Residenz – Residenzstadt – Metropole – Zentraler Ort. Probleme ihrer Definition und Charakterisierung," in *Metropolen im Wandel. Zentralität in Ostmitteleuropa an der Wende vom Mittelalter zur Neuzeit*, eds Evamaria Engel, Karen Lambrecht and Hanna Nogossek (Berlin: Akademie Verlag, 1995), pp. 11–31.
2 The notion of *medium regni* was identified by Bernát L. Kumorovitz, "Buda (és Pest) 'fővárossá' alakulásának kezdetei," [The beginnings of the formation of Buda (and Pest) as 'capital'] *Tanulmányok Budapest Múltjából* 18 (1971), pp. 7–57. For an overview of the idea of the *medium regni*, see András Kubinyi, "Preface: From the 'Middle of the Country' to the Capital," in *Medium regni*, pp. 5–8; György Györffy, *Pest–Buda kialakulása. Budapest története a honfoglalástól az Árpád-kor végi székvárossá alakulásáig* [The formation of Pest-Buda. The history of Budapest from the Hungarian conquest to its late Árpádian-period formation as capital] (Budapest, Akadémiai, 1997), p. 223.
3 Klaus Neitmann, "Was ist eine Residenz? Methodische Überlegungen zur Erforschung der spätmittelalterlichen Residenzbildung," in *Vorträge und Forschungen zur Residenzenfrage* (Residenzenforschung, 1), ed. Peter Johanek (Sigmaringen: J. Thorbecke, 1990), pp. 11–43,

in the early fifteenth century (lasting up to the Ottoman conquest), and its status as a capital city before that time is debatable.[4] Here I will investigate Buda's status through some contemporary references to 'capital' features – particularly those manifested in certain important events – and the self-assessment of Buda citizens.

Early fourteenth-century sources undoubtedly identify Buda as a royal seat. In 1308, the *Anonymi Descriptio Europae Orientalis* described Buda as the seat of the Hungarian kingdom and largest city.[5] In the same year, King Charles I wrote that he had transferred governance of the kingdom to Buda and taken up residence in the city together with his prelates and barons.[6] These two items of information do not have exactly the same meaning. The *Descriptio* calls Buda the "seat of the realm", rather than *sedes regis* or *regia*, i.e. "the seat of the king". There is also a problem with the expression *civitas principalis*, which may seem to correspond to "capital city", but actually denotes a category, as is clear from an urban decree of 1405 which mentions the *civitates principaliores*, i.e. the "more principal cities."[7] The same category existed in Poland, whose development was similar to Hungary's. Indeed, Polish historians have identified six main cities denoted as *civitates principaliores* in the late Middle Ages.[8]

Further complicating the issue is a Hungarian-language source from the first half of the sixteenth century: "Szeged is a large city in Hungary; what is more, it is the king's capital city [*fő várasa*]."[9] Since Szeged was never the king's

---

here pp. 41–42; Winfried Eberhard, "Metropolenbildung im östlichen Mitteleuropa. Eine vorläufige Diskussionsbilanz," in *Metropolen im Wandel. Zentralität in Ostmitteleuropa an der Wende vom Mittelalter zur Neuzeit*, eds Evamaria Engel, Karen Lambrecht and Hanna Nogossek (Berlin: Akademie Verlag, 1995), pp. 277–282, here p. 281.

4   The question has a long historiography. Cf. Albert Gárdonyi, "Magyarország középkori fővárosa," [The medieval capital of Hungary] *Századok* 78 (1944), pp. 219–231. Scholarship up to the beginning of the 1990s is summarized in the different studies published in the exhibition catalogue: *Budapest im Mittelalter*; see also above, note 2.

5   "…ubi est sedes regni, que est maxima civitatum […] in tota Ungaria" – ÁMTF, iv, p. 606.

6   "…suscepto regni nostri gubernaculo in Budensem civitatem nostram principalem […] venissemus" – ÁMTF, iv, p. 606. Cf. Erzsébet Ladányi, "Libera villa, civitas, oppidum. Terminologische Fragen in der ungarischen Städteentwicklung," *Annales Universitatis Scientiarum Budapestinensis de Rolando Eötvös Nominatae. Sectio historica* 18 (1977), pp. 3–43.

7   Ladányi, "Libera villa," pp. 23–24.

8   Maria Bogucka and Henryk Samsonowicz, *Dzieje miast i mieszczaństwa w Polsce przedrozbiorowej* [The history of towns and the bourgeoisie until the partitions of Poland] (Wrocław–Warsaw–Łódź: Zakład Narodowy im. Ossolińskich, 1986), pp. 106 and 120.

9   *Memoria Rerum. A Magyarországon legutóbbi László király fiának legutóbbi Lajos királynak születése óta esett dolgok emlékezete (Verancsics-évkönyv)* [The memory of the things that happened in Hungary since the birth of the last King Ladislas's most recent son, King Louis (Verancsics journal)] (Bibliotheca historica), ed. József Bessenyei (Budapest: Magyar Helikon, 1981), p. 16.

capital, we must interpret the term *civitas principalis*, or its equivalent *civitas capitalis*, or the German *Hauptstadt,* or the Hungarian *fő város* [in medieval sources, and as distinct from modern *főváros*] as meaning "a prime city", rather than "capital" in the usual modern sense. The same may be said for some foreign countries.[10]

Nonetheless, the charter of Charles I may indeed convey the sense of "capital city". The wording is clear: the king had taken over government and arrived in his *civitas principalis,* Buda. We can refer back to our other source from 1308 which, as we have seen, mentions Buda as the *sedes regni*. This also has a foreign analogy: in 1166, Frederick Barbarossa called Aachen *caput et sedes regni Theutonici* ("head and seat of the kingdom of the Germans"). Although this statement uses the same term, *sedes regni*, it relates to Aachen Cathedral, the site of coronations, and to the fact that the German king resided there for a while.[11]

The same could not apply to Buda, because what later became the capital was at most an auxiliary coronation site, and a coronation there was indeed challenged. So despite having definitely credible sources, we cannot give a clear answer for 1308. There are no further sources I know of before the second half of the fifteenth century which mention Buda as a royal seat, and even then, perhaps significantly, they link the city to the king (*rex*) rather than to the kingdom (*regnum*). The reference from 1308 thus has a somewhat uncertain connection, but nonetheless tells us much.

The first piece of later information is from 1468. Buda's former protonotary wrote a letter to the town of Bardejov, stating that "His royal highness and the other judges of the realm have deemed Buda to be the royal throne". (But they nonetheless suppress its rights...)[12] Matthias himself, in an undated charter, says of Buda that it is "the seat and throne of the royal office" and the capital of the realm.[13] The same occurs in almost identical form in another charter: "Buda is practically the seat and throne of the royal office".[14]

---

10   Engel and Lambrecht, "Hauptstadt," pp. 12–17.
11   Engel and Lambrecht, "Hauptstadt," p. 13.
12   "...civitas Budensis a regia Maiestate et aliis eiusdem regni assessoribus scribitur solium regale". See Béla Iványi, *Bártfa szabad királyi város levéltára*, i [Archive of the free royal town of Bardejov] (Budapest: MTA, 1910), no 1760.
13   "...quae est sedes et solium Regiae dignitatis, Caputque Regni nostri." See Martinus Georgius Kovachich, *Formulae solennes styli in cancellaria...* (Pest: Typis Matthiae Trattner, 1799), p. 531.
14   "...quasi sedes est solium dignitatis Regni existit" – Kovachich, *Formulae*, p. 531.

All sources use the word *solium* to mean the royal throne. Its primary meaning is indeed throne, official seat, chair with a back, and even denotes the royal office. Most medieval Hungarian vocabularies translate it as the seat of the king or queen,[15] but the Schlägl Word List, dated to around 1405, gives it the meaning of "hall", and thus considers it identical to the word *aula*.[16] Since *aula* also means royal court, *solium* may also mean the same, because, as we have seen, it also occurs with the word *sedes*, which definitely means a seat.

Before going any further, it should be mentioned that several charters from the second half of the thirteenth and first half of the fourteenth centuries call Székesfehérvár the king's *locus cathedralis*.[17] *Cathedra* can also mean seat, throne or even royal office; denoting in the adjectival form, "belonging to the royal seat".[18] The great Austrian historian Heinrich Koller regarded Árpádian-period Székesfehérvár as a Carolingian-type capital, and rightly pointed out that "Székesfehérvár held the royal throne and the right to crown the kings of Hungary, and was the city where Hungarian kings were buried."[19] Koller thus saw the royal throne as being most important (cf. Aachen). What makes this interesting is that Pope John XXII mentioned in a 1321 bull Óbuda (i.e. not Buda) as the royal seat, the *locus cathedralis*.[20] Whereas the expression *cathedralis* in Székesfehérvár can be linked to the constitutionally crucial royal throne – the *cathedra*, held in the coronation church there – the term is problematic in the case of Óbuda, which did not effectively serve even as a royal seat or residence in 1321.

Up to now we have encountered in relation to Buda two related, but subtly distinct words, or three if we include Óbuda: *solium*, *sedes* and *cathedra*. Now comes the most important text. It is preserved in a charter issued on

---

15   Jolán Berrár and Sándor Károly, *Régi magyar glosszárium. Szótárak, szójegyzékek és glosszák egyesített szótára* [Old Hungarian glossary. Combined word list of dictionaries and glossaries] (Budapest: Akadémiai, 1984), p. 638.

16   Berrár and Károly, *Glosszárium*, p. 692.

17   For this information, see Gárdonyi, "Főváros," p. 221. Székesfehérvár is also described in the same document as *civitas regalis sedis* and *regni metropolis*.

18   *Lexicon Latinitatis Medii Aevi Hungariae*, ii/1, ed. János Harmatta (Budapest: Akadémiai, 1991), pp. 72–73.

19   Heinrich Koller, "A székesfehérvári királyi trónszék kérdése," [The question of the royal throne of Székesfehérvár] in *Székesfehérvár évszázadai*, ii. *Középkor* [The centuries of Székesfehérvár. Middle Ages], ed. Alán Kralovánszky (Székesfehérvár: Fejér Megyei Múzeumok Igazgatósága, 1972), pp. 7–20, here p. 16.

20   "Veteri Bude loco videlicet cathedrali ipsius regis" – quoted in Gárdonyi, "Főváros," p. 222, note 17.

behalf of the Buda city council in 1498, and expresses the self-assessment of the Buda citizenry. It conveys in its very prolixity their conception of the city as a 'capital'.

"The almighty God [...] has raised up this city of Buda (to which, by virtue of its honored and notable situation and foundation, for as long as it has existed, the kings of Hungary, the prelates, and no less the barons and higher nobles and magnates of the said kingdom have gathered together and customarily reside there) to the extent that as the other towns of the said kingdom of Hungary call this city of Buda the royal seat and royal throne, they make their way and meet together there."[21]

This text thus considers the *solium regale thronusque regius* to be the city itself. We thus have a fourth expression of similar meaning, expressing 'royal' with a separate word. This could be the effect of customary medieval legal language, saying the same thing in several different ways, or it could be a deliberate distinction. For example, *solium* could carry the sense of 'hall', i.e. *aula*, and therefore ultimately mean 'court'; it is difficult to decide now. We can, however, be sure of at least two claims for Buda made by its council: the city was the residence of the king and the great dignitaries, and it was also the leader of other towns in Hungary, providing support to the Hungarian urban estate. We should add that there is every indication that this form of words was not new for the Buda Council. In two petitions to the pope in 1497 to extend the rights of the parish of the Church of Our Lady in Buda Castle, the priest, Paul Wann, attempted to prove the significance of his church with a text almost identical to that of the 1498 document. Since it is unlikely that the city notary would have used petitions to the pope written by the priest a year before and not including reference to the royal throne, there must have been an original text in circulation from which both the priest and the council drew.

In his petition of 13 May 1497, Wann quoted the "honored and eminent situation and foundation" of his church, the permanent residence of the king, and something not mentioned in the 1498 charter: "there is a large gathering here of

---

21 MNL OL DF 254 980. The text of the charter is partially published in Frigyes Pesty, *A szörényi bánság és Szörény vármegye története*, iii, *Oklevéltár*, i [The history of the Banate of Severin and Severin county. Documents] (Budapest: MTA Könyvkiadó, 1878), p. 124. "... altissimus Deus [...] hanc ipsam civitatem Budensem (ad quam propter honorificum et notabilem situm ac fundationem reges Hungariae pro tempore existentes prelatique et nichilominus barones et prestantiores dicti regni Hungariae nobiles et magnates convenire et communiter residere consueverunt) adeo prefecit, ut quemadmodum eadem ipsa civitas Budensis inter ceteras istius regni civitates solium regale thronusque regius appellatur, sic etiam eedem civitates dicti regni Hungariae ad ipsam recursum habent et confluuntur."

nobles, traders and assorted other persons from various parts of the world."[22] Wann received the title of archdeacon for his parish and the right to give a prelate's blessing in the absence of a prelate. On 15 June 1497, he petitioned the pope to have this restriction relaxed, stating that since the Hungarian kings mostly kept their seat in Buda and several prelates followed the court, it was rare for there not to be a prelate to celebrate mass on a feast day, and so this restriction should apply only in the event of a papal legate or of the bishop of Veszprém being present.[23]

Another item concerning Buda as the royal seat comes from a request for papal assistance written by Louis II on 29 June 1521, during Suleiman's campaign against Belgrade. The king stated that after taking Belgrade, the Sultan threatened to advance on Buda "where my royal seat is."[24] Here again the word *sedes* appears, but he does not call Buda itself the "seat", saying rather that is where his seat is. This could of course be a stylistic device, but it may also mean something more. Another example may allow us to propose a further hypothesis.

We have documentary evidence linking the city of Buda with the royal seat (in 1308 the "seat of the realm") and statements by city officials proudly

---

22   *Monumenta Romana Episcopatus Vesprimiensis*, iv (1492–1526), ed. Vilmos Fraknói (Budapest: Római Magyar Történeti Intézet, 1907), 77–78: "...cum ecclesia beate Marie virginis Vespremiensis diocesis, *ad quam propter honorificum et notabilem situm ac fundationem et singularem ac solempnem divini cultus celebrationem, que in ea cothidie fit, pro eo, quod reges Hungariae pro tempore existentes* in opido Bude hujusmodi *residere consueverunt*, ex diversis mundi partibus maximus nobilium, mercatorum et aliarum diversarum personarum concursus habetur, in partibus illis notabilis et admodum insignis existat..." (italics mine, AK). It is obvious that merchants did appear in the original text: reference to them in particular as churchgoers does not make any sense, unlike the fact that the city was a royal center. (Underlined are the parts of the 1498 arenga that go back to the original text.) Wann, whose name appears in the charters in different forms (in these supplications, in the form "Bani") was the son of Conrad Wann (schoolmaster and later councillor of Buda) and the nephew of Paul Wann (professor of theology at Vienna, later canon of Passau), whose first name he received. See Alfons Huber and András Kubinyi, "Egy budai iskolamester pályája a XV. század második felében," [The career of a schoolmaster in the second half of the fifteenth century] in *A magyar iskola első évszázadai (996–1526)* [The first centuries of schooling in Hungary, 996–1526], ed. Katalin G. Szende (Győr: Győr-Moson-Sopron Megyei Múzeumok Igazgatósága, 1996), pp. 51–60.

23   "...in opido Budensi huiusmodi reges Hungarie pro tempore existentes, cum eorum curiam quamplures antistites sequuntur, pro maiori parte temporis residere solent, raro contingere possit, quod in dicta ecclesia, dum misse solempniter celebrantur, aliquis antistes presens non sit." – MREV, iv, pp. 82–83.

24   "Budam, ubi mihi regia sedes est, recte perventurum minatur" – *Epistolae procerum regni Hungariae*, i, ed. Georgius Pray (Pressburg: Belnay, 1806), p. 143.

declaring Buda to be the "royal seat and throne". Medieval etiquette was symbolic, and state occasions such as coronations, burials and ritual royal entries were the visual manifestations of the monarch's standing. "As power became a matter of appearances in the late Middle Ages, there was a need for agreement, and to obtain that in an era when not everybody could read, the visual media were crucial, and knowingly employed," wrote the French historian, Colette Beaune.[25]

In search of clues to settle the "seat issue", we will examine how royal power was manifested on special occasions in Buda. First, however, we must mention an extraordinary event. In 1458, the newly-elected King Matthias was in the custody of George of Poděbrady in Prague, and Emperor Frederick III had not returned the Holy Crown to Hungary. An agreement was reached with George enabling the king to come home, but there could be no coronation with the Holy Crown. The dignitaries of the land declined to stage a coronation using the crown from the St Stephen's head reliquary, as had been done for Wladislas I, and chose a different and somewhat surprising route. It certainly succeeded, because Matthias' royal power was not held in doubt, although – as Werbőczy recorded – the charters of privilege issued before his coronation in 1464 were only accepted by the courts because he subsequently confirmed them.[26]

Bonfini described the new king's entry into Buda from Bohemia. On his approach, the king was met by a procession of prelates, magnates and nobles, the city judge and his officers, members of every clerical body – carrying the sacrament and singing hymns – and the entire people, welcoming him with acclamation and hurrahs. The Jews, carrying Moses's tablets, were among the first to greet the king, requesting confirmation of their privileges. At the city gate, the burghers received Matthias, who swore, at the request of the judge, never to violate their privileges. Matthias promised the same to the prelates and barons before they admitted him to the castle. After he had made his entry, he was led into the Church of Our Lady. As he passed by the City Hall, the prisoners held inside were released. In the church he gave thanks to God and the Virgin Mary, the protector of Hungary, and promised to uphold the "sacred rights". From there, he was led into the royal palace, while in the streets, alleyways and market places the people applauded and exalted him. As he sat in the palace, he turned his attention to arranging the affairs of state.[27]

---

25   Colette Beaune, "Les structures politiques comparées de l'occident médiéval (1250–1350). Le prince," in *XIVe et XVe siècles: crises et genèses* (Peuples et civilisations), ed. Jean Favier (Paris: Presses universitaires de France, 1996), pp. 3–37, here p. 29.

26   DRMH, v, p. 261 (*Tripartitum*, ii, 14 [47]).

27   Bonfini, *Decades*, III-IX-152–160 (pp. 216–217).

It was an event which had been carefully composed in every detail, and Bonfini's description is as revealing as it is colorful. The king's oaths to uphold privileges, and his confirmation of privileges, starts with the Jews, but in their case no royal oath was taken. The procedure continued with oaths confirming the privileges of the city of Buda, then of the prelates and barons, and finally the confirmation of "sacred rights", which was made in the church. This is a logical order of ceremony, starting with those of lowest rank and ending with the confirmation of the highest dignitaries' privileges. The only confusion arises with the oath to the prelates and barons, which Bonfini places before the entry to the castle, but which could only have taken place after the church ceremony. As important as the triple oath was the giving of thanks in church, especially to the Blessed Virgin, patron of Hungary, whom Matthias especially revered.[28]

The public and the city clergy were also involved in the ceremony. The king was received by a church procession and a public *acclamatio*. Bonfini even suggests that the new king may have ridden around the city, because he was applauded on the streets and in the market place. To a certain extent, the general amnesty was already a kingly act. The formalities ended with Matthias swearing an oath to uphold privileges, and then he – having been acknowledged as king by the church estate, the barons, the nobles, the city burghers, the commoners and even the Jews, i.e. every stratum of society – sat down in the palace and arranged the affairs of state, i.e. participated in the government of the kingdom.

Two things were intertwined in this highly theatrical event – in the sense of a public spectacle following a script – of 14 February 1458: elements of the coronation ritual for which the crown was not needed,[29] and the *entrée*, a ritual followed by kings throughout medieval Europe. Kings enacted particularly grand *entrées* upon their return to the capital city after their coronation.[30] Matthias's 1458 entry to Buda thus had precedents – even in Hungary, as we will see. The entry pageant which Buda staged in his honor also demonstrates the city's significance. There was, however, something else. The king sat down in

---

28 On Matthias' special devotion to the Virgin Mary, patron of Hungary, see András Kubinyi, *Főpapok, egyházi intézmények és vallásosság a középkori Magyarországon* [Prelates, ecclesiastical institutions and piety in medieval Hungary] (METEM, 22) (Budapest: METEM, 1999), pp. 335–339.

29 Cf. Erik Fügedi, *Uram, királyom... A XV. századi Magyarország hatalmasai* [My Lord, my King...the powerful men of fifteenth-century Hungary] (Budapest: Akadémiai, 1974), pp. 52–71. Fügedi supposes he took the second oath in the royal palace (ibid., p. 54), but in light of the information discussed above this is unlikely.

30 Beaune, "Les structures politiques," pp. 35–36.

the palace to arrange the affairs of state. This may well provide explanation for the detailed treatment of the royal seat and throne.

The earliest manifestations of Buda's significance and of the king's entry to the city were the events following the death of Andrew III. Foreign sources record Wenceslas, son of the king of Bohemia, as being led into Buda by the citizenry and the nobles after his election as king.[31] The Styrian Rhyming Chronicle relates that the clergy processed before the young Wenceslas as he arrived in Buda and he was led, as the bells rang, into the Church of Our Lady. "He was taken up to the altar in the chancel [...], that his election as king be evident to the people." He was then crowned at Székesfehérvár and taken home to Buda.[32] Seeing the rising strength of Charles of Anjou, the other claimant to the throne, Wenceslas' father, the king of Bohemia, came to visit his son in Buda in 1304. He expressed a wish to see his son in royal robes, and so for the procession into church for the festive mass, Wenceslas was dressed in St Stephen's mantle, furnished with St Stephen's sword and spurs, and St Stephen's Holy Crown was placed on his head. After the mass, the clergy escorted the king to his palace with hymns, and there he gave a banquet for the barons and the Hungarian lords.[33] Afterwards, the king of Bohemia took his son together with the Hungarian crown jewels to Bohemia, where Wenceslas renounced the Hungarian throne in favor of Otto Wittelsbach. When Otto came to Hungary, he brought the crown with him and his first destination was Buda, where the citizenry received him and swore an oath of loyalty.[34] He returned to Buda after his coronation at Székesfehérvár. This was described in the Illuminated Chronicle with the words, "From there [Székesfehérvár], he went to Buda and on the feast day, in royal pomp, with the Holy Crown on his head and, with a great number of people on horseback, he processed along all of the streets to display to everybody that he was the lawful king."[35]

Buda's status might be thought to have been inflated in the turbulent times of the early fourteenth century, especially because the king was living there,

---

31 ÁMTF, iv, p. 601.
32 "...uf dem altar in dem kor huoben si in empor [...] dass den Hüten wurde offenbaere, daz er ze kunig erweit waere" – *Catalogus fontium historiae Hungariae aevo ducum et regum ex stirpe Arpad descendentium*, iii, ed. Albinus Franciscus Gombos (Budapest: Szent István Akadémia, 1938, repr. Budapest: Nap, 2005), pp. 1905–1906 [henceforth: CFH].
33 CFH, iii, pp. 1914–1916.
34 CFH, iii, pp. 1936.
35 "Inde Budam veniens et in die sollempni in decore regio, coronam sanctam habens in capite, per omnes plateas et vicos incidebat eques cum populo copioso, ut cunctis se esse regem legittimum publicaret" – Alexander Domanovszky, ed., *Chronici Hungarici compositio saeculi XIV*, in SRH, i, pp. 217–505, here p. 483 (cap 191).

but there were similar events in the 1340s, when the king lived in Visegrád. Louis I, after inheriting the throne from his father and being crowned at Székesfehérvár, also went to Buda, where "...the entire population and the citizenry, the clergy and every monk received him with great reverence and respect, as befits his royal highness." Then he returned to Visegrád.[36] The same may have happened with other kings. Both Sigismund[37] and his son-in-law Albert[38] hurried to Buda after their coronation at Székesfehérvár. We may presume that both were admitted with same high ceremony as the others, i.e. that the customary *entrée* took place. Entries of new queens followed a similar program. Queen Beatrice arrived in Buda on Sunday, 15 December 1476. Some way outside the city, the Jews again, in ceremonial dress, received the monarch's new wife. One mile from the town, the prelates, barons and the burghers of Buda and of other towns awaited the royal couple as they approached on horseback. Despite the falling snow, a brief tournament was held on the field beneath the city, and then they made their entry. Once again, there was a procession of the clergy, the monks of the city's monasteries, and the guilds, carrying relics. The Eucharist was followed by the sound of 67 trumpeters. There are contemporary descriptions giving details of the procession and of the ornate costumes. The route again led to the Church of Our Lady, where a *Te Deum* was sung. Once again, there was an amnesty for prisoners. Then the royal couple remounted their horses and dismissed their escort in front of the palace.[39] The wife of Wladislas II, Anne de Foix (Queen Anne of Candale), made a similar entry.[40]

---

36 "...ibi ab omni populo ac civibus et clero virisque religiosis omnibus cum magna reverentia et honore est susceptus, prout regiam decet maiestatem" – *Chronici Hungarici*, p. 505 (cap. 212).

37 ZsO, i, p. 3 (no 4) (he still issued charters on 1 April in Székesfehérvár, then on the 4 April in Buda).

38 József Teleki, *Hunyadiak kora Magyarországon*, x [The age of the Hunyadis in Hungary] (Pest: Emich, 1853), pp. 10–11. (Albert informed Friedrich, the prince of Austria, of the coronation at Székesfehérvár on 9 January 1438, from Buda.) Louis II, crowned already during the life of his father was not been brought to the funeral at Székesfehérvár, but 23 March 1516, at Easter, he was carried around the city, both before and after the holy mass. See Gusztáv Wenzel, "Marino Sanuto Világkrónikájának Magyarországot illető tudósításai, iii," [The Hungarian references in the World Chronicle of Marino Sanuto] *Magyar Történelmi Tár* 13 [25] (1878), pp. 3–390, here pp. 42–43.

39 Stephanus Katona, *Historia critica regum Hungariae*, xvi (Buda: Weingand & Koepf, 1793), pp. 60–61; Béla Borsa, "Reneszánszkori ünnepségek Budán," [Renaissance festivities in Buda] *Tanulmányok Budapest Múltjából* 10 (1943), pp. 13–51, here pp. 46–47.

40 Henrik Marczali, "Candale i Anna, II. Ulászló neje, magyarországi útjának és a menynyegzői ünnepségek leírása," [The description of the Hungarian journey and the wedding

The entries of kings and queens thus had a set choreography, in which Buda and its citizens played no small role. The king (and his queen) had to be crowned in Székesfehérvár, but afterwards went to Buda to receive homage from the citizens of the capital city as a kind of confirmation of their lawful rule. The citizenry expressed their homage outside the city after the new king – according to the record of Matthias's entry – promised to uphold their privileges. The ceremony also had a religious component, which took place in the main parish church of the city, and the procession which received the king was also primarily, if not exclusively, ecclesiastical.

There is ample evidence demonstrating that the king rode round the city, although this may not have been at the same time as the entry ceremony. Then, there was the release of prisoners held in the City Hall. Having ridden around the city and with the *Te Deum* sung, Matthias immediately went to the private chambers of his palace. Beatrice, however, was taken by the king to her chambers immediately after the *Te Deum* in the church. It is possible that the queen was tired or that the snow made riding difficult. The progress through the city did take place, however, a few days after the church wedding in the Church of Our Lady and – perhaps significantly – on the day after the consummation of the marriage. Our source writes: "Afterwards, they went from the castle on a golden sleigh, drawn by a fine white horse, and drove all round the city."[41] (It was the end of December!).

Ceremonial entries in Medieval Europe were not restricted to such constitutionally important, post-coronation events.[42] In Buda, they were held on customary occasions, with a prescribed choreography, and the citizens of Buda played their part. Article 7 of the *Ofner Stadtrecht* provided that if the king went to war or was abroad for an extended period, then upon his return, as he approached the City Hall, everybody – men and women, young and old, and all of the clergy of the churches and monasteries – were to go before him in procession, with flags, the Eucharist and burning candles, dressed respectably. The judge and persons of authority were required to ride before him and "receive him with honor and escort him to the castle (i.e. the royal palace), where the city judge shall humbly take his leave".[43] As we have seen, leave was taken of the new Queen Beatrice at the palace gate.

---

ceremonies of Anna of Candale, wife of Wladislas II] *Magyar Történelmi Tár* 11 [25] (1877), pp. 97–113.

41 "Darnach fueren Sy heraus der pürg in die statt auf dem guldin Schlitten vnd ain schon weyss ross darjnn, vnd fueren in der stat vmb" – Borsa, "Ünnepségek," p. 52.
42 See note 30.
43 OSt, p. 61 (cap. 7).

The citizens of Buda played a similar role in royal entries as citizens of other European capitals, a role whose constitutional significance was probably related to Buda citizens' rights and obligations in the coronation ceremony at Székesfehérvár. Article 6 of the *Ofner Stadtrecht*, written in the first half of the fifteenth century, provided that upon the coronation of a king or queen, the city judge and several councillors and notables, together with their retinues, should travel to Székesfehérvár and guard the front door of the coronation church during the ceremony. Afterwards, they were to escort the king and queen to their residence.[44] What was set down as an obligation in the opening articles was repeated as an explicit right in Article 166, in a slightly shorter form: "...and nobody shall occupy the front gate of the Church of Our Lady in Székesfehérvár except the men of Buda, who shall guard it in armor until the coronation ends."[45] The men of Buda exercised this right, and a description of Beatrice's coronation confirms the level of trust invested in them: "...the men of Buda seized and occupied the church door, because they are at liberty to grant or deny admission to the coronation."[46] The citizens of the capital city (and we can be sure of that title by now) were therefore responsible for security at the Székesfehérvár coronation. This is partially related to the role of the Buda citizenry in royal departures. There is much less surviving information on this, consisting essentially of no more than a foreign ambassadorial report on Matthias's wedding. The king set out with a large retinue from Buda to Székesfehérvár for the reception and coronation of his wife. The Jews had an interesting role. At the king's command, they rode into the inner castle, led by Mendel, their prefect, who gave a speech at the well. The ambassador's report gives a detailed account of the ornate clothes of the 31-strong mounted Jewish delegation, and their long silvered swords. Then the king mounted his horse to ride from the palace with his retinue, behind the Jews, towards Székesfehérvár. The source finds it necessary to mention that the Jews took a different route to Székesfehérvár. It mentions the ornately-dressed prelates and barons in the royal retinue, and the "Buda citizens, also in their finery."[47] The choreography

---

44   OSt, p. 61 (cap. 7).
45   "Vnntcz an daß forderst Portal an vnßer frawen kirchen zu weisenpûrg sol nymant ynne haben, dye ofner, dy sullenn yn irem harnâsch hutten vncz das dy kronung verpracht wirt" – OSt p. 119 (cap. 166).
46   "...darnach haben dy burger von ofen die kirchtur eingenommen vnd besetztt, wann sy die freyhaitt haben, wen Sy hinein zue der krönung lassen, oder nicht" – Borsa, "Ünnepségek," p. 45.
47   "...die burger der stat zue ofen die auch kostlich waren, Ettllich in Samatt vnd Seyden die anndem kostlich in Harnasch, vnd all mit Strauss vedernn die tzugen all vor dem künig aus der Statt" – Borsa, "Ünnepségek," pp. 44–45.

was the same. The Jews received the approaching royal couple first, and were the first to leave the palace. The place of the citizenry in the procession is not clear, but the escort definitely left Buda before the king. The men of Buda in ceremonial armor were clearly those who had to guard the door of the coronation church.

The king's burial was another important state occasion because, as has been noted by a French historian, a medieval king died in public.[48] Although most late medieval kings were buried in Székesfehérvár, Buda also had a place in the funeral ceremony. Illustrative of this is the death and burial of Charles I. He died in his Visegrád residence and was first laid out and mourned in the parish church there. Then he was taken by boat to Buda, the "truly famous city." The citizenry and clergy of Buda, in funeral attire, processed down to the Danube. The body was taken into the city – presumably the Church of Our Lady – and prayers were said, and psalms sung, night and day. Only on the third day did the funeral procession set out for Székesfehérvár.[49] Wladislas II, who died in Buda on 13 March 1516, was also laid out in the palace for everyone to see. On 16 March (Palm Sunday), he was taken in procession to the "holy church" (clearly the Church of Our Lady) and next day, the 17th, the funeral procession started out for Székesfehérvár. At the same time, the remains of his wife Queen Anne, who had been buried in St Sigismund's chapter, were exhumed and taken by separate carriage to the royal burial church.[50]

The Buda citizenry thus played an important part in royal entries, departures and burials. This raised their self-esteem, as may be gauged from their description of the city in the 1498 arenga as *solium regale thronusque regius*. The Church of Our Lady in Buda (the parish church of the German population) had a distinguished place in all of these events. It was where the most important constitutional acts took place. (The Buda diets, however, were usually held in the Franciscan Church of St John.) Its locally-elected priest was – according to Article 21 of the *Ofner Stadtrecht* – the first among the four highest office-bearers of the city (*obristen amptleüt*),[51] even though there were three other parish churches in the city: the Hungarians' Church of St Mary Magdalene in

---

48 Beaune, "Les structures politiques," pp. 33–35.
49 Johannes de Thurocz, *Chronica Hungarorum*, i, eds Elisabeth Galántai, Julius Kristó (Bibliotheca Scriptorum Medii Recentisque Aevorum. Series Nova, 7) (Budapest: Akadémiai, 1985), pp. 156–157 (cap. 128).
50 Luis Neustadt, "Die letzten Stunden des Königs Wladislaw II," *Ungarische Revue* 4 (1884), pp. 38–42. The body of Queen Anna, after its exhumation had been taken in a procession to the Church of Our Lady, accompanied by barons and commons. See Wenzel, "Sanuto," p. 42.
51 OSt, p. 66 (cap. 21).

the Castle, the Church of St Peter the Martyr in the suburb of the same name, and St Gerard's Church in Alhéviz.[52]

We find another indication of the significance of the German parish church in Paul Wann's petition, and there were other events that demonstrate the distinctive role of the church and the city populace. In late 1476, János Dengelegi Pongrác, voivode of Transylvania, died suddenly during the ceremonies for King Matthias's wedding. He was one of the highest dignitaries of the land and closest relative – first cousin – of the king, his mother having been Regent John Hunyadi's sister. The Hungarian barons – and again the citizens of Buda – took his body in procession to the Church of Our Lady, where a requiem was held. Despite being the parish church of the German population, it was where the funeral was held for the voivode, the monarch's close relative.[53]

Buda differed from most European capitals in not being an episcopal seat. Nevertheless, it is recorded as being an ecclesiastical center, enjoying an exemption which made it subject to the jurisdiction of the archbishop of Esztergom, despite belonging to the diocese of Veszprém. Although the primate naturally had his diocesan and archiepiscopal seat in Esztergom,[54] there is a question surrounding the legatine tribunal over which he presided in his capacity as papal legate. There are records of him (occasionally) making judgments in Buda. The earliest of these date from the time when András Chesius, provost of Čazma and doctor of canon law, was acting legate. He held court "in the customary time and place for hearing legatine matters," in the Buda house of the archbishop of Esztergom.[55]

---

52   Kubinyi, *Anfänge Ofens*, pp. 34–42.
53   Borsa, "Ünnepségek," p. 50, where the ceremony is discussed in detail.
54   Cf. György Bónis, "Az egyházi bíráskodás fejlődése a Mohács előtti Magyarországon," [The development of ecclesiastical jurisdiction in Hungary before the battle of Mohács] in idem, *Szentszéki regeszták. Iratok az egyházi bíráskodás történetéhez a középkori Magyarországon* [Registers from the Holy See. Documents on the history of ecclesiastical jurisdiction in medieval Hungary] (Jogtörténeti Tár, i/1), ed. Elemér Balogh (Szeged: József Attila Tudományegyetem Állam- és Jogtudományi Karának Tudományos Bizottsága, 1997), pp. 621–658.
55   MNL OL DF 232 528 (1519). This lawsuit was connected to the mysterious death and inheritance of Zsigmond Ernuszt, bishop of Pécs. For the adjudication of Chesius in Buda in issues relating to the bishopric of Transylvania and the claims of the archbishopric of Kalocsa, see Károly Szabó, "Az Erdélyi Múzeum eredeti okleveleinek kivonatai, 1231–1540, iv," [The summary of the original charters of the Transylvanian Museum] *Történelmi Tár* 13 (1890), pp. 328–359, here p. 341 (no 476) (1515); Bónis, *Szentszéki regeszták*, no 4196 (1517). Unfortunately Bónis, when editing the volume, did not always give the place of issue of the charters. It has thus proved impossible so far to track the beginnings of the legatine court of the primate in Buda.

There were other occasions, of no constitutional import, in which Buda and its citizens also had a prominent presence. One was carnival, when the king always held a great and expensive reception. Unfortunately, the only surviving royal accounts relating to carnival time are for 1494–1495 and 1525. In 1495, when the king was waging a campaign against Lőrinc Újlaki, he held a carnival in Pécs, with a banquet on Shrove Tuesday (3 March).[56] In 1494, Wladislas II was in Buda on Shrove Tuesday, which fell on 11 February, and he invited the citizens of Buda and their wives to a carnival banquet. 42 pints (about 70.5 litres) of expensive Madeira wine was served at the dinner, and the royal understeward added 34 florins of his own to meet the expenses of the reception.[57] On Shrove Tuesday in 1525 (28 February), Louis II also gave a banquet, but invited the papal legate cardinal, the prelates and the barons rather than the citizens. Then, too, Madeira wine was bought, as were crystal glasses, knives and lamps.[58]

The invitation of the Buda citizens (which must have meant the city council and other leading personages) with their families could not have been a unique occasion. There is no information concerning Buda, but we know that Matthias invited the "ladies" to his Viennese court in 1488, and had them taken home at night at the city's expense. The event is twice mentioned in the Vienna municipal accounts, first between the end of March and the middle of May, and then on 31 August, which was a Sunday.[59] These records can be interpreted in two ways. We know that the courtesans of the city were present at the receptions of Matthias's predecessors, Albert and Ladislas V,[60] and so perhaps they were the ladies "taken home." More likely, however, the king gave a reception for the lady citizens, which would be consistent with Sigismund's giving a dinner in the Bourbon Palace for the noble and most respectable ladies of Paris when he stayed there.[61] Whatever the details, it seems that the citizens of Buda expected

---

56   Johann Christian von Engel, *Geschichte des ungrischen Reichs und seiner Nebenländer*, I (Halle: Johann Jacob Gebauer, 1797), p. 71.
57   Engel, *Geschichte des ungrischen*, I, pp. 83 and 87.
58   Vilmos Fraknói, "II. Lajos király számadási könyve, 1525. január 12–július 16," [The account book of Louis II, 12 January 1525 – July 16 1525] *Magyar Történelmi Tár* [NS] 10 [22] (1876), pp. 47–236.
59   Vienna, Wiener Stadt- und Landesarchiv, OKA Rechnungen 1, 49. Bd., 37^v and 69^v.
60   Brigitte Rath, "Prostitution und spätmittelalterliche Gesellschaft im österreichisch–süddeutschen Raum," in *Frau und spätmittelalterlicher Alltag* (Veröffentlichungen des Instituts für mittelalterliche Realienkunde Österreichs, 9 = Österreichische Akademie der Wissenschaften, Philosophisch–historische Klasse, Sitzungsberichte, 473) (Vienna: Verlag der Österreichischen Akademie der Wissenschaften, 1986), pp. 553–571, here p. 569.
61   *Journal d'un bourgeois de Paris de 1405 à 1449*, ed. Colette Beaune (Paris: Poche, 1990), p. 92.

the occasional festive invitation (together with their families) from the king. Buda citizens were naturally spectators at the frequent chivalric tournaments and horse races. The latter featured the king's specially-bred racehorses. The horse races were held in the *stadium*, whose location is unknown. The city judge and his men were charged with guarding the prizes for the winners set up in the *stadium*. It was regarded as a great popular holiday, when Gypsies and the barons' musicians provided the music.[62] There is every sign that it was up to the city council to organize the race. In Vienna, the "scarlet horse race" (*Scharlachrennen*), whose name derived from the winner's prize of a bolt of scarlet broadcloth, was held twice a year. One of the races in 1486 was postponed because Matthias, then lord of Vienna, was at war and unable to attend.[63]

It is no surprise that Buda became the first city of the realm and had special rights. Around 1440, the city managed to become the permanent location of the *tárnokszék*, the court of the Lord Chief Treasurer or *tavernicus* and the appeal court for the seven most privileged cities in Hungary, among which Buda law applied. The court had to gather in the city of Buda (i.e. not in the royal palace), and Buda law was applied in its proceedings. There are several surviving copies of the reference book of tavernical law (*ius tavernicale*), which was based on Buda law.[64] Article 17 of the statutes of the seven cities, laid down in 1456, stated that since Buda was the capital city, where the affairs of nobles were judged and summonses could be issued with ease, the Lord Chief Treasurer always had to keep a deputy in the city to issue the summonses.[65] Another description of the customs of the *tárnokszék* puts the same thing differently: "...since the city of Buda is held to be pre-eminent, where the inhabitants of the realm settle all of their affairs," there should always be a representative of the tavernical law court there.[66]

Buda was therefore clearly the capital, the pre-eminent city of the realm. The courts which were competent in the affairs of the nobility sat there, a fact which also justified the permanent presence of the appeal court serving the

---

62   Fraknói, "II. Lajos király," pp. 83, 156, 161, 163 and 169.
63   Vienna, Wiener Stadt- und Landesarchiv, Urkunden, no 5152.
64   Imre Szentpétery, ifj., "A tárnoki ítélőszék kialakulása," [The formation of the court of law of the *tavernicus*] *Századok* [Supplementum] 68 (1934), pp. 510–590; Štefánia Mertanová, *Ius tavernicale: štúdie o procese formovania práva tavernických miest v etapách vyvoja tavernickeho súdu v Uhorsku, 15–17. stor* [Studies in the legal development of the tavernical towns in the period of the development of the tavernical court, fifteenth–seventeenth centuries] (Bratislava: Veda, Vydavateľstvo Slovenskej akadémie vied, 1985), *passim*.
65   Szentpétery, "A tárnoki," p. 589.
66   "Nach dem Ofenstadt die furnembste gennenet wirdt unnd alle Sachen des Lands Einwohnern darinnen gehandelt werden" – Mertanová, *Ius tavernicale*, p. 158.

principal cities of the kingdom. It should be noted that by 1498 at the latest, but almost certainly earlier, Buda acquired the right to judge criminal cases from all over the country. There are records of many robbers, nobles among them, being held prisoner or sentenced to death by the Buda municipal court. King Wladislas (of Poland and Hungary) granted a similar right to Cracow (the capital of Poland) and Lviv in 1444. We do not know whether Wladislas was following the Hungarian example or vice-versa.[67] The amnesty granted on the occasion of royal entrances may well have been connected with this right.

I have attempted to clear up the question of Buda's status as capital city and royal seat through clues from contemporary linguistic usage, 'official' titles (including the city's self-evaluation) and events related to the city, but some doubt remains. Buda's citizens – sometimes represented by the judge and council – and its main parish church certainly played a major constitutional role after the turn of the thirteenth and fourteenth centuries. This was recognized by the king and advertised in special occasions and ceremonies. The king's way of honoring his capital city was to occasionally entertain its citizens and their wives. We must also consider, however, the definition of the functions of capital, royal residence and garrison put forward by the great German economic historian, Georg von Below, in the early twentieth century. In a dispute with Werner Sombart, who saw these functions as having major roles in the development of the city, he claimed that the capital was the permanent location of the central authorities, the residence was the current monarch's favorite abode, and the 'garrison town' was a regular station of some units of a standing army. Below's conclusion, however, somewhat takes us aback: according to him, none of these existed in the Middle Ages. Or at least we cannot describe cities as such at the time of their formation (which does not apply to the late medieval period).[68]

There is another, rarely mentioned fact: Buda was indeed a garrison town in the late Middle Ages, where most of the elite military unit of the kingdom, the royal militia known as the *aulici* (the 'household army') were stationed,[69] and was also the location of the arsenal and cannon foundry.[70]

---

67   Kubinyi, *Budapest*, pp. 170–171.
68   Georg von Below, *Probleme der Wirtschaftsgeschichte eine Einführung in das Studium der Wirtschaftsgeschichte* (Tübingen: J.C.B. Mohr, 1926.), pp. 499–500.
69   András Kubinyi, "A királyi udvar élete a Jagelló-korban," [The life of the court in the age of the Jagiellonian Period] in *Kelet és Nyugat között. Történeti tanulmányok Kristó Gyula tiszteletére* [Between East and West. Historical studies in honor of Gyula Kristó], ed. László Koszta (Szeged: Szegedi Középkorász Műhely, 1995), pp. 309–335, here p. 321.
70   Engel, *Geschichte des ungrischen*, pp. 98–107.

Most historians, like Below, use the term capital city to mean a concentration of political authorities, including the government, parliament, highest court and embassies.[71] This definition of course relates to the modern age, but the same idea can be seen, if with some inherent contradictions, in Peter Moraw's account of Prague as a royal center during the reign of Charles IV. Although he denies that the "city as capital" can be a historical topic for the era of Charles IV, he claims that the presence in Prague of a financial authority – working independently of the itinerant Emperor – was "a clear expression in Bohemia and beyond that Prague was a central location with a capital-city function."[72]

By this criterion, what makes a city a capital is the presence of offices of state and royal courts which act and make judgments even the absence of the monarch. Indeed the statutes of the tavernical court of 1456 called Buda the capital because it was the judicial center of the realm. As we have seen, Buda's labels *sedes*, *solium*, *thronus* and so forth, may be interpreted – from at least the time of Matthias – as meaning that it was the royal seat from which he governed and where he sat in judgment. Matthias was recognized as king by taking the oath, performing the *entrée* and, most importantly, sitting in the palace and arranging the affairs of state. The only trouble is that for most of the fourteenth century, the royal courts and court chapel were located in the permanent royal residence of Visegrád, even when the king himself was absent, so that the residence could also be the seat of institutions which operated independently of the king's presence.[73]

The answer is to be sought at the turn of the thirteenth and fourteenth centuries, the turbulent period of interregnum. That was when Buda became a royal seat[74] and capital city, and it was by then, at the latest, that the citizenry of Buda managed to secure the rights that they subsequently enjoyed until 1541, unchallenged even by Charles I and Louis I when they took up residence in Visegrád. It is true that Visegrád was also part of the *medium regni*, the king's 'home ground', but from the time that Sigismund returned the royal residence to Buda (where it remained until the Ottoman era), the city became the capital and royal seat, contributing to the rise of its economic power.

---

71   Engel and Lambrecht, "Hauptstadt," p. 16.
72   Peter Moraw, "Zur Mittelpunktfunktion Prags im Zeitalter Karls IV," in *Europa slavica – Europa orientalis. Festschrift für Herbert Ludat zum 70. Geburtstag* (Osteuropastudien der Hochschulen des Landes Hessen. Reihe, i. Gießener Abhandlungen zur Agrar- und Wirtschaftsforschung des europäischen Ostens, 100), eds Klaus-Detlev Grothusen and Klaus Zernack (Berlin: Duncker & Humblot, 1980), pp. 445–489, here p. 474.
73   Kubinyi, *Főpapok*, pp. 306–307.
74   Györffy, *Pest-Buda*, pp. 223–228.

PART 5

Court Culture of a 'Capital'

∴

CHAPTER 16

Made for the King: Sigismund of Luxemburg's Statues in Buda and Their Place in Art History

*Szilárd Papp**

A major find of sculpture, almost as much as a hoard of treasure, sets off a wave of excitement among academics and the public for a while. Things discovered underground, spectacularly separated from their original context, hinting at dark mysteries or possibly links to an emblematic building or person, have just what is needed for a media sensation. Accidental discovery and the fragmented state of the objects only intensify the sense of mystery. For those engaged in serious study, the significance of these archaeological finds rests on somewhat different criteria: whether they substantially expand our knowledge of similar material, how much they change the accepted historical view, and whether they throw light on unknown areas or fill major gaps in our knowledge. The biggest medieval sculpture finds, such as the fragments of the chancel of Cologne Cathedral, the torsos of Notre-Dame in Paris and the Bern statuary,[1] have all satisfied both public and academic expectations.

Standing alongside these is the 1974 find of Gothic sculpture in Buda. At the time, it was a sensation among academics and the public alike, although political circumstances conspired to keep it within the country's borders for a while. The Hungarian public had more than just an ephemeral interest in the find

---

Translated by Alan Campbell.

* The numbers of the statues referred here are the same as in the following publications: László Zolnay, "Der gotische Skulpturenfund von 1974 in der Burg von Buda,"*Acta Historiae Artium* 22 (1976), pp. 173–331, here pp. 263–327; László Zolnay and Ernő Marosi, *A budavári szoborlelet* [Buda statue finds] (Budapest: Corvina, 1989), pp. 131–156 and 172–175. I acknowledge the useful information provided by András Végh while writing this article, and I am also grateful to Ernő Marosi for his comments on the text. The study was published in a slightly different format in Hungarian as "A király műhelye. Luxemburgi Zsigmond budavári szobrai és művészettörténeti helyzetük," [The king's workshop. The statues of Sigismund of Luxemburg in the Buda Castle and their art historical position] *Művészettörténeti Értesítő* 63 (2014), pp. 1–37.

1 On Cologne, see *Verschwundenes Inventarium. Der Skulpturenfund im Kölner Domchor*, ed. Ulrike Bergmann (Cologne: Stadt Köln – Schnütgen-Museum, 1984); on Paris: François Giscard d'Estaing, Michel Fleury and Alain Erlande-Brandenburg, *Notre-Dame de Paris. Les rois retrouvés* (Paris: J. Cuénot, 1977); on Bern, see Franz-Josef Sladeczek, *Der Berner Skulpturenfund. Die Ergebnisse der kunsthistorischen Auswertung* (Bern: Benteli, 1999).

thanks to the archaeologist who made the discovery, László Zolnay. His writing was directed at a broad audience, well beyond the confines of his profession, with excursions into imaginative literature. For art historians, the discovery from this period of court art on a level which surpassed the bravest of dreams, took them completely by surprise and presented them with an enormous long-term task. Nowadays, however, with the change of circumstances, the Buda statuary has lost much of its motivational power and has almost completely lapsed into obscurity among the public. Although Ernő Marosi, the art historian who worked most intensively with the figures at the time, repeatedly pointed out the need for further research, archaeologists and art historians today tend to see the story as either already told or as hidden in an impenetrable mist. As a result, the Buda fragments have not been the subject of substantial investigation for several decades and – much more so than their west European counterparts – remain surrounded by archaeological and historical uncertainties beyond what the nature of such finds makes inevitable.

A few facts serve to illustrate the unfortunate condition of the material. On the archaeological side, the difficult conditions of the 1974 excavation allowed little more than an emergency rescue, leaving basic questions unanswered. It is an outstandingly large collection, and excavations carried out in the Buda Castle District from time to time are regularly adding to it. The figures have been the subject of many publications, but in fact, they have never been catalogued in detail and their restoration is at best incomplete. Partly owing to these circumstances, but also because of where they were found, many art historical issues also remain obscure. We do not know where the statues were intended for, or exactly where they were erected. We do not know to what extent the assemblage as a whole remained unfinished, and we only have guesses as to their subject matter and categorization. They cannot be consistently dated, and the time and circumstances of their destruction remains indeterminate.

Compounding these dilemmas is the obscurity surrounding European sculpture in this era owing to uncertainties in methodology and other basic problems, not to mention the difficulties arising from national-based approaches. This may be one reason why foreign art historians, with one or two exceptions, avoid making any statements about the find despite its relatively high level of familiarity. As a result, the Buda statuary has not really found its place in the European or even (East-)Central European art of this period.[2]

---

2   This is well indicated by the fact that its detailed analysis is regularly left out of the overviews of Central European art recently published outside Hungary. See for instance: *Prag und die grossen Kulturzentren Europas in der Zeit der Luxemburger 1310–1437*, eds Markéta Jarošová, Jiří Kuthan and Stefan Scholz (Prague: Togga, 2008); *Kunst als Herrschaftsinstrument.*

Another inhibiting factor is the sheer quantity of comparative material which has been included – with varying degrees of justification – in the studies. It is distributed through several different regions of Europe and has by now swelled to a quantity that could not possibly be studied by one person except via illustrations. The dangers of this as regards three-dimensional objects need hardly to be explained. In several respects, then, assessments of the Buda statuary, partly owing to broader problems of sculpture from this period, continue to fluctuate widely and sometimes embrace extreme notions.[3]

Böhmen und das Heilige Römische Reich unter den Luxemburgern im europäischen Kontext, eds Jiří Fajt and Andrea Langer (Berlin–Munich: Deutscher Kunstverlag, 2009); *Art and Architecture around 1400. Global and Regional Perspectives*, eds Marjeta Ciglenečki and Polona Vidmar (Maribor: Faculty of Arts, 2012).

3   The most important literature of the sculpture-find comprises: László Zolnay and Ernő Szakál, *Der gotische Skulpturenfund in der Burg von Buda* (Budapest: Corvina, 1976); Zolnay, *Der gotische Skulpturenfund*; Ernő Marosi, "Vorläufige kunsthistorische Bemerkungen zum Skulpturenfund von 1974 in der Burg von Buda," *Acta Historiae Artium* 22 (1976), pp. 333–373; László Zolnay, "Az 1967–1975. évi budavári ásatásokról s az itt talált gótikus szoborcsoportról," [On the excavations at the Buda Castle between 1967 and 1975 and the Gothic statue ensemble found there] *Budapest Régiségei* 24, no 3 (1977), pp. 3–164; and 24, no 4 (1977), pp. 1–239; Gyöngyi Török, "Einige unbeachtete Holzskulpturen des weichen Stils in Ungarn und ihre Beziehungen zu dem Skulpturenfund in der Burg von Buda," *Acta Historiae Artium* 27 (1981), pp. 209–224; Michael Viktor Schwarz, *Höfische Skulptur im 14. Jahrhundert. Entwicklungsphasen und Vermittlungswege im Vorfeld des Weichen Stils*, i–ii (Worms: Wernersche Verlagsgesellschaft, 1986), ii, pp. 444–468; Ernő Marosi, "König Sigismund von Ungarn und Avignon," in *Orient und Okzident im Spiegel der Kunst. Festschrift Heinrich Gerhard Franz zum 70. Geburtstag*, eds Günther Brucher and Wolfgang T. Müller (Graz: Akademische Druck- und Verlagsanstalt, 1986), pp. 229–249; Zolnay and Marosi, *A budavári szoborlelet*; Ernő Marosi, "Die Skulpturen der Sigismundszeit in Buda und die Anschaulichkeit der Kunst des frühen 15. Jahrhunderts," in *Internationale Gotik in Mitteleuropa* (Kunsthistorisches Jahrbuch Graz, 24), eds Götz Pochat and Brigitte Wagner (Graz: Akademische Druck- und Verlagsanstalt, 1990), pp. 182–195; Michael Viktor Schwarz, "Das Budaer Ritteratelier und der Anfang des Weichen Stils in der venezianischen Skulptur," in *Internationale Gotik*, pp. 269–280; Ernő Marosi, "Zu 'Werkstatt' und 'Künstler' in der Skulpturenreihe der Sigismundszeit von Buda," in *Der Meister von Großlobming*, ed. Arthur Saliger (Vienna: Galerie, 1994), pp. 56–63; Lothar Schultes, "Der Skulpturenfund von Buda und der Meister von Großlobming," in *Sigismund von Luxemburg. Kaiser und König im Mitteleuropa 1387–1437*, eds Josef Macek, Ernő Marosi and Ferdinand Seibt (Warendorf: Fahlbusch, 1994), pp. 293–306; Michael Viktor Schwarz, "König Sigismund als Mäzen und der Weiche Stil in der Skulptur," in *Sigismund von Luxemburg. Kaiser und König*, pp. 307–338; András Végh, "Gotische Statuen aus dem Königspalast von Buda," in *Hans Multscher. Bildhauer der Spätgotik in Ulm*, eds Brigitte Reinhardt and Michael Roth (Ulm: Süddeutsche Verlagsgesellschaft, 1997), pp. 71–85; Ernő Marosi, "A budavári Zsigmond-kori szobrok kérdései huszonkét év (és a Szent Zsigmond templom feltárásai) után,"

It is crucial to find out what we can say for certain about the location and circumstances of the find, what proportion of the figures have survived, and how they can be classified. This knowledge will determine the conclusions which may be drawn with confidence or with reasonable reliability. The way in which these issues have been regarded has gone through considerable changes since the first assessments of the find in 1974, owing partly to archaeological finds since then and partly to reassessments of old finds. This study reviews the present state of research into the remains and attempts to formulate questions and lines of research that might yield more results.

Locations and Circumstances of the Find

The medieval city of Buda, lying on a rocky plateau that runs roughly parallel with the Danube in a north-south direction, was founded by Béla IV after the Mongol invasion of 1241–1242. The modest royal palace at the southern end of the plateau, as is discussed in other studies of this volume,[4] only began to develop into a proper king's residence in the second half of the fourteenth century (Fig. 16.1). The largest find of statues (1974) was located on land belonging to the civilian town. The find lay directly to the north of the castle and within a hundred meters of the palace. We know that King Sigismund effected major changes to this district in the second half of his reign. Court barons involved in the government of the kingdom increasingly acquired land there, and it also contained several buildings belonging to the king.[5]

A recent reassessment of the excavation documents has established that the place where the statuary was found in 1974 was definitely not an internal courtyard or water reservoir as previously thought, but a cellar on an urban building plot, over which there stood a building or perhaps part of it.[6]

[Questions on the Sigismund-age statues at Buda after twenty-two years (and the excavations of the Saint Sigismund church)] *Budapest Régiségei* 33 (1999), pp. 93–101; András Végh, "Skulpturenfunde aus der Zeit Sigismunds aus dem Umfeld des Königspalastes von Buda," in *Sigismundus Rex et Imperator*, pp. 219–224; Michael Viktor Schwarz, "König Sigismunds höfischer Traum. Die Skulpturen für die Burg in Buda," in *Sigismundus Rex et Imperator*, pp. 225–235.

4 See the studies by Károly Magyar and András Végh in the present volume and the literature quoted there.

5 On the history of the quarter, see András Végh, "Középkori városnegyed a királyi palota előterében. A budavári Szent György tér és környezetének története a középkorban," [Medieval quarter in the forefront of the royal palace. The history of the Szent György Square and its surroundings in the Middle Ages] *Tanulmányok Budapest Múltjából* 31 (2003), pp. 7–42.

6 On its evaluation with earlier literature, see Végh, "Skulpturenfunde aus der Zeit Sigismunds".

The same study found that the thick, homogeneous infill containing the statues was not brought in from elsewhere, but appeared when the building burned down, consisting mostly of material which fell from the upper floor or floors when the cellar roof collapsed. From almost fifty coins found there, the collapse may be dated to the two decades in the middle of the fifteenth century.[7] The finds have also revealed what the building was used for before it burned down. The various stages of completion of some of the statues and other finds related to stone carving leave little doubt that the site excavated in 1974 was the workshop, or more accurately, part of the premises used by the craftsmen who were making the statues.[8] There were no direct clues to stone carving (debris, tools) found beside the statues, and so the workshop itself was most likely housed in a different part of the building, and the room or rooms above the cellar were mostly used for storage.[9] Although a few related statues have turned up in the vicinity of the building and the plot, this is satisfactorily explained by the frequent and drastic disturbance of the area, including the cellar. It is also important to note that most of the statues made by the sculpture workshop were never installed.

Nonetheless, some pieces previously found on the area of the royal castle have links to the 1974 find, some by virtue of their workmanship and style, others more directly. Among them are a corbel with a female head (no 70) and a fragment of another female head (unlisted) found in a very significant place: a recess in the wall of the palace chapel.[10] Then there is a fragment of hands clasped together in prayer, also found in the chapel, with a fracture surface that fits a female saint, showing signs of repair, which was found in the 1974 find from the cellar described above. The hand gesture suggests a statue of Mary

---

7   Imre Bodor, "Az 1974-ben feltárt budavári szoborleletet kísérő pénzleletek," [The coin finds that accompanied the Buda statue finds from 1974] *Budapest Régiségei* 33 (1999), pp. 89–92; Végh, "Skulpturenfunde aus der Zeit Sigismunds," p. 221.

8   The local production of the statues is confirmed by their material. This is Sarmatian soft limestone from the surroundings of Buda (Budafok-Nagytétény, Kőbánya), but the solidity of the material of the statues differs significantly: see Jenő Boda, "A budavári ásatásokkal kapcsolatban feltárt Anjou-kori szobortöredékek kőzetanyagának vizsgálata," [The scientific analysis of the Angevin-Period statue fragment-finds from the castle of Buda] *Budapest Régiségei* 24 (1977), pp. 222–227.

9   The workshop itself was probably situated in the street wing of the building. This area cannot be investigated any further as a new annex to the Baroque palace was built here in the 1960s.

10 László Gerevich, *A budai vár feltárása* [The excavation of the castle of Buda] (Budapest: Akadémiai, 1966), p. 168 and 207, table ix/1 and 2; idem, *The Art of Buda and Pest in the Middle Ages* (Budapest: Akadémiai, 1971), pp. 72–73, pic. xlviii/123, li/132; Zolnay and Marosi, *A budavári szoborlelet*, Fig. 16.26.

(no 32).¹¹ Also having links with the palace is the upper part of a drinking fountain, with figurative decoration, whose shape and size match it to two through-drilled pillar trunks from the 1974 find.¹² Although the severely deteriorated medieval palace was finally demolished and its remains levelled to make way for the new Baroque palace in the early eighteenth century, spreading the fragments out and possibly mixing them with material from the city, it would be difficult to divorce the medieval provenance of these pieces from the palace area. Some of the statues associated with the 1974 find must therefore have been destroyed in the palace, i.e. where they were intended for, and not in the workshop. Which buildings or parts of the palace they were in can only be guessed at even in the best case from the archaeological data. Candidates, in principle, are the Angevin-period chapel, the New Palace building incorporating the enormous hall built by Sigismund on the north area, or another of his constructions, the ostentatious Csonka (i.e. "Incomplete") Tower.¹³ As is hinted by a later source stating that Palatine Mihály Ország (1458–1484) ordered the re-gilding of a statue of Sigismund on a gate tower that the king had built, there could have been statues anywhere.¹⁴

A find in 1994/95 adjusted and extended in many ways the picture sketched out so far. In the same part of medieval Buda, about a hundred and fifty meters north of the sculpture workshop, Sigismund founded a collegiate chapter consecrated to the Virgin Mary and St Sigismund, immediately before 1410. The event bore great similarity to the foundation sixty years before of the Frauenkirche in Nuremberg by his father, Charles IV. The two buildings are strikingly similar in floor plan and dimensions, and the construction of the new chapel was what most influenced the changes in the district of Buda mentioned above.¹⁵ A large waste pit five meters from the south wall of the

---

11   Végh, "Skulpturenfunde aus der Zeit Sigismunds," p. 222; *Sigismundus Rex et Imperator*, pp. 327–328 (Cat. 4.19, by Imre Takács).

12   *Budapest im Mittelalter*, p. 476 (Cat. 323, by Emese Nagy). It should be pointed out that the stone material of the pillars (sweetwater hard limestone) differs in composition from the upper part.

13   On these buildings of the castle, see most recently Sándor Tóth, "Die Gebäude des Budaer Königspalastes zur Zeit Sigismunds von Luxemburg," in *Sigismundus Rex et Imperator*, pp. 200–218. The planned erection of at least some of the statues in an architectonic structure is implied by two figural consoles (nos 1 and 2) and a baldachin-fragment (no 69 of the 1974-finds) and one console with a female head found previously in the castle (no 70).

14   Jolán Balogh, *A művészet Mátyás király udvarában*, i [Art in the court of King Matthias] (Budapest: Akadémiai, 1966), p. 137.

15   Bernát L. Kumorovitz, "A budai várkápolna és a Szent Zsigmond prépostság történetéhez," [On the construction history of the chapel of the castle of Buda and the St Sigismund

nave, discovered during the excavation of the foundations and surroundings of the provostry, which was destroyed during the Ottoman era, yielded finds that clearly originated in this church. These consisted of many architectural fragments, heaps of stained glass and glazed roof tiles, some furnishings, and more than two hundred, mostly small statue shards. They were disposed of some time in the second quarter of the sixteenth century, after the church suffered serious damage during the four sieges and multiple capture of Buda by the Ottomans.[16] Many of the pieces retrieved were small statues of terracotta and possibly artificial stone, but there were also stone torsos whose style at first inspection links them to the 1974 find. The most striking examples are remains of a Man of Sorrows and a fragment of a drapery-clad figure.[17] One of the most important lessons the chapel finds have to tell is that the sculpture workshop uncovered in 1974 worked for places other than the palace alone. Indeed, we at present know of many more fragments with apparent links to St Sigismund's Church than of statues we can be sure were erected in the palace. This only confirms, however, that it was a court workshop working to royal orders, and is entirely consistent with the location of the workshop within the city.[18] Another fundamental conclusion drawn from the more recent find, one related to the time of the church's construction, leads us into the question of dating.

chapter] *Tanulmányok Budapest Múltjából* 15 (1963), pp. 109–149; András Végh, "Beiträge zur Geschichte des neueren Kollegiat-Stiftes zu Unserer Lieben Frau oder St. Sigismund von Buda (Ofen)," *Acta Archaeologica Academiae Scientiarum Hungaricae* 50 (1998), pp. 215–231.

16 *A budavári Szent Zsigmond templom és gótikus szobrai* [The St Sigismund church of Buda and its Gothic statues], eds Gergely Buzás and István Feld (Budapest: BTM, 1996); István Feld, "Beszámoló az egykori budai Szent Zsigmond templom és környéke feltárásáról," [Report on the excavation of the St Sigismund's Church and its surroundings] *Budapest Régiségei* 33 (1999), pp. 35–50.

17 Gergely Buzás, "A budai Szent Zsigmond templom kőfaragványai," [The stone fragments of the St Sigismund's Church of Buda] *Budapest Régiségei* 33 (1999), pp. 51–65; on the two statues, see Dóra Sallay, "A budai Szent Zsigmond prépostság Fájdalmas Krisztus-szobránakikonográfiája," [The iconography of the Suffering Christ statue of the St Sigismund's Chapter] *Budapest Régiségei* 33 (1999), pp. 123–139; *Sigismundus Rex et Imperator*, pp. 319–320 (Cat. 4.13, by Imre Takács). For some fragments of the somewhat stylistically independent terracotta and artificial stone figures, see *Sigismundus Rex et Imperator*, pp. 317–319 (Cat. 4.10 and 4.11, by Imre Takács).

18 The plot of the workshop may have very well been a royal property, or the king could have rented it out. Either way, this does not mean that the workshop or some of its members did not also produce pieces for others. Apart from the immediate neighborhood, parts of the statues were only found at the sites of Sigismund's constructions and no parts are known to be of urban provenance.

Operational Time Frame of the Sculpture Workshop

Because the Buda statues are not the subject of any specific written source, a debate has raged ever since their discovery as to when they were carved. At first, they were placed towards the end of the reign of King Louis I and the following years, but the interpretation of a fragment of a Bohemian king's helmet decoration definitely shifted the dating to the reign of Sigismund.[19] A proposed link to the Battle of Nicopolis in 1396 was supported only by speculative historical hypothesis and shaky style constructions. Every other tangible argument clearly pointed to a later stage, the middle or second half of Sigismund's reign.[20] The still-uncertain stylistic associations of the statues are not really worth bringing into the matter of their date, and neither are they necessary. Historical records of Sigismund's rule and the king's journeys, contracts with craftsmen and information on the construction of Buda Palace and St Sigismund's Church, where the statues were to be housed, give much more specific and satisfactory information on when the workshop operated.[21]

Sigismund, a member of the house of Luxemburg, ascended the Hungarian throne following the demise of the Angevin kings, and the difficulties arising from the change of dynasty put a heavy burden on both the first decade of his reign and a part of the second. The last Angevin king of Hungary, Louis the Great, made arrangements for his succession a few years before his death in 1382, by betrothing one of his daughters to Sigismund. Nevertheless, Sigismund

---

19 On the earlier dating, see Zolnay, "Der gotische Skulpturenfund," pp. 243–246; on the dating from the 1380s to the first third of the fifteenth century, see Marosi, "Vorläufige kunsthistorische Bemerkungen zum Skulpturenfund," pp. 352–369; for the second and third decade of the fifteenth century, see Zolnay and Marosi, *A budavári szoborlelet*, pp. 96 and 109–110 (by Ernő Marosi). On the helmet-decoration found ten meters from the finds of 1974, see László Zolnay, "A Luxemburg-ház kőcímere és kőkorona-töredék a budavári ásatás leletei között," [The stone armor of the Luxemburg dynasty and stone crown-fragment amongst the finds at the excavation of the Buda castle] *Művészettörténeti Értesítő* 25 (1976), pp. 218–233, here pp. 218 and 229–232; Imre Holl, "Heraldikai megjegyzések," [Some heraldic notes] *Archaeologiai Értesítő* 111 (1984), pp. 109–114, here pp. 109–111. It is to be noted, however, that Sigismund used the Bohemian helmet decoration with lime tree leaves as margrave of Brandenburg from 1373. See *Sigismundus Rex et Imperator*, p. 180 (Cat. 3.1, by Tünde Wehli).

20 On the supposition of the Nicopolis connection, see Schwarz, *Höfische Skulptur*, pp. 444–468; on criticism of it, see Ernő Marosi's review, see *Acta Historiae Artium* 34 (1989), pp. 63–64.

21 In the dating of the statues it was mostly Ernő Marosi who considered this historical data. See for instance: Zolnay and Marosi, *A budavári szoborlelet*, pp. 97–109; Marosi, "Die Skulpturen der Sigismundszeit," pp. 185–186.

only managed to have himself crowned in 1387, after combating the claims to the throne raised by Louis of Orleans, brother of Charles VI of France, who enjoyed the support of Louis's widow, and by Charles Durazzo of Naples and his son Ladislas. The country sank into civil war, putting a squeeze on royal revenues. In these bleak circumstances, mere coronation was not enough. Uprisings against the king broke out in the south of the country until the 1390s. The defeat at Nicopolis in 1396, from which Sigismund only just escaped with his life and took six months to get home, again cast his precarious rule in jeopardy. In his absence, some of the barons invited Ladislas of Durazzo (also known as Ladislas of Naples) to make a return. Sigismund managed to put down this rebellion in early 1397, but the increasing influence of foreigners in government prompted a section of the Hungarian nobility to incarcerate the king for six months in 1401. Highly-placed barons took advantage of another of the king's absences in 1402 by again offering the Hungarian crown to Ladislas of Durazzo, who landed with an army on the coast of the Hungarian province of Dalmatia and was crowned in Zadar by the archbishop of Esztergom. Sigismund succeeded in quelling the rebellion in 1403–1404, and his rule was never challenged again. It was only after the end of this long series of vexations that the king could engage in the peaceful pursuit of large-scale building – building his realm as well as commissioning new architectural constructions.[22] For our present theme, his most important building project was the major expansion of the Buda royal palace complex. There are varying opinions as to the condition in which Sigismund took possession of the royal residence built by Louis the Great, whether he did any building at the beginning of his rule, and, if so, what he built. The archaeological observations mostly permit several interpretations, including the possibility that Louis did not finish the project before he died and that building continued afterwards, possibly extending into the start of Sigismund's reign. This must, however, have been limited to the southern area which Louis had already covered (the Little Court and the Great or Inner Court). It could hardly have involved an enormous set of statuary of such a high standard.[23] This is supported by the observations of the envoy of

22 Elemér Mályusz, *Kaiser Sigismund in Ungarn 1387–1437* (Budapest: Akadémiai, 1990), pp. 7–69; Jörg K. Hoensch, *Kaiser Sigismund. Herrscher an der Schwelle zur Neuzeit 1368–1437* (Munich: C.H. Beck, 1996), pp. 48–118; István Draskóczy, "Sigismund von Luxemburg und Ungarn," in *Sigismundus Rex et Imperator*, pp. 11–23, here pp. 11–16.

23 On the different assessment of the periodization of the construction works, see among more recent works: Emese Nagy, "Die gotische Architektur im Königpalast von Buda," in *Budapest im Mittelalter*, pp. 236–250, here pp. 240–241; Imre Holl, "A budai palota középkori építéstörténetének kérdései," [Questions on the construction history of the Buda palace in the Middle Ages] *Budapest Régiségei* 31 (1997), pp. 79–99, here pp. 82–83; Károly

Francesco Gonzaga, prince of Mantua, who wrote in 1395 of the Buda court (*curia*) that it was so wretched it hardly deserved the name, although he does not say whether he refers to its buildings or the courtly life that took place in them.[24] It is also confirmed by the chronological pattern of documents referring to the palace.[25] The almost complete absence of such sources from before about 1410, and the very large number thereafter cannot be explained purely in terms of the random survival of manuscripts. Sigismund's gradual transfer of his seat from Visegrád to Buda around 1408 may, likewise, be interpreted in terms of the readiness of the palace to accommodate him, although it is probable that the palace complex still at this time comprised mostly Angevin-period buildings.[26] Recent research, however, is unanimous in concluding that architecture of truly international significance could only have started after the first decade of the new century.

The earliest definite record of the construction of St Sigismund's Church is from 1410. It comes in a papal document which mentions the foundation of the provostry and Sigismund's commencement of construction at great expense.[27] In 1411, the king acquired building timber from Austria *zu unserm Bau* via a Buda burgher, for the hefty sum of a thousand florins.[28] There are references to various payments between 1409 and 1424, some related to stipends lasting several years and concerning *magister Petrus architector maiestatis*, the king's special Buda stonemason Egyed (*specialis lapicida nostre maiestatis Budensis*), the sculptor Peter Kytel (*sculptor imaginum*), who was probably based in Buda, and another Peter of Buda, a maker of water pipes (*aqueductor*

    Magyar, *A budai középkori királyi palota építészeti együttesének változásai (1340–1440) európai kitekintésben*, unpublished PhD dissertation [The history of the architectural ensemble of the medieval palace of Buda (1340–1440) in European perspective] (Budapest: ELTE, 2008), pp. 85–105 and 179–180; Tóth, "Die Gebäude des Budaer Königspalastes," pp. 213–214.

24   Lajos Thallóczy, *Mantovai követjárás Budán 1395* [A Mantovese embassy in Buda, 1395] (Budapest: Magyar Tudományos Akadémia, 1905), pp. 76 and 110.

25   A critical analysis of these separate sources is yet to be done.

26   Márta Kondor, "Hof, Residenz und Verwaltung: Ofen und Blindenburg in der Regierungszeit König Sigismunds – unter besonderer Berücksichtigung der Jahre 1410–1419," in *Kaiser Sigismund (1368–1437) – Urkunden und Herrschaftspraxis eines europäischen Monarchen*, ed. Karel Hruza and Alexandra Kaar (Vienna–Cologne–Weimar: Böhlau, 2012), pp. 215–233, esp. pp. 223–227.

27   *Vetera monumenta historica Hungariam sacram illustrantia*, i, ed. Augustinus Theiner (Rome–Paris–Pest–Vienna: Typis Vaticanis, 1859), pp. 187–189.

28   *Regesta imperii*, xi, *Die Urkunden Kaiser Sigmunds (1410–1437)*, ed. Wilhelm Altmann (Innsbruck: Wagner, 1896), p. 3 (no 31).

noster in Buda).²⁹ There are records of the foreign craftsmen the king contracted in French and German lands during his extensive travels after 1414. He sent from Cologne in 1414 at least seven stonemasons to the kingdom, together with carpenters and roofers.³⁰ In 1416, he arranged for a payment of 1000 Rhenish florins to a Nuremberg pipesmith (*rorsmid*) called Hartman, for laying on water to the Buda Hill.³¹ In 1418, he contracted a stonemason from Tübingen and one from Stuttgart, with dozens of assistants, two carpenter brothers from Augsburg with assistants, and a well-maker from Augsburg.³² Sigismund made these contracts when he was in Augsburg and Regensburg, all of them in October, some with identical wording. The contracts differ in details, but they agree on the day upon which the craftsmen had to join the king's service, that they worked for annual and not occasional pay, and that they had to perform their commissions in Hungary. One case reveals their place of work more closely, for we learn that an assistant to the Augsburg carpenters died in the same year as he was contracted – in Buda.³³ Some of the contracts made in France also show that Sigismund set at least some of the foreign craftsmen to work on his building project in Buda. The Chronicle of St Denis notes that during his extended stay in Paris in 1416, Sigismund entertained the idea of sending a large number (300!) of famous craftsmen from France to Hungary.³⁴ A member of his retinue, István Rozgonyi, wrote that it was for Buda that Sigismund

29 Kemény Lajos: "Zsigmond király budai építkezéseihez," [On the constructions of King Sigismund] *Történelmi Tár* 18 (1895), pp. 205–206; Jenő Házi, *Sopron sz. kir. város története*, i/2 [The history of the free royal town of Sopron] (Sopron: Székely, Szabó és Társa Könyvnyomdája, 1923), pp. 221–222 (no 254); Imre Takács, "Petrus Kytel, ein Bildhauer König Sigismunds," in *Sigismundus Rex et Imperator*, pp. 236–238.
30 Volker Liedke, "Meister Dietrich, König Sigismunds Baumeister und Meister Rapolt von Köln," *Ars Bavarica* 3 (1975), pp. 18–20.
31 *Regesta imperii*, xi, p. 134 (no 1967).
32 *Regesta imperii*, xi, p. 255 (nos 3621, 3622, 3623, 3624 and 3635) and 258 (nos 3670 and 3671).
33 Henrik Horváth, *Zsigmond király és kora* [King Sigismund and his age] (Budapest: Budapest Székesfőváros, 1937), p. 109.
34 *Chronique du Religieux de Saint-Denys contenant le règne de Charles VI de 1380 à 1422*, v–vi, ed. M.L. Bellaguet (Paris: Edition du Comité des travaux historiques et scientifiques, 1994), pp. 746–747. I acknowledge information provided by Sándor Csernus on the text of the chronicle, for which see Sándor Csernus, "Francia források Zsigmond párizsi tartózkodásáról (1416. március)," [French sources on Sigismund's residence in Paris (March 1416)] in *Kelet és nyugat között. Történeti tanulmányok Kristó Gyula tiszteletére* [Between East and West. Studies in honor of Gyula Kristó], ed. László Koszta (Szeged: Szegedi Középkorász Műhely, 1995), pp. 103–140, here p. 116.

contracted goldsmiths and other craftsmen in Paris.[35] A report by Bertrandon de la Broquière, agent of Philip the Good of Burgundy, tells us that a considerable number of these craftsmen were builders.[36] Bertrandon visited Buda and Pest in 1433, and mentioned six to eight French masons' families, one from Bray-sur-Somme, as living in Pest. They had settled in the city to work on Sigismund's building projects and were out of work at the time. Bertrandon also mentioned a French prototype of a tower with a boom above the Danube. Destruction of the buildings renders it impossible to assess the complete accuracy of these observations, but the king was clearly collecting architectural models when, during his travels in 1414 and 1415, he obtained views of the Ospedale della Scala in Siena and – more importantly for the present discussion – the pope's palace in Avignon.[37] Sigismund's chronicler, Eberhard Windecke, found it important to note in connection with his return to Buda from his six-and-a-half-year West-European diplomatic tour in 1419 that "there stood his building, since he had ordered a very costly building, as I think that no one has ever had such a wonderful, useful and precious edifice built."[38] In a manuscript completed in Esztergom in 1418–1419, a member of Sigismund's retinue in Constance, Winand von Steeg, disparaged the king's enormously costly palace-building venture.[39]

Some of these records can of course be only circumstantially linked to the building work in Buda. There is, however, good reason for including them here, since we know of no other contemporary royal building project in Hungary of remotely comparable magnitude or quality, which argues in favor of their relevance. Taken together, the sources clearly mark out the period of Sigismund's building operations in Buda. Given his political position, the work could hardly have started before the second half of the first decade of the fifteenth century,

---

35   Antal Áldásy, "Rozgonyi István levele Párizsból 1416 márczius 14-ről," [The letter of István Rozgonyi from Paris on 14 March 1416] *Történelmi Tár* 3 (1902), pp. 575–577.

36   *Le Voyage d'Outremer de Bertrandon de la Broquière premier écuyer tranchant et conseiller de Philippe le Bon, duc de Bourgogne*, ed. Ch. Schefer (Paris: Leroux, 1892), pp. 234–237.

37   Ernő Marosi, "König Sigismund von Ungarn und Avignon," in *Orient und Okzident im Spiegel der Kunst. Festschrift Heinrich Gerhard Franz zum 70. Geburtstag*, eds Günther Brucher and Wolfgang T. Müller (Graz: Akademische Druck- und Verlagsanstalt, 1986), pp. 229–249.

38   "und lag do sin buwe, wann er gar einen costlichen buwe liess machen, wann ich mein, das ie kein mönschenbilde einen solichen weudelichen nützlichen costlichen buwe…" See *Eberhart Windeckes Denkwürdigkeiten zur Geschichte des Zeitalters Kaiser Sigmunds*, ed. Wilhelm Altmann (Berlin: Gaertner, 1893), p. 109.

39   Aloys Schmidt and Hermann Heimpel, *Winand von Steeg (1371–1453), ein mittelrheinischer Gelehrter und Künstler und die Bilderhandschrift über Zollfreiheit des Bacharacher Pfarrweins auf dem Rhein aus dem Jahr 1426* (Munich: Verlag der Bayerischen Akademie der Wissenschaften, 1977), p. 18.

and must have been at its peak in the 1410s and the early 1420s. We have relatively precise information about when it came to an end. Several sources tell us that the new buildings in Buda were not completed, and this fact tallies with the large proportion of the statues which were never erected.[40] One of the main reasons for this must have been that in the second half of the 1420s, because of his imperial plans and the Bohemian situation Sigismund's attention shifted to Pressburg, on the western border of the realm. The castle and palace he built for his new seat had comparable dimensions to those in Buda, but with architecture of markedly different style.[41] As reported by Broquière, the king stopped building in Buda in the 1430s at the latest. We can thus be quite sure that the sculpture workshop operated during the approximately twenty years between 1405/10–1425/30. No sources tell us whether the work was continuous in the period, or when the various groups of sculptures were made, even in relation to each other. Nor have stylistic observations so far yielded any guidance.[42]

Classification of the Statues by Material, Size, and Theme

The approximately three thousand fragments recovered from the 1974 excavation have yielded compilations of about sixty separate figures to which may be added half a dozen more figures from the finds in St Sigismund's Church. The still unidentified pieces are so small and so few that they can have no major influence on the overall picture. It is clear from thematic considerations that the statues form only a fraction of the whole, or at least of those that were planned.

A self-evident method of classification started immediately upon the discovery of what was a very large find. By the criteria of material, size and theme, the statues fell into two basic groups. These largely corresponded with what also seemed to be a two-way split by style criteria.[43] There is a 'secular' (also known as 'knight figure') series of relatively large pieces, and one of saints,

---

40   *Le Voyage d'Outremer*, p. 234; Bonfini, *Decades*, III-III-343–350 (p. 75).

41   Szilárd Papp, "Die neue Residenz Sigismunds in Pressburg," in *Sigismundus Rex et Imperator*, pp. 239–245.

42   In this respect, Sigismund's contracts with Parisian and German masters, dating from the second half of the 1410s should be taken into account as they coincide with the historical dating of the costumes on the statues (unlikely to be from before 1415). See *Magyarországi művészet 1300–1470 körül*, i, ed. Ernő Marosi (Budapest: Akadémiai, 1987), p. 240 (by Éva Kovács). Ernő Marosi emphasized the role of the West European travels of Sigismund between 1412 and 1419 in the statues. See Zolnay and Marosi, *A budavári szoborlelet*, pp. 107–109.

43   Zolnay, "Der gotische Skulpturenfund," pp. 208–214; Marosi, "Vorläufige kunsthistorische Bemerkungen zum Skulpturenfund," pp. 338–343.

which are smaller. This led to the hypothesis that they were intended for different buildings, one secular and one ecclesiastical. Although the rigidity of this division was always open to doubt, and publications increasingly pointed to a crossover between the two groups,[44] this approach went as far as postulating that there were two independent workshops working alongside each other in Buda (an *Apostelatelier* and a *Ritteratelier*).[45] This is clearly contradicted by the location of the 1974 find, i.e. that the statues were all deposited in the same workshop building. But the two-way division of a set of statues within one workshop poses fundamental problems of its own and several considerations imply a much more complex internal relationship. Unfortunately, any classification of such a fragmentary and unfinished set of statues generates more problems than it can resolve.

There is only one set of statues in the ensemble which can be clearly be delineated by most criteria. It comprises standing figures, approximately 85 cm-high, in non-secular costume, carved from dense, close-grained limestone (Figs 16.13, 16.16, 16.17, 16.19 and 16.23). They mostly share stocky proportions, a block-like overall outline, (nearly) vertical and static posture, and clearly composed but ample and busy costume, with highly characteristic soft modeling of thick materials, such as the kind of pleat that might be made by drawing a finger through soft clay. Central to the astonishingly fine detail is the use of the toothed chisel. Furthermore, certain deviations from these characteristics show that at least three masons worked on the surviving pieces of the series. The torsos of at least eight figures (nos 25, 26, 28, 31, 33, 35, 36, 55/56) stand on bases evoking an undulating surface (a cloud?), many of them wearing shoes, with some barefoot, while the surviving heads, a few of which wear hoods (nos 28, 33, 55, 56) bolster the conviction that we are looking at apostles and/or prophets (Figs 16.2 and 16.21).[46] As regards their intended location, it is not clear whether they are a single ensemble or fragments of different series intended for different places. Neither can we tell whether their intended surroundings were secular or ecclesiastical. Possibly linked to them, to judge by size, material and working, are a praying female saint (no 32) – whose hand was discovered in the palace chapel – and a Madonna figure (no 30) which stands on a markedly different geometrical base and whose style contrasts with the identifiable, relatively coherent formal repertoire of the others (Fig. 16.25).[47]

---

44   See for instance Zolnay and Marosi, *A budavári szoborlelet*, pp. 87–96 (the relevant part is by Ernő Marosi).
45   Schwarz, *Höfische Skulptur*, pp. 457–468.
46   A book in a bag held in the hand points further to this (no 33).
47   A female saint or the Virgin Mary does not require an apostle/prophet cycle; moreover, there are other arguments that this statue was intended to be free-standing.

We now come to the other statues via a female figure (no 20), which serves as a kind of transition. Originally 120–125 cm high including its missing head, it is surprisingly similar to the Madonna (no 30), but has a symmetrical pose and is more fragmented. This second group is considerably larger, but surrounded by much greater uncertainties. The statues are generally made of coarser limestone of somewhat uneven density. The surfaces show rare signs of working by toothed chisel and their bases largely have the same shape as the Madonna's, although one or two have undulating surfaces.[48] They belong to at least three or four orders of size, which in itself suggests several cycles.[49] The vast majority of the group (e.g. nos 4, 5, 14, 18, 19, 22, 34), are men wearing fashionable court attire or, in one or two cases, armor (Figs 16.3, 16.4, 16.7 and 16.29). There are much fewer women (e.g. nos 9, 17, 20), and these stand out as a consequence of their strikingly simple and far-from-courtly clothes. Usually included among these are at least one youth holding a helmet (no 29), two bishop figures – one in a semi-finished state – (nos 6, 16), two crouched console figures (nos 1 and 2, prophets/apostles?) and some other torsos which are difficult to determine (Figs 16.5 and 16.34). There are a great many head fragments, and they clearly belong to the headless figures. Many heads of similar size show similar faces with mustaches and some of these wear various kinds of headgear of an obviously secular type (e.g. nos 8, 42, 44, 53, 57, 61) (Figs 16.6 and 16.31). On two fragments, the hair is tied up with a roll of cloth (Nos 45 and 46) (Fig. 16.11). The female heads are either bereft of hair ornament or headgear or are covered with simple headscarves (e.g. nos 48, 49, 50, 70).

Sadly, only a very small number of attributes associated with these statues have been found, and these are of a general character. A crown (no 62), an orb and the Hungarian coat of arms with the double cross (no 15) have a variety of potential associations, as does a long and unfortunately empty banderole. The bottom of a vessel or jar fragment held in the left hand alludes to a religious representation.[50] A fur hat with a peak, regarded as an attribute of Sigismund, and its appearance on a head with a mustache and round beard suggests an association with the king. There is another example of such a hat as a standalone object, whose working suggests it as having been held in the hand or

---

48 The use of the toothed chisel does not necessarily point to different stone-cutting practices, since it may be that its use was dictated by the quality of the stone.

49 With the heralds it seems obvious that within one representation there may be figures of different sizes. On the problem of comparing the sizes because of the fragmented state of the statues, see: Marosi, "Vorläufige kunsthistorische Bemerkungen zum Skulpturenfund," pp. 340–343.

50 On the two latter, see Zolnay and Marosi, *A budavári szoborlelet*, pics 89–90.

else lying discarded on the ground (nos 43, 68).[51] These may allude to specific representations of the monarch, but may also have been Bible-based cryptoportraits related to him.

The royal commission, the finding of remains alluding to Sigismund, and representations of luxury court costume were seized on by researchers keen to propose that these sculptures were part of a secular program connected with the king himself. The ensemble would have been intended to express Sigismund's power in some way, either promoting a genealogical and dynastic connection, or by representing figures from the court and the highest ranks of nobility.[52] The most tangible clues to such a program are the pages holding the armorial bearings. These could not have been isolated statues. No matter how ardently we would like to know, however, we cannot identify the underlying theme any more precisely. The fragmented state of the ensemble is not the only problem. Some of the examples that suggest themselves as analogies, most of them French, are also fragmentary or known only from written sources, and their themes are also uncertain. Moreover, a patron of such a level, aspiring to the imperial title, could be expected to deviate somewhat from precursors, demanding some kind of independent iconography, perhaps adapted to his own sovereign position.[53] As to where the sculptures were to be located, St Sigismund's Church cannot be ruled out. Parallels for this include the statuary cycles in the Grand Chapel (*beau pilier*) of Amiens Cathedral and the nave doors of the Stephansdom in Vienna,[54] although the program is more likely to have been intended for Sigismund's enormous new palace. A king who had only acquired the crown through struggle and at the price of great difficulties,

---

51   On the fur hat as characteristic of Sigismund, see Elfriede Regina Knauer, "Kaiser Sigismund. Eine ikonographische Nachlese," in *Festschrift für Otto von Simson zum 65. Geburtstag*, ed. Lucius Grisebach and Konrad Renger (Frankfurt am Main–Berlin–Vienna: Propyläen Verlag, 1977), pp. 173–196, here pp. 183–186; Ulrike Jenni, "Das Porträt Kaiser Sigismunds in Wien und seine Unterzeichnung," in *Sigismund von Luxemburg. Ein Kaiser in Europa*, eds Michel Pauly and François Reinert (Mainz am Rhein: Philipp von Zabern, 2006), pp. 285–300, here pp. 288–290.

52   Marosi, "Vorläufige kunsthistorische Bemerkungen zum Skulpturenfund," pp. 364–366; Zolnay and Marosi, *A budavári szoborlelet*, pp. 114–116 (by Ernő Marosi).

53   For a possible antitype of the program, see Schwarz, "König Sigismunds höfischer Traum," pp. 230–232.

54   Aurélien André, "Le Beau Pilier de la cathédrale Notre-Dame d'Amiens. Sa place dans l'iconographie politique du XIVe siècle," *Bulletin de la Société des antiquaires de Picardie* 167 (2003), pp. 543–565; *Geschichte der bildenden Kunst in Österreich*, ii. *Gotik*, ed. Günther Brucher (Munich–London–New York: Prestel, 2000), pp. 353–355 (Cat. 96 and 97, by Lothar Schultes).

over a protracted period, could be expected to aim for a strong statement of his legitimacy in the capital of his kingdom.[55]

Not all of the pieces of the 'secular' part of the ensemble, however, may be assigned to such a program. Arguing against this are the varying dimensions and the timeless costume of the female figures, almost totally devoid of fashion, in sharp contrast to the males. The most probably allusion is to saints.[56] The unsettling gesture of a male figure (no 34) consistently determined as a herald – with a raised right arm – is reminiscent of the battle-axe-wielding hand, which is customary on representations of the eleventh-century Hungarian king, St Ladislas. Moreover, the uncertain posture and court costume of the figure match the St Ladislas figure of Sigismund's gold florins so faithfully that the coin could have served as the sculptor's model (Figs 16.7 and 16.8).[57] As one of Sigismund's predecessors on the Hungarian throne, the holy king's representation could of course also fit into a dynastic program, but another torso, surviving only from the waist down, identified by research as a heraldic supporter (no 7), has distinct allusions to a biblical theme (Fig. 16.9). The figure has his left foot inclined outwards, with the heel raised, and must have been leaning slightly forward, a posture which occasionally occurs on representations of the Adoration of the Magi, where one of the wise men kneels before the child. Confirming this cautious interpretation is the prominently-represented pouch hanging from the belt – a reference to wealth – and an almost ubiquitous

---

55 On the Parisian statue-cycles of Charles V with regard to a legitimization problem of somewhat different origin, see Uwe Bennert, "Ideologie in Stein. Zur Darstellung französischer Königsmacht im Paris des 14. Jahrhunderts," in *Opus Tessellatum. Modi und Grenzgänge der Kunstwissenschaft. Festschrift für Cornelius Claussen*, eds Katharina Corsepius and Daniela Mondini (Hildesheim: Olms, 2004), pp. 153–163, here pp. 156–163.

56 Cf. Éva Kovács, "Viselet Zsigmond korában," [Costume in the age of Sigismund] in *Művészet Zsigmond király korában 1387–1437*, I [Art in the age of Sigismund, 1387 to 1437], eds László Beke, Ernő Marosi and Tünde Wehli (Budapest: MTA Művészettörténeti Kutató Csoport, 1987), pp. 226–234, here pp. 226–227.

57 On the coins: *Sigismundus Rex et Imperator*, p. 191 (Cat. 3.24, 3.25, by Csaba Tóth). On the iconography of St Ladislas, see Ernő Marosi, "Der heilige Ladislaus als Ungarischer Nationalheiliger. Bemerkungen zu seiner Ikonographie im 14–15. Jh.," *Acta Historiae Artium* 33 (1987–1988), pp. 211–256; Terézia Kerny, "László király ikonográfiája," [The iconography of St Ladislas] in *Magyar Művelődéstörténeti Lexikon. Középkor és kora újkor*, VI [The lexicon of Hungarian intellectual history. Middle Ages and Early Modern Period], ed. Péter Kőszeghy (Budapest: Balassi, 2006), pp. 411–453; on his widespread cult in the age of Sigismund, Terézia Kerny, "Szent László-kultusz a Zsigmond-korban," [The cult of St Ladislas in the age of Sigismund] in *Művészet Zsigmond király korában*, I, pp. 353–363; Béla Zsolt Szakács, "Saints of the Knights – Knights of the Saints: Patterns of Patronage at the Court of Sigismund," in *Sigismund von Luxemburg. Ein Kaiser in Europa*, pp. 319–330.

accessory of one of the kings – usually the one kneeling – in early Netherlandish art. Also in the Netherlands, there are many cases of kings represented with a fur hat, sometimes combined with a crown, on the ground or held in the hand and some figures with hair wound in a cloth. A standard component of the scene was the jar of frankincense or myrrh in the hand of a king or of his servant. Most of these may be seen, for example, in the central panel of Rogier van der Weyden's Columba altar (Fig. 16.10).[58] It is therefore reasonable to infer that part of the 'secular' ensemble actually belonged to such a representation. In the surviving examples of the scene from that period, the (king) figures were almost mandatorily dressed in court costume identical to the Buda knight figures, in *huque* or *journade*.[59] In addition, monarchs of the fourteenth and fifteenth centuries preferred to have themselves dressed as the kingly figures of Epiphany representations, and partly owing to a remark by Windecke, this has been proposed most often in connection with Sigismund.[60] Such a statue cycle in Buda would have been most suited to a prominent location in St Sigismund's Church, possibly the main door.

Style, Type, and Motif Origins

Although it is obviously a type, there is a surprising similarity between the head of a male figure with his hair tied in a roll of cloth, his mouth open in awe (no 46), and a king's head on the right wing of another Rogier work, the Bladelin Triptych, made two or three decades later than the statues (Figs 16.11 and 16.12).[61] It exemplifies the basic problems of the Buda ensemble's style connections. Like those of the sculpture of the time, these largely boil down to

---

58 Dirk De Vos, *Rogier van der Weyden. The Complete Works* (Antwerp: Harry N. Abrams, 1999), pp. 276–284.
59 The possibility has already been raised by László Zolnay. See idem and Marosi, *A budavári szoborlelet*, p. 44.
60 Bertalan Kéry, *Kaiser Sigismund. Ikonographie* (Vienna–Munich: Schroll, 1972), pp. 157–173; Friedrich B. Polleross, *Das sakrale Identifikationsporträt. Ein höfischer Bildtypus vom 13. bis zum 20. Jahrhundert* (Worms: Werner, 1988), pp. 177–194; Gerhard Schmidt, *Malerei der Gotik. Fixpunkte und Ausblicke*, ed. Martin Roland (Graz: Akademische Druck- und Verlagsanstalt, 2005), pp. 329–340 and 348; Götz Pochat, "Zur Genese des Porträts," in *Sigismundus Rex et Imperator*, pp. 124–142, here pp. 137–141.
61 De Vos, *Rogier van der Weyden*, pp. 242–248; at the same place on another king-bust which may be a portrait of Sigismund. See: Elfriede Knauer, "A Cubiculo Augustorum. Bemerkungen zu Rogier van der Weydens Bladelin-Altar," *Zeitschrift für Kunstgeschichte* 33 (1970), pp. 332–339, here p. 338.

two basic questions: whether it is possible to distinguish aspects of individual modeling from the more or less self-evident types and motifs, and whether we can trace, directly or indirectly, the development of the types and motifs.

On the Buda statues, suspicion is aroused by designs that seem unique to one craftsman (or perhaps workshop). Such are the strongly-projecting, winding, undetailed hair bundles (e.g. nos 46, 52) and perhaps beards and hair formed from spaghetti-like strands on the apostle/prophet series (nos 28, 56) (Figs 16.2, 16.11, 16.13 and 16.17). To date, however, nothing produced in the workshop has been convincingly linked to previous work by any particular craftsman, a fact that may be related to the severely fragmented state of material from the time. Secondly, quite apart from their high quality and the burst of novelty they brought to Central European sculpture, the mode of composition of the craftsmen who worked in Buda can best be described as a professional combination of types and motifs, procedures based on the guiding principles of contemporary sculpture.[62] This shows up strikingly in the face of the *chaperone* male head (No 54) and the series of mustached heads (e.g. nos 8, 22, 53, 57, 61) (Figs 16.6 and 16.31).[63]

Such coincidences of type and motif form the basis for a good proportion of the analogies suggested for the statues, characteristically supported by stylistic criticism of a rather old-fashioned, literary kind. As a result, it is often difficult to tell from where the pieces in each sequence originate stylistically, whether the connections are direct or indirect, and whether the analogies stand in a linear sequence of development or represent parallel phenomena. Almost every scholar who has addressed this morphological jumble has come up with a different explanation. Some, using the statues and their analogies as points of reference for other constructions, such as historical connections, geographical

---

62   On the sculpting method, see Roland Recht, "Motive, Typen, Zeichnung. Das Vorbild in der Plastik des Spätmittelalters," in *Skulptur des Mittelalters. Funktion und Gestalt*, eds Friedrich Möbius and Ernst Schubert (Weimar: Böhlau, 1987), pp. 354–384; Herbert Beck and Horst Bredekamp, "Kompilation der Form in der Skulptur um 1400," *Städel-Jahrbuch* 6 (1977), pp. 129–157.

63   On the type of the *chaperon* face, see for instance the St Wenceslas statue in the St Vitus's Cathedral at Prague (*Umění* 47, no 5 [1999], cover image), or the St James statue at the parish church of Steyr (Beck and Bredekamp, *Kompilation der Form in der Skulptur*, pic. 19.). On the one with mustache, see one of the drawings of Pisanello (*Sigismundus Rex et Imperator*, p. 365 [Cat. 4.74]), a St Sigismund statue from Tyrol (*Die Parler und der Schöne Stil 1350–1400. Europäische Kunst unter den Luxemburgern* 3 vols, ed. Anton Legner [Cologne: Museen der Stadt Köln, 1978], ii, p. 439), or the bust of Louis of Bavaria on the tomb model of Multscher in Munich (*Hans Multscher. Bildhauer der Spätgotik in Ulm*, eds Brigitte Reinhardt and Michael Roth [Ulm: Süddeutsche Verlagsgesellschaft, 1997], p. 303.)

links or national fixations, have put forward interpretations to suit their own purposes. The resulting uncertainties and fluctuations of opinion show up spectacularly in the chaotic avalanche of analogies for the ensemble or certain of its pieces, involving all kinds of schools, and sometimes of an author resolutely discussing a statue as the representative of first one style movement and then of another.

Researchers are agreed on one thing: the style of the Buda statuary is not homogeneous. It is a mix of various distinct trends. This in itself tells us something about the organization of the workshop: there was no monopoly on style, no leading master whose style all members of the workshop had to adapt. There is nothing exceptional about this in late Gothic sculpture.[64] It also suggests that following a more or less coherent style was not a matter of overriding concern for the patron, i.e. not necessarily a means for conveying a fixed identity of himself and of his reign.

I

The less problematic of the two identified groups has also found more agreement among researchers as regards its stylistic origins. The series of small apostle/prophet statues is clearly the work of artists who studied in western lands far from Buda, in northern France or the southern Netherlands. One favorite area is French court sculpture. In this respect, Schwarz has concentrated on Beauneveu and his 'disciples' in the period up to 1400, while Heinrichs-Schreiber, looking through Vincennes spectacles, refers to works around the turn of the century.[65] Marosi saw the art of Paris and the French ducal centers as having only an indirect influence on the series. It may have found its way to Buda via craftsmen – particularly from Brabant and the Lower Rhine – belonging to generations active around or after 1400.[66] The principal task is not, however, to reduce the question to a choice of candidate versions. If our determination of the origins of the Buda figures is ever to go further than mere dates and places, we need to find closer, more 'personalized' parallels, and decide which of the existing proposals have real substance. Within the

---

64 Gerhard Schmidt, *Gotische Bildwerke und ihre Meister*, i (Vienna–Cologne–Weimar: Böhlau, 1992) pp. 347–352.
65 Schwarz, *Höfische Skulptur*, pp. 457–460; Ulrike Heinrichs-Schreiber, *Vincennes und die höfische Skulptur. Die Bildhauerkunst in Paris 1360–1420* (Berlin: Reimer, 1997), pp. 230–233.
66 Marosi, "Vorläufige kunsthistorische Bemerkungen zum Skulpturenfund," pp. 345–352; Zolnay and Marosi, *A budavári szoborlelet*, pp. 93–96.

present boundaries, it is only a slight exaggeration to say that good type and motif analogies – and fairly close style analogies – to the Buda statues can be found almost anywhere. The reasons for this lie in the art works available for comparison. There is so little surviving sculpture from the areas involved that the main trends may not even be visible, and there was also a close interrelationship at that time between French and southern Netherlandish sculpture. Consequently, great uncertainties remain concerning where things appeared first and which area served as the source for other areas, although at the moment the money seems to be on Paris.[67] In any case, to the extent that an overall picture can be compiled from the tiny surviving fragments, it suggests a multitude of variants rather than a coherent style.[68] A form of this multiplicity shows up in the Buda series, which seem to display a kind of compilation of the style variations from the source area. At present, then, considering how much of the surviving material has not yet been studied, we cannot characterize the figures in terms of the style of any named artist or well-defined group of objects of Franco-Flemish sculpture.

A good example of this is the Buda apostle statue determined as St Bartholomew (no. 28, Fig. 16.13). Several authors have noted that the motion of this figure sets it apart from the others in the series, which have more traditional poses.[69] Although its lower body basically stands frontally, the upper body turns markedly to the side, suggesting a relationship with another figure – so much so, indeed, that the head is in profile and the dynamic motion is counterbalanced by the outstretched right hand. This truly little-known pose effectively coincides with that of Sluter's Madonna of Dijon, for which the St Donatian Madonna of Bruges or associated work may have served as a model, not to mention the thirteenth-century statue of Ecclesia in Strasbourg Munster[70]

---

67 On the unquestionable primacy of Paris, see Robert Didier, "Probleme der Kunst in Belgien zwischen 1350 und 1410/1420," in *Die Parler und der Schöne Stil*, i, pp. 78–79; Heinrichs-Schreiber, *Vincennes und die höfische Skulptur*, pp. 134–143. See however even more recently, Christian Bodiaux, "Le portail de l'Hôtel de ville de Bruxelles. Icône de la sculpture Bruxelloise vers 1400," *Städel-Jahrbuch* [NS] 18 (2001), pp. 7–29; Frits Scholten, "Sculpture in the Burgundian Netherlands, 1380–1450," in *The Road to Van Eyck*, eds Stephan Kemperdick and Friso Lammerste (Rotterdam: Museum Boijmans van Beuningen, 2012), pp. 69–75, here p. 70.

68 Georg Zeman, "Rezension von Heinrichs-Schreiber, *Vincennes und die höfische Skulptur*," *Kunstchronik* 51 (1998), pp. 129–135, here pp. 134–135.

69 Marosi, "Zu 'Werkstatt' und 'Künstler' in der Skulpturenreihe," p. 59; *Sigismundus Rex et Imperator*, 322 (Cat. 4.15, by Imre Takács).

70 *Die Parler und der Schöne Stil*, i, pp. 82–83 (by Robert Didier and John Steyaert); Renate Prochno, *Die Kartause von Champmol. Grablege der burgundischen Herzöge 1364–1477* (Berlin: Akademie Verlag, 2002), p. 29.

(Fig. 16.14). An accurate analogy to Bartholomew's seemingly-unique spaghetti-like hair and beard has been identified in the statues of the chancel of St Martin's Church in Halle, near Brussels, but the same appears of an apostle or prophet figure in Boston, whose origins have been traced to Burgundy or Paris, and its style to between those of Sluter and Beauneveu[71] (Fig. 16.15).

If we still hold out some hope of determining the more specific background to the apostle/prophet series of the Buda statuary, we should do more than merely seek independent style/type analogies. We have to take these together with compositional motifs, detail motifs, surface treatments and peculiarities of technique, and extend the search beyond sculpture to other art forms, particularly goldsmith's works. Serving to support this are some examples which have not received sufficient – or indeed any – attention in the literature. These, in my opinion, could narrow down the currently broad spectrum. One is the Boston statue. The form of the beard, the transparent composition of folds on the clothes and the motif of the open mantle on the chest put it considerably closer to the Buda pieces (e.g. nos 25, 36) than the Halle statues, whose clothes bear almost no similarity to those in Buda[72] (Figs 16.15–17). Somewhat at odds with the block-like outlines and stumpy proportions, the drapery of the Buda figures has a materiality which bears particular comparison with Sluter's door statues in Dijon and the prophet and angel figures of the Moses Fountain. Despite the crowded folds in the heavy, thick material, they display a clear spatial structure and their surface elaboration is dominated by an almost dough-like softness. The correspondence also shows up in many of the motifs: the arrangement of the folds on the back of the female saint (no 43) and of St Catherine on the Champmol Door; the mantle detail held up by the right arm of a male saint (no 25) and by the left arm of the prophet Jeremiah; and the drapery billowing out above the belts of the male saints (nos 25 and 36) and of the angels of the Moses Fountain[73] (Figs 16.16–18). Also notable is the

---

71 See Marosi, "Vorläufige kunsthistorische Bemerkungen zum Skulpturenfund," pp. 348–349, pic. 10. On the statue at Boston, see Robert Didier and Roland Recht, "Paris, Prague, Cologne et la sculpture de la seconde moitié du XIVe siècle. À propos de l'exposition des 'Parler' à Cologne," *Bulletin Monumental* 138 (1980), pp. 173–219, here pp. 192–193; *Gothic Sculpture in America*, i, *The New England Museums*, ed. Dorothy Gillerman (New York–London: Garland, 1989), pp. 30–33 (Cat. 18, by Anne M. Morganstern); *Art from the Court of Burgundy. The Patronage of Philip the Bold and John the Fearless. 1364–1419* (Cleveland–Paris: Cleveland Museum of Art and Réunion des musées nationaux, 2004), p. 316 (Cat. 121, by Todd Herman).

72 Marosi, "Vorläufige kunsthistorische Bemerkungen zum Skulpturenfund," p. 350.

73 For the first pair of analogies, see Zolnay and Marosi, *A budavári szoborlelet*, pic. 22 and Kathleen Morand, *Claus Sluter: Artist at the Court of Burgundy* (London–Austin:

rare technique of roughening with a chisel to distinguish the tunic of another male saint (no 35) from the smooth-carved surface of the rest of the drapery. The inside of the clothing of certain mourners on the tomb of Philip the Bold displays the same technique (Figs 16.19 and 20).[74] A similar surface effect is visible on the beard of a Buda head (no 55) whose close precursor – in terms of style as well as this technique – is one of the most prominent pieces of Parisian goldsmiths' art from around 1400. The so-called Matthias Corvinus Calvary in Esztergom from 1402/1403, which has also been linked to Sluter, includes a prophet head whose facial expression and the state of mind it displays is on the same level as we see on the Buda head[75] (Figs 16.21 and 22). Parisian ronde-bosse enamels from that period as well as fifteenth-century Burgundian stone carving long preserved the same method that we have already seen: somewhat illogical creases which look as if they were made by drawing a finger through wet clay.[76] This was the method used when the garments of a prophet or apostle were carved on an early fifteenth-century corbel from Bourges (now kept in the Louvre), the head of which also very closely resembles one of the torsos from Buda (no 33)[77] (Figs 16.23 and 24). The same type of head appears on another sculpture from the Louvre depicting God the Father, likewise from Bourges, from the early fifteenth century.[78] There is a striking similarity in composition, and to some extent in style, between the principal view of the

---

University of Texas Press, 1991), table 10. No photo of the above-mentioned detail of the male saint, no 25, has been published. A similar detail on Jerome can be found. See ibid., table 51.

74   *Sigismundus Rex et Imperator*, p. 321 (Cat. 4.14, by Imre Takács) and Morand, *Claus Sluter*, table 122, 126 and 144.

75   Éva Kovács, *L'âge d'or de l'orfèvrerie parisienne au temps des princes de Valois* (Dijon–Budapest: Balassi, 2004), pp. 37 and 47; on the possible connection to the Matthias Corvinus Calvary and the Moses well at Dijon, see Gerhard Schmidt, "Rezension von Morand, *Claus Sluter*," *Kunstchronik* 46 (1993), pp. 139–146 and 152–159, here pp. 145–146.

76   *Paris 1400. Les arts sous Charles VI*, eds Elisabeth Taburet-Delahaye and François Avril (Paris: Réunion des musées nationaux, 2004), pp. 178–179 (Cat. 97 and 98, by Elisabeth Taburet-Delahaye); Pierre Quarré, *Höhepunkte burgundischer Bildhauerkunst im späten Mittelalter* (Fribourg–Würzburg: Popp, 1978), e.g. pics 7, 26, 44, 51 and 94. In the Buda material the most salient appearance of this feature is at the right-hand side and the bottom of the costume of Bartholomew. It may originate in (miniature-) painting. See e.g. in the book of hours of Jean de Berry: *Paris 1400*, pp. 300–301 (Cat. 188).

77   *Les Belles heures du duc de Berry*, ed. Hélène Grollemund and Pascal Torres (Paris: Réunion des musées nationaux, 2012) p. 388 (Cat. 6, by Pierre-Yves Le Pogam).

78   Theodor Müller, *Sculpture in the Netherlands, Germany, France and Spain 1400 to 1500* (Harmondsworth: Penguin, 1966), p. 16, pic. 25A.

praying female saint (no 32) and a statue of similar theme, probably from a Parisian workshop, in the parish church of Villers-Saint-Paul (Oise).[79]

In my view, these examples seem to show that the Buda statues were influenced above all by French royal and ducal art of around 1400.[80] Such an intensive and diverse relationship concentrated on one region and period cannot, I think, be demonstrated for the sculpture of any other area; at most we find only parallel phenomena elsewhere. Like the apostle statues from Bec (Eure; now in Bernay) and the Boston statue, the Buda series stands in relation to or derivative of the sculpture of the main French centers in a way that cannot yet be clearly discerned.[81] Let us not forget, however, that the Buda sculptors may have taken elements from these centers to compile their own unique variant without parallel elsewhere, and this makes our work today all the more difficult. Further and more thorough research into the Buda statues in the hope of better determining their origins could usefully draw on the body of knowledge of French sculpture which has greatly expanded in the several decades since the first publication of the principal research on the Buda find. Indeed, the benefits may not all be one way. The Buda statuary could be an important auxiliary source for filling some of the many gaps in our knowledge of French court sculpture. Confirmation of all this would lend greater credibility to the reports of craftsmen hired by King Sigismund during his stay in Paris in 1416, and to the inference that they included sculptors as well as the goldsmiths. This also has consequences for the dating of this section of the sculpture ensemble.

II

Determining the origins of the other statues in the Buda ensemble presents somewhat greater difficulties. This is also reflected in the literature, where differences of opinion on this issue are much deeper. The first art historical treatment outlined a broad Central European background, citing examples

79 *Sigismundus Rex et Imperator*, pp. 327–328 (Cat. 4.19, by Imre Takács) and *Paris 1400*, p. 152 (Cat. 77A – by Françoise Baron).
80 i.e. at the moment Heinrichs-Schreiber's argument seems to me the most likely. It is notable that apart from the apostle/prophet cycle, he attributes a French origin to objects from the "lay" group. See further below.
81 On Bernay, see Georg Troescher, *Die burgundische Plastik des ausgehenden Mittelalters und ihre Wirkungen auf die europäische Kunst*, i (Frankfurt am Main: Prestel, 1940), pp. 72–73; Schwarz, *Höfische Skulptur*, pp. 201–202 and 457; *Paris 1400*, pp. 316–318 (Cat. 197, by Béatrice de Chancel-Bardelot).

mainly from Vienna, Prague, Poland and eastern Germany.[82] It also mentioned a group of statues of Styrian provenance which still bears the name of the place it was found, Grosslobming. This Austrian statuary later became the authoritative point of reference for the origins of the Buda pieces, so much so that the possibility of the same artist has been proposed.[83] There were even attempts to ascribe the whole Buda statuary, including the apostle/prophet series, to followers of the Grosslobming Master.[84] Michael Viktor Schwarz was on his own when he rejected this construction and sought the source of the statues somewhere else entirely. As with the apostle/prophet series, he proposed a set of French precursors, basically associated with Guy de Dammartin, and above all the statues made for the Palais de Justice and Tour Maubergeon in Poitiers around 1390.[85] Later, he judged the exclusiveness of this connection to be too one-sided, and took in a broader area of French court sculpture, but he remained emphatic in his conclusions regarding the Grosslobming statues, saying they could only be derivative of those in Buda.[86]

First of all, we should be clear that this part of the Buda ensemble is no more coherent in terms of style than it is in terms of material, size and theme. The idea that it forms a definite style group alongside the apostle/prophet series is a misleading simplification which recurs frequently in the literature, albeit stated with somewhat less confidence nowadays. In fact, the very distinguishing feature of the 'remainder ensemble' is the impossibility of treating it as a coherent whole.

The prime example is the Madonna statue (no 30), which researchers have always preferred – or have been forced – to treat somewhat separately because of features that are unusual in Central Europe (Fig. 16.25). The figure has at least two immediately striking features. The first is the pose. It displays pillar-like verticality from the waist down, despite the slight inward inclination of the left leg. The folds in the clothes, the outline of this narrower part and even the drapery hanging from the arms on each side all serve to emphasize this verticality. Above this, the upper body bends outward and the head bends strongly inward. The second is the drapery, built up by the contrast of folds with the flat

---

82   Marosi, "Vorläufige kunsthistorische Bemerkungen zum Skulpturenfund," pp. 355–364.
83   See thus: Zolnay and Marosi, *A budavári szoborlelet*, pp. 87–92 (by Ernő Marosi); Schultes, "Der Skulpturenfund von Buda".
84   *Der Meister von Großlobming*, ed. Arthur Saliger (Vienna: Galerie, 1994), pp. 172, 176, 179 and 180 (Cat. 42, 44, 45 and 46, by Arthur Saliger).
85   Schwarz, *Höfische Skulptur*, pp. 460–468.
86   Schwarz, "König Sigismund als Mäzen"; Schwarz, "König Sigismunds höfischer Traum," pp. 232–235.

surfaces from which they abruptly project, effectively without transitions; the folds are not drawn together, and the effect is somewhat less than harmonious, especially underneath. As Ernő Marosi pointed out a long time ago, the composition and iconography of the statue are of French origin and can be traced to much earlier precursors from the first half of the fourteenth century.[87] It is worth investigating whether they derive from a specific type, such as the "Poissy", particularly favored in court circles, or another version, represented by Jeanne d'Evreux's Madonna in the Louvre (Fig. 16.26).[88] Certainly, various derivatives of earlier French types were still current in this area in the second half of the century and even around 1400, including such masterpieces as the group of Madonnas linked to the Beauneveu circle and the Mary of the Wilton diptych, which has even greater resonance with the Buda statues (Fig. 16.27).[89] Very typical of these is the treatment of the child as an independent figure hardly touching his mother's body; this is also an important characteristic of the Buda Madonna. The face and hair of the latter, or rather what remains of them, can quite easily be traced to French examples. Although we cannot at present name a parallel to the highly-modeled cloth folds, the kind of contrast described above is typical, with some difference in emphasis, of French examples from the end of the century. Although French types always served as models for Central Europe, the Buda statue is much closer to the French pieces than to any other surviving examples in Central Europe.[90] The Buda Madonna thus fits into the apostle/prophet series on the basis of material, dimensions

87   Zolnay and Marosi, *A budavári szoborlelet*, pp. 89 and 145–146.
88   On the Poissy-type, see for example Robert Didier, "Contribution à l'étude d'un type de Vierge française du XIVe siècle. A propos d'un réplique de la Vierge de Poissy à Herresbach," *Revue des Archéologues et historiens d'art de Louvain* 3 (1970), pp. 49–72; Robert Suckale, "Überlegungen zur Pariser Skulptur unter König Ludwig dem Heiligen (1236–70) und König Philipp dem Schönen (1285–1314)," in idem, *Das mittelalterliche Bild als Zeitzeuge* (Berlin: Lukas, 2002), pp. 123–171, here pp. 152–160; on the Virgin Mary of Jeanne d'Evreux, see *Les fastes du Gothique. Le siècle de Charles v* (Paris: Réunion des musées nationaux, 1981), pp. 232–233 (Cat. 186, by Danielle Gaborit-Chopin); *Le trésor de Saint-Denis*, ed. Daniel Alcouffe (Paris and Dijon: Faton, 1991), pp. 246–254 (Cat. 51, by Danielle Gaborit-Chopin).
89   On the former group, see Susie Nash, "'A maistre Andrieu Biaunevue, de faire j ymagine de Nostre Dame.' Carving the Virgin and Child," in *"No Equal in any Land": André Beauneveu, Artist to the Courts of France and Flanders*, ed. Susie Nash (London: Holberton, 2007), pp. 66–105, here pp. 83–101; on the French origin of the Wilton diptych, on its identification with an illuminator working for Jean de Berry, see Ulrike Igl, *Das Wiltondiptychon. Stil und Ikonographie* (Berlin: Akademie, 1996), pp. 25–45.
90   On the Central European debt to the Poissy-type, see Markus Hörsch, "Paris – Prag – Würzburg. Die Madonna in Nordheim am Main und ihre Kunstgeschichtliche Stellung,"

and surface treatment, and we should look in a similar direction for its stylistic precursors. We have no real reason to assume any intermediary pieces from Central Europe, such as the 'Beautiful Madonnas', not to mention the Grosslobming figures, with which – as a comparison with the Mary statue clearly shows – there is absolutely no link at all[91] (Figs 16.25 and 16.33). Any correlations with Central European art rather betray knowledge of similar western prototypes, even in the case of the Falkenstein Madonna, whose identical details make it truly comparable to the Buda statue.[92]

There are figures other than the Madonna for which an attempt to find Central European precursors or intermediaries would be unnecessary even if there were any candidates. Schwarz has drawn a very convincing comparison of a Buda knight figure (no 14) with a former figure from the St-Yves Chapel in Paris (John V, prince of Brittany) and figures of the Tour Maubergeon in Poitiers, representing about a dozen people, almost certainly courtiers (Fig. 16.28).[93] Like the Buda figure and its companion piece (no 19), they feature a stocky, block-like monumentality, enhanced by striking verticality, and an 'individual' position of the hands (Fig. 16.29). The figures also have identical and similarly formed clothing. This is more than an equivalent representation type. There can be no further doubt that the source for these Buda torsos is to be sought here. If the statues had been discovered somewhere in Austria or Bohemia instead of Buda, there would hardly be an art historian who would not immediately cite western, and specifically French, precursors. We also find a significant similarity to the Buda figures in characteristics of the *beau pilier* statues in Amiens, the heroes of the La Ferté-Milon chateau in Pierrefonds, and a knight figure allegedly from Sainte-Chapelle in Bourges (Fig. 16.30).[94] Not only do these

---

in *Künstlerische Wechselwirkungen in Mitteleuropa*, eds Jiří Fajt and Markus Hörsch (Ostfildern: Thorbecke, 2006), pp. 27–51, esp. pp. 31–34.

91   It is also telling that the Buda Madonna holds her child on her right arm, while putting her weight on the same side., This posture is exceptional for the 'Beautiful Madonnas' from Central Europe while it is frequently used in the French context. See: See Schmidt, *Gotische Bildwerke*, p. 310.

92   See here Lothar Schultes, "Der Meister von Großlobming und die Wiener Plastik des schönen Stils," *Wiener Jahrbuch für Kunstgeschichte* 39 (1986), pp. 1–40, here pp. 17–20, pic. 32.

93   Schwarz, *Höfische Skulptur*, pp. 463–464; Schwarz, "König Sigismund als Mäzen," p. 316.

94   For better images of the statues of Amiens: Claire Richter Sherman, *The Portraits of Charles V of France (1338–1380)* (New York: New York University Press for the College Art Association of America, 1969), pic. 53–57; on the castle-statues: Heinrichs-Schreiber, *Vincennes und die höfische Skulptur*, pp. 205–209; *Paris 1400*, pp. 220 and 222–223 (Cat. 133, by Françoise Baron). On the figure of uncertain dating which may represent Louis de

French figures share the most visible and basic features of the Buda torsos, they are arranged in a similar program, which has also been proposed, and with good reason, to those in Buda. Block-like monumentality also appears in other representational types in the French court sculpture of the time, such as the sculpture of Jean de Cambrai.[95] We might propose that this pose and monumentality originally derive from French court tomb sculpture, where it is strikingly characteristic of the figures throughout the fourteenth and into the fifteenth centuries. Since the Buda statues date from the second and third decades of the fifteenth century, the idea that they form an organic progression from the examples we have discussed, mostly dating from around 1400 or after, is quite reasonable. It also seems unnecessary to look beyond French territory in connection with the two figurative consoles (nos 1, 2).[96] As regards the type, the motifs and – to a fairly high degree – even the style, we could cite pertinent analogies from Amiens and Poitiers, or even Dijon or Vincennes.[97]

Although console figures of this type were not unknown in Central Europe, the French examples also belong to a series and display clearer style relations. We thus have good reason to look westward for the direct origins. There is another Buda type which is quite well known both here and there, associated with a specific motif. To determine the place whence they came to Buda, we have to rely on truly minute clues. We have already encountered the series of mustached heads among the Buda finds. Their uniform faces definitely suggest a type (e.g. nos 53, 57 and 61) (Fig. 16.31). To the modern observer, the faces have

Châtillon, which is now kept in the parish church of Morogues (Cher), see Theodor Müller, *Sculpture in the Netherlands, Germany, France and Spain 1400 to 1500* (Harmondsworth: Penguin, 1966), p. 16, pic. 24B; Stephen K. Scher, "Un problème de la sculpture en Berry: les statues de Morogues," *Revue de l'Art* 13 (1971), pp. 11–24, here pp. 16–24 and Anne Adrian, "Le banc d'oeuvre de Morogues," in *Une fondation disparue de Jean de France, duc de Berry*, eds Béatrice de Chancel-Bardelot and Clémence Raynaud (Bourges: Musée du Berry, 2004), pp. 90–101, here pp. 96–99.

95   On his œuvre in details, see Georg Zeman, "Studien zur Skulptur am Hof des Jean de Berry. Stilfragen," *Wiener Jahrbuch für Kunstgeschichte* 48 (1995), pp. 165–214, here pp. 185–203.

96   Zolnay and Marosi, *A budavári szoborlelet*, pic. 1–4.

97   See the console of the *beau pilier* under Charles v in the cathedral of Amiens, see *Bildindex der Kunst und Architektur* (Marburg) no 171.568; for Poitiers, see Schwarz, "König Sigismund als Mäzen," pp. 316–317, pic. 55; on the console under St John the Baptist at the portal of the Champmol at Dijon, see Morand, *Claus Sluter*, pic. 19; on the consoles mostly at the sacristy of the Sainte-Chapelle at Vincennes, see Alain Erlande-Brandenburg, "Aspects du mécénat de Charles v. La sculpture décorative," *Bulletin Monumental* 130 (1972), pp. 303–345, here p. 323, pic. 25–26. Cf. Zolnay and Marosi, *A budavári szoborlelet*, p. 132 (by Ernő Marosi).

a dreamy, almost listless, inward-looking gaze, which presumably served to display a kind of high social status or court position. A much more forceful parallel than any put forward hitherto, and one which also embraces the angular head form and the slightly balloon-like puffiness, is the head of the Goldenes Rössl's Charles VI and his helmet-carrying knight (Fig. 16.32).[98] Clear examples of how this head type and facial expression spread beyond the 'court' themes of French sculpture are the heads of certain statues of the Amiens *beau pilier*.[99] In this light, the later Tyrolean and Pisanello analogies for the Buda statues we encountered above are better explained, and the head of Louis the Bavarian on Multscher's tomb model figure in Munich is an example of how this type, traceable to similar French sources, could also have appeared elsewhere – as we will discuss below.[100]

Gerhard Schmidt has drawn attention to a motif which was relatively widespread among statues from, or linked to Vienna around 1400, but was unknown elsewhere in Central Europe. It is found on standing figures, and consists of a hand holding up a corner of the mantle in front of the body. It almost certainly came to Austria from French sculpture.[101] A clear example in Buda is the now handless, outstretched left arm of a knight figure; underneath, the mantle runs upwards towards a peak (no 4).[102] Although we cannot tell from the fragments of the torso exactly how the motif was executed, comparison with the Austrian series is enough to establish that it came to Buda from Vienna. A point to ponder, however, is that it appears in Vienna solely on female saints, whereas similar motifs on late-fourteenth-century French Madonnas seem to derive from court figures, such as those of the Amiens *beau pilier* and the Poitiers Tour Maubergeon.[103]

We now face some specific questions concerning the very marked French connections of the 'secular' statues in Buda. 1. Are they traceable to a Central European context, particularly the Grosslobming group, according to the

---

98 *Das Goldene Roessl. Ein Meisterwerk der Pariser Hofkunst um 1400*, ed. Reinhold Baumstark (Munich: Bayerisches Nationalmuseum, 1995), tables 20, 25 and 26.
99 Sherman, *The Portraits of Charles V*, pic. 53 and 54.
100 On the sculpture of Multscher with its archetype in the French court, together with further literature, see Manfred Tripps, "Die stilistischen Quellen für Multschers Kunst," in idem, *Hans Multscher. Meister der Spätgotik. Sein Werk, Seine Schule, Seine Zeit* (Leutkirch: Heimatpflege Leutkirch, 1993), pp. 22–29; Hartmut Krohm, "Hans Multscher und die westeuropäische Kunst um 1400," in *Hans Multscher. Bildhauer der Spätgotik in Ulm*, pp. 61–70.
101 Schmidt, *Gotische Bildwerke*, pp. 307–308 and 343–345.
102 Zolnay and Marosi, *A budavári szoborlelet*, pic. 69.
103 Schmidt, *Gotische Bildwerke*, p. 343; Heinrichs-Schreiber, *Vincennes und die höfische Skulptur*, p. 217.

still-dominant view of the origin of their style? 2. Did these elements spread solely within the workshop, borrowed from the masters of the apostle/prophet series?[104] 3. Or should we look to at least partially direct French precursors even for the 'secular series'?

The main stumbling block in approaching these questions is how the secular statues of the Buda group relates to the Grosslobming figures. The Styrian group is still the subject of many uncertainties. For example, only recently has it emerged – in a catalogue entry of a handbook, almost as an aside – that their location in the third-order church in the five-street village where they (or at least most of them) were found was due to a secondary placement, probably during a rearrangement around 1500.[105] Other relevant facts are the lack of homogeneity within the ensemble, the considerable differences in height between the comparable figures, the differences in the shape of their bases, and the evident fluctuations in their quality, not to mention the somewhat less than completely convincing argument for their possible localization in Vienna. Further compounding the difficulties of determination is that some have been put together from fragments, resulting in considerable retouching and no doubt some additions.[106]

The first point to consider when comparing the Grosslobming figures with the Buda statues is that, as we have already seen, their average quality lags behind that of the Buda ones.[107] This shows up well in some direct juxtapositions: the Mary statues; knight figure (no 5) with the Grosslobming St John the Evangelist (which has some strikingly clumsy features); and the Buda bishop (no 16) with the Grosslobming bishop (Figs 16.4, 16.25 and 16.33). The differences between the Marys are clear and immediately obvious, but to show up the fundamental differences in composition and style we will take the bishops as our examples, because they are usually called upon to prove the closeness of the relationship (Figs 16.34 and 35). A fruitful point of reference is another figure, the bishop statue from the Bergenfahrer Chapel in Lübeck, from after 1406 (Fig. 16.36).[108]

---

104 Previous scholarship has already pointed out that masters of different erudition working in the same workshop inevitably take over each other's techniques and style. See Marosi, "Zu 'Werkstatt' und 'Künstler' in der Skulpturenreihe."

105 *Geschichte der bildenden Kunst in Österreich*, pp. 375–377 (Cat. 131, by Lothar Schultes); see also here the earlier literature, especially Schultes, "Der Meister von Großlobming".

106 See thus the suspiciously modern expression of St John: Schultes, "Der Meister von Großlobming," p. 107.

107 See thus Zolnay and Marosi, *A budavári szoborlelet*, p. 145 (by Ernő Marosi); Schwarz, "König Sigismund als Mäzen," pp. 310–312.

108 Anna Elisabeth Albrecht, *Steinskulptur in Lübeck um 1400. Stiftung und Herkunft* (Berlin: Reimer, 1997), pp. 119–120, pic. 122 and 124.

Although the Buda and Grosslobming figures share the same contrapposto pose, what is truly striking is the lack of any other similarities. The posture of the two statues immediately conveys a fundamental difference: the very slight contrapposto of the Buda figure may be described as a natural posture motif, whereas the other falls well within the artificial, exaggerated zone so typical of Central European sculpture of around 1400. The way their bodies relate to their clothes is also revealing. The clothes tend to conceal and obscure the body of the Grosslobming figure, while emphasizing that of the Buda figure. The Lübeck bishop's hardly-perceptible contrapposto, its 'flesh and blood' figure and even its outline all put it closer to the Buda statue. Whereas the awkward lower part of the Grosslobming figure, with its busy folds, and the improbably tapering upper body with sloping shoulders distinctly draw our attention to the head of the statue, the Buda and Lübeck figures have a much more balanced main aspect, giving our gaze free rein to follow each part. Comparison of the heads yields a similar result. Although some motifs are shared (short hair falling over the ears, wrinkles and bags under the eyes), they appear on the Grosslobming bishop in a rigid and lifeless overall composition whose effect, despite the surviving paint, is somewhat 'artificial'. This contrasts with the Buda bishop with his lively surface and dreamy, introverted gaze, even if the facial expression reminiscent of the knights' heads is less expressive of internal characteristics.[109] In this respect, too, the Lübeck figure lies closer.

The Lübeck example, although I would not claim any direct relation with Buda, throws some light on the serious differences between the Buda and Grosslobming figures.[110] These are not overridden by the coincidences of detail – like the partially-similar armor and identical border decoration – which have been used to infer identity of style, overlapping workshops and even the work of the same craftsmen.[111] The strenuous pursuit of a Grosslobming link

---

109   On a similar assessment of the two bishop figures, see Schwarz, "König Sigismund als Mäzen," pp. 310–312; *Sigismundus Rex et Imperator*, pp. 328–329 (Cat. 4.20, by Imre Takács).

110   The bishop of Lübeck has not come into sight accidentally in connection with Buda. With regard to the stylistic predecessors of these figures the same uncertainty prevails in the literature as in the case of the Buda statues. Though attention has recently been drawn to the Lower Saxon connections, some elements of the Franco–Flemish impact, long present in the literature, cannot be denied. Albrecht, *Steinskulptur in Lübeck*, pp. 123–134.

111   Zolnay and Marosi, *A budavári szoborlelet*, pp. 87–88 (by Ernő Marosi). The similar representation of the armor is less the consequence of the identity of style or of the same workshop but rather of the same period. The border decoration in question was not exceptional in the period either, see for instance the Madonna statue of Třeboň (Wittingau) or the contemporaneous St Michael fresco of Tarpa (north-eastern Hungary). Karl Heinz

seems a cul-de-sac for research into the Buda statues, and if there is any relationship, it is more likely to be in the other direction, as proposed by Schwarz. That, however, seems to be ruled out by the dating. The dating of the Grosslobming ensemble has always been subject to wide fluctuations, the most recent estimate being circa 1395. Any date subsequent to the Buda figures would have to be at the opposite extreme from those given in the 1994 Grosslobming exhibition catalogue entries, i.e. 1375–1385/90.[112] This largely detaches the Grosslobming 'ballast' from the Buda ensemble, but has little real relevance in any case. The two ensembles do retain a relationship, but one of a different kind, showing up chiefly through motifs. Lothar Schultes has tried to assert French precursors to the style of the Austrian statues. Some of his examples may seem exaggerated, but there is certainly a clear western relationship in the case of the composition of the St George statue,[113] and the context of the Grosslobming pieces – Lower Austrian sculpture from around 1400 – certainly drew on western sources.[114] It is more likely that Franco-Flemish sculptural influences arrived independently in Austria and Hungary around 1400, with only a small time difference. Another pointer to independent impulses is that, for me at least, the French influence is perceptibly stronger and more direct in Buda, even for the knight figure series, than in Vienna.

The close French connections to part of the knight series, for which the above examples seem to provide good evidence, exclude or at least challenge the theory that craftsmen of various backgrounds were working in the same workshop and influencing each other. Much more likely is the state of affairs alluded to by the chronicler of Saint Denis, that Sigismund, during his sojourn in Paris in 1416, "frequently mentioned what really commendable things he

---

Clasen, *Der Meister der Schönen Madonnen* (Berlin–New York: de Gruyter, 1974), pic. 237; Tibor Kollár, ed., *Falfestészeti emlékek a középkori Magyarország északkeleti megyéiből* [Wall-paintings from the northeastern part of medieval Hungary] (Budapest: Teleki, 2009) p. 421. Though the form in question of the border decoration is currently unknown from elsewhere, these kinds of border decorations were typical elements in the sculpture of the second half of the fourteenth century (see e.g. the figures of the royal sepulchers of the Saint Vitus at Prague or the figures of the Moses-well at Dijon).

112 For the two extremes, see *Der Meister von Großlobming*, p. 105 and 121 (by Arthur Saliger).
113 Schultes, "Der Meister von Großlobming," pp. 5–8. In respect of the statues from Grosslobming Heinrichs-Schreiber was unable to demonstrate any clear French parallels. See Ulrike Heinrichs-Schreiber, "Die Bedeutung der französisch-höfischen Bildhauerkunst für den Meister von Großlobming," in *Der Meister von Großlobming*, pp. 8–30, esp. pp. 23–24.
114 Schultes, "Der Meister von Großlobming," pp. 13, 19–20 and 27; Schmidt, *Gotische Bildwerke*, pp. 301–310.

saw in that kingdom; since he considered these artisans better than anyone else, he convoked with the king's consent three hundred of the better skilled ones from Paris and elsewhere, and sent them to Hungary."[115] The important information here is "from Paris and elsewhere", i.e. the relation of the apostle/prophet series with the other statues is determined not so much by different style origins – French and Central European – as by the diverse, multifaceted French (and possibly Netherlandish) art of around 1400. Heinrichs-Schreiber's work on the direct effects on Central Europe of the French court sculpture of the time is relevant here. Although he mentioned the traditional style-division of the Buda statues, he instinctively included some of the knight figures among his examples rather than restricting himself to the apostle/prophet series.[116] It would therefore definitely be worthwhile engaging in further research into the knight figures, but shifting from ad hoc hypotheses to "time-consuming, methodical style criticism."[117] Even though comparable western sculpture is highly fragmentary, knowledge of the surviving pieces covers a much wider spectrum now than it did thirty or forty years ago, when the interpretation of the Buda statues which holds sway today was born. And as has been proposed for the apostle/prophet series, it is important to emphasize that the knight figures could make valuable contributions to the highly fragmentary picture of French court art and/or Netherlandish art and its reconstruction.

As regards the style origins of at least some of the knight figures, we come back to the evidence for a western orientation. At present, we cannot say precisely which section or what proportion of the group this relationship holds for.[118] Is it possible, as Schwarz asserts in his 'reverse' construction, that International Gothic, so dominant in Central Europe around 1400, was not in any way a factor in these 'secular' figures (because they themselves engendered the style)? No other author apart from Schwarz today would dare give a definite "yes" to this question, whatever the dating. Looking through the statues,

---

115   "Sepius eciam seriose recitans que in regno commendabiliora viderat, dum artifices mechanicorum operum judicaret cunctis aliis preferendos, rege (i.e. Charles VI) consenciente, Parisiis et alibi trecentos ex pericioribus congregari statuit, et in Hungariam misit..." – *Chronique de Saint-Denis*, pp. 746–747; Csernus, "Francia források," p. 116.

116   Heinrichs-Schreiber, *Die Bedeutung der französisch-höfischen Bildhauerkunst*, p. 25; Heinrichs-Schreiber, *Vincennes und die höfische Skulptur*, pp. 230–233, pic. 316 and 317.

117   See here Marosi, "A budavári Zsigmond-kori szobrok," p. 97.

118   In the evaluation of the Buda finds, those from San Marco in Venice, firstly included by Schultes certainly deserve more attention (Schultes, "Der Meister von Großlobming," pp. 29–30). However, we have to agree with Schwarz that these statues on account of their present state and difficulties of access can only be evaluated with considerable uncertainty. See Schwarz, "Das Budaer Ritteratelier".

some seem to display familiar, indeed to some extent definitive schemas of Central European sculpture from that time. This is particularly striking with the arrangement of folds in clothing (nos 9, 13, 72) and the mostly-headscarved female heads (nos 49, 70), as was pointed out in respect of the scattered fragments uncovered in Buda Castle even before 1974.[119] Since the pieces mentioned above, with one exception, are also made up of scattered fragments, their affinities with the devices of the Beautiful Madonnas might just be explained by the earlier view that not all of them were products of the workshop.[120] Be that as it may, the revision of the Grosslobming connection has re-opened the question regarding possible Central European precursors to the knight series, and of whence this layer of style came to Buda, and by what route. The above, however, prompts another question concerning the origin of the Beautiful Madonnas/soft style: can these devices, too, be derived directly from French precursors, and, if so, to what extent?

We do not, as yet, have satisfactory answers to these questions. Certainly, Central European prototypes in general have received much more attention in the literature on the Buda ensemble than is warranted by analysis of the statues. The types, motifs and styles primarily and definitively point to western, French precursors, permitting little other explanation than a conscious choice by the patron. Sigismund always had very definite objectives, and as he traveled throughout almost all Europe, he would hardly have made up his mind on the basis of immediate impressions. His choice seems much more likely to have been guided by well-considered – and not entirely aesthetic – aims. If true, it is striking and noteworthy that he did not follow in the steps of his father, Charles IV, or of his brother, Wenceslas, and that he declined to draw on the monumental sculpture which was theoretically close at hand – that of Central Europe, particularly Prague.[121] There were of course other aspects of his royal display where he made a similar departure.[122] He preferred what was in a sense the more 'traditional' approach of following the French court

---

119 Dénes Radocsay, "Die schönen Madonnen und die Plastik in Ungarn," *Zeitschrift des Deutschen Vereins für Kunstwissenschaft* 23 (1969), pp. 49–60.

120 The relationship of the scattered fragments with the products of the workshop may be eventually established by analysis of the materials.

121 For the apparently one-sided or at least questionable treatment of Sigismund's imperial display, see: Wilfried Franzen, "Römischer Kaiser und König von Böhmen – Rückkehr zu Prager Vorbilder," in *Karl IV. Kaiser von Gottes Gnaden. Kunst und Repräsentation des Hauses Luxemburg 1310–1437*, ed. Jiří Fajt (Munich: Deutscher Kunstverlag, 2006), pp. 595–607.

122 See on this *Sigismundus Rex et Imperator*.

mode, as his father had done early in his reign.[123] Whether there lay behind this choice an old, Central European monarch's reflex, possibly supported by the similar artistic orientation of his royal predecessors of French origin (the Angevin dynasty), we do not know.[124] Nonetheless, this concept of royal display could easily be interpreted in terms of the imperial universalism which Sigismund so often declared. This reached a peak while he was in Paris, where on several occasions he most definitely promoted imperial supremacy against the absolute sovereignty enjoyed by the French monarch in his own country. His moves at that time, which turned out to be of somewhat fleeting success, were designed to proclaim the change in the situation since Emperor Charles IV's visit to Paris in 1378. No longer was he content to engage with the French king as merely an equal.[125] Thus Sigismund may have intended his royal display, too, as a means of competition with the court, which was still of prime importance for the art of the continent, and for a short time, he may even have taken the lead. This is suggested by certain characteristics of the Buda statuary which went beyond the level of style current in Paris in the early fifteenth century.[126] This possibility takes us to the question of the statues' own subsequent influence.

Afterlife

The most fascinating dilemma concerning the influence of the Buda ensemble, and one which has been long lurking in the literature without express

---

123 On the mostly French-orientated representation of Charles IV at the beginning of his reign, see Jiří Fajt, "Karl IV., 1316–1378. Von der Nachahmung zu einem neuen kaiserlichen Stil. Entwicklung und Charakter der herrscherlichen Repräsentation Karls IV. von Luxemburg," in *Karl IV. Kaiser von Gottes Gnaden. Kunst und Repräsentation des Hauses Luxemburg 1310–1437*, ed. Jiří Fajt (Munich: Deutscher Kunstverlag, 2006), pp. 41–75, here pp. 42–56.
124 On this orientation, see Ernő Marosi, "Itinerarien mittelalterlicher Künstler," in *Gotika v Sloveniji. Nastajanje kulturnega prostora med Alpami, Panonijo in Jadranom*, ed. Janez Höfler (Ljubljana: Narodna galerija v Ljubljani, 1995), pp. 17–25, here p. 23; Imre Takács, "Königshof und Hofkunst in Ungarn in der späten Anjouzeit," in *Sigismundus Rex et Imperator*, pp. 68–86, here pp. 76–78.
125 Sándor Csernus, "Zsigmond és a Hunyadiak a középkori francia történetírásban," [Sigismund and the Hunyadi family in medieval French historiography] *Századok* 132 (1998), pp. 47–127, here pp. 80–86; idem, "Sigismund von Luxemburg und die französische Geschichtsschreibung," in *Sigismundus Rex et Imperator*, pp. 487–493, here p. 493.
126 Heinrichs-Schreiber, *Vincennes und die höfische Skulptur*, p. 232.

formulation, is whether the Buda statues could have contributed to a departure from the International Gothic in Central European sculpture and the emergence of a new phase, and, if so, in what way.[127] To answer this question, we must clearly establish which characteristics of the Buda figures not only differ from the traditional style of Central Europe but also presage subsequent developments. So far, hardly any preparatory work has been carried out that might facilitate answering this highly complex question. Here we will look at only three possible examples of the influence of the Buda statues. Some appear clear and tangible, others offer little further promise, but further investigation could be fruitful.

Considering that many of the statues are unfinished and never left the workshop, which means that they could not have been widely known in their own time, one question touching on their influence is what happened to the craftsmen involved in making them. The most obvious answer is that they stayed where they were and worked for other patrons in Hungary. There are definite signs of this in architecture. In the middle of the century, the building of Hunedoara Castle for John Hunyadi, regent between 1446 and 1453, involved some obviously French elements which are unknown anywhere else in Hungary. The castle also features the armorials of the Valois family.[128] This development unavoidably brings to mind the French stonemason families whom Broquière met in Pest in 1433. They had been without work for some time, owing to Sigismund's cancellation of the construction work in Buda. There is also an indication of continuity in sculpture, if only at one single point. A series of fragments of red marble tombs from the 1430s are known to have been made in the same workshop, obviously in Buda. The artist responsible for the ensemble is referred to as the "Master of the Stibor tomb" after the principal – i.e. most intact – figure, the tomb of Stibor II of Stiboric (d. 1434).[129] Although the fragmentary remnants, the diverse material and the different representational functions of the tomb figure make comparison difficult, close

---

127 Apart from Hungarian scholarship these views were emphatically expressed at the Multscher-exhibition at Ulm in 1997 where before the works attributed to Multscher, ten fragments represented the Buda ensemble in the catalogue; however, the studies refrained from discussing the problem (*Hans Multscher. Bildhauer der Spätgotik in Ulm*).

128 Radu Lupescu, *Vajdahunyad vára a Hunyadiak korában*, unpublished PhD-Dissertation [The castle of Hunedoara in the age of the Hunyadi family] (Budapest: ELTE, 2006), pp. 159–166.

129 Pál Engel, Pál Lővei and Lívia Varga, "Grabplatten von ungarischen Magnaten aus dem Zeitalter der Anjou-Könige und Sigismundus von Luxemburg," *Acta Historiae Artium* 30 (1984), pp. 33–63, here pp. 36, 38, 40, 42 and 47–50 (cat. 9–11); *Sigismundus Rex et Imperator*, pp. 347–348 (cat. 4.51, by Pál Lővei); Pál Lővei, "A Stibor-síremlékek mestere," [The master of the Stibor tombstones] *Budapest Régiségei* 33 (1999), pp. 103–121.

links can be discerned among the motifs and indeed the style, particularly of the heads. It is difficult to imagine that the craftsmen in the workshop who made these tomb statues did not have close connections with the 'secular' Buda figures.[130]

Attempts to ascribe to the Buda statuary's sphere of influence Hungarian relics which quite easily fit into the "Beautiful" or "Soft" style of Central European International Gothic are much more uncertain and difficult to assess. Some of these are second- and third-grade, mostly wooden statues, many of obscure date and provenance.[131] If we accept that this style characterized only a very narrow section of the Buda statuary, then we might well ask of these (wooden) statues why such a widespread style should have come particularly from Buda. Such an oversimplified view of relations at the time clearly stems from the nature of the surviving material, which is even more fragmentary in Hungary than in neighboring areas. A clue to the greater complexity of affairs is offered by four stone relics dating from the same period, the first quarter of the fifteenth century, and linked to Sibiu, one of the principal towns of Transylvania. Three have already been long known internationally (Pietà and Mater Dolorosa, Sibiu, Museul Național Brukenthal; Calvary group, Sibiu, Chapel of the Holy Cross); the fourth has been described only recently (torso of standing figure, Sibiu, Museul Național Brukenthal). They are of uneven quality, and display at least two, and more probably three, different style variants. This multiplicity of stylistic links is also apparent from differences in the possible provenance of these examples: the inscription on the Calvary tells of an Austrian link; the Pietà is most often treated as a Bohemian import (although a Hungarian or Austrian provenance has also been proposed); finally, particular devices on the recently-published torso display striking coincidences with certain pieces of the Buda statuary.[132]

The craftsmen of Sigismund's sculpture workshop could of course have left the country when work in Buda stopped. They may have returned to where they had worked before or found commissions nearby, in Central Europe. One such case may have been that of Hans Multscher, whose work is regarded by art historians as giving the definitive impulse to Central European sculpture's departure from the International Gothic style. Multscher's early work has long

---

130 Marosi, "Vorläufige kunsthistorische Bemerkungen zum Skulpturenfund," p. 362; Zolnay and Marosi, *A budavári szoborlelet*, pp. 110–111 (by Ernő Marosi); Ernő Marosi, "Das künstlerische Erbe der Zeit Sigismunds. Auftakt zur Spätgotik," in *Sigismundus rex et Imperator*, pp. 558–564, here pp. 562–563.
131 Radocsay, "Die schönen Madonnen," and Török, "Einige unbeachtete Holzskulpturen".
132 *Sigismundus Rex et Imperator*, pp. 569–574 (Cat. 7.6–7.9, by Imre Takács).

been recognized as displaying a general Franco-Flemish influence. In recent decades, this influence has been narrowed down to French – specifically Parisian – work of the end of the fourteenth and early fifteenth centuries.[133] The name of the Swabian master has also been linked to the Buda statuary.[134] In addition to Multscher's part of the elector series in Ulm Rathaus, to which Buda provides much clearer parallels of iconography and motif than does Vienna,[135] Ernő Marosi saw a link to Multscher's early works in the Franco-Flemish style of the apostle/prophet series, and alluded to Multscher in connection with certain features of the knight figures.[136] Multscher's works date from the late 1420s and early 1430s, i.e. immediately following – not at the same time as – the Buda statues. The links between them involve more, however, than a common style and similar devices. Sigismund nurtured close, if not always cordial, relations with the patrons of Multscher's works, Duke Louis VII (the Bearded) of Bavaria-Ingolstadt (r. 1413–1443) and the city of Ulm. Louis belonged for a while to the French court and led the French delegation to the Council of Constance, where he was one of the main supporters of Sigismund's proposals. He prepared and financed the king's journey to France in 1415–1416 and stayed for several extended periods in the Buda court – for example serving Sigismund's daughter – during the second phase of the palace's reconstruction.[137] Sigismund's multi-faceted and partly personal connections with Ulm reached

---

133   Sabine Reisner and Peter Steckhan, "Ein Beitrag zur Grabmalvisier Hans Multschers für Herzog Ludwig den Bärtigen," in *Das geschnitzte und gemalte Bild auf den altaren stehen ist nutzlich und christenlich. Aufsätze zur süddeutschen Skulptur und Malerei des 15. und 16. Jahrhunderts*, ed. Rupert Schreiber (Messkirch: Gmeiner, 1988), pp. 9–74; Hartmut Krohm, "Hans Multscher und die westeuropäische Kunst um 1400," in *Hans Multscher. Bildhauer der Spätgotik in Ulm*, pp. 61–70; Heinrichs-Schreiber, *Vincennes und die höfische Skulptur*, pp. 233–235.
134   The earliest: Török, "Einige unbeachtete Holzskulpturen".
135   Cf. *Hans Multscher. Bildhauer der Spätgotik in Ulm*, pp. 288–289 (by Michael Roth).
136   The Holy Trinity relief of Sandizelland and the sepulchral monument of Louis the Bearded are here relevant. See Zolnay and Marosi, *A budavári szoborlelet*, p. 152; Marosi, "Die Skulpturen der Sigismundszeit," p. 183; Marosi, "Das künstlerische Erbe der Zeit Sigismunds," p. 562. On the works of Multscher reviewed here, see *Hans Multscher. Bildhauer der Spätgotik in Ulm*, pp. 283–299 and 302–306 (Cat. 14A–E and 16 – by Michael Roth, Rainer Kahsnitz and Evamaria Popp); Manfred Tripps, "Hans Multschers Frankfurter Gnadenstuhl. Ehemaliges Herzstück einer Vierge Ouvrante?" *Zeitschrift für württembergische Landesgeschichte* 58 (1999), pp. 99–111.
137   Windecke, p. 177; *Allgemeine Deutsche Biographie*, xix (Leipzig: Duncker & Humblot, 1884), pp. 504 and 506; *Neue Deutsche Biographie*, xv (Berlin: Duncker & Humblot, 1987) p. 362.

a peak just around 1430, and this intensive, fruitful relationship found expression in Multscher's statues for the town hall.[138]

So numerous and concrete are these connections that we cannot avoid wondering whether Multscher's early art might also be approached from a Buda perspective. What such an investigation might bring is an open question. Nevertheless, by admitting such a possibility we necessarily concede that the output of Sigismund's Buda workshop "[…] may be regarded as of greater significance than some sculptures which, for many decades, have held the spotlight in investigations into the art of around 1400".[139]

Conclusions

The present study provides a survey of research initiatives concerning the Buda sculpture find in the last forty years since its discovery. Furthermore, it aims to clarify and in some respect complement the results that have been achieved so far, and suggests possible directions for future investigations. By now it can be stated with certainty that the statuary ensemble was made in the 1410s and 1420s on King Sigismund of Luxemburg's commission in order to embellish his monumentally expanded royal residence, the palace of Buda. The statues were not intended for a single building, but for different parts of the palace complex, and some were placed in the St Sigismund church, a collegiate chapter founded by the king in the castle area. The thematic range was also more complex than it had been previously assumed: besides Sigismund himself and persons connected to his reign as well as series of apostles and prophets, it has been possible to identify further saints and probably also figures of an Epiphany representation.

The style of the ensemble is not homogeneous. The erudition of its masters reflects first and foremost the art of French royal and princely courts, although stylistic features of Central European provenance can also be observed. The latter are, however, much less dominant than previous scholarship had assumed, and their appearance can hardly be explained with the influence of that circle of artwork, the so-called statues of Grosslobming, which had been considered so fundamental for Buda up till now.

---

138 Michael Roth, "Reichsstadt und Kaiser. Der Skulpturenschmuck am Ulmer Rathaus," in *Hans Multscher. Bildhauer der Spätgotik in Ulm*, pp. 87–102, esp. pp. 98–100.
139 See thus Schwarz, "König Sigismunds höfischer Traum," p. 235.

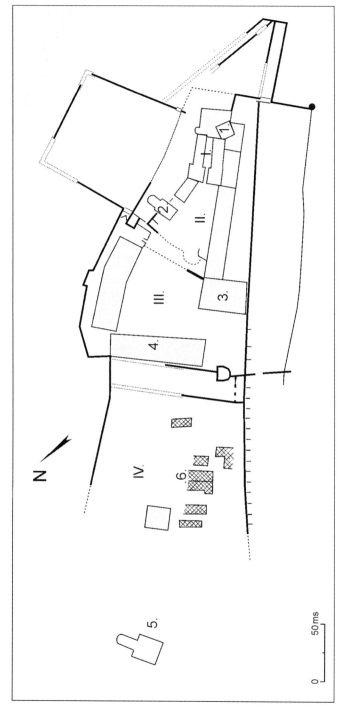

FIGURE 16.1 Buda, the southern end of the Castle Hill with the buildings of the royal palace and the find spots of the statues (1: The so-called Small Court; 11. The so-called Grand or Inner Court; 111. The so-called Sigismundian or Second Court; 1V. The so-called Northern Forecourt; 1. Stephen Tower 2. Palace chapel 3. The so-called Incomplete Tower 4. The Grand palace of Sigismund 5. St Sigismund chapel 6. The find spot of the 1974 statue finds) (research by K. Magyar)

FIGURE 16.2   *Fragment of an apostle's/prophet's head (BTM, No 56)*

FIGURE 16.6   Chaperone *male head (BTM, No 54)*

FIGURE 16.3   Torso of a knight figure (BTM, No 22)

FIGURE 16.4   *Torso of a knight figure (BTM, No 5)*

FIGURE 16.5   *Figure of a helmet-carrying herald* (BTM, No 29)

MADE FOR THE KING 431

FIGURE 16.7   *Saint Ladislas (?) (BTM, No 34)*

FIGURE 16.8
Gold coin of King Sigismund (1402–1437), reverse side (Hungarian National Museum)

FIGURE 16.9
Torso of a royal (?) figure (BTM, No 7)

FIGURE 16.10   *Rogier van der Weyden: Columba altar, central panel, detail*
MUNICH, ALTE PINAKOTHEK

FIGURE 16.11   *Fragment of a head with its hair tied up with a roll of cloth* (BTM, No 46)

FIGURE 16.12
Rogier van der Weyden: Bladelin Triptych, right wing, detail
BERLIN, GEMÄLDEGALERIE, STAATLICHE MUSEEN ZU BERLIN – PREUßISCHER KULTURBESITZ; PHOTO: JÖRG P. ANDERS

FIGURE 16.13   *Saint Bartholomew (?)* (BTM, *No 28*)

FIGURE 16.14   *Claus Sluter: Madonna (Dijon, former Carthusian church)*

FIGURE 16.16   *Torso of an apostle/prophet (BTM, No 25)*

FIGURE 16.15 *Torso of an apostle/prophet*
BOSTON, MUSEUM OF FINE ARTS

FIGURE 16.17 *Torso of an apostle/prophet* (BTM, No 36)

FIGURE 16.18   *Claus Sluter: Angel (Dijon, former Carthusian church, calvary)*

FIGURE 16.19   *Torso of an apostle/prophet* (BTM, *No 35*)

MADE FOR THE KING 441

FIGURE 16.20   *Mourner on the tomb of Philip the Bold*, detail
DIJON, MUSÉE DES BEAUX-ARTS

FIGURE 16.22
Detail of a prophet from the so-called Matthias calvary
ESZTERGOM CATHEDRAL TREASURY PHOTO: ATTILA MUDRÁK

FIGURE 16.21
Head fragment of an apostle/prophet (BTM, No 55)

MADE FOR THE KING 443

FIGURE 16.23   *Torso of an apostle/prophet* (BTM, No 33)

FIGURE 16.24   *Console with the figure of a prophet/apostle*
PARIS, MUSÉE DU LOUVRE

FIGURE 16.25   *Madonna* (BTM, *No 30*)

FIGURE 16.26 *The Madonna of Jeanne d'Evreux*
PARIS, MUSÉE DU LOUVRE

FIGURE 16.27 *Wilton diptych, right wing, detail*
LONDON, NATIONAL GALLERY

FIGURE 16.29   *Torso of a knight figure* (BTM, No 19)

FIGURE 16.28 *Courtier figure*
POITIERS, TOUR MAU-
BERGEON; PHOTO:
© BILDARCHIV FOTO
MARBURG

FIGURE 16.30 *Courtier (Morogues [Cher], parish church)*

FIGURE 16.31   *Fragment of a* Chaperone *male head* (BTM, No 61)

FIGURE 16.32
Charles VI, king of France, detail from the Goldenes Rössl (Altötting, former Stiftskirche)

FIGURE 16.33 *Mary from the Annunciation ensemble*
FRANKFURT AM MAIN, STÄDTISCHE GALERIE
LIEBIEGHAUS

FIGURE 16.34   *Torso of a bishop* (BTM, *No 16*)

FIGURE 16.35 *Bishop*
VIENNA, ÖSTER-
REICHISCHE GALERIE
BELVEDERE;
PHOTO: INSTITUT FÜR
KUNSTGESCHICHTE DER
UNIVERSITÄT WIEN,
FOTOSAMMLUNG, INV.
NO 158 165

FIGURE 16.36 *Bishop from the Bergenfahrer chapel*
LÜBECK, MUSEUM FÜR
KUNST- UND KULTUR-
GESCHICHTE; PHOTO:
©FOTOARCHIV DER HANSE-
STADT LÜBECK – ST.
ANNEN-MUSEUM

CHAPTER 17

The Court of the King and Queen in Buda in the Jagiellonian Age

Orsolya Réthelyi

The association between the court of the kings of Hungary and the city of Buda became final when King Sigismund chose Buda as the royal residence sometime between 1405 and 1408 and moved there – with the main royal offices – from Visegrád, which had been the royal residence of the Angevin kings. Even though the itinerant character of medieval royal life did not cease completely, the close association of Buda with the royal court came to be ever closer during the fifteenth century down to 1526. In this article the court of the kings and queens of late medieval Hungary will be discussed in relation to Buda. By the term court we usually understand an institution comprising the extended household of a ruler. Nevertheless, there is general agreement in scholarship that the definition of a medieval and early modern court is difficult not only because of the complexity of the term and its changing form, but also due to the fluidity of the court itself, which was also noted by contemporaries.[1]

To reflect some of this conceptual complexity a number of different aspects of the court will be discussed without any claim to comprehensiveness. The subject will include the court as the center of royal administration and jurisdiction; the personnel of the court; the relative position of the courts of the king and the queen; questions of languages and ethnicity, size and location; and, finally, the court as a cultural center. I will not discuss here the issue of 'the palace' (*palatium*), which in my sources denotes a place or an edifice rather than a group of people.[2] Although situating the subject in the broader context of the fifteenth and early sixteenth century, I will focus on the Jagiellonian

---

1 The question is discussed in great detail by Malcolm Vale, *The Princely Court: Medieval Courts and Culture in North-West Europe, 1270–1380* (Oxford: Oxford University Press, 2001), pp. 15–33, esp. p. 16. For a clear and useful overview of the recent changes in theoretical approaches and methods in early modern court studies, see Jeroen Duindam, "Early Modern Court Studies: an Overview and a Proposal," in *Historiographie an europäischen Höfen (16.–18. Jahrhundert): Studien zum Hof als Produktionsort von Geschichtsschreibung und historischer Repräsentation*, eds Markus Völkel and Arno Stroymeyer (Berlin: Duncker & Humblot, 2009), pp. 37–60.
2 On the Buda palace and its functional division, see Károly Magyar's article in the present volume.

period (1490–1526), comprising the reigns of Wladislas II and his son, Louis II, kings of Hungary and Bohemia.[3]

Court and Administration

The royal household differed from other great medieval households in that besides the domestic functions and the administration of the household, its officials were responsible for the governance of the realm and the two functions were not separated.[4] This meant that certain household offices obtained immense political influence. In some countries the major household offices eventually became hereditary and honorary titles of rank, and did not necessarily imply attendance at court, but since influence was strongly connected to physical closeness to the lord, these offices lost importance.[5] The relationships between the terms household and court is a distinction which was already made by contemporaries. However, while the concept of the royal household can be described and understood with ease, the concept of the court changed its meaning in medieval as well as modern use. There seems to be an agreement, however, that the 'material infrastructure' of princely courts was provided by the household.[6] In the court and the administration of the late medieval kingdom of Hungary, the chief governing body was the royal council consisting officially of all the *barones* (major aristocrats) *et prelates* of the realm. This group of some 60–70 people was obviously too large to manage the day-to-day tasks, which was done by a smaller group of 8–10 people forming a kind of inner council making decisions about those issues of domestic and foreign policy

---

3 In the following description I rely greatly on the findings of András Kubinyi, "A királyi udvar a késő középkori Magyarországon," [The royal court in late medieval Hungary] in *Idővel paloták...: Magyar udvari kultúra a 16–17. században* [Palaces in time...Hungarian court culture in the sixteenth and seventeenth centuries], eds Nóra Etényi and Ildikó Horn (Budapest: Balassi, 2005). pp. 13–32, and András Kubinyi, "Alltag und Fest am ungarischen Königshof der Jagellonen: 1490–1526," in *Alltag bei Hofe* (Residenzenforschung, 5), ed. Werner Paravicini (Sigmaringen: Thorbecke 1995), pp. 197–215.

4 Rainer A. Müller, *Der Fürstenhof in der frühen Neuzeit* (Munich: Oldenbourg, 2004), p. 18.

5 Aloys Winterling, "'Hof'. Versuch einer idealtypischen Bestimmung anhand der mittelalterlichen und frühneuzeitlichen Geschichte" in *Hof und Theorie. Verstehen durch Erklären eines historischen Phänomens*, eds Reinhardt Butz, Jan Hirschbiegel and Dietmar Willoweit (Cologne: Böhlau, 2004), pp. 77–90, here p. 84.

6 Vale, *The Princely Court*, p. 14.

which did not need parliamentary sanction.[7] When the sovereign was in Buda the royal council held its sessions in the palace.

Permanent members were the holders of chief governmental offices: the palatine, the judge royal (*iudex curiae*), the so called "master of the treasury" (*magister tavernicorum*), the steward of the royal court (*magister curiae*), the chancellor and some of the prelates. The role of the lord chancellor (*aulae regiae cancellarius*) was the most influential in the royal council, because he kept the royal seals. He was also the supervisor of the chancellery, which meant that all documents passed through his hands, giving him the opportunity to control and influence the administration. He was appointed by the king, but also had to take into account the opinions of the prelates and barons. He was helped in his work by the notaries of the chancellery. The secretaries of the king should not be counted among the staff of the chancellery, although they did help out with the work there. They were appointed by the king and were often also councillors (*secretarius et consiliarius*); they were typically sophisticated individuals, often with a university education, and frequently from middle class burgher or even peasant background. Kubinyi compares them to the educated councillors appearing in increasing number in the royal councils of Western Europe.[8] In this period the court of justice included three central offices, two of them – the palatine and the judge royal – were magnates, the third was a professional who represented the king (*personalis praesentiae regiae in iudiciis locumtenens*). He was also the keeper of the judicial seal. Four legal professionals (*prothonotarii*) assisted the judges, one each for the palatine and the judge royal, and two for the king's *personalis*.

When the king presided over the court session, it took place within the palace, but it is unknown exactly where the location was. It is possible that in other cases the court held sessions in the city of Buda.[9] The *curia militaris* was the central link between the court as organ of judgment and as household. Originally it counted as a separate court for the royal household, and later on, cases of honor belonged to this court. The parties were obliged to appear in person, not represented by lawyers and ordeal by single combat was often the decisive means of judgment. Judgment was brought by the king, who was in practice represented by the judge royal, or by the royal steward. From the time of the economic reforms of Matthias Corvinus in 1464–1468, the financial matters of the kingdom were managed by the royal treasurer (*thesaurarius*) and his

---

7 Pál Engel, *The Realm of St Stephen, a History of Medieval Hungary, 895–1526* (London–New York: I.B. Tauris, 2001), pp. 352–353.
8 Kubinyi, "A királyi udvar," p. 20.
9 Kubinyi, "A királyi udvar," pp. 16–17.

familiares. It is unclear whether this took place in the palace or in the town of Buda. The royal treasury – where the *Libri Regii*, i.e. copies of the royal charters of donation, and other treasures, including the armor of the king, were kept – was in the charge of the *tavernici*, and was in the royal palace beside the Stephen's Tower.[10]

The Personnel of the Court

The royal household proper was then for the personal service of the king. With some resemblance to the differentiation between gentle and menial servants, Kubinyi divided this group into three sub-categories: (1) The court nobility, who – in a system similar to western courts – received salary according to the number of horses, that is armed horsemen, who accompanied them on campaigns. (The group could include non-noble burghers, who had the same rights as the nobles once they were on the king's pay-list.) (2) The body of menial servants, who were usually non-noble, including ushers, grooms, waggoners, tailors, gunsmiths, shoemakers, painters, etc. (3) A miscellaneous third group included the royal secretaries, the personnel of the chapel, the physicians, astronomers, musicians, hunting personnel, etc. and was characterized by not belonging to either of the first two groups. The situation was further complicated by the relationship between the royal court and the personnel of the Buda Castle. The Buda Castle was under the jurisdiction of the castellan (*castellanus castri Budensis*) and the royal estate manager (*provisor curiae castri Budensis*, *udvarbíró* in Hungarian). Kubinyi argued that although the royal court resided predominantly in Buda, the castle's personnel should not be formally regarded as part of the royal household, even though the *provisor curiae* was responsible for the management of all the royal estates. As such, he was the superior of the royal dispenser (*dispensator regius*), who in turn was the master of the personnel of the royal kitchen and cellar.[11] All members of the household were on the royal pay-roll and received a salary from the king.

The court nobility served in one of the departments of the household, but it is often difficult to delineate these departments. Some of them are more visible, others hardly discernible from the records. The most visible and populous department was that of the chamber. The account book of 1525 mentions the names of 73 gentlemen of the chamber (*cubicularii*), who apparently served the king in groups of eight. In the same source there is record of 18 gentlemen

---

10   See Károly Magyar's article in the present volume.
11   Kubinyi, "A királyi udvar," pp. 20–21.

of the table (*dapiferi*), but the other departments cannot be pinpointed. The court nobility can also be categorized according to rank. According to the order of hierarchy in the Jagiellonian era, members of the court nobility (*aulici*) were either pages (*parvulus, aprodianus*), squires (*adolescens*), or belonged to the group of court *familiares* (*aulae familiaris*). As reflected in the terms of their salary, the court nobility had a military function. A distinction was made between the court light cavalry (*aulicus huzaro*), a term which emerged in the Jagiellonian period and the other group, presumably consisting of knights in heavy armor. Both groups were stationed either at the royal court in Buda or in the castles in the border region. The two groups together constituted the *banderium* of the king.[12] The court offered possibilities of social advancement and positions were hotly contested. Offices were often given to people the king and his advisers wanted to entice, or tie to the king. Individuals often entered the court through the support of relatives: we have examples of families from which three or four members were among the court nobility at the same time.[13]

The main four court officials of the Jagiellonian royal household were the master of the doorkeepers (*magister ianitorum regalium*), who also served as the steward (*magister curiae regiae*), the master carver (*magister dapiferorum/ structorum regalium*), the master cup-bearer (*magister pincernarum/pocillatorum regalium*) and the master of the horse or marshal (*magister agazonum regalium*).[14] The holders of these offices ranked as "genuine barons" (*veri barones regni*) of the realm.[15] In contrast to many countries these offices never became hereditary in Hungary; the king had the power of appointing and terminating them. It is not clear to what extent the chief offices required regular attendance at court. In our period the office of the marshal, the master carver and the master cupbearer seem to have become ceremonial functions which were practiced on the occasion of important events while the everyday tasks

---

12 Kubinyi, "A királyi udvar," pp. 24–25. The number of the court nobles together with their *familiares* amounted to a thousand men. The king was required to have a body of 1000 knights under his banner, according to paragraph 21 of the laws of 1498. See DRMH, iv, pp. 100–103.

13 Kubinyi, "Alltag und Fest," p. 207. "Was a position at Maximilian's court hotly competed or not? The evidence so far suggests that even menial posts had to be purchased with bribes worth up to five years in expected salaries." See Gerhard Benecke, *Maximilian I, 1459–1519: An Analytical Biography* (London–Boston: Routledge – Kegan Paul, 1982), p. 111.

14 András Kubinyi, "Alltag und Fest," p. 202.

15 Martyn Rady, "Rethinking Jagiełło Hungary, 1490–1526," *Central Europe* 3 (2005), pp. 3–18, here pp. 12–13.

were delegated to a deputy officer.[16] Both the steward and the relatively new office of the royal master of the chamber (*magister cubiculariorum*, created by Wladislas II in 1490) had actual tasks in the household, implying their presence. The steward also had an important political function in the royal council; after debating an issue he was responsible for asking every member individually for their opinion before a decision was reached, as well as officially announcing the decision. However, neither officer can be considered as the formal leader of the household, since the master of the chamber who, according to the 1523 reform proposals, was responsible for the valuables and the personal safety of the king, was not lower in rank than the steward.

A further characteristic specific to the Jagiellonian royal court was that both Wladislas and Louis were kings of both Hungary and Bohemia. While a separate royal court existed in Prague, both kings were served by court nobles from both kingdoms. In addition to Czechs, a number of Poles were also in the court because of the Polish roots of the dynasty and the close family ties with the king of Poland. According to the calculations of Kubinyi, these non-Hungarian subjects made up slightly more than half of the court nobility under Louis II. The two groups of subjects stood under the leadership of their own stewards (*magister curiae*).[17] This virtually even distribution of the court offices between people from the Hungarian and Bohemian crowns is no coincidence. It is rather a reflection of a Letter of Majesty (*Majestätsbrief*) issued by King Wladislas in 1510, in which he promised his Bohemian subjects that members of both crowns would be evenly represented in the courts of both of his children.[18]

The King's and Queen's Courts

Analyses of the form and function of the courts of queens has a shorter history and the basic categories are much less developed than investigations of the royal court. This is partly due to the fact that the queen's household is often

---

16 It is described that at the wedding of Matthias Corvinus the most powerful magnates served the royal couple at the table: *Regis Ungariae Matthiae nuptiae, et coronationis regiae atque illorum postea ingressus in Budam a Palatini comitis legato diligenter descripta*. Given in Johann Georg Schwandtner, *Scriptores rerum Hungaricum varii*, i (Vienna: Impensis Ioannis Pauli Kraus, 1746), pp. 519–527.

17 Kubinyi, "A királyi udvar," p. 24.

18 Franz Palacký, *Geschichte von Böhmen: Größtentheils nach Urkunden und Handschriften. Fünfter Band: Das Zeitalter der Jagelloniden. Zweite Abtheilung: König Wladislaw II und König Ludwig I. Von 1500 bis 1526.* (Prague: In Commission bei Friedrich Tempsky, 1867), pp. 194–195.

'hidden'. The queen consort is always understood in relation to the king and her position and power defined in comparison to his. In many cases there are no queens beside the kings for long stretches of time, without this influencing the kingdom in any significant manner. Furthermore, the queen's household seems in many cases to have melded together with the king's, only showing its own characteristics when the king and queen resided in different locations. Scholarship has only recently begun addressing the question whether a certain queen had a separate household.[19] A further question is whether a queen indeed had her own court. This depends largely on what we mean by household and court, which is not a clear-cut matter.[20]

One of the central points of distinction in all studies of the courts of queen consorts is the relationship of their court or household to that of the king. Students of this matter speak of varieties, ranging from an 'autonomous organization' to an administration subordinated or simply submerged in the royal court.[21] Even in the well-researched English material, rich in sources, there is no consensus on the degree of independence in organization and personnel of the queen's court, conventionally described as her *curia et hospicium* in the late medieval accounts.[22] The households of queens were usually organized like those of the king, with a parallel system of separate court officials and servant body. The main difference in the personal element was the presence of a group of women, in English termed ladies-in-waiting, in German sources and literature referred to as the *Frauenzimmer*.[23] In the queen's *familia*, therefore, one may expect a great diversity of people, noble and non-noble, men and women,

---

19   The first such study to my knowledge is that of Hilda Johnstone on the households of the queens of England: eadem, "The Queen's Household," in *Chapters in the Administrative History of Mediaeval England. The Wardrobe, the Chamber and the Small Seals*, v, ed. T.F. Tout (Manchester–New York: Manchester University Press, 1930), pp. 231–289.

20   Recently, the Residenzen-Kommission has dedicated a conference and a volume to the question of courts and women. See *Das Frauenzimmer. Die Frau bei Hofe in Spätmittelalter und früher Neuzeit* (Residenzenforschung, 11), eds Jan Hirschbiegel and Werner Paravicini (Stuttgart: Thorbecke, 2000).

21   C.M. Woolgar, *The Senses in Late Medieval England* (New Haven: Yale University Press, 2007), p. 229.

22   J.L. Laynesmith, *The Last Medieval Queens: English Queenship 1445–1503* (Oxford: Oxford University Press, 2005), p. 224.

23   Anja Kircher-Kannemann, "Organisation der Frauenzimmer im Vergleich zu männlichen Höfen," in *Das Frauenzimmer. Die Frau bei Hofe in Spätmittelalter und früher Neuzeit* (Residenzenforschung, 11), eds Jan Hirschbiegel and Werner Paravicini (Stuttgart: Thorbecke, 2000), pp. 235–246. I will use both terms.

officers and menial servants, locals with frequently different ethnic and cultural background and people brought with her from her own home country.

As the court of the queen is relatively less known, it is worth giving a concise overview of the queens of Hungary and their court at Buda during the fifteenth and early sixteenth centuries. Due to historical circumstances, the years in which the Buda royal court lacked a residing queen outnumbered by far the periods in which a queen was present: only in 26 of the 86 years between 1440 and 1526 did a queen reside in the court.[24] Most importantly, this meant that customs relating to the presence of a queen at the court had very little continuity, and so traditions had not much time to develop and sink in. It also meant a quite dramatic change in court life every time a queen appeared. We have evidence that the household personnel of the kings in the Jagiellonian period were male, down to the servants in charge of washing the dishes or the clothes.[25] The advisory and administrative members of the court were of course also men, thus in the absence of a queen the court was almost exclusively male. However, when a queen appeared in addition to bringing her own retinue and advisors, her ladies-in-waiting and their servants also accompanied her, as well as attracting ladies from the local nobility. This female element in itself must have changed the everyday life at the court. The arrival of the members a new queen's household must have resulted in tensions in the court's life, especially so, if – as in the case of the royal court of Hungary – the presence of queens was interrupted by long periods when no queens resided at the court.[26]

The queen's household or court was the basis of her power.[27] In the model that developed in Hungary, the economy of the queen's court was based on the reginal estates. Evidence points to an independent management of the estates by late medieval queens of Hungary.[28] These estates were exceptionally

---

24   András Kubinyi, "The Court of Queen Mary of Hungary and Politics between 1521 and 1526," in *Mary of Hungary*, pp. 13–25, here p. 13.

25   Kubinyi, "Alltag und Fest," pp. 209–211.

26   For a detailed discussion of the topic, see Orsolya Réthelyi, "Ambiguous Loyalties? Mary as Queen of Hungary (1521–1526)," in *Marie de Hongrie. Politique art et culture sous la Renaissance aux Pays-Bas* (Monographies du Musée royal de Mariemont, 17) (Binche: Musée Royal de Mariemont, 2008), pp. 13–24.

27   Martin Kintzinger, "Die zwei Frauen des Königs. Zum politischen Handlungsspielraum von Fürstinnen im europäischen Spätmittelalter," in *Das Frauenzimmer*, pp. 377–398, here p. 385.

28   Spiess argues for two models in Europe for the financing of the reginal household. "It is obvious that the two models entailed quite different roles for respective queens. In England and Castile the queens were relatively wealthy landowners with considerable

large, even in international comparison.[29] Her possession of extremely lucrative estates made the queen one of the largest landowners of the kingdom. Through her domains the queen might obtain significant economic and political weight; whether she made use of this possibility depended chiefly on her personality, intelligence, and ambitions. The queen also had the right of patronage over the religious institutions on her lands and could make use of this for the construction of a power base.

A crucial development regarding the development of the queen's power and court was connected with Sigismund's second wife, Barbara of Cilli (1390/1392–1451).[30] While it is unclear to what extent a group of estates was designated as belonging to the queen in the previous centuries, the first grant given as dower to Barbara already refers to specific "reginal estates" (Óbuda, Csepel, Kecskemét, etc.). In relation to the city of Buda the estate of Óbuda deserves special attention. The royal castle and its incomes had been granted to the dowager Queen Elizabeth by her son, Louis I, in 1343 and had been part of the body of the reginal estates (*civitas reginalis*) up to the end of the Middle Ages. Charter evidence testifies to the enduring importance of Óbuda as a center for the queens of Hungary up to 1526.[31]

The position of Queen Elizabeth (1409–1442) is significant because as daughter of King Sigismund she claimed to have the power of a queen in her own right.[32] Queen Elizabeth had her own chancellery and court officials. She obtained all the possessions that had once belonged to her mother Barbara

---

revenues at their disposal and had their own administrative staffs and their own councils. In Germany, by contrast, the queen was financially completely dependent on her husband. See Karl-Heinz Spiess, "European Royal Marriages in the Late Middle Ages: Marriage treaties, questions of income, cultural transfer," *Majestas* 13 (2005), pp. 7–21, here pp. 19–20.

29 Amalie Fössel, *Die Königin im mittelalterlichen Reich. Herrschaftsausübung, Herrschaftsrechte, Handlungsspielräume* (Stuttgart: Thorbecke, 2000), pp. 78–79.

30 Amalie Fössel, "Barbara von Cilli. Ihre frühen Jahre als Gemahlin Sigismunds und ungarische Königin," in *Sigismund von Luxemburg. Ein Kaiser in Europa. Tagungsband des internationalen historischen und kunsthistorischen Kongresses in Luxemburg, 8.–10 Juni 2005*, eds Michel Pauly and François Reinert (Mainz am Rhein: Philipp von Zabern, 2006), pp. 95–112.

31 István Kenyeres, *Uradalmak és végvárak. A kamarai birtokok és a törökellenes határvédelem a 16. században* [Lordships and border castles. Estates of the Hungarian Chamber and the anti-Ottoman border protection in the sixteenth century] (Habsburg Történeti Monográfiák, 2) (Budapest: Új Mandátum, 2008), p. 62.

32 Mályusz adduces many examples of this. See Elemér Mályusz, "Az első Habsburg a magyar trónon," [The first Habsburg on the Hungarian throne] *Aetas* 9, no 1 (1994), pp. 120–150, here pp. 124–125. Analyzing the coronation ceremony of Elizabeth, János M. Bak comes to

and was given further estates, as well as 20,000 florins per year to cover the costs of her household. After her husband's death, in an attempt to ensure the succession of her yet unborn child she feigned to accept the suggestion of the diet to marry King Wladislas III of Poland (the future Wladislas I, as king of Hungary), but at the same time made plans to steal the Holy Crown of Hungary and escape to the relatives of her deceased husband.[33] A fascinating account written by Helene Kottanerin, member of the queen's *Frauenzimmer* tells of how the crown was stolen from the treasury of the stronghold in Visegrád. The unique source also gives a valuable insight into the working and dynamics of the female household around the queen and shows how it might be manipulated for political ends by an authoritative queen.

In the last fifty years of the medieval Hungarian kingdom, four queens resided at the royal court. Twelve years after the death of his first wife Catherine of Poděbrady (1449–1464),[34] Matthias Corvinus married Beatrice of Aragon (1457–1508), daughter of King Ferrante I of Naples. Unfortunately no comprehensive modern study has been made of her household.[35] Anne of Foix (1484–1506), daughter of Gaston II de Foix, count of Candale, and Catherine de Foix, was a cousin of the French queen, Anne of Brittany, and a member of the French royal court. Sources about her are scarce, probably due to the mere four years she spent in Hungary as queen consort of King Wladislas II, from her arrival to Buda in 1502 until her premature death in 1506.[36] A precious

---

the conclusion that she cannot be considered a queen in her own right: idem, *Königtum und Stände in Ungarn im 14.–16. Jahrhundert* (Wiesbaden: Franz Steiner, 1973), p. 169.

33 James Ross Sweeney, "The Tricky Queen and Her Clever Lady-in-Waiting: Stealing the Crown to Secure Succession, Visegrad 1440," *East Central Europe – L'Europe du Centre Est* 20–23 (1993–1996), pp. 87–100, here pp. 90–95; *Die Denkwürdigkeiten der Helene Kottanerin (1439–1440)* (Wiener Neudrucke, 2), ed. Karl Mollay (Vienna: Österreichischer Bundesverlag für Unterricht, Wissenschaft und Kunst Wien, 1971).

34 Orsolya Réthelyi, "King Matthias on the Marriage Market," in *Matthias Corvinus, the King*, pp. 247–250, here p. 248.

35 Albert Berzeviczy, *Beatrix királyné. Történelmi élet- és korrajz* [Queen Beatrice. Historical biography and her era] (Budapest: Magyar Történelmi Társulat, 1908). The Italian version of the monograph was published under the title of *Beatrice d'Aragona* (Milan: Corbaccio, 1931).

36 Lajos Kropf, "Anna királyné, II. Ulászló neje," [Queen Anne, wife of Wladislas II] *Századok* 29 (1895), pp. 689–709; Gusztáv Wenzel, "II. Ulászló magyar és cseh királynak házas élete, 1501–1506," [The married life of Wladislas II, king of Hungary and Bohemia] *Századok* 11 (1877), pp. 727–757; Josef Macek, *Tři ženy krále Vladislava* [The three wives of King Ladislas] (Prague: Mladá fronta, 1991); Attila Györkös, "II. Ulászló házassága és a francia diplomácia," [The marriage of Wladislas II and the French diplomacy] *Acta Academiae Agriensis* 39 (2012), pp. 89–102.

exception, which also describes the city of Buda, is the detailed report by the herald in the service of the French Queen Anne of Brittany, Pierre Choque, which gives an account of Anne's journey, the festivities in the Italian city states, and the queen's coronation and arrival to Buda.[37] Very little is known of the queen's actual income and next to nothing about her household, its expenses, or its relation to the royal court.[38] The names of a few of her officials are known: her secretary was János Gosztonyi and her estates were managed by Johannes Melakh de Gozon.[39] Certain charters give evidence of estate management activities by the queen and tempting details on further administrative bodies.

Recent studies on the court of Mary of Hungary (1505–1558), daughter of Philip of Castile and Juana of Castile, and queen consort of Louis II, show a reginal institution that can be compared to those of other late medieval queens' courts of Europe in terms of size, form, function, and even inherent problems.[40] The extent of Mary's influence on politics, despite the short period of her reign, was significant. Two factors played a decisive role in the power of Mary of Hungary, both of which expressed themselves in the queen's household.

One of these was the vast size of the reginal domain. Mary recognized the potential and utilized the possibilities provided by her estates, both financially and politically. The second factor was the right to appoint members to court functions. Besides being an obvious means to exercise patronage and win supporters, authority over appointments also meant a personally selected, close body of loyal followers around the queen. Several members of the queen's household and officials seem to have played a significant role in the political events of the diets of 1525–1526. It is conceivable that the queen had a free hand in appointments because those forces at the court which wished to strengthen the authority of the king realized that her political ambitions and intelligence backed by the weight of the reginal estates could act as a stabilizing factor in the kingdom.

37 Antoine Le Roux de Lincy, "Discours des cérémonies du mariage d'Anne de Foix, de la maison de France, avec Ladislas VI, roi de Bohême, précédé du discours du voyage de cette reine dans la seigneurie de Venise, le tout mis en écrit du commandant d'Anne, reine de France, duchesse de Bretagne, par Pierre Choque, dit Bretagne, l'un de ses rois d'armes. Mai 1502," *Bibliothèque de l'École des Chartes* 21 and 22 (1861), pp. 156–185 and 422–439.

38 There are extant charters relating to the queen's estate management, but no overall study has been made of these.

39 See: *La succession de Jean de Gozon: grand maître de la maison du roi de Hongrie* (Rodez: Impr. P. Carrère, [1965]).

40 Orsolya Réthelyi, *Mary of Hungary in Court Context, 1521–1531*, unpublished PhD dissertation (Budapest: Central European University, 2010).

Language and Ethnicity at the Court

The kingdom of Hungary had a long tradition of linguistic plurality due to the presence of different ethnic groups in the area speaking a number of different languages.[41] Buda can be placed in the list of Central European residential towns, like Prague and Cracow, in which a combination of a German and a local population made up the majority of the town population. The court resembled the city by also being a forum of linguistic interaction.

Despite the tradition of a multi-ethnic and linguistically pluralist society in the kingdom, however, the late medieval period was characterized by a growth of a frequently expressed ethnic intolerance. Hungary was by no means exceptional, since this seems to be a general phenomenon of the age with the same signs discernible in Bohemia as well as in the Holy Roman Empire.[42] It is interesting to see how one of the most important documents expressing this ideology, a strongly propagandistic charter summarizing the demands of the nobility at the diet of 1505, also refers to language as the mark of 'national' unity.

The increased use of the vernacular in official diplomatic relations is also an important feature of the age. In the selection of diplomats sent to the Hungarian court, knowledge of the Hungarian language was desirable. That the Czech lords delivered their speeches in their own vernacular at the Hungarian court in the Jagiellonian decades was not surprising since the royal court at Buda counted as the royal court for Bohemia as well. More significant is the use of Polish by the official delegate of the king of Poland, the Chancellor Szydłowiecki at the diplomatic summit in 1523.[43]

In one of the two Letters of Majesty (*Majestätsbrief*) issued to the Bohemian estates by Wladislas in 1510 in the Czech language, the king proclaimed:[44]

---

41 András Kubinyi, "Zur Frage der Toleranz im mittelalterlichen Königreich Ungarn," in *Toleranz im Mittelalter* (Vorträge und Forschungen, 45), eds Alexander Patschovsky and Harald Zimmermann (Sigmaringen: J. Thorbecke, 1998). pp. 187–206; J[ános] M. Bak, "Linguistic Pluralism in Medieval Hungary," in *The Culture of Christendom: Essays in Medieval History in Commemoration of Dennis L.T. Bethell.*, ed. Marc Anthony Meyer (London: The Hambledon Press, 1993), pp. 269–280.

42 Václav Bůžek, "Strangers in Their Own Country: King Louis II (Jagiello) and Mary of Hungary's Stay in Bohemia at the Turn of 1522–1523," in *Mary of Hungary*, pp. 63–68; András Kubinyi, "Az 1505. évi rákosi országgyűlés és a szittya ideológia," [The diet of Rákos in 1505 and the 'Scythian' ideology] *Századok* 140 (2006), pp. 361–374.

43 Krzysztof Szydłowiecki, *Szydłowiecki kancellár naplója 1523-ból* [The diary of Chancellor Szydłowiecki from 1523], ed. István Zombori (Budapest: METEM, 2004).

44 Both Letters of Majesty were issued on 11 January 1510 and they were considered the basis for the succession of the Habsburg House to the throne of Bohemia. See Palacký, *Geschichte von Böhmen*, p. 195 note 151.

Therefore we have decided, and with this charter confirm that our heirs will be raised in a place which is suitable and to which subjects of both the Hungarian and the Bohemian crowns have equally easy and free access. Furthermore, we pledge to keep with them an equal number of subjects, both men and women, from Bohemia and Hungary, so that they thereby freely learn both languages, Hungarian and Czech, so each crown may use their own language to negotiate and speak of their needs to the Royal Majesties.[45]

Later evidence from the court of Louis II corroborates the promise given in the Letter of Majesty in respect of the more or less even distribution of Bohemians and Hungarians. Wladislas was of Polish origin and a number of courtiers were from the kingdom of Poland. His brother Sigismund, later king of Poland, had spent three years at the court of Wladislas in Buda between 1498 and 1501. According to Kubinyi's calculations, the Polish element in the household of Louis II was approximately ten percent. The wife of Wladislas, Anne de Foix, was French, and brought with her some of her French personnel, although she died a few weeks after Louis's birth. Louis's sister, Anne, was three years old at this time. There must therefore have been some French linguistic influence at the court, although no letters of either royal children attest to their written knowledge of French.

Buda was to a great extent made up of German speakers, not to mention the presence at the court and in the young king's immediate vicinity of Wladislas's nephew, George of Brandenburg, who brought with him a specific German linguistic and cultural influence. Several autograph letters of both Louis and Anne to the brother of George, Casimir of Brandenburg, have survived written in German, attesting to their knowledge of the written language.[46] Several autograph letters written in Latin also attest to the Latin knowledge of the young king.[47] Louis must have had a considerable command of the language of diplomacy, Italian as well, as noted by the delegates of the Venetian Republic. According to the report of Lorenzo Orio, which in view of what we know, we have no reason to doubt, King Louis was proficient in six languages: Hungarian, Czech, Polish, French, Italian and Latin.[48] That the knowledge of Hungarian was

---

45   I have used the German translation (instead of the Czech original) provided by Palacký, *Geschichte von Böhmen*, p. 195.
46   The letters were written between 1519 and 1525. See thus MNL OL DF 267 662, 267 658, DF 267 659, etc.
47   See for instance the autograph letter written by the then fourteen-year-old Louis to Casimir of Brandenburg, 13 July 1520, Buda: MNL OL DF 267 661.
48   Vincenzo Guidoto, another diplomat, mentions his knowledge of German in place of French.

vital at the royal court is demonstrated by a letter written by reginal counsellor, Schneidpöck, about an unnamed relative of Gabriel Salamanca, who obtained a position as Carver in the household of Mary of Hungary. After the appointment Schneidpöck tells Salamanca to put pressure on his relative to learn Hungarian.[49]

A further important root for linguistic variety in the royal courts was the arrival of queen consorts, who usually came from abroad. It was generally accepted that their native language was different, but they were also expected to learn the language of their new country as soon as possible. This is most clearly expressed in the tractate *De institutione vivendi* by Diomede Carafa, an excellent source for the practical working and the social dynamics of the queen's court is the late Middle Ages.[50] Diomede Carafa – a learned diplomat of the Neapolitan court and the childhood tutor of Beatrice of Aragon, queen consort to Matthias Corvinus – wrote a work containing a list of practical advice for the young queen. According to its prologue, the *De institutione vivendi*, written in the form of a "Queen's mirror", was composed at the request of Beatrice and given to her upon her departure from Naples. Carafa advised Beatrice in the matter of language in his usual practical manner:

> You can be certain that you will have grave difficulties in communication with your husband as well as with the people – especially the women – until you learn their language. So have somebody, who knows the language, ride beside you every day of the journey to learn the basics. Once you have arrived you will learn the language with ease from the women in your household.[51]

Mobility, Size, and Relation with Civic Buda

Even though the Jagiellonian kings were sovereigns of both Hungary and Bohemia, Buda was their principal residence. The king had separate institutions for

---

[49] Correspondence between Johann Schneidpöck and Gabriel Salamanca, 18 April 1524–29 April 1524. Vienna, Haus-, Hof- und Staatsarchiv, Österreichische Staatsarchiv, Grosse Correspondenz fasc. 25/b. Quoted by Kubinyi, "The Court of Queen Mary," p. 16.

[50] Diomede Carafa, *Memoriale a Beatrice d'Aragona Regina d'Ungheria*, ed. B. Croce (Naples: [n. p.], 1894). A new publication of both the Italian and Latin version of the text, together with a Hungarian translation, was published in 2006. See Diomede Carafa, *De institutione vivendi* (Budapest: OSZK, 2006).

[51] Carafa, *De institutione vivendi*, p. 41.

the government of Bohemia and a separate Czech chancellery. When he held court in Bohemia, his regent in Hungary was the palatine. This makes the reign of the Jagiellonian kings an interesting case for the mobility of the court at the end of the Middle Ages. In the period between 1521 and 1526, the royal couple and their households spent two longer periods away from the royal residence of Buda. On 26 February 1522 they left Buda and traveled to Prague to attend to matters of state and have Mary crowned queen of Bohemia.[52] After a longer period spent in Prague and a shorter stay in the Moravian Olomouc, they returned to Buda more than a year later, at the end of April 1523. Unfortunately there is no record of the royal couple spending a period apart, which might make it easier to distinguish their separate households.

It is notoriously difficult to calculate court sizes and because different researchers have different criteria as to whom belongs within and without the court comparisons are not always meaningful.[53] Kubinyi calculated the size of the royal household at about 450–500 people, excluding the royal council, the judges of the royal court of justice, the chapel and the court of the queen, and the "horses", i.e. men in arms serving the court nobility. These people were not all present at the court simultaneously, since a significant number of them performed military service in the border region. If one includes the royal council, the chancellery, and the law court, this number approaches a thousand people.[54] This is rather a large number in comparison with the contemporary Habsburg royal courts, that of Maximilian in 1519, amounting to above 450 people, and that of Ferdinand in 1527/28 amounting to about 360 people.[55] However, these other calculations only count those people directly on the prince's payroll, which makes the comparison difficult. The court of the kings of England, by comparison, had 400 to 700 servants in the fourteenth century, about 800 during the reign of Henry VI, and continued growing during the sixteenth and seventeenth centuries.[56] Charles V of Habsburg's itinerant court

---

52   Norbert C. Tóth, "A királyi pár Csehországban 1522–1523," [The royal couple in Bohemia 1522–1523] in *"Köztes-Európa" vonzásában: Ünnepi tanulmányok Font Márta tiszteletére* [In the pull of *Zwischeneuropa*. Studies in honor of Márta Font], eds Dániel Bagi, Tamás Fedeles and Gergely Kiss (Pécs: Kronosz, 2012), pp. 83–96.

53   Paul-Joachim Heinig, "How large was the Court of Emperor Frederick III?," in *Princes, Patronage and the Nobility: The Court at the Beginning of the Modern Age, c. 1450–1650*, eds Ronald G. Asch and Adolf M. Birke (New York: Oxford University Press, 1991), pp. 139–156.

54   Kubinyi, "A királyi udvar," p. 25; idem, "Alltag und Fest," p. 206.

55   Alfred Kohler, *Ferdinand I. 1503–1564. Fürst, König und Kaiser* (Munich: C.H. Beck, 2003), pp. 137–141.

56   C.M. Woolgar, *The Great Household in Late Medieval England* (New Haven: Yale University Press, 1999), p. 11.

amounted to between 1000 and 2000 members.[57] Nevertheless, the information we have, taken with the necessary doses of salt, suggests that the household of King Louis was more numerous than that of Ferdinand.

The residential function of Buda had important consequences for the city itself, which can be seen for instance in the high number of citizens coming from the court nobility. Recent research by András Végh on the topography of Buda has shown that during the fifteenth century up to 1526, a significant number of members of the court nobility owned real estate in Buda. Both the higher nobility – who were expected to take part in the royal council as barons of the realm–and those members of nobility, who had offices in the royal and reginal court, owned houses in the city. This influenced Buda directly, because by becoming citizens through their ownership of real estate they also paid civic taxes, at least up to 1492, when their houses were exempted from taxes by law. The royal palace at the southern end of the city made this part attractive to the nobility, but the houses of nobles and court officials can be found in all parts of the area of the *castrum*. The function of royal residence naturally also influenced the presence of trade and craftsmen in the town of Buda. It can be generally said that the majority of those citizens involved in trade or the crafts relied on the purchasing power of the royal court and the visiting nobility. The relatively high percentage of arms manufacturers and craftsmen of luxury products also points in this direction.[58]

The Royal Court as a Religious and Cultural Center

The requirements of princely display in the competition between royal courts, the presence of highly trained men of letters and diplomats, and visitors from many backgrounds and languages made royal courts traditionally the place where culture and the arts flourished and new ideas appeared. This was also true of the royal court of Buda, where in different periods royal and reginal patronage resulted in high points in the cultural life of the later middle ages.[59] The arrival of a queen to the court was often associated with a reform in court customs and the thriving of the arts. In the case of Beatrice of Aragon, we have the evidence of the humanist Italian historian, Antonio Bonfini, who lived at

---

57   Jeroen Duindam, *Vienna and Versailles: the Courts of Europe's Major Dynastic Rivals, 1550–1780* (Cambridge: Cambridge University Press, 2003), p. 36.
58   Végh, *Buda*, i, pp. 318–321.
59   For some of the recent results see among others the catalogues of three recent exhibitions in Hungary: *Mary of Hungary*; *Sigismundus Rex et Imperator*; *Matthias Corvinus, the King*.

the court as a reader to Beatrice and was commissioned by King Matthias to write a chronicle of the Hungarians.[60] In an elaborate comparison of the king's court before the arrival of the queen to the court with a queen, he attributes most civilizing measures to the influence of Beatrice. He describes the court of Matthias alone as simple, lacking in ceremony, where lords and soldiers had free access to their king. In contrast the arrival of the queen resulted in an intensification of court ceremonial, and at the table, in limitations to the accessibility of the king, in a rich cultural and artistic life, and in an increased expenditure. From other sources we know details such as Beatrice introducing the use of the fork at the royal table. Galeotto Marzio, another court humanist also comments on how the Hungarians still ate from a common dish taking the meat with their hands and using a piece of bread, while south of the River Po individual plates were used.[61] The Renaissance splendour and the patronage of arts, literature, sciences, architecture typifying the court of King Matthias, which certainly were present in the court already before the arrival of the queen, intensified significantly from the second half of the 1470s.[62]

In the early sixteenth century after the arrival of Mary of Hungary to Buda again one can see a flowering of art and intellectual activity. At the request of the queen, her husband King Louis II invited Thomas Stoltzer, the most talented musician of the region, to fill the post of choirmaster (*magister capellae*) of the queen's chapel. He stayed in her service up to 1526 and during the years spent in Buda, Stoltzer set Martin Luther's recently written German translation of the Psalms to music, at the request of the young queen. These are considered the first non-Latin polyphonic Psalms in the history of music. The painter, Hans Krell, from the Franconian town of Crailsheim, was present at the court in Buda from 1522. He accompanied the king and queen on their journeys and was active in Prague and Pressburg, as well as in Buda. Beside the portraits he made of the royal couple and various courtiers, he also made decorations for tournaments, hunting, ceremonial banquets, and masks to be worn at masked festivities, alongside being engaged in purely artisan work. His accounts give a glimpse of a lively courtly culture at the royal court of Buda from a period in

---

60 Bonfini, *Decades*, I.
61 Galeotto Marzio, *De egregie, sapienter et iocose dictis ac factis Mathiae regis*, ed. Ladislaus Juhász (Leipzig: B.G. Teubner, 1934.), cap. 17.
62 Árpád Mikó, "Queen Beatrice of Aragon" in *Matthias Corvinus, the King*, pp. 251–265, here pp. 251–253. András Kubinyi, *Matthias Rex* (Budapest: Balassi, 2008), p. 132; *The Dowry of Beatrice: Italian Maiolica Art and the Court of King Matthias. Exhibition Catalogue*, eds Gabriella Balla and Zsombor Jékely (Budapest: Iparművészeti Múzeum, 2008).

which the details of everyday life are difficult to reconstruct due to the lack of sufficient sources.[63]

In the same period the ideas of Christian humanism and the teachings of the early reformation also found their way to the royal court very early. The acknowledged poet and diplomat, Jacobus Piso, provost, royal and reginal secretary, who had been the teacher of the young Louis II, played a crucial role in establishing contacts between Hungarian humanists and Erasmus. As a result Elek Thurzó, royal treasurer, Stanislaus Thurzo, bishop of Olomouc, Johannes Thurzo, bishop of Wrocław, Johannes Antoninus, the court physician of Louis II, and Johannes Henckel, the court chaplain of Queen Mary, among others, exchanged frequent letters with Erasmus, as well as maintaining an intensive correspondence with each other. The erudite humanist Johannes Henckel, from Levoča, persuaded Erasmus to write the tract *Vidua Christiana* for the queen as consolation after the death of her husband in 1526. Queen Mary, and several others in her environment, demonstrated a receptive attitude towards the idea of humanist Christianity and new church doctrines. Her correspondence demonstrates that she had read some of Luther's works herself. Luther, like Erasmus, sent a work of consolation, the *Vier tröstliche Psalmen an die Königin zu Hungern*, to the young widowed queen, much to the displeasure of her Habsburg family.[64]

When one tries to form a picture of the everyday religious life of the royal court one is hindered by the lack of basic sources for such reconstruction, the account books for daily expenses within the royal court, of which source type only three fragments have survived from the Jagiellonian period.[65] The

---

63   Kurt Löcher, "Der Maler Hans Krell aus Crailsheim in den Diensten des Markgrafen Georg von Brandenburg-Ansbach und König Ludwigs II. Von Ungarn," *Jahrbuch des historischen Vereins für Mittelfranken* 97 (1994–1995), pp. 151–186.

64   Zoltán Csepregi, "Court Priests in the Entourage of Queen Mary of Hungary," in *Mary of Hungary*, pp. 49–61; Hans Martin Rothkegel, *Der lateinische Briefwechsel des Olmützer Bischofs Stanislaus Thurzó. Eine ostmitteleuropäische Humanistenkorrespondenz der ersten Hälfte des 16. Jahrhunderts* (Hamburger Beiträge zur neulateinischen Philologie, 5) (Münster–Hamburg: Lit, 2007); Ute Monika Schwob, "Der Ofener Humanistenkreis der Königin Maria von Ungarn," *Südostdeutsches Archiv* 17/18 (1974/1975), pp. 50–73; *Oláh Miklós levelezése* [The letters of Miklós Oláh] (Magyar történelmi emlékek, i. Okmánytár, 25), ed. Arnold Ipolyi (Budapest: MTA Könyvkiadó Hivatala, 1875).

65   Johann Christian von Engel, ed., "Fragmentum libri rationarii super erogationibus aulae regis Hungariae Ludovici II," in *Monumenta Ungrica* (Vienna: Sumptibus Nicolai Doll, Bibliopolae, 1809), pp. 187–236. The list of the expenditure of the royal court during a period of five months from 1525 was edited by Vilmos Fraknói, "II. Lajos király számadási könyve, 1525. január 12–július 16," [The account book of Louis II, 12 January 1525 – July

account books allow us a glimpse of the celebration of religious feasts in the first half of 1525 (12 January to 16 July). This permits a view on at least a part of the liturgical year, including the important liturgical feasts of Candlemas (2 February), the Feast of Annunciation (25 March), Holy Week (9–16 April), Pentecost and the Feast of Corpus Christi (15 June). The king heard High Mass in the royal chapel on Candlemas.[66] As many as 44 candles had to be bought for the procession on the feast decorated with tin flowers and red bands, which were to be consecrated in the chapel.[67] The king specially sent for a canon of Székesfehérvár to sing the Mass of Good Friday, who, several weeks later, was paid ten florins for the service. The king heard Mass with great ceremony and placed three florins in gold on the altar on Palm Sunday, Maundy Thursday and Easter Sunday.[68] The account book records the ritual of setting up the Holy Sepulchre which was lit with 25 candles of different sizes and sealed with red sealing wax on Good Friday.[69] Fraknói discusses this as an "ancient and specific ritual of the Hungarian church, not paralleled in other countries", but it shows close resemblance to the ritual of burying the Cross and Host in the Easter Sepulchre traditionally performed in the western Church on Good Friday.[70] The Feast of Corpus Christi was elaborately celebrated with the throne of the king set up at a square in the Buda Castle covered with a canopy. From this point the king watched while the Blessed Sacrament was carried in procession by twelve squires with torches. More squires carried the relics, crucifixes and gilded pictures, or perhaps sculptures from the royal chapel on decorated wooden structures while flowers were strewn on the ground before them. The rector of the chapel, Master Albert was given money for buying incense to fumigate the Sacrament. The account book contains no evidence of theatrical

---

16 1525] *Magyar Történelmi Tár* [NS] 10 [22] (1876), pp. 47–236. The account book of the brother of Prince Sigismund, later Sigismund, king of Poland, who lived at the royal court of his brother Wladislas for a few years was edited by Adorján Divéky, *Zsigmond lengyel herczeg budai számadásai, 1500–1502, 1505* (Magyar Történelmi Tár, 26) [The accounts of Sigismund, Polish prince at Buda, 1500–1502, 1505] (Budapest: MTA, 1914).

66 Also called: Purification of the Blessed Virgin (Greek Hypapante), observed 2 February: Fraknói, "II. Lajos király," p. 68.
67 Fraknói, "II. Lajos király," p. 69.
68 As well as on Candlemas and Pentecost.
69 Fraknói, "II. Lajos király," pp. 142–143.
70 Cf. a description of the ritual in the contemporary court of Henry VIII, Fiona Kisby, "'When the King Goeth a Procession': Chapel Ceremonies and Services, the Ritual Year, and Religious Reforms at the Early Tudor Court, 1485–1547," *Journal of British Studies* 40 (2001), pp. 44–75, here p. 63.

performances during the procession.[71] It is assumed that much of the everyday private devotional practice of both the king and queen took place in the oratories of their respective private chambers, as this was the general practice in contemporary courts.

Conclusion

Through the analysis of a wide range of sources and with numerous parallels from western court studies, we can conclude that the court of the late medieval Hungarian kings was in every way comparable to the courts of other European sovereigns. In his eminent study on the court of the dukes of Burgundy, Werner Paravicini lists the functions typically filled by a princely residence, ranging from supplying the everyday necessities of the court, safety, courtly display, legitimation of the sovereign, integration and communication, and administration.[72] It is not difficult to see that the city of Buda, as a royal residence, was influenced and shaped in its topography, as well as in its economic and social development, by every aspect of these residential functions. Research is still needed to establish as precisely as possible from the scant sources available how this happened and in which period, but it is safe to say that late medieval Buda owes much of its character to the relationship between the court and the town.

---

[71] For a discussion of the Corpus Christi Feast and procession in the late Middle Ages see Miri Rubin, *Corpus Christi: The Eucharist in Late Medieval Culture* (Cambridge: Cambridge University Press, 1992).

[72] Werner Paravicini, "The Court of the Dukes of Burgundy: a Model for Europe?" in *Princes, Patronage, and the Nobility: The Court at the Beginning of the Modern Age*, eds Ronald G. Asch and Adolf M. Birke (Oxford: Oxford University Press, 1991), pp. 69–102.

CHAPTER 18

Buda as a Center of Renaissance and Humanism

Valery Rees

During recent years, many scholars have been re-examining aspects of cultural life in Hungary in the late fifteenth and early sixteenth centuries. In particular, interest has focused on those literary works and artistic commissions that reflect the clear influence of Classical antiquity. An exhibition mounted by the Budapest History Museum in Florence in 2013, *Mattia Corvino e Firenze*, gave a clear demonstration of the extensive and pervasive links between Florence and Hungary from the days of Emperor Sigismund to the last days of the house of Hunyadi.[1] Without a doubt, the richest period of interconnectedness belongs to the reign of Matthias Corvinus in Hungary and the government of Lorenzo the Magnificent in Florence. Artefacts commissioned by these two great leaders held pride of place among the exhibits, but on their own they are insufficient to answer the question that is of central importance to this volume, namely, whether Buda can be considered alongside the cities of Italy, France and the German lands as a place where the reawakening of interest in ancient Greece and Rome blossomed into what may be truly called a sense of 'rebirth', or Renaissance.[2] This article will consider the wider context in which these artefacts of high value and high fashion were acquired. It will first propose some general features that characterize a Renaissance city and will then relate the new displays of magnificence to a changing background of values and ideas.

---

1 See the excellent and scholarly exhibition catalogue, *Mattia Corvino e Firenze. Arte e Umanesimo alla Corte del re di Ungheria*, eds Péter Farbaky *et al.* (Florence: Giunti, 2013).
2 The literature on this topic is now extensive. Those most accessible to an international readership include: *Matthias Corvinus, the King*; *Italy & Hungary*; *A Star in the Raven's Shadow. János Vitéz and the Beginnings of Humanism in Hungary*, ed. Ferenc Földesi (Budapest: National Széchényi Library, 2008); András Kubinyi, *Matthias Rex* (Budapest: Balassi, 2008); *Infima Aetas Pannonica. Studies in Late Medieval Hungarian History*, eds Péter E. Kovács and Kornél Szovák (Budapest: Corvina, 2009); Tibor Klaniczay, *Alle origini del movimento accademico ungherese* (Ister. Collana di studi ungheresi, 125) (Alessandria: Edizioni dell'Orso, 2010 [based on original Hungarian version of 1993]). The older literature is amply surveyed in these volumes.

Some Characteristics of a Renaissance City

While the history of Renaissance thought in Italy is not without its own complexities and controversies, it is generally agreed that the rise of Renaissance humanism in northern Italy was accompanied by a change in status of independent city states in Italy, such as Florence, Siena, Brescia, Venice and Milan. It is also agreed that the so-called humanist aspirations were enthusiastically embraced by citizens conscious that they were standing in the tradition of the ancients. In each of these North Italian cities, we see the rise of an educated and articulate class of men serving the state administration, chancellors, lawyers, orators and poets, and we see a degree of freedom from feudal impositions or baronial control. The language of public discourse becomes refined in style, purged of many medieval accretions. Clarity of expression was held to foster clarity of thought, and Cicero's open-minded approach to ancient philosophy, evident in his *De finibus*, *Academica* or *Tusculanae Disputationes*, encouraged a spirit of exploration long before the re-engagement with Greek texts. Certainly the study of Ciceronian Latin rather than Theocritus's *Idyll* and Peter Lombard's sentences made for a different kind of education. Schools teaching the *studia humanitatis*, so well suited to the new requirements of public life, began to supplement if not replace the older church schools, focused on *studia divinitatis*, that had served the needs of feudal institutions and canon law. Whether or not the similarities with republican Rome were as extensive as their advocates implied, it was true that the North Italian cities had established themselves as communes independent of imperial control, generally on the basis of the wealth derived from mercantile activity, from the wool trade, silk, banking or overseas trade. In doing so they had evolved an ethos that we can readily identify as humanist and that they interpreted as a re-awakening, or rebirth.

In southern Italy, the narrative is rather different. The political structures of kingship and baronial control in Naples and of papal authority in Rome display a greater continuity with medieval forms of government. Yet no one doubts the existence of Renaissance culture within the court in Naples, where new forms of literature, art and music flourished, and in the papal court at Rome where learning, architecture, art, poetry and music received unstinting patronage from a succession of popes from Nicholas V onwards. From 1444, with the publication of Flavio Biondo's *De Roma instaurata*, the ruins of ancient Rome became once more a living presence and historical writing took on new form.

In southern Italy, therefore, and also in some ducal states in the north – Ferrara, Mantua, Urbino, Sforza Milan and perhaps even Florence under the

Medici from Lorenzo onwards – Renaissance humanism presents itself as a movement rooted in the revival of antiquity, but under monarchic or quasi-monarchic patronage. Educational and literary undertakings flourished, from the humanist schools of Vittorino da Feltre and Guarino[3] to the libraries of Pope Nicholas V, Alfonso of Naples and Federico da Montefeltro.[4] From the 1450s onwards we see a new level of engagement with the building techniques and architectural ornamentation of antiquity that allowed an expression of magnificence. Along with the grand literary and architectural projects went a new status for painting and sculpture and for other decorative arts from garden design to book illumination.[5]

Whether in the north or the south, among all who could afford it, collecting works of art and books, new and old, became a passion. Poets, playwrights, historians and artists were inspired to take themes from classical antiquity rather than religion, while the philosophy of the ancients – be it Aristotelian, Platonic, Stoic or even Epicurean – found new exponents.

Does Buda Fit This Pattern?

If this was the pattern for Renaissance developments in Italy, how much of it can be applied also to Buda? Hungary as a kingdom enjoyed considerable independence, both from the Emperor and from the papacy, yet its government remained monarchic in form. János Bak, in numerous studies, has been at pains to point out the medieval continuities of political life in terms of royal institutions, administration and the law.[6] We should not look for institutional

---

3   For educational treatises of this period, see Craig W. Kallendorf, *Humanist Educational Treatises* (Cambridge, Mass.: Harvard University Press, 2002).

4   For the excitement of book collecting, see Phyllis Walter Goodhart Gordan, *Two Renaissance Book Hunters: the Letters of Poggius Bracciolini to Nicolaus de Niccolis* (New York: Columbia University Press, 1974, repr. 1991). The bibliography on early libraries is too extensive to review here.

5   The leading art theorist was Leon Battista Alberti, whose buildings were as influential as his principal writings, *De re aedificatoria* (1443–1452) and *De pictura* (1435). On gardens, there is an extensive literature. See, for example: Amanda Lillie, *Florentine Villas in the Fifteenth Century: An Architectural and Social History* (New York: Cambridge University Press, 2005); and eadem, "Fiesole: *Locus Amoenus* or Penitential Landscape?," *I Tatti Studies: Essays in the Renaissance* 11 (2007), pp. 11–55. On book illumination, see ed. Jonathan J.G. Alexander, *The Painted Page. Italian Renaissance Book Illumination 1450–1550* (Munich: Prestel, 1994).

6   See, for example, János M. Bak, "The Kingship of Matthias Corvinus. A Renaissance State?," in *Matthias Corvinus and the Humanism in Central Europe*, eds Tibor Klaniczay and József

humanism, but we may at least find within the institutions of government and the church individuals who were inspired by humanist ideals. It is also important to distinguish between Buda and other parts of the country, so I shall not discuss evidence related to educational advances in Esztergom or Oradea, except insofar as students of these schools were later active in Buda.

In economic terms, Buda like many other Hungarian cities and towns in the fifteenth century enjoyed flourishing trade.[7] In Buda at least this was accompanied by a growth in the number of artisanal workshops. Buda also had a prosperous community of Jews, as described in the account of Matthias's marriage in 1476.[8] Many leading Italian families established trading branches in Buda, importing fine fabrics and luxury goods for the royal court and the nobility. Notable among these were the Gondi and the Giugni, but many others participated in a constantly changing pattern of family alliances. The profits of their labours were generally channelled back to Italy.[9] On the Hungarian side, it was trade in agricultural and primary produce that continued to dominate: cattle, wine and grain. It was another primary product, wool, that had been the basis for Florentine growth, but the rise of Florentine economic power

---

Jankovics (Budapest: Balassi, 1994), pp. 37–47. See also Leslie S. Domonkos, "The Hungarian Royal Chancellery 1458–90: Was it a center of Humanism?" in *Triumph in Adversity. Studies in Hungarian Civilization in Honor of Professor Ferenc Somogyi on the Occasion of his Eightieth Birthday* (East European Monographs, 253), eds Steven Bela Vardy and Agnes Huszar Vardy (New York: East European Monographs, 1988), pp. 97–111.

7   On economic history, see Erik Fügedi, *Kings, Bishops, Nobles and Burghers in Medieval Hungary* (Variorium) ed. János M. Bak (Aldershot: Ashgate, 1986); Zsigmond Pál Pach, *Hungary and the European Economy in Early Modern Times* (Variorum) (Aldershot: Ashgate, 1994); *East-Central Europe in Transition: From the Fourteenth to the Seventeenth Century*, eds Antoni Maczak, Henryk Samsonowicz and Peter Burke (Cambridge: Cambridge University Press, 1985). See also works listed in note 2 above and István Draskóczy's article in the present volume.

8   See the report of the Imperial Count Palatine's envoy, *Regis Ungariae Matthiae nuptiae, et coronationis regiae atque illorum postea ingressus in Budam a Palatini comitis legato diligenter descripta*, included in Johann Georg Schwandtner, *Scriptores rerum Hungaricum varii*, i (Vienna: Impensis Ioannis Pauli Kraus, 1746), pp. 519–527.

9   Recent research is concerned mainly with the early part of the fifteenth century: see Krisztina Arany, "Generations Abroad: Florentine Merchant Families in Hungary in the First Half of the Fifteenth Century," in *Generations in Towns: Succession and Success in Pre-Industrial Urban Societies*, eds Finn-Einar Eliassen and Katalin Szende (Newcastle-upon-Tyne: Cambridge Scholars, 2009), pp. 129–153 and Katalin Prajda, "Florentine Merchant Companies Established in Buda at the Beginning of the 15th Century," *Mélanges de l'École française de Rome – Moyen Âge* 125, no 1 (2013). Online publication: http://mefrm.revues.org/1062 (last accessed: 15 January 2015).

rested on the mercantile aspects of the wool trade, namely high-quality cloth production as well as banking in the service of international transactions. A further factor special to Hungary was the yield of the gold and silver mines of the northern mountain districts. These provided an important component of royal income, and allowed the king to fund major cultural projects as well as military strength. Even if the country lacked the more widespread accumulations of capital enjoyed in Italy by families involved in banking and in trade in manufactured goods,[10] under Matthias royal wealth was such that it was not unrealistic for the king to compare himself with those rulers of Ferrara, Florence and Rome that had played host to the potentates of all Europe and Byzantium, and to be a most generous patron of culture and the arts.[11]

The cultural changes happening in Italy therefore began to have their effect in Hungary surprisingly soon, with royal patronage as a major vector of change. Factors resisting change were still formidable: in the context of book culture, Anna Boreczky recently concluded that "the occasionally very open-minded and far-reaching ambitions of János Vitéz, King Matthias and some high priests and aristocrats had an impact on a relatively narrow circle of intellectuals" but that "the urban culture of late fifteenth-century citizens cherishing their own deep-rooted contacts was unaffected by the Italian Renaissance, a culture which was still felt to be basically alien."[12] While this may be true among citizen groups, others have tracked the diffusion of interest in Renaissance culture within the ruling elites,[13] and to some extent, at least through buildings and public works, fashions, music and applied arts, a general influence on public taste may be detectable. As far as other barriers are concerned, since Latin had always been the language of learning, there was no language barrier against the introduction of new intellectual directions from Italy. Furthermore, the vast majority of early humanist work did not involve any challenge to the teachings of the church. Though Lorenzo Valla had challenged the Donation of Constantine, attacking the very basis of temporal power for the Church, most scholars

---

10　Hungary in the late medieval period did not have its own equivalent of the great Italian or German banking families. Indeed in the sixteenth century it was the Fuggers of Augsburg who developed the mines.

11　The obvious comparison is with the Medici family whose role at the Council of Ferrara/Florence was celebrated in the famous paintings of Benozzo Gozzoli in the Medici Chapel. But in 1424 the Byzantine Emperor had sought aid at the Hungarian court and in the 1470s Matthias had been constantly involved in military expeditions to hold back the Turks.

12　Anna Boreczky, "Book Painting in Hungary in the Age of János Vitéz," in *A Star in the Raven's Shadow*, pp. 25–45, here p. 45.

13　*Uralkodók és corvinák* [Potentates and corvinas], ed. Orsolya Karsay (Budapest: OSZK, 2002).

were content to expand horizons and could absorb new ideas within existing religious frameworks. After all, it was the Orthodox Church in the Byzantine world that had kept alive the heritage of the Greeks even when it had been lost to the west, and a great representative of that church, Cardinal Bessarion, who championed Greek scholarship in Italy.

Humanist Initiatives in Buda

The earliest humanist impulses in Hungary were principally related to the royal court and were concerned with education. When Pier Paolo Vergerio accompanied Emperor Sigismund to Buda in 1418, he had already taught the arts, medicine and law in Padua, Florence and Bologna, and had set out his educational ideals in a treatise for an earlier patron, Ubertino of Carrara. This thoroughly humanist treatise, entitled *De ingenuis moribus et liberalibus adulescentiae studiis liber*, written in 1403–1404, was the first of its kind.[14] Vergerio lays great emphasis on training in morals and manners, with physical exercise and military pursuits taking their place alongside a rigorous training in letters. Drawing on Quintilian, Plutarch and Basil, Vergerio recreates an educational approach that includes rhetoric, poetry, music, mathematics, astronomy and medicine with the addition, where appropriate, of history and law. The study of Virgil will provide a sound introduction, while the models of conduct proposed for continued study and application include Alexander, Cicero, Caesar and Augustus. The aim throughout is towards virtue and nobility of conduct, which may both be achieved through discipline and understanding. Some students, he adds, will be suited to natural science and moral philosophy, while others may be ripe for metaphysics.

Vergerio remained in Hungary after the death of Sigismund in 1437, dying in Buda in 1444. His influence on education was actively continued by János Vitéz (1408–1472), first in his episcopal court at Oradea, then at Esztergom when he became archbishop. The education of the young Hunyadi princes was entrusted to his care. It may well be that Matthias was to be educated for a distinguished career in the church, not as a ruler of the country. The assumption was that his brother Ladislas, who was 10–12 years his senior, would inherit their father's political role, under the young king, Ladislas V, but the elder brother fell victim to political intrigue and was beheaded in Buda, on the orders of Ladislas V, on 16 March 1457.

---

14 Edited and translated in Kallendorf, *Humanist Educational Treatises*, pp. 2–91.

On 23 November of the same year the young king himself died, and Matthias was elected as his successor. In the early years of his reign Vitéz was his close adviser. Vitéz initiated the new university, the Academia Istropolitana at Pressburg, inviting Giovanni Gatti and Regiomontanus (Johannes Müller of Königsberg) to teach there in 1467, setting a high standard of teaching in theology, mathematics and astronomy.[15] In 1471, John Argyropoulos accepted an invitation to leave Florence and teach Greek there, although as events turned out he canceled his journey and went instead to Rome.

Another significant venture backed jointly by Vitéz and the provost of Buda, László Karai, was the invitation to the German-speaking Andreas Hess to come and set up a printing press in Buda. Buda was thus one of the earliest cities outside Italy to have its own printing press, though it appears to have been both small and short-lived. In 1472, from his press located in Buda near the castle (perhaps in László Karai's house), Hess produced a *Chronica Hungarorum* as well as some small items central to the humanist program, such as St Basil's letter on reading the ancient poets, Xenophon's *Apology of Socrates*, and a few religious texts. However the enterprise appears to have closed the following year.

The new university in the north of the country did not survive the fall of Vitéz, and the Buda press did not last long after it, but their demise did not halt educational change. We know that an active *studium* continued at the Dominican cloister in Buda, led by the eminent German theologian Petrus Niger (1434–1483) and for which university status was sought in the 1480s. Niger was noted for his attempts to promote the study of Hebrew and Greek in connection with biblical exposition. There was also a modest but influential flow of students returning from time spent in the Hungarian communities at various universities in Italy or at the famous universities of Cracow and Vienna. On their return they often took up employment in the institutional underpinnings of the royal court, especially the chancellery, where elegant Latinity was highly valued. This pattern continued into the sixteenth century. A late example is Augustine Moravus of Olomouc, who studied in both Padua and Cracow before entering the chancellery of Wladislas II in Buda in 1494, remaining

---

15   Tibor Klaniczay, "Egyetem Magyarországon Mátyás korában," [University in Hungary in the time of Matthias] *Irodalomtörténeti Közlemények* 94 (1990), pp. 575–611. Regiomontanus became the first chancellor of this *Academia Istropolitana*. On Giovanni Gatti, resident in Hungary from 1466 to 1467, see John Monfasani, "Giovanni Gatti of Messina: A Profile and an Unedited Text," in *Filologia umanistica per Gianvito Resta II*, eds V. Fera and G. Ferraú (Padua: Antenore, 1997), pp. 1315–1338, reprinted in John Monfasani, *Greeks and Latins in Renaissance Italy* (Variorum) (Aldershot: Ashgate, 2004).

associated with it until 1511 while becoming a highly influential churchman and humanist, and encouraging poets in a *Sodalitas Litterarum Danubiana*.[16]

University education in and of itself was no guarantee of a humanist outlook. Certain faculties of the universities of Padua and Bologna remained resolutely Aristotelian and scholastic throughout the period, so every case must be taken on its own merits. Perhaps more important was the steady refinement of Latin usage that was taking place, together with the opportunities to cultivate lasting friendships in humanist circles that were provided by periods of study abroad.

In 1479 and again in 1487, Marsilio Ficino was invited to teach philosophy in Buda, specifically the philosophy of Plato, but on both occasions he felt obliged to decline.[17] His work, however, was ably promoted by a younger friend of his, Francesco Bandini, who was resident at the royal court from 1476, and to whom Ficino sent a steady flow of his newly published works for the king to read.[18]

16   For documents relating to university education in Hungary, see Laszló Szögi, *Régi magyar egyetemek emlékezete* (Budapest: Eötvös Loránd Tudományegyetem, 1995). On the education of churchmen, see József Köblös, *Az egyházi középréteg Mátyás és a Jagellók korában* [Midddle class ecclesiastical society in the age of King Matthias and the Jagiellonian kings] (Budapest: MTA Történettudományi Intézete, 1994). On Augustin of Olomouc, see: Jacqueline Glomski, *Patronage and Humanist Literature in the Age of the Jagiellons* (Toronto: University of Toronto Press, 2007); Lubomir Konečný, "Augustine Käsenbrot of Olomouc. His Golden Bowl in Dresden and the Renaissance Revival of 'Poetic' Bacchus," *Artibus et Historiae* 24, no 48 (2003), pp. 185–197; Péter Ekler, "Augustinus Moravus Olomucensis levele Laki Thuz Jánosnak," [A letter of Augustinus Moravus Olomucensis to János Laki Thuz] *Magyar Könyvszemle* 128 (2012), pp. 478–480 and idem, "Classical Literature as a Model and Standard in the *De modo Epistolandi* of Augustinus Moravus Olomucensis," in *Investigatio Fontium*, ed. László Horváth (Budapest: ELTE Eötvös Kollégium, 2014), pp. 159–169). I am indebted to Péter Ekler for this. See also *Augustinus Moravus Olomuciensis*, eds. Péter Ekler and Farkas Gábor Kiss (Budapest: Institute for Literary Studies, Hungarian Academy of Sciences and National Széchényi Library, 2015).

17   *The Letters of Marsilio Ficino*, 10 vols (London: Shepheard-Walwyn, 1975–2015); iii, 39; vii, 48; viii, 6 [henceforth: Ficino, *Letters*] (references to this edition are by volume and letter number). See also Valery Rees, "Marsilio Ficino and the Rise of Philosophic Interests in Buda," in *Italy & Hungary*, pp. 127–148; eadem, "Four Ficino Codices from the Corvina Library," in *Corvina Augusta. Die Handschriften des Königs Matthias Corvinus in der Herzog August Bibliothek Wolfenbüttel* (Supplementum Corvinianum, iii), eds Edina Zsupán and Christian Heitzmann (Budapest: OSZK, 2014), pp. 163–177.

18   Ficino, *Letters*, iii, 39 and vii, 48. On Bandini's biography, see Paul Oskar Kristeller, "An Unpublished Description of Naples by Francesco Bandini," *Romanic Review* 33 (1942), pp. 290–306, reprinted in idem, *Studies in Renaissance Thought and Letters* (Rome: Edizioni di storia e letteratura, 1956), pp. 395–410 and ibid., "Francesco Bandini and his consolatory dialogue upon the death of Simone Gondi," pp. 411–435. See also Rózsa Feuer-Tóth,

Ficino's first contact had been with Vitéz's nephew, Janus Pannonius, around 1465, when both were in their early thirties. Janus was by then bishop of Pécs, though he lived mainly at court in Buda and was a trusted member of the royal chancellery. He first met Ficino while in Florence on his way to or from a diplomatic mission in Rome. Pannonius had already studied in Italy for seven years from the age of thirteen, under Guarino of Verona in Ferrara. There he won fame as the most outstanding pupil of his generation in literary studies. A training in canon and civil law at the University of Padua followed, and on returning home in 1458 he soon won favor at the court of the new king, Matthias. On 5 August 1469, some years after their first meeting, Ficino sent Pannonius one of the early manuscript copies of his commentary on Plato's *Symposium* (published later with his Plato translations in 1484). In the dedication Ficino addresses Pannonius affectionately as a fellow Platonist, and Pannonius wrote a poem admiring Ficino as Plato's reincarnation.[19] Ficino especially hoped that Pannonius would find the work pleasing and would introduce it appropriately in his own land.

Pannonius was one of the few people besides Ficino to take an active interest in the writings of Plotinus and, in another of his poems, *Ad animam suam*, he celebrates a Plotinian descent of the soul through the starry spheres, receiving gifts from the planets it passes as it enters the body, as well as musing on the relationship of soul and body during life and its existence thereafter.[20]

Pannonius befriended various humanist scholars and poets in Italy, and it was at his invitation that the eccentric humanist from Umbria, Galeotto Marzio, first came to Buda in 1461. After a short initial visit he returned, with Pannonius, in 1465 and stayed until 1471 in the service of the king. In 1477, when Galeotto was in trouble in Italy with the ecclesiastical authorities on account of views expressed in his audacious *De incognitis vulgo*, it appears to have been Matthias who helped to secure his release. Galeotto visited Buda again in 1478,

---

Art and Humanism in Hungary in the Age of Matthias Corvinus, ed. Péter Farbaky (Budapest: Akadémiai, 1990).

19 For the text of Ficino's dedication letter, see Paul Oskar Kristeller, *Supplementum Ficinianum*, i (Florence: Olschki, 1937), pp. 87–88. Janus Pannonius, *Epigrams*, in *Opera Latine et Hungarice*, i, eds Sándor V. Kovács and Győző Csorba (Budapest: Tankönyvkiadó, 1972), p. 228 (no 236). On Pannonius more generally, see Marianna D. Birnbaum, *Janus Pannonius, Poet and Politician* (Zagreb: Jugoslavenska akademija znanosti i umjetnosti, 1981); Enikő Békés, *Janus Pannonius. Selected Bibliography* (Budapest: Balassi, 2006).

20 See László Jankovits, "Plato and the Muses at the Danube: Platonic Philosophy and Poetry in Janus Pannonius' *Ad Animam Suam*," in *Acta Conventus Neo-Latini Bonnensis*, ed. Rhoda Schnur (Tempe: Arizona Center for Medieval and Renaissance Studies, 2006), pp. 379–387.

clearly thriving in the atmosphere of the court.[21] He served for a while as royal librarian, and was followed in this task by another Italian, Taddeo Ugoleto of Parma. Taddeo had also arrived in Hungary in 1465. He later became tutor to the young prince, John Corvin (b. 1473). The selection of this notable Italian scholar as tutor to the prince reflects the care given to his education. Beatrice had failed to provide a legitimate heir after some years of marriage, so Matthias designated John as his heir, despite his illegitimate birth, and he took the necessary steps to provide him with an appropriate education.[22]

Taddeo is best known, however, for his work as librarian, where his knowledge of both Latin and Greek enabled him to make important progress in expanding the Corvina library. He undertook visits to many other libraries. While in Florence in 1485–1486, he set up a workshop under the supervision of Naldo Naldi, specifically to increase the production of books for Buda. He worked closely with Angelo Poliziano, who remained in Italy, and with Bartolommeo della Fonte, who eventually visited Hungary in 1489.

Another friend of Pannonius educated in Italy was Péter Garázda (c.1440–1507) who studied in Ferrara and Florence. Garázda remained in Italy in 1465 when Pannonius returned home, but was on his way back in 1471 when he heard news of his friend's fall. Following the discovery of their plot against the king, Vitéz was placed under house arrest, and Pannonius fled, dying of consumption the following spring. For the next few years, those with Italian connections were held in suspicion at the royal court in case of any connection with the conspirators. Péter Garázda therefore stayed on in Padua. On his return in 1476, he became a canon and later provost of Esztergom. In 1478 he became principal of the cathedral school at Pécs, and in 1483 dean of Nitra, so he remained without real influence in Buda, but brought humanist educational practices to his own provincial schools.[23] While our main focus in this

---

21   Enikő Békés, "Galeotto Marzio and the Court of King Matthias Corvinus ('De egregie, sapienter, iocose dictis ac factis regis Mathiae')," *Studi Umanistici Piceni* 29 (2009), pp. 287–296.

22   Much has also been made of Matthias's own relatively obscure origins and Bonfini was quick to provide him with testimony of an ancient lineage. At the time he became king, the elective nature of the Hungarian monarchy and his family's proven contribution to good rule was sufficient to establish his claims at home. By the 1480s, however, he may have felt more sensitive about his status – and certainly about his son's status – vis-à-vis Italian princes. The *Libellus de Corvinae domus origine* that Bonfini wrote for the king in 1486 is lost, but much of its material probably survives in his *Decades*, III–IV and III–IX.

23   Klára Pajorin, "The First Humanists at Matthias Corvinus' Court, the Early Inspirers of Flaunting Wealth and Power," in *Matthias Corvinus, the King*, pp. 139–146, here p. 142; Alessandro Daneloni, "Nota sul soggiorno a Firenze dell'umanista ungherese Peter Garazda,"

essay is on Buda, it is in such provincial schools that we find more compelling evidence for long-term educational change.

Closer to the court were two other members of the same circle: Miklós Bátori (1435–1506) and Péter Váradi (1450–1501). Bátori, a cousin of the king, had studied in Bologna[24] and became successively bishop of Srijem and Vác, spending the years after the disgrace of 1471 in quiet pursuit of letters and learning in his bishopric. After 1476 he was able to return to Buda, bringing his influence to bear on educational matters there. It was Bátori who, on the king's behalf and through Bandini, invited Ficino to come and teach in Hungary in 1479 and 1487.[25] He befriended Bandini and offered him a refuge from Buda during the plague.[26]

Péter Váradi, another student sent to Bologna by Vitéz in 1465, became a member of the royal chancellery in 1475, rising rapidly thereafter to become both the king's secretary and chancellor in 1479. This gave him influence in both domestic and diplomatic affairs. Unlike Garázda and Bátori, he was of humble origins. Yet through his abilities he earned a high position, becoming archbishop of Kalocsa in 1480, before his own fall from grace in 1484. A rapid rise of this kind through education and ability rather than birth was becoming more frequent under a humanist educational system.[27] This in itself is a sign of some social change.

Between 1477 and 1479, Ficino included Váradi in correspondence on astrology, sending him his *Disputatio contra iudicium astrologorum*.[28] Ficino was aware of the considerable attention being given to astronomy in Buda. Regiomontanus had been present at court from 1467 to 1471 and continued his associations with Matthias even after he left. In 1468 Regiomontanus had been joined by Martin Bylica, another distinguished mathematician, who

---

Rinascimento 61 (2001), pp. 259–264; Sándor V. Kovács, "Garázda Péter élete és költészete," [The poetry of Péter Garázda] *Irodalomtörténeti Közlemények* 61 (1957), pp. 48–62.

24 Dennis E. Rhodes, "Battista Guarini and a Book at Oxford," *Journal of the Warburg and Courtauld Institutes* 37 (1974), pp. 349–353. Rhodes cites Eugenio Koltay-Kastner, "L'umanesimo italiano in Ungheria," *La Rinascita* 2 (1939), pp. 10–55, here p. 39–40 to claim that Bátori studied under Ficino in Florence, but there is no trace of this in Ficino's account of his students (see: Ficino, *Letters*, x, 27 [in press]).

25 Ficino, *Letters*, vi, 30. See also ibid., iii, 39 and vii, 48.

26 Kristeller, "Francesco Bandini".

27 On humanist education, see István Mészáros, *A humanizmus és a reformáció-ellenreformáció nevelésügye a 15–16. században* [Humanist education and the Reformation–Counter-Reformation in the fifteenth–sixteenth centuries] (Budapest: Tankönyvkiadó, 1984).

28 Ficino, *Letters*, iii, 37.

remained in Buda as astronomer royal and parish priest.[29] An astronomical ceiling adorned the library in the royal palace, where the king's collection of mathematical instruments was probably also housed.[30]

Next to the library in the palace complex stood the royal chapel, which became a center for music highly praised by many visitors. We should not underestimate the influence of church music, as the daily liturgical round was a constant feature of life at court. Secular music was also a constant presence, in the form of singing and dancing to accompany the numerous splendid banquets, as well as on more intimate occasions.[31] The renowned lutenist Pietro Bono and the Flemish composer Johannes de Stokem both spent time in Buda, and numerous letters from Queen Beatrice relate to the engagement of musicians of the first rank.[32] The high place accorded to music can be considered an indicator of courtly sophistication. For Ficino, the appreciation of fine music brought with it an openness to heavenly influences and to the mathematics of the *Timaeus*.[33] When Ficino sent his *Life of Plato* to the Hungarian court, he included in the preface an imaginary conversation between Plato and himself:

---

29   Darin Hayton, "Martin Bylica at the Court of Matthias Corvinus: Astrology and Politics in Renaissance Hungary," *Centaurus* 49 (2007), pp. 185–198.

30   Jolán Balogh, *Művészet Mátyás király udvarában*, 2 vols [Art at the court of King Matthias] (Budapest: Magyar Nemzeti Galéria, 1966), i, p. 448; Stéphane Toussaint, "Ficino, Archimedes and the Celestial Arts: Modern Outlines of Ficino's Magic," in *Marsilio Ficino: his Theology, his Philosophy, his Legacy*, eds M.J.B. Allen and V.R. Rees (Leiden: Brill, 2002), pp. 307–326.

31   Klára Pajorin, "Asztali művelődés és szórakozás Mátyás király udvarában," [Education at the table and amusement in the court of King Matthias] in *"Ritrar parlando il bel." Tanulmányok Király Erzsébet tiszteletére* [Studies in honor or Erzsébet Király], eds Eszter Szegedi and Dávid Falvay (Budapest: L'Harmattan, 2011), pp. 287–298; Balogh, *A művészet*, i, pp. 445–447 and 684–689.

32   Beatrice had her own musical education as a girl under the outstanding music theorist Johannes Tinctoris. See Allan Atlas, *Music at the Aragonese Court of Naples* (Cambridge: Cambridge University Press, 1985). For the most recent findings on Tinctoris, see Ron Woodley, "Johannes Tinctoris: Biographical Outline," online: http://earlymusictheory.org/Tinctoris/Tinctoris/BiographicalOutline/# (last accessed: 5 February 2015). See also Árpád Mikó, "Queen Beatrice of Aragon," in *Matthias Corvinus, the King*, pp. 251–265, here pp. 252–253. Louis A. Waldman gives some details of the engagement of two members of the Florentine polyphonic choir in idem, "Commissioning Art in Florence for Matthias Corvinus," in *Italy & Hungary*, pp. 427–501, here p. 442.

33   The importance of music in Ficino's thinking is evident in his *Timaeus* commentary, in several letters (see Ficino, *Letters*, i, 90 and vii, 76), and in the fact that he was himself an accomplished player. See most recently Jacomien Prins, *Echoes of an Invisible World. Marsilio Ficino and Francesco Patrizi on Cosmic Order and Music Theory* (Leiden: Brill

I said, 'O Plato, will you seek again your ancestral and native seat of Athens?' But he immediately exclaimed, 'O unjust fate! Alas, nowhere do I have an ancestral home! O iron age! in which brutal Mars has laid in ruins the Attic citadels of Pallas. Therefore, Marsilio, not into unhappy Greece, but into Hungary shall I go for refuge. For there flourishes the great King Matthias, who, sustained at once by a wonderful power and wisdom in these years of manifest decline, will provide once more a sanctuary to the wise and powerful Pallas, that is, the philosophic schools of the Greeks.'[34]

There is no doubt that word of the artistic and intellectual life of Buda had reached Florence.

Italian influences were numerous in Buda and there were many Italians resident in the city, including Francesco Bandini to whom the above preface was addressed. Bandini was a member of the Queen's retinue but was increasingly influential with the king in cultural matters and the arts, to which I shall return below. To Queen Beatrice are credited changes to the etiquette of court life and the introduction of new styles, new fashions and new foods. Not everyone saw these as good, some Hungarians complaining, for example, of reduced access to the king. The queen was also involved in the major beautification of royal residences during the 1480s.[35] But it is hard to assess how these changes in courtly life or in aesthetic standards might have affected the lives of the citizens of Buda.[36]

[in press]) and eadem, *Marsilio Ficino Commentaries on Plato, Timaeus* (Cambridge, Mass.: Harvard University Press [in press]).

34 Ficino, *Letters*, iii, 38. "Ad hunc ego conversus o plato inquam patrias ne avitasque sedes repetes athenarum. At ille repente o fatum excalmavit iniquum. Nulla mihi prohdolor: nulla usquam restat patria domus. O ferrea secula quibus mars ille sevissimus atticas diruit palladis arces. Non igitur in miseram graeciam, sed in pannoniam, Marsili, me conferam. Ibi enim floret magnus rex ille Mathias, qui mira quadam potentia simul et sapientia fretus certis relabentibus annis aedem potenti sapientique palladi, hoc est graecorum gymnasia reparabit. Ibidem praeterea penes regem ipsum pannoniae foelicissimum foeliciter vivit: bandinus ille meus" – idem, *Epistolarum* (Venice: Hieronymus Blondus, 1495) fol. 97ᵛ. The letter is undated, but can be attributed to the period between early 1478 and the spring of 1479.

35 See especially Árpád Mikó, "Beatrice d'Aragona e il primo rinascimento in Ungheria," in *Italy & Hungary*, pp. 409–425.

36 Some of these aspects are discussed in Valery Rees, "A Woman of Valour," in *Matthias Rex 1458–1490: Hungary at the Dawn of the Renaissance,* eds Iván Horváth *et al.* (Budapest: Eötvös Loránd University Faculty of Humanities, Centre des hautes études de la Renaissance, 2013). Published so far as e-book: http://renaissance.elte.hu/?page_id=369 (last accessed: 25 February 2015).

Engagement with the Platonic Circle in Florence

An illuminating exchange published in Ficino's correspondence illustrates a level of interest among members of the court in Buda in the work of the Platonic circle in Florence. Dating from around 1485, it purports to be from Janus Pannonius, and various attempts have been made to identify the sender.[37] The writer claims to have been a student in Florence prior to 1463 and to be in Buda at the time of writing. None of the candidates for authorship presented so far meets both those criteria. But whoever its author was, the letter at least attests to active engagement in Buda with the ideas that Ficino was promoting. In particular, it concerns the proper relationship between philosophy and religion, it raises questions related to providence and free will and it expresses some anxiety about astrology, which was enjoying a Renaissance of its own both in Florence and Buda.[38] Ficino's reply stresses the importance of Greek philosophy not as a substitute for the Christian religion but for its perfection:

> First of all, we should not, as a general rule, look for Christian precepts in those who preceded the coming of Christ; nor ought we to believe that men with keen and philosophically inclined minds can ever be attracted and led, step by step, to perfect religion by any bait other than that of philosophy. For keen intellects entrust themselves to reason alone, and when they hear reason from a religious philosopher they at once gladly admit religion in general. Indeed, when they have been instructed in this, they are more easily led to a finer and more specific form of religion.[39]

His own endeavors are to be seen as part of this process, uncovering ancient wisdom to affirm faith and refute error, for all who are "prepared to listen to it with an open mind." He also relates human minds to celestial minds, which are universal

---

37 Ficino, *Letters*, vii, 18 and pp. 200–201. See also more recently Péter Kőszeghy, "Dubitatio utrum opera philosophica regantur fato an providentia," *Irodalomtörténeti Közlemények* 115 (2011), pp. 168–173. I thank Edina Zsupán for drawing this article to my attention.

38 Ficino, *Letters*, vii, 19 is his reply. For my discussion of its authorship, see pp. 200–201 of that volume; on its significance, see Michael. J.B. Allen, *Synoptic Art: Marsilio Ficino on the History of Platonic Interpretation* (Florence: Olschki, 1998), pp. 1–24. On Ficino's astrology, see: Cesare Vasoli, "Ficino e l'astrologia," in idem, *Quasi sit deus: Studi su Marsilio Ficino* (Lecce: Conte, 1999), pp. 281–299, and my paper presented to the Renaissance Society of America in April 2013 "A Fine Balance – Marsilio Ficino on the stars in the 1490s," (to be published). On astrology, see notes 28 and 29 above.

39 Ficino, *Letters*, vii, 19.

first causes, and therefore he cannot help but see the movements of the heavens as indicative, with Providence guiding such work rather than Fate.[40]

In June 1489, a famous series of public debates on free will and the origins of evil took place between the Dominicans and Franciscans in Florence, before an audience of leading citizens. Niccolò de Mirabilibus, an Italian born in Cluj, was the main Dominican speaker. He was at the time the senior teacher (*regente*) of the Florentine Dominican School at Santa Maria Novella. A redoubtable adversary led the Franciscan side: Giorgio Benigno of Ragusa (Dubrovnik). Thus both protagonists were originally from cities under Hungarian sovereignty, and both were friends of Ficino.

By July, 1489, both men had produced books in print justifying their positions, and the Franciscan claimed victory. Not long after, and perhaps only by coincidence rather than on account of the defeat, Niccolò was transferred to Buda, where he became head of the Dominican academy. Ficino's letter to the king written on Niccolò's behalf was a glowing commendation. Besides likening him to a reincarnation of Thomas Aquinas, Ficino jests that:

> Your Niccolò dwells with you, while our Niccolò at the same time lives with us. His voice still rings out in the school and the echo resounds from their very walls…for we longed for the presence of this great man so much that, in answer to our desire, he never appeared to leave us.[41]

Niccolò remained in Buda for some years, publishing a work on Providence in 1493.

While the writings of Ficino gave a new philosophical perspective, they were not the only option. Aristotelian philosophy and science flourished too, and were perhaps more germane to the interests of those trained in the universities. What Ficino provided, however, was a basis for Christian engagement with Platonic and Neoplatonic philosophy, just as Thomas Aquinas had provided the foundation for studying Aristotelian science two centuries before. Ficino's own works, as already mentioned, were included in the Corvina Library, and it would appear from Ficino's letters that Bandini was able to introduce some level of study of Platonic thought at least among the more educated members of the court.[42] Antonio Bonfini later described these interests in his *Symposion*

---

40   Ficino, *Letters*, vii, 19.
41   Ficino, *Letters*, viii, 19.
42   Ficino, *Letters*, vi, 30 and vii, 11, 14, 33 and 37. Bandini had been on intimate terms with Ficino prior to his exile from Florence in 1473 or 1474. After that date, their relationship is an epistolary one. Although we have only one side of the correspondence, it seems to

de virginitate et pudicitia coniugali of 1484–1485, depicting a courtly life where intelligent conversation on philosophical topics was highly prized. This work (see more below) won him royal favor and a place at court. Besides the Corvinas, Ficino's *Three Books on Life* survived, but not as a Corvina for it had not left Florence before Matthias died in April 1490, and it was therefore recycled for presentation to Lorenzo de' Medici. However, the third book of this work, printed in 1489, is dedicated to Matthias and consists of the most controversial portions of his commentary on Plotinus, removed from the main Plotinus volume. Ficino's choice of patron for this section reflects his perception of the king's likely support for bold new thinking on the theology of the ancients.[43] His translation of Iamblichus' *Mysteries of the Syrians and Egyptians*, the subject of a letter to the librarian Taddeo Ugoleto, was certainly made available in Buda, and indeed was later cited by Bonfini for the dedication letter of his *Rerum Ungaricarum decades* when it was presented to Matthias's successor in 1492 (see below).[44]

In the very first letter Ficino had sent to the king (the preface to his third book of letters, dated 1st October, 1480), he had expressed a widely held hope that Matthias would prove to be a "philosopher-king" in the Platonic sense of uniting wisdom and power for the benefit of all.[45] The importance of philosophy for a ruler is a recurrent theme:

> Philosophy, to express it in a few words, is the ascent of the mind from the lower regions to the highest, and from darkness to light. Its origin is an impulse of the divine mind; its middle steps are the faculties and disciplines which we have described; and its end is the possession of the highest good. Its fruit is the right government of men.[46]

---

reflect a warm relationship. Ficino recognized Bandini's talents in gaining the king's ear, asks favors for others when needed, and makes it clear that Bandini is to be Plato's herald and defender in the Hungarian court.

[43] For a more detailed discussion, see Valery Rees, "Marsilio Ficino and the Rise of Philosophic Interest in Buda," in *Italy & Hungary*, pp. 127–148.

[44] Ficino, *Letters*, viii, 22; idem (transl.), Iamblichus, *De mysteriis Aegyptiorum, Chaldaeorum, Assyriorum* (and other works) (*editio princeps*: Venice: Aldus Manutius, 1497, facsimile repr. Paris, 2006). Antonio Bonfini, *Rerum Hungaricarum decades* (Basle: Brenner, 1543), f. a.4. For further publication details, see note 52 below.

[45] "Exhortatio ad bellum contra barbaros" – Ficino, *Letters*, ii, 1.

[46] Ficino, *Letters*, iii, 18 and p. 31. Originally an introduction to Plato's *Philebus* (before 1474), this letter together with his *Life of Plato* is found in a volume dedicated to Matthias.

Matthias in his turn was keen that his wisdom and power should also take visible form. Hence he was keen to display all the latest developments in the arts and to build a capital that would reflect his *magnificentia*. If Bandini played an important part in fostering philosophic interests in Buda, no less significant was the role he played in helping the king and queen to transform the physical environment of the capital.[47] Bandini became the king's adviser on art and architectural matters, and served as intermediary with the many Italian artists and craftsmen working in the city. Outstanding among these were the architect Chimenti Camicia and the sculptor Giovanni Dalmata.[48] The palace in Buda underwent costly renovations, using prodigious quantities of fine red marble, while white marble sculptures by leading Italian artists adorned its halls. Woodwork and tiling, all executed to a very high standard, called for the employment of more local craftsmen. All of these aspects have been studied in detail, and reported in publications mentioned earlier.[49] The surviving tabernacle of the medieval parish church of Pest shows that the program of beautification was not limited to the royal court alone but also included buildings open to a wider public.[50]

Besides the building commissions effected through Bandini, he also turned to other ways of achieving lasting fame. This included a rewriting of history. In 1486, Antonio Bonfini, an Italian from the Marches, had presented himself at court hoping for work. Matthias first appointed him as Queen's Reader, impressed no doubt by the idealized version of the intellectual life of his own court described in the *Symposion*.[51] In a series of dramatized dialogues Bonfini attempts to display the erudition and wisdom of the king and the bright intelligence of his queen through Socratic conversations covering philosophy,

---

47 The last letter from Ficino to Bandini is from 6 December 1489. Bandini's own surviving letters are few, and the latest is dated 1 July 1488. See Kristeller, "Francesco Bandini," pp. 424–429.

48 Péter Farbaky, "Recent Research on Early Renaissance Art in Hungary," in *Italy & Hungary*, pp. 73–93.

49 See note 2. Of special interest in this regard are the contributions of Árpád Mikó, Louis Waldman, Dániel Pócs and Johannes Röll in *Italy & Hungary* and of Péter Farbaky, András Végh, Eszter Kovács and Gabriella Fényes in *Matthias Corvinus, the King* (Section ix).

50 Other surviving examples include decorative elements in the cathedrals of Esztergom and Alba Iulia as well as the altar at Diósgyőr.

51 Antonio Bonfini, *Symposion de virginitate et pudicitia coniugali* [composed in 1484–1485 and presented in manuscript in Vienna, January 1487.], ed. Stephanus Apró (Budapest: K.M. Egyetemi Nyomda, 1943). See also Klára Pajorin, "La rinascita del symposio antico e la corte di Mattia Corvino," in *Italia e Ungheria all'epoca dell'Umanesimo Corviniano*, eds Sante Graciotti and Cesare Vasoli (Florence: Olschki, 1994), pp. 179–228.

mathematics, astronomy, religion, history, geography and the arts. Other interlocutors include the queen's two brothers, two Hungarian bishops and two humanists, Galeotto Marzio and Nicolaus Pamphilus. In Book III, Bonfini acknowledges the interests and achievements of Hungarians (*Symposion*, iii, 13–14) before unfolding neo-platonic teachings, Greek cosmology and astronomy.

Matthias soon commissioned from Bonfini the first fully "modern" (i.e. humanist) history of Hungary, extending its roots to the classical past.[52] He also engaged him to translate the bold architectural work written for the prince of Milan around 1461, Filarete's *De architectura*. Bandini had obtained a copy of this in 1489 and the king was so keen to read it that he had Bonfini translate it into Latin (Fig. 18.1).[53]

When the rebuilding of the palace in Buda was nearing completion, Matthias planned to undertake a more grandiose project that would redesign an entire section of the capital as an ideal town, taking his inspiration, as other princes had done, mainly from Alberti, but he was affected, too, by the extraordinary illustrations found in Filarete's treatise.[54] Amongst these are two images which show plans for a *House of Virtues and Vices*. These appear to have inspired Matthias's ideas for a new university building (Figs 18.2–18.3).

The proposed university building was described later by Gáspár Heltai, based on an anonymous description of what little remained by way of legend and material foundations.[55] Whether or not this was linked to plans for obtaining papal recognition for the Dominican school of Buda as a fully-fledged

---

52 Bonfini, *Rerum Ungaricarum decades*. This was not completed during Matthias's lifetime, but four decades were presented to Wladislas Jagiello in 1492; a further half of the fifth decade, bringing the subject covered up to 1496, was completed before Bonfini's own death in 1502. The first edition (Basle, 1543) contains only the first three Decades. Johannes Sambucus added the remaining sections for a second edition (Basle, 1568). German and Hungarian translations were available from 1545 and 1575 respectively. The critical edition is: Bonfini, *Decades*.

53 Antonius Averulinus, *De architectura libri xxv, ex Italico traducti et Matthiae regi dicati ab Antonio de Bonfinis*, Venice, Biblioteca Nazionale Marciana, MS Lat. VIII, 2 (formerly 2796). See Csaba Csapodi and Klára Csapodiné G., *Bibliotheca Corviniana: the Library of King Matthias Corvinus of Hungary* (Budapest: Helikon, 1969), plates 89 and 90, and more recently *Matthias Corvinus, the King*, pp. 331–333.

54 A facsimile edition of the original Italian text, complete with illustrations, was published by J.R. Spencer, *Treatise on Architecture being the Treatise by Antonio di Piero Averulino, Known as Filarete*, 2 vols (New Haven: Yale University Press, 1965). For discussion of this work in the Hungarian context, see Alessandro Scafi, "Filarete e l'Ungheria: l'utopia universitaria di Mattia Corvino," *Storia dell'arte* 81 (1994), pp. 137–168.

55 *Descriptio fabricate academicae, quam Matthias Corvinus Budae fuit molitus*, Budapest, ELTE Egyetemi Könyvtár, Kézirattár Coll. Kaprinayana MS B., vol. lviii, pp. 82–83. This

FIGURE 18.1   *Frontispiece for Antonio Averulino,* De architectura libri xxv, ex Italico traducti et Matthiae regi dicati ab Antonio de Bonfinis, *Venice, Biblioteca Nazionale Marciana,* MS Lat. VIII, *2 (formerly 2796).*

university is uncertain. The account speaks of the intention of housing the new *Athenaeum* in a seven-storey domed structure. Each of the liberal arts would occupy its own floor. This does not comply exactly with Filarete's illustration but the similarities are striking. Foundations were apparently laid on the banks of the Danube towards Óbuda, with an ideal town quarter around it, containing student hostels, masters' homes and other related buildings. It thus seems likely that the king still nurtured hopes of an academy modeled somewhat on the reputation of Ficino's academy in Florence, where the classical tradition was being studied in depth to reveal its hidden stores of knowledge. Such an academy could not fail to attract the foremost scholars and Buda would perhaps have become a powerful center of learning had the king lived long enough to realise his plans.

Looking to the Future

At the Dominican school in Buda, a new generation of churchmen was being educated, creating new circles where the *studia humanitatis* were highly valued. We know frustratingly little about the individuals concerned, but new research is gradually opening up a more extensive understanding of education

anonymous description can only be dated approximately, to before 1574. Heltai's *Chronika az magyarok viselt dolgairol* was first published in 1575.

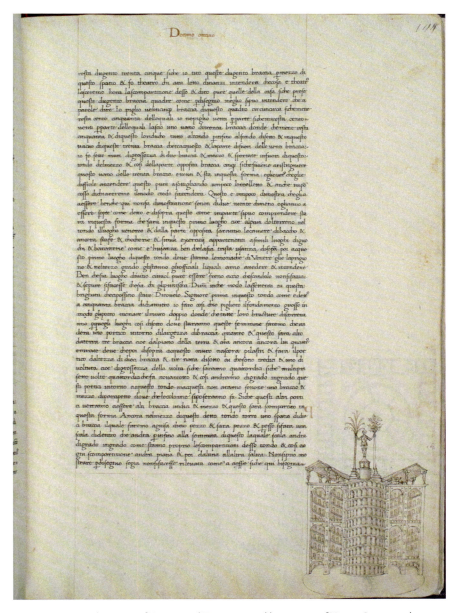

FIGURE 18.2 *The House of Virtues and Vices, crowned by a statue of Virtue. Cutaway plan. Antonio Averulino,* Trattato di Architettura, *Florence, Biblioteca Nazionale. Cod. Magliabecchianus. Book XVIII, f. 144r.*

FIGURE 18.3 *The House of Virtues and Vices, plan and elevation. Antonio Averulino,* Trattato di Architettura, *Florence, Biblioteca Nazionale. Cod. Magliabecchianus. Book XVIII, f. 145r.*

in the early sixteenth century. While visiting scholars, artists, craftsmen and merchants from Italy had undoubtedly played a large part in the beginnings of Buda's Renaissance, Bonfini's proud claim that Matthias tried to create another Italy is wide of the mark.[56] Although Matthias may have had personal ambitions to become Emperor, it was not a second Italy that was his aim, nor a second Greece. What was required was for the classical past to enliven the present and to assure the future. This went further than establishing his own or his son's legitimation by connecting with the classical past.[57] So many of Matthias's choices and policies indicate a genuine belief in the virtues handed down from ancient times. His success in passing on a strong and resilient kingdom to his heirs was, however, less than he had hoped, for he could not foresee his own premature death or the extraordinary struggles that followed.

In the Jagiellonian period and the subsequent division of Hungary after Mohács, Buda lost many of its gains and humanist endeavors took different forms. Several scholars went to study at Wittenberg, imbibing the precepts of Erasmus and Melanchthon. Hungarian appears as a language of prayer, with a Hungarian–Latin dictionary (1538) and the first Hungarian grammar (1539) paving the way for New Testament translations by Gábor Pesti (the four

---

56 "Pannoniam alteram Italiam reddere conabatur" – Bonfini, *Decades*, IV–VII–87 (p. 135).

57 The fact that Matthias was not descended from a royal line has often been evinced in this connection. See note 22 above.

Gospels, published in Vienna, 1536), János Sylvester (the whole New Testament, Sárvár, 1541) and Benedek Komjáthy (St Paul's Epistles, Cracow, 1553). In Transylvania the Unitarian (Anti-trinitarian) preacher, Gáspár Heltai, established his own printing press in Cluj and produced a Hungarian translation of Bonfini's *Decades* under the title *Chronika az magyarok viselt dolgairol*. By 1590, the full text of the Bible in Hungarian and published by the Calvinist Gáspár Károli (Vizsoly, 1590). In the west of the country, Catholic education was supported by the great humanist statesman Miklós Oláh (1493–1568), and later restored again under Péter Pázmány (1570–1637) in Trnava; Protestant education developed with a new college at Sárospatak (founded in 1531).[58] Latin continued as the main language of learning, government and religion, at least in the west, while Transylvania had to focus on other priorities even to survive.

Buda lost its predominance during this period, but the seeds that had been laid bore fruit elsewhere. Meanwhile, although later generations have marveled at the fine works of Renaissance art that have recently come to light, to many contemporaries it was the restoration of a pure and elegant Latin that mattered most.[59] On this count, Buda held its own among the nations, preserving Latin fluency longer than most.

Conclusion

The kingdom of Hungary and its capital city, Buda, suffered many vicissitudes during the sixteenth century. However, examining changes wrought during the closing decades of the fifteenth reveals many of the characteristics of a Renaissance city. Behind the displays of magnificence and the acquisition of priceless books and works of art lay some far-reaching innovations. Matthias Corvinus was energetic in his pursuit of humanist goals, be it personal qualities and virtues or the latest advances in science and philosophy. In court life, in education and the arts, Buda certainly enjoyed some of the reawakening of ancient ideas and values to which we give the name Renaissance.

---

58 On Oláh, see Cristina Neagu, *Servant of the Renaissance: the Poetry and Prose of Nicolaus Olahus* (Oxford–New York: Peter Lang, 2004).

59 See Patrick Baker, "*De viris illustribus* and the Self-conception of Italian Humanism in the 15th century," in *Acta Conventus Neo-Latini Upsaliensis. Proceedings of the Fourteenth International Congress of Neo-Latin Studies (Uppsala 2009)*, ed. Astrid Steiner-Weber (Leiden: Brill, 2012), pp. 189–198; Patrick Baker, *Humanism through the Looking Glass* (Cambridge, Mass.: Harvard University Press [in press]).

PART 6

Buda beyond Buda

∴

CHAPTER 19

Buda: From a Royal Palace to an Assaulted Border Castle, 1490–1541

László Veszprémy

The present study aims to focus on the surprisingly intense presence of Buda in late medieval Latin and Ottoman historiography, and its political-military background. The basic factor behind both issues was the radical transformation of the Central European concert of powers, the permanent fight for supremacy between the Habsburgs and the Ottomans before and especially after the fatal battle at Mohács, 1526, and finally the Ottoman occupation of the city in 1541.

Chroniclers of Late Medieval Buda

The turn of the fifteenth to sixteenth centuries can be regarded as the beginning of a totally new era in historiography: more and more historians turned up in Buda and consequently the history of the royal seat can be reconstructed in the detailed context of Hungarian and European history. No doubt the person who most intimately combined the two eras is the Italian-born Antonio Bonfini, who was commissioned to write a chronicle of Hungarian history by the court, first under the rule of King Matthias Corvinus and then under King Wladislas II. In his magisterial historical work he traced the country's history from the beginnings to 1496. In October 1492 he was raised to the ranks of the Hungarian nobility. Following his death in 1502 he was buried, in accordance with his testament, in the cemetery of Óbuda at St Margaret's Chapel on the site of the present-day St Peter and St Paul Parish Church. He had spent the decisive years of his life in the Hungarian capital; and we have him to thank for the most detailed description of the Renaissance palace built under King Matthias. Bonfini was the first historian to put Hungarian history in the organic texture of universal history. Due to its acknowledged historical and rhetorical qualities his work became from its first full edition in Basle in 1568 one of the most widespread handbooks on Hungarian history and it was reprinted and translated several times, and even later augmented with an appendix.[1]

---

[1] Bonfini, *Decades*. Based on the Basle edition (Basle: ex officina Oporiniana [per Bartholomaeum Franconem, et Paulum Quecum, sumptibus partim successorum Oporini, partim

Beside the comprehensive national chronicle the new genre of autobiographical diary was introduced by János Kakas, a citizen of Buda; a kind of *Liber memorialis*, his work has been transmitted to us in the *Almanach nova* of Johann Stoeffler and Jacob Pflaumen, printed in Venice in 1504.[2] Understandably, because the author lived in Buda, he saw the city not as an outsider and he records many incidents which would have been appreciated only by local residents. Thus we learn from him that in 1506 the queen died and was buried in Buda;[3] that in April 1512 twenty-four houses were destroyed by fire; and that in the same year István Bátori, *ban* of Temes, put 3000 Turks to flight on the southern border of the country and sent the heads of 160 of them to the king in Buda.[4]

A decisive historic importance is attributed to Buda by the court chaplain of Louis II, king of Hungary and later of King John I Szapolyai, György Szerémi, the chronologically last medieval historian of the town, in his work entitled *On the Loss of Hungary*, written in Latin ca. 1545, in which he relates events from the 1450s to 1543.[5] In 1526 Szerémi as court chaplain accompanied King Louis II as he was about to leave for the battlefield at Mohács, but returned in time to avoid the fateful battle. Nevertheless, he did not flee before the Ottomans from Buda but joined John Szapolyai, at that time voivode of Transylvania, who was elected and crowned as king of Hungary in November 1526. In his chronicle the city of Buda and the ongoing internal struggle for its possession are set at the center of the account. This is partly because his work was written in the years when the troops both of Szapolyai, who was supported by the

---

Sigismundi Feirabent], 1568). For the later editions and translations see Péter Kulcsár, *Inventarium de operibus litterariis ad res Hungaricas pertinentibus ab initiis usque ad annum 1700* (Budapest: Balassi – OSZK, 2003), pp. 81–82.

2 *Almanach noua plurimis annis venturis in seruientia per Ioannem Stoefflerinum Iustingemsem et Iacobum Pflaumen Vlmensem accuratissime supputata...* (Venice: Petrus Liechtensteyn, 1504 die 2 Ianuarij).

3 Queen Anne of Foix-Candale (1484–1506) was buried in St Sigismund's Church in the Castle of Buda; but after the death of her husband in 1516 her body was exhumed and buried again with him at Székesfehérvár (Fehérvár), the customary necropolis of the Hungarian kings.

4 András Kubinyi, "Budai Kakas János és történeti feljegyzései," [The historical notes of János Budai Kakas] *Tanulmányok Budapest Múltjából* 18 (1971), pp. 59–79.

5 Georgius Sirmiensis, *Epistola de perditione regni Hungarorum* (Monumenta Hungariae Historica. Scriptores, 1), ed. Gusztáv Wenzel (Pest: Eggenberger, 1857), p. 1. Already in the first sentence is stated that "I, Georgius Sirmiensis, the chaplain of Kings Louis and John, lived in Buda for more than twenty years" (*Ego Georgius Sirmiensis capellanus Ludovici Regis et Joannis in regione Budensi plus quam viginti annis residenciam habui*). For this chronicle see *Repertorium fontium historiae Medii Aevi: Fontes, D – E – F – Gez* (Rome: Istituto storico italiano per il Medio Evo, 1976), pp. 690–691.

Ottomans, and of the rival Habsburg king, Ferdinand I, fought with each other for possession of the town. A constant theme throughout Szerémi's work is his focus on those places and objects that reminded him and his audience of the once unified kingdom of Hungary, and beside the Holy Crown he apparently found this in the symbolic walls of Buda. There can be no doubt that at that time Buda was still the center of the country, and as reported several times by Szerémi the most important events were all somehow connected with it.

The point of interest in Szerémi's work is not the amount of information it contains or authenticity of it, but rather its radical break with the forms of traditional historical narration. With Szerémi's work a new genre appears in Hungarian historiography that can be called *Zeitgeschichte* with subjective overtones. Its documentary value stems from the fact that the fantastic stories and gossip it records were alive among his contemporaries and were accepted by them as valid and decisive explanations for the sudden changes and unexpected tragedies of early-sixteenth-century Hungarian history. Here we find for the first time a text in which what is spread as gossip about events is subsequently considered as history by the author. Again and again he refers to his own prophecies that came to pass in reality as well as to superstitions and rumor, for example, that the Ottoman sultan himself acted as a spy, participating in the Corpus Christi procession in Buda – something that of course never happened – or that on leaving for the battle of Mohács, King Louis II entrusted the citizens of Buda with the responsibility to bathe his puppies twice a week while he was absent.[6]

The First Occupation of Buda by the Ottomans, 1526

On 29 August 1526 the army of the king of Hungary, Louis II, encountered the army of the Ottoman Sultan Suleiman I the Magnificent on the battlefield of Mohács. The battle ended with a catastrophic defeat of the Hungarians and with the death of the king and the majority of the secular and ecclesiastical elite.[7] The news of the defeat at Mohács and of an impending siege of the town

---

6 Georgius *Sirmiensis, Epistola*, p. 118.
7 Géza Perjés, *The Fall of the Medieval Kingdom of Hungary: Mohács 1526 – Buda 1541* (War and society in East Central Europe, 26 = Atlantic studies on society in change, 56 = East European Monographs, 255) (Boulder: East European monographs, 1989); Gábor Ágoston, "Mohács," in *The Seventy Great Battles of All Time*, ed. Jeremy Black (London: Thames & Hudson, 2005), pp. 100–112; János B. Szabó and Ferenc Tóth, *Mohács 1526. Soliman le Magnifique prend pied en Europe centrale* (Paris: Économica, 2009).

found the commanders of the castle of Buda totally unprepared. Most of the castle-guard and the artillery had been taken for use in the battle so there was no possibility of successfully protecting the castle. Queen Mary and the papal legate, Antonio Giovanni da Burgio, who were staying in the castle, were informed of the tragedy on the day following the defeat and immediately decided to flee. The Ottomans approached the city and the castle from the direction of Kelenföld, following the military road on the right side of the Danube, and occupied Buda without any fight. They set up their camp south of the town in Kelenföld and on 14 September the Sultan ordered 300 of his people to set the city (but not the castle) on fire. Terrified by the death of their main protector, the king, practically the only inhabitants remaining in the city were by 8 September Jews. According to the Ottoman historian Ferdi,[8] they appealed to the Sultan for mercy. The symbolic keys of the city were presented to the invaders by Joseph, son of Solomon, and for this the Jews were treated with special mercy.[9] They remembered even in the 1550s that they were transported south on ships along the Danube and were settled not as slaves but as taxpaying citizens in Thessaloniki and other parts of the Ottoman Empire.[10] These events were mostly neglected by Szerémi, who chose to record only how the German citizens fled with torches in their hands and safeguarded their treasures on hearing the news of the lost battle at Mohács, and how Queen Mary departed with fifty cavalrymen.[11] Astonishingly enough, his Chapter 26 seems to show

8   Ferdi Efendi, Tarih-i-sahib kamun Sultan *Suleyman* (*Süleymanname*), [The History of Sultan *Suleiman* the Lawgiver]. Hungarian transl. József Thúry, *Török történetírók*, 2 vols [Ottoman chroniclers] (Budapest: MTA, 1893–1896), ii, p. 71; English transl. of the relevant paragraphs in *Jewish Budapest. Monuments, Rites, History* (Atlantic Studies on Society in Change, 101), ed. Géza Komoróczy (Budapest: CEU Press, 1999), p. 22.
9   See Katalin Szende, "Scapegoats or Competitors? The Expulsion of Jews from Hungarian Towns in the Aftermath of the Battle of Mohács, 1526," in *Religious and Ethnic Identities in the Process of Expulsion and Diaspora Formation*, ed. John Tolan (Turnhout: Brepols 2015), pp. 51–83. The number of the Jews mentioned by Ferdi as 2000 should be regarded as an overestimate. The information of the Austrian humanist Cuspinianus that the Jews fought bravely against the Ottomans also seems to be fictitious. See Johannes Cuspinianus, *Oratio protreptica ad Sacri Romani Imperii principes et proceres*… (Vienna: Joannes Singrenius, 1527), fol. B III^v (Budapest, OSZK Régi Nyomtatványok Tára [Department of Old Prints] Röpl. 60), English transl. in *Jewish Budapest*, p. 22.
10 Hans Dernschwam, *Tagebuch einer Reise nach Konstantinopel und Kleinasien (1553–1555)*, ed. Franz Babinger (Munich – Leipzig: Duncker & Humblot, 1923), p. 110. On the Jews as taxpayers see Aryeh Schmuelewitz, *The Jews of the Ottoman Empire in the late Fifteenth and the Sixteenth Century* (Leiden: Brill, 1984), pp. 81–127; *Jewish Budapest*, pp. 24–25, cited by Szende, "Scapegoats".
11 Georgius Sirmiensis, *Epistola*, pp. 122–125.

no knowledge of the ships that carried the royal treasury and archives and sank in the Danube at Esztergom.[12] Neither does he give any details concerning the setting on fire of Buda, although he was an eyewitness of the event. The removal of the local Jews by the Turks is not recorded in Hungarian sources but only in Ottoman chronicles and charters.[13]

Much more detailed and less unbiased descriptions have survived on Buda's capture in Ottoman historiography. Kemalpaşazâde (d. 1534), the renowned court historiographer, scholar and poet devoted a separate work to the battle of Mohács entitled *Mohaç-name*. He described Buda as "a very large and old town...that with its invincible castle belongs to the wonders of the world. No enemy has ever managed to enter it and occupy it...."[14] According to his account, the arrival of the sultan had turned the whole area into a garden of roses and he also mentions that "from the beautiful palace of the wicked king" he took a lot of booty, among other things two big cannons seized by John Hunyadi in 1456 at Belgrade from the troops of Sultan Mehmed II the Conqueror when the latter was fleeing from the walls of the castle. These cannons and three beautiful statues were loaded on ships to be sent to Istanbul. Evidently the possession of Turkish trophies was scandalous in the eyes of the Ottomans. We are informed in detail of the sultan's stay at Buda, of his banquets in the palace, of his interest in listening to musicians and their remuneration, and of his visit to the famous royal hunting lodge not far from Buda. The Ottoman chronicler counts 4700 years from the alleged foundation of Buda, thus emphasizing its ancient roots. He states also as a fact that the sultan deliberately saved the castle from being set on fire by his soldiers.

12   Zuzana Ludiková, "The Fate of Buda's Ecclesiastical Treasuries," in *Mary of Hungary*, pp. 129–136.
13   Johannes Heinrich Mordtmann, *Adalék Buda 1526-iki elfoglalásához* [A contribution to the capture of Buda in 1526] (A Konstantinápolyi Magyar Tudományos Intézet közleményei, 3) (Budapest – Istanbul: A konstantinápolyi Magyar Tudományos Intézet, 1918). Later German chronicles, for example that of Nuremberg in 1568, mention, without any historical basis, a horrifying massacre of the Jews in Buda: see Béla Iványi, "Buda és Pest sorsdöntő évei, 1526–1541," [The fateful years of Buda and Pest, 1526–1541] *Tanulmányok Budapest Múltjából* 9 (1941), pp. 32–84, here p. 34 note 13.
14   Kemalpaşazâde, also called Ibn Kemal, Ibn Kemal Paşa, or Şemseddin Ahmet ibn Süleyman ibn Kemal Paşa, xxx, 114–115, in Hungarian translation: *Török történetírók*, i, pp. 255–256; for a French translation with mistakes, see Pavet de Courteille, *Histoire de la campagne de Mohacz par Kemal Pacha Zadeh* (Paris: Imprimerie impériale, 1859). A later Ottoman source, the *Diaries of Suleiman*, attests to the transport of arms, guns and statues from Buda. *Török történetírók*, i, p. 318, on 7th day of the year 932.

We also learn of further statues, those of Hercules, Diana and Apollo, re-erected in Istanbul that originated from the Hungarian royal palace, as attested by Peçevi (1, 99).[15] The history of these statues became a common topic of contemporary humanist literature thanks to the summaries of Ascanio Centario and Paolo Giovio.[16] It was also Peçevi who confirmed that the candelabra of the Buda churches came to Constantinople as booty and were still on display in the Ayasofya mosque – former Hagia Sophia – in Istanbul.[17] The Church of Our Lady in Buda was held in a special esteem even among Ottoman historiographers: the occupation of the town in 1541 was completed and symbolized by the transformation of the church into a mosque. The statues and wall paintings which were considered idolatrous were removed from the church walls and a mihrab was installed in it.[18] After a sojourn of sixteen days in Buda the Turks quit the city, crossed the Danube and the Great Hungarian Plain and left the country, leaving just a strip of land in the south occupied.

---

15 Peçuyli İbrahim Efendi (1572–1650) was born in the south-western part of present day Hungary, in Pécs, hence his name, Peçevi, literally "from the city of Pécs". Peçevi Efendi is famous for his two-volume book *Tarih-i Peçevi* ("Peçevi's History") on the history of the Ottoman Empire, which is the main work of reference for the period 1520–1640.

16 Ottó Béla Kelényi, "A török Buda a keresztény Nyugat közvéleményében," [Ottoman Buda in the public opinion of the Christian West] *Tanulmányok Budapest Múltjából* 5 (1936), pp. 34–101; Jolán Balogh, *A művészet Mátyás király udvarában*, i [Art at the court of King Matthias] (Budapest: Akadémiai, 1966), pp. 138–140. Cited prints: Ascanio Centario, *Commentarii della guerra di Transilvania* (Vinegia: Appresso Gabriel Giolito de' Ferrari, 1565); the book of Paulus Jovius (Paolo Giovio) entitled *Commentario de le cose de' Turchi* was written at the request of Emperor Charles v, edited in 1532 in Rome, and later translated into several languages. For a critical edition, see Paolo Giovio, *Commentario de le cose de' Turchi* (Quaderni di Schede Umanistiche, 10), ed. Lara Michelacci (Bologna: CLUEB, 2005). See also Margaret Meserve's review in *Renaissance Quarterly* 60 (2007), pp. 158–160.

17 Nicolaus Istvánffy, *Regni Hungarici Historia* (Cologne: Sumptibus Henrici Rommerskirchen, 1724), pp. 82–83 and 85; *Matthias Corvinus und die Renaissance in Ungarn* (Katalog der Niederösterreichischen Landesmuseums NF, 118) (Vienna: Niederösterreichisches Landesmuseum, 1982), pp. 313–314 (no 263). For Peçevi's history see *Török történetírók*, i, p. 257, with a German translation in Joseph von Karabacek, *Zum orientalischen Altertumskunde* (Vienna: A. Hölder, 1913), p. 93. On one of the candelabra, some lines in Turkish testify that they originate from the church of Buda. According to art historian Jolán Balogh they had probably come from the Royal Palace and not from the Church of Our Lady, as misleadingly suggested by the Turkish inscription. Balogh, *Művészet*, i, pp. 144–145.

18 Celâlzâde Mustafa Çelebi (ca. 1490–1567), "Levels of the Dominions and Grades of Professions," in *Török történetírók*, ii, p. 231. *Encyclopaedic Historiography of the Muslim World*, i, eds N.K. Singh and A. Samiuddin (Delhi: Global Vision Publishing House, 2004), p. 213.

But their influence in Hungarian internal affairs increased continuously from then on and the final occupation of the country was merely a question of time.

The Second Occupation of Buda in the Reign of John Szapolyai, 1529

After the battle of Mohács the issue of the possession of Buda and its frequent sieges stood in the forefront of interest. Compared to earlier periods, a remarkable amount of information about the city is preserved in contemporary chronicles, charters, correspondence and memoirs. The first to arrive in Buda in the autumn of 1526 and to occupy the town was John Szapolyai. By 16 December his rival Ferdinand had advanced only as far as Pressburg;[19] his troops took possession of Pressburg and Trnava in July of the following year, and after occupying Győr, Komárno and Visegrád they threatened to capture Buda as well. Ferdinand's agents hired 33 gunboats from the Danube fleet of Baranya County in southern Hungary; ten of them succeeded in reaching Csepel Island, south of Buda. King John deployed a chain barrage over the Danube against them which they broke through and succeeded in joining the Habsburg army. But in any case, with his relatively small army of two or three thousand, Szapolyai would have been in no position to oppose the army of Ferdinand. He probably came to the right decision when he fled from Buda voluntarily and let the city pass into the possession of Ferdinand – then already king of Hungary – without firing a shot.

Ferdinand marched to the castle and palace on 20 August, a day of symbolic meaning, being the feast of the first Hungarian King, St Stephen, accompanied by a few German dukes and two thousand magnificently-armed men to admire what had been left intact by the people of the Ottoman sultan.[20] According to an account by his marshal Wilhelm von Waldburg-Trauchburg, he went directly to the Church of Our Lady to celebrate *Te Deum* and then he moved

---

19   Kubinyi, *Budapest*, pp. 207–214 and 227–231; Lajos Fekete and Lajos Nagy, "Budapest története a török korban," [History of Budapest in the Ottoman period] in *Bp. tört.*, ii, pp. 335–436, here pp. 199–206 and 337–338; Géza Pálffy, *The Kingdom of Hungary and the Habsburg Monarchy in the Sixteenth Century* (CHSP Hungarian studies series, 18 = East European monographs, 735) (Boulder: East European monographs, 2010), pp. 37–48.

20   Caspar Ursinus Velius (d. 1539) turned up in Buda for the first time in 1525 as a guest of the local humanist circle, and later accompanied Ferdinand to Buda in 1527. He was appointed Ferdinand's court historian and provided a vivid description of these events; see Balogh, *Művészet*, i, pp. 159–160. The standard edition is Casparis Ursini Velii, *De Bello Pannonico Libri decem* (Vienna: Trattner, 1762, repr. Whitefish: Kessinger, 2009).

on to the royal palace.[21] Meanwhile, an alliance between the Szapolyai party and the Ottomans was beginning to take shape. This brought about a decisive change in the balance of military forces as well as in the struggle for the throne in Hungary and for Buda. In May 1529, Sultan Suleiman personally embarked on a campaign against Vienna via Hungary. The main goal of the Habsburg high command was to protect Vienna; consequently they sent only a couple of hundred soldiers to guard Buda.

In the history of Buda Castle this was the first serious siege fought with firearms – and perhaps that was the reason why it was extremely short. No serious fortification work had been carried out since 1526, so for an army well-equipped with fire power the castle did not prove difficult to conquer. On 26–27 August the sultan had Buda encircled and the siege commenced. Between 5 and 7 September the walls were destroyed by the intensive cannon and gun fire of the Ottoman army and the Ottoman batteries placed on Gellért Hill also proved to be highly effective.[22] In recording some hearsay, Szerémi described the superiority of the Ottomans during the siege in 1529: on landing their cannons, they warned the local inhabitants to look to protect themselves because the cannons would cause an earthquake. Szerémi only mentioned two shots being fired, and – at least as he reports – the defenders did not wait for the third one but chose to surrender instead.[23] Nevertheless, the defenders succeeded in driving back the Ottomans even after they had launched several attacks. According to Celâlzâde Mustafa Çelebi's florid and an exaggerated description, "the army attacking the castle and every side of the walls was like the sea. The war cries and the noise of the fighters for the cause of Belief reached up to the blue sky… Cannons thundered and guns were booming everywhere…."[24] The military preparedness of the sultan's army, the uninterrupted attacks and the – at that time still unusual – physical and psychological destruction caused by the artillery had the desired effect. The German mercenaries accepted the Ottomans' call for surrender and handed over the castle to them on 8 September. Thereupon Buda came – thanks to the Turks – into the possession of King John Szapolyai, who drove out the German-speaking population as potential allies of the Habsburgs.[25] After that, order was maintained in Buda and its surroundings by Ottoman auxiliaries.

21   For the contemporary description of Waldburg, see Iványi, "Buda és Pest," p. 4.
22   *Török történetírók*, ii, pp. 220–230; see also Imre Holl, "Feuerwaffen und Stadtmauern. Angaben zur Entwicklung der Wehrarchitektur des 15. Jahrhunderts," *Acta Archaeologica Academiae Scientiarum Hungaricae* 33 (1981), pp. 201–243.
23   Georgius Sirmiensis, *Epistola*, p. 261.
24   *Török történetírók*, ii, pp. 220–230.
25   The fethname of the campaign in 1529, *Török történetírók*, i, p. 387; see also *Török történetírók*, ii, pp. 220–230; Georgius Sirmiensis, *Epistola*, pp. 259–266.

Szerémi also recorded King John's enthronement in the royal palace, in contradiction to Hungarian custom and the practice of coronation in Székesfehérvár. According to the Ottoman ceremony, which was conducted partly in a Slavic language, King John was seated on an ornate Turkish chair and at the end "Allah, Allah, Allah" was cried three times.[26] The sieges between 1526 and 1529 were also recorded in world chronicles; the first mention can be found in the work by Sebastian Franck von Wörd, which was completed by 1531.[27] These decades also saw the birth of historical memoirs in Hungarian: an anonymous chronicle on the events after 1526, another on the Habsburg siege of Buda in 1541 by Tamás Bornemissza, and a third one on the last days of King John Szapolyai by Gábor Mindszenti.[28]

The Siege of 1530 by Habsburg Troops. The First Successful Defense of Buda Castle

Best prepared of all the attempts to recover the city was the siege of 1530. An army of approximately ten thousand German, Austrian, Spanish, Czech and – naturally – Hungarian soldiers led by General Wilhelm von Roggendorf[29] arrived beneath the walls of Buda Castle on 31 October.[30] In the meantime the three thousand Turks sent from Constantinople under the leadership of the Venetian Lodovico Gritti,[31] together with some 800 armed Serbs and Turks

---

26   Georgius Sirmiensis, *Epistola*, pp. 262–263.
27   On the fall of Buda, see Sebastian Franck von Wörd, *Chronica, Zeitbuch und Geschichtsbibel* (Strasbourg: Balthasar Beck 1531), largely a compilation on the basis of the Nuremberg Chronicle (1493), with six editions up to 1585.
28   Dezső Véghelyi, ed., "Mohachy veszedelem után való szép emlékezetre való dolog," [History of Hungary after the battle at Mohács] *Győri történelmi és régészeti füzetek* 2 (1863), pp. 166–170; Tamás Bornemissza, *Emlékezés Buda veszéséről* [Account on the loss of Buda] in *Verancsics Antal m. kir. helytartó, esztergomi érsek összes munkái, 2. Történelmi dolgozatok magyar nyelven 1504–1566* [Complete works of Antal Verancsics, royal lieutenant and archbishop of Esztergom. Historical studies in Hungarian, 1504–1566] (Monumenta Hungariae Historica, ii. Scriptores, 3), ed. László Szalay (Pest: Akadémiai, 1857), pp. 193–203; Gábor Mindszenti, *Diárium öreg János király haláláról* [Diary on the last days of old King John] (Budapest: Magyar Helikon, 1977). See also the bibliography in Kulcsár, *Inventarium*, pp. 85, 350 and 675.
29   Wilhelm Freiherr von Roggendorf (1481–1541). During the siege of Vienna in 1529 by the Turks he served as commander of the heavy cavalry. He resigned in 1539, but returned as commander of the siege of Buda in 1541.
30   Istvánffy, *Historia*, pp. 106–107.
31   Lodovico Gritti, illegitimate son of Andrea Gritti, Venetian doge 1523–1538, an adventurer, diplomat and politician, minister of Sultan Suleiman I, intimate advisor of Pargalı

who came by water, joined the Buda garrison troops in support of King John. At the same time there were few gunners in the castle – the sources mention only two – and it was, moreover, found impossible to store enough food for the newly arriving soldiers. As to the Danube, the defenders had to be satisfied with the help of a total of 22 gunboats. The attackers were, however, hindered by the weather, which turned cold and wet, and by Gritti's successful defense of the castle.[32]

Roggendorf issued orders for an overall attack on 10 November. The siege was launched at three points: from the northeast (the so-called Kammerhof), from the east (the site of present-day Matthias Church) and from the Gellért Hill in the southwest. The attack from the south–west was unexpectedly successful; four banners were set on the bastions and the besiegers almost mounted the ramparts. But the defenders cleverly mobilized the reserves they had set up at Szent György Square and were able to drive back the besiegers.[33] Szerémi reports the unsuccessful siege in a very realistic way, adding many details; for example, the chaplains of the king loaded the handguns themselves and gave them to the king, John Szapolyai, who killed four armed boatmen firing from the walls of the castle.[34]

Cutting the food supplies of the castle would have been another option for the besiegers, but for that they would have needed far more soldiers and to have had the Danube as well under their complete control. Nevertheless, the royal secretary Menyhért Ölyvedi managed to catch a fresh fish for the king every day – a deed he was later ennobled for. Even more soldiers would have been necessary to drive back the relief troops of the Turks whose advance was first reported on 20 November. This day became a turning point in the history of the siege, and also in the process of the gradual Ottoman occupation of Hungary. The overall attack planned for that day was canceled, and on 22 November the army set out on its way back to Vienna.

From the record we can draw the conclusion that the attackers withdrew from the city in panic, since their sick and injured soldiers were captured by the soldiers of King John who then had them massacred. They also set off in pursuit of the German armed boatmen, but the latter had enough time to

---

Ibrahim Pasha, the Grand Vizier, and first royal treasurer and later governor of Hungary 1530–1534, appointed by King John.

32   *Török történetírók*, ii, pp. 85–86.
33   Istvánffy, *Historia*, pp. 106–107; *Török történetírók*, ii, pp. 85–86.
34   Georgius Sirmiensis, *Epistola*, pp. 280–294; see also an anonymous print entitled *Oppugnatio Budensis per exercitum Ferdinandi regis anno 1530*, kept in the Wrocław Ossolineum, XVI.O.8327 Available online: www2.oss.wroc.pl/old/pn/kalendarium.html (last accessed 14 March 2015), mentioned by Kubinyi, *Budapest*, p. 230.

put ashore six cannons at Káposztásmegyer and rout their enemies. Even the contemporary German sources agreed that after the siege ended the Austrians left "suffering ridicule and...without money".[35] King John rewarded the citizens of Buda with privileges. In the wording formulated by Werbőczy, these charters stress that during the fifty days of the siege the citizens of Buda passed the test of fidelity, as they had suffered famine, were reduced to eating horse meat, endured the devastation of the cannons of the enemy and sacrificed their wine-casks in order to strengthen the walls of the city. For all this, the king raised each citizen to noble rank and added a lion holding a red banner to the coat of arms of the city.[36]

The Sieges of Buda and Pest in 1540 and 1541

The year 1540 brought an unforeseen turn of events. In June King John died, and his new wife, the Polish king's daughter Isabella, asked King Ferdinand to support her infant son. But after this son had been elected king of Hungary as John Sigismund by the Hungarian diet on the Field of Rákos, Ferdinand ordered General Leonhard Freiherr von Vels on 9 September to occupy Buda by force.[37]

Vels reached Buda on 21 October and this time, too, his army first tried to reach the walls from the north. But following the last siege of 1530, the castle was now strongly fortified and well supplied with artillery and large quantities of ammunition and food. The activity of a number of Italian military architects in the service of King John, including the famous Domenico da Bologna is convincingly documented.[38] Although the ramparts and bastions recently built by King John did not follow exactly the classical Italian-type patterns of the time, they proved their worth during the sieges and some parts were still in

---

35   The words of Melchior Hauff, cited by Kubinyi, *Budapest*, pp. 209 and 230 note 43.
36   Kubinyi, *Budapest*, pp. 210 and 212.
37   Istvánffy, *Historia*, pp. 142–144; Peter Ratkoš, "Memoar habsburského zoldniera Hauffeho (1526–1543)," *Sborník Filozofickej Fakulty Univerzity Kamenského. Historica* 17 (1966), pp. 141–158; referred to by Kubinyi, *Budapest*, pp. 230–231. See also Iványi, "Buda és Pest," pp. 54–62.
38   King John donated a house in Buda to Dominico da Bologna; the donation was later endorsed by King Ferdinand on 26 August 1540. See Klára P. Kovács, "Itáliai építész 'az ellenkirályok' szolgálatában. Domenico da Bologna életrajzához, 1540," [An Italian architect in the service of the anti-kings. Additions to the career of Dominico de Bologna, 1540] *Erdélyi Múzeum* 74, no 3 (2012), pp. 103–115; Leone Andrea Maggiorotti and Florio Banfi, *Le fortificazioni di Buda e di Pest e gli architetti militari italiani*. Offprint (Rome: Atti dell'Istituto di Architettura Militare, [1935]), pp. 32, 34 and 51–52.

use in the seventeenth and eighteenth centuries.[39] In spite of the fact that the number of the besiegers might have reached as high as 10,000 in the meantime, after a few days of military activity they started to withdraw along the Danube towards Vienna on 1 November, having left behind a strong garrison in Pest. Surprisingly, they managed to defend the city of Pest against both the Ottoman and Hungarian troops, until April of the following year. The reason for this might be that until the very last moment Ferdinand hoped that Queen Isabella and György Fráter (George Martinuzzi, 1482–1551), as the infant king's guardian, would concede him Buda after negotiations instead of forcing a bloody siege. Accordingly, in his letter of 20 September 1540 he advised General Vels to lure György Fráter and above all the citizens of Buda – either by money or by other means – over to him.[40]

In 1541 King Ferdinand again made an attempt to conquer Buda, making the most of the long-resisting bridgehead of Pest. Already in February he had imposed taxes on his subjects to cover the costs of the campaign, and in mid-April he appointed von Roggendorf head of the army. The commander was at that time 60 years old and ill, but he knew Buda very well. This time the march from Vienna of a strong army of 25,000 Austrian, German, Bohemian and Moravian soldiers was not slowed down by sieges, Esztergom and Visegrád already being controlled by the Habsburg king. They reached Óbuda with their thirty huge bombards and camped there on 3 May.[41]

Unlike in 1540, the unsuccessful negotiations aiming at the surrender of the castle were followed by a heavy siege. After three days of intensive cannon fire first the so-called water castle on the Danube bank was reduced to ruins, thus cutting off the water supply of the castle. In a sign of increasing professionalism, a map of Buda was sent to Vienna to help the war council decide which

---

39   Florio Bánfi, "Domenico da Bologna architetto della fortezza di Buda," *L'Archiginnasio* 30 (1935), pp. 56–71; András Végh, "A középkori várostól a török erődig," [From medieval town to Ottoman fortress] *Budapest Régiségei* 31 (1997), pp. 295–313, here pp. 297–299; Mihály Détshy, "Adatok Joannes Maria Speciecasa hadiépítész életpályáról," [Information on the career of the military engineer Joannes Maria Speciecasa] in *Emlékkönyv Gerő László nyolcvanötödik születésnapjára. Tanulmányok* [Studies in honor of the 85th birthday of László Gerő], ed. Nóra Pamer (Budapest: Országos Műemlékvédelmi Hivatal, 1994), pp. 227–234. More recently István Feld, "A magyarországi építészet Szapolyai János korában," [Architecture in Hungary in the age of János Szapolyai] in *Tanulmányok Szapolyai Jánosról és a kora újkori Erdélyről* [Studies on the age of János Szapolyai and Early Modern Transylvania] (Studia Miskolcinensia, 5), eds József Bessenyei, Zita Horváth and Péter Tóth (Miskolc: Miskolci Egyetem BTK, 2004), pp. 71–90, here pp. 71–73.
40   Iványi, "Buda és Pest," pp. 54 and 57.
41   Istvánffy, *Historia*, pp. 144–148.

side the castle should be attacked from. In spite of its apparent lack of success, after three months the siege began to have a psychological effect. Contrary to the intentions of György Fráter and despite receipt of a letter from the sultan promising Ottoman military support, the council of Buda Castle secretly decided to put an end to the siege and capitulate. During the night of 14 June, two detachments of German soldiers were let in through the little gate near the Church of Our Lady; but being unable to speak Hungarian they were easily detected. Roggendorf bore a great responsibility for the failure of this action. Had he sent Hungarian soldiers instead of the Germans, the night-posts at the City Hall might more easily have been deceived.

Meanwhile the army of the sultan set out from Istanbul in the spring of 1541, and after a very slow march arrived at Buda, in the vicinity of Kelenföld, on 10 June. First the Ottomans reinforced their position on the northern shore of Csepel Island with artillery to prevent hostile actions from the Habsburg fleet. Some minor clashes were still taking place between the Ottoman and Hungarian cavalry in the foreground of Gellért Hill when the sultan left Belgrade in July. During the battles in the foreground of Csepel Island a German gunboat sank in the Danube.[42] But the forces of King Ferdinand were once more forced to withdraw by the large Ottoman army, and in the night of 21 August they crossed over to the Pest bank of the Danube. These dramatic events were described by the Nuremberg *Meistersinger* Hans Sachs (d. 1576) in three songs, and later by Sebestyén Tinódi Lantos (d. 1556) in a Hungarian one.[43]

The Ottomans attacked both on land and water, causing the army they encountered severe losses, while Ferdinand's army tried to cross the Danube. The commander, Roggendorf, was lying in his tent suffering from a gunshot wound from which he eventually died on his way back to Vienna. The German fleet escaped, but the infantry numbering several thousand men who were left behind on the other bank were slaughtered or taken prisoner. According to the lively description in the diary of Sultan Suleiman, in the darkness of the night Muslims and *giaour*, true believers and infidels, fought so hard "that the true believers could only be told from the inhabitants of hell by the light of firing cannons or the flash of swords."[44]

---

42   The boat was brought to the surface in 1873 together with its weapons and handed over to the Hungarian National Museum: see Tibor Kovács S., "A Kopaszi-zátonyi fegyverek," [The arms from Kopaszi Shallow] *Folia Archeologica* 43 (1994), pp. 251–277.
43   Rochus von Liliencron, *Die historische Volkslieder der Deutschen*, iv (Leipzig: Vogel, 1869), pp. 164–167; for Tinódi see: *Régi magyar költők tára*, iii [Collection of old Hungarian poets], ed. Áron Szilády (Budapest: MTA, 1881), pp. 270–276.
44   *Diaries of Suleiman*, in Hungarian in *Török történetírók*, i.

29 August 1541 – Buda Becomes the Border Castle of Islam

When the Sultan and his imperial army[45] arrived in Buda on 26 August, the Hungarian lords, courting his favor, handed over to him 600 German and Bohemian captives, whose massacre was watched by the Sultan from his tent. On 29 August, the fifteenth anniversary of the battle of Mohács, the heir of King John, his infant son John Sigismund was cordially received by the Sultan in his tent while the Ottoman troops withdrew peacefully to Buda Castle pretending to visit it. But the head of the Janissaries ordered them to collect the weapons of the Buda citizens and to take possession of the strategically important points of the castle, starting with the gates.[46] Those who remained in the city were forced to leave and robbed of their valuables, although they had been promised they would be allowed to keep them. The Ottomans took possession of Buda for good and made it the center of a new province, the Buda vilayet, and at the same time the new Buda pasha was appointed. They turned the Church of Our Lady into a mosque and moved the sultan's tent to Szent György Square. On 2 September the muezzins called for prayer from the tower of the Church of Our Lady as the sultan was riding to the castle through the Logodi Gate. The castle of Buda became part of the Ottoman world. According to sixteenth-century descriptions, on the walls by the gate called Vienna Gate (*Bécsi kapu*) huge weapons and the bones of prehistoric beasts were displayed. The weapons were later attributed by the Ottomans to Sultan Murad IV, but by the Hungarians to a knight of legendary strength in the court of King Louis I, Miklós Toldi.[47]

The fate of Buda could not be reversed by the next unsuccessful siege by the Christians in 1542. On the contrary, as a logical consequence of the Buda fiasco the nearby fortresses of Esztergom, Tata and Székesfehérvár fell as well. The fall of Buda resulted in the creation and firm establishment of an Ottoman

---

45   See the report of Antonio Mazza, edited by Albert Nyáry, "Buda 1541. évi bevételéről Mazza Antal egykorú jelentése," [The contemporary account of Antonio Mazza on the capture of Buda in 1541] *Történelmi Tár* 8 [20] (1875), pp. 190–240.

46   Istvánffy, *Historia*, pp. 149–151.

47   First described in 1573, see József László Kovács, *Ungnád Dávid konstantinápolyi utazásai* [The travels of Dávid Ungnád to Constantinople] (Budapest: Szépirodalmi, 1986), p. 115; for the original German text, see *Stephan Gerlachs deß Aeltern Tage-Buch der von zween glorwürdigsten römischen Kaysern, Maximiliano und Rudolpho, beyderseits den Andern dieses Nahmens an die ottomanische Pforte zu Constantinopel [...] Gesandtschafft*, ed. Samuel Gerlach Zunner (Frankfurt am Main: Johann David Zunner, 1674); recently Balázs Sudár, "A Bécsi-kapu átdöfött pajzsa és a szultáni kar ereje," [The shield at the Gate of Vienna and the strength of the Sultan's arm] *Keletkutatás* 2009 (Fall), pp. 91–100.

occupation zone in the center of Hungary. Buda became a bulwark of Islam, rather than, as before, a bulwark of Christendom.

Epilogue

Alhough a man of modest education, György Szerémi compared the battles of the Turks and the Hungarians to the Trojan War. As might be expected, he sympathized with the Trojans and identified the Hungarians and Hungary, especially Buda, with Troy. This is a late and most probably coincidental continuation of the first attempts from the age of King Louis the Great to link the Hungarians to the literary tradition of Troy, a fabrication very popular all over Europe, or of the claims of Robert de Clari around 1210, who maintained that the Turks, having captured Troy, thereafter became the enemies of the Franks. Szerémi compared the great number of corpses thrown into the Danube following the unsuccessful siege of 1541 by the Christians, to the number of the dead at Troy, and the fate of Bálint Török,[48] captured by the Ottomans, to that of Hector leaving Troy for good and hastening to his own destruction. He even remarks in the same chapter that the numerous ethnic groups present in the Ottoman military camps might be compared to those at the siege of Troy, and it is certainly not by chance that in this very chapter, in enumerating literary examples, he refers to Óbuda under its literary Latin name Sicambria.

Another who cited the tradition of Troy was Jean Lemaire de Belges (c. 1473–c. 1525). He also affirmed that *Bude en Hongrie, enlaquelle est le siege royal, et un tres fort avantmur pour la chretienté conter les Turcz*.[49] Likewise the archbishop of Kalocsa, Francis Frangepán (Franjo Frankapan), at the imperial diet in Regensburg in 1541 stressed the defensive role of Buda to the German envoys, who had become very anxious about the western Ottoman advance.[50] But already in 1529 the situation had changed radically, and even more so in 1541, as the role of the bastion of Christendom passed from Buda to the kingdom of Hungary under the Habsburg kings. Buda was re-occupied by the Christians only in 1686.

---

48   The most important references to the Homeric world in Szerémi's work are Georgius Sirmiensis, *Epistola*, pp. 332, 351, 361, 366 and 400.
49   Kelényi, "A török Buda," *p* 35; For the Hungarian medieval Sicambria tradition, see Alexandre Eckhardt, *De Sicambria à Sans-Souci. Histoires et légendes franco-hongroises* (Paris – Budapest: Presses universitaires de France, 1943).
50   Kelényi, "A török Buda," p. 42.

In a humanist anthology from 1544, Johann Lange evoked the former kings of Hungary, Louis the Great, Sigismund of Luxemburg and Matthias, in a very striking simile. He stated that if they turned up from Elysium and saw their former great seat, they would return to Elysium in despair.[51] In contrast, later chroniclers and above all travelers tried to find traces of the former medieval golden age of Buda, and with their descriptions they often help present-day researchers to locate and reconstruct the lost and mostly destroyed world of medieval monuments in Buda.[52]

51 "O lux, o magnum nostrae decus, inclyta Buda/Pannoniae, o regum, Caesaridumque parens" – cited by Bálint Lakatos, "Pannoniae luctus – egy humanista antológia és a törökellenes Habsburg–lengyel összefogás kísérlete," [Pannoniae luctus – a humanist anthology and the question of a Habsburg-Polish anti-Ottoman coalition] *Irodalomtörténeti Közlemények* 112 (2008), pp. 15–44; see further, *Pannoniae luctus: Quo principum aliquot, et insignium virorum mortes, aliique funesti casus deplorantur* (Cracow: Hieronymus Vietor, 1544).

52 Balogh, *Művészet*, i, *passim*.

CHAPTER 20

The Last Medieval King Leaves Buda

Antonín Kalous

The Hungarian throne had been for thirty-six years occupied by the Bohemian line of the Polish-Lithuanian royal dynasty of the Jagiellonians. Ever since 1490, when Wladislas II succeeded the deceased Matthias Corvinus, Buda had become the Jagiellonians' principal court and the center of their rule in the two kingdoms. The inhabitants of Bohemia now had to get used to the fact that their king was resident in Buda (the Moravians, Silesians and Lusatians having had a few years under the rule of Matthias Corvinus to grow accustomed to Buda being the center of administration). Thus the city with the court was not only the capital of Hungary, it now in part fulfilled a similar function for the Kingdom of Bohemia. It was attracting a significant number of Bohemians, Moravians and Silesians both as courtiers and also as soldiers.[1]

Self-evidently, late medieval sovereigns who held two kingdoms had to be at least sometimes on the move. Matthias was away from Buda very often, mainly for the purposes of war. He spent considerable time in Moravia and Silesia when he was conducting the war against the heretics, and also in Lower Austria when he invaded the lands of the Emperor. After his definitive conquest of the Czech lands he visited them rarely; conversely, after his success in Austria he settled in Vienna. However, as Kubinyi indicates, he did not move his capital (with all the administration and library, which stayed in Buda), but rather kept

---

1 For a general overview, see Pál Engel, *The Realm of St. Stephen. A History of Medieval Hungary, 895–1526* (London–New York: I.B. Tauris, 2001), pp. 298–371. The rule of Matthias as king of Hungary is described by András Kubinyi, *Matthias Rex* (Budapest: Balassi, 2008) and idem, *Matthias Corvinus: Die Regierung eines Königreichs in Ostmitteleuropa 1458–1490* (Herne: Tibor Schäfer Verlag, 1999); for Matthias as king of Bohemia, see Antonín Kalous, *Matyáš Korvín (1443–1490): Uherský a český král* [Matthias Corvinus (1443–1490): King of Hungary and Bohemia] (České Budějovice: Veduta, 2009), esp. pp. 122–222; for the Jagiellonian period, see András Kubinyi, "Historische Skizze Ungarns in der Jagiellonenzeit," in idem, *König und Volk im spätmittelalterlichen Ungarn: Städteentwicklung, Alltagsleben und Regierung im mittelalterlichen Königreich Ungarn* (Herne: Tibor Schäfer, 1998), pp. 323–366; Martyn Rady, "Rethinking Jagiełło Hungary (1490–1526)," *Central Europe* 3 (2005), pp. 3–18; for the Jagiellonians in the Czech lands, see Josef Macek, *Jagellonský věk v českých zemích (1471–1526)*, i [The Jagiellonian age in the Czech lands (1471–1526)] (Prague: Academia, 1992), pp. 180–262 and 292–318. For Bohemians and Moravians in the Buda court see Antonín Kalous, "Bohemians and Moravians in the court of Matthias Corvinus," in *Matthias Corvinus, the King*, pp. 65–75.

traveling between the two cities, as his itinerary demonstrates.[2] His successors on the throne did not conduct wars in the western and northwestern borders of the realm as Matthias had done (apart from Wladislas, and then only at the very beginning of his reign in Hungary). The kingdom of Bohemia was clearly not a frequent destination for Wladislas after he moved to Buda. After that time, i.e. from 1490, he visited Prague only three times. The last of these occasions, in 1509, was connected with the coronation of the two-year old child prince, Louis.[3]

The rule of King Louis is not generally regarded as a strong one. Hungary was controlled by various political factions and holders of land and court offices. The slightly stronger position of the king and the new queen started to be felt only in the 1520s. King Louis was at the center of attention for papal diplomacy from the very beginning of his reign, on account of the need to coordinate action against the Ottomans. Many letters of Pope Leo X showed great interest in events in Hungary. The church was one of the stabilizing factors in the country; at least, we might think that was the conclusion of Louis's father Wladislas before he died, and why he named the pope and the Roman church the guardian of the young king.[4] Even though Leo X did not particularly like the then papal legate in Hungary and archbishop of Esztergom, Tamás Bakóc, he left him to represent the Curia in Hungary. In 1518, when dispatching four legates to the European powers, Leo X did not want to send any legate to Hungary,[5] even though after Wladislas's death he planned to send (but probably did not) a new nuncio *cum potestate legati de latere*, Roberto Latino Orsini, the bishop-elect of Reggio di Calabria.[6] Yet the activity of papal diplomats continued, and

---

2   Kubinyi, *Matthias*, p. 210; Katalin Szende, "'Proud Vienna Suffered Sore...' Matthias Corvinus and Vienna, 1457–1490," in *Matthias Corvinus, the King*, pp. 381–391, here p. 382. Cf. Richárd Horváth, *Itineraria regis Matthiae Corvini et reginae Beatricis de Aragonia* (História könyvtár. Kronológiák, adattárak, 12 = Subsidia ad historiam medii aevi Hungarie inquirendam, 2) (Budapest: História – MTA Történettudományi Intézete, 2011).

3   Macek, *Jagellonský věk*, i, p. 293; František Šmahel, "Korunovační rituály, ceremonie a festivity české stavovské monarchie 1471–1526," [Coronation rituals, ceremonies and festivities of the Czech estates monarchy, 1471–1526] in *Rituály, ceremonie a festivity ve střední Evropě 14. a 15. století* [Rituals, ceremonies and festivities in fourteenth- and fifteenth-century Central Europe], eds Martin Nodl and František Šmahel (Prague: Filosofia, 2009), pp. 154–158.

4   Paride de Grassi, *Il diario di Leone X,* ed. Mariano Armellini (Rome: Cuggiani, 1884), p. 34.

5   *Nova scriptorum ac monumentorum...collectio,* i, ed. Christ[ophus] Godofredus Hoffmannus (Leipzig: Sumptibus haered. Lanckisianorum, 1731), p. 403 (Excerpta ex Paridis de Grassis... Diario curiae Romanae).

6   Antonín Kalous, *Plenitudo potestatis in partibus? Papežští legáti a nunciové ve střední Evropě na konci středověku (1450–1526)* [Papal legates and nuncios in late medieval Central Europe

in the following years we hear of nuncios and even two legates *de latere,* the Dominican Cardinal Tommaso De Vio and Cardinal Lorenzo Campeggi. Both of them stayed with the king at the royal court in Buda or elsewhere for longer periods of time, represented papal interests in the region, took part in political negotiations and reported back to Rome.[7] The crucial reports for the last years of Louis's reign, however, come from the papal nuncio, Antonio Giovanni da Burgio, who was present in Hungary between 1524 and 1526. From him we learn of the internal matters of the Kingdom of Hungary (negotiations over representation in the diet), but also details of the life of the court and of the preparations for war against the Turks.

As ruling king, Louis left Buda for a longer period only once, when together with his wife, Mary of Habsburg, he spent some time in his other kingdom. He was away visiting the Kingdom of Bohemia and Prague for a whole year from February 1522 to April 1523.[8] By that time, ties between the two kingdoms were fairly well established and communication functioned effectively enough, although the estates of all the Czech lands would have preferred Louis (as indeed they had his father) to leave the palace in Buda and move to Prague, which had no resident king since 1490. Nevertheless, Louis was accepted as their king, and he was thus able, at least to some extent, to use the resources of the kingdom of Bohemia for whatever purposes he wished, within the limits of the estates' liberties.

The king's trip to Bohemia and Moravia in 1522–1523 gave the opportunity to deal with problems regarding the administration of the country, and also the occasion for the coronation of the queen; in addition, it was an opportunity for recruiting an army and assembling military machines, to which the king clearly refers in a letter to the citizens of Braşov, one of his last letters from Buda before he left for Prague.[9] Even in Moravia, on the way to Prague, Louis continued

---

(1450–1526)] (Brno: Matice moravská, 2010), p. 371 (with further references); Grassi, *Il diario*, p. 34.

7   Kalous, *Plenitudo potestatis,* pp. 377–382 (with further references).
8   Václav Bůžek, "Strangers in their own country: King Louis II (Jagiello) and Mary of Hungary's stay in Bohemia at the turn of 1522–1523," in *Mary of Hungary*, pp. 63–67; Šmahel, "Korunovační rituály," pp. 158–162; Norbert C. Tóth, "A királyi pár Csehországban 1522–1523," [The royal couple in Bohemia 1522–1523] in *"Köztes-Európa" vonzásában: Ünnepi tanulmányok Font Márta tiszteletére* [In the pull of *Zwischeneuropa*. Studies in honor of Márta Font], eds Dániel Bagi, Tamás Fedeles and Gergely Kiss (Pécs: Kronosz, 2012), pp. 83–96.
9   "...ire nos ad Bohemiam oportuit, unde propediem redibimus et tantas copias tormentaque bellica nobiscum ducemus..." – *Politikatörténeti források Bátori István első helytartóságához (1522–1523)* [Political and historical sources for the first regency of István Bátori (1522–1523)] (A Magyar Országos Levéltár Kiadványai, ii. Forráskiadványok, 50), ed. Norbert C. Tóth (Budapest: Magyar Országos Levéltár, 2010), pp. 34–35 (no 12).

to refer to the topic in his letters back home to the regent, the palatine István Bátori.[10] The king was keenly interested in soldiers and weaponry and kept an eye out for them even during his entry into the country and the capital. In Čáslav, one of the Bohemian royal cities, for example, he writes that he saw only very few unarmed people welcoming him, for "those who did not have breastplates and helmets, were carrying huge shields or guns or spears," and even in Prague he found armed people everywhere in the streets "from the gate to the bridge."[11] After news from Hungary of the danger posed by the progress of the Turks, Louis kept writing to the threatened regions that he was very diligently searching for reinforcements in all the Czech lands, and with the help of his brother-in-law, Duke Ferdinand, also in Austria.[12] Like his predecessors before, the king was not surprisingly willing to draw on the military strength of the Czech lands in his doomed conflict against the advancing Ottomans.

The sources collected by Norbert C. Tóth provide details of the taxes demanded of the Hungarian royal towns, the thirtieth and other financial sources.[13] Louis turned to his royal cities not only for money and soldiers, but also for specialists – matters for which King Matthias had previously also become heavily dependent on the towns.[14] Louis – represented here by his regent in 1522, the palatine István Bátori – asked Košice as well as Bardejov to supply him with gun-founders, their assistants, and a considerable quantity of gunpowder.[15] The king referred to his efforts to gain support for war against the Ottomans even during his journey home from Prague. The Austrian envoy reported that Louis had written to various princes of the Empire as well as to the duke of Austria to ask for cannons and gunpowder; he also had money collected in Bohemia to permit an army to be recruited as soon as possible.[16] On his way back through Moravia, he ordered twenty-five harquebuses (i.e. smaller cannons, *pixides barbate*) from the town of Olomouc.[17]

---

10 "In Moravia nunc dieta celebratur pro huiusmodi auxiliis ordinandis, in qua reliquimus prepositum Albensem et Franciscum Balassa, qui res nostras illic solicitent. Nam sine conventu generali tractari hec negocia non potuerunt, ea autem commissione eos illic reliquimus, ut aliquam partem gentium, quas Moravi daturi sunt, quam citissime versus Hungariam mittendam curent." – C. Tóth, *Politikatörténeti források*, pp. 50–52 (no 30).
11 C. Tóth, *Politikatörténeti források*, pp. 55–56 (no 34).
12 C. Tóth, *Politikatörténeti források*, pp. 61–63 (no 40).
13 C. Tóth, *Politikatörténeti források*, pp. 70–88 (nos 48–51, 53–56, 60–62 and 65–68).
14 Kubinyi, *Matthias*, pp. 172–187.
15 C. Tóth, *Politikatörténeti források*, pp. 145–146 (nos 129 and 130).
16 "Conclusum est, quod rex scribat ad diversos principes imperii et eitam ad serenitatem vestram pro habendis artellariis et pulveribus etc." – C. Tóth, *Politikatörténeti források*, pp. 203–204 (no 181).
17 C. Tóth, *Politikatörténeti források*, p. 226 (no 201).

Apart from soldiers, arms and military material, it seems the king was anxious to enlist divine protection for the kingdom through the acquisition of long desired relics. The head of St Paul the Hermit, whose body had been laid to rest entire at Budaszentlőrinc, in the vicinity of Buda, in 1381, had been lost sometime during the fifteenth century, but the king was able to find it in the principal Czech Castle of Karlštejn, where a considerable number of relics were kept along with the royal insignia. There is no clear evidence that the translation of the head of St Paul was directly connected with the Ottoman threat, but the possibility has been raised and discussed in modern literature.[18] Clearly it was regarded as an act of significance, as both the king and the bishop of Vác, László Szalkai, reported the translation in their letters to Bátori.[19]

Even though Louis was actively engaged in collecting help for the defense of Hungary, his Hungarian subjects wanted him to come home again and resume rule of the country. János Gosztonyi, bishop of Győr, wrote towards the end of February 1523:

> O most serene king, all – the great, the middling and the small – cry with one spirit and one mouth, they raise their voices, their weeping eyes testifying that your majesty should return and rule your kingdoms with law and sword....

The king should not allow others to usurp his power in the kingdom; and if the king did not return, there was no hope for the defense and safety (*salutis*) of the country;

> If [your majesty] is willing to use your authority, your power, your dignity, all would be willing to die in your service, if need be, for they declare that in the will of God they did not crown anyone else but your majesty, and into no other's hands did they consecrate the sword, sceptre, orb, justice and authority which represent the kingdom, but only [into the hands] of your majesty.[20]

---

18   Orsolya Réthelyi, *Mary of Hungary in Court Context (1521–1531)*, unpublished PhD dissertation (Budapest: Central European University, 2010), pp. 170–171. Cf. also Lajos Pásztor, *A magyarság vallásos élete a Jagellók korában* [Hungarian religious life in the Jagiellonian age] (Budapest: Királyi Magyar Egyetemi Nyomda, 1940), pp. 96–97.

19   C. Tóth, *Politikatörténeti források*, pp. 189–190 (nos 172 and 173).

20   "Serenissime rex, omnes uno animo, uno ore magni, mediocres et parvi clamant, vociferant oculis lacrimantibus testantibus, ut maiestas vestra reddeat et iure et ense regna sua gubernet, protegat et quod non patiatur ullo modo, quod aliquis alios precipiat, gubernet bona sua, proventus suos dissipet, regna sua distrahat, sed quod solus sit rex, solus dominus et non permittat auctoritatem suam, dignitatem suam ab aliis usurpary, sicuti

The text of the letter, which continues at considerable length, clearly shows the subjects' ideas and expectations of the ideal king and the need felt for his presence in the country. He was called on to defend the land against every danger, be it the threat of internal conflict or the external menace of the Ottomans. Expectations were high, but the subjects were willing to follow their king, if he fulfilled his role.

When Louis left Buda for the last time in 1526, it was not for the purpose of visiting his other kingdom, nor was he traveling to his summer house even though it was July and the weather was hot; it was not even for hunting. By July of that year he had used all possible means to put together an army capable of withstanding the renewed Ottoman attack. The situation in Hungary in 1526 is described in detail by Burgio, the papal nuncio, in his letters to Rome, which are preserved in the Vatican Secret Archives.[21] Burgio was very active in Hungary and at the royal court; his letters to Rome were read in the papal consistory in Rome and were surely the cause of some emotion. The tension before the decisive battle can be felt in the entries of the consistorial diary.[22] Burgio was

hucusque fuit, quia si maiestas vestra hoc non fecerit, nulla est in eis spes defensionis et salutis, si autem vult uti auctoritate, potentia sua, dignitate sua, volunt omnes, si opus erit, penes maiestatem vestram mori, quia dicunt, quod ipsi et voluntate Dei neminem alium coronarunt, quam maiestatem vestram et ad nullius alterius manus gladium, sceptrum, pomum, iustitiam, auctoritatem regnum representantia consecrarunt, quam ad solius maiestatis vestre." – C. Tóth, *Politikatörténeti források*, p. 177 (no 163).

21 Vatican, Archivio Segreto Vaticano (ASV), Segr. Stato, Germania, vol. 55; published in *Relationes oratorum pontificiorum* (Monumenta Vaticana historiam regni Hungariae illustrantia ii/1), ed. Vilmos Fraknói (Budapest: Franklin, 1884); basic literature about Mohács is gathered in *Mohács* [The battle of Mohács] (Nemzet és Emlékezet), ed. János B. Szabó (Budapest: Osiris, 2006); a brief summary appears in idem, *A mohácsi csata* [The battle of Mohács] (2nd ed. Budapest: Corvina, 2011); and idem and Ferenc Tóth, *Mohács, 1526: Soliman le Magnifique prend pied en Europe centrale* (Paris: Economica, 2009); for the inner situation in Hungary, see András Kubinyi, "Hungary's power factions and the Turkish threat in the Jagiellonian period (1490–1526)," in *The Fight Against the Turk in Central-Europe in the First Half of the 16th Century*, ed. István Zombori (Budapest: METEM, 2004), pp. 115–145; András Kubinyi, "The Court of Queen Mary of Hungary and Politics between 1521 and 1526," in *Mary of Hungary*, pp. 13–25.

22 ASV, Arch Concist., Acta Vicecanc., vol. 3; published in Antonín Kalous, "Elfeledett források a mohácsi csatáról: Antonio Burgio pápai nuncius jelentései és azok hadtörténeti jelentősége," [Forgotten sources for the battle of Mohács: The reports of the papal nuncio Antonio Burgio and their importance for military history] *Hadtörténelmi Közlemények* 120 (2007), pp. 603–622, here pp. 616–621; idem, *Plenitudo potestatis*, pp. 399–406; and recently in *Consistorialia Documenta Pontificia de Regnis Sacrae Coronae Hungariae (1426–1605)* [Collectanea Vaticana Hungariae, i/7], eds Péter Tusor and Gábor Nemes

most probably also the author of other reports preserved outside the archives in manuscripts of the Vatican Library.[23]

After a period of preparation Louis decided to lead his army into the field. This happened on 20 July 1526 and the event was a huge pageant, which could to some extent be compared to the celebrated army parade of Matthias Corvinus in Wiener Neustadt in 1487.[24] King Louis was not leaving the city in haste in his attempt to stop the proceeding Ottoman army but in a most dignified manner. Even though we cannot speak of manoeuvres as in the case of Wiener Neustadt (described in detail by Bonfini), the disposition of the army as it marched out is quite clearly reported. It was arrayed for ceremonial departure for war. At its head there were about 600 Bohemians, Moravians, and Silesians; next came the light cavalry; in third place, the heavy cavalry; fourth, the barons, nobles, and other lords; fifth, the king himself with the German guard (*la guardia del re*) of fifty men; sixth, the royal standard; seventh, four horses for the king; eighth, further heavy cavalry; ninth, the infantry and the artillery at the flanks; and tenth and at the end, some 800 wagons with provisions. Altogether there were some 4000 horses, slightly over 3000 infantrymen, and for each ten infantrymen a wagon with provisions, wagons which – most importantly – could be turned into powerful wagon castles (*castello*), i.e. a defensive circle of wagons (as had been used to great effect by the Czech Hussites). Every fifty infantrymen would have had a common flag. The details aside, it is clear that the king's presence in the middle of his army was meant to be solemn and symbolic for the expectations of his struggle.[25]

(Budapest–Rome: [Pázmány Péter Katolikus Egyetem Egyháztörténeti Kutatócsoportja], 2011), pp. 59–67.

23   Vatican, Biblioteca Apostolica Vaticana (BAV), Vat. lat. 3924, *passim*; a number of the texts are published in Kalous, "Elfeledett," pp. 611–616; idem, "The politics of Church unification: Efforts to reunify the Utraquists and Rome in the 1520s," in *Friars, Nobles and Burghers – Sermons, Images and Prints. Studies of Culture and Society in Early-Modern Europe. In Memoriam István György Tóth*, eds Jaroslav Miller and László Kontler (Budapest–New York: Central European University Press, 2010), pp. 191–197; idem, *Plenitudo potestatis*, pp. 385–399.

24   Bonfini, *Decades*, IV-VIII-78–106 (pp. 152–154); see also, Gyula Rázsó, "The Mercenary Army of King Matthias Corvinus," in *From Hunyadi to Rákóczi: War and Society in Late Medieval and Early Modern Hungary,* eds János M. Bak and Béla K. Király (Brooklyn: Social Science Monographs, 1982), pp. 125–140, with the chart following p. 140.

25   The full description of the event is preserved in BAV, Vat. lat. 3924, fol. 257^r– 257^v; published in Franz Palacky, *Literarische Reise nach Italien im Jahre 1837* (Prague: Kronberger's Witwe und Weber, 1838), pp. 120–122; Kalous, "Elfeledett," pp. 613–615, with the sketch on p. 607; and idem, *Plenitudo potestatis*, pp. 388–390; see: Fig. 20.1. It is not quite clear who

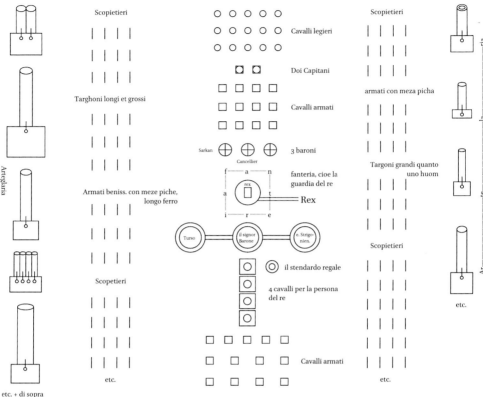

FIGURE 20.1 *The pageant of Louis II's army when leaving Buda on 20 July 1526*
BIBLIOTECA APOSTOLICA VATICANA, VAT. LAT. 3924, FOL. 257ᵛ, REDRAWN BY THE AUTHOR

Let us start from the king. King Louis, as the crucial figure of the day, appeared outside the castle clad in gold and the tawny color of a lion (*leonato*; see below); his horse was also richly harnessed, the harness itself being the gift of

---

the author of the description was: either Antonio Burgio, or possibly Giovanni Verzelio, a papal messenger or courier who brought money to Burgio and stayed for some time in Hungary, and who in one of his letters to Jacobo Sadoleto writes (Fraknói, *Relationes*, p. 424 [no 114] the following: "Mando a Vostra Reverendissima Signoria la uscita del Re da Buda aponcto, con che ordine è andato. Saranno un poco più o meno gente, di quello io pongo, chè non gli ho aponto noverati. In verità furono molti Signori bene in ordine, con bellissimi fornimenti et richi, et pennache sino in terra bellissimi").

Queen Mary.[26] As he exited the royal palace, the king stopped immediately outside its walls and entered the Church of St Sigismund. Standing in one of the streets close to the royal palace, the church offered a place for ceremonies of significance staged in the transitional zone between the two worlds. Since the times of King Matthias Corvinus (and especially after his second marriage to Beatrice of Aragon), access to the royal court had started to become more complicated for common people. St Sigismund's then offered a possibility for the people to meet the king, as a report from 1484 makes clear: meeting the king in the church during the vespers was the only possibility available when it was desired to hand him a supplication sent by the city of Bardejov.[27] In 1514 the church was the place where the crusade against the Turks was proclaimed by the cardinal and papal legate, Tamás Bakóc.[28] So now similarly, King Louis was using the church for symbolic communication with his subjects. Even though he could have done so earlier in the privacy of the royal palace (and most probably did), he now dismounted his horse, entered St Sigismund's Church and fell in front of the high altar and prayed for the success of his campaign.[29] The role of the king as a leader and defender of the country was thus displayed; he was the king, willing to risk his life for the country, for which he asked heavenly protection, thus fulfilling the expectations and demands of his subjects expressed in the letter of János Gosztonyi in 1523, given above.[30]

---

26 On Mary and her court, see *Mary of Hungary; Maria von Ungarn (1505–1558): Eine Renaissancefürstin*, eds Martina Fuchs and Orsolya Réthelyi (Münster: Aschendorff, 2007) and Réthelyi, *Mary of Hungary*.

27 András Kubinyi, "Alltag und Fest am ungarischen Königshof der Jagellonen 1490–1526," in idem, *König und Volk im spätmittelalterlichen Ungarn*, pp. 184–215, here p. 189; idem, "Courtiers and Court Life in the Time of Matthias Corvinus," in *Matthias Corvinus, the King*, pp. 21–34, here p. 22; András Végh, "Adatok a budai kisebb Szűz Mária, más néven Szent Zsigmond templom alapításának történetéhez," [Information on the history of the foundation of the smaller Church of the Virgin Mary or St Sigismund's Church in Buda] *Budapest Régiségei* 33 (1999), pp. 25–34, here p. 32, note 25; see also József Laszlovszky, "Crown, Gown and Town: Zones of Royal, Ecclesiastical and Civic Interaction in Medieval Buda and Visegrád," in *Segregation – Integration – Assimilation: Religious and Ethnic Groups in the Medieval Towns of Central and Eastern Europe* (Historical Urban Studies), eds Derek Keene, Balázs Nagy and Katalin Szende (Farnham: Ashgate, 2009), pp. 179–203, and Károly Goda, "Buda Festiva: Urban Society and Processional Culture in a Medieval Capital City," *Czech and Slovak Journal of Humanities. Historica* 1, no 2 (2011), 58–79.

28 Végh, "Adatok," pp. 32–33.

29 Kalous, "Elfeledett," p. 614; idem, *Plenitudo potestatis*, p. 389. – "…e quando fu alla chiesa di sant Sigismondo, smonto, e fece al quanto oratione inante laltare grande…".

30 Cf. Ernst H. Kantorowicz, *The King's Two Bodies: A Study in Mediaeval Political Theology* (Princeton: Princeton University Press, 1997), pp. 259–260 (first published in 1957).

As he ceremonially departed from the city in the midst of his army, the king was surrounded by the royal guard. András Kubinyi has remarked that this may be the first instance when the Hungarian royal guard is specifically mentioned, although we may presume that it goes back at least to the reign of Matthias Corvinus.[31] The figure of the king was complemented by the fifty German and Hungarian members of the guard, arrayed in garments of red, white and tawny hue, and by the royal standard and four pages on armored horses who followed the king and his guard. The sovereign himself was probably accompanied by the closest members of his entourage from the time when he left the royal palace, when he stopped at St Sigismund's, and when he exited the gate of the city. The sketch of the army, which is preserved together with its description in the manuscript of the Vatican Library, additionally shows some important personalities around the king. They may have accompanied the sovereign from the palace onwards. The significance of the moment was underlined by the presence of Ambrus Sárkány, judge royal (*iudex curiae*), István Brodarics, the royal chancellor, Elek Thurzó, master of the treasury (*magister tavernicorum*), as well as one of the most important personalities in the land after the king, the archbishop of Esztergom, László Szalkai and the papal nuncio, Antonio Burgio (*il signor Barone*). In the array of the army, the first two were accompanied by a further baron and preceded the king; the latter three followed the king and his guard, but preceded the royal standard.

So the first part of the ceremony must have occurred in the streets of Buda leading from the castle past the Church of St Sigismund's and towards one of the gates of the city. Most probably this was the Jewish Gate, the one closest to the church and at the same time the only gate of the city that led to an open space.[32] In the field outside there was enough room for the army to muster and even to proceed in the aforementioned order, with the cavalry and the king in the middle flanked by the infantry and the artillery; the army would then be able to march between the hills in the direction of Tolna on the right-hand side of the Danube, where it was planned that it should meet up with the other anti-Ottoman forces. It is possible that the king had a chance to proceed solemnly through the streets of Buda, as is described in the case of previous royal entries, e.g. of Matthias Corvinus in 1458, or Matthias with Beatrice, his new wife, in 1476 – where in both cases they stopped at the main parish church of the city, the Church of Our Lady.[33] The ceremonial departure

---

31 Kubinyi, "Courtiers," p. 22.
32 Végh, *Buda*, i, pp. 59–60.
33 Kalous, *Matyáš*, pp. 53 and 295. Cf. Goda, "Buda Festiva," pp. 67–68. Unfortunately, the report of the entry of King Wladislas in 1490 lacks detail. See Bonfini, *Decades*, IV-X-20–34 (pp. 191–192).

of Matthias Corvinus and his court in 1476 as he went to Székesfehérvár to meet his new wife Beatrice of Aragon is not described in detail as far as the procession through the city is concerned, even though there are three contemporary descriptions from eyewitnesses.[34] There are, however, no references in the sources to such a procession in the present case; indeed, if King Louis had wanted to exit the city through some other gate, he would have faced difficulties (due to the terrain and the built-up areas) when riding outside around the city to meet up with his army (which due to its size must have camped in the field to the west of the city).

The soldiers themselves varied in type and origin. First of all, the center of the army consisted mostly of horsemen. Its first group, however, contained foot soldiers, who had been recruited in Bohemia, Moravia, and Silesia. These 600 infantrymen were followed by 2500 light cavalrymen, and after these came a formation of 600 heavy cavalry led by two captains. Their horses were armored down to their knees, the horsemen all clad in tawny with green coats and armed with lances.[35] These three groups of soldiers formed the vanguard of the army on the march, for they were followed by the king and his suite, as described earlier. The horsemen (heavy cavalry) that followed were this time clad in coats of various colors and armed with bladed weapons (*arme bianche*).[36] The use of tawny color (*leonato;* the color of a lion) is significant. The king was dressed in a combination of gold and tawny, his guard wore tawny, red and white and the preceding heavy cavalry tawny and green. The lion color recalls the symbolism of a lion as a royal beast, underlining the significance of the fact that the king himself was going to war.

The center of the procession was flanked by various types of infantry. The sketch of the layout of the army describes the infantry as gunmen (*scopetieri*), [footmen with] long and large shields (i.e. pavises in the Czech style; *targhoni longi et grossi; targhoni grandi quanto un huom[o]*), and footmen armed with pikes (*armati con meza picha; armati benissimi con meze piche, longo ferro*). Thus we can see that the infantry was bringing to war all the military innovations of the age, including Hussite techniques.[37] As for the constitution

---

34 The most detailed report (with many descriptions of the clothes) is published in Béla Borsa, "Reneszánszkori ünnepségek Budán," [Renaissance festivities in Buda] *Tanulmányok Budapest Múltjából* 10 (1943), pp. 13–53, here pp. 44–45.
35 Kalous, "Elfeledett," p. 614; idem, *Plenitudo potestatis,* pp. 389–390.
36 Kalous, "Elfeledett," p. 615; idem, *Plenitudo potestatis,* p. 389.
37 Analyzed by László Veszprémy, "The State of Military Affairs in East-Central Europe, 1380–c. 1520s," in *European Warfare, 1350–1750,* eds Frank Tallett and D.J.B. Trim (Cambridge–New York: Cambridge University Press, 2010), pp. 96–109, here p. 109.

of the army, the nationalities explicitly mentioned in the description are – unsurprisingly – Hungarians, as well as Germans, who constituted the king's guard, and Bohemians, Moravians, and Silesians, who were infantrymen. It is clear that in addition to the resources of the kingdom of Hungary, Louis heavily relied on his Bohemian subjects.

In keeping with the latest innovations, the army was equipped with heavy artillery, which had only recently begun to be used in field battles. The sketch shows nine cannons, two of which have more than one barrel. According to another source, the Hungarians lost some eighty-five large cannons in the battle of Mohács, which was a considerable number, but still about three times less than what the Ottomans used in the battle.[38] The cannons could have been sent by individual Hungarian or Czech cities – as noted above, they were asked to do so for earlier campaigns – or even produced in Buda. The existence of a royal gun foundry in the city is attested through archaeological finds, dating from the late fifteenth and early sixteenth centuries, and the activity of a gunfoundry master is confirmed in written documents from the early years of Louis' reign, but it apparently ended "a few years" before 1518.[39] There is preserved, however, a letter of *magister bombardarius Johannes Mauthier*, which clearly refers to the intention of refounding the gun foundry or restarting production, since he asked the king for a financial and material support. The letter is not dated, but it may be inferred that it was written at the end of 1525 or beginning of 1526.[40] Possibly, then, the cannons were the production of the new Buda gun foundry, which may, like the original one, have been somewhere in the vicinity of the royal palace.

Alas, all the military innovations were to no avail, and the campaign ended with the defeat and death of the king on 29 August 1526, in the vicinity of the little town of Mohács close to the Danube. Queen Mary, after she learned the devastating news a day later, did not delay and left Buda together with her court and made for Pressburg. Sultan Suleiman entered the city, which was

38   Kalous, "Elfeledett," p. 612; idem, *Plenitudo potestatis*, p. 387; Stephanus Brodericus, *De conflictu Hungarorum cum Solymano Turcarum imperatore ad Mohach historia verissima*, ed. Petrus Kulcsár (Budapest: Akadémiai, 1985), p. 57, states that all the cannons were lost. Cf. Gábor Ágoston, "Empires and Warfare in East-Central Europe, 1550–1750: the Ottoman–Habsburg rivalry and military transformation," in *European Warfare, 1350–1750*, eds Frank Tallett and D.J.B. Trim (Cambridge–New York: Cambridge University Press, 2010), pp. 110–143, here p. 117.
39   Végh, *Buda*, i, p. 152; Károly Belényesy, "Remains of a Royal Gun Foundry in Buda from the turn of the Fifteenth Century," in *Matthias Corvinus, the King*, pp. 348–350.
40   Kalous, "Elfeledett," pp. 615–616, for discussion of the dating see pp. 607–609; idem, *Plenitudo potestatis*, pp. 397–399.

completely abandoned but for few inhabitants (notably the Jews, who handed the keys to the Sultan), on 11 September. The city was plundered and burned, and after a ten-day stay the Ottoman army set out on its homeward journey.[41] Reportedly, the queen in Pressburg was visited by Ottoman envoys, who expressed the Sultan's sympathy for her misfortune.[42] This could have been not only a courtesy, but also an indication that the death of the king and seizure of the country had not been his intention. Normally the first stage of Ottoman conquest would mean keeping the local administration and bringing the country into a condition of dependency.[43] This can be seen in Suleiman's early departure from Buda and his later backing of János Szapolyai, one of the two contending kings.

Even though Buda passed into Ottoman hands for a longer period only in 1541 (although briefly also in the 1529 campaign), the period of grand court life and ceremonies was ended by the first incursion of the Ottomans. King Louis had gathered an army which was intended to stop the Sultan; he had prayed and displayed his glory, but all in vain. Buda lost its position as the capital of medieval Hungary, and in the longer term the capital shifted to Pressburg, which became the Habsburg seat of the kingdom.

41　Kubinyi, *Budapest*, pp. 200–201; Géza Pálffy, "New Dynasty, New Court, New Political Decision-Making: A Decisive Era in Hungary – The decades following the Battle of Mohács 1526," in *Mary of Hungary*, pp. 27–39, here pp. 27–28.

42　Kalous, *Elfeledett*, p. 621; idem, *Plenitudo potestatis,* p. 405, "…cardinalis Cibo…legit litteras…, quibus significabat tyrannum Turcarum misisse oratores suos ad reginam Ungarię existentem apud Possonium ad condolendum de morte regis Ungarię eius mariti."

43　Cf. Halil Inalcik, "Ottoman Methods of Conquest," *Studia Islamica* 2 (1954), pp. 103–129.

CHAPTER 21

Buda and the Urban Development of East Central Europe

Katalin Szende

The introductory essay of the present volume on medieval Buda poses the question "How relevant?" Now that the reader has reached this final article, we hope that he or she will not only feel persuaded by the arguments presented there, but has reached conclusions of his or her own upon the subject. Here I intend to take up two further, seemingly contradictory questions: 'How typical?' and 'How unique?' In other words, my aim will be to sum up the common traits and the individual features of medieval Buda and contextualize them within the trends of urban development in the high and late Middle Ages in general, and in comparison with a number of other cities and towns in East Central Europe in particular.[1]

The reasons for selecting certain particular cities to be compared with Buda relate to the many functions medieval Buda fulfilled as a social, economic, governmental and religious center, and – first and foremost – as the royal residence and emerging capital of Hungary. Some of the cities considered below, notably Prague, Cracow, Wrocław and Vienna, have already been referred to in several articles in this volume and indeed in numerous other publications, both on account of their direct contacts to Buda and in light of their evident comparability. To complete the circle around the Carpathian Basin, however, it is also useful to consider the princely seats and eventual capitals of Hungary's eastern and southern neighbors: the Romanian principalities (Moldavia and Wallachia), and the kingdoms of Serbia and Bosnia. Cities and towns to be taken into account for these regions include Siret, Suceava, Curtea de Argeș, Târgoviște, Bucharest, Stari Ras, Bobovac, Kraljeva Sutjeska, Belgrade and

---

1 There is not room here to provide a comprehensive bibliographic overview. Let me just refer to a major monograph and two recently edited volumes: Eberhard Isenmann, *Die deutsche Stadt im Mittelalter, 1150–1550* (Cologne–Vienna: Böhlau, 2012); *Europäische Städte im Mittelalter*, eds Ferdinand Opll, Christoph Sonnlechner (Innsbruck–Vienna–Bozen: Studien Verlag, 2009), and *Stadtgründung und Stadtwerdung. Beiträge von Archäologie und Stadtgeschichtsforschung* (Beiträge zur Geschichte der Städte Mitteleuropas, 22), ed. Ferdinand Opll (Linz: Österreichischer Arbeitskreis für Stadtgeschichtsforschung, 2011), which have a good coverage of urban development in the Central European lands as well as of general issues and the pertinent literature.

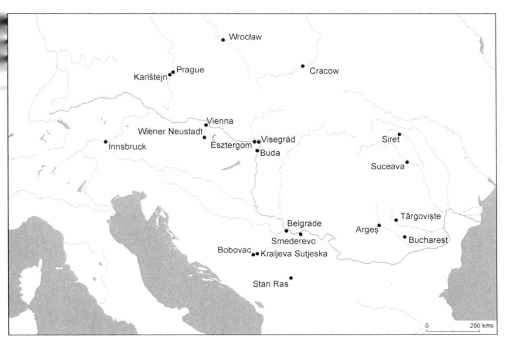

FIGURE 21.1   Residences referred to in the article

Smederevo (Fig. 21.1).[2] Their inclusion is all the more justified as they maintained intensive contacts with Hungary in the Middle Ages, being partners in or targets of diplomatic, military, commercial and ecclesiastic activities and, at times, of expansion.

An impressive amount of research has been devoted to all these centers individually, and there have been a number of studies published that compare two or more of these cities to each other.[3] In order to avoid confusing the

---

2   The best overview on the general trends of urban development in these lands, including Serbia and Bosnia, is given by Laurenţiu Rădvan, *At Europe's Borders: Medieval Towns in the Romanian Principalities* (East Central and Eastern Europe in the Middle Ages, 450–1450, 7) (Leiden: Brill, 2010). Unless indicated otherwise, my information on this region relies on this volume.

3   Some comparative studies include: Derek Keene, "England and Poland. Medieval Metropolises Compared," in *Britain and Poland-Lithuania: Contact and Comparison from the Middle Ages to 1795*, ed. Richard Unger. (Leiden: Brill, 2008), pp. 147–164; *Breslau und Krakau im Hoch- und Spätmittelalter. Stadtgestalt, Wohnraum, Lebensstil* (Städteforschung, A 87), ed. Eduard Mühle (Vienna–Cologne: Böhlau, 2014); Zoë Opačić, "Architecture and Ceremony in Cracow and Prague, 1335–1455," in *Medieval Art, Architecture and Archaeology in Cracow and Lesser*

reader with a plethora of details, I will concentrate here only on those particular natural and man-made features that defined the urban character and topography of the settlements in question; and then, their association with church organization, royalty, and political power.

Strategic Location

More than any other factor, Buda's growth and prosperity was determined by its location on the bank of the Danube. This was not a feature unique to it: no major city (or even biggish town) in medieval Europe was ever able to grow and prosper that lacked access to a seaport or a major, and preferably navigable, river close by. Riverside location was definitive for the cities west and north of Buda: Vienna on the Danube, Prague on the Vltava, Wrocław on the Oder, Cracow on the Vistula. South of the Carpathians, Curtea de Argeş and Târgovişte were located on two tributaries of the Danube, the Argeş and the Ialomiţa respectively; and Siret stood by the river of the same name. Suceava also lies close to its eponymous river, but its site on a plateau was chosen rather for its potential as a stronghold. Likewise, the Serbian and Bosnian centers in the mountainous areas of the Balkans were valued for their defensibility and not so much for their riverside locations. Interestingly, with the last two capitals of the Serbian state, Belgrade and Smederevo, the focus of gravity shifted to the Danube there as well.[4]

For landlocked entities such as the Carpathian Basin, land routes were also crucial arteries of communication, and the ferry places and trans-shipment ports where these routes crossed or connected to the main rivers multiplied the importance of any settlement built beside them.[5] This was another factor in Buda's favor and a feature that it shared with several of the cities listed above. It was of no little importance, however, how broad the river was and how easy it was to ford. Along the course of the Danube the easternmost permanent bridge throughout the Middle Ages was the stone bridge at Regensburg, built

---

Poland (British Archaeological Association Conference Transactions, 37), eds Agnieszka Rożnowska-Sadraei and Tomasz Węcławowicz (Leeds: Maney, 2014), pp. 95–117.

4   Sima Ćirković, "Unfulfilled Autonomy: Urban Society in Serbia and Bosnia," in *Urban Society of Eastern Europe in Premodern Times*, ed. Bariša Krekić (Berkeley: University of California Press, 1987), pp. 158–185; *The Cultural Treasury of Serbia*, ed. Jovan Janićejević (Belgrade: Idea, 2002), *passim*.

5   Peter Csendes, "Die Stadt im Strassennetz," in *Stadt. Strom – Strasse – Schiene. Die Bedeutung des Verkehrs für die Genese der mitteleuropäischen Städtelandschaft,* ed. Alois Niederstätter (Linz: Österreichischer Arbeitskreis für Stadtgeschichtsforschung, 2001), pp. 55–66.

in the mid-twelfth century. Further downstream the river was either too broad, as at Buda, or too divided, as at Vienna, to make the building of permanent bridges (or even durable pontoon bridges) feasible or worthwhile.[6]

In other cases, where rivers typically narrower and shallower than the Danube at Buda allowed the construction of a permanent bridge, it made a huge difference to the communication networks. It enabled the continuous use of land routes and strengthened the connection between the settlements on either riverbank. Bridges like the Judith and later the Charles Bridge over the Vltava at Prague (Fig. 21.2) were typically sponsored by monarchs residing in the city, the former in this case by Wladislas II (1158–1172), who named the city's first stone bridge after his wife, and the latter by Emperor Charles IV (1346–1378), who showed no reluctance to call the remodeled bridge after himself. In Cracow the building of a stone bridge over the Vistula became essential after the foundation of a substantial new settlement on the south bank in 1335. The latter was the initiative of King Kazimierz the Great (1333–1370) and was commemorated by the name of the new town, Kazimierz, as well as by the term *pons regalis* for the bridge.[7] (Fig. 21.3) But at Buda no such plans could be realistically pursued until as late as the mid-nineteenth century. Before that, passage over the river was provided by ferries, the ferrymen being united in a special association under archaic conditions of royal control.[8] In the case of the Romanian and Serbian seats situated at the upper reaches of their respective rivers the routes of communication led rather through the valleys parallel to the rivers. Watercourses were crossed by ferries or at fords, or occasionally on bridges built of wooden planks by bridge workers recruited at the princes' command.[9]

Islands represented a major hindrance to the crossing of rivers wherever the current was not strong enough to remove alluvial deposits, and this could have a negative impact on urban development. For instance, the five separate and

---

6 Peter Schmied, "Regensburg liegt gar schön. Die Gegend musste eine Stadt herlocken," in *Europäische Städte*, pp. 351–364; Peter Csendes, "Urban Development and Decline on the Central Danube, 100–1600," in *Towns in Decline, AD 100–1600*, ed. Terry R. Slater (Aldershot: Ashgate, 2000), pp. 137–153.
7 Opačić, "Architecture," p. 96.
8 András Kubinyi, "Die Anfänge des städtischen Handwerks in Ungarn," in *La formation et le développement des metiers au moyen âge (V^e–XIVe siècles)*, eds László Gerevich and Ágnes Salamon (Budapest: Akadémiai, 1977), pp. 139–153.
9 Laurenţiu Rădvan, "Between Free Passage and Restriction. Roads and Bridges in the Towns of Wallachia and Moldavia (16th–18th century)," in *Towns and Communication*, i. *Communication in Towns*, ed. Neven Budak (Zagreb: Leykam International, 2009), pp. 101–117, here pp. 108–110.

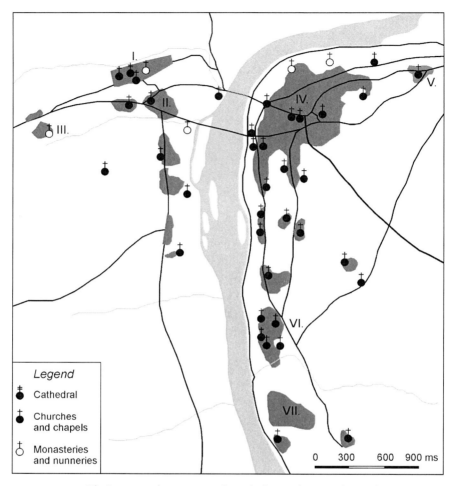

FIGURE 21.2 *The Prague agglomeration in the early thirteenth century (I: Castle; II: Suburbium (later Malá Strana); III: Strahov; IV: Old Town (Staré Mesto); V: Vicus Teutonicum; VI: Suburbium of Vyšehrad; VII: Vyšehrad)*

unstable arms of the Danube at Vienna made it extremely difficult to cross the river there, and even to protect the inhabited lands.[10] Buda's site was fortunate in this respect: it was located along a short but very convenient stretch of the Danube where there was direct access between the left and the right bank. This enabled Buda to form an agglomeration with its twin city, Pest. Prague and Cracow also benefited from a direct connection between both riverbanks.

10   Severin Hohensinner *et al.*, "Changes in Water and Land: the Reconstructed Viennese Riverscape from 1500 to the Present," *Water History* 5 (2013), pp. 145–172.

FIGURE 21.3
Medieval Cracow: the Wawel, the Old Town, Okół, Kazimierz, and Kleparz

Islands could nevertheless be integrated into the urban fabric in various ways or accommodate functions complementing the settlements on the mainland. The relatively small Margaret Island (the medieval *Insula leporum*, i.e. Hares' Island), situated between Buda and Óbuda and conveniently separated from the cities on either riverbank, was an ideal site for ecclesiastical establishments (monasteries), for pilgrimage to the grave of the holy Princess Margaret, and, when need arose, for political negotiations.[11] One of the two major islands in the Oder at Wrocław, the *Dominsel*, was likewise used as an ecclesiastical enclave housing the cathedral and a cluster of monasteries and chapels (Fig. 21.4);[12] Kazimierz, a civic settlement with a royally founded Augustinian friary and

---

11 See Gábor Klaniczay's article in the present volume; on the location and its environment, see András Vadas, "Long-Term Perspectives on River Floods. The Dominican Nunnery on Margaret Island (Budapest) and the Danube River," *Interdisciplinaria Archaeologica – Natural Sciences in Archaeology* 4, no 1 (2013), pp. 73–82.

12 Jerzy Piekalski, *Von Köln nach Krakau. Der topographische Wandel früher Städte* (Bonn: Habelt, 2001), pp. 141–158.

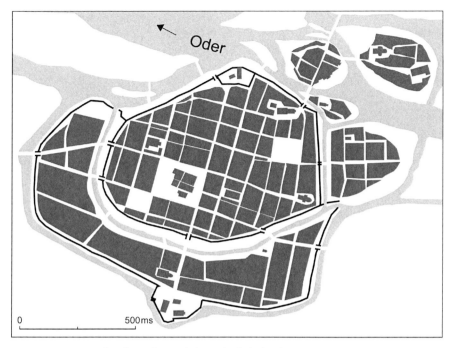

FIGURE 21.4   Medieval Wrocław with the Cathedral Island

later a significant Jewish population, was built on a major island of the Vistula east of Cracow. Numerous other examples could be quoted (Fig. 21.3).

Nature endowed Buda with a further special water-related feature, the hot springs which welled up north and south of the Castle Hill and which were beneficial medicinally as well as for industrial purposes; in addition, by keeping the surface of the river free of ice they allowed watermills and fishermen to work and operate even in the coldest winters. This is, to the best of my knowledge, an advantage that none of the other neighboring princely seats (except for Esztergom, one of Buda's functional predecessors) could boast of. As a distant parallel, the hot springs at Aachen, the favorite seat of Charlemagne and some of his successors, also made it an ideal winter residence;[13] nevertheless Aachen never developed into a fixed capital or a city on the scale of Prague, Cracow, or even Buda.

13   Derek Keene, "Capital Cities in Medieval Europe," in *Håkonshallen 750 Years. Royal Residence and National Monument*, eds Øystein Brekke and Geir Atle Ersland (Oslo: Dreyers Forlag, 2013), pp. 123–156, here p. 128.

As we move further away from the river and into the hinterland, what strikes the eye is the variability of the terrain. Buda, like most other Central European princely seats, was located at the contact zone between hilly and plain areas and was thus able to draw on the resources of different regions. Human geographers have long established the advantages of such locations for market exchange. Often the hilltop used for erecting a royal castle (the Wawel in Cracow, the Hradčany in Prague and the Castle Hill in Buda) was the last peak in a range extending down to the riverbank. The sizes of the hilltops, however, often limited the possibility for expansion. Still higher elevations restricted even more the inhabitable area and the resources for provisioning, as was the case with Curtea de Argeș, the early seat of the Wallachian princes, or with Visegrád, the fourteenth-century residence of the Hungarian kings, not to mention the mountainous environment of the Bosnian royal seats. An exceptional need for security, namely the safekeeping of the imperial regalia, led Charles IV in 1348 to commission one of the most emblematic royal strongholds of Central Europe, Karlštejn Castle. On this location about 30 km southwest of Prague, a promontory somewhat resembling the site of the Upper Castle at Visegrád, no more than a small village could be placed under the fortification.

Buda's environs did not offer overly much space for expansion either, but Óbuda further north, and especially Pest on the flat left bank, were ideally placed for facilitating settlement growth. Pest provided space for mills, tanneries, and a cattle market, but also for meetings of the diets of the realm.[14] Indeed, the composite structure of most Central European capitals can be accounted for by their varied terrain, as we shall see when discussing the topography of these cities' built-up areas. In Buda's broader hinterland, the Pilis royal forest was the most dominant feature. The importance of hunting in projecting royal prestige has long been recognized for many European monarchs. The concept of the Royal Forest as a legal entity was, however, often associated with the itinerant ruler and not so closely tied to the capital. Areas such as Vincennes near Paris or Windsor near London were set aside for hunting, but Buda's location was even more fortunate in this respect, with the Pilis reaching practically to the king's doorstep.[15] The forest kept together the center of the realm, the *medium regni*, from the inside, while the bending Danube framed it from the outside.

In the vast forested lands of the inner Balkans and the outer range of the Carpathians securing areas for hunting was less of a challenge. Nevertheless,

---

14   See the study by János M. Bak and András Vadas in the present volume, with references to European comparisons.
15   See the study by Péter Szabó in the present volume.

control of the forests was an important royal or princely prerogative in the Romanian principalities as much as in Serbia and Bosnia, as testified by royal or princely privileges given to mining settlements allowing them to cut down trees according to their needs.[16] The close proximity of forests, however, was so common everywhere that it did not play any particular role when it came to choosing sites for princely seats.

Besides natural endowments, often pre-existing man-made facilities played a role in determining the sites of medieval cities and princely seats. Prehistoric settlers had already discovered which sites were most suitable for human habitation; but it was first and foremost the remains left behind by the Romans that most impressed their medieval successors. In Western Europe and in the Holy Roman Empire one finds cases of 'natural' continuity determined by the geographical setting, but also deliberate revivals. The prime example of the latter was Paris, where the Merovingian king Clovis consciously chose as his residence the palace of Julian, the last of the Constantinian emperors, on the Île de la Cité (another important island!).[17]

However, in East Central Europe the Roman heritage did not have a decisive impact in the long run. Prague, Wrocław or Cracow became just as significant centers as Vienna or Belgrade that had been part of the *Imperium Romanum*, being the sites of the legionary camps of Vindobona and Singidunum respectively. Buda in this respect was in an intermediate position: the Roman predecessor Aquincum, likewise a seat of a legion, had a strong impact on Óbuda, and the suburban parts of Buda by the Danube and the road along the riverbank were in use in Roman times.[18] However, the area of the Castle Hill and much of Pest (apart from the small fortress of Contra Aquincum, already in the *Barbaricum*) were 'green-field developments' of the Middle Ages, as were all the seats in the countries surrounding Hungary to the north, east and south.

To recapitulate the issues of location and environment: Buda shared many common features with other Central European royal and princely seats, such as being located by a major watercourse, at a stretch favorable for crossing; being embedded in the network of land routes; and having the advantage of an elevated point for building a fortified seat. It was also centrally placed within the realm, a consideration likewise relevant when, for instance, the site of Stari Ras in Serbia was chosen or when the seat of Wallachia was moved from Curtea de Argeş to Târgovişte, and subsequently to Bucharest. The main

16   Rădvan, *At Europe's Borders*, p. 92 note 19.
17   Philippe Lorentz and Dany Sandron, *Atlas de Paris au moyen âge. Espace urbain, habitat, société, religion, lieux de pouvoir* (Paris: Parigramme, 2006), pp. 19–23.
18   See the studies by Enikő Spekner and András Végh in the present volume.

impediment was the hilly terrain which limited territorial growth, a drawback which could be partly compensated, as in the case of Prague, by expanding to the opposite riverbank; but in Buda's case the lack of a permanent link in the form of a bridge due to the width of the Danube here made this less of a possibility. The presence of hot springs and the closeness of the royal forest were, however, advantages that few other seats enjoyed.

Urban Layout

The need for a residence (or residences) belongs to the ruler's dignity and can always be traced back to the period of state foundation – a process that took place at different times in the different states of Central Europe. In consequence, the challenges and solutions were also different. The castles of Cracow and Prague were both erected on hilltops in the course of the tenth century, with the significant difference that in case of the latter the size and shape of the hilltop allowed for substantial settlements on the slopes of the Castle Hill (the Hradčany and Malá Strana); in contrast, the Wawel in Cracow only had room to accommodate a princely residence plus a small number of ecclesiastical establishments. The civic quarters (Okół) had to be relegated to the back side of the hill, further away from the river (Figs 21.2–21.3).

Hungarian royal seats had common traits with both of these cities.[19] The first residence, Esztergom, had more in common with Cracow, with the castle hill providing just enough room for the cathedral, its chapter, another collegiate church, and the royal palace. The scarcity of space became apparent when King Béla IV, aghast at the total destruction of the civic quarters by the Mongols in 1241–1242, attempted – quite unsuccessfully – to move the whole population to the Castle Hill. This experience probably contributed to his eventual decision to give up Esztergom as a royal seat.[20] Buda, in its turn, shows more similarity with Prague, because the Castle Hill was in both cases long and broad enough to contain a royal residence as well as a civic quarter. The big difference was, however, that Prague Castle was already fortified before any civic settlement was established, whereas in Buda the castle at the southern tip of the hill was in all likelihood only built as a later addition, partly by

---

19   See the study by Károly Magyar in the present volume, with ample literature on Prague and Cracow.

20   See in more detail: Katalin Szende and András Végh, "Royal Power and Urban Space in Medieval Hungary," in *Lords and Towns in Medieval Europe: Maps and Texts*, eds Anngret Simms and Howard B. Clarke (Farnham: Ashgate 2015, pp. 255–286).

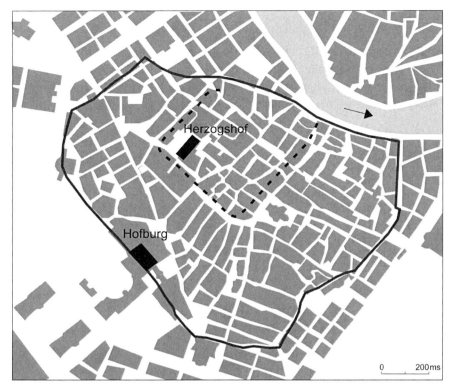

FIGURE 21.5   Medieval Vienna with the old (Herzogshof) and new (Hofburg) princely residences

expropriating and demolishing a good number of urban houses.[21] Here the entire hilltop was perceived as an extended castle, in which the burghers' houses were included, the king's early 'town house', the thirteenth-century *Kammerhof* on the north-eastern part of the hilltop, being but one of them.[22]

In some Central European seats the princely residences lay on flat land: in Wrocław on an island protected by the arms of the Oder (just as the Cité in Paris was by the Seine) (Fig. 21.4); in Vienna the first court (Herzogshof), built in the mid-twelfth century, was situated within the perimeter of the Roman legionary camp and defended by the ancient walls (Fig. 21.5). This arrangement reminds one of Óbuda's castle (Budavára), where the first royal house

21 Cf. Susan Reynolds, *Before Eminent Domain: Toward a History of Expropriation of Land for the Common Good* (Chapel Hill: UNC Press, 2010).

22 See the articles by András Végh and Károly Magyar in the present volume. See also András Végh, "Urban Development and Royal Initiative in the Central Part of the Kingdom of Hungary in the 13th–14th centuries: Comparative Analysis of the Development of the Towns of Buda and Visegrád," in *Stadtgründung und Stadtwerdung*, pp. 431–446.

was likewise built within the circuit of the late Roman fortifications (even if not inside the former camp area). The parallel continues in the early thirteenth century, when both residences were rebuilt on new and more peripheral sites compared to their predecessors. The big difference was, however, that Vienna's Hofburg leaned against a town wall encircling the entire built-up area of its time, whereas Óbuda as a medieval town was never fortified.[23]

In this sense Óbuda resembles the seats of some Romanian principalities which were likewise not encircled by town walls. The establishing of the rulers' seats during the fourteenth and fifteenth centuries is attested either in chronicles, as in the case of Siret,[24] or by archaeological evidence as with Curtea de Argeș and Târgoviște. In Suceava (Fig. 21.6) there were simultaneously two princely residences: a palace in the very center of the settlement, next to the market place, and a stronghold on higher ground further east.[25] Town walls encircling virtually the entire inhabited area are attested only for Suceava and Târgoviște. The early princely seats in Serbia and Bosnia included a fortified citadel (Gradina in Stari Ras) or palaces (Bobovac, Sutjeska), but no walls around the settlement below them.[26] All these princely buildings played a dominant role in the creation and spatial structuring of the settlements around them. The two latest seats of medieval Serbia, Belgrade and Smederevo (Fig. 21.7), built and fortified in the face of the Ottoman threat, united the castles and the surrounding settlements by the strongest possible bonds. Even these extraordinary efforts proved to be futile against the Ottoman military machinery; but that is already a different story.[27]

The construction of town walls often accompanied the founding of new towns, especially in disorderly areas and near frontiers; in this respect Buda displays parallels to various other regions in thirteenth-century Europe. At the same time, town walls could serve the display of status rather than defence. There were many different intentions behind town foundations, from aggressive military expansion (Edward I in Wales) through the fighting of heresy (Louis IX in southern France) to the colonization of new lands and the establishing

---

23 See Enikő Spekner's article in the present volume and István Feld, "Ecilburg und Ofen – zur Problematik der Stadtburgen in Ungarn," *Castrum Bene* 6 (1999), pp. 73–88.

24 *Siret/Sereth. Atlas istoric al orașelor din România/Städtegeschichteatlas Rumäniens* (Serie A: Moldova, Fasc. 2), ed. Dan Dumitru Iacob (Bucharest: Editura Enciclopedică, 2010). The remains of the princely residence that was located supposedly in the vicinity of the orthodox church of the Holy Trinity have not been identified by archaeological research.

25 *Suceava/Suczawa. Atlas istoric al orașelor din România/Städtegeschichteatlas Rumäniens* (Serie A: Moldova, Fasc. 1), ed. Mircea D. Matei (Bucharest: Editura Enciclopedică, 2005), p. 9/IX.

26 *The Cultural Treasury of Serbia*, pp. 476–477.

27 David Norris, *Belgrade: A Cultural History* (Oxford: Oxford Univresity Press, 2009), pp. 4–9.

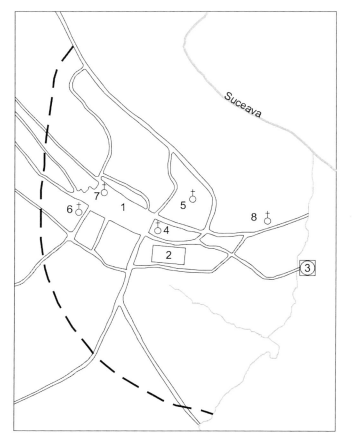

FIGURE 21.6   Suceava in the fifteenth century after Laurențiu Rădvan (1: Marketplace [Piața Principala]; 2. Ruler's palace; 3: Stronghold [Cetatea de Scaun]; 4: Catholic church around 1400 [later Biserica Sf. Dumitru]; 5. Catholic church after 1475 [destroyed]; 6: St Simeon [later Biserica Sf. Cruce]; 7: St. Mary [destroyed]; 8. Biserica Sf. Georghe [Mirauți])

of trading outposts (the Teutonic Order in Pomerania), or the consolidation of rulership in already established realms.[28] Town foundations or extensions in Central Europe in the thirteenth and fourteenth centuries fall into this latter category of 'internal colonization'. It has been debated how far the ravages of the Mongol invasion of 1241–1242 and their much feared reappearance in the

28   Keith Lilley, *City and Cosmos: The Medieval World in Urban Form* (London: Reaktion Books, 2009), pp. 45–53; Roman Czaja, "Die Anfänge Preußischer Hansestädte im Lichte historischen und archäologischen Quellen: Danzig/Gdańsk, Elbing/Elbląg, Thorn/Toruń," in *Stadtgründung und Stadtwerdung*, pp. 59–74.

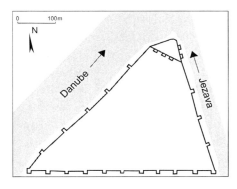

FIGURE 21.7
Smederevo, castle and walls built between
1428 and 1459

second half of the century contributed to the impetus to establish new towns. The current consensus is that it may have acted at times as a catalyst, accelerating the course of events, but without changing them fundamentally.[29]

The new center of Wrocław is a case in point (Fig. 21.4). It is attested in several sources that the city suffered major destruction from the Mongols and it was following this that the new, regularly planned settlement on the left bank of the Oder with its grid plan and impressive market square took shape. Recent research has made it clear, however, that the location of new settlers (*locatio* being the actual word used by contemporaries) and the transformation of the episcopal and princely seat into a predominantly commercial city had been initiated by Henry the Bearded, duke of Silesia (1201–1238) already in the decades preceding the Mongols, and the ensuing development continued well into the next century.[30]

Cracow's new town developed north of the first civic *suburbium* of Okół, due to the impetus of the first *locatio* in the 1220s; the regularly re-planned town was chartered by Bolesław the Chaste in 1257 (Fig. 21.3). Subsequent events, including the devastation by the Mongol army, showed many similarities to the Silesian case. One reason for the building of the town walls under Wenceslas II, king of Bohemia (1278–1305), remembered as the ruler who "surrounded the whole city of Cracow with walls,"[31] was to withstand a possible repeated Mongol attack; yet

---

29   See the studies collected in *Rechtsstadtgründungen im mittelalterlichen Polen* (Städteforschung, A 81), ed. Eduard Mühle (Cologne–Vienna: Böhlau, 2011).

30   Piekalski, *Von Köln*, pp. 172–176; Benedykt Zientara, *Heinrich der Bärtige und seine Zeit. Politik und Gesellschaft im mittelalterlichen Schlesien* (Munich: Oldenbourg, 2002); Jerzy Rozpędowski, "Breslau zur Zeit der ersten Lokation," in *Rechtsstadtgründungen*, pp. 127–138, esp. Fig. 1 on p. 135.

31   "civitatem Cracoviensem ex integro muravit" – see: Opačić, "Architecture," p. 95; Jerzy Wyrozumski, "Eine Gründung oder mehrere Gründungen Krakaus nach deutschem Recht?" in *Rechtsstadtgründungen*, pp. 245–274.

the outside threat only speeded up processes that had already set roots. The grid model applied in the new town proved to be so successful that it was copied in laying out the northern suburb, Kleparz, and a century later in Kazimierz.[32] The foundation of the New Town of Prague by Charles IV in 1348 likewise followed the principle of a regularly planned settlement, but on an even grander scale.[33]

These examples indicate that founding new towns or restructuring/relocating existing settlements was not restricted in space and time to areas affected by the Mongol invasion but was a regular practice in Central Europe from the 1220s onwards. There were hundreds of larger or smaller urban settlements planted all over Bohemia, Moravia, Silesia, and the various Polish provinces, the best-known examples being, besides the ones already cited, Plzeň (Pilsen), České Budějovice (Budweis), Sandomierz, Toruń (Thorn) and Poznań (Posen). Most of them fulfilled their founders' intentions in consolidating their dominance over their territories. New settlers were attracted by the "equal opportunities" embodied in the newly laid out, identically sized burgage plots, and the clearly defined rights and obligations based on their ownership. The regular grid plan was apparently the most efficient way of accommodating these plots as basic units of urban society and economy.[34]

In the case of the princely seats of the Romanian principalities, Serbia and Bosnia, the existing written or cartographic sources seldom allow definitive statements to be made about the internal settlement structures, but recent archaeological and topographic research has thrown some light on these questions. Wherever it has been possible to identify streets as well as public and private buildings, what was striking about the internal structure has been "the apparently unplanned distribution of buildings and plots in the built-up areas."[35] This irregularity can be regarded as a reflection of the heterogeneous social and legal standing of the local population. More recent research, however, has also identified cases where at least certain parts of the towns were regularly planned, in accordance with the ruler's intentions. The surroundings

---

32 *Krakow. Atlas Historyczny Miast Polskich/Historical Atlas of Polish Towns* (Vol. V. Part 1), ed. Zdzysław Noga (Cracow: Towarzystwo Miłośników Historii, 2007).

33 Vilém Lorenc, *Das Prag Karls IV. Die Prager Neustadt* (Stuttgart: SNTL, 1982); Paul Crossley and Zoë Opačić, "Prague as a New Capital," in *Prague: the Crown of Bohemia. Exhibition Catalogue*, eds Barbara Drake Boehm and Jiří Fajt (New Haven: Yale University Press, 2005), pp. 59–73.

34 Piekalski, *Von Köln*, pp. 170–194; Bogusław Krasnowolski, "Muster urbanistischer Anlagen in Lokationsstädten in Kleinpolen. Forschungsstand, Methoden, und Versuch einer Synthese," in *Rechtsstadtgründungen*, pp. 275–322; Keith Lilley, *Urban Life in the Middle Ages 1000–1450* (Basingstoke: Palgrave, 2002), pp. 148–163 and 192–211.

35 Rădvan, "Between Free Passage," p. 102.

of Suceava's royal palace from Petru I's reign (1375–1391) onwards is one such example (Fig. 21.6), the area of St Mary's Church in Târgoviște another; both of them were connected to the presence of Saxon settlers.[36] Fixed legal conditions based on royal statutes were likewise set down in the case of the mining towns of Serbia and Bosnia; the physical surroundings of these settlements, however, determined by the location of the mineral resources in mountainous regions, did not allow the implementation of any sort of grid layout.[37]

Town foundations and urban layout in Hungary in general and in Buda in particular seem to have shown features of both of these models. The first and most immediate reaction to the shock of 1241–1242, and especially to Béla IV's flight to the Dalmatian coast and the cities that he saw on his way, was the foundation of the town of Gradec on a hilltop overlooking the eleventh-century bishop's seat of Zagreb.[38] This can be considered Béla's first experiment with a planned new town, where the reconstructed layout of equal-sized plots follows a checker-board plan, slightly adjusted to the irregularities of the terrain.[39]

The new city of Buda on the Castle Hill, as it was conceived probably a few years later, was likewise a direct result of the "fear of the Mongols". As King Béla stated in his letter to the pope around 1250, he had no choice but to build fortifications along the Danube to protect the whole of Christendom: "for it is the river of resistance."[40] Buda, partly a relocation of Pest and Óbuda, and partly a brand new fortified town, was one among these strongholds.[41] This is why the city wall, a full ring of defensive structures made of solid stone surrounding the entire hilltop, was the primary built feature of the new settlement.

36 Rădvan, *At Europe's Borders*, pp. 296 and 536, with references to the Romanian literature.
37 Ćirković, "Unfulfilled autonomy," pp. 161–175; Kovačević-Kojić, Desanka. "Le développement économique des agglomérations urbaines sur le territoire actuel de la Yougoslavie du XIIIe au XVe siècle," in *Actes du IIe Congrès International des études du sud-est européen*, ii. *Histoire* (Athens: [N.p.], 1972), pp. 167–185; Dubravko Lovrenović, "Medieval Bosnia and Central European Culture: interweaving and acculturation," *Forum Bosnae* 15 (2002), pp. 207–237.
38 Klaus-Detlev Grothusen, *Entstehung und Geschichte Zagrebs bis zum Ausgang des 14. Jahrhunderts: ein Beitrag zum Städtewesen Südosteuropas im Mittelalter* (Wiesbaden: Harrasowitz, 1967); Ludwig Steindorff, "Das mittelalterliche Zagreb – ein Paradigma der mitteleuropäischen Stadtgeschichte," *Südosteuropa Mitteilungen* 35 (1995), pp. 135–145; on the foundation in the context in Béla IV's new urban policy: Szende and Végh, "Royal power", pp. 269–279.
39 Vladimir Bedenko, *Zagrebački Gradec. Kuća i grad u srednjem vijeku* [The Gradec of Zagreb. House and town in the Middle Ages] (Zagreb: Školska knjiga, 1989).
40 "haec est enim aqua contradictionis" – Cf. CD, iv/2, pp. 218–224.
41 On the legal aspects of relocation or foundation, see Martyn Rady's study in the present volume.

The shape of the plateau thus encircled excluded the implementation of any grid plan, but a systematic process of plot layout was nevertheless carried out, the regular-sized plots measured out in parallel rows following the line of the walls to cover the whole available area.[42] The regular layout can be followed, often better than on the surface, in the arrangement of the cellars cut into the soft limestone of the hill.[43] Later royal interventions did not fundamentally disturb the system, but they increasingly encroached on the town by continuous northward extensions of the royal palace, while in its foreground a sort of 'buffer zone' of ecclesiastical establishments was introduced.[44]

Bolder plans yet may have been envisaged for Pest, where the flat terrain lent itself more readily to the expansion of the built-up area. Although there is no explicit written evidence for it, it is perhaps not unreasonable to assume that the extension of the town walls of Pest owed much to King Sigismund's patronage and that in so doing the monarch may have been seeking to emulate his father's achievement in the New Town of Prague.[45] The final, somewhat better documented, yet never implemented medieval restructuring of the Hungarian capital, was Matthias Corvinus's bold plan to redesign a section of Buda as an ideal Renaissance city – a project that would have connected Buda to Italian urbanism rather than Central Europe, but which never came to fruition.[46]

To round off this comparative overview of urban layouts, however sketchy, one further feature deserves mention. Many significant royal seats in Central Europe were not unified single settlements, but conglomerates of settlements of different sizes and legal standings, each of them enjoying autonomy

---

42   See the study by András Végh in the present volume and the works referred to there.

43   Balázs Szabó, "A budavári barlangpincék kialakításának oka és eddigi funkcióinak vizsgálata a 13. századi (első) telekosztás tükrében," [The formation of cave cellars in Buda Castle and their functions with regard to the first plot allocation in the thirteenth century] *Mérnökgeológia – Kőzetmechanika 2013* [Engineering geology – rock mechanics], ed. Á. Török *et al.* (Budapest: BME, 2014), pp. 241–276.

44   On the extensions of the palace, see the articles by Károly Magyar and Szilárd Papp in the present volume. The buffer zone is described by József Laszlovszky, "Crown, Gown and Town. Zones of Royal, Ecclesiastical and Civic Interaction in Medieval Buda and Visegrád," in *Segregation – Integration – Assimilation. Religious and Ethnic Groups in the Medieval Towns of Central and Eastern Europe* (Historical Urban Studies), eds Derek Keene, Balázs Nagy and Katalin Szende (Farnham: Ashgate, 2009), pp. 179–203.

45   On Prague see note 33, above. The analogy with Pest was first suggested in Katalin Szende, "Geschichte und Archäologie bei der Erforschung der mittelalterlichen Stadtentwicklung in Ungarn – Die Ebenen der Zusammenarbeit," in *Geschichte und Archäologie: Disziplinäre Interferenzen*, eds Armand Baeriswyl, Martina Stercken and Dölf Wild (Zurich: Chronos, 2009), pp. 193–202, here p. 199.

46   See the study by Valery Rees in the present volume.

and having their own separate governance. The prime examples of extensive agglomerations in Central Europe besides Buda are Prague, Cracow, and, later, Berlin and Warsaw.[47] These structures were the result not simply of geographical fragmentation or protracted development over time, but more specifically of the division of roles and activities, secular and sacred alike, which allowed the preservation of a complex system of legal autonomies. As far as the princely seats south and east of the Carpathian Basin are concerned, this compartmentalization cannot be observed in the same way. Since there were seldom defensive circuits around the settlements, and their administrative autonomy was not particularly strong or exclusive, there were no limits set to expansion, and, even with low population density, "towns seemed to occupy vast tracts of land in the eye of the visiting foreigner."[48]

Sacred Sites and Ecclesiastic Institutions

Recent research has pointed out the role of complex settlement structures in the sacralization of urban landscapes and in the expanded display of royal authority in many parts of Europe.[49] Having examined the issues of the city's site selection and layout and compared them with the neighboring royal and princely seats, I shall now turn to the questions of ecclesiastical foundations and sacrality and show how these offer yet another angle from which to approach the specific traits of Buda's medieval development.

In terms of ecclesiastical hierarchy, Buda ranks surprisingly low: it was not the seat of an archbishopric or bishopric throughout its medieval history – in fact, it was not until 1993 that Budapest became an adjunct seat of the archdiocese of Esztergom. This mismatch between political and ecclesiastical status, however, is not unheard of in medieval Central Europe, at least as far as archbishoprics are concerned. In Poland the only medieval archbishopric was founded in Gniezno, and the church organization of the Czech lands was governed until 1344 from the archbishopric of Mainz, while the Austrian provinces were under the authority of Passau and Salzburg respectively. Even so,

---

47 György Székely, "Städtische Agglomeration im Osten Mitteleuropas (13.–15. Jh.): Berlin, Buda, Prag, Krakau," in *Mittelalterliche Häuser und Strassen in Mitteleuropa*, eds Márta Font and Mária Sándor (Budapest–Pécs: MTA, 2000), pp. 9–16.
48 Rădvan, "Between free passage," p. 103.
49 Zoë Opačić, "The Sacred Topography of Medieval Prague," in *Sacred Sites and Holy Places*, eds Sæbjørg Walaker Nordeide and Stefan Brink (Turnhout: Brepols, 2013), pp. 253–281; Opačić, "Architecture."

bishoprics were founded in all the important seats around the turn of the tenth century, including Cracow, Wrocław and Prague, the latter being elevated to the rank of archbishopric in 1344 due to the efforts of Charles IV. The exception to prove the rule was Vienna, where, after unsuccessful attempts in the previous centuries, a diocese was established as late as 1469 under Frederick III of Habsburg, who simultaneously acquired the same status from the pope for his favorite seat, Wiener Neustadt.[50] This example makes the contrast with Buda even more striking. The explanation lies in part with the late foundation of Buda, but especially in the fact that the church hierarchy of Hungary was so firmly based on the archdiocese of Esztergom, the archbishop of which had the exclusive right of crowning the king, that no ruler considered it advisable to initiate any changes to the existing structures.

The low status of Buda in ecclesiastical matters stands out also in comparison with princely and royal seats further east or south. In the Romanian principalities during the state formation processes in the fourteenth century both early seats, Siret in Moldavia (Fig. 21.8) and Curtea de Argeş in Wallachia, became seats of Catholic bishoprics, founded in 1371 and 1381 respectively, with the strong involvement of the Franciscan order. In the long run, however, sees of the Metropolitan Orthodox Church became dominant. The first Orthodox see at Curtea de Argeş was established in 1359 and transferred in 1517 to Târgovişte, the new capital; Suceava in Moldavia obtained a see at the same time. Each of these changes was initiated by the respective princes.[51] In Serbia, sees of the autocephalous Orthodox Church, founded around 1220, were located instead in large monasteries (Žiča, Gračanica, and others) and not in cities, their strong connection to the ruling family being manifest through personal control and patronage of these monasteries.[52]

To westerners, both medieval and modern, Buda's small number of parish churches, the main form of ecclesiastical organization 'on the ground', may seem surprising for a major city, especially compared to the more than one hundred medieval parishes in London, or even to the seven to nine parishes in many small French towns.[53] This should not be taken, however, as a sign

---

50   Peter Csendes and Ferdinand Opll, *Wien. Geschichte einer Stadt*, i. *Von den Anfängen bis zur ersten Türkenbelagerung (1529)* (Cologne–Vienna–Weimar: Böhlau, 2001), p. 323; Richard Perger, "Die Ungarische Herrschaft über Wien 1485–1490 und ihre Vorgeschichte," *Wiener Geschichtsblätter* 45 (1990), pp. 53–87.

51   Rădvan, *At Europe's Borders*, pp. 244–245 (Curtea de Argeş); 301 (Târgovişte); 530 (Siret) and 537–541 (Suceava).

52   Ćirković, "Unfulfilled Autonomy," p. 160. An Orthodox bishopric was also established in the wealthy mining town of Novo Brdo.

53   Marie-Madeleine de Cevins, *L'Église dans les villes hongroises à la fin du Moyen Âge (vers 1320 – vers 1490)* (Publications de l'Institut Hongrois de Paris – Université de Szeged/

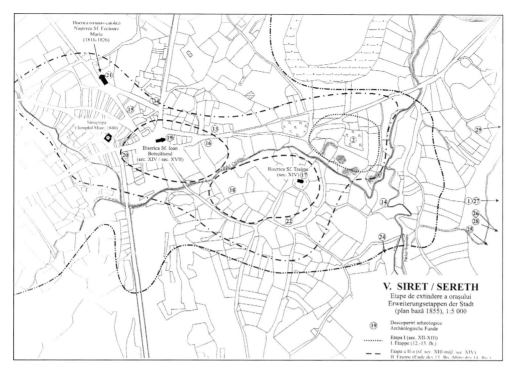

FIGURE 21.8   *Siret in the fourteenth and fifteenth centuries*

of any 'underdevelopment' of the parish system, but rather as a product of the period when they took shape. In settlement landscapes with a rich and continuous tradition since the tenth century, like the agglomeration on both banks of the Vltava between Prague Castle and the other early royal center, Vyšehrad, about 3.5 km further south, more than two dozen churches were established (Fig. 21.2).[54]

In general terms, the number of parishes depended on whether growth in the cities in question took place before or after the impact of Gregorian Reform around 1100. Post-reform bishops tended to restrict the foundation of parochial churches so that they would have sufficient funds to maintain the clergy and the cure of souls. In contrast, in the thirteenth century the 'norm' for new towns all over Europe was one parish per town, and any higher number than that usually means that the town had an earlier origin or composite

Dissertationes, 1) (Budapest–Paris–Szeged: METEM, 2003), Ch. 1 ("Les insuffisances du réseau paroissial"), pp. 23–48.

54   Piekalski, *Von Köln*, pp. 105–110 and Fig. 35.

structure.[55] Thus large towns in the thirteenth century which had grown up after the reform could have fewer parish churches than smaller towns which had developed earlier. Even Vienna, elevated to a ducal seat in 1137 by Leopold IV of Babenberg, followed a similar pattern. Soon after the parish church dedicated to St Stephen (the later Stephansdom) became the main parish, the earlier churches that had up to then fulfilled parish functions (the Ruprechtkirche, the Petruskirche and the Maria am Gestade church) were donated to the Schottenstift (Fig. 21.5).[56] Regarding Silesia and Little Poland (represented by Wrocław and Cracow in our sample), recent research has been intent on identifying stages of a 'nucleation' process of the urban population around a few, topographically well-positioned parish churches – fewer than in the first phases of settlement.[57] In Buda, the four parishes had distinct functions: Our Lady's in the middle of the hilltop (a.k.a. the "Matthias Church"), the only church that had parish rights at the time of the city's foundation, served the German population. St Peter Martyr's was built for the inhabitants of the Danube suburb, and, somewhat later, St Mary Magdalene's on the northern end of the hilltop won parish rights for the Hungarian community. The fourth parish, that of St Gerard's, became part of Buda's church network when the suburb of Alhévíz (*Calidae Aquae Inferiores*) was placed under Buda's jurisdiction.[58]

In the Romanian princely seats the situation was even more complex. Catholic and Orthodox parishes and parish churches were established side by side as part of the princes' settlement policy, and in Siret and Suceava the Armenian communities also had their own churches.[59] In Orthodox Serbia, Catholic parishes were established instead in the mining towns and not in the princely seats, whereas in Bosnia the fourteenth- and fifteenth-century kings embraced Catholicism and put the Franciscan Order in charge of the parish system in their own seats as well as in other towns.

---

55 András Kubinyi, "Stadt und Kirche in Ungarn im Mittelalter," in *Stadt und Kirche* (Beiträge zur Geschichte der Städte Mitteleuropas, 13), ed. Franz-Heinz Hye (Linz: Österreichischer Arbeitskreis für Stadtgeschichtsforschung, 1995), pp. 179–197.

56 See the entries on these churches in Felix Czeike, *Historisches Lexikon Wien* (Vienna: Kremayr & Scheriau, 1992–2004). Online version: www.wien.gv.at/wiki/index.php/Sakralbau (last accessed: 5 January 2015).

57 Marek Słoń, "Fundatio civitatis. Städtische Lokation und kirchliches Stiftungsprogramm in Breslau, Krakau und Posen," in *Rechtsstadtgründungen*, pp. 107–126.

58 See András Végh's article in the present volume.

59 Rădvan, *At Europe's Borders,* pp. 245 (Curtea de Argeş); 301 (Târgovişte); 530–533 (Siret) and 537–541 (Suceava).

Religious orders were the third main contributor to the ecclesiastical landscape of the cities.[60] These operated in the loosely defined spiritual (and physical) space between the rulers and the burghers, between 'crown and town'. An intricate network of monasteries and nunneries, collegiate chapters and convents developed in all the cities under review. They included the old Benedictine nunnery beside St George's Church in Prague and the Premonstratensian abbey in Strahov, connected to the episcopal see, and a number of princely foundations, such as the Benedictine abbey at Tyniec near Cracow, the monastery of the Augustinian canons on Sand Island in Wrocław and the Schottenstift, an abbey of Irish monks in Vienna. A further characteristic feature was the presence of military orders in practically all early Central European seats where Latin Christianity was predominant. Foundations such as the Hospitallers in Prague, the Teutonic Order in Vienna, or the Knights of the Holy Sepulchre in Wrocław testify to the sponsorship of princely patrons who were actively involved in supporting the Crusaders.[61]

A new wave of monastic foundations, namely the appearance of the mendicant orders in the first decades of the thirteenth century, coincided with the foundation and spatial reorganization of cities and towns in Central Europe. The results are seen in the settlement in the 1220s–1230s of both the Franciscans and the Dominicans in Prague, Cracow, Wrocław and Vienna on exceptionally favorable sites compared to their locations in West European cities, more frequently within than outside the city walls, often in already existing parish churches which were then re-dedicated in consequence. A further common feature was the intensive royal or princely involvement in these early mendicant foundations, in contrast to cities in Western Europe where such friaries were established with strong civic participation. This may be taken to reflect conscious princely foundation programs which aimed at enhancing the status of their seats through the settling of these new orders. The topographic expression of this intention may have been the intermediate position of the friaries along roads that connected the princely residence to the city center, like in the above mentioned cases of Cracow, Wrocław and Vienna.[62]

60   Piekalski, *Von Köln,* pp. 127–134.
61   See selected studies in *Monarchische und adlige Sakralstiftungen im mittelalterlichen Polen,* ed. Eduard Mühle (Stiftungsgeschichten, 9) (Berlin: Akademie, 2012), esp. József Dobosz, "Herzogliche und adlige Stiftungstätigkeit im Piastischen Polen des 12. Jahrhunderts," ibid., pp. 201–268, here p. 249.
62   Słoń, "Fundatio civitatis," pp. 115–125; Piekalski, *Von Köln,* pp. 228–230; Béla Zsolt Szakács, "Early Mendicant Architecture in Medieval Hungary," in *Monastic Architecture and the City* (CES Contexto, Debates, 6 [June 2014]), ed. Caterina Almeida Marado (Coimbra: Centre for Social Studies – Associate Laboratory University of Coimbra, 2014), pp. 23–34.

In Buda and its agglomeration the traditional monastic orders were absent due to Buda's relatively late foundation (apart from an insignificant Premonstratensian provostry on Margaret Island and the wealthy Hospitaller convent of Felhévíz, between Óbuda and Buda – a good parallel to the houses of the military orders mentioned above). In contrast there was an overwhelming presence of the mendicants: before the 1280s there were no less than three Dominican and four Franciscan friaries in the agglomeration embracing Buda, Pest and Óbuda, to which can be added the houses of the Austin friars and the Carmelites. All were founded with strong royal patronage.[63] The wealthiest religious houses, however, were not these but two nunneries, the Dominicans on Margaret Island and the Poor Clares of Óbuda. The latter was the only one in the Buda agglomeration with a female founder, namely Elizabeth Piast (1305–1380), but there is a parallel in the Franciscan nunneries established a century earlier by Agnes of Bohemia (1211–1282, cousin of St Elizabeth of Hungary) in Prague and by her sister, Anne (1204–1265), duchess of Silesia, in Wrocław. The most peculiar feature of Buda's monastic landscape was, however, the presence of an eremitic (!) order, the Paulines. It must be more than a coincidence that the center of this order, which had previously possessed three important houses in the Pilis royal forest, moved closer to Buda during the fourteenth century, when the palace at the southern end of the Castle Hill was extended.[64]

The mendicant orders, particularly the Franciscans, were present in princely seats in Wallachia, Moldavia and Bosnia as well. In Moldavia and Bosnia they went beyond their 'customary' missionary activities and – in the absence of secular clergy – formed parishes of Latin Christianity,[65] and in Siret even a bishop's see. The friaries relied for patronage not only on the rulers of the neighboring Catholic countries, Poland and Hungary, but also on members of the local princely families. In Siret, for instance, the Dominicans were invited by Petru I's mother, Margaret. From the fifteenth century, the importance of the Orthodox monasteries, however, clearly outweighed that of any other religious establishment. In Târgoviște, the four monasteries in the vicinity of the city had encroached so much on urban land by the early sixteenth century that "their presence begins to alter the normal course of urban development".[66]

---

63 See the details in Beatrix F. Romhányi's article in this volume.
64 Besides Beatrix F. Romhányi's and András Végh's articles in this volume, see Zsuzsa Eszter Pető, *The Medieval Landscape of Pauline Monasteries in Pilis Forest*, unpublished MA thesis (Budapest: Central European University, 2014). Available online: http://goya.ceu.hu/search/aPet%C5%91%2C%20Zsuzsa (last accessed 5 January 2015).
65 Lovrenović, "Medieval Bosnia," pp. 215–217.
66 Rădvan, *At Europe's Borders,* pp. 530 (Siret) and 301 (Târgoviște).

The importance of Orthodox monasteries was even more apparent in medieval Serbia, where they often performed functions otherwise characteristic of the urban milieu. In Stari Ras, Sopoćani monastery was apparently more important than the settlement itself, being now the only part of it that survives as a standing building. As explained above, bishoprics were often founded in monasteries instead of in cities, and other important princely foundations, including Gradac, established by Queen Helen of Anjou (1236–1314), were not part of an urban setting, implying that the sites of ecclesiastic centers did not necessarily presuppose an urban environment.[67]

Our overview of church structures and their place in urban development raises the interesting question whether the low status of Buda in terms of ecclesiastical hierarchy was in itself a disadvantage. Certainly for the urban community it meant greater autonomy in the election of parish priests and the management of church properties compared to other localities in medieval Hungary that were bishops' sees. For the kings, however, the absence of a cathedral must have often entailed missed opportunities for royal representation. This disadvantage was especially obvious in comparison with Prague and Cracow, where the presence of patron saints like St Wenceslas or St Stanislas and the their relics, as well as of dynastic burial sites in the respective cathedrals, provided strong sacral legitimization for the ruling monarchs.

While royal burials might reinforce the status of capital cities, the rulers' selection of their burial site was also heavily influenced by personal choices and associations, dynastic or regional loyalties. Some of the later Árpád rulers were indeed buried in the Buda agglomeration, notably Stephen V in the Dominican nunnery on Margaret Island in 1272 and Andrew III at the Buda Franciscans in 1301, but none of the later kings followed their examples. Even King Sigismund, the ruler who invested perhaps the greatest financial resources in developing Buda and Pest, chose for his first wife Mary of Anjou, and indeed for himself, a burial site in the cathedral and pilgrimage site of Oradea, beside the holy king St Ladislas. Buda's other great promoter, Matthias Corvinus, was interred at Székesfehérvár, where St Stephen and St Emeric also rested. Székesfehérvár also retained its importance as the only legitimate coronation site throughout the Middle Ages, with an auxiliary role played by the Buda burghers there.[68]

---

67 *The Cultural Treasury of Serbia*, pp. 461–463 and 477–479.
68 See the article by András Kubinyi in the present volume.

Royal Seat and Capital City

In medieval Europe the status of royal seats and capital cities was not as fixed and embedded as is customary in modern times. It was rather defined by a loose combination of functions, including, in Derek Keene's formulation, "the formal residence or periodic presence of a ruler or ruling body responsible for the territory; some form of administrative and judicial bureaucracy; stores of money and other resources; and a population that could provide fighting men, and [...] crowds ready to acclaim and legitimate rulers".[69] This flexible definition is particularly useful in Buda's case, given that the city became the capital of Hungary during the fourteenth century despite long periods during which the ruler was absent.[70] A full-scale comparative discussion that treated all four aspects of Keene's definition in respect of the royal and princely seats surveyed so far would exceed the framework of the present study, but a few selected examples may serve to shed light on features that Buda fully or partially shared with other Central European capitals.

The material presented in this volume refers mainly to the first, residential aspect; but the second, administrative function is just as important. Previous scholarship, most notably the branch called *Residenzenforschung*, has already demonstrated that during the slow transformation from itinerant to resident kingship, offices and officials became settled at an earlier stage than the monarchs themselves.[71] By the time capital cities became synonymous with 'centers of political life' in the early modern period, the centralization and bureaucratization of states had already been accomplished.[72] In the period examined here, however, signs of stability are still more or less occasional. As the clustering of royal or princely seats and residences within each polity shows [see Fig. 21.1], settling for a definite location of a 'capital city' did not happen until the late Middle Ages or even beyond. In this respect Hungary shares many similarities with the principalities east and south of it. The example of

---

69 Keene, "Capital Cities," p. 125.
70 See András Kubinyi's study in the present volume.
71 Werner Paravicini, "Getane Arbeit, künftige Arbeit: Fünfundzwanzig Jahre Residenzen-Kommission," in *Städtisches Bürgertum und Hofgesellschaft*, ed. Jan Hischbiegel (Residenzenforschung, 25) (Ostfildern: Thorbecke, 2011), pp. 11–22; József Laszlovszky and Katalin Szende, "Cities and Towns as Princely Seats: Medieval Visegrád in the Context of Royal Residences and Urban Development in Europe and Hungary," in *The Medieval Royal Town at Visegrád: Royal Centre, Urban Settlement, Churches* (Archaeolingua – Main Series, 32), eds József Laszlovszky, Gergely Buzás and Orsolya Mészáros (Budapest: Archaeolingua, 2014), pp. 9–44.
72 Peter Clark and Bernard Lepetit, "Introduction," in *Capital Cities and their Hinterlands in Early Modern Europe* (Aldershot: Ashgate, 1996), pp. 2–7.

Visegrád, where the private residences of the main judges and other dignitaries of the realm also served as agencies of state administration, still displays the archaic pattern of personal bonds between ruler and his confidants.[73] This was probably also the model that prevailed in the case of the Serbian, Bosnian, Moldavian and Wallachian seats. For example, when the Moldavian princely court was transferred from Siret to Suceava, the great boyars and the high clergy also moved to the vicinity of the new seat. In Wallachia, the alternating use of Bucharest and Târgoviște as principal cities in the sixteenth century depending on political allegiances likewise presupposed an administrative structure that was not tied to a single site.[74] But to understand how unstable the selection of rulers' seats was as late as the turn of the fifteenth century, one can also remember the example of the Habsburg residences: Frederick III (1440–1493) preferred Wiener Neustadt, whereas his son, Maximilian I (1493–1519) held his court for strategic reasons in Innsbruck rather than in Vienna.[75]

In Buda it was the move of Sigismund's court from Visegrád around 1408–1410, followed afterwards by his long and frequent absences from the country, that catalyzed the emergence of administrative offices independent of the presence of the traveling ruler, a development favored by Buda's already undisputed dominance in trade and economy. In fact, the palace and the institutions of royal government as well as the houses of the men entrusted with the main offices ended up dominating the whole Castle Hill.[76] Buda's administrative stabilization was foreshadowed by Prague, where both the imperial and Bohemian royal offices set up under Charles IV, functioned independently of the presence of the ruler.[77] A similar process took place in the case of Vienna under Charles's son-in-law and rival, Duke Rudolf IV of Habsburg (1358–1365), and under Casimir the Great (1333–1370) in the case of Cracow.

It is not coincidental that all three rulers mentioned above founded universities in their respective residential cities, which turned out, among others, qualified administrators for the court and state offices.[78] It may be symptomatic of the lack of concentrating all efforts on a single center that Louis I's

---

73   Orsolya Mészáros, "Topography and Urban Property Translactions," in *The Medieval Royal Town at Visegrád*, pp. 125–178.

74   Rădvan, *At Europe's Borders,* pp. 257–258 and 535.

75   Peter Moraw, "Zur Mittelpunktfunktion Prags im Zeitalter Karls IV," in *Europa slavica – Europa orientalis. Festschrift für Herbert Ludat zum 70. Geburtstag,* eds Klaus-Detlev Grothusen and Klaus Zernack (Berlin: Duncker & Humblot, 1980), pp. 445–489, here pp. 446–447, on Vienna being the least favorable of possible choices.

76   See Martyn Rady's article in the present volume.

77   Moraw, "Zur Mittelpunktfunktion," pp. 459 and 485.

78   Enno Bünz, "Die Universität zwischen Residenzstadt und Hof im späten Mittelalter. Wechselwirkung und Distanz, Integration und Konkurrenz," in *Städtisches Bürgertum*

similar attempt at founding a university in 1367 was connected to the bishop's seat Pécs and not Buda or Visegrád, and it did not have the same intellectual impact either. When Sigismund founded a short-lived university closer to the capital, it was at Óbuda and not in Buda itself, which shows the limits of centralization in this case, too. Matthias Corvinus's *Academia Istropolitana* came to be founded by the Danube (*Ister*), but in Pressburg, and only his last attempt, the upgrading of the Dominican *Studium generale*, was attached to the city of Buda itself.[79]

Besides the increasing role of sedentary administration, temporary assemblies (*Hoftage, Reichstage*) also enhanced the centrality of the cities in or beside which they were held. These can be perceived as in a way reversing the model of itinerant kingship: it was now not the ruler who visited his subjects in the realm, but the nobility who traveled to meet the king.[80] The symbolic role of the ruler's mobility did not cease with the stabilization of his residence, however, but rather took on new forms. His arrival at the royal seat or leaving it – alive or dead – (the *adventus* and *exitus*) gained new meaning in the late medieval period, enhancing the importance of the cities as theaters where these performances were arranged and which provided their chief audience. In Prague and Cracow, Charles IV and Casimir III introduced ceremonial processions on a grand scale.[81] In Buda, it was again Sigismund who set the stage for such ceremonies, and his spiritual heir, Matthias Corvinus, followed suit.[82] It is both symbolic and typical that Louis II on his departure for the battlefield of Mohács left the Hungarian capital – forever – following the same ceremonial route as the royal entries did, except in the opposite direction.[83] In the princely and royal residences east and south of Buda, processions were strictly confined to the ecclesiastical domain, a custom to which the rulers themselves conformed.

The example of processions shows that the rulers' presence in their capitals did not have to be continuous, but it did need to make itself visible.

---

und Hofgesellschaft (Residenzenforschung, 25), ed. Jan Hischbiegel (Ostfildern: Thorbecke, 2011), pp. 229–254; Csendes and Opll, *Wien*, pp. 130–135.

79 Jerzy Wyrozumski, "Die ältesten Universitätsgründungen Mitteleuropas in vergleichender Hinsicht," in *Die ungarische Universitätsbildung und Europa*, eds Márta Font and László Szögi (Pécs: Pécsi Tudományegyetem, 2001), pp. 23–32; and several studies in *Universitas Budensis 1395–1995*, eds László Szögi and Júlia Varga (Budapest: ELTE Levéltára, 1997).

80 Moraw, "Zur Mittelpunktfunktion," pp. 452–453, and see also the study by János Bak and András Vadas in the present volume.

81 Opacic, "Architecture," pp. 109–111.

82 Károly Goda, "Buda Festiva: Urban Society and Processional Culture in a Medieval Capital City," *Czech and Slovak Journal of Humanities* 2 (2011), pp. 58–79.

83 See the study by Antonín Kalous in the present volume.

For example, Charles IV only spent about one-third of his regnal period in "his" Prague,[84] but his activity during these years was testified by a large number of foundations and ceremonies. Calculations of the itineraries of Sigismund or Matthias Corvinus suggest that they spent even less time personally present in the capital,[85] even though their names are intimately connected with major building projects centered on Buda palace.[86]

The renovation of the palaces was a necessary precondition for, but not a guarantee of, the ruler's presence. It also frequently happened that subsequent generations abandoned lavishly refurbished castles in favor of new residences, as when Wenceslas IV moved out of Hradčany to the Old Town of Prague. Sigismund was even more restless in his nature and pursuits. As the high status but unfinished sculptures at Buda show, he was capable of abandoning a project even as construction reached its peak – an enormous waste of resources, one can only think...[87]

One project he did complete was the great ceremonial hall in Buda palace. Such halls were not only necessary for formal assemblies and diplomatic meetings but were also symbols of prestige and important expressions of authority and power all over Europe: places where monarchs imposed justice and where great assemblies of the king's most powerful supporters were held.[88] As such, they are perhaps the appropriate note on which to close this comparative survey. Until the early fifteenth century Buda palace lacked a hall comparable to the Grand Salle on the Île de la Cité in Paris or to Westminster Hall in London. By adding this particular element and on a scale commensurate with these imposing models, Sigismund demonstrated the economic and political capital that had accumulated in his realm. Buda, in spite of being a late starter, had now caught up with the older residences. The city thus became one of the mightiest capitals in Central Europe and a model for other royal seats in the region.

---

84 Moraw, "Zur Mittelunktfunktion," p. 455.
85 Such calculations can be based on: Pál Engel and Norbert C. Tóth, *Itineraria regum et reginarum (1382–1438)* (Subsidia ad historiam medii aevi Hungariae inquirendam, 1) (Budapest: MOL, 2005) and Richárd Horváth, *Itineraria regis Matthiae Corvini et reginae Beatricis de Aragonia* (História könyvtár. Kronológiák, adattárak, 12 = Subsidia ad historiam medii aevi Hungarie inquirendam, 2) (Budapest: História – MTA Történettudományi Intézete, 2011).
86 See Károly Magyar's article in the present volume.
87 See Szilárd Papp's article in the present volume.
88 Zoë Opačić, "Fit for a King: Håkonshallen and Contemporary Royal Residences," in *Håkonshallen 750 Years. Royal Residence and National Monument*, eds Øystein Brekke and Geir Atle Ersland (Oslo: Dreyers Forlag, 2013), pp. 45–75.

Appendices

Appendix 1: List of the Kings of Medieval Hungary

Árpád dynasty
Stephen I (Saint) 1000–1038
Peter Orseolo 1038–1041 and 1044–1046
Samuel Aba 1041–1044
Andrew I 1046–1060
Béla I 1060–1063
Salamon 1063–1074
Géza I 1074–1077
Ladislas I (Saint) 1077–1095
Coloman (the Learned) 1095–1116
Stephen II 1116–1131
Béla II (the Blind) 1131–1141
Géza II 1141–1162
Stephen III 1162–1172
Béla III 1172–1196
Emeric 1196–1204
Ladislas III 1204–1205
Andrew II 1205–1235
Béla IV 1235–1270
Stephen V 1270–1272
Ladislas IV (the Cuman) 1272–1290
Andrew III 1290–1301

Přemysl dynasty
Wenceslas 1301–1305

Wittelsbach dynasty
Otto 1305–1307

Angevin dynasty
Charles I (Robert) 1301–1342
Louis I (the Great) 1342–1382
Mary 1382–1395
Charles II (the Short) 1385–1386

Luxemburg dynasty
Sigismund 1387–1437

Habsburg dynasty
Albert 1437–1439
Ladislas V (Postumus) 1440–1457

Jagiellonian dynasty
Wladislas I (Warneńczyk) 1440–1444

Hunyadi dynasty
Matthias Corvinus 1458–1490

Jagiellonian dynasty
Wladislas II 1490–1516
Louis II 1516–1526

Szapolyai dynasty
John I 1526–1540
John II Sigismund 1540–1551 and 1556–70; Prince of Transylvania, 1570–1571

Habsburg dynasty
Ferdinand I 1526–1564

Appendix 2: The Privilegial Charter of the Town of Pest Issued by Béla IV, 24 November 1244

In nomine sancte trinitatis et individue unitatis Amen. Bela Dei gratia Hungarie, Dalmatie, Croatie, Rame, Servie, Gallicie, Lodomerie Comanieque rex in perpetuum. Omnibus Christi fidelibus presentem paginam inspecturis salutem in omnium salvatore. Cum in multitudine populorum regum ac principum gloria sumpmopere attendatur, non inmerito regalis decrevit sublimitas suos subditos provisionibus amplioribus ordinare, ut populus sibi serviens et fidelitate et numero augeatur. Ad universorum igitur notitiam presentium ac posterorum harum tenore volumus pervenire, quod cum tempore persecutionis Tartarorum, quorum impetus et sevitia Domino permittente grave dispendium intulit regno nostro, hopsites nostri de Pesth privilegium super ipsorum libertate confectum et concessum ammisissent, nos seriem libertatis memorate, cum esset notoria, duximus renovandam et presentibus annotandam, que talis est, videlicet quod in expeditionem, in quam personaliter ibimus, debent nobiscum mittere decem milites decenter armatos. Item infra limites regni nostri ab omni tributo, salva tricesima et salvo iure ecclesie Budensis, quantum ad tributa de salibus exigenda, sunt exempti. Item de vineis eorundem cibriones nullatenus exigantur. Item nullus principum nostrorum violentum (!) descensum facere possit super eos, nec aliquid contra eorundem recipere voluntatem, sed descendens iusto pretio sibi necessaria debeat comparare. Item nullus hospes ex ipsis possessiones suas vel domos vendere valeat alicui extraneo, nisi in eadem villa volenti a modo habitare. Item quicumque ex ipsis sine herede decesserit, possessiones suas dimittendi facultatem habeat, cui volet. Item quicumque ex eis possessiones emerit, si per annum et diem nullus ipsum super hoc impetierit, de cetero eas sine contradictione aliqua possideat pacifice et quiete. Item habeant liberam electionem plebani, cum eorum ecclesia vacaverit, nec plebanus vicarios constituat eis invitis. Item ipsi maiorem ville sibi eligant quem volent et nobis electum presentent, qui omnes causas eorum mundanas debeat iudicare. Sed si per ipsum debita iustitia alicui non fuerit exhibita, ipse villicus et non villa debeat conveniri coram nobis, vel illo, cui duxerimus committendum. Item vicepalatinus violenter descendere non possit super eos, nec eosdem iudicare. Item omnia, que eis post recessum Tartarorum possint sine contradictione qualibet possidere. Item quicumque cum eis habitare voluerint habentes ibidem possessiones, cum eis debeantur servitia debita exercere. Item duellum inter eos non iudicetur, sed secundum quantitatem et qualitatem commissi, super quo quis impetitor purgationem exhibeat congruentem. Item cum impetiti fuerint per quempiam, ab aliquo extraneo non possint produci testes contra eos, nisi ex ipsis vel aliis habentibus consimilem libertatem. Item tam terram Kuer, quam eis de novo contulimus, quam alias, quas prius habuerunt, dividant in communi habita contemplatione facultatis cuiuslibet, quantam possit facere araturam, ne terre supradicte inculte remaneant et inanes. Item naves et carine descendentes et ascendentes cum mercibus et curribus apud eos descendant et forum sicut prius habeant cottidianum. Item Minor Pesth ultra Danubium sita, quantum ad naves ascendentes et descendentes et cibriones non solvendos consimili gaudeat libertate. Item homo magistri thawarnicorum nostrorum non debeat stare cum monetariis inter ipsos, si unus ex ipsa villa fidedignus illis associetur, qui super receptionem monete regalis curam adhibeat pervigilem et undique diligentem. Ut autem huius prenotate libertatis series salva semper et inconcussa perseveret in posterum, nec aliquo successu temporum possit aliquatenus retractari, presentem eisdem paginam duximus concedendam caractere bulle nostre auree perhenniter roboratam. Verum quia exhibitio privilegii ipsorum existentis sub aurea bulla propter viarum discrimina esse periculosa videbatur, transcriptum eiusdem de verbo ad verbum sub munimine dupplicis sigilli nostri consessimus, tantam presentibus fidem volentes adhiberi, ut ad exhibitionem illius nullatenus compellantur. Datum per manus venerabilis patris Benedicti Colocensis archiepiscopi, aule nostre cancellarii, venerabili patre Stephano archiepiscopo Strigoniensi, Bartholomeo Quinqueecclesiensi, Cleto Agriensi, Stephano Zagrabiensi, Blasio Chanadiensi, Artolpho Ultrasilvano epsicopis, ecclesias Dei salubriter gubernantibus, Vincencio in episcopum ecclesie Waradiensis electo et confirmato, Iauriensi et Wesprimiensi sedibus vacantibus, Ladislao palatino et comite Simigiensi, Dionisio bano et duce totius Sclavonie, Matheo magistro thawarnicorum a comite Posoniensi, Demetrio iudice curie et comite Musuniensi, Laurentio waiawada Ultrasilvano, Rolando magistro dapiferorum et comite Suppruniensi, Mauritio magistro pincernarum et comite Iauriensi, Stephano magistro agazonum et comite de Orbaz, Arnoldo comite Nitriensi, Herrico Ferrei Castri ac ceteris magistratus et comitatus regni nostri tenentibus, anno ab incarnatione Domini millesimo ducentesimo quadragesimo quarto, regni autem nostri anno nono et octavo Kalendas Decembris.

In a transcript from 1496. Bratislava, Archiv Mesta Bratislavy, no 2173 (= MNL OL DF 240 797), edition: BTOE I. pp. 41–43 and EFHU iii/2, pp. 39–41.

Select Bibliography on the History of Medieval Buda

Altmann, Julianna, Biczó, Piroska, Buzás, Gergely, Horváth, István, Kovács, Annamária, Siklósi, Gyula and Végh, András, *Medium regni. Medieval Hungarian Royal Seats* (Budapest: Nap, 1999)

Benkő, Elek and Orosz, Krisztina, eds, *In medio regni Hungariae. Régészeti, művészettörténeti és történeti kutatások "az ország közepén"* [Archaeological, art historical and historical research in the middle of the kingdom] (Budapest: MTA Bölcsészettudományi Kutatóközpont, 2015)

Berza, László, ed., *Budapest történetének bibliográfiája*, 7 vols [Bibliography of the History of Budapest] (Budapest: Fővárosi Szabó Ervin Könyvtár, 1963–1974)

Biegel, Gerd, ed., *Budapest im Mittelalter. Ausstellungskatalog* (Veröffentlichungen des Braunschweigischen Landesmuseums, 62) (Braunschweig: Braunschweigisches Landesmuseum, 1991)

Engel, Pál, *The Realm of St. Stephen. A History of Medieval Hungary, 895–1526* (London–New York: I.B. Tauris, 2001)

Farbaky, Péter and Waldman, Louis A., eds, *Italy & Hungary: Humanism and Art in the Early Renaissance* (Florence: Villa i Tatti, 2011)

Farbaky, Péter, Spekner, Enikő, Szende, Katalin and Végh, András, eds, *Matthias Corvinus, the King. Tradition and Renewal in the Hungarian Royal Court 1458–1490* (Budapest: Budapest History Museum, 2008)

Farbaky, Péter, Szalay, Olga and Farbakyné Deklava, Lilla, eds, *Mátyás-templom: a budavári Nagyboldogasszony-templom évszázadai, 1246–2013: kiállítási katalógus* [Matthias church: centuries of the Church of Our Lady at Buda Castle, 1246–2013] (Budapest: Budapesti Történeti Múzeum – Budapest-Vári Nagyboldogasszony Főplébánia, 2015)

Font, Márta and Sándor, Mária, eds, *Mittelalterliche Häuser und Strassen in Mitteleuropa* (Varia Archaeologica Hungarica, 9) (Budapest–Pécs: Archäologisches Institut der UAW, 2000)

Fügedi, Erik, "Topográfia és városi fejlődés a középkori Óbudán," [Topography and urban development in medieval Óbuda] *Tanulmányok Budapest Múltjából* 13 (1959), pp. 7–57.

Gárdonyi, Albert and Kumorovitz L., Bernát, eds, *Budapest történetének okleveles emlékei*, 3 vols in 4 parts [Charters to the history of Budapest] (Budapest: A Székesfőváros kiadása – BTM, 1936–1988)

Gerevich, László, *The Art of Buda and Pest in the Middle Ages* (Budapest: Akadémiai, 1971)

———, ed., *Budapest története*, 5 vols [The history of Budapest] (Budapest: Budapest Főváros Tanácsa, 1975–1980)

———, ed., *Towns in Medieval Hungary* (Budapest: Akadémiai, 1990)

Gönczi, Katalin, *Ungarisches Stadtrecht aus europäischer Sicht. Die Stadtrechtsentwicklung im spätmittelalterlichen Ungarn am Beispiel Ofen* (Frankfurt am Main: Klostermann, 1997)

Györffy, György, *Az Árpád-kori Magyarország történeti földrajza*, 4 vols [in progress] Historical geography of Hungary in the Árpád period] (Budapest: Akadémiai, 1963–1998)

———, *Pest–Buda kialakulása. Budapest története a honfoglalástól az Árpád-kor végi székvárossá alakulásáig* [The formation of Pest-Buda. The history of Budapest from the Hungarian conquest to its late Árpádian-period formation as capital] (Budapest, Akadémiai, 1997)

Gyürky, Katalin H., *Das mittelalterliche Dominikanerkloster in Buda* (Fontes Archaeologici Hungariae) (Budapest: Akadémiai, 1981)

Holl, Imre, *Fundkomplexe des 15.–17. Jahrhunderts aus dem Burgpalast von Buda.* (Varia Archaeologica Hungarica 17) (Budapest: Archäologisches Institut der UAW, 2005)

Keene, Derek, Nagy, Balázs and Szende, Katalin, eds, *Segregation – Integration – Assimilation. Religious and Ethnic Groups in the Medieval Towns of Central and Eastern Europe* (Historical Urban Studies) (Farnham: Ashgate, 2009)

Kenyeres, István, ed., *A budai mészárosok középkori céhkönyve és kiváltságlevelei – Zunftbuch und Privilegien der Fleischer zu Ofen aus dem Mittelalter* (Források Budapest közép– és kora újkori történetéhez, 1/Quellen zur Budapester Geschichte im Mittelalter und in der frühen Neuzeit, 1) (Budapest: BFL – BTM, 2008)

Kubinyi, András, *Die Anfänge Ofens* (Osteuropastudien der Hochschulen des Landes Hessen. Reihe i. Giessener Abhandlungen zur Agrar- und Wirtschaftsforschung des europäischen Ostens, 60) (Berlin: Duncker & Humblot, 1972)

———, ed., *Elenchus fontium historiae urbanae* (Elenchus fontium historiae urbanae, iii/2) (Budapest: Balassi, 1997)

———, *Tanulmányok Budapest középkori történetéről*, 2 vols [Studies in the history of medieval Budapest] (Várostörténeti Tanulmányok), eds Kenyeres, István, Kis, Péter and Sasfi, Csaba (Budapest: BFL, 2009)

Kumorovitz, L. Bernát, "Buda (és Pest) 'fővárossá' alakulásának kezdetei," [The formation of Buda (and Pest) as 'capital' of Hungary] *Tanulmányok Budapest Múltjából* 18 (1971), pp. 7–57.

Magyar, Károly, "Residenzen des Königs und der Königin," in *Maria von Ungarn (1505–1558): Eine Renaissancefürstin*, eds Martina Fuchs and Orsolya Réthelyi (Münster: Aschendorff, 2007), pp. 381–399.

Mollay, Károly, ed., *Das Ofner Stadtrecht. Eine deutschsprachige Rechtssammlung des 15. Jahrhunderts aus Ungarn* (Monumenta Historica Budapestinensia, 1) (Budapest: Akadémiai, 1959)

Rady, Martyn C., *Medieval Buda: A Study of Municipal Government and Jurisdiction in the Kingdom of Hungary* (East European Monographs, 182) (Boulder: East European Monographs, 1985)

Réthelyi, Orsolya, Romhányi, Beatrix F., Spekner, Enikő and Végh, András, eds, *Mary of Hungary: The Queen and Her Court 1521–1531* (Budapest: Budapest History Museum, 2005)

Spekner, Enikő, *Hogyan lett Buda a középkori Magyarország fővárosa? A budai királyi székhely története a 12. század végétől a 14. század közepéig* [How did Buda become the capital of medieval Hungary? The history of the Buda seat from the end of the twelfth to the mid-fourteenth century] (Monumenta Historica Budapestinensia, 17) (Budapest: BTM, 2015)

Takács, Imre, ed., *Sigismundus Rex et Imperator. Kunst und Kultur zur Zeit Sigismunds von Luxemburg 1387–1437* (Budapest–Mainz am Rhein: Philipp von Zabern, 2006)

Végh, András, *Buda város középkori helyrajza*, 2 vols (Monumenta Historica Budapestinensia, 15–16) [The topography of medieval Buda] (Budapest: Budapesti Történeti Múzeum, 2006–2008)

———, "Les synagogues de Buda (XIVe et XVe siècles): fouilles récentes," in *Archéologie du judaïsme en France et en Europe. Colloque international, Paris, 14 et 15 janvier 2010*, eds Salmona, Paul and Sigal, Laurence (Paris: La Découverte, 2011), pp. 215–224.

———, "Urban Development and Royal Initiative in the Central Part of the Kingdom of Hungary in the 13th–14th centuries: Comparative Analysis of the Development of the Towns of Buda and Visegrád," in *Stadtgründung und Stadtwerdung. Beiträge von Archäologie und Stadtgeschichtsforschung* (Beiträge zur Geschichte der Städte Mitteleuropas, 22), ed. Opll, Ferdinand (Linz: Österreichischer Arbeitskreis für Stadtgeschichtsforschung, 2011), pp. 431–446.

———, *Buda, Part I, to 1686* (Hungarian Atlas of Historic Towns, 4) (Budapest: BTM – PPKE, 2015)

Index of Geographic Names

Aachen 288, 322, 368, 369, 532
Abda 280
Adrianopolis (Edirne) 355
Alba Iulia (Gyulafehérvár, Weissenburg) 488fn
Alhévíz (part of present-day Budapest) 192, 197, 379, 546
Altlublau, *see* Stará Ľubovňa
Altofen, *see* Óbuda
Altötting 448
Amberg 283
Amiens 402, 413–415
Aquincum (part of present-day Budapest) 1, 18, 26, 27, 32, 72, 76, 81, 93, 94fn, 97, 110, 176, 186, 236, 238, 534
Arad 324
Argeş (river) 528
Augsburg 265, 283, 295, 297, 397
Austria 97, 258, 280, 282, 293–296, 347, 353–354, 359, 396, 413, 415, 418, 513, 516
Avignon 164fn, 244–245, 398

Bamberg 99fn, 195
Banská Bystrica (Besztercebánya, Neusohl) 279, 292, 295fn
Banská Štiavnica (Selmecbánya, Schemnitz) 279, 295
Baranya County 218, 503
Bardejov (Bártfa, Bartfeld) 53, 59, 319, 336, 368, 516, 521
Basle (Basel) 16, 292fn, 343, 360fn, 497
Bavaria 97, 144, 282, 347, 359, 405fn, 424
Bec (Bernay) 410
Bécsújhely, *see* Wiener Neustadt
Belgrade (Nándorfehérvár) 342, 371, 501, 509, 526, 528, 534, 537
Berlin 433, 543
Bern 387
Besenyő (part of present-day Budapest) 174, 180
Besztercebánya, *see* Banská Bystrica
Biograd na Moru (Tengerfehérvár) 323
Black Sea 355
Blocksberg (Brocken) (mountain) 252
Bobovac 526, 537

Bohemia 144, 145, 149, 155, 156, 196, 234, 278, 279, 283, 285, 308, 327, 338, 350–353, 357–358, 363, 364, 372, 374, 383, 413, 453, 457, 463–466, 513–516, 523, 539–540, 548
Bologna 15, 245, 477, 479, 482, 507
Bosnia 251, 333, 349, 354, 359, 360fn, 526, 527fn, 528, 534, 537, 540–541, 546, 548
Boston 408, 410, 437
Bourges 409, 413
Brabant 406
Braşov (Brassó) 515
Bratislava, *see* Pressburg
Brescia 473
Breslau, *see* Wrocław
Brno (Brünn) 283
Bruges 261, 284, 298, 407
Brünn, *see* Brno
Brussels 308, 408
Bucharest 526, 534, 551
Budafelhévíz (part of present-day Budapest) 2, 5, 76–78
Budakalász 82, 113
Budaörs 222
Budaszentlőrinc (part of present-day Budapest) 32–33, 247–250, 361, 517
Budweis, *see* České Budějovice

Čáslav (Tschaslau) 516
Castle District (part of present-day Budapest) 34–35, 39, 41–43, 46, 109, 162, 177, 179, 184, 188–192, 194, 197, 201–202, 207, 388
Castle Hill (part of present-day Budapest) 532–535, 541, 548, 551
Cenad (Marosvár, Csanád) 232, 235
České Budějovice (Budweis) 540
Cheb (Eger/Bohemia) 283
City Park (part of present-day Budapest) (Városliget) 26–27
Clarendon 150–151
Cluj (Kolozsvár, Klausenburg) 57, 315, 486, 493
Cologne (Köln) 261, 281, 283–286, 288–289, 387, 397

INDEX OF GEOGRAPHIC NAMES 563

Comagena 97fn
Constance (Konstanz) 398, 424
Constantinople 85, 349, 355, 357, 361, 365, 502, 505
Contra Aquincum (part of present-day Budapest) 72, 81, 534
Cracow (Kraków) 15, 76, 135, 137, 139–140, 151, 154, 156, 167–168, 170, 203, 261, 284, 297, 322, 353, 361, 382, 463, 478, 493, 526, 528–535, 539, 543–544, 547, 549, 551–552
Crailsheim 468
Csanád, see Cenad
Csatka 219
Csepel Island 78, 84, 88, 183, 214fn, 326, 349–349, 358, 364, 503, 509
Csillaghegy (part of present-day Budapest) 113
Csőt (part of present-day Budapest) 208fn, 214
Curtea de Argeş 528, 533–534
Czestochowa 248

Dalmatia 238, 322, 395, 541
Danube (river) 1–6, 20, 41, 49, 51, 53, 71–72, 74, 76, 78–82, 87, 90, 97fn, 100, 103, 107fn, 116, 124fn, 127, 133, 135, 148, 150, 154, 160, 169, 173–177, 179–181, 184, 186–188, 192, 194, 197, 202, 205–207, 218, 228, 230–234, 236–238, 243–244, 255, 268, 273, 275, 278–281, 287, 298, 304fn, 307, 327, 329, 331, 336–337, 341, 347–348, 355, 378, 390, 398, 490, 500–503, 506, 508–509, 511, 522, 524, 528–531, 533–535, 541, 546, 552
Danzig, see Gdańsk
Debrecen 253, 358
Dijon 407–408, 414, 418fn, 435, 439, 441
Diósgyőr (part of present-day Miskolc) 358, 488
Dömös 118–119, 347
Dresden 58, 479fn
Drinápoly, see Edirne
Dubrovnik (Ragusa) 68, 486
Dunaszekcső 82
Duvno 322

Edirne (Drinápoly) 84
Edirne, see Adrianopolis

Eger/Bohemia, see Cheb
Eisenach 103
Eperjes, see Prešov
Erdély, see Transylvania
Esztergom (Gran) 3, 60, 71, 75–76, 84–85, 115, 118–119, 121, 133–135, 139, 140, 143, 144, 154, 174–175, 185–186, 201, 209, 215, 218, 227, 243, 279, 283, 323–324, 328, 335, 337, 347–348, 364, 366, 379, 395, 398, 409, 442, 475, 477, 481, 501, 508, 510, 514, 522, 532, 535, 543–544
Etzelburg, "Attila's town" 76, 78fn, 84, 96, 99–100, 103

Fedémes (part of present-day Csobánka) 119
Fehéregyháza (part of present-day Budapest) 74, 101fn, 111, 113, 219, 223, 227
Felhévíz (part of present-day Budapest) 2, 5, 62, 76–78, 90, 169, 174–175, 177, 191–192, 197, 204, 214–215, 222–223, 226–228, 236, 258, 265fn, 268, 275, 548
Felsőtárkány 220
Fermo 327
Ferrara 473, 476, 480–481
Flanders 268, 283, 292
Florence (Firenze) 261, 265, 363, 472–473, 476–478, 480–481, 484–487, 490–492
Frankfurt am Main 261, 265, 296, 322, 343, 449
Fünfkirchen, see Pécs
Füzítő (part of present-day Almásfüzítő) 280

Gallipoli (Gelibolu) 355
Gdańsk (Danzig) 284, 538fn
Gelibolu, see Gallipoli
Genoa 265, 298
Gercse (part of present-day Budapest) 176, 223
Gnesen, see Gniezno
Gniezno (Gnesen) 322, 346, 543
Gračanica 544
Gran, see Esztergom
Great Hungarian Plain 71, 279, 502
Grosslobming 411, 413, 415–418, 420, 425
Großwardein, see Oradea
Gubacs (part of present-day Budapest) 184, 222

Győr (Raab)   279–280, 326, 503, 517
Gyulafehérvár, *see* Alba Iulia

Halle   408
Hares' Island, *see* Margaret Island
Harz (mountains)   252
Hermannstadt, *see* Sibiu
Holdvilág-árok (valley; part of present-day Pomáz)   111–112, 114
Holy Roman Empire   54, 56, 58–59, 278, 298, 322, 342, 346, 362, 463, 534
Hradčany (part of present-day Prague)   135, 170fn, 196fn, 533, 535, 553
Hunedoara (Vajdahunyad)   422
Huy   283

Ialomiţa (river)   528

Jasna Góra (part of present-day Czestochowa)   248
Jászberény   104fn
Jenő (part of present-day Budapest)   76, 174, 180, 186, 191
Jerusalem   75, 347

Kalocsa   482, 511
Kána (part of present-day Budapest)   205, 218, 223
Káposztásmegyer (part of present-day Budapest)   506
Karlštejn (Karlstein)   196, 246, 517, 533
Kaschau, *see* Košice
Kassa, *see* Košice
Kecskemét   460
Kékes (part of present-day Pilisszentlászló)   219–220
Kelenföld (part of present-day Budapest) (Kreenfeld)   12, 87, 169, 192, 206, 234, 236, 304, 500, 509
Kerepes (part of present-day Budapest)   78fn, 328
Kesztölc   119–120
Kevélyek (mountains)   127
Kiev (Kijev)   82
Kispest (part of present-day Budapest)   87–90, 174, 177, 179, 184, 187, 191–192
Klausenburg, *see* Cluj
Köln, *see* Cologne
Kolozsvár, *see* Cluj

Komárno (Révkomárom)   120fn, 125fn, 134fn, 503
Konstanz, *see* Constance
Körmöcbánya, *see* Kremnica
Košice (Kassa, Kaschau)   53, 57, 59, 184, 279, 285, 290, 319, 516
Kovácsi (part of present-day Esztergom)   119
Kövérföld (part of present-day Budapest)   181
Kraków, *see* Cracow
Kreenfeld, *see* Kelenföld
Kraljeva Sutjeska   526
Kremnica (Körmöcbánya, Kremnitz)   279, 290
Kutná Hora (Kuttenberg)   145, 308

Lád, *see* Sajólád
Legnica (Liegnitz)   149fn, 351
Leipzig   58, 60
Lemberg, *see* Lviv
Leutschau, *see* Levoča
Levoča (Lőcse, Leutschau)   11fn, 184fn, 469
Liegnitz, *see* Legnica
Little Poland   546
Lőcse, *see* Levoča
Logod (part of present-day Budapest)   192, 200
Low Countries   283, 287, 289, 297
Lübeck   58–59, 84, 99, 348, 416–417, 451
Lviv (Lemberg)   297, 382

Madár Hill (part of present-day Budapest)   177, 180
Magdeburg   58–59
Mainz   283, 543
Malá Strana (part of present-day Prague)   170fn, 530, 535
Mantua   396, 473
Marchegg   353
Margaret Island (part of present-day Budapest) (Margit-sziget, Hares' Island)   32, 62, 122, 174–175, 177, 180–181, 183, 186, 189, 191, 204–205, 207, 209–210, 214, 221, 226–227, 230–231, 236, 239, 246–247, 251, 253–254, 258fn, 259, 531, 548–549
Maros (river) (Mureș)   82, 88
Maros, *see* Nagymaros
Marosvár, *see* Cenad

INDEX OF GEOGRAPHIC NAMES 565

Mechelen   261
Megyer (part of present-day
    Budapest)   78, 176
Milan (Milano)   245, 473, 489
Mohács   3, 6, 64, 250, 278, 314, 342, 379fn,
    492, 497–501, 503, 510, 518fn, 524, 552
Moldau, see Vltava
Moldavia   526, 529fn, 544, 548, 551
Morava (river)   353
Moravia   149fn, 154–155, 258, 278–279, 285,
    353–354, 513, 515–516, 523, 540
Morogues   414fn, 447
Moson (part of present-day
    Mosonmagyaróvár)   279
Munich (München)   415, 432
Mureș, see Maros

Nagymaros (Maros)   124fn, 148fn
Nagyszeben, see Sibiu
Nagyszombat, see Trnava
Nagyvárad, see Oradea
Nándor (part of present-day Budapest)   177,
    215
Nándor Hill (part of present-day
    Budapest)   187
Nándorfehérvár, see Belgrade
Naples (Napoli)   149, 192, 245, 291, 395, 461,
    465, 473–474, 479fn
Neusohl, see Banská Bystrica
Neutra, see Nitra
Nikopol (Nicopolis, Nikápoly)   333, 394–395
Nitra (Nyitra, Neutra)   78, 481
Nové Město (part of present-day
    Prague)   170fn, 535
Nuremberg (Nürnberg)   200, 265, 278, 281,
    283–287, 289, 291–292, 295–298, 314,
    322, 343, 392, 397, 501fn, 505fn, 509
Nyék (part of present-day Budapest)   33
Nyitra, see Nitra

Óbuda (part of present-day Budapest)
    (Altofen, Vetus Buda)   1–5, 15, 17, 20–21,
    25fn, 26, 32–33, 52, 54, 61–62, 65,
    67fn, 71–81, 83–87, 89–99, 101fn,
    103–104, 107–114, 124, 133, 141–144,
    169–170, 172–177, 182, 184–186, 189–191,
    193–194, 196, 198, 204–205, 207, 208fn,
    209, 210, 211fn, 212, 213, 216, 219–221, 223,
    226–228, 236, 238–240, 255–256, 259fn,
    273–274, 277, 278fn, 328, 347–349, 364, 366,
    369, 460, 490, 497, 508, 511, 531, 533–534,
    536–537, 541, 548, 552
Óbudai Island (part of present-day
    Budapest)   72, 174
Ödenburg, see Sopron
Oder (river)   528, 531, 536, 539
Okół (part of present-day Cracow)   531, 535,
    539
Olomouc (Olmütz)   322, 466, 469, 478,
    479fn, 516
Ólubló, see Stará Ľubovňa
Ópusztaszer (Szer)   322
Oradea (Várad, Nagyvárad,
    Großwardein)   279, 289–290, 328, 333fn,
    334fn, 358, 475, 477, 549
Ottoman Empire   6, 500, 502fn

Paderborn   346
Padua (Padova)   154fn, 477–481
Palota (part of present-day Budapest)   184
Pannonhalma   218, 322
Párdi (part of present-day Budapest)   184
Paris   31, 102, 115, 141, 149, 151, 167fn, 224, 380,
    387, 397–398, 406–408, 410, 418–419,
    421, 443, 445, 533–534, 536, 553
Passau   360, 543
Patak Forest   119
Pécs (Fünfkirchen)   15, 252, 379fn, 380,
    480–481, 502fn, 552
Pest (part of present-day Budapest)   1–5, 7,
    17–18, 20–21, 25fn, 26, 51, 52–53,
    55, 61, 63–65, 71–72, 75–76, 80–83,
    86–91, 94, 116, 124, 169–170, 172–178,
    180–185, 187–193, 195–197, 200, 203,
    204–209, 211–214, 216, 219–222, 226–227,
    232, 235–236, 238–239, 253–254,
    255–259, 271, 273, 274, 276–277, 278fn,
    279, 285, 288, 290, 293fn, 294, 297–298,
    303–305, 315fn, 319, 325–330, 334–338,
    340–343, 366fn, 398, 422, 488, 507–509,
    530, 533–534, 541–542, 548–549, 556
Peszérd (part of present-day Esztergom)   119
Petrovaradin (Pétervárad,
    Peterwardein)   205–206, 218
Pettau, see Ptuj
Philippopolis (Plovdiv)   355
Pierrefonds   413
Pilis (mountains)   2, 6, 121, 220

Pilis County   111–120, 122–129, 174, 204, 533, 548
Pilismarót   113
Pilisszentkereszt   119–120, 349fn
Pilisszentlászló   119
Pilisszentlélek   119, 120fn
Pilisvörösvár   127
Pilsen, see Plzeň
Plovdiv, see Philippopolis
Plzeň (Pilsen)   540
Po (river)   468
Poitiers   411, 413–415, 447
Poland   149, 157, 248, 278, 285, 290, 292, 297, 322fn, 323, 327, 340fn, 343, 346, 350–354, 357–358, 360–361, 363–364, 367, 382, 411, 457, 461, 463–464, 470fn, 527, 528fn, 543, 546, 548
Pomáz   111–112, 127
Pomerania   360, 538
Poznań (Posen)   540
Pozsony County   122
Pozsony, see Pressburg
Prague   3, 15, 76, 82, 115, 116fn, 135, 136, 139–140, 149, 151, 154–155, 157, 167–168, 170, 181fn, 184fn, 190, 196fn, 197fn, 203, 250, 283–284, 292, 322, 337, 346, 353, 372, 383, 405fn, 408fn, 411, 418fn, 420, 457, 463, 466, 468, 514–516, 526, 528–530, 532–535, 540, 542–545, 547–549, 551–553
Prešov (Eperjes, Preschau)   11fn, 59, 319
Pressburg (Bratislava, Pozsony)   3, 11fn, 15, 53, 57, 59, 62, 64, 78, 153, 251, 280fn, 283, 285–288, 292–294, 298, 314, 318–319, 329, 333, 336–338, 343, 357, 399, 468, 478, 503, 524–525, 552
Prussia   278, 292
Ptuj (Pettau)   279, 292, 294

Quedlinburg   346

Raab, see Győr
Radkersburg   295
Ragusa, see Dubrovnik
Rákos (fields; part of present-day Budapest)   3, 173, 181, 183, 322, 325–331, 337, 340–342, 344, 507
Rákos (river)   72, 174

Ravensburg   295
Regensburg   80, 265, 279–281, 284, 298, 397, 511, 528
Reims   141
Révkomárom, see Komárno
Rhine (river)   102, 283, 406
Rome   16, 245, 346, 472–473, 476, 478, 480, 515, 518
Rusovce (Oroszvár)   287

Salzburg   543
Sandomierz   351, 540
Sankt Gallen   295
Sárospatak   493
Sárvár   493
Schemnitz, see Banská Štiavnica
Segesd   220
Seine (river)   58, 536
Selmecbánya, see Banská Štiavnica
Serbia   6, 205, 359, 362, 526, 527fn, 534, 537, 540–541, 544, 546, 549
Sibiu (Szeben, Nagyszeben, Hermannstadt)   288, 295, 423
Sibrik Hill (part of present-day Visegrád)   121, 147
Sicambria, legendary seat of Attila   76, 96, 102–103, 511
Sicily   142
Siebenbürgen, see Transylvania
Siena   398, 473
Siklós   78
Singidunum (Roman predecessor of present-day Belgrade)   534
Siret   526, 528, 537, 544–546, 548, 551
Smederevo (Szendrő)   526, 528, 537, 539
Solymár   119
Sopron (Ödenburg)   53, 59, 179fn, 286, 288, 293–294, 319
Soroksár (part of present-day Budapest)   222
Srem, see Srijem
Sremska Mitrovica (Szávaszentdemeter)   482
Srijem (Srem, Szerémség)   285
St Denis   141, 397
Stará Ľubovňa (Ólubló, Altlublau)   358
Stari Ras   526, 534, 537, 549
Stavelot-Malmedy   117
Strasbourg   284, 407

INDEX OF GEOGRAPHIC NAMES   567

Stuhlweißenburg, see Székesfehérvár
Stuttgart   397
Styria   374, 411, 416
Suceava   526, 528, 537–538, 541, 544,
    546, 551
Sutjeska   526, 537
Swabia   16, 282, 424
Szabolcs County   334
Szabolcs   323
Szávaszentdemeter, see Sremska Mitrovica
Szeben, see Sibiu
Szeged   82, 253, 328–329, 332, 334, 338, 367
Székesfehérvár (Stuhlweißenburg)   3, 32,
    71, 75–78, 84, 86, 113, 115, 133, 140–141,
    144, 179, 184–185, 197, 222, 232, 279, 294,
    323–324, 328, 332, 335, 338, 343, 347,
    353, 366, 369, 374–378, 470, 498fn, 505,
    510, 523, 549
Szendrő, see Smederevo
Szenterzsébetfalva (part of present-day
    Budapest)   88, 169, 175, 193, 207, 329
Szentháromságfalva (part of present-day
    Budapest)   174, 177, 191
Szentjakabfalva (part of present-day
    Budapest)   77, 169, 174, 176–177
Szentlőrinc (part of present-day
    Budapest)   184, 219
Szentmihály (part of present-day
    Budapest)   184
Szer, see Ópusztaszer
Szerémség, see Srijem

Tarcal   323
Târgoviște   526, 528, 534, 537, 541, 544,
    548, 551
Taschental (part of present-day
    Budapest)   194, 197, 199, 207, 210
Telki   205, 218
Temesvár, see Timișoara
Tengerfehérvár, see Biograd na Moru
Tétény (part of present-day Budapest)   327
Thessaloniki   9, 500
Thorn, see Toruń
Tihany   98, 217, 266, 272, 274
Timișoara (Temesvár)   14, 122, 225,
    332–333, 350
Titel   78
Tolna   333, 338, 522

Tolna County   218
Toruń (Thorn)   540
Tótfalu (part of present-day Budapest)   6,
    44fn, 194, 197
Tournai   284
Transaquincum   72
Transylvania (Siebenbürgen, Erdély)   2, 46,
    82, 258, 261, 268, 279, 288–290, 296, 315,
    338, 355, 379, 493, 498, 556
Trenčín (Trencsén)   251, 279, 351
Trnava (Nagyszombat, Tyrnau)   59, 184fn,
    279, 283, 286, 319, 493, 503
Troy   96, 102, 511
Tschaslau, see Čáslav
Tübingen   397
Tulln   97fn
Tyniec (part of present-day Cracow)   547
Tyrnau, see Trnava

Újbécs (part of present-day Budapest)   83,
    88, 175, 180, 186, 193
Ulm   295, 298, 422fn, 424
Umbria   480
Urbino   158, 160fn, 473
Üröm   176

Vác   122, 175, 482, 517
Vajdahunyad, see Hunedoara
Várad, see Oradea
Váralja (part of present-day Budapest)   44
Varna   333–334
Városliget, see City Park
Venice (republic)   248
Venice (Venezia)   265, 278–280, 285, 292,
    294, 298, 363, 419fn, 473, 490, 498
Veszprém   175, 185, 215fn, 217, 279, 371, 379
Vetus Buda, see Óbuda
Vidin   356
Vienna (Wien)   3, 15, 67fn, 184, 190, 261, 265,
    278–281, 283–288, 292–298, 336, 354,
    380–381, 402, 411, 415–416, 418, 424,
    451, 478, 493, 504, 506, 508–510, 513,
    526, 528–530, 534, 536, 544, 546–547,
    551
Villers-Saint-Paul   410
Vincennes   406, 414, 533
Vindobona (Roman predecessor of
    Vienna)   534

Visegrád   2, 71, 115, 120–124, 129, 133, 143,
    147–151, 153–154, 156, 162, 172, 192, 196,
    283, 287, 308, 347, 350–353, 360–361,
    364–365, 375, 378, 383, 396, 452, 461,
    503, 508, 523, 533, 551–552
Víziváros, *see* Water Town
Vizsoly   493
Vltava (river) (Moldau)   135, 197fn,
    528–529, 545
Vyšehrad (part of present-day
    Prague)   530, 545

Wallachia   526, 533–534, 544, 548, 551
Warsaw   543
Water Town (part of present-day Budapest)
    (Víziváros)   4, 33

Wawel Hill (part of present-day
    Cracow)   137, 156fn
Weissenburg, *see* Alba Iulia
Westminster (part of present-day
    London)   141, 145, 154fn, 553
Wiener Neustadt (Bécsújhely)   294–296, 519,
    544, 551
Windsor   533
Wittenberg   16, 351, 492
Wrocław (Breslau)   283–284, 297–298, 353,
    469, 506fn, 526, 528, 531, 532, 534, 536,
    539, 544, 546–548

Zadar (Zára)   322fn, 395
Zagreb   279, 306, 541
Žiča   544

Index of Personal Names*

Aba, Amádé, palatine of Hungary   330
Adalbert, bishop of Prague, saint   134, 136, 346
Aeneas, mythical figure   102
Agnes of Bohemia, daughter of King Ottokar I, saint   548
Aimoin, chronicler   102
Ákos Master, chronicler   78
Albert II, duke of Austria   354
Albert of Wittelsbach, duke of Bavaria   357
Albert, duke of Austria, later king of Hungary   354
Alberti, Leon Battista, architect   474fn
Alexander the Great, Ancient ruler   477
Álmos, brother of King Coloman, prince   118
Álmos, prince of the Magyars   101
Andreas, prior of the Buda Carmelite friary   244
Andrew II, king of Hungary   85–86, 143, 205, 324, 349
Andrew III, king of Hungary   122, 144, 172–173, 182, 208, 281, 324, 328–330, 374, 549
Andrew-Zoerard, hermit, saint   233
Anna of Schweidnitz (Świdnica), queen consort to Charles IV, Holy Roman emperor   354
Anne de Foix, queen consort to Wladislas II, king of Hungary and Bohemia   375, 464
Anne of Brittany, duchess of Brittany   461–462
Anne of Candale, see Anne de Foix
Anne of the Palatinate, queen consort to Charles IV, Holy Roman emperor   354
Anonymus, chronicler   74, 78, 82–84, 100–101, 103, 105, 186fn, 325
Ansbert, chronicler   84, 99, 348
Antoninus, Johannes, humanist   469
Apa of the Becsegergely kindred, comes of Bodrog County and ban   205
Arany, János, poet   104–107, 114
Argyropoulos, John, humanist   478

Arnold of Lübeck, chronicler   84, 99, 348
Árpád, grand prince of the Magyars   74, 101, 111–112, 214
Artemios, saint   242
Arthur, legendary king   92
Ascanio Centario, chronicler   502
Attila, leader of the Huns   76, 84, 94, 96–101, 103, 106–107, 109, 113–114, 348
Augustine Moravus of Olomouc, humanist   478
Augustus, Roman emperor   477
Averulino, Antonio, architect   490, 491, 492

Bakács, István   62fn, 66
Bakóc, Tamás, archbishop of Esztergom   514, 521
Bandini, Francesco, humanist   479, 482, 484, 486, 487fn, 488–489
Bánfi family   316
Barbara of Cilli, queen consort to Sigismund, Holy Roman emperor   192, 460
Basil of Caesarea, theologian, saint   477, 478
Bátori, István, regent of Hungary   339, 498, 515fn, 516–517, 522
Bátori, Miklós, humanist, bishop of Vác   482
Batu, Khan, Mongol ruler   87
Beatrice of Aragon, queen of Hungary and Bohemia, wife of Matthias Corvinus and Wladislas II   9, 163, 165, 375–377, 461, 465, 467–468, 481, 483–484, 521–523
Beatrice of Luxemburg, queen consort to Charles I, king of Hungary   245
Beaune, Colette   372
Beauneveu, André, sculptor   406, 408, 412
Béla I, king of Hungary   119
Béla II, king of Hungary   324
Béla III, king of Hungary   84, 100, 120–121, 135, 348, 349fn
Béla IV, king of Hungary   1, 55, 63, 71, 87, 89–91, 94, 121–122, 135, 143, 147, 174, 176,

---

*   Kings listed here are numbered according to their reign in Hungary.

181, 186, 205–210, 214, 238–240, 255, 259, 280, 304–306, 390, 535, 541
Benedict XI, *see* Boccasini, Nicholas
Benedict, hermit, saint   233
Bernardi family   267
Bertrandon de la Broquière, Burgundian diplomat   9, 258, 398
Bessarion, Basilius, humanist and theologian   477
Billa, noble lord from Bular   83
Biondo, Flavio, humanist   473
Bleda, Hun leader, brother of Attila   94, 106
Boccasini, Nicholas (later Pope Benedict XI), papal legate   329
Bolesław I Chrobry, king of Poland   346
Bolesław III the Generous (Rozrzutny), duke of Legnica   351
Bolesław the Chaste, high duke of Poland   539
Bonfini, Antonio, chronicler   158, 160–162, 164, 166, 372–373, 467, 481fn, 486–490, 492–493, 497, 519
Bono, Pietro, alchemist   483
Boreczky, Anna   476
Boris, pretender to the Hungarian throne   347
Bornemissza, Tamás, burgher of Buda, chronicler   505
Branda da Castiglione, humanist, cardinal   360, 362
Brodarics, István, royal chancellor, chronicler   522
Budó, Jusztin   65
Bylica, Martin, astronomer and physician   482

Caesar, Julius, Roman politician   477
Camicia, Chimenti, architect   488
Campeggi, Lorenzo, cardinal   515
Carafa, Diomede, cardinal   465
Casimir III (the Great), king of Poland   149, 154, 156, 351–354, 357, 551, 552
Casimir of Brandenburg, margrave of Bayreuth   464
Catherine de Foix, countess of Candale   461
Catherine of Alexandria, saint   247, 408
Catherine of Poděbrady, queen consort to Matthias, king of Hungary   32, 461
Celâlzâde Mustafa, chronicler   502fn, 504
Cesarini, Giuliano, cardinal   208

Charles Durazzo of Naples, *see* Charles II (the Short)
Charles I, king of Hungary   2, 122, 124, 146fn, 148–150, 173, 175, 182fn, 187, 211, 241, 244, 281–283, 327, 330, 331, 350–353, 367–368, 374, 378, 383
Charles II (the Short), Charles Durazzo, king of Hungary   332, 395
Charles IV, Holy Roman emperor   154–155, 196, 200, 246, 248, 351–355, 357, 383, 392, 420–421, 529, 533, 540, 544, 551–553
Charles V, Holy Roman emperor   151, 403fn, 414fn, 466, 502fn
Charles VI, king of France   395, 415, 419fn, 448
Chesius, András, provost of Čazma   379
Choque, Pierre, chronicler   462
Cicero, Ancient author   473, 477
Cilli, Barbara, *see* Barbara of Cilli
Clovis, king of the Franks   102fn, 534
Coloman (the Learned), king of Hungary   118, 323
Conrad III, king of the Germans   347
Conrad of Masovia, high duke of Poland   156
Cordatus, Conrad, Protestant preacher   16
Corvin, John, son of King Matthias I   340, 481
Cosmas, saint   242
Csák, Máté, palatine of Hungary   173, 182fn, 329, 350
Csanádi, Albert, poet and Pauline monk   225
Csánki, Dezső   17–18, 65

da Burgio, Antonio Giovanni, papal legate and nuncio in Hungary   500, 515
Dalmata, Giovanni, sculptor   488
Damian, saint   242
de La Vigne, Nicolas Marcel, military engineer   261
Demetrios Kydones, Byzantine chancellor   356
Dengelegi, Pongrác János, voivode of Transylvania   379
Długosz, Jan, chronicler   352, 358–359
Domenico da Bologna, architect   507
Dominici, Giovanni, archbishop of Dubrovnik, cardinal   245–246
Druget family   173, 175, 182fn

INDEX OF PERSONAL NAMES 571

Ebenhauser, Lorenz, burgher of Vienna   296
Edlasperg, Peter, burgher of Buda   295, 297
Edward I, king of England   106, 537
Eliade, Mircea   229
Elizabeth of Bosnia (Kotromanić), queen consort to Louis I, king of Hungary   354, 460
Elizabeth of Hungary, saint   352, 548
Elizabeth of Luxembourg, daughter of Emperor Sigismund   460
Elizabeth, Piast, queen consort to Charles I, king of Hungary   193, 198–199, 211, 245, 353, 355, 548
Emeric, son of Stephen I, saint   85, 135, 232–233, 349, 549
Eötvös, József   320
Erasmus, Desiderius, humanist   469, 492
Eric VII of Pomerania, king of Denmark   360
Ernest, duke of Austria   359
Evlia Celebi, traveler   252
Eysvogel, Ulrich, burgher of Nuremberg   284
Eyza 'the Saracen', comes of Pilis County   122, 124fn

Federico da Montefeltro, lord of Urbino   474
Fekete Nagy, Antal   66
Ferdinand I, king of Hungary and Bohemia   55–56, 63, 298, 466–467, 499, 503, 507–509, 516
Ferrante I of Naples, king of Naples   461
Ficino, Marsilio, humanist   478–480, 482–483, 485–488, 490
Filarete, *see* Averulino, Antonio
Forster family   267
Francio, mythical figure   102
Francis of Prague, chronicler   352
Frangepán, Francis, archbishop of Kalocsa   511
Frankapan, Franjo, *see* Frangepán, Francis
Fráter, György (George Martinuzzi), archbishop of Esztergom, regent   508–509
Frederick I Barbarossa, Holy Roman emperor   84, 348–349, 368
Frederick II Hohenstaufen, Holy Roman emperor   142
Frederick III (the Fair), duke of Austria and king of Germany   282

Frederick III, Holy Roman emperor   336, 363, 372, 544, 551
Freiberger family   267
Freiberger, Wolfgang, judge of Buda   6
Fügedi, Erik   19, 373fn
Fugger family   267
Fugger, Jacob, burgher of Nuremberg   297

Gailsam family   267, 293
Garády, Sándor   33
Garázda, Péter, provost of Esztergom, humanist   481–482
Gárdonyi, Albert   18, 64fn, 65
Garinus, general master of the Dominicans, hagiographer   244–245
Gaston II de Foix, count of Candale   461
Gatti, Giovanni, theologian   478
Gellért, *see* Gerhard
Gentile Particino da Montefiore, cardinal, legate   248, 330–331
Gentilis, *see* Gentile Particino da Montefiore
George Litteratus   314
George of Brandenburg, margrave of Brandenburg-Ansbach   16, 464
George of Poděbrady, king of Bohemia   363, 372
George Sphrantzes, historiographer   361
George, canon of Veszprém   217
George, saint   199, 254, 311, 335, 418
Gerard, *see* Gerhard
Gerevich, László 19, 27–30, 33, 66, 145fn, 146fn, 151fn
Gerhard (Gerard), saint, bishop of Cenad   225, 232–235, 252, 254
Gerhard van Tyl, burgher of Buda   285
Gerz Ilyās, legendary figure   251–252, 254
Géza I, king of Hungary   79
Géza II, king of Hungary   78–79, 85, 118, 347
Géza, grand prince of the Magyars   75, 133, 140
Giovanni Conversini da Ravenna, humanist   355
Giovanni Gherardi da Prato, humanist   246
Giovio, Paolo, humanist   502
Giugni family   475
Gondi family   475
Gonzaga, Francesco, prince of Mantua   396
Gosztonyi, János, bishop of Győr   462, 517, 521

Gregory of Tours, bishop of Tours, chronicler   102
Gregory X, pope   240
Gritti, Lodovico, regent of Hungary   505–506
Grynaeus, Simon, rector of the church school at Buda   16
Guarino of Verona, humanist   474, 480
Guy de Dammartin, sculptor   411
Gyöngyösi, Gregorius, general of the Pauline order   225–226, 248, 250
Györffy, György   19, 66–67, 329

Hadnagy, Bálint, Pauline monk, chronicler   225, 249
Hadrian, provost of the Buda chapter   84
Haller family   267
Haller, Hans, burgher of Buda   296
Haller, Ruprecht, burgher of Nuremberg and Buda   296
Hartvik, bishop of Győr, hagiographer   233
Heimbach family   286
Heinrichs-Schreiber, Ulrike   406, 419
Helen of Anjou, queen consort to Stephen Uroš I, king of Serbia   549
Heltai, Gáspár, chronicler   489, 493
Henckel, Johann, court chaplain of Queen Mary of Hungary   16, 469
Henrik of the Héder clan, palatine of Hungary   173
Henry II (Jasomirgott), duke of Austria   347
Henry Preussel, knight, rector of Buda   306
Henry the Bearded, high duke of Poland   539
Henry the Lion, duke of Bavaria   347
Henry VI, king of England   466
Henszlmann, Imre   32
Herdegger, Vorchtel, burgher of Nuremberg   284
Hermann of Cilli, ban of Slavonia-Croatia   214
Hervoja of Spalato (Hrvoje Vukčić Hrvatinić), ban of Croatia and grand duke of Bosnia   359
Hess, Andreas, printer   478
Himfy, Benedict, ban of Bulgaria   123
Horváth, Henrik   27
Hrvoje Vukčić Hrvatinić, *see* Hervoja of Spalato
Hunor, mythical figure   107

Hunyadi, John, regent of Hungary   163, 335, 379, 422, 501
Hunyadi, Ladislas, ban of Croatia-Dalmatia   163, 166, 477

Iamblichus, Ancient philosopher   487
Isabella Jagiello, queen consort to John Szapolyai, king of Hungary   56, 507–508

Jánossy, Dénes   66
Janus Pannonius, bishop of Pécs, humanist   480, 485
Japhet, Biblical figure   100
Jean de Cambrai, sculptor   414
Jean Lemaire de Belges, chronicler   511
Jeanne d'Evreux, queen consort to Charles IV, king of France   412, 445
Joachim, master of the treasury   122
Johannes Carpentarius, provincial prior of the Carmelites   225
Johannes de Stokem, composer   483
Johannes Melakh de Gozon, court official of Queen Anne de Foix   462
Johannes Rasor, judge of Buda   312
Johannes, compilor of the *Ofner Stadtrecht*   310
John I Szapolyai, king of Hungary   55–56, 63–64, 168, 222, 297–298, 324, 341, 498, 503–507
John of Luxemburg, king of Bohemia   149, 283, 351, 353
John Sigismund, prince of Transylvania   507, 510
John V Palaiologos, Byzantine emperor   355, 361–362, 364–365
John V, prince of Brittany   415
John VIII Palaiologos, Byzantine emperor   361–362, 364–365
John XXII, pope   369
Jolanta (Violant) of Hungary, queen consort to James I, king of Aragón   88
Jordanes, chronicler   103
Joseph II, Austrian emperor   104fn
Juana of Castile, queen of Castile   462
Juncker, Peter, *see* Edlasperg, Peter

Kakas, János, burgher of Buda, author of a memoir   498
Kaltenhauser family   296

INDEX OF PERSONAL NAMES 573

Kammerer, Ulrich, burgher of Buda 291
Karai, László, provost of the Buda
  chapter 478
Károli, Gáspár, Calvinist pastor and Bible
  translator 493
Kemalpaşazâde, chronicler 501
Kenderesi, Balázs, Hungarian nobleman 222
Kisfaludy-Stróbl, Zsigmond, sculptor 254
Kochaim family 293
Koller, Heinrich 369
Komjáthy, Benedek, Bible translator 493
Komjáthy, Miklós 66
Kont, Nicolas, palatine of Hungary 211
Kottanerin, Helene, author of a memoir 461
Kraft, Bertold, burgher of Nuremberg 284
Kratzer, Friedrich, councillor of Buda 281, 290
Krell, Hans, painter 468
Kriemhild, literary figure 97fn
Krúdy, Gyula, writer 92
Kubinyi family 316
Kubinyi, András 3, 19–20, 30, 66, 273, 366–383, 454–455, 457, 464, 466, 513, 522
Küküllei, János, chronicler 245
Kumorovitz, L. Bernát 18, 30, 66–67
Kurszán, chieftain 74
Kuzsinszky, Bálint 26–27
Kytel, Peter, sculptor 396

Lackfi, Dénes, voivode of Transylvania 355
Ladislas I, king of Hungary, saint 42, 78, 199, 403, 431, 549
Ladislas IV (the Cuman), king of Hungary 55, 208, 241, 305, 326
Ladislas of Durazzo, king of Naples and claimant to the Hungarian throne 192, 291, 395
Ladislas of Naples, *see* Ladislas of Durazzo
Ladislas V (Postumus), king of Hungary 280, 335–337, 380, 477
Ladislas, rector of Buda 307
Ladislas, son of Peter Juncker, burgher of Buda 295
Lange, Johann, humanist 512
Lebmester, Niklas, burgher of Buda 291
Lehel, chieftain 104fn
Leo III, pope 346
Leo X, pope 514

Leopold IV of Babenberg, duke of Bavaria 546
Leopold VI, duke of Austria 280
Lorand, judge of Buda 309
Lorenzo the Magnificent, ruler of the Florentine Republic 472, 474, 487
Louis I (the Great), king of Hungary 2, 8, 15, 109, 147, 149, 150fn, 154, 157, 192, 193–194, 196–199, 210, 214, 235, 241, 246, 248, 281, 283–284, 288, 308, 331, 352–357, 365, 375, 383–384, 394–395, 460, 510–512, 551
Louis II, king of Hungary and Bohemia 10, 15, 60, 222, 342, 371, 380, 453, 457, 462, 464, 467–469, 498–499, 514–516, 518–521, 523–525, 552
Louis IX, saint, king of France 537
Louis of Orleans, brother of Charles VI, king of France 395
Louis VII (the Bearded), duke of Bavaria-Ingolstadt 415, 424
Louis VII, king of France 347
Lubenau, Reinhard, traveler 261
Luther, Martin, theologian 16–17, 468–469

Magog, Biblical figure 100
Magor, mythical figure 107
Mair family 296
Mályusz, Elemér 66
Manichaites, George, chancellor of John V, Byzantine emperor 356
Manuel I Komnenos, Byzantine emperor 80fn,
Manuel II Palaiologos, Byzantine emperor 356, 362
Marcellus, prior provincial of the Dominicans in Hungary 241, 243
Margaret Capet, wife of Béla III 84
Margaret, daughter of Béla IV, Dominican nun, saint 122, 210–211, 224–225, 233, 236–237, 240–247, 251, 254, 531
Margaret, mother of Petru I 548
Mark of Nuremberg, burgher of Buda 291
Marosi, Ernő 388, 406, 412, 424
Martin, abbot of the Bakonybél abbey 50, 218
Martinus Oppaviensis, Dominican friar, chronicler 234
Martinuzzi, George, *see* Fráter, György

Mary of Hungary, governor of the Habsburg Netherlands, queen consort to Louis II, king of Hungary and Bohemia   15–16, 21, 31, 462, 465–466, 468–469, 500, 515, 521, 524
Mary of Hungary, queen consort to Charles II, king of Naples   46, 245, 331
Mary, Laskaris, queen consort to Béla IV, king of Hungary   121, 147
Mary, queen of Hungary, wife of Sigismund of Luxembourg   196, 549
Marzio, Galeotto, humanist   468, 480, 489
Matthias I, king of Hungary   7, 9, 21, 32, 59, 109, 157, 159–167, 214, 241, 246, 283, 292–295, 333, 337–341, 363, 368, 372–373, 376–377, 379–381, 383, 409, 454, 457fn, 461, 465, 468, 472, 475–478, 479fn, 480–482, 484, 487–489, 492–493, 497, 513–514, 516, 519, 521–523, 542, 549, 552–553
Mauthier, Johannes, bombardier   524
Maximilian I, Holy Roman emperor   456fn, 466, 551
Mediomontanus (Czimbalmos), János, theologian   253
Mehmed II, sultan   501
Meistaler, Hans, burgher of Nuremberg   296
Melanchthon, Philipp theologian   492
Mendel, family   9, 377
Michael, brother of John V, Byzantine emperor   356
Mikó, Gábor   341
Mikod, ban of Severin   306
Mindszenti, Gábor, author of a memoir   505
Mollay, Károly   19
Molnár, Ferenc   104fn
Moraw, Peter   383
Moses, Biblical figure   229, 372, 408, 418fn
Muhr, Hans, sculptor   97fn
Multscher, Hans, sculptor   405fn, 415, 422fn, 423–425
Murad IV, sultan   510

Nagy, Emese   30
Nagy, Lajos   18fn, 27
Nagylaki Jaksics, Gergely   107fn
Naldi, Naldo, humanist   481
Niccolò de Mirabilibus, Dominican vicar general   486

Nicholas V, pope   473–474
Nicholas, archbishop of Esztergom   122
Nicholas, rector of Buda   307–308, 309fn
Niger, Petrus, theologian   15, 224, 478
Nogin, Mihail, sculptor   97fn

Odo of Deuil (Diogilo), chaplain of Louis VII, king of France, chronicler   347
Oecolampadius, Johannes, theologian, reformer   16
Oláh, Miklós, archbishop of Esztergom   337, 493
Oliver, comes of Pilis County   122
Ölyvedi, Menyhért, royal secretary   506
Orio, Lorenzo, Venetian diplomat   464
Orsini, Roberto Latino, archbishop of Reggio di Calabria   514
Ország, Mihály (Gúti), palatine of Hungary   392
Osvald of Lasko, Franciscan vicar, preacher   14, 225
Oszvald, Arisztid   66
Otto I, Holy Roman emperor   346
Otto II, Holy Roman emperor   346
Otto III, Holy Roman emperor   346
Otto of Freising, bishop of Freising, chronicler   347
Otto Wittelsbach of Bavaria, duke of Bavaria, king of Hungary   97fn, 144, 173, 374
Ottokar I, king of Bohemia   143, 327

Pálczán, Péter, judge of Buda   64
Pálóczi, László, chief justice of Hungary   335fn
Pamphilus, Nicolaus (Bátori, Miklós [?], bishop of Vác)   489
Paravicini, Werner   471
Paul the Hermit, saint   214, 225, 248, 250–251, 517
Pázmány, Péter, archbishop of Esztergom   493
Peçevi, İbrahim, chronicler   252, 502
Pelbart of Temesvár, Franciscan friar, preacher   14, 225
Pemfflinger family   267, 294
Pemfflinger, Hans, judge of Buda   295
Pemfflinger, Mark, judge royal of Sibiu   295
Perényi family   316
Pesti, Gábor, Bible translator   492

INDEX OF PERSONAL NAMES

Peter II of Courtenay, Latin emperor   349
Peter Lombard, bishop of Paris, theologian   473
Peter Orseolo, king of Hungary   204
Peter, abbot of Szenttrinitás abbey   215fn, 218
Peterman, prefect of Buda   307–308
Petronella, patroness of the Kána abbey   205
Petru I, prince of Moldavia   541, 548
Philip I of Castile, duke of Burgundy   462
Philip le Bel   167fn
Philip the Bold, duke of Burgundy   409, 441
Philip the Good, duke of Burgundy   398
Philip, bishop of Fermo   327
Philip, comes of Pilis County   122
Pipo of Ozora, *see* Scolari, Filippo
Pius II, pope   246
Plato, Ancient philosopher   479–480, 483–484, 487fn
Plotinus, Ancient philosopher   480, 487
Plutarch, Ancient historian   477
Podhraczky, József   17, 64
Podmaniczky, John, chamberlain   222
Poliziano, Angelo, humanist   481
Preussel (Preuchul), Henry, rector of Buda   306

Quintilian, Ancient author   477

Rácz, György   352
Rady, Martyn   20, 303–321
Ráskai, Lea, Dominican nun, codex copier   224, 247
Regiomontanus (Johannes Müller of Königsberg), astronomer   478, 482
Reichel, Peter, head of the Buda minting chamber   291fn
Remus, brother of Romulus   106
Révay family   56
Révay, Ferenc, court judge   56
Révay, János, bishop of Szepes   56
Robert Courtenay, Latin emperor   349
Rómer, Flóris   32
Romulus, Ancient king of Rome   106
Rozgonyi, István, comes of Temes County   397
Rudolf I of Saxe-Wittenberg, prince-elector of Saxony   149fn, 351
Rudolf I, king of Germany   326–327

Rudolf IV, duke of Austria   286, 551
Rupert I, count palatine of the Rhine   357

Sachs, Hans, poet   509
Salamanca, Gabriel, archchancellor of Ferdinand I   465
Salamon, Ferenc   17, 65
Salamon, king of Hungary   97, 325fn
Samuel Aba, king of Hungary   232
Sashegyi, Sándor   111–114
Schedel, Hartmann, cartographer, humanist   13–14, 164–165
Schneidpöck, Hans, imperial diplomat   465
Schön, Erhard, engraver   50, 144, 165–166
Schönwiesner, István   32
Schulek, Frigyes   42, 45fn
Schultes, Lothar   418
Schürstab, Leopold, burgher of Nuremberg   284, 286
Schwarz, Michael Viktor   406, 411, 413, 418–419
Scolari, Filippo (Pipo of Ozora), chief treasurer   291
Siebenlinder, Hans, judge of Buda   291
Sigismund I, king of Poland   223, 464, 470fn
Sigismund, king of Hungary and Bohemia, Holy Roman emperor   2, 15, 21, 31, 49, 55, 67–68, 109, 123–124, 150fn, 153–154, 157–160, 163–164, 166, 168, 192, 196, 200, 278, 286–288, 291, 310, 312, 332–333, 336, 343, 358, 360–365, 375, 380, 383, 387, 390, 392, 394–399, 401–404, 410, 418, 420–426, 431, 452, 460, 472, 477, 512, 542, 549, 551–553
Simon, bishop of Zagreb   250
Simon of Kéza, chronicler   76fn, 103, 106, 235
Sluter, Claus, sculptor   407–409, 414, 435, 439
Soběslav I, king of Bohemia   136
Sombart, Werner   382
Somi family   316
Sophia of Halshany (Sonka Olshanskaya), queen consort to Wladislas II, king of Poland   361
Söptei, Peter, burgher of Buda, notary   221, 223
Sövényházi, Márta, Dominican nun, codex copier   247
Speratus, Paul, Protestant preacher   16
Stadler, Hans, burgher of Buda   291

Stanislas of Szczepanów, bishop of
   Cracow, saint   139, 549
Stefan Lazarević, despot of Serbia   359, 362
Stephen I, king of Hungary, saint   75, 77, 114,
   119, 133, 140, 147, 185, 232–233, 323fn,
   332fn, 374, 503, 549
Stephen III, king of Hungary   140fn, 348
Stephen of Anjou, brother of King Louis I,
   duke of Slavonia   151
Stephen V, king of Hungary   147fn, 240, 306,
   324fn, 549
Stibor II of Stiboric, comes of Máramaros
   County   422
Stoeffler, Johann, humanist   498
Stoltzer, Thomas, court chaplain   16, 468
Stoss, Andreas, sculptor   225
Stoss, Veit, sculptor   225
Suleiman I, sultan   9, 251, 371, 499, 504,
   505fn, 509, 524–525
Sybenlinder, János, notary of Buda   268
Sylvester, János, Bible translator   493
Szalkai, László, bishop of Vác   517, 522
*Széchényi, Ferenc, founder of the Hungarian
   National Museum and the National Széché-
   nyi Library*   26, 104
Székely, György   67
Szerecsen, János, burgher of Buda,
   chamberlain   267
Szerémi, György, court chaplain,
   chronicler   489–500, 504–506, 511
Szerencsés, Imre, treasury official   10, 222
Szilágyi, Mihály, regent of Hungary
   337fn, 338
Szörényi, Levente   114
Szydłowiecki, Krzysztof, count of Szydłowiec,
   diplomat   463

Taddeo Ugoleto of Parma, humanist,
   librarian   481, 487
Taksony, grand prince of the Magyars   82
Taurinus, Stephanus, chronicler   14
Than, Mór, painter   107
Theocritus, Ancient poet   473
Theoderic the Great, king of the
   Ostrogoths   99
Thomas Aquinas, theologian, saint   486
Thomas, comes of Pilis county, bishop of
   Vác   122
Thuróczy, John, chronicler   106, 352

Thurzó, Elek, chief justice of
   Hungary   469, 522
Thurzó, János, entrepreneur, mayor of
   Cracow   297
Thurzó, Johannes, bishop of
   Wrocław   469
Thurzó, Stanislaus, bishop of Olomouc   469
Tino di Camaino, sculptor   245
Toldi, Miklós, chivalric hero   252, 510
Tolnai, Máté, abbot of Pannonhalma
   abbey   218
Tommaso De Vio, theologian, cardinal   515
Török, Bálint, ban of Belgrade   511
Tóth, Norbert, C.   322fn, 516
Töttös of Becse, master of the
   doorkeepers   123
Töttös, László, master of the cupbearers   338
Tucher family   296
Turkovith, Nicholas, judge of Buda   17
Turner, Victor   238
Tvrtko II, king of Bosnia   359

Ubertino I of Carrara, lord of Padua   477
Újlaki, Lőrinc, duke of Bosnia   380
Ulrich of Cilli, count of Celje   336
Urban III, pope   118
Urban V, pope   355–356
Urban VI, pope   245

Valla, Lorenzo, humanist   476
van der Bach family   283
van der Bach, Jakob, burgher of Buda   283
van der Weyden, Rogier, painter   404,
   432–433
Váradi, Péter, archbishop of Kalolcsa,
   humanist   482
Végh, András   21, 30fn, 31fn, 48fn, 169–203,
   204fn, 209–210, 273, 387fn, 467
Vels, general   507–508
Vergerio, Pier Paolo, nuncio, humanist   477
Verzelio, Giovanni, papal messenger   520fn
Vico, Enea, engraver   238–239
Viollet-le-Duc, Eugène   93fn
Virgil, Ancient author   477
Vitéz, János, archbishop of Esztergom,
   humanist   339, 476–478, 480–482
Vittorino da Feltre, humanist   474
Vogelweider family   267
von Below, Georg   382

INDEX OF PERSONAL NAMES

von Vels, Leonhard Freiherr, chief commandant of King Ferdinand I in Hungary   507
Vorchtel family   284, 286
Vörösmarty, Mihály, poet   105
Vratislas I, duke of Bohemia   135

Walter, rector of Buda   306–308
Wann, Paul, parish priest of the Our Lady church of Buda   370–371, 377, 379
Wenceslas I, Duke of Luxembourg   420
Wenceslas I, saint   136, 234, 549
Wenceslas II, king of Bohemia   145fn, 156, 539
Wenceslas III of Bohemia, king of Poland and Bohemia, claimant to the Hungarian throne   144, 173, 374
Wenceslas IV, king of Bohemia and Germany   145fn, 155, 355, 358, 374, 553
Werbőczy, Stephen, palatine of Hungary   372, 507
Werner, rector of Buda   87–88, 90, 183, 307, 382
Wilhelm von Roggendorf, Habsburg military commander   505
Wilhelm von Waldburg-Trauchburg, Habsburg military commander   503

Windecke, Eberhard, chronicler   359fn, 360–361, 398, 404
Wladislas I Łokietek, king of Poland   156
Wladislas I, king of Hungary and Poland   332, 334–335, 372, 461
Wladislas II (Jogaila), king of Poland   358–361
Wladislas II, duke of Bohemia   529
Wladislas II, king of Hungary and Bohemia   155, 157, 161–162, 276, 340, 363, 375, 378, 380, 382, 453, 457, 461, 463–464, 478, 489fn, 497, 513–514, 522fn
Wladislas Jagiello, *see* Wladislas II, king of Hungary and Bohemia
Wulving (Ulving), councillor of Buda   175, 199

Xenophon, Ancient historian   478
Yolanda de Courtenay, queen consort to Andrew II, king of Hungary   349

Zichy family   94
Zolnay, László   19, 388

Printed in the United States
By Bookmasters